Corner House Publishers

SOCIAL SCIENCE REPRINTS

General Editor MAURICE FILLER

FOLK-LORE OF SHAKESPEARE

FOLK-LORE

OF

SHAKESPEARE

BY THE

Rev. T. F. THISELTON DYER, M.A. Oxon.

AUTHOR OF "BRITISH POPULAR CUSTOMS, PAST AND PRESENT," ETC.

CORNER HOUSE PUBLISHERS

WILLIAMSTOWN, MASSACHUSETTS 01267

1983

FIRST PUBLISHED IN ENGLAND
ABOUT 1883 THIS IS AN EXACT
REPRINT OF THE AMERICAN EDITION
PUBLISHED BY HARPER'S IN 1884.

REPRINTED 1978

BY

CORNER HOUSE PUBLISHERS

SECOND PRINTING 1983

ISBN 0–87928–088–3

Printed in the United States of America

PREFACE.

IT would be difficult to overestimate the value which must be attached to the plays of Shakespeare in connection with the social life of the Elizabethan age. Possessed of a rich treasury of knowledge of a most varied kind, much of which he may be said to have picked up almost intuitively, he embellished his writings with a choice store of illustrations descriptive of the period in which he lived. Apart, too, from his copious references to the manners and customs of the time, he seems to have had not only a wide knowledge of many technical subjects, but also an intimate acquaintance with the folk-lore of bygone days. How far this was the case may be gathered from the following pages, in which are collected and grouped together, as far as arrangement would permit, the various subjects relating to this interesting and popular branch of our domestic history. It only remains for me to add that the edition of the poet's plays made use of is the "Globe," published by Messrs. Macmillan.

T. F. THISELTON DYER.

CONTENTS.

viii   CONTENTS.

FOLK-LORE OF SHAKESPEARE.

CHAPTER I.

FAIRIES.

THE wealth of Shakespeare's luxuriant imagination and glowing language seems to have been poured forth in the graphic accounts which he has given us of the fairy tribe. Indeed, the profusion of poetic imagery with which he has so richly clad his fairy characters is unrivalled, and the " Midsummer-Night's Dream " holds a unique position in so far as it contains the finest modern artistic realization of the fairy kingdom. Mr. Dowden, in his " Shakspere Primer " (1877, pp. 71, 72) justly remarks : " As the two extremes of exquisite delicacy, of dainty elegance, and, on the other hand, of thick-witted grossness and clumsiness, stand the fairy tribe and the group of Athenian handicraftsmen. The world of the poet's dream includes the two—a Titania, and a Bottom the weaver—and can bring them into grotesque conjunction. No such fairy poetry existed anywhere in English literature before Shakspere. The tiny elves, to whom a cowslip is tall, for whom the third part of a minute is an important division of time, have a miniature perfection which is charming. They delight in all beautiful and dainty things, and war with things that creep and things that fly, if they be uncomely ; their lives are gay with fine frolic and delicate revelry." Puck, the jester of fairyland, stands apart from the rest, the recognizable " lob of spirits," a rough, " fawn-faced, shock-pated little fellow, dainty-limbed shapes around him." Judging, then, from the elaborate account

which the poet has bequeathed us of the fairies, it is evident
that the subject was one in which he took a special interest.
Indeed, the graphic pictures he has handed down to us of

> " Elves of hills, brooks, standing lakes and groves ;
>   And ye, that on the sands with printless foot,
>   Do chase the ebbing Neptune, and do fly him
>   When he comes back ; you demy-puppets that
>   By moonshine do the green-sour ringlets make
>   Whereof the ewe not bites," etc.,

show how intimately he was acquainted with the history
of these little people, and what a complete knowledge he
possessed of the superstitious fancies which had clustered
round them.   In Shakespeare's day, too, it must be remembered, fairies were much in fashion ; and, as Johnson remarks,
common tradition had made them familiar.   It has also been
observed that, well acquainted, from the rural habits of his
early life, with the notions of the peasantry respecting these
beings, he saw that they were capable of being applied to a
production of a species of the wonderful.   Hence, as Mr.
Halliwell Phillipps[1] has so aptly written, " he founded his
elfin world on the prettiest of the people's traditions, and
has clothed it in the ever-living flowers of his own exuberant
fancy."   Referring to the fairy mythology in the " Midsummer-Night's Dream," it is described by Mr. Keightley[2] as
an attempt to blend " the elves of the village with the fays
of romance."   His fairies agree with the former in their
diminutive stature—diminished, indeed, to dimensions in-
appreciable by village gossips—in their fondness for dancing, their love of cleanliness, and their child-abstracting
propensities.   Like the fays, they form a community, ruled
over by the princely Oberon and the fair Titania.   There
is a court and chivalry ; Oberon would have the queen's
sweet changeling to be a " knight of his train, to trace the
forests wild."   Like earthly monarchs, he has his jester,
" that shrewd and knavish sprite called Robin Goodfellow."

---

[1] " Illustrations of the Fairy Mythology of ' A Midsummer-Night's
Dream,' " 1845, p. xiii.

[2] " Fairy Mythology," p. 325.

Of the fairy characters treated by Shakespeare may be mentioned Oberon, king of fairyland, and Titania, his queen. They are represented as keeping rival courts in consequence of a quarrel, the cause of which is thus told by Puck (" Midsummer-Night's Dream," ii. 1):

> " The king doth keep his revels here to-night:
> Take heed the queen come not within his sight;
> For Oberon is passing fell and wrath,
> Because that she as her attendant hath
> A lovely boy, stolen from an Indian king;
> She never had so sweet a changeling;
> And jealous Oberon would have the child
> Knight of his train, to trace the forests wild;
> But she perforce withholds the loved boy,
> Crowns him with flowers and makes him all her joy;
> And now they never meet in grove or green,
> By fountain clear, or spangled starlight sheen," etc.

Oberon first appears in the old French romance of " Huon de Bourdeaux," and is identical with Elberich, the dwarf king of the German story of Otnit in the " Heldenbuch." The name Elberich, or, as it appears in the " Nibelungenlied," Albrich, was changed, in passing into French, first into Auberich, then into Auberon, and finally became our Oberon. He is introduced by Spenser in the " Fairy Queen " (book ii. cant. i. st. 6), where he describes Sir Guyon:

> " Well could he tournay, and in lists debate,
> And knighthood tooke of good Sir Huon's hand,
> When with King Oberon he came to faery land."

And in the tenth canto of the same book (stanza 75) he is the allegorical representative of Henry VIII. The wise Elficleos left two sons,

> " of which faire Elferon,
> The eldest brother, did untimely dy;
> Whose emptie place the mightie Oberon
> Doubly supplide, in spousall and dominion."

" Oboram, King of Fayeries," is one of the characters in Greene's " James the Fourth." [1]

---

[1] Aldis Wright's " Midsummer-Night's Dream," 1877, Preface, pp. xv. xvi.; Ritson's " Fairy Mythology," 1875, pp. 22, 23.

The name Titania for the queen of the fairies appears to have been the invention of Shakespeare, for, as Mr. Ritson [1] remarks, she is not "so called by any other writer." Why, however, the poet designated her by this title, presents, according to Mr. Keightley, [2] no difficulty. "It was," he says, "the belief of those days that the fairies were the same as the classic nymphs, the attendants of Diana. The fairy queen was therefore the same as Diana, whom Ovid (Met. iii. 173) styles Titania." In Chaucer's "Merchant's Tale" Pluto is the king of faerie, and his queen, Proserpina, "who danced and sang about the well under the laurel in January's garden." [3]

In "Romeo and Juliet" (i. 4) she is known by the more familiar appellation, Queen Mab. "I dream'd a dream to-night," says Romeo, whereupon Mercutio replies, in that well-known famous passage—

"O, then, I see Queen Mab hath been with you,"

this being the earliest instance in which Mab is used to designate the fairy queen. Mr. Thoms [4] thinks that the origin of this name is to be found in the Celtic, and that it contains a distinct allusion to the diminutive form of the elfin sovereign. *Mab*, both in Welsh and in the kindred dialects of Brittany, signifies a child or infant, and hence it is a befitting epithet to one who

"comes
In shape no bigger than an agate-stone
On the fore-finger of an alderman."

Mr. Keightley suggests that Mab may be a contraction of Habundia, who, Heywood says, ruled over the fairies; and another derivation is from Mabel, of which Mab is an abbreviation.

Among the references to Queen Mab we may mention Drayton's "Nymphidia :"

---

[1] Essay on Fairies in "Fairy Mythology of Shakspeare," p. 23.
[2] "Fairy Mythology," 1878, p. 325.
[3] Notes to "A Midsummer-Night's Dream," by Aldis Wright, 1877, Preface, p. xvi.
[4] "Three Notelets on Shakespeare," pp. 100–107.

> " Hence Oberon, him sport to make
> (Their rest when weary mortals take,
> And none but only fairies wake),
>   Descendeth for his pleasure:
> And Mab, his merry queen, by night
> Bestrides young folks that lie upright," etc.

Ben Jonson, in his " Entertainment of the Queen and Prince at Althrope," in 1603, describes as " tripping up the lawn a bevy of fairies, attending on Mab, their queen, who, falling into an artificial ring that there was cut in the path, began to dance around."   In the same masque the queen is thus characterized by a satyr:

> " This is Mab, the mistress fairy,
> That doth nightly rob the dairy,
> And can help or hurt the cherning
> As she please, without discerning," etc.

Like Puck, Shakespeare has invested Queen Mab with mischievous properties, which " identify her with the night hag of popular superstition," and she is represented as

> " Platting the manes of horses in the night."

The merry Puck, who is so prominent an actor in " A Midsummer-Night's Dream," is the mischief-loving sprite, the jester of the fairy court, whose characteristics are roguery and sportiveness.   In his description of him, Shakespeare, as Mr. Thoms points out, " has embodied almost every attribute with which the imagination of the people has invested the fairy race; and has neither omitted one trait necessary to give brilliancy and distinctness to the likeness, nor sought to heighten its effect by the slightest exaggeration.   For, carefully and elaborately as he has finished the picture, he has not in it invested the 'lob of spirits' with one gift or quality which the popular voice of the age was not unanimous in bestowing upon him."   Thus (ii. 1) the fairy says:

> " Either I mistake your shape and making quite,
> Or else you are that shrewd and knavish sprite,
> Call'd Robin Goodfellow: are you not he
> That frights the maidens of the villagery;

> Skim milk; and sometimes labour in the quern,
> And bootless make the breathless housewife churn;
> And sometime make the drink to bear no barm;
> Mislead night-wanderers, laughing at their harm?
> Those that Hobgoblin call you, and sweet Puck,
> You do their work, and they shall have good luck:
> Are not you he?"

The name " Puck " was formerly applied to the whole race of fairies, and not to any individual sprite—*puck*, or *pouke*, being an old word for devil, in which sense it is used in the " Vision of Piers Plowman:"

> " Out of the poukes pondfold
> No maynprise may us feeche."

The Icelandic *puki* is the same word, and in Friesland and Jutland the domestic spirit is called Puk by the peasantry. In Devonshire, Piskey is the name for a fairy, with which we may compare the Cornish Pixey. In Worcestershire, too, we read how the peasantry are occasionally " poake-ledden," that is, misled by a mischievous spirit called *poake*. And, according to Grose's " Provincial Glossary," in Hampshire they give the name of Colt-pixey to a supposed spirit or fairy, which, in the shape of a horse, neighs, and misleads horses into bogs. The Irish, again, have their Pooka, [1] and the Welsh their Pwcca—both words derived from Pouke or Puck. Mr. Keightley [2] thinks, also, that the Scottish *pawkey*, sly, knowing, may belong to the same list of words. It is evident, then, that the term Puck was in bygone years extensively applied to the fairy race, an appellation still found in the west of England. Referring to its use in Wales, " there is a Welsh tradition to the effect that Shakespeare received his knowledge of the Cambrian fairies from his friend Richard Price, son of Sir John Price, of the Priory of Brecon." It is even claimed that Cwm Pwcca, or Puck Valley, a part of the romantic glen of the Clydach, in Breconshire, is the original scene of the " Midsummer-Night's Dream." [3]

Another of Puck's names was Robin Goodfellow, and one

---

[1] See Croker's " Fairy Legends of South of Ireland," 1862, p. 135.

[2] " Fairy Mythology," 1878, p. 316.

[3] Wirt Sikes's " British Goblins," 1880, p. 20.

of the most valuable illustrations we have of the "Mid-summer-Night's Dream" is a black-letter tract published in London, 1628, under the title of "Robin Goodfellow: His Mad Pranks, and Merry Jests, full of honest mirth, and is a fit medicine for melancholy."[1] Mr. Halliwell-Phillipps,[2] speaking of Robin Goodfellow, says, "there can be no doubt that in the time of Shakespeare the fairies held a more prominent position in our popular literature than can be now concluded from the pieces on the subject that have descended to us." The author of "Tarlton's News out of Purgatory," printed in 1590, assures us that Robin Goodfellow was "famosed in every old wives chronicle for his mad merry pranks;" and we learn from "Henslowe's Diary" that Chettle was the writer of a drama on the adventures of that "merry wanderer of the night." These have disappeared; and time has dealt so harshly with the memory of poor Robin that we might almost imagine his spirit was still leading us astray over massive volumes of antiquity, in a delusive search after documents forever lost; or, rather, perhaps, it is his punishment for the useless journeys he has given our ancestors, misleading night-wanderers, "and laughing at their harm."[3] He is mentioned by Drayton in his "Nymphidia:"

> "He meeteth Puck, which most men call
> Hob-goblin, and on him doth fall," etc.,

"hob being the familiar or diminutive form of Robert and Robin, so that Hobgoblin is equivalent to Robin the Goblin, *i.e.*, Robin Goodfellow."[4] Burton, in his "Anatomy of Melancholy," alludes to him thus: "A bigger kinde there is of them, called with us hobgoblins and Robin Goodfellows, that would, in superstitious times, grinde corne for a mess of milk, cut wood, or do any manner of drudgery work." Under his

---

[1] This is reprinted in Hazlitt's "Fairy Tales, Legends, and Romances, illustrating Shakespeare and other English Writers," 1875, p. 173.

[2] "Illustrations of the Fairy Mythology of the Midsummer-Night's Dream," printed for the Shakespeare Society, p. viii.

[3] See Brand's "Pop. Antiq.," 1849, vol. ii. pp. 508–512.

[4] Thoms's "Three Notelets on Shakespeare," p. 88.

name of Robin Goodfellow, Puck is well characterized in Jonson's masque of "Love Restored."[1]

Another epithet applied to Puck is "Lob," as in the "Midsummer-Night's Dream" (ii. 1), where he is addressed by the fairy as

> "Thou lob of spirits."[2]

With this we may compare the "lubber-fiend" of Milton, and the following in Beaumont and Fletcher's "Knight of the Burning Pestle" (iii. 4): "There is a pretty tale of a witch that had the devil's mark about her, that had a giant to be her son, that was called Lob-lye-by-the-Fire." Grimm[3] mentions a spirit, named the "Good Lubber," to whom the bones of animals used to be offered at Manseld, in Germany. Once more, the phrase of "being in," or "getting into Lob's pound," is easy of explanation, presuming Lob to be a fairy epithet—the term being equivalent to Poake-ledden or Pixy-led.[4] In "Hudibras" this term is employed as a name for the stocks in which the knight puts Crowdero:

> "Crowdero, whom in irons bound,
> Thou basely threw'st into *Lob's pound*."

It occurs, also, in Massinger's "Duke of Milan" (iii. 2), where it means "behind the arras:"

> "Who forc'd the gentleman, to save her credit,
> To marry her, and say he was the party
> Found in Lob's pound."

The allusion by Shakespeare to the "Will-o'-the-Wisp," where he speaks of Puck as "sometime a fire," is noticed elsewhere, this being one of the forms under which this fairy was supposed to play his midnight pranks.

Referring, in the next place, to the several names of Shakespeare's fairies, we may quote from "The Merry Wives of Windsor" (iv. 3), where Mrs. Page speaks of

---

[1] See Nares's Glossary, vol. ii. p. 695.

[2] Mr. Dyce considers that Lob is descriptive of the contrast between Puck's square figure and the airy shapes of the other fairies.

[3] "Deutsche Mythologie," p. 492.

[4] See Keightley's "Fairy Mythology," pp. 318, 319.

" urchins, ouphes, and fairies "—urchin having been an appellation for one class of fairies.   In the " Maydes' Metamorphosis " of Lyly (1600), we find fairies, elves, and urchins
separately accommodated with dances for their use.   The
following is the *urchin's* dance :

> " By the moone we sport and play,
>   With the night begins our day;
>   As we frisk the dew doth fall,
>   Trip it, little urchins all,
>   Lightly as the little bee,
>   Two by two, and three by three,
>   And about goe wee, goe wee."

In " The Tempest " (i. 2) their actions are also limited to
the night :

> " Urchins
>   Shall, for that vast of night that they may work,
>   All exercise on thee."

The children employed to torment Falstaff, in " The Merry
Wives of Windsor " (iv. 4), were to be dressed in these fairy
shapes.

Mr. Douce regards the word *urchin*, when used to designate a fairy, as of Celtic origin, with which view Mr. Thoms[1]
compares the *urisks* of Highland fairies.

The term *ouphe*, according to Grimm, is only another
form of the cognate *elf*, which corresponds with the Middle
High-German *ulf*, in the plural *ulve*.   He further proves the
identity of this *ulf* with *alp*, and with our English *elf*, from
a Swedish song published by Asdwiddson, in his " Collection
of Swedish Ballads," in one version of which the elfin king
is called Herr *Elfver*, and in the second Herr *Ulfver*.

The name *elf*, which is frequently used by Shakespeare, is
the same as the Anglo-Saxon *alf*, the Old High-German and
the Middle High-German *ulf*.   " Fairies and elvs," says
Tollet, " are frequently mentioned together in the poets
without any distinction of character that I can recollect."

The other fairies, Peas-blossom, Cobweb, Moth, and Mustard-
seed probably owe their appellations to the poet himself.

---

[1] " Three Notelets on Shakespeare," pp. 79–82.

How fully Shakespeare has described the characteristics of the fairy tribe, besides giving a detailed account of their habits and doings, may be gathered from the following pages, in which we have briefly enumerated the various items of fairy lore as scattered through the poet's writings.

Beauty, then, united with power, was one of the popular characteristics of the fairy tribe. Such was that of the " Fairy Queen " of Spenser, and of Titania in " A Midsummer-Night's Dream." In " Antony and Cleopatra " (iv. 8), Antony, on seeing Cleopatra enter, says to Scarus:

> " To this great fairy I'll commend thy acts,
> Make her thanks bless thee."

In " Cymbeline " (iii. 6), when the two brothers find Imogen in their cave, Belarius exclaims:

> " But that it eats our victuals, I should think
> Here were a fairy." [1]

And he then adds:

> " By Jupiter, an angel! or, if not,
> An earthly paragon! behold divineness
> No elder than a boy."

The fairies, as represented in many of our old legends and folk-tales, are generally noticeable for their beauty, the same being the case with all their surroundings. As Sir Walter Scott,[2] too, says, " Their pageants and court entertainments comprehended all that the imagination could conceive of what were accounted gallant and splendid. At their processions they paraded more beautiful steeds than those of mere earthly parentage. The hawks and hounds which they employed in their chase were of the first race. At their daily banquets, the board was set forth with a splendor which the proudest kings of the earth dared not aspire to, and the hall of their dancers echoed to the most exquisite music."

Mr. Douce[3] quotes from the romance of " Lancelot of the

---

[1] Showing, as Mr. Ritson says, that they never ate.
[2] " Letters on Demonology and Witchcraft," 1831, p. 121.
[3] " Illustrations of Shakespeare," p. 115.

Lake," where the author, speaking of the days of King Arthur, says, "En celui temps estoient appellees faees toutes selles qui sentre-mettoient denchantemens et de charmes, et moult en estoit pour lors principalement en la Grande Bretaigne, et savoient la force et la vertu des paroles, des pierres, et des herbes, parquoy elles estoient tenues et jeunesse et en beaulte, et en grandes richesses comme elles devisoient."

"This perpetual youth and beauty," he adds, "cannot well be separated from a state of immortality;" another characteristic ascribed to the fairy race. It is probably alluded to by Titania in "A Midsummer-Night's Dream" (ii. 1):

> "The human mortals want their winter here."

And further on (ii. 1), when speaking of the changeling's mother, she says:

> "But she, being mortal, of that boy did die."

Again, a fairy addresses Bottom the weaver (iii. 1)—

> "Hail, mortal!"

—an indication that she was not so herself. The very fact, indeed, that fairies "call themselves *spirits*, ghosts, or shadows, seems to be a proof of their immortality." Thus Puck styles Oberon "king of shadows," and this monarch asserts of himself and his subjects—

> "But we are spirits of another sort."

Fletcher, in the "Faithful Shepherdess," describes (i. 2)—

> "A virtuous well, about whose flow'ry banks
> The nimble-footed fairies dance their rounds,
> By the pale moonshine, dipping oftentimes
> Their stolen children, so to make them free
> From dying flesh, and dull mortality."

Ariosto, in his "Orlando Furioso" (book xliii. stanza 98) says:

> "I am a fayrie, and to make you know,
> To be a fayrie what it doth import,
> We cannot dye, how old so e'er we grow.
> Of paines and harmes of ev'rie other sort
> We taste, onelie no death we nature ow."

An important feature of the fairy race was their power of vanishing at will, and of assuming various forms. In "A Midsummer-Night's Dream" Oberon says:

> "I am invisible,
> And I will overhear their conference."

Puck relates how he was in the habit of taking all kinds of outlandish forms; and in the "Tempest," Shakespeare has bequeathed to us a graphic account of Ariel's eccentricities. "Besides," says Mr. Spalding,[1] "appearing in his natural shape, and dividing into flames, and behaving in such a manner as to cause young Ferdinand to leap into the sea, crying, 'Hell is empty, and all the devils are here!' he assumes the forms of a water nymph (i. 2), a harpy (iii. 3), and also the Goddess Ceres (iv. 1), while the strange shapes, masquers, and even the hounds that hunt and worry the would-be king and viceroys of the island, are Ariel's 'meaner fellows.'" Poor Caliban complains of Prospero's spirits (ii. 2):

> "For every trifle are they set upon me;
> Sometimes like apes, that mow and chatter at me,
> And after bite me; then like hedgehogs which
> Lie tumbling in my bare-foot way, and mount
> Their pricks at my footfall; sometime am I
> All wound with adders, who, with cloven tongues
> Do hiss me into madness."

That fairies are sometimes exceedingly diminutive is fully shown by Shakespeare, who gives several instances of this peculiarity. Thus Queen Mab, in "Romeo and Juliet," to which passage we have already had occasion to allude (i. 4), is said to come

> "In shape no bigger than an agate stone
> On the fore-finger of an alderman."[2]

---

[1] "Elizabethan Demonology," p. 50.

[2] Agate was used metaphorically for a very diminutive person, in allusion to the small figures cut in agate for rings. In "2 Henry IV." (i. 2), Falstaff says: "I was never manned with an agate till now; but I will inset you neither in gold nor silver, but in vile apparel, and send you back again to your master, for a jewel." In "Much Ado About Nothing" (iii. 1) Hero speaks of a man as being "low, an agate very vilely cut."

And Puck tells us, in " A Midsummer-Night's Dream " (ii. 1), that when Oberon and Titania meet,

> "they do square, that all their elves, for fear,
> Creep into acorn cups, and hide them there."

Further on (ii. 3) the duties imposed by Titania upon her train point to their tiny character:

> " Come, now a roundel and a fairy song;
> Then, for the third part of a minute, hence;
> Some to kill cankers in the musk-rose buds,
> Some war with rere-mice for their leathern wings,
> To make my small elves coats."

And when enamoured of Bottom, she directs her elves that they should—

> " Hop in his walks and gambol in his eyes;
> Feed him with apricocks and dewberries,
> With purple grapes, green figs, and mulberries;
> The honey bags steal from the humble-bees,
> And for night tapers crop their waxen thighs
> And light them at the fiery glow-worm's eyes,
> To have my love to bed, and to arise;
> And pluck the wings from painted butterflies
> To fan the moonbeams from his sleeping eyes."

We may compare, too, Ariel's well-known song in " The Tempest " (v. 1):

> " Where the bee sucks, there suck I:
> In a cowslip's bell I lie;
> There I couch when owls do cry,
> On the bat's back I do fly
> After summer merrily,
> Merrily, merrily shall I live now
> Under the blossom that hangs on the bough."

Again, from the following passage in " The Merry Wives of Windsor " (iv. 4) where Mrs. Page, after conferring with her husband, suggests that—

> " Nan Page my daughter, and my little son,
> And three or four more of their growth, we'll dress
> Like urchins, ouphes, and fairies, green and white,
> With rounds of waxen tapers on their heads,
> And rattles in their hands "

it is evident that in Shakespeare's day fairies were supposed
to be of the size of children. The notion of their diminu-
tiveness, too, it appears was not confined to this country,[1]
but existed in Denmark,[2] for in the ballad of " Eline of Vil-
lenskov " we read :

> " Out then spake the smallest Trold ;
>   No bigger than an ant ;—
> Oh ! here is come a Christian man,
>   His schemes I'll sure prevent."

Again, various stories are current in Germany descriptive
of the fairy dwarfs ; one of the most noted being that relating to Elberich, who aided the Emperor Otnit to gain the
daughter of the Paynim Soldan of Syria.[3]

The haunts of the fairies on earth are generally supposed
to be the most romantic and rural that can be selected ;
such a spot being the place of Titania's repose described by
Oberon in " A Midsummer-Night's Dream " (ii. 1) :[4]

> " a bank where the wild thyme blows,
> Where oxlips and the nodding violet grows,
> Quite over-canopied with luscious woodbine,
> With sweet musk-roses and with eglantine :
> There sleeps Titania some time of the night,
> Lull'd in these flowers with dances and delight ;
> And there the snake throws her enamell'd skin,
> Weed wide enough to wrap a fairy in."

Titania also tells how the fairy race meet

> " on hill, in dale, forest, or mead,
> By paved fountain, or by rushy brook,
> Or in the beached margent of the sea."

In " The Tempest " (v. 1), we have the following beautiful
invocation by Prospero :

> " Ye elves of hills, brooks, standing lakes, and groves ;
> And ye, that on the sands with printless foot
> Do chase the ebbing Neptune, and do fly him
> When he comes back—"

---

[1] See Grimm's " Deutsche Mythologie."
[2] Thoms's " Three Notelets on Shakespeare," 1865, pp. 38, 39.
[3] See Keightley's " Fairy Mythology," 1878, p. 208.
[4] See also Thorpe's " Northern Mythology," 1852, vol. iii. p. 32, etc.

Their haunts, however, varied in different localities, but their favorite abode was in the interior of conical green hills, on the slopes of which they danced by moonlight. Milton, in the "Paradise Lost" (book i.), speaks of

> "fairy elves,
> Whose midnight revels, by a forest side
> Or fountain, some belated peasant sees,
> Or dreams he sees, while overhead the moon
> Sits arbitress, and nearer to the earth
> Wheels her pale course, they, on their mirth and dance
> Intent, with jocund music charm his ear;
> At once with joy and fear his heart rebounds."

The Irish fairies occasionally inhabited the ancient burial-places known as tumuli or barrows, while some of the Scottish fairies took up their abode under the "door-stane" or threshold of some particular house, to the inmates of which they administered good offices.[1]

The so-called fairy-rings in old pastures[2]—little circles of a brighter green, within which it was supposed the fairies dance by night—are now known to result from the out-spreading propagation of a particular mushroom, the fairy-ringed fungus, by which the ground is manured for a richer following vegetation. An immense deal of legendary lore, however, has clustered round this curious phenomenon, popular superstition attributing it to the merry roundelays of the moonlight fairies.[3] In "The Tempest" (v. 1) Prospero invokes the fairies as the "demy-puppets" that

> "By moonshine do the green-sour ringlets make,
> Whereof the ewe not bites; and you, whose pastime
> Is to make midnight-mushrooms."

---

[1] Gunyon's "Illustrations of Scottish History, Life, and Superstitions," p. 299.

[2] Chambers's "Book of Days," vol. i. p. 671.

[3] Among the various conjectures as to the cause of these verdant circles, some have ascribed them to lightning; others maintained that they are occasioned by ants. See Miss Baker's "Northamptonshire Glossary," vol. i. p. 218; Brand's "Pop. Antiq.," 1849, vol. ii. pp. 480–483; and also the "Phytologist," 1862, pp. 236–238.

In " A Midsummer-Night's Dream " (ii. 1), the fairy says :

> " I do wander everywhere,
> Swifter than the moon's sphere ;
> And I serve the fairy queen,
> To dew her orbs upon the green."

Again, in the " Merry Wives of Windsor " (v. 5), Anne Page says :

> " And nightly, meadow-fairies, look, you sing
> Like to the Garter's compass, in a ring ;
> The expressure that it bears, green let it be,
> More fertile-fresh than all the field to see."

And once in " Macbeth " (v. 1), Hecate says :

> " Like elves and fairies in a ring."

Drayton, in his " Nymphidia " (l. 69–72), mentions this superstition :

> " And in their courses make that round,
> In meadows and in marshes found,
> Of them so called the fayrie ground,
> Of which they have the keeping."

Cowley, too, in his " Complaint," says :

> " Where once such fairies dance, no grass does ever grow."

And again, in his ode upon Dr. Harvey :

> " And dance, like fairies, a fantastic round."

Pluquet, in his " Contes Populaires de Bayeux," tells us that the fairy rings, called by the peasants of Normandy " Cercles des fées," are said to be the work of fairies.

Among the numerous superstitions which have clustered round the fairy rings, we are told that when damsels of old gathered the May dew on the grass, which they made use of to improve their complexions, they left undisturbed such of it as they perceived on the fairy-rings, apprehensive that the fairies should in revenge destroy their beauty. Nor was it considered safe to put the foot within the rings, lest they should be liable to the fairies' power.[1] The " Athenian

---

[1] Douce's " Illustrations of Shakespeare," p. 112.

Oracle" (i. 397) mentions a popular belief that " if a house be built upon the ground where fairy rings are, whoever shall inhabit therein does wonderfully prosper."

Speaking of their dress, we are told that they constantly wore green vests, unless they had some reason for changing their attire. In the " Merry Wives of Windsor" (iv. 4) they are spoken of as—

> " Urchins, ouphes, and fairies, green and white."

And further on (v. 4):

> " Fairies, black, grey, green, and white."

The fairies of the moors were often clad in heath-brown or lichen-dyed garments, whence the epithet of " Elfin-grey."[1]

The legends of most countries are unanimous in ascribing to the fairies an inordinate love of music; such harmonious sounds as those which Caliban depicts in " The Tempest" (iii. 2) being generally ascribed to them :

> " The isle is full of noises,
> Sounds and sweet airs, that give delight and hurt not.
> Sometimes a thousand twangling instruments
> Will hum about mine ears, and sometime voices
> That, if I then had waked after long sleep,
> Will make me sleep again."

In the " Midsummer-Night's Dream " (ii. 3), when Titania is desirous of taking a nap, she says to her attendants:

> " Come, now a roundel, and a fairy song."

And further on (iii. 1) she tells Bottom :

> " I'll give thee fairies to attend on thee,
> And they shall fetch thee jewels from the deep,
> And sing, while thou on pressed flowers dost sleep."

The author of " Round About our Coal Fire "[2] tells us that "they had fine musick always among themselves, and danced in a moonshiny night, around, or in, a ring."

---

[1] Ritson's " Fairy Mythology," 1878, pp. 26, 27.
[2] Quoted by Brand, " Pop. Antiq.," vol. ii. p. 481.

They were equally fond of dancing, and we are told how they meet—

"To dance their ringlets to the whistling wind;"

and in the "Maydes' Metamorphosis" of Lyly, the fairies, as they dance, sing:

"Round about, round about, in a fine ring a,
Thus we dance, thus we dance, and thus we sing a,
Trip and go, to and fro, over this green a,
All about, in and out, for our brave queen a," etc.

As Mr. Thoms says, in his "Three Notelets on Shakespeare" (1865, pp. 40, 41), "the writings of Shakespeare abound in graphic notices of these fairy revels, couched in the highest strains of poetry; and a comparison of these with some of the popular legends which the industry of Continental antiquaries has preserved will show us clearly that these delightful sketches of elfin enjoyment have been drawn by a hand as faithful as it is masterly."

It would seem that the fairies disliked irreligious people; and so, in "Merry Wives of Windsor" (v. 5), the mock fairies are said to chastise unchaste persons, and those who do not say their prayers. This coincides with what Lilly, in his "Life and Times," says: "Fairies love a strict diet and upright life; fervent prayers unto God conduce much to the assistance of those who are curious hereways," *i. e.*, who wish to cultivate an acquaintance with them.

Again, fairies are generally represented as great lovers and patrons of cleanliness and propriety, for the observance of which they were frequently said to reward good servants, by dropping money into their shoes in the night; and, on the other hand, they were reported to punish most severely the sluts and slovenly, by pinching them black and blue.[1] Thus, in "A Midsummer-Night's Dream" (v. 1), Puck says:

"I am sent, with broom, before,
To sweep the dust behind the door."

---

[1] Brand's "Pop. Antiq.," 1849, vol. ii. p. 483.

In "Merry Wives of Windsor" (v. 5), Pistol, speaking of the mock fairy queen, says:

> "Our radiant queen hates sluts and sluttery;"

and the fairies who haunt the towers of Windsor are enjoined:

> "About, about,
> Search Windsor Castle, elves, within and out:
> Strew good luck, ouphes, on every sacred room:
>   *   *   *   *   *
> The several chairs of order look you scour
> With juice of balm and every precious flower."

In Ben Jonson's ballad of "Robin Goodfellow"[1] we have a further illustration of this notion:

> "When house or hearth doth sluttish lie,
> I pinch the maidens black and blue,
> The bed clothes from the bed pull I,
> And lay them naked all to view.
>   'Twixt sleep and wake
>   I do them take,
> And on the key-cold floor them throw;
>   If out they cry,
>   Then forth I fly,
> And loudly laugh I, ho, ho, ho!"

In "Round About our Coal Fire," we find the following passage bearing on the subject: "When the master and mistress were laid on the pillows, the men and maids, if they had a game at romps, and blundered up stairs, or jumbled a chair, the next morning every one would swear 'twas the fairies, and that they heard them stamping up and down stairs all night, crying, 'Waters lock'd, waters lock'd!' when there was no water in every pail in the kitchen." Herrick, too, in his "Hesperides," speaks of this superstition:

> "If ye will with Mab find grace,
> Set each platter in his place;
> Rake the fire up, and set
> Water in, ere sun be set,

---

[1] Halliwell-Phillipps's "Illustrations of Fairy Mythology," p. 167; see Douce's "Illustrations of Shakespeare," pp. 122, 123.

> Wash your pales and cleanse your dairies,
> Sluts are loathesome to the fairies :
> Sweep your house ; who doth not so,
> Mab will pinch her by the toe."

While the belief in the power of fairies existed, they were supposed to perform much good service to mankind. Thus, in " A Midsummer-Night's Dream " (v. 1), Oberon says :

> " With this field-dew consecrate,
>   Every fairy take his gait ;
>   And each several chamber bless,
>   Through this palace, with sweet peace ;
>   And the owner of it blest,
>   Ever shall in safety rest "—

the object of their blessing being to bring peace upon the house of Theseus. Mr. Douce[1] remarks that the great influence which the belief in fairies had on the popular mind " gave so much offence to the holy monks and friars, that they determined to exert all their power to expel these imaginary beings from the minds of the people, by taking the office of the fairies' benedictions entirely into their own hands ;" a proof of which we have in Chaucer's " Wife of Bath :"

> " I speke of many hundred yeres ago ;
>   But now can no man see non elves mo,
>   For now the grete charitee and prayeres
>   Of limitoures and other holy freres
>   That serchen every land and every streme,
>   As thikke as motes in the sonne beme,
>   Blissing halles, chambres, kichenes, and boures,
>   Citees and burghes, castles highe and toures,
>   Thropes and bernes, shepenes and dairies,
>   This maketh that ther ben no faeries :
>   For ther as wont to walken was an elf
>   Ther walketh now the limitour himself."

Macbeth, too (v. 8), in his encounter with Macduff, says :

> " I bear a charmed life, which must not yield
>   To one of woman born."

---

[1] " Illustrations of Shakespeare," pp. 126, 127.

In the days of chivalry, the champion's arms were ceremoniously blessed, each taking an oath that he used no charmed weapon. In Spenser's "Fairy Queen" (book i. canto 4) we read:

> "he bears a charmed shield,
> And eke enchanted arms, that none can pierce."

Fairies were amazingly expeditious in their journeys. Thus, Puck goes "swifter than arrow from the Tartar's bow," and in "A Midsummer-Night's Dream" he answers Oberon, who was about to send him on a secret expedition:

> "I'll put a girdle round about the earth
> In forty minutes."

Again, the same fairy addresses him:

> "Fairy king, attend, and mark:
> I do hear the morning lark.
>   *Oberon.* Then, my queen, in silence sad,
> Trip we after the night's shade:
> We the globe can compass soon,
> Swifter than the wand'ring moon."

Once more, Puck says:

> "My fairy lord, this must be done with haste,
> For night's swift dragons cut the clouds full fast,
> And yonder shines Aurora's harbinger," etc.

It was fatal, if we may believe Falstaff in "Merry Wives of Windsor" (v. 5), to speak to a fairy: "They are fairies; he that speaks to them shall die."

Fairies are accustomed to enrich their favorites; and in "A Winter's Tale" (iii. 3) the shepherd says: "It was told me I should be rich by the fairies;"[1] and in "Cymbeline" (v. 4), Posthumus, on waking and finding the mysterious paper, exclaims:

> "What fairies haunt this ground? A book? O rare one!
> Be not, as is our fangled world, a garment
> Nobler than that it covers," etc.

----

[1] See Croker's "Fairy Legends and Traditions of the South of Ireland, p. 316.

At the same time, however, it was unlucky to reveal their acts of generosity, as the shepherd further tells us: "This is fairy gold, boy; and 'twill prove so; up with't, keep it close, home, home, the next way. We are lucky, boy; and to be so still requires nothing but secrecy."

The necessity of secrecy in fairy transactions of this kind is illustrated in Massinger and Field's play of "The Fatal Dowry," 1632 (iv. 1),[1] where Romont says:

> "But not a word o' it; 'tis fairies' treasure,
> Which, but reveal'd, brings on the blabber's ruin."

Among the many other good qualities belonging to the fairy tribe, we are told that they were humanely attentive to the youthful dead.[2] Thus Guiderius, in "Cymbeline," thinking that Imogen is dead (iv. 2), says:

> "With female fairies will his tomb be haunted,
> And worms will not come to thee;"[3]

there having been a popular notion that where fairies resorted no noxious creature could be found.

In the pathetic dirge of Collins a similar allusion is made:

> "No wither'd witch shall here be seen,
> No goblin lead their nightly crew;
> The female fays shall haunt the green,
> And dress thy grave with pearly dew."

It seems, however, that they were also supposed to be malignant; but this, "it may be," says Mr. Ritson, "was merely calumny, as being utterly inconsistent with their general character, which was singularly innocent and amiable." Thus, when Imogen, in "Cymbeline" (ii. 2), prays on going to sleep,

> "From fairies and the tempters of the night,
> Guard me, beseech ye,"[4]

---

[1] See Brand's "Pop. Antiq.," vol. ii. p. 493.

[2] Ritson's "Fairy Mythology of Shakespeare," 1875, p. 29.

[3] Some copies read *them*.

[4] We may compare Banquo's words in "Macbeth" (ii. 1):

> "Restrain in me the cursed thoughts that nature
> Gives way to in repose."

it must have been, says Mr. Ritson,[1] the *incubus* she was so afraid of.

Hamlet, too, notices this imputed malignity of the fairies (i. 1):

> " Then no planet strikes,
> Nor fairy takes, nor witch hath power to charm."[2]

That the fairies, however, were fond of indulging in mischievous sport at the expense of mortals is beyond all doubt, the merry pranks of Puck or Robin Goodfellow fully illustrating this item of our fairy-lore. Thus, in " A Midsummer-Night's Dream " (ii. 1) this playful fairy says:

> " I am that merry wanderer of the night.
> I jest to Oberon and make him smile,
> When I a fat and bean-fed horse beguile,
> Neighing in likeness of a filly foal:
> And sometime lurk I in a gossip's bowl,
> In very likeness of a roasted crab;
> And when she drinks, against her lips I bob,
> And on her wither'd dewlap pour the ale.
> The wisest aunt, telling the saddest tale,
> Sometime for three-foot stool mistaketh me;
> Then slip I from her bum, down topples she,
> And ' tailor ' cries, and falls into a cough."

A fairy, in another passage, asks Robin:

> " Are you not he
> That frights the maidens of the villagery,
>   *   *   *   *   *
> Mislead night-wanderers, laughing at their harm ?"

We have already mentioned how Queen Mab had the same mischievous humor in her composition, which is described by Mercutio in " Romeo and Juliet " (i. 4):

> " This is that very Mab
> That plats the manes of horses in the night,
> And bakes the elflocks in foul sluttish hairs,
> Which, once untangled, much misfortune bodes."

---

[1] " Fairy Mythology," pp. 27, 28.

[2] In " Comedy of Errors " (iv. 2) some critics read:

> " A fiend, a fairy, pitiless and rough."

Another reprehensible practice attributed to the fairies was that of carrying off and exchanging children, such being designated changelings.[1]   The special agent in transactions of the sort was also Queen Mab, and hence Mercutio says:

> " She is the fairies' midwife."

And " she is so called," says Mr. Halliwell-Phillipps, " because it was her supposed custom to steal new-born babes in the night and leave others in their place."   Mr. Steevens gives a different interpretation to this line, and says, " It does not mean that she was the midwife to the fairies, but that she was the person among the fairies whose department it was to deliver the fancies of sleeping men in their dreams, those children of an idle brain."

---

[1] This superstition is fully described in chapter on *Birth*.

CHAPTER II.

WITCHES.

IN years gone by witchcraft was one of the grossest forms of superstition, and it would be difficult to estimate the extent of its influence in this and other countries. It is not surprising that Shakespeare should have made frequent allusions to this popular belief, considering how extensively it prevailed in the sixteenth and seventeenth centuries; the religious and dramatic literature of the period being full of it. Indeed, as Mr. Williams[1] points out, "what the vulgar superstition must have been may be easily conceived, when men of the greatest genius or learning credited the possibility, and not only a theoretical but possible occurrence, of these infernal phenomena." Thus, Francis Bacon was "not able to get rid of the principles upon which the creed was based. Sir Edward Coke, his contemporary, the most acute lawyer of the age, ventured even to define the devil's agents in witchcraft. Sir Thomas Browne and Sir Matthew Hale, in 1664, proved their faith—the one by his solemn testimony in open court, the other by his still more solemn sentence." Hence, it was only to be expected that Shakespeare should introduce into his writings descriptions of a creed which held such a prominent place in the history of his day, and which has made itself famous for all time by the thousands of victims it caused to be sent to the torture-chamber, to the stake, and to the scaffold. Thus he has given a graphic account of the celebrated Jeanne D'Arc, the Maid of Orleans, in " 1 Henry VI.," although Mr. Dowden[2] is of opinion that this play was written by one or more authors, Greene

---

[1] "Superstitions of Witchcraft," 1865, p. 220.
[2] "Shakspere Primer," 1877, p. 63.

having had, perhaps, a chief hand in it, assisted by Peele and Marlowe.   He says, " It is a happiness not to have to ascribe to our greatest poet the crude and hateful handling of the character of Joan of Arc, excused though to some extent it may be by the occurrence of view in our old English chronicles."

Mr. Lecky,[1] too, regards the conception of Joan of Arc given in " 1 Henry VI." as " the darkest blot upon the poet's genius," but it must be remembered that we have only expressed the current belief of his day—the English vulgar having regarded her as a sorceress, the French as an inspired heroine.   Talbot is represented as accusing her of being a witch, serving the Evil One, and entering Rouen by means of her sorceries (iii. 2):

> " France, thou shalt rue this treason with thy tears,
>   If Talbot but survive thy treachery.
>   Pucelle, that witch, that damned sorceress,
>   Hath wrought this hellish mischief unawares,
>   That hardly we escaped the pride of France."

Further on (v. 3) she is made to summon fiends before her, but she wishes them in vain, for they speak not, hanging their heads in sign of approaching disaster :

> " Now help, ye charming spells and periapts ;
>   And ye choice spirits that admonish me
>   And give me signs of future accidents.
>   You speedy helpers, that are substitutes
>   Under the lordly monarch of the north,
>   Appear and aid me in this enterprise."

But she adds :

> " See, they forsake me !   Now the time is come
>   That France must vail her lofty-plumed crest,
>   And let her head fall into England's lap.
>   My ancient incantations are too weak,
>   And hell too strong for me to buckle with :
>   Now, France, thy glory droopeth to the dust."

Finally, convicted of practising sorcery, and filling " the

---

[1] " Rationalism in Europe," 1870, vol. i. p. 106.

world with vicious qualities," she was condemned to be burned. Her death, however, Sir Walter Scott[1] says, "was not, we are sorry to say, a sacrifice to superstitious fear of witchcraft, but a cruel instance of wicked policy, mingled with national jealousy and hatred. The Duke of Bedford, when the ill-starred Jeanne fell into his hands, took away her life in order to stigmatize her memory with sorcery, and to destroy the reputation she had acquired among the French."

The cases of the Duchess of Gloucester and of Jane Shore, also immortalized by Shakespeare, are both referred to in the succeeding pages.

The Witch of Brentford, mentioned by Mrs. Page in "The Merry Wives of Windsor" (iv. 2), was an actual personage, the fame, says Staunton,[2] "of whose vaticinations must have been traditionally well known to an audience of the time, although the records we possess of her are scant enough. The chief of them is a black-letter tract, printed by William Copland in the middle of the sixteenth century, entitled "Jyl of Braintford's Testament," from which it appears she was hostess of a tavern at Brentford.[3] One of the characters in Dekker and Webster's "Westward Ho"[4] says, "I doubt that old hag, Gillian of Brainford, has bewitched me."

The witches in "Macbeth" are probably Scottish hags. As Mr. Gunnyon remarks,[5] "They are hellish monsters, brewing hell-broth, having cats ·and toads for familiars, loving midnight, riding on the passing storm, and devising evil against such as offend them. They crouch beneath the gibbet of the murderer, meet in gloomy caverns, amid earthquake convulsions, or in thunder, lightning, and rain." Coleridge, speaking of them, observes that "the weird sisters are as true a creation of Shakespeare's as his Ariel and Caliban —fates, fairies, and materializing witches being the elements. They are wholly different from any representation of witches

---

[1] "Demonology and Witchcraft," 1881, pp. 192, 193.
[2] "Shakespeare," 1864, vol. ii. p. 161.   [3] See Dyce's "Glossary," p. 51.
[4] Webster's Works, edited by Dyce, 1857, p. 238.
[5] "Illustrations of Scottish History, Life, and Superstition," 1879, p. 322.

in the contemporary writers, and yet presented a sufficient external resemblance to the creatures of vulgar prejudice to act immediately on the audience. Their character consists in the imaginative disconnected from the good, they are the shadowy obscure and fearfully anomalous of physical nature, elemental avengers without sex or kin."

It has been urged, however, by certain modern critics, that these three sisters, "who play such an important part in 'Macbeth,' are not witches at all, but are, or are intimately allied to, the Norns or Fates of Scandinavian paganism."[1] Thus, a writer in the *Academy* (Feb. 8, 1879) thinks that Shakespeare drew upon Scandinavian mythology for a portion of the material he used in constructing these characters, and that he derived the rest from the traditions of contemporary witchcraft; in fact, that the "sisters" are hybrids between Norns and witches. The supposed proof of this is that each sister exercises the special function of one of the Norns. "The third," it is said, "is the special prophetess, while the first takes cognizance of the past, and the second of the present, in affairs connected with humanity. These are the tasks of Urda, Verdandi, and Skulda. The first begins by asking, 'When shall we three meet again?' The second decides the time: 'When the battle's lost and won.' The third the future prophesies: 'That will be ere the set of sun.' The first again asks, 'Where?' The second decides: 'Upon the heath.' The third the future prophesies: 'There to meet with Macbeth.'"

It is further added that the description of the sisters given by Banquo (i. 3) applies to Norns rather than witches:

> "What are these
> So wither'd and so wild in their attire,
> That look not like the inhabitants o' the earth,
> And yet are on't? Live you? or are you aught
> That man may question? You seem to understand me,
> By each at once her chappy finger laying
> Upon her skinny lips: you should be women,
> And yet your beards forbid me to interpret
> That you are so."

---

[1] Spalding's "Elizabethan Demonology," 1880, p. 86.

But, as Mr. Spalding truly adds, "a more accurate poetical counterpart to the prose descriptions given by contemporary writers of the appearance of the poor creatures who were charged with the crime of witchcraft could hardly have been penned." Scot, for instance, in his "Discovery of Witchcraft" (book i. chap. iii. 7), says: "They are women which commonly be old, lame, bleare-eied, pale, fowle, and full of wrinkles; they are leane and deformed, showing melancholie in their faces." Harsnet, too, in his "Declaration of Popish Impostures" (1603, p. 136), speaks of a witch as "an old weather-beaten crone, having her chin and knees meeting for age, walking like a bow, leaning on a staff, hollow-eyed, untoothed, furrowed, having her limbs trembling with palsy, going mumbling in the streets; one that hath forgotten her paternoster, yet hath a shrewd tongue to call a drab a drab."

The beard, also, to which Shakespeare refers in the passage above, was the recognized characteristic of the witch. Thus, in the "Honest Man's Fortune" (ii. 1), it is said, "The women that come to us for disguises must wear beards, and that's to say a token of a witch." In the "Merry Wives of Windsor" (iv. 2), Sir Hugh Evans says of the disguised Falstaff: "By yea and no, I think the 'oman is a witch indeed: I like not when a 'oman has a great peard; I spy a great peard under her muffler."

It seems probable, then, that witches are alluded to by Shakespeare in "Macbeth," the contemporary literature on the subject fully supporting this theory. Again, by his introduction of Hecate among the witches in "Macbeth" (iii. 5), Shakespeare has been censured for confounding ancient with modern superstitions. But the incongruity is found in all the poets of the Renaissance. Hecate, of course, is only another name for Diana. "Witchcraft, in truth, is no modern invention. Witches were believed in by the vulgar in the time of Horace as implicitly as in the time of Shakespeare. And the belief that the pagan gods were really existent as evil demons is one which has come down from the very earliest ages of Christianity."[1] As far back as the fourth

---

[1] "Notes to Macbeth" (Clark and Wright), 1877, p. 137.

century, the Council of Ancyra is said to have condemned the pretensions of witches; that in the night-time they rode abroad or feasted with their mistress, who was one of the pagan goddesses, Minerva, Sibylla, or Diana, or else Herodias.[1] In Middleton's "Witch," Hecate is the name of one of his witches, and she has a son a low buffoon. In Jonson's "Sad Shepherd" (ii. 1) Maudlin the witch calls Hecate, the mistress of witches, "Our dame Hecate." While speaking of the witches in "Macbeth," it may be pointed out that[2] "the full meaning of the first scene is the fag-end of a witch's Sabbath, which, if fully represented, would bear a strong resemblance to the scene at the commencement of the fourth act. But a long scene on such a subject would be tedious and uninteresting at the commencement of the play. The audience is therefore left to assume that the witches have met, performed their conjurations, obtained from the evil spirits the information concerning Macbeth's career that they desired to obtain, and perhaps have been commanded by the fiends to perform the mission they subsequently carry through." Brand[3] describes this "Sabbath of the witches as a meeting to which the sisterhood, after having been anointed with certain magical ointments, provided by their infernal leader, are supposed to be carried through the air on brooms," etc. It was supposed to be held on a Saturday, and in past centuries this piece of superstition was most extensively credited, and was one of the leading doctrines associated with the system of witchcraft.

Referring, in the next place, to the numerous scattered notices of witches given by Shakespeare throughout his plays, it is evident that he had made himself thoroughly acquainted with the superstitions connected with the subject, many of which he has described with the most minute accuracy. It appears, then, that although they were sup-

---

[1] Scot's "Discovery of Witchcraft," 1584, book iii. chap. 16. See Douce's "Illustrations of Shakespeare," p. 235.

[2] "Elizabethan Demonology," pp. 102, 103. See Conway's "Demonology and Devil-lore," vol. ii. p. 253.

[3] "Pop. Antiq.," 1849, vol. iii. p. 8.

posed to possess extraordinary powers, which they exerted in various ways, yet these were limited, as in the case of Christmas night, when, we are told in "Hamlet" (i. 1), "they have no power to charm." In spite, too, of their being able to assume the form of any animal at pleasure, the tail was always wanting. In "Macbeth" (i. 3), the first witch says:

> "And, like a rat without a tail,
> I'll do, I'll do, and I'll do."

One distinctive mark, also, of a were-wolf, or human being changed into a wolf, was the absence of a tail. The cat was said to be the form most commonly assumed by the familiar spirits of witches; as, for instance, where the first witch says, "I come, Graymalkin!"[1] (i. 1), and further on (iv. 1), "Thrice the brinded cat hath mew'd." In German legends and traditions we find frequent notice of witches assuming the form of a cat, and displaying their fiendish character in certain diabolical acts. It was, however, the absence of the tail that only too often was the cause of the witch being detected in her disguised form. There were various other modes of detecting witches: one being "the trial by the stool," to which an allusion is made in "Troilus and Cressida" (ii. 1), where Ajax says to Thersites,

> "Thou stool for a witch!"

—a practice which is thus explained in Grey's "Notes" (ii. 236): "In one way of trying a witch, they used to place her upon a chair or a stool, with her legs tied cross, that all the weight of her body might rest upon her seat, and by that means, after some time, the circulation of the blood would be much stopped, and her sitting would be as painful as the wooden horse; and she must continue in this pain twenty-four hours, without either sleep or meat; and it was no wonder that, when they were tired out with such an ungodly trial, they would confess themselves many times guilty to free themselves from such torture."

Again, it was a part of the system of witchcraft that draw-

---

[1] Graymalkin—a gray cat.

ing blood from a witch rendered her enchantments ineffectual. Thus, in " 1 Henry VI." (i. 5), Talbot says to the Maid of Orleans:

> " I'll have a bout with thee ;
> Devil or devil's dam, I'll conjure thee :
> Blood will I draw on thee, thou art a witch."

An instance of this superstition occurred some years ago in a Cornish village, when a man was summoned before the bench of magistrates and fined, for having assaulted the plaintiff and scratched her with a pin. Indeed, this notion has by no means died out. As recently as the year 1870, a man eighty years of age was fined at Barnstaple, in Devonshire, for scratching with a needle the arm of a young girl. He pleaded that he had " suffered affliction " through her for five years, had had four complaints on him at once, had lost fourteen canaries, and about fifty goldfinches, and that his neighbors told him this was the only way to break the spell and get out of her power."[1]

It was, also, a popular belief that a great share of faith was a protection from witchcraft. Hence, in the " Comedy of Errors " (iii. 2), Dromio of Syracuse says of Nell :

> " if my breast had not been made of faith and my heart of steel,
> She had transform'd me to a curtail-dog, and made me turn i' the wheel."

In order, moreover, to check the power of witches, it was supposed to be necessary to propitiate them, a ceremony which was often performed. It is alluded to further on in the same play (iv. 3), where Dromio of Syracuse says—

> " Some devils ask but the parings of one's nail,
> A rush, a hair, a drop of blood, a pin,
> A nut, a cherry-stone ;"

and in " Macbeth " we read of their being propitiated by gifts of blood. Witches were supposed to have the power of creating storms and other atmospheric disturbances—a notion to which much prominence is given in " Macbeth."

---

[1] Henderson's " Folk-Lore of Northern Counties," p. 181.

Thus, the witches elect to meet in thunder, lightning, or rain. They are represented as being able to loose and bind the winds (v. 3), to cause vessels to be tempest-tossed at sea. Hence Macbeth addresses them (iv. 1):

> " Though you untie the winds, and let them fight
> Against the churches; though the yesty waves
> Confound and swallow navigation up;
> Though bladed corn be lodged and trees blown down;
> Though castles topple on their warders' heads;
> Though palaces and pyramids do slope
> Their heads to their foundations; though the treasure
> Of nature's germins tumble all together,
> Even till destruction sicken."

Thus, by way of illustration, we may quote a curious confession made in Scotland, about the year 1591, by Agnes Sampson, a reputed witch. She vowed that "at the time his majesty [James VI.] was in Denmark, she took a cat and christened it, and afterwards bound to each part of that cat the chiefest parts of a dead man, and several joints of his body; and that in the night following, the said cat was conveyed into the midst of the sea, by herself and other witches, sailing in their riddles, or crieves, and so left the said cat right before the town of Leith, in Scotland. This done, there arose such a tempest in the sea, as a greater hath not been seen, which tempest was the cause of the perishing of a boat or vessel coming from the town of Brunt Island to the town of Leith, wherein were sundry jewels and rich gifts, which should have been presented to the new Queen of Scotland at his majesty's coming to Leith. Again, it is confessed that the said christened cat was the cause of the king's majesty's ship, at his coming forth of Denmark, having a contrary wind to the rest of the ships then being in his company, which thing was most strange and true, as the king's majesty acknowledged." It is to this circumstance that Shakespeare probably alludes in "Macbeth" (i. 3), where he makes the witch say:

> " Though his bark cannot be lost,
> Yet it shall be tempest-toss'd."

Witches were also believed to be able to sell or give winds, a notion thus described in Drayton's " Moon-Calf" (865):

> " She could sell winds to any one that would
> Buy them for money, forcing them to hold
> What time she listed, tie them in a thread,
> Which ever as the seafarer undid
> They rose or scantled, as his sails would drive
> To the same port whereas he would arrive."

So, in " Macbeth " (i. 3):

> " 2 *Witch*. I'll give thee a wind.
> 1 *Witch*. Thou'rt kind.
> 3 *Witch*. And I another."

Singer quotes from Sumner's " Last Will and Testament:"

> " In Ireland, and in Denmark both,
> Witches for gold will sell a man a wind,
> Which, in the corner of a napkin wrapp'd,
> Shall blow him safe unto what coast he will."

At one time the Finlanders and Laplanders drove a profitable trade by the sale of winds. After being paid they knitted three magical knots, and told the buyer that when he untied the first he would have a good gale; when the second, a strong wind; and when the third, a severe tempest.[1]

The sieve, as a symbol of the clouds, has been regarded among all nations of the Aryan stock as the mythical vehicle used by witches, nightmares, and other elfish beings in their excursions over land and sea.[2] Thus, the first witch in " Macbeth " (i. 3), referring to the scoff which she had received from a sailor's wife, says:

> " Her husband's to Aleppo gone, master o' the Tiger:
> But in a sieve I'll thither sail." [3]

---

[1] Olaus Magnus's " History of the Goths," 1638, p. 47. See note to " The Pirate."

[2] See Hardwick's " Traditions and Folk-Lore," pp. 108, 109; Kelly's " Indo-European Folk-Lore," pp. 214, 215.

[3] In Greek, ἐπὶ ῥιπους πλἐιν, " to go to sea in a sieve," was a proverbial expression for an enterprise of extreme hazard or impossible of achievement. — Clark and Wright's " Notes to Macbeth," 1877, p. 82.

Stories of voyages performed in this way are common enough in Germany. A man, for instance, going through a corn-field, finds a sieve on the path, which he takes with him. He does not go far before a young lady hurries after him, and hunts up and down as if looking for something, ejaculating all the time, " How my children are crying in England!" Thereupon the man lays down the sieve, and has hardly done so ere sieve and lady vanish. In the case of another damsel of the same species, mentioned by Mr. Kelly, the usual exclamation is thus varied: " My sieve rim! my sieve rim! how my mother is calling me in England!" At the sound of her mother's voice the daughter immediately thinks of her sieve. Steevens quotes from the " Life of Doctor Fian," "a notable sorcerer," burned at Edinburgh, January, 1591, how that he and a number of witches went to sea, " each one in a *riddle or cive*." In the " Discovery of Witchcraft," Reginald Scot says it was believed that " witches could sail in an egg-shell, a cockle or muscleshell, through and under the tempestuous seas." Thus, in " Pericles " (iv. 4), Gower says:

> " Thus time we waste, and longest leagues make short;
> Sail seas in cockles, have, and wish but for't."

Their dance is thus noticed in " Macbeth " (iv. 1):

> " I'll charm the air to give a sound
> While you perform your antic round."

Witches also were supposed to have the power of vanishing at will, a notion referred to in " Macbeth " (i. 3), where, in reply to Banquo's inquiry as to whither the witches are vanished, Macbeth replies:

> " Into the air; and what seem'd corporal melted
> As breath into the wind."

In his letter to his wife he likewise observes: " They made themselves air, into which they vanished." Hecate, in the third act, fifth scene, after giving instructions to the weird host, says:

> " I am for the air; this night I'll spend
> Unto a dismal and a fatal end."

To this purpose they prepared various ointments, concerning which Reginald Scot[1] says: "The devil teacheth them to make ointment of the bowels and members of children, whereby they ride in the air and accomplish all their desires. After burial they steal them out of their graves and seethe them in a caldron till the flesh be made potable, of which they make an ointment by which they ride in the air." Lord Bacon also informs us that the "ointment the witches use is reported to be made of the fat of children digged out of their graves, of the juices of smallage, wolfbane, and cinquefoil, mingled with the meal of fine wheat; but I suppose the soporiferous medicines are likest to do it, which are henbane, hemlock, mandrake, moonshade — or rather nightshade—tobacco, opium, saffron,"[2] etc.　These witch recipes, which are very numerous, are well illustrated in Shakespeare's grim caldron scene, in "Macbeth" (iv. 1), where the first witch speaks of

> "grease that's sweaten
> From the murderer's gibbet."

We may compare a similar notion given by Apuleius, who, in describing the process used by the witch, Milo's wife, for transforming herself into a bird, says: "That she cut the lumps of flesh of such as were hanged."[3]

Another way by which witches exercise their power was by looking into futurity, as in "Macbeth" (i. 3), where Banquo says to them:

> "If you can look into the seeds of time,
> And say which grain will grow and which will not,
> Speak then to me."

Charles Knight, in his biography of Shakespeare, quotes a witch trial, which aptly illustrates the passage above; the

---

[1] "Discovery of Witchcraft," 1584, book iii. chap. i. p. 40; see Spalding's "Elizabethan Demonology," p. 103.

[2] See Brand's "Pop. Antiq.," vol. iii. pp. 8–10.

[3] Douce, "Illustrations of Shakespeare," p. 245, says: "See Adlington's Translation (1596, p. 49), a book certainly used by Shakespeare on other occasions."

case being that of Johnnet Wischert, who was "indicted for passing to the green-growing corn in May, twenty-two years since, or thereby, sitting thereupon tymous in the morning before the sun-rising; and being there found and demanded what she was doing, thus answered, I shall tell thee; I have been piling the blades of the corn. I find it will be a dear year; the blade of the corn grows withersones [contrary to the course of the sun], and when it grows sonegatis about [with the course of the sun], it will be a good, cheap year."

According to a common notion firmly believed in days gone by, witches were supposed to make waxen figures of those they intended to harm, which they stuck through with pins, or melted before a slow fire. Then, as the figure wasted, so the person it represented was said to waste away also. Thus, in "Macbeth" (i. 3), the first witch says:

> "Weary sev'n-nights, nine times nine,
> Shall he dwindle, peak, and pine."

Referring to the histories of the Duchess of Gloucester and of Jane Shore, who were accused of practising this mode of witchcraft, Shakespeare, in "2 Henry VI." (i. 2), makes the former address Hume thus:

> "What say'st thou, man? hast thou as yet conferr'd
> With Margery Jourdain, the cunning witch,
> With Roger Bolingbroke, the conjurer?
> And will they undertake to do me good?"

She was afterwards, however, accused of consulting witches concerning the mode of compassing the death of her husband's nephew, Henry VI. It was asserted that "there was found in the possession of herself and accomplices a waxen image of the king, which they melted in a magical manner before a slow fire, with the intention of making Henry's force and vigor waste away by like insensible degrees."

A similar charge was brought against Jane Shore, the mistress of Edward IV., by Richard, Duke of Gloucester. Thus, in "King Richard III." (iii. 4), Gloucester asks Hastings:

> "I pray you all, tell me what they deserve
> That do conspire my death with devilish plots

> Of damned witchcraft, and that have prevail'd
> Upon my body with their hellish charms?"

And he then further adds:

> "Look how I am bewitch'd; behold mine arm
> Is, like a blasted sapling, wither'd up:
> And this is Edward's wife, that monstrous witch,
> Consorted with that harlot, strumpet Shore,
> That by their witchcraft thus have marked me."

This superstition is further alluded to in " King John " (v. 4) by Melun, who, wounded, says:

> "Have I not hideous death within my view,
> Retaining but a quantity of life,
> Which bleeds away, even as a form of wax
> Resolveth from his figure 'gainst the fire?"

And, again, in " The Two Gentlemen of Verona " (ii. 4), Proteus says:

> "for now my love is thaw'd;
> Which, like a waxen image 'gainst a fire,
> Bears no impression of the thing it was."[1]

Images were frequently formed of other materials, and maltreated in some form or other, to produce similar results —a piece of superstition which still prevails to a great extent in the East. Dubois, in his " People of India " (1825), speaks of magicians who make small images in mud or clay, and then write the names of their animosity on the breasts thereof; these are otherwise pierced with thorns or mutilated, " so as to communicate a corresponding injury to the person represented." They were also said to extract moisture from the body, as in " Macbeth " (i. 3):

> "I will drain him dry as hay."

Referring to the other mischievous acts of witches, Steevens quotes the following from " A Detection of Damnable Driftes Practised by Three Witches, etc., arraigned at Chelmisforde, in Essex, 1579:" " Item—Also she came on a tyme to the house of one Robert Lathburie, who, dislyking

---

[1] See Henderson's " Folk-Lore of the Northern Counties," 1879, p. 181.

her dealyng, sent her home emptie; but presently after her departure his hogges fell sicke and died, to the number of twentie." Hence in "Macbeth" (i. 3) in reply to the inquiry of the first witch:

> "Where hast thou been, sister?"

the second replies:

> "Killing swine."

It appears to have been their practice to destroy the cattle of their neighbors, and the farmers have to this day many ceremonies to secure their cows and other cattle from witchcraft; but they seem to have been most suspected of malice against swine. Harsnet observes how, formerly, " A sow could not be ill of the measles, nor a girl of the sullens, but some old woman was charged with witchcraft." [1]

Mr. Henderson, in his "Folk-Lore of the Northern Counties" (1879, p. 182), relates how a few years ago a witch died in the village of Bovey Tracey, Devonshire. She was accused of "overlooking" her neighbors' pigs, so that her son, if ever betrayed into a quarrel with her, used always to say, before they parted, "Mother, mother, spare my pigs."

Multiples of three and nine were specially employed by witches, ancient and modern. Thus, in "Macbeth" (i. 3), the witches take hold of hands and dance round in a ring nine times—three rounds for each witch, as a charm for the furtherance of her purposes: [2]

> "Thrice to thine and thrice to mine,
> And thrice again, to make up nine.
> Peace! the charm's wound up."

The love of witches for odd numbers is further illustrated (iv. 1), where one of them tells how

> "Thrice and once the hedge-pig whined,"

this being the witches' way of saying four times.

In Fairfax's "Tasso" (book xiii. stanza 6) it is said that

> "Witchcraft loveth numbers odd."

---

[1] See *Pig*, chap. vi.
[2] "Notes to Macbeth," by Clark and Wright, 1877, p. 84.

This notion is very old, and we may compare the following quotations from Ovid's " Metamorphoses " (xiv. 58):

> " Ter novies carmen magico demurmurat ore."

And, again (vii. 189–191):

> " Ter se convertit ; ter sumtis flumine crinem
> Irroravit aquis ; ternis ululatibus ora
> Solvit."

Vergil, too, in his " Eclogues " (viii. 75), says:

> " Numero deus impare gaudet."

The belief in the luck of odd numbers is noticed by Falstaff in the " Merry Wives of Windsor " (v. 1):

> " They say there is divinity in odd numbers, either in nativity, chance, or death !"

In " King Lear " (iv. 2) when the Duke of Albany tells Goneril,

> " She that herself will sliver and disbranch
> From her material sap, perforce must wither
> And come to deadly use "—

he alludes to the use that witches and enchanters were commonly supposed to make of withered branches in their charms.[1]

Among other items of witch-lore mentioned by Shakespeare may be noticed the common belief in the intercourse between demons and witches, to which Prospero alludes in the " Tempest " (i. 2):

> " Thou poisonous slave, got by the devil himself
> Upon thy wicked dam, come forth !"

This notion is seriously refuted by Scot in his " Discovery of Witchcraft " (book iv.), where he shows it to be " flat knavery."

The offspring of a witch was termed " Hag-seed," and as such is spoken of by Prospero in the " Tempest " (i. 2).

Witches were also in the habit of saying their prayers

---

[1] See Jones's " Credulities, Past and Present," 1880, pp. 256–289.

backwards; a practice to which Hero refers in " Much Ado About Nothing" (iii. 1), where, speaking of Beatrice, she says:

> " I never yet saw man,
> How wise, how noble, young, how rarely featured,
> But she would spell him backward."

Familiar spirits [1] attending on magicians and witches were always impatient of confinement.[2] So in the " Tempest" (i. 2) we find an illustration of this notion in the following dialogue:

> "*Prospero.* What is't thou canst demand?
> *Ariel.* My liberty.
> *Prospero.* Before the time be out? No more."

Lastly, the term " Aroint thee " (" Macbeth," i. 3), used by the first witch, occurs again in " King Lear" (iii. 4), " Aroint thee, witch, aroint thee." That *aroint* is equivalent to "away," " begone," seems to be agreed, though its etymology is uncertain.[3] " Rynt thee " is used by milkmaids in Cheshire to a cow, when she has been milked, to bid her get out of the way. Ray, in his " Collection of North Country Words" (1768, p. 52), gives " Rynt ye, by your leave, stand handsomely, as rynt you witch, quoth Bessie Locket to her mother. Proverb, Chesh." Some connect it with the adverb " aroume," meaning " abroad," found in Chaucer's " House of Fame " (book ii. stanza 32):

> " That I a-roume was in the field."

Other derivations are from the Latin *averrunco:* the Italian *rogna*, a cutaneous disease, etc.

How thoroughly Shakespeare was acquainted with the

---

[1] Allusions to this superstition occur in " Love's Labour's Lost" (i. 2), " love is a familiar ;" in " 1 Henry VI." (iii. 2), " I think her old familiar is asleep; and in " 2 Henry VI." (iv. 7), " he has a familiar under his tongue."

[2] See Scot's " Discovery of Witchcraft," 1584, p. 85.

[3] See Dyce's " Glossary," pp. 18, 19.

system of witchcraft is evident from the preceding pages, in which we have noticed his allusions to most of the prominent forms of this species of superstition. Many other items of witch-lore, however, are referred to by him, mention of which is made in succeeding chapters.[1]

---

[1] " Notes to Macbeth " (Clark and Wright), pp. 81, 82.

CHAPTER III.

GHOSTS.

FEW subjects have, from time immemorial, possessed a wider interest than ghosts, and the superstitions associated with them in this and other countries form an extensive collection in folk-lore literature. In Shakespeare's day, it would seem that the belief in ghosts was specially prevalent, and ghost tales were told by the firelight in nearly every household. The young, as Mr. Goadby, in his " England of Shakespeare," says (1881, p. 196), " were thus touched by the prevailing superstitions in their most impressionable years. They looked for the incorporeal creatures of whom they had heard, and they were quick to invest any trick of moon-beam shadow with the attributes of the supernatural." A description of one of these tale-tellings is given in the " Winter's Tale " (ii. 1):

> "*Her.* What wisdom stirs amongst you ?   Come, sir, now
> I am for you again : pray you, sit by us,
> And tell's a tale.
>   *Mam.*   Merry or sad shall't be ?
>   *Her.* As merry as you will.
>   *Mam.*   A sad tale's best for winter :
> I have one of sprites and goblins.
>   *Her.*   Let's have that, good sir.
> Come on, sit down : Come on, and do your best
> To fright me with your sprites : you're powerful at it.
>   *Mam.* There was a man,—
>   *Her.*   Nay, come, sit down ; then on.
>   *Mam.* Dwelt by a churchyard : I will tell it softly ;
> Yond crickets shall not hear it.
>   *Her.*   Come on, then,
> And give't me in mine ear."

The important part which Shakespeare has assigned to the ghost in " Hamlet " has a special value, inasmuch as it illustrates many of the old beliefs current in his day respecting their history and habits. Thus, according to a popular notion, ghosts are generally supposed to assume the exact appearance by which they were usually known when in the material state, even to the smallest detail of their dress. So Horatio tells Hamlet how, when Marcellus and Bernardo were on their watch (i. 2),

> "A figure like your father,
> Arm'd at point, exactly, cap-a-pe,
> Appears before them, and with solemn march
> Goes slow and stately by them."

Further on, when the ghost appears again, Hamlet addresses it thus:

> "What may this mean,
> That thou, dead corse, again, in complete steel,
> Revisit'st thus the glimpses of the moon,
> 'Making night hideous."

In the graphic description of Banquo's ghost in "Macbeth" (iii. 4), we have a further allusion to the same belief; one, indeed, which is retained at the present day with as much faith as in days of old.

Shakespeare has several allusions to the notion which prevailed in days gone by, of certain persons being able to exorcise or raise spirits. Thus, in "Cymbeline" (iv. 2), Guiderius says over Fidele's grave:

> "No exorciser harm thee."

In "Julius Cæsar" (ii. 1), Ligarius says:

> "Soul of Rome!
> Brave son, derived from honourable loins!
> Thou, like an exorcist, hast conjured up
> My mortified spirit. Now bid me run,
> And I will strive with things impossible;
> Yea, get the better of them."

In "All's Well that Ends Well" (v. 3) the king says:

> "Is there no exorcist
> Beguiles the truer office of mine eyes?
> Is't real that I see?"

This superstition, it may be added, has of late years gained additional notoriety since the so-called spiritualism has attracted the attention and support of the credulous. As learning was considered necessary for an exorcist, the schoolmaster was often employed. Thus, in the " Comedy of Errors " (iv. 4), the schoolmaster Pinch is introduced in this capacity.

Within, indeed, the last fifty years the pedagogue was still a reputed conjurer. In " Hamlet " (i. 1), Marcellus, alluding to the ghost, says:

> " Thou art a scholar; speak to it, Horatio."

And in " Much Ado About Nothing " (ii. 1), Benedick says:

> " I would to God some scholar would conjure her."

For the same reason exorcisms were usually practised by the clergy in Latin ; and so Toby, in the " Night Walker " of Beaumont and Fletcher (ii. 1), says:

> " Let's call the butler up, for he speaks Latin,
> And that will daunt the devil."

It was also necessary that spirits, when evoked, should be questioned quickly, as they were supposed to be impatient of being interrogated. Hence in " Macbeth " (iv. 1) the apparition says:

> " Dismiss me. Enough !"

The spirit, likewise, in " 2 Henry VI." (i. 4) utters these words:

> " Ask what thou wilt. That I had said and done !"

Spirits were supposed to maintain an obdurate silence till interrogated by the persons to whom they made their special appearance.[1] Thus Hamlet, alluding to the appearance of the ghost, asks Horatio (i. 2):

> " Did you not speak to it ?"

---

[1] We may compare the words " unquestionable spirit" in " As You Like It " (iii. 2), which means " a spirit averse to conversation."

Whereupon he replies:

> " My lord, I did ;
> But answer made it none : yet once, methought
> It lifted up its head and did address
> Itself to motion, like as it would speak."

The walking of spirits seems also to have been enjoined by way of penance. The ghost of Hamlet's father (i. 5) says:

> " I am thy father's spirit,
> Doom'd for a certain term to walk the night,
> And for the day confin'd to fast in fires,
> Till the foul crimes done in my days of nature
> Are burnt and purg'd away."

And further on (iii. 2) Hamlet exclaims:

> " It is a damned ghost that we have seen."

This superstition is referred to by Spenser in his " Fairy Queen " (book i. canto 2):

> " What voice of damned ghost from Limbo lake
> Or guileful spright wand'ring in empty ayre,
> Sends to my doubtful eares these speeches rare ?"

According to a universal belief prevalent from the earliest times, it was supposed that ghosts had some particular reason for quitting the mansions of the dead, " such as a desire that their bodies, if unburied, should receive Christian rites of sepulture, that a murderer might be brought to due punishment," etc.[1] On this account Horatio (" Hamlet," i. 1) invokes the ghost:

> " If there be any good thing to be done,
> That may to thee do ease and grace to me,
> Speak to me."

And in a later scene (i. 4) Hamlet says:

> " Say, why is this ? wherefore ?   What should we do ?"

The Greeks believed that such as had not received funeral rites would be excluded from Elysium ; and thus the wan-

---

[1] Douce's " Illustrations of Shakespeare," pp. 450, 451.

dering shade of Patroclus appears to Achilles in his sleep, and demands the performance of his funeral. The younger Pliny tells a story of a haunted house at Athens, in which a ghost played all kinds of pranks, owing to his funeral rites having been neglected. A further reference to the superstition occurs in "Titus Andronicus" (i. 1), where Lucius, speaking of the unburied sons of Titus, says:

> "Give us the proudest prisoner of the Goths,
> That we may hew his limbs, and, on a pile,
> *Ad manes fratrum* sacrifice his flesh,
> Before this earthy prison of their bones;
> That so the shadows be not unappeased,
> Nor we disturbed with prodigies on earth."

In olden times, spirits were said to have different allotments of time, suitable to the variety and nature of their agency. Prospero, in the "Tempest" (i. 2), says to Caliban:

> "Be sure, to-night thou shalt have cramps,
> Side-stitches that shall pen thy breath up; urchins
> Shall, for that vast [1] of night that they may work,
> All exercise on thee."

According to a popular notion, the presence of unearthly beings was announced by an alteration in the tint of the lights which happened to be burning—a superstition alluded to in "Richard III." (v. 3), where the tyrant exclaims, as he awakens:

> "The lights burn blue.—It is now dead midnight,
> Cold fearful drops stand on my trembling flesh—
>   *   *   *   *   *
> Methought the souls of all that I had murder'd
> Came to my tent."

So in "Julius Cæsar" (iv. 3), Brutus, on seeing the ghost of Cæsar, exclaims:

> "How ill this taper burns! Ha! who comes here?"

It has been a wide-spread belief from the most remote

---

[1] Vast, *i. e.*, space of night. So in "Hamlet" (i. 2):
"In the dead waste and middle of the night."

period that ghosts cannot bear the light, and so disappear at the dawn of day; their signal being the cock-crow.[1] The ghost of Hamlet's father says (i. 5):

> " But, soft! methinks I scent the morning air;
> Brief let me be "—

and—

> " Fare thee well at once.
> The glow-worm shows the matin to be near,
> And 'gins to pale his uneffectual fire:
> Adieu, adieu! Hamlet, remember me."

Again, in " King Lear" (iii. 4), Edgar says: " This is the foul fiend Flibbertigibbet: he begins at curfew, and walks till the first cock."

The time of night, as the season wherein spirits wander abroad, is further noticed by Gardiner in " Henry VIII." (v. 1):

> " Affairs, that walk,
> As they say spirits do, at midnight."

It was a prevalent notion that a person who crossed the spot on which a spectre was seen became subject to its malignant influence. In " Hamlet " (i. 1), Horatio says, in reference to the ghost:

> " But soft, behold! lo, where it comes again!
> I'll cross it, though it blast me."

Lodge, in his " Illustrations of British History " (iii. 48), tells us that among the reasons for supposing the death of Ferdinand, Earl of Derby (who died young, in 1594), to have been occasioned by witchcraft, was the following: " On Friday there appeared a tall man, who twice crossed him swiftly; and when the earl came to the place where he saw this man, he fell sick."

Reginald Scot, in his " Discovery of Witchcraft " (1584), enumerates the different kinds of spirits, and particularly notices white, black, gray, and red spirits. " So in " Macbeth " (iv. 1), " black spirits " are mentioned — the charm

---

[1] See p. 104.

song referred to (like the one in act iv.) being found in Middleton's " Witch " (v. 2):

> " Black spirits and white,
> Red spirits and gray;
> Mingle, mingle, mingle,
> You that mingle may."

A well-known superstition which still prevails in this and foreign countries is that of the " spectre huntsman and his furious host." As night-time approaches, it is supposed that this invisible personage rides through the air with his yelping hounds; their weird sound being thought to forbode misfortune of some kind. This popular piece of folk-lore exists in the north of England under a variety of forms among our peasantry, who tenaciously cling to the traditions which have been handed down to them.[1] It has been suggested that Shakespeare had some of these superstitions in view when he placed in the mouth of Macbeth (i. 7), while contemplating the murder of Duncan, the following metaphors:

> " And pity, like a naked new-born babe,
> Striding the blast, or heaven's cherubim, horsed
> Upon the sightless couriers of the air,
> Shall blow the horrid deed in every eye,
> That tears shall drown the wind !"

Again, in " The Tempest " (iv. 1), Prospero and Ariel are represented as setting on spirits, in the shape of hounds, to hunt Stephano and Trinculo. This species of diabolical or spectral chase was formerly a popular article of belief. As Drake aptly remarks,[2] " the hell-hounds of Shakespeare appear to be sufficiently formidable, for, not merely commissioned to hunt their victims, they are ordered, likewise, as goblins," to—

> "grind their joints
> With dry convulsions; shorten up their sinews

---

[1] See Hardwick's " Traditions, Superstitions, and Folk-lore," 1872, pp. 153–176.

[2] " Shakespeare and His Times," vol. i. p. 378.

With aged cramps; and more pinch-spotted make them
Than pard or cat o' mountain.
    Ariel.   Hark, they roar!
    Prospero. Let them be hunted soundly."

TRANSMIGRATION OF SOULS.

Shakespeare has several references to the old superstitious belief in the transmigration of souls, traces of which may still be found in the reverence paid to the robin, the wren, and other birds. Thus, in "The Merchant of Venice" (iv. 1), Gratiano says to Shylock:

> "Thou almost makest me waver in my faith
> To hold opinion with Pythagoras
> That souls of animals infuse themselves
> Into the trunks of men: thy currish spirit
> Govern'd a wolf, who, hang'd for human slaughter,
> Even from the gallows did his fell soul fleet,
> And, whilst thou lay'st in thy unhallow'd dam,
> Infused itself in thee; for thy desires
> Are wolfish, bloody, starved, and ravenous."

Caliban, when remonstrating with the drunken Stephano and Trinculo, for delaying at the mouth of the cave of Prospero, instead of taking the magician's life ("Tempest," iv. 1), says:

> "I will have none on't: we shall lose our time,
> And all be turn'd to barnacles, or to apes."

In "Hamlet" (iv. 5), in the scene where Ophelia, in her mental aberration, quotes snatches of old ballads, she says: "They say the owl was a baker's daughter! Lord, we know what we are, but know not what we may be." [1]

Again, in "Twelfth Night" (iv. 2), there is another reference in the amusing passage where the clown, under the pretence of his being "Sir Topas, the curate," questions Malvolio, when confined in a dark room, as a presumed lunatic:

---

[1] See *Owl*, chap. vi.

"*Mal.* I am no more mad than you are : make the trial of it in any constant question.

Clo. What is the opinion of Pythagoras concerning wild fowl ?

Mal. That the soul of our grandam might haply inhabit a bird.

Clo. What thinkest thou of his opinion ?

Mal. I think nobly of the soul, and no way approve his opinion.

Clo. Fare thee well.   Remain thou still in darkness : thou shalt hold the opinion of Pythagoras ere I will allow of thy wits, and fear to kill a woodcock lest thou dispossess the soul of thy grandam."

Although this primitive superstition is almost effete among civilized nations, yet it still retains an important place in the religious beliefs of savage and uncivilized communities.

CHAPTER IV.

DEMONOLOGY AND DEVIL-LORE.

THE state of popular feeling in past centuries with regard to the active agency of devils has been well represented by Reginald Scot, who, in his work on Witchcraft, has shown how the superstitious belief in demonology was part of the great system of witchcraft. Many of the popular delusions of this terrible form of superstition have been in a masterly manner exposed by Shakespeare; and the scattered allusions which he has given, illustrative of it, are indeed sufficient to prove, if it were necessary, what a highly elaborate creed it was. Happily, Shakespeare, like the other dramatists of the period, has generally treated the subject with ridicule, showing that he had no sympathy with the grosser opinions shared by various classes in those times, whether held by king or clown. According to an old belief, still firmly credited in the poet's day, it was supposed that devils could at any moment assume whatever form they pleased that would most conduce to the success of any contemplated enterprise they might have in hand; and hence the charge of being a devil, so commonly brought against innocent and harmless persons in former years, can easily be understood. Among the incidental allusions to this notion, given by Shakespeare, Prince Hal ("1 Henry IV.," ii. 4) tells Falstaff "there is a devil haunts thee in the likeness of an old fat man;" "an old white-bearded Satan." In the "Merchant of Venice" (iii. 1) Salanio, on the approach of Shylock, says: "Let me say 'amen' betimes, lest the devil cross my prayer, for here he comes in the likeness of a Jew."

Indeed, "all shapes that man goes up and down in" seem to have been at the devil's control, a belief referred to in "Timon of Athens" (ii. 2):

"*Var. Serv.* What is a whoremaster, fool?

Fool. A fool in good clothes, and something like thee. 'Tis a spirit: sometime 't appears like a lord; sometime like a lawyer; sometime like a philosopher, with two stones moe than's artificial one: he is very often like a knight; and, generally, in all shapes that man goes up and down in from fourscore to thirteen, this spirit walks in."

A popular form assumed by evil spirits was that of a negro or Moor, to which Iago alludes when he incites Brabantio to search for his daughter, in "Othello" (i. 1):

> "Zounds, sir, you are robb'd; for shame, put on your gown;
> Your heart is burst, you have lost half your soul;
> Even now, now, very now, an old black ram
> Is tupping your white ewe. Arise, arise!
> Awake the snorting citizens with the bell,
> Or else the devil will make a grandsire of you.
> Arise, I say."

On the other hand, so diverse were the forms which devils were supposed to assume that they are said occasionally to appear in the fairest form, even in that of a girl (ii. 3):

> "When devils will the blackest sins put on,
> They do suggest at first with heavenly shows."

So in "The Comedy of Errors" (iv. 3) we have the following dialogue:

"*Ant. S.* Satan, avoid! I charge thee, tempt me not!

Dro. S. Master, is this mistress Satan?

Ant. S. It is the devil.

Dro. S. Nay, she is worse, she is the devil's dam; and here she comes in the habit of a light wench; and thereof comes that the wenches say, 'God damn me;' that's as much as to say, 'God make me a light wench.' It is written, they appear to men like angels of light."

(Cf. also "Love's Labour's Lost," iv. 3.) In "King John" (iii. 1) even the fair Blanch seemed to Constance none other than the devil tempting Lewis "in likeness of a new untrimmed bride."

Not only, too, were devils thought to assume any human shape they fancied, but, as Mr. Spalding remarks,[1] "the forms

---

[1] "Elizabethan Demonology," p. 49.

of the whole of the animal kingdom appear to have been at
their disposal; and, not content with these, they seem to
have sought for unlikely shapes to appear in"—the same
characteristic belonging also to the fairy tribe.

Thus, when Edgar is trying to persuade the blind Gloucester that he has in reality cast himself over the cliff, he describes the being from whom he is supposed to have just
departed:

> " As I stood here below, methought his eyes
> Were two full moons; he had a thousand noses,
> Horns whelk'd and wav'd like the enridged sea:
> It was some fiend."

Again, Edgar says (" King Lear," iii. 6): " The foul fiend
haunts poor Tom in the voice of a nightingale "—the allusion probably being to the following incident related by
Friswood Williams: " There was also another strange thing
happened at Denham about a bird. Mistris Peckham had
a nightingale which she kept in a cage, wherein Maister Dibdale took great delight, and would often be playing with it.
The nightingale was one night conveyed out of the cage,
and being next morning diligently sought for, could not be
heard of, till Maister Mainie's devil, in one of his fits (as it
was pretended), said that the wicked spirit which was in this
examinate's sister had taken the bird out of the cage and
killed it in despite of Maister Dibdale." [1]

Even the shape of a fly was a favorite one with evil spirits, so much so, that the term " fly " was a popular synonym
for a familiar. In " Titus Andronicus " (iii. 2) there is an
allusion to this belief, where Marcus, being rebuked by Titus
for having killed a fly, gives as his reason:

> " It was a black ill-favour'd fly,
> Like to the empress' Moor: therefore I kill'd him."

Mr. Spalding gives the following illustrations of the superstition: " At the execution of Urban Grandier, the famous
magician of London, in 1634, a large fly was seen buzzing

---

[1] Harsnet's " Declaration of Egregious Popish Impostures," p. 225.

about the stake; and a priest promptly seizing the opportunity of improving the occasion for the benefit of the onlookers, declared that Beelzebub had come in his own proper person to carry off Grandier's soul to hell. In 1664 occurred the celebrated witch trials which took place before Sir Matthew Hale. The accused were charged with bewitching two children, and part of the evidence against them was that flies and bees were seen to carry into their victims' mouths the nails and pins which they afterwards vomited."

Once more, another form devils assumed was that of a dead friend. Thus "Hamlet" (i. 4), when he confronts the apparition, exclaims:

> "Angels and ministers of grace defend us!
> Be thou a spirit of health, or goblin damn'd,
> Bring with thee airs from heaven, or blasts from hell,
> Be thy intents wicked, or charitable,
> Thou com'st in such a questionable shape
> That I will speak to thee"—

for, as Mr. Spalding remarks, "it cannot be imagined that Hamlet imagined that a 'goblin damned' could actually be the spirit of his dead father; and, therefore, the alternative in his mind must be that he saw a devil assuming his father's likeness—a form which the Evil One knew would most incite Hamlet to intercourse."

The same idea seems present in Horatio's mind:

> "What, if it tempt you toward the flood, my lord,
> Or to the dreadful summit of the cliff,
> That beetles o'er his base into the sea,
> And there assume some other horrible form,
> Which might deprive your sovereignty of reason,
> And draw you into madness?"

Once more, in the next act (ii. 2), Hamlet again expresses his doubts:

> "The spirit that I have seen
> May be the devil: and the devil hath power
> To assume a pleasing shape; yea, and, perhaps,
> Out of my weakness and my melancholy,
> As he is very potent with such spirits,
> Abuses me to damn me."

In the Elizabethan times, too, no superstitious belief exerted a more pernicious and baneful influence on the credulous and ignorant than the notion that evil spirits from time to time entered into human beings, and so completely gained a despotic control over them as to render them perfectly helpless. Harsnet, in his " Declaration of Egregious Popish Impostures" (1603), has exposed this gross superstition; and a comparison of the passages in " King Lear," spoken by Edgar when feigning madness, with those given by Harsnet, will show that Shakespeare has accurately given the contemporary belief on the subject. Mr. Spalding also considers that nearly all the allusions in " King Lear" refer to a youth known as Richard Mainey, a minute account of whose supposed possession has been given by Harsnet.

Persons so possessed were often bound and shut up in a dark room, occasionally being forced to submit to flagellation—a treatment not unlike that described in " Romeo and Juliet" (i. 2):

> " Not mad, but bound more than a madman is;
> Shut up in prison, kept without my food,
> Whipp'd and tormented."

In the " Comedy of Errors" (iv. 4) we have an amusing scene, further illustrative, probably, of the kind of treatment adopted in Shakespeare's day:

> " *Courtesan.* How say you now? is not your husband mad?
> *Adriana.*   His incivility confirms no less—
>   Good doctor Pinch, you are a conjurer;
>   Establish him in his true sense again,
>   And I will please you what you will demand.
> *Luciana.*   Alas, how fiery and how sharp he looks!
> *Courtesan.* Mark how he trembles in his ecstasy!
> *Pinch.*   Give me your hand, and let me feel your pulse.
> *Ant. E.*   There is my hand, and let it feel your ear.
> *Pinch.*   I charge thee, Satan, hous'd within this man,
>   To yield possession to my holy prayers,
>   And to thy state of darkness hie thee straight:
>   I conjure thee by all the saints in heaven."

Pinch further says:

> " They must be bound, and laid in some dark room."

As Brand remarks,[1] there is no vulgar story of the devil's having appeared anywhere without a cloven foot. In graphic representations he is seldom or never pictured without one. In the following passage, where Othello is questioning whether Iago is a devil or not, he says (v. 2):

> "I look down towards his feet;—but that's a fable.—
> If that thou be'st a devil, I cannot kill thee."

Dr. Johnson gives this explanation: "I look towards his feet to see if, according to the common opinion, his feet be cloven."

In Massinger's "Virgin Martyr" (iii. 3), Harpax, an evil spirit, following Theophilus in the shape of a secretary, speaks thus of the superstitious Christian's description of his infernal enemy:

> "I'll tell you what now of the devil:
> He's no such horrid creature; cloven-footed,
> Black, saucer-ey'd, his nostrils breathing fire,
> As these lying Christians make him."

GOOD AND EVIL DEMONS.

It was formerly commonly believed that not only kingdoms had their tutelary guardians, but that every person had his particular genius or good angel, to protect and admonish him by dreams, visions, etc.[2] Hence, in "Antony and Cleopatra" (ii. 3), the soothsayer, speaking of Cæsar, says:

> "O Antony, stay not by his side:
> Thy demon,—that's thy spirit which keeps thee,—is
> Noble, courageous, high, unmatchable,
> Where Cæsar's is not; but, near him, thy angel
> Becomes a fear, as being o'erpower'd."

Thus Macbeth (iii. 1) speaks in a similar manner in reference to Banquo:

---

[1] "Pop. Antiq.," 1849, vol. ii. pp. 517–519.
[2] Ibid. vol. i. pp. 365–367.

> "There is none but he
> Whose being I do fear; and, under him,
> My Genius is rebuked; as, it is said,
> Mark Antony's was by Cæsar."

So, too, in "2 Henry IV." (i. 2), the Chief-justice says:

> "You follow the young prince up and down, like his ill angel."

We may quote a further reference in "Julius Cæsar" (iii. 2), where Antony says:

> "For Brutus, as you know, was Cæsar's angel."

"In the Roman world," says Mr. Tylor, in his "Primitive Culture" (1873, vol. ii. p. 202), "each man had his 'genius natalis,' associated with him from birth to death, influencing his action and his fate, standing represented by its proper image, as a *lar* among the household gods and at weddings and joyous times, and especially on the anniversary of the birthday when genius and man began their united career, worship was paid with song and dance to the divine image, adorned with garlands, and propitiated with incense and libations of wine. The demon or genius was, as it were, the man's companion soul, a second spiritual Ego. The Egyptian astrologer warned Antonius to keep far from the young Octavius, 'For thy demon,' said he, 'is in fear of his.'"

The allusion by Lady Macbeth (i. 5), in the following passage, is to the spirits of Revenge:

> "Come, you spirits
> That tend on mortal thoughts, unsex me here,
> And fill me, from the crown to the toe, top-full
> Of direst cruelty!"

In Nash's "Pierce Pennilesse" we find a description of these spirits and of their office. "The second kind of devils which he most employeth are those northern *Martii*, called the *Spirits of Revenge*, and the authors of massacres and seed-men of mischief; for they have commission to incense men to rapine, sacrilege, theft, murder, wrath, fury, and all manner of cruelties; and they command certain of the southern spirits to wait upon them, as also great Arioch, that is termed the Spirit of Revenge." In another passage we are further told how "'the spirits of the aire will mixe themselves with thunder and lightning, and so infect the clime where they raise any tempest, that suddenly great mortalitie shall ensue of the inhabitants." "Aerial spirits or devils," according to Burton's "Anatomy of Melancholy," "are such as keep quarter most part in the aire, cause many tempests, thunder and lightnings, tear oakes, fire steeples, houses, strike men and beasts," etc. Thus, in "King John" (iii. 2), the Bastard remarks:

> "Now, by my life, this day grows wondrous hot;
> Some airy devil hovers in the sky,
> And pours down mischief."

It was anciently supposed that all mines of gold, etc., were guarded by evil spirits. Thus Falstaff, in "2 Henry IV." (iv. 3), speaks of learning as "a mere hoard of gold kept by a devil." This superstition still prevails, and has been made the subject of many a legend. Thus, it is believed by the peasantry living near Largo-Law, Scotland, that a rich mine of gold is concealed in the mountain. "A spectre once appeared there, supposed to be the guardian of the mine, who, being accosted by a neighboring shepherd, promised to tell him at a certain time and on certain conditions, where 'the gowd mine is in Largo-Law,' especially enjoining that the horn sounded for the housing of the cows at the adjoining farm of Balmain should not blow. Every precaution having been taken, the ghost was true to his tryst; but, unhappily, when he was about to divulge the desired secret, Tammie Norrie, the cowherd of Balmain, blew a blast, whereupon the ghost vanished, with the denunciation:

> 'Woe to the man that blew the horn,
> For out of the spot he shall ne'er be borne.'

The unlucky horn-blower was struck dead, and, as it was found impossible to remove the body, a cairn of stones was raised over it." [1]

---

[1] See Jones's "Credulities, Past and Present," 1880, p. 133.

Steevens considers that when Macbeth (iii. 2) says:

> "Good things of day begin to droop and drowse;
> Whiles night's black agents to their preys do rouse,"

he refers to those demons who were supposed to remain in their several places of confinement all day, but at the close of it were released; such, indeed, as are mentioned in "The Tempest" (v. 1), as rejoicing "to hear the solemn curfew," because it announced the hour of their freedom.

Among other superstitions we may quote one in the "Merchant of Venice" (iii. 1), where Salanio says: "Let me say 'amen' betimes, lest the devil cross my prayer."

Of the devils mentioned by Shakespeare may be noted the following:

Amaimon is one of the chief, whose dominion is on the north side of the infernal gulf. He might be bound or restrained from doing hurt from the third hour till noon, and from the ninth hour till evening. In the "Merry Wives of Windsor" (ii. 2) Ford mentions this devil, and in "1 Henry IV." (ii. 4) Falstaff says: "That same mad fellow of the north, Percy; and he of Wales, that gave Amaimon the bastinado, and made Lucifer cuckold." [1]

The north was always supposed to be the particular habitation of bad spirits. Milton, therefore, assembles the rebel angels in the north. In "1 Henry VI." (v. 3), La Pucelle invokes the aid of the spirits:

> "Under the lordly monarch of the north."

Barbason. This demon would seem to be the same as "Marbas, alias Barbas," who, as Scot[2] informs us, "is a great president, and appeareth in the forme of a mightie lion; but at the commandment of a conjurer cometh up in the likeness of man, and answereth fullie as touching anything which is hidden or secret." In the "Merry Wives of Windsor" (ii. 2) it is mentioned by Ford in connection with Lucifer, and

---

[1] See Scot's "Discovery of Witchcraft," 1584, p. 393; Douce's "Illustrations of Shakespeare," p. 264.   [2] Ibid. p. 378.

again in " Henry V." (ii. 1) Nym tells Pistol: " I am not Barbason; you cannot conjure me."

The names of the several fiends in " King Lear," Shakespeare is supposed to have derived from Harsnet's " Declaration of Egregious Popish Impostures" (1603).

Flibbertigibbet, one of the fiends that possessed poor Tom, is, we are told (iv. 1), the fiend " of mopping and mowing, who since possesses chambermaids and waiting-women." And again (iii. 4), " he begins at curfew, and walks till the first cock; he gives the web and the pin."

Frateretto is referred to by Edgar (iii. 6): " Frateretto calls me; and tells me, Nero is an angler in the lake of darkness. Pray, innocent, and beware the foul fiend."

Hobbididance is noticed as " prince of dumbness" (iv. 1), and perhaps is the same as Hopdance (iii. 6), " who cries," says Edgar, " in Tom's belly for two white herring."

Mahu, like *Modo*, would seem to be another name for " the prince of darkness" (iii. 4), and further on (iv. 1) he is spoken of as the fiend " of stealing;" whereas the latter is described as the fiend " of murder." Harsnet thus speaks of them: " Maho was general dictator of hell; and yet, for good manners' sake, he was contented of his good nature to make show, that himself was under the check of Modu, the graund devil in Ma(ister) Maynie."

Obidicut, another name of the fiend known as Haberdicut (iv. 1).

Smulkin (iii. 4). This is spelled Smolkin by Harsnet.

Thus, in a masterly manner, Shakespeare has illustrated and embellished his plays with references to the demonology of the period; having been careful in every case—while enlivening his audience—to convince them of the utter absurdity of this degraded form of superstition.

CHAPTER V.

NATURAL PHENOMENA.

MANY of the most beautiful and graphic passages in Shakespeare's writings have pictured the sun in highly glowing language, and often invested it with that sweet pathos for which the poet was so signally famous. Expressions, for instance, such as the following, are ever frequent: "the glorious sun" ("Twelfth Night," iv. 3); "heaven's glorious sun" ("Love's Labour's Lost," i. 1); "gorgeous as the sun at midsummer" ("1 Henry IV.," iv. 1); "all the world is cheered by the sun" ("Richard III.," i. 2); "the sacred radiance of the sun" ("King Lear," i. 1); "sweet tidings of the sun's uprise" ("Titus Andronicus," iii. 1), etc. Then, again, how often we come across passages replete with pathos, such as "thy sun sets weeping in the lowly west" ("Richard II.," ii. 4); "ere the weary sun set in the west" ("Comedy of Errors," i. 2); "the weary sun hath made a golden set" ("Richard III.," v. 3); "The sun, for sorrow, will not show his head" ("Romeo and Juliet," v. 3), etc. Although, however, Shakespeare has made such constant mention of the sun, yet his allusions to the folk-lore connected with it are somewhat scanty.

According to the old philosophy the sun was accounted a planet,[1] and thought to be whirled round the earth by the motion of a solid sphere, in which it was fixed. In "Antony and Cleopatra" (iv. 13), Cleopatra exclaims:

> "O sun,
> Burn the great sphere thou mov'st in! darkling stand
> The varying shore o' the world."

Supposing this sphere consumed, the sun must wander in

---

[1] Singer's "Shakespeare," vol. x. p. 292.

endless space, and, as a natural consequence, the earth be involved in endless night.

In " 1 Henry IV." (i. 2), Falstaff, according to vulgar astronomy, calls the sun a "wandering knight," and by this expression evidently alludes to some knight of romance. Mr. Douce[1] considered the allusion was to " The Voyage of the Wandering Knight," by Jean de Cathenay, of which the translation, by W. Goodyeare, appeared about the year 1600. The words may be a portion of some forgotten ballad.

A pretty fancy is referred to in " Romeo and Juliet" (iii. 5), where Capulet says:

> " When the sun sets, the air doth drizzle dew;
> But for the sunset of my brother's son
> It rains downright."

And so, too, in the " Rape of Lucrece:"

> " But as the earth doth weep, the sun being set."

" That Shakespeare thought it was the air," says Singer,[2] " and not the earth, that drizzled dew, is evident from many passages in his works. Thus, in ' King John ' (ii. 1) he says: ' Before the dew of evening fall.'" Steevens, alluding to the following passage in " A Midsummer-Night's Dream" (iii. 1), " and when she [*i. c.*, the moon] weeps, weeps every little flower," says that Shakespeare "means that every little flower is moistened with dew, as if with tears; and not that the flower itself drizzles dew."

By a popular fancy, the sun was formerly said to dance at its rising on Easter morning—to which there may be an allusion in " Romeo and Juliet" (iii. 5), where Romeo, addressing Juliet, says:

> " look, love, what envious streaks
> Do lace the severing clouds in yonder east;
> Night's candles are burnt out, and jocund day
> Stands tiptoe on the misty mountain tops."

We may also compare the expression in "Coriolanus" (v. 4):

---

[1] "Illustrations of Shakespeare," 1839, pp. 255, 256.
[2] Singer's "Shakespeare," vol. viii. p. 208.

> " The trumpets, sackbuts, psalteries, and fifes,
>   Tabors, and cymbals, and the shouting Romans,
>   Make the sun dance."

Mr. Knight remarks, there was " something exquisitely beautiful in the old custom of going forth into the fields before the sun had risen on Easter Day, to see him mounting over the hills with tremulous motion, as if it were an animate thing, bounding in sympathy with the redeemed of mankind." [1]

A cloudy rising of the sun has generally been regarded as ominous—a superstition equally prevalent on the Continent as in this country.   In " Richard III." (v. 3), King Richard asks:

> " Who saw the sun to-day ?
>   *Ratcliff.*   Not I, my lord,
>   *K. Richard.* Then he disdains to shine ; for, by the book
> He should have braved the east an hour ago :
> A black day will it be to somebody."

" The learned Moresin, in his ' Papatus,' " says Brand, [2] " reckons among omens the cloudy rising of the sun." Vergil, too, in his first Georgic (441–449), considers it a sign of stormy weather : [3]

> " Ille ubi nascentem maculis variaverit ortum
>   Conditus in nubem, medioque refugerit orbe,
>   Suspecti tibi sint imbres ; namque urget ab alto
>   Arboribusque satisque Notus pecorique sinister,
>   Aut ubi sub lucem densa inter nubila sese
>   Diversi rumpent radii, aut ubi pallida surget,
>   Tithoni croceum linquens Aurora cubile,
>   Heu, male tum mitis defendet pampinus uvas :
>   Tam multa in tectis crepitans salit horrida grando."

A red sunrise is also unpropitious, and, according to a well-known rhyme :

> " If red the sun begins his race,
>   Be sure the rain will fall apace."

---

[1] See Knight's " Life of Shakespeare," 1843, p. 63.

[2] " Pop. Antiq.," 1849, vol. iii. p. 241.

[3] See Swainson's " Weather-Lore," 1873, p. 176, for popular adages on the Continent.

This old piece of weather-wisdom is mentioned by our Lord in St. Matthew, xvi. 2, 3: "When it is evening, ye say, It will be fair weather: for the sky is red. And in the morning, It will be foul weather to-day, for the sky is red and lowring." Shakespeare, in his "Venus and Adonis," thus describes it:

> "a red morn, that ever yet betoken'd
> Wreck to the seaman, tempest to the field,
> Sorrow to shepherds, woe unto the birds,
> Gusts and foul flaws to herdmen and to herds."

Mr. Swainson[1] shows that this notion is common on the Continent. Thus, at Milan the proverb runs, "If the morn be red, rain is at hand."

Shakespeare, in "Richard II." (ii. 4), alludes to another indication of rain:

> "Thy sun sets weeping in the lowly west,
> Witnessing storms to come, woe and unrest."

A "watery sunset" is still considered by many a forerunner of wet. A red sunset, on the other hand, beautifully described in "Richard III." (v. 3)—

> "The weary sun hath made a golden set,"—

is universally regarded as a prognostication of fine weather, and we find countless proverbs illustrative of this notion, one of the most popular being, "Sky red at night, is the sailor's delight."

From the earliest times an eclipse of the sun was looked upon as an omen of coming calamity; and was oftentimes the source of extraordinary alarm as well as the occasion of various superstitious ceremonies. In 1597, during an eclipse of the sun, it is stated that, at Edinburgh, men and women thought the day of judgment was come.[2] Many women swooned, much crying was heard in the streets, and in fear some ran to the kirk to pray. Mr. Napier says he remembers

---

[1] "Weather-Lore," pp. 175, 176.
[2] Napier's "Folk-Lore of West of Scotland," 1879, p. 141.

" an eclipse about 1818, when about three parts of the sun
was covered. The alarm in the village was very great, in-
door work was suspended for the time, and in several families
prayers were offered for protection, believing that it por-
tended some awful calamity; but when it passed off there
was a general feeling of relief." In " King Lear " (i. 2),
Gloucester remarks : " These late eclipses in the sun and
moon portend no good to us : though the wisdom of nature
can reason it thus and thus, yet nature finds itself scourged
by the sequent effects ; love cools, friendship falls off, brothers
divide ; in cities, mutinies ; in countries, discord ; in palaces,
treason ; and the bond cracked 'twixt son and father."
Othello, too (v. 2), in his agony and despair, exclaims :

> " O heavy hour !
> Methinks it should be now a huge eclipse
> Of sun and moon, and that the affrighted globe
> Should yawn at alteration."

Francis Bernier[1] says that, in France, in 1654, at an eclipse
of the sun, " some bought drugs against the eclipse, others
kept themselves close in the dark in their caves and their
well-closed chambers, others cast themselves in great multitudes into the churches ; those apprehending some malign
and dangerous influence, and these believing that they were
come to the last day, and that the eclipse would shake the
foundations of nature."[2]

In " 3 Henry VI." (ii. 1), Shakespeare refers to a curious
circumstance in which, on a certain occasion, the sun is reported to have appeared like three suns. Edward says, " do
I see three suns ?" to which Richard replies :

> " Three glorious suns, each one a perfect sun ;
> Not separated with the racking clouds,
> But sever'd in a pale clear-shining sky.
> See, see ! they join, embrace, and seem to kiss,
> As if they vow'd some league inviolable :

---

[1] Quoted in Southey's " Commonplace Book," 1849, 2d series, p. 462.
[2] See Tylor's " Primitive Culture," 1871, vol. i. pp. 261, 296, 297, 321.

Now are they but one lamp, one light, one sun,
In this the heaven figures some event."[1]

This fact is mentioned both by Hall and Holinshed; the latter says: "At which tyme the sun (as some write) appeared to the Earl of March like *three sunnes*, and sodainely joyned altogether in one, upon whiche sight hee tooke such courage, that he fiercely setting on his enemyes put them to flight." We may note here that on Trinity Sunday three suns are supposed to be seen. In the "Mémoires de l'Académie Celtique" (iii. 447), it is stated that " Le jour de la fête de la Trinité, quelques personne vont de grand matin dans la campagne, pour y voir levre trois soleils à la fois."

According to an old proverb, to quit a better for a worse situation was spoken of as to go " out of God's blessing into the warm sun," a reference to which we find in " King Lear" (ii. 2), where Kent says:

"Good king, that must approve the common saw,
Thou out of heaven's benediction com'st
To the warm sun."

Dr. Johnson thinks that Hamlet alludes to this saying (i. 2), for when the king says to him,

" How is it that the clouds still hang on you?"

he replies,

" Not so, my lord; I am too much i' the sun,"

i. e., out of God's blessing.

This expression, says Mr. Dyce,[2] is found in various authors from Heywood down to Swift. The former has:

" In your running from him to me, yee runne
Out of God's blessing into the warme sunne;"

and the latter:

---

[1] In " 3 Henry VI." (ii. 1), Edward says:

" henceforward will I bear
Upon my target three fair shining suns."

[2] " Glossary to Shakespeare," p. 283.

"*Lord Sparkish*. They say, marriages are made in heaven; but I doubt, when she was married, she had no friend there.

Neverout. Well, she's got out of God's blessing into the warm sun."[1]

There seems to have been a prejudice from time immemorial against sunshine in March; and, according to a German saying, it were "better to be bitten by a snake than to feel the sun in March." Thus, in "1 Henry IV." (iv. 1), Hotspur says:

> "worse than the sun in March,
> This praise doth nourish agues."

Shakespeare employs the word "sunburned" in the sense of uncomely, ill-favored. In "Much Ado" (ii. 1), Beatrice says, "I am sunburnt;" and in "Troilus and Cressida" (i. 3), Æneas remarks:

> "The Grecian dames are sunburnt, and not worth
> The splinter of a lance."

Moon. Apart from his sundry allusions to the "pale-faced," "silver moon," Shakespeare has referred to many of the superstitions associated with it, several of which still linger on in country nooks. A widespread legend of great antiquity informs us that the moon is inhabited by a man,[2] with a bundle of sticks on his back, who has been exiled thither for many centuries, and who is so far off that he is beyond the reach of death. This tradition, which has given rise to many superstitions, is still preserved under various forms in most countries; but it has not been decided who the culprit originally was, and how he came to be imprisoned in his lonely abode. Dante calls him Cain; Chaucer assigns his exile as a punishment for theft, and gives him a thorn-bush to carry, while Shakespeare also loads him with the thorns, but by way of compensation gives him a dog for a companion. In "The Tempest" (ii. 2), Caliban asks Stephano whether he has "not dropped from heaven?" to which he answers, "Out o' the moon, I do assure thee: I was the man i' the moon when time was." Whereupon Caliban

---

[1] Ray gives the Latin equivalent "Ab equis ad asinos."

[2] Baring-Gould's "Curious Myths of the Middle Ages," 1877, p. 190.

says: "I have seen thee in her and I do adore thee: my mistress show'd me thee, and thy dog and thy bush." We may also compare the expression in "A Midsummer-Night's Dream" (v. 1), where, in the directions for the performance of the play of "Pyramus and Thisbe," Moonshine is represented "with lanthorn, dog, and bush of thorn." And further on, in the same scene, describing himself, Moonshine says: "All that I have to say, is, to tell you that the lanthorn is the moon; I, the man in the moon;[1] this thorn-bush, my thorn-bush; and this dog, my dog."

Ordinarily,[2] however, his offence is stated to have been Sabbath-breaking—an idea derived from the Old Testament. Like the man mentioned in the Book of Numbers (xv. 32), he is caught gathering sticks on the Sabbath; and, as an example to mankind, he is condemned to stand forever in the moon, with his bundle on his back. Instead of a dog, one German version places him with a woman, whose crime was churning butter on Sunday. The Jews have a legend that Jacob is the moon, and they believe that his face is visible. Mr. Baring-Gould[3] says that the "idea of locating animals in the two great luminaries of heaven is very ancient, and is a relic of a primeval superstition of the Aryan race." The natives of Ceylon, instead of a man, have placed a hare in the moon; and the Chinese represent the moon by "a rabbit pounding rice in a mortar."[4]

From the very earliest times the moon has not only been an object of popular superstition, but been honored by various acts of adoration. In Europe,[5] in the fifteenth century, "it was a matter of complaint that some still worshipped the new moon with bended knee, or hood or hat removed. And to this day we may still see a hat raised to her, half in

---

[1] Cf. "Love's Labour's Lost" (v. 2): "Yet still she is the moon, and I the man."

[2] Fiske, "Myths and Mythmakers," 1873, p. 27.

[3] "Curious Myths of the Middle Ages," 1877, p. 197.

[4] Douce's "Illustrations of Shakespeare," 1839, p. 10.

[5] For further information on this subject, see Tylor's "Primitive Culture," 1873, vol. i. pp. 288, 354–356; vol. ii. pp. 70, 202, 203.

conservatism and half in jest. It is with deference to silver
as the lunar metal that money is turned when the act of
adoration is performed, while practical peasant wit dwells
on the ill-luck of having no piece of silver when the new
moon is first seen." Shakespeare often incidentally alludes
to this form of superstition. To quote one or two out of
many instances, Enobarbus, in "Antony and Cleopatra"
(iv. 9), says:

> "Be witness to me, O thou blessed moon!"

In "Love's Labour's Lost" (v. 2) the king says:

> "Vouchsafe, bright moon, and these thy stars, to shine,
> Those clouds removed, upon our watery eyne."

Indeed, it was formerly a common practice for people to address invocations to the moon,[1] and even at the present day
we find remnants of this practice both in this country and
abroad. Thus, in many places it is customary for young
women to appeal to the moon to tell them of their future
prospects in matrimony,[2] the following or similar lines being
repeated on the occasion:

> "New moon, new moon, I hail thee:
> New moon, new moon, be kind to me;
> If I marry man or man marry me,
> Show me how many moons it will be."

It was also the practice to swear by the moon, to which we
find an allusion in "Romeo and Juliet" (ii. 2), where Juliet
reproves her lover for testifying his affections by this means:

> "O, swear not by the moon, the inconstant moon,
> That monthly changes in her circled orb,
> Lest that thy love prove likewise variable."

And again, in "The Merchant of Venice" (v. 1), where
Gratiano exclaims:

> "By yonder moon I swear you do me wrong."

We may note here that the inconstancy[3] of the moon is

---

[1] See Brand's "Pop. Antiq.," vol. iii. pp. 142, 143.
[2] See "English Folk-lore," pp. 43, 44.
[3] "Primitive Culture," 1873, vol. i. pp. 354, 355.

the subject of various myths, of which Mr. Tylor has given the following examples: Thus, an Australian legend says that Mityan, the moon, was a native cat, who fell in love with some one else's wife, and was driven away to wander ever since. A Slavonic legend tells us that the moon, king of night, and husband of the sun, faithlessly loved the morning star, wherefore he was cloven through in punishment, as we see him in the sky. The Khasias of the Himalaya say that the moon falls monthly in love with his mother-in-law, who throws ashes in his face, whence his spots.[1]

As in the case of the sun, an eclipse of the moon was formerly considered ominous. The Romans[2] supposed it was owing to the influence of magical charms, to counteract which they had recourse to the sound of brazen instruments of all kinds. Juvenal alludes to this practice in his sixth Satire (441), when he describes his talkative woman:

> " Jam nemo tubas, nemo æra fatiget,
> Una laboranti poterit succurrere lunæ."

Indeed, eclipses, which to us are well-known phenomena witnessing to the exactness of natural laws, were, in the earlier stages of civilization, regarded as " the very embodiment of miraculous disaster." Thus, the Chinese believed that during eclipses of the sun and moon these celestial bodies were attacked by a great serpent, to drive away which they struck their gongs or brazen drums. The Peruvians, entertaining a similar notion, raised a frightful din when the moon was eclipsed,[3] while some savages would shoot up arrows to defend their luminaries against the enemies they fancied were attacking them. It was also a popular belief that the moon was affected by the influence of witchcraft, a notion referred to by Prospero in " The Tempest " (v. 1), who says:

> " His mother was a witch, and one so strong
> That could control the moon."

---

[1] The words " moonish " (" As You Like It," iii. 2) and " moonlike " (" Love's Labour's Lost," iv. 3) are used in the sense of inconstant.

[2] See Douce's " Illustrations of Shakespeare," 1839, p. 18.

[3] Tylor's " Primitive Culture, vol. i. p. 329.

In a former scene (ii. 1) Gonzalo remarks: " You are gentlemen of brave mettle; you would lift the moon out of her
sphere."   Douce [1] quotes a marginal reference from Adlington's translation of " Apuleius " (1596), a book well known
to Shakespeare: " Witches in old time were supposed to be
of such power that they could put downe the moone by
their inchantment." [2]   One of the earliest references to
this superstition among classical authorities is that in the
" Clouds" of Aristophanes, where Strepsiades proposes the
hiring of a Thessalian witch, to bring down the moon and
shut her up in a box, that he might thus evade paying his
debts by a month.   Ovid, in his " Metamorphoses " (bk. xii.
263), says:

> " Mater erat Mycale; quam deduxisse canendo
>   Sæpe reluctanti constabat cornua lunæ."

Horace, in his fifth Epode (45), tells us:

> " Quæ sidera excantata voce Thessala,
>   Lunamque cælo deripit." [3]

Reverting again to the moon's eclipse, such a season, being considered most unlucky for lawful enterprises, was held
suitable for evil designs.   Thus, in " Macbeth " (iv. 1), one
of the witches, speaking of the ingredients of the caldron,
says:

> " Gall of goat, and slips of yew,
>   Sliver'd in the moon's eclipse."

As a harbinger of misfortune it is referred to in " Antony
and Cleopatra," where (iii. 13), Antony says:

> " Alack, our terrene moon
> Is now eclipsed; and it portends alone
> The fall of Antony!"

Milton, in his " Paradise Lost " (bk. i. 597), speaks much in
the same strain:

---

[1] " Illustrations of Shakespeare," 1839, p. 16.

[2] See Scot's " Discovery of Witchcraft," 1584, pp. 174, 226, 227, 250.

[3] For further examples, see Douce's " Illustrations of Shakespeare,"
p. 17.

> "as when the sun new-risen
> Looks through the horizontal misty air
> Shorn of his beams, or from behind the moon
> In dim eclipse, disastrous twilight sheds
> On half the nations."

And in "Lycidas," he says of the unlucky ship that was wrecked:

> "It was that fatal and perfidious bark
> Built in the eclipse."

Its sanguine color is also mentioned as an indication of coming disasters in "Richard II." (ii. 4), where the Welsh captain remarks how:

> "The pale-faced moon looks bloody on the earth."

And its paleness, too, in "A Midsummer-Night's Dream" (ii. 2), is spoken of as an unpropitious sign.

According to a long-accepted theory, insane persons are said to be influenced by the moon; and many old writers have supported this notion. Indeed, Shakespeare himself, in "Othello" (v. 2), tells how the moon when

> "She comes more nearer earth than she was wont,
> And makes men mad."

Dr. Forbes Winslow, in his "Light: its Influence on Life and Health," says that "it is impossible altogether to ignore the evidence of such men as Pinel, Daquin, Guislain, and others, yet the experience of modern psychological physicians is to a great degree opposed to the deductions of these eminent men." He suggests that the alleged changes observed among the insane at certain phases of the moon may arise, not from the direct, but the indirect, influence of the planet. It is well known that certain important meteorological phenomena result from the various phases of the moon, such as the rarity of the air, the electric conditions of the atmosphere, the degree of heat, dryness, moisture, and amount of wind prevailing. It is urged, then, that those suffering from diseases of the brain and nervous system, affecting the mind, cannot be considered as exempt from the operation of agencies that are admitted to affect patients afflicted with other maladies. Dr. Winslow further adds, that "an intelligent lady, who occupied for about five years the position of matron in my establishment for insane ladies, has remarked that she invariably observed among them a greater agitation when the moon was at its full." A correspondent of "Notes and Queries" (2d series, xii. 492) explains the apparent aggravated symptoms of madness at the full moon by the fact that the insane are naturally more restless on light than on dark nights, and that in consequence loss of sleep makes them more excitable. We may note here, that in "Antony and Cleopatra" (iv. 9) Enobarbus invokes the moon as the "sovereign mistress of true melancholy."

The moisture of the moon is invariably noticed by Shakespeare. In "Hamlet" (i. 1) Horatio tells how

> "the moist star,
> Upon whose influence Neptune's empire stands,
> Was sick almost to doomsday with eclipse."

In "A Midsummer-Night's Dream" (ii. 1) Titania says:

> "Therefore the moon, the governess of floods,
> Pale in her anger, washes all the air,
> That rheumatic diseases do abound."

And in "The Winter's Tale" (i. 2) Polixenes commences by saying how:

> "Nine changes of the watery star hath been
> The shepherd's note, since we have left our throne
> Without a burthen."

We may compare, too, the words of Enobarbus in "Antony and Cleopatra" (iv. 9), who, after addressing the moon, says: "The poisonous damp of night disponge upon me." And once more, in "Romeo and Juliet" (i. 4), we read of the "moonshine's watery beams."

The same idea is frequently found in old writers. Thus, for instance, in Newton's "Direction for the Health of Magistrates and Studentes" (1574), we are told that "the moone is ladye of moisture." Bartholomæus, in "De Proprietate Rerum," describes the moon as "mother of all humours,

minister and ladye of the sea."[1]   In Lydgate's prologue to
his "Story of Thebes" there are two lines not unlike those
in "A Midsummer-Night's Dream," already quoted:

> "Of Lucina the moone, moist and pale,
>   That many shoure fro heaven made availe."

Of course, the moon is thus spoken of as governing the tides,
and from its supposed influence on the weather.[2]   In " 1 Henry IV." (i. 2) Falstaff alludes to the sea being governed "by
our noble and chaste mistress, the moon;" and in " Richard III." (ii. 2) Queen Elizabeth says:

> "That I, being govern'd by the watery moon,
>   May send forth plenteous tears to drown the world."

We may compare, too, what Timon says ("Timon of Athens," iv. 3):

> "The sea's a thief, whose liquid surge resolves
>   The moon into salt tears."

The expression of Hecate, in " Macbeth " (iii. 5):

> "Upon the corner of the moon
>   There hangs a vaporous drop profound,"

seems to have been meant for the same as the *virus lunare*
of the ancients, being a foam which the moon was supposed
to shed on particular herbs, when strongly solicited by enchantment. Lucan introduces Erictho using it ("Pharsalia,"
book vi. 669): " Et virus large lunare ministrat."

By a popular astrological doctrine the moon was supposed
to exercise great influence over agricultural operations, and
also over many "of the minor concerns of life, such as the
gathering of herbs, the killing of animals for the table, and
other matters of a like nature."   Thus the following passage
in the "Merchant of Venice" (v. 1), it has been suggested,
has reference to the practices of the old herbalists who attributed particular virtues to plants gathered during partic-

---

[1] See Douce's "Illustrations of Shakespeare," 1839, p. 116.
[2] See Swainson's "Weather-Lore," 1873, pp. 182–192.

ular phases of the moon and hours of the night. After Lorenzo has spoken of the moon shining brightly, Jessica adds:

> "In such a night
> Medea gather'd the enchanted herbs,
> That did renew old Æson."

And in " Hamlet " (iv. 7) the description which Laertes gives
of the weapon-poison refers to the same notion:

> "I bought an unction of a mountebank,
> So mortal that, but dip a knife in it,
> Where it draws blood no cataplasm so rare,
> Collected from all simples that have virtue
> Under the moon, can save the thing from death."

The sympathy of growing and declining nature with the
waxing and waning moon is a superstition widely spread,
and is as firmly believed in by many as when Tusser, in his
" Five Hundred Points of Good Husbandry," under " February" gave the following advice:

> "Sow peason and beans in the wane of the moon,
> Who soweth them sooner, he soweth too soon,
> That they with the planet may rest and arise,
> And flourish, with bearing most plentifull wise."

Warburton considers that this notion is alluded to by Shakespeare in "Troilus and Cressida" (iii. 2), where Troilus, speaking of the sincerity of his love, tells Cressida it is,

> "As true as steel, as plantage to the moon,
> As sun to day, as turtle to her mate."

There is a little doubt as to the exact meaning of plantage
in this passage. Nares observes that it probably means anything that is planted; but Mr. Ellacombe, in his " Plant-lore
of Shakespeare " (1878, p. 165), says "it is doubtless the
same as plantain."

It appears that, in days gone by, "neither sowing, planting, nor grafting was ever undertaken without a scrupulous
attention to the increase or waning of the moon."[1] Scot, in

---

[1] See Tylor's " Primitive Culture," 1873, vol. i. p. 130; " English Folk-
Lore," 1878, pp. 41, 42.

his " Discovery of Witchcraft," notes how " the poore hus-
bandman perceiveth that the increase of the moone maketh
plants fruitful, so as in the full moone they are in best
strength; decaieing in the wane, and in the conjunction do
utterlie wither and vade."

It was a prevailing notion that the moon had an attending
star—Lilly calls it " Lunisequa;" and Sir Richard Hawkins,
in his " Observations in a Voyage to the South Seas in 1593,"
published in 1622, remarks: " Some I have heard say, and
others write, that there is a starre which never separateth
itself from the moon, but a small distance." Staunton considers that there is an allusion to this idea in " Love's Labour's Lost " (iv. 3), where the king says:

> " My love, her mistress, is a gracious moon :
> She an attending star, scarce seen a light."

The sharp ends of the new moon are popularly termed
horns—a term which occurs in " Coriolanus " (i. 1)—

> " they threw their caps
> As they would hang them on the horns o' the moon."

It is made use of in Decker's " Match me in London " (i.):

> " My lord, doe you see this change i' the moone ?
> Sharp hornes doe threaten windy weather."

When the horns of the moon appear to point upwards the
moon is said to be like a boat, and various weather prognostications are drawn from this phenomenon.[1] According to
sailors, it is an omen of fine weather, whereas others affirm it
is a sign of rain—resembling a basin full of water about to
fall.

Among other items of folk-lore connected with the moon
we may mention the moon-calf, a false conception, or fœtus
imperfectly formed, in consequence, as was supposed, of the
influence of the moon. The best account of this fabulous
substance may be found in Drayton's poem with that title.
Trinculo, in " The Tempest " (ii. 2), supposes Caliban to be a
moon-calf: " I hid me under the dead moon-calf's gaberdine."

---

[1] See Swainson's " Weather-Lore," pp. 182, 183.

It has been suggested that in calling Caliban a moon-calf Shakespeare alluded to a superstitious belief formerly current, in the intercourse of demons and other non-human beings with mankind. In the days of witchcraft, it was supposed that a class of devils called Incubi and Succubi roamed the earth with the express purpose of tempting people to abandon their purity of life. Hence, all badly deformed children were suspected of having had such an undesirable parentage.[1]

A curious expression, "a sop o' the moonshine," occurs in "King Lear" (ii. 2), which probably alludes to some dish so called. Kent says to the steward, "Draw, you rogue; for, though it be night, yet the moon shines; I'll make a sop o' the moonshine of you."

There was a way of dressing eggs, called "eggs in moonshine," of which Douce[2] gives the following description: "Eggs were broken and boiled in salad oil till the yolks became hard. They were eaten with slices of onion fried in oil, butter, verjuice, nutmeg, and salt." "A sop in the moonshine" must have been a sippet in this dish.[3]

Planets. The irregular motion of the planets was supposed to portend some disaster to mankind. Ulysses, in "Troilus and Cressida" (i. 3), declares how:

> "when the planets
> In evil mixture, to disorder wander,
> What plagues and what portents! what mutiny!
> What raging of the sea! shaking of earth!
> Commotion in the winds! frights, changes, horrors,
> Divert and crack, rend and deracinate
> The unity and married calm of states
> Quite from their fixture."

Indeed, the planets themselves were not thought, in days gone by, to be confined in any fixed orbit of their own, but ceaselessly to wander about, as the etymology of their name demonstrates. A popular name for the planets was "wan-

---

[1] See Williams's "Superstitions of Witchcraft," pp. 123–125; Scot's "Discovery of Witchcraft," bk. iv. p. 145.

[2] "Illustrations of Shakespeare," 1839, p. 405.

[3] Nares's "Glossary," 1872, vol. ii. p. 580.

dering stars," of which Cotgrave says, "they bee also called wandering starres, because they never keep one certain place or station in the firmament." Thus Hamlet (v. 1), approaching the grave of Ophelia, addresses Laertes:

> "What is he, whose grief
> Bears such an emphasis? whose phrase of sorrow
> Conjures the wandering stars, and makes them stand
> Like wonder-wounded hearers?"

In Tomkis's "Albumazar" (i. 1) they are called "wanderers:"

> "Your patron Mercury, in his mysterious character
> Holds all the marks of the other wanderers."

According to vulgar astrology, the planets, like the stars, were supposed to affect, more or less, the affairs of this world, a notion frequently referred to by old writers. In "Winter's Tale" (ii. 1), Hermione consoles herself in the thought—

> "There's some ill planet reigns:
> I must be patient till the heavens look
> With an aspect more favourable."

In "1 Henry VI." (i. 1), the Duke of Exeter asks:

> "What! shall we curse the planets of mishap
> That plotted thus our glory's overthrow?"

Again, King Richard ("Richard III.," iv. 4):

> "Be opposite all planets of good luck
> To my proceeding."

And once more, in "Hamlet" (i. 1), Marcellus, speaking of the season of our Saviour's birth, says, "then no planets strike."

That diseases, too, are dependent upon planetary influence is referred to in "Timon of Athens" (iv. 3):

> "Be as a planetary plague, when Jove
> Will o'er some high-viced city hang his poison
> In the sick air: let not thy sword skip one."

"Fiery Trigon" was a term in the old judicial astrology, when the three upper planets met in a fiery sign—a phenomenon which was supposed to indicate rage and contention. It is mentioned in "2 Henry IV." (ii. 4):

"*P. Hen.* Saturn and Venus this year in conjunction! what says the almanac to that?

Poins. And, look, whether the fiery Trigon, his man, be not lisping to his master's old tables."

Dr. Nash, in his notes to Butler's "Hudibras," says: "The twelve signs in astrology are divided into four *trigons* or triplicities, each denominated from the connatural element; so they are three fiery [signs], three airy, three watery, and three earthy:"

> Fiery—Aries, Leo, Sagittarius.
> Airy—Gemini, Libra, Aquarius.
> Watery—Cancer, Scorpio, Pisces.
> Earthly—Taurus, Virgo, Capricornus.

Thus, when the three superior planets met in Aries, Leo, or Sagittarius, they formed a *fiery trigon;* when in Cancer, Scorpio, and Pisces, a watery one.

Charles's Wain was the old name for the seven bright stars of the constellation Ursa Major. The constellation was so named in honor of Charlemagne; or, according to some, it is a corruption of chorles or churl's, *i. e.*, rustic's, wain. Chorl is frequently used for a countryman, in old books, from the Saxon ceorl. In "1 Henry IV." (ii. 1), the Carrier says, "Charles' wain is over the new chimney."

Music of the spheres. Pythagoras was the first who suggested this notion, so beautifully expressed by Shakespeare in the "Merchant of Venice" (v. 1):

> "There's not the smallest orb which thou behold'st,
>   But in his motion like an angel sings,
>   Still quiring to the young-eyed cherubins."

Plato says that a siren sits on each planet, who carols a most sweet song, agreeing to the motion of her own particular planet, but harmonizing with the other seven. Hence Milton, in his "Arcades," speaks of the "celestial Sirens' harmony, that sit upon the nine enfolded spheres."

Stars. An astrological doctrine, which has kept its place in modern popular philosophy, asserts that mundane events are more or less influenced by the stars. That astronomers should have divided the sun's course into imaginary signs of the Zodiac, was enough, says Mr. Tylor,[1] to originate astrological rules "that these celestial signs have an actual effect on real earthly rams, bulls, crabs, lions, virgins." Hence we are told that a child born under the sign of the Lion will be courageous; but one born under the Crab will not go forth well in life; one born under the Waterman is likely to be drowned, and so forth. Shakespeare frequently alludes to this piece of superstition, which, it must be remembered, was carried to a ridiculous height in his day. In "Julius Cæsar" (i. 2), Cassius says:

> "The fault, dear Brutus, is not in our stars,
> But in ourselves, that we are underlings."

In the following passage in "Twelfth Night" (i. 3):

> "*Sir Tob.*   Were we not born under Taurus?
> *Sir And.* Taurus! that's sides and heart.
> *Sir Tob.* No, sir; it is legs and thighs."

"Both the knights," says Mr. Douce ("Illustrations of Shakespeare," p. 54), "are wrong in their astrology, according to the almanacs of the time, which make Taurus govern the neck and throat."

Beatrice, in "Much Ado about Nothing" (ii. 1), says: "there was a star danced, and under that was I born;" Kent, in "King Lear" (iv. 3), remarks,

> "It is the stars,
> The stars above us, govern our conditions;"

and once more, in "Pericles" (i. 1), King Antiochus, speaking of the charming qualities of his daughter, says:

> "Bring in our daughter, clothed like a bride,
> For the embracements even of Jove himself:
> At whose conception, till Lucina reign'd,
> Nature this dowry gave, to glad her presence,
> The senate-house of planets all did sit,
> To knit in her their best perfections."[2]

---

[1] "Primitive Culture," vol. i. p. 131.

[2] Cf. "Richard III." (iv. 4); "1 Henry IV." (i. 1, iii. 1); "Antony and Cleopatra" (iii. 13); "The Tempest" (i. 2); "Hamlet" (i. 4); "Cymbeline" (v. 4); "Winter's Tale" (iii. 2); "Richard II." (iv. 1).

Throughout the East, says Mr. Tylor,[1] "astrology even now remains a science in full esteem. The condition of mediæval Europe may still be perfectly realized by the traveller in Persia, where the Shah waits for days outside the walls of his capital till the constellations allow him to enter; and where, on the days appointed by the stars for letting blood, it literally flows in streams from the barbers' shops in the streets. Professor Wuttke declares that there are many districts in Germany where the child's horoscope is still regularly kept with the baptismal certificate in the family chest." Astrology is ridiculed in a masterly manner in "King Lear" (i. 2); and Warburton suggests that if the date of the first performance of "King Lear" were well considered, "it would be found that something or other had happened at that time which gave a more than ordinary run to this deceit, as these words seem to indicate—'I am thinking, brother, of a prediction I read this other day, what should follow these eclipses.'" Zouch,[2] speaking of Queen Mary's reign, tells us that "Judicial astrology was much in use long after this time. Its predictions were received with reverential awe; and even men of the most enlightened understandings were inclined to believe that the conjunctions and oppositions of the planets had no little influence in the affairs of the world."

The pretence, also, of predicting events, such as pestilence, from the aspect of the heavenly bodies—one form of medical astrology—is noticed in "Venus and Adonis:"

> "Long may they kiss each other, for this cure!
> O, never let their crimson liveries wear!
> And as they last, their verdure still endure,
> To drive infection from the dangerous year!
>   That the star-gazers, having writ on death,
>   May say, the plague is banish'd by thy breath!"

Heroes were in ancient times immortalized by being placed among the stars, a custom to which Bedford refers in "1 Henry VI." (i. 1):

---

[1] "Primitive Culture," vol. i. p. 131; see Brand's "Popular Antiquities," 1849, vol. iii. pp. 341–348.
[2] "Walton's Lives," 1796, p. 113, note.

> " A far more glorious star thy soul will make
> Than Julius Cæsar."

And, again, " Pericles " (v. 3) exclaims :

> " Heavens make a star of him."

On a medal of Hadrian, the adopted son of Trajan and Plotina, the divinity of his parents is expressed by placing a star over their heads ; and in like manner the medals of Faustina the Elder exhibit her on an eagle, her head surrounded with stars.[1]

In " 2 Henry IV." (iv. 3) a ludicrous term for the stars is, " cinders of the elements ;" and in " Merchant of Venice " (v. 1) they are designated " candles of the night."

Meteors. An elegant description of a meteor well known to sailors is given by Ariel in " The Tempest " (i. 2):

> " sométime I'd divide
> And burn in many places ; on the topmast,
> The yards, and bowsprit, would I flame distinctly,
> Then meet and join."

It is called, by the French and Spaniards inhabiting the coasts of the Mediterranean, St. Helme's or St. Telme's fire ; by the Italians, the fire of St. Peter and St. Nicholas. It is also known as the fire of St. Helen, St. Herm, and St. Clare. Douce[2] tells us that whenever it appeared as a single flame it was supposed by the ancients to be Helena, the sister of Castor and Pollux, and in this state to bring ill luck, from the calamities which this lady is known to have caused in the Trojan war. When it came as a double flame it was called Castor and Pollux, and accounted a good omen. It has been described as a little blaze of fire, sometimes appearing by night on the tops of soldiers' lances, or at sea on masts and sailyards, whirling and leaping in a moment from one place to another. According to some, it never appears but after a tempest, and is supposed to lead people to suicide by drowning. Shakespeare in all probability consulted Bat-

---

[1] Douce's " Illustrations of Shakespeare," 1839, p. 397.
[2] Ibid. p. 3.

man's "Golden Books of the Leaden Goddes," who, speaking of Castor and Pollux, says : " They were figured like two
lampes or cresset lightes—one on the toppe of a maste, the
other on the stemme or foreshippe." He adds that if the
first light appears in the stem or foreship and ascends upwards, it is a sign of good luck ; if " either lights begin at the
topmast, bowsprit," or foreship, and descends towards the
sea, it is a sign of a tempest. In taking, therefore, the latter
position, Ariel had fulfilled the commands of Prospero, and
raised a storm.[1] Mr. Swainson, in his "Weather-Lore" (1873,
p. 193), quotes the following, which is to the same purport :

> " Last night I saw Saint Elmo's stars,
>   With their glittering lanterns all at play,
>   On the tops of the masts and the tips of the spars,
>   And I knew we should have foul weather that day."

Capell, in his " School of Shakespeare" (1779, iii. 7), has
pointed out a passage in Hakluyt's " Voyages " (1598, iii. 450),
which strikingly illustrates the speech of Ariel quoted above :
" I do remember that in the great and boysterous storme of
this foule weather, in the night, there came vpon the toppe
of our maine yarde and maine maste, a certaine little light,
much like unto the light of a little candle, which the Spaniards called the Cuerpo-Santo, and said it was St Elmo, whom
they take to bee the aduocate of sailers. . . . This light continued aboord our ship about three houres, flying from maste
to maste, and from top to top ; and sometimes it would be
in two or three places at once." This meteor was by some
supposed to be a spirit ; and by others " an exhalation of
moyst vapours, that are ingendered by foul and tempestuous
weather."[2] Mr. Thoms, in his " Notelets on Shakespeare"
(1865, p. 59), says that, no doubt, Shakespeare had in mind
the will-o'-the-wisp.[3]

Fire-Drake, which is jocularly used in " Henry VIII." (v. 4)

---

[1] See Brand's " Pop. Antiq.," 1849, vol. iii. p. 400.

[2] Purchas, " His Pilgrimes " (1625, pt. i. lib. iii. p. 133), quoted by Mr.
Aldis Wright in his " Notes to The Tempest," 1875, p. 86.

[3] See Puck as Will-o'-the-Wisp ; chapter on " Fairy-Lore."

for a man with a red face, was one of the popular terms for the will-o'-the-wisp,[1] and Burton, in his "Anatomy of Melancholy," says: "Fiery spirits or devils are such as commonly work by fire-drakes, or ignes fatui, which lead men often in flumina et præcipitia." In Bullokar's "English Expositor" (1616), we have a quaint account of this phenomenon: "Firedrake; a fire sometimes seen flying in the night like a dragon. Common people think it a spirit that keepeth some treasure hid, but philosophers affirme it to be a great unequal exhalation inflamed betweene two clouds, the one hot, the other cold, which is the reason that it also smoketh, the middle part whereof, according to the proportion of the hot cloud being greater than the rest, maketh it seem like a bellie, and both ends like unto a head and taill."[2] White, however, in his "Peripateticall Institutions" (p. 156), calls the fiery-dragon or fire-drake, "a weaker kind of lightning. Its livid colors, and its falling without noise and slowly, demonstrate a great mixture of watery exhalation in it. . . . 'Tis sufficient for its shape, that it has some resemblance of a dragon, not the expresse figure.'

Among other allusions to the will-o'-the-wisp by Shakespeare, Mr. Hunter[3] notices one in "King Lear" (iii. 4), where Gloster's torch being seen in the distance, the fool says, "Look, here comes a walking fire." Whereupon Edgar replies, "This is the foul fiend, Flibbertigibbet; he begins at curfew, and walks till the first cock." "From which," observes Mr. Hunter, "Flibbertigibbet seems to be a name for the will-o'-the-wisp. Hence the propriety of 'He *begins at curfew*, and walks till the crowing of the cock,' that is, is

---

[1] See "Notes and Queries," 5th series, vol. x. p. 499; Brand's "Pop. Antiq.," 1849, vol. iii. p. 410; Nares's "Glossary," vol. i. p. 309.

[2] A "fire-drake" appears to have been also an artificial firework, perhaps what is now called a serpent. Thus, in Middleton's "Your Five Gallants" (1607):

"But, like fire-drakes,
Mounted a little, gave a crack and fell."

[3] "New Illustrations of the Life, Studies, and Writings of Shakespeare," vol. ii. p. 272.

seen in all the dark of the night." It appears that when Shakespeare wrote, " a walking fire " was a common name for the *ignis fatuus*, as we learn from the story of " How Robin Goodfellow lead a company of fellows out of their way:" "A company of young men, having been making merry with their sweethearts, were, at their coming home, to come over a heath ; Robin Goodfellow, knowing of it, met them, and to make some pastime hee led them up and downe the heathe a whole night, so that they could not get out of it, for hee went before them in the shape of a *walking fire*, which they all saw and followed till the day did appear ; then Robin left them, and at his departure spake these words :

> " ' Get you home, you merry lads,
> Tell your mammies and your dads,
> And all those that newes desire
> How you saw a walking fire,
> Wenches, that doe smile and lispe,
> Use to call me willy-wispe.' "

Another allusion to this subject occurs in " The Tempest " (iv. 1), where Stephano, after Ariel has led him and his drunken companions through " tooth'd briers, sharp furzes, pricking goss and thorns," and at last " left them i' the filthy mantled pool," reproaches Caliban in these words : " Monster, your fairy, which you say is a harmless fairy, has done little better than played the Jack with us "—that is, to quote Dr. Johnson's explanation of this passage, " he has played Jack-with-a-lanthorn, has led us about like an *ignis fatuus*, by which travellers are decoyed into the mire." [1] Once more, when Puck, in " A Midsummer-Night's Dream " (iii. 1), speaks of the various forms he assumes in order to " mislead night wanderers, laughing at their harm," he says :

> " Sometime a horse I'll be, sometime a hound,
> A hog, a headless bear, sometime a fire."

Shakespeare, no doubt, here alludes to the will-o'-the wisp,

---

[1] See Thoms's " Notelets on Shakespeare," p. 59.

an opinion shared by Mr. Joseph Ritson,[1] who says: "This Puck, or Robin Goodfellow, seems likewise to be the illusory candle-holder, so fatal to travellers, and who is more usually called 'Jack-a-lantern,'[2] or 'Will-with-a-wisp,' and 'Kit-with-the-candlestick.'" Milton, in "Paradise Lost" (book ix.), alludes to this deceptive gleam in the following lines:

> "A wandering fire
> Compact of unctuous vapour, which the night
> Condenses, and the cold environs round,
> Kindled through agitation to a flame,
> Which oft, they say, some evil spirit attends,
> Hovering and blazing with delusive light,
> Misleads th' amaz'd night-wanderer from his way
> To bogs and mires, and oft through pond and pool."[3]

This appearance has given rise to a most extensive folk-lore, and is embodied in many of the fairy legends and superstitions of this and other countries. Thus, in Germany, Jack-o'-lanterns are said to be the souls of unbaptized children, that have no rest in the grave, and must hover between heaven and earth. In many places they are called land-measurers, and are seen like figures of fire, running to and fro with a red-hot measuring rod. These are said to be persons who have falsely sworn away land, or fraudulently measured it, or removed landmarks.[4] In the neighborhood of Magdeburg, they are known as "Lüchtemännekens;" and to

---

[1] "Fairy Mythology," edited by Hazlitt, 1875, p. 40.

[2] Among the many other names given to this appearance may be mentioned the following: "Will-a-wisp," "Joan-in-the-wad," "Jacket-a-wad," "Peg-a-lantern," "Elf-fire," etc. A correspondent of "Notes and Queries" (5th series, vol. x. p. 499) says: "The wandering meteor of the moss or fell appears to have been personified as Jack, Gill, Joan, Will, or Robin, indifferently, according as the supposed spirit of the lamp seemed to the particular rustic mind to be a male or female apparition." In Worcestershire it is called "Hob-and-his-lanthorn," and "Hobany's," or "Hobnedy's Lanthorn."

[3] Mr. Ritson says that Milton "is frequently content to pilfer a happy expression from Shakespeare—on this occasion, 'night-wanderer.'" He elsewhere calls it "the friar's lantern."

[4] Thorpe, "Northern Mythology," 1852, vol. iii. pp. 85, 158, 220.

cause them to appear, it is sufficient to call out " Ninove, Ninove." In the South Altmark they are termed "Dickepôten;" and if a person only prays as soon as he sees one, he draws it to him; if he curses, it retires. In some parts, too, a popular name is "Huckepôten," and "Tuckbolde." The Jack-o'-lanterns of Denmark[1] are the spirits of unrighteous men, who, by a false glimmer, seek to mislead the traveller, and to decoy him into bogs and moors. The best safeguard against them, when they appear, is to turn one's cap inside out. A similar notion occurs in Devonshire with regard to the Pixies, who delight in leading astray such persons as they find abroad after nightfall; the only remedy to escape them being to turn some part of the dress. In Normandy these fires are called " Feux Follets," and they are believed to be cruel spirits, whom it is dangerous to encounter. Among the superstitions which prevail in connection with them, two, says Mr. Thoms,[2] are deserving of notice: " One is, that the *ignis fatuus* is the spirit of some unhappy woman, who is destined to run *en furolle*, to expiate her intrigues with a minister of the church, and it is designated from that circumstance La Fourlore, or La Fourolle." Another opinion is, that Le Feu Follet is the soul of a priest, who has been condemned thus to expiate his broken vows of perpetual chastity; and it is very probable that it is to some similar belief existing in this country, at the time when he wrote, that Milton alludes in " L'Allegro," when he says:

> " She was pinched and pulled, she said,
>   And he by Friar's Lanthorn led."

In Brittany the " Porte-brandon " appears in the form of a child bearing a torch, which he turns like a burning wheel; and with this, we are told, he sets fire to the villages, which are suddenly, sometimes in the middle of the night, wrapped in flames.

The appearance of meteors Shakespeare ranks among omens, as in " 1 Henry IV." (ii. 4), where Bardolph says:

[1] " Notelets on Shakespeare," pp. 64, 65.
[2] Ibid.

" My lord, do you see these meteors? do you behold these exhalations? What think you they portend?" And in " King John " (iii. 4), Pandulph speaks of meteors as " prodigies and signs." The Welsh captain, in " Richard II." (ii. 4), says:

> " 'Tis thought the king is dead ; we will not stay.
> The bay-trees in our country are all wither'd,
> And meteors fright the fixed stars of heaven."

Comet. From the earliest times comets have been superstitiously regarded, and ranked among omens. Thus Thucydides tells us that the Peloponnesian war was heralded by an abundance of earthquakes and comets; and Vergil, in speaking of the death of Cæsar, declares that at no other time did comets and other supernatural prodigies appear in greater numbers. It is probably to this latter event that Shakespeare alludes in " Julius Cæsar " (ii. 2), where he represents Calpurnia as saying:

> " When beggars die, there are no comets seen ;
> The heavens themselves blaze forth the death of princes."

Again, in " 1 Henry VI." (i. 1), the play opens with the following words, uttered by the Duke of Bedford :

> " Hung be the heavens with black, yield day to night !
> Comets, importing change of times and states,
> Brandish your crystal tresses in the sky,
> And with them scourge the bad revolting stars
> That have consented unto Henry's death !"

In " Taming of the Shrew " (iii. 2), too, Petruchio, when he makes his appearance on his wedding-day, says:

> " Gentles, methinks you frown :
> And wherefore gaze this goodly company,
> As if they saw some wondrous monument,
> Some comet, or unusual prodigy ?"

In " 1 Henry IV." (iii. 2), the king, when telling his son how he had always avoided making himself " common-hackney'd in the eyes of men," adds:

> " By being seldom seen, I could not stir
> But, like a comet, I was wonder'd at."

Arcite, in the "Two Noble Kinsmen" (v. 1), when addressing the altar of Mars, says:

> "Whose approach
> Comets forewarn." [1]

Dew. Among the many virtues ascribed to dew was its supposed power over the complexion, a source of superstition which still finds many believers, especially on May morning. All dew, however, does not appear to have possessed this quality, some being of a deadly or malignant quality. Thus Ariel, in "The Tempest" (i. 2), speaks of the "deep brook" in the harbor:

> "where once
> Thou call'dst me up at midnight to fetch dew
> From the still vex'd Bermoothes."

And Caliban (i. 2), when venting his rage on Prospero and Miranda, can find no stronger curse than the following:

> "As wicked dew as e'er my mother brush'd,
> With raven's feather from unwholesome fen
> Drop on you both!"

It has been suggested that in "Antony and Cleopatra" (iii. 12) Shakespeare may refer to an old notion whereby the sea was considered the source of dews as well as rain. Euphronius is represented as saying:

> "Such as I am, I come from Antony:
> I was of late as petty to his ends
> As is the morn-dew on the myrtle leaf
> To his grand sea."

According to an erroneous notion formerly current, it was supposed that the air, and not the earth, drizzled dew—a notion referred to in "Romeo and Juliet" (iii. 5):

> "When the sun sets, the air doth drizzle dew."

And in "King John" (ii. 1):

> "Before the dew of evening fall."

---

[1] See Proctor's "Myths of Astronomy:" Chambers's "Domestic Annals of Scotland," 1858, vol. ii. pp. 410–412; Douce's "Illustrations of Shakespeare," pp. 364, 365.

Then there is the celebrated honey-dew, a substance which has furnished the poet with a touching simile, which he has put into the mouth of "Titus Andronicus" (iii. 1):

> "When I did name her brothers, then fresh tears
> Stood on her cheeks; as doth the honey-dew
> Upon a gather'd lily almost wither'd."

According to Pliny, "honey-dew" is the saliva of the stars, or a liquid produced by the purgation of the air. It is, however, a secretion deposited by a small insect, which is distinguished by the generic name of aphis.[1]

Rainbow. Secondary rainbows, the watery appearance in the sky accompanying the rainbow, are in many places termed "water-galls"—a term we find in the "Rape of Lucrece" (1586–89):

> "And round about her tear-distained eye
> Blue circles stream'd, like rainbows in the sky:
> These water-galls in her dim element
> Foretell new storms to those already spent."

Horace Walpole several times makes use of the word: "False good news are always produced by true good, like the water-gall by the rainbow;" and again, "Thank heaven it is complete, and did not remain imperfect, like a water-gall."[2] In "The Dialect of Craven" we find "Water-gall, a secondary or broken rainbow. *Germ.* Wasser-galle."

Thunder. According to an erroneous fancy the destruction occasioned by lightning was effected by some solid body known as the thunder-stone or thunder-bolt. Thus, in the beautiful dirge in "Cymbeline" (iv. 2):

> "*Guid.* Fear no more the lightning flash,
> *Arv.* Or the all-dreaded thunder-stone."

Othello asks (v. 2):

> "Are there no stones in heaven
> But what serve for the thunder?"

---

[1] See Patterson's "Insects Mentioned by Shakespeare," 1841, p. 145.
[2] "Letters," vol. i. p. 310; vol. vi. pp. 1, 187.—Ed. Cunningham.

And in " Julius Cæsar " (i. 3), Cassius says :

> " And, thus unbraced, Casca, as you see,
> Have bared my bosom to the thunder-stone."

The thunder-stone is the imaginary product of the thunder, which the ancients called *Brontia*, mentioned by Pliny (" Nat. Hist." xxxvii. 10) as a species of gem, and as that which, falling with the lightning, does the mischief. It is the fossil commonly called the Belemnite, or finger-stone, and now known to be a shell.

A superstitious notion prevailed among the ancients that those who were stricken with lightning were honored by Jupiter, and therefore to be accounted holy. It is probably to this idea that Shakespeare alludes in " Antony and Cleopatra " (ii. 5) :

> " Some innocents 'scape not the thunderbolt." [1]

The bodies of such were supposed not to putrefy; and, after having been exhibited for a certain time to the people, were not buried in the usual manner, but interred on the spot where the lightning fell, and a monument erected over them. Some, however, held a contrary opinion. Thus Persius (sat. ii. l. 27) says :

> " Triste jaces lucis evitandumque bidental."

The ground, too, that had been smitten by a thunderbolt was accounted sacred, and afterwards enclosed ; nor did any one even presume to walk on it. Such spots were, therefore, consecrated to the gods, and could not in future become the property of any one.

Among the many other items of folk-lore associated with thunder is a curious one referred to in " Pericles " (iv. 3): "Thunder shall not so awake the bed of eels." The notion formerly being that thunder had the effect of rousing eels from their mud, and so rendered them more easy to be taken in stormy weather. Marston alludes to

---

[1] Douce's " Illustrations of Shakespeare," 1839, p. 369.

this superstition in his satires ("Scourge of Villainie," sat. vii.):

> "They are nought but eeles, that never will appeare
> Till that tempestuous winds or thunder teare
> Their slimy beds."

The silence that often precedes a thunder-storm is thus graphically described in "Hamlet" (ii. 2):

> "'we often see, against some storm,
> A silence in the heavens, the rack stand still,
> The bold winds speechless, and the orb below
> As hush as death, anon the dreadful thunder
> Doth rend the region.'"

Earthquakes, around which so many curious myths and superstitions have clustered,[1] are scarcely noticed by Shakespeare. They are mentioned among the ominous signs of that terrible night on which Duncan is so treacherously slain ("Macbeth," ii. 3):

> "the obscure bird
> Clamour'd the livelong night: some say, the earth
> Was feverous and did shake." .

And in "1 Henry IV." (iii. 1) Hotspur assigns as a reason for the earthquakes the following theory:

> "Diseased nature oftentimes breaks forth
> In strange eruptions; oft the teeming earth
> Is with a kind of colic pinch'd and vex'd
> By the imprisoning of unruly wind
> Within her womb; which, for enlargement striving,
> Shakes the old beldam earth, and topples down
> Steeples, and moss-grown towers."

Equinox. The storms that prevail in spring at the vernal equinox are aptly alluded to in "Macbeth" (i. 2):

> "As whence the sun 'gins his reflection
> Shipwrecking storms and direful thunders break,
> So from that spring, whence comfort seem'd to come,
> Discomfort swells."

—the meaning being: the beginning of the reflection of the

---

[1] See Tylor's "Primitive Culture," vol. i. pp. 364–367.

sun is the epoch of his passing from the severe to the milder
season, opening, however, with storms.

Wind. An immense deal of curious weather-lore[1] has been
associated with the wind from the earliest period; and in
our own and foreign countries innumerable proverbs are
found describing the future state of the weather from the
position of the wind, for, according to an old saying, " every
wind has its weather." Shakespeare has introduced some
of these, showing how keen an observer he was of those
every-day sayings which have always been much in use, especially among the lower classes. Thus the proverbial wet
which accompanies the wind when in the south is mentioned
in " As You Like It " (iii. 5):

> " Like foggy south, puffing with wind and rain."

And again, in " 1 Henry IV." (v. 1):

> " The southern wind
> Doth play the trumpet to his [*i. e.*, the sun's] purposes;
> And by his hollow whistling in the leaves
> Foretells a tempest, and a blustering day."

A popular saying to the same effect, still in use, tells us that:

> " When the wind is in the south,
> It is in the rain's mouth."

Again, in days gone by, the southerly winds were generally
supposed to be bearers of noxious fogs and vapors, frequent
allusions to which are given by Shakespeare. Thus, in " The
Tempest " (i. 2), Caliban says:

> " a south-west blow on ye
> And blister you all o'er."

A book,[2] too, with which, as already noticed, Shakespeare
appears to have been familiar, tells us, " This southern wind
is hot and moist. Southern winds corrupt and destroy;
they heat, and make men fall into the sickness." Hence, in

---

[1] See Swainson's " Weather-Lore."

[2] Batman upon Bartholomæus—" De Proprietatibus Rerum," lib. xi.
c. 3.

"Troilus and Cressida" (v. 1), Thersites speaks of "the rotten diseases of the south;" and in "Coriolanus" (i. 4), Marcius exclaims:

> "All the contagion of the south light on you."

Once more, in "Cymbeline" (ii. 3), Cloten speaks in the same strain: "The south fog rot him."

Flaws. These are sudden gusts of wind. It was the opinion, says Warburton, "of some philosophers that the vapors being congealed in the air by cold (which is the most intense in the morning), and being afterwards rarefied and let loose by the warmth of the sun, occasion those sudden and impetuous gusts of wind which were called 'flaws.'" Thus he comments on the following passage in "2 Henry IV." (iv. 4):

> "As humorous as winter, and as sudden
> As flaws congealed in the spring of day."

In "2 Henry VI." (iii. 1) these outbursts of wind are further alluded to:

> "And this fell tempest shall not cease to rage
> Until the golden circuit on my head,
> Like to the glorious sun's transparent beams,
> Do calm the fury of this mad-bred flaw."

Again, in "Venus and Adonis" (425), there is an additional reference:

> "Like a red morn, that ever yet betoken'd
> Wreck to the seaman, tempest to the field,
>   Sorrow to shepherds, woe unto the birds,
>   Gusts and foul flaws to herdmen and to herds."

In the Cornish dialect a *flaw* signifies primitively a cut.[1] But it is also there used in a secondary sense for those sudden or cutting gusts of wind.[2]

Squalls. There is a common notion that "the sudden storm lasts not three hours," an idea referred to by John of Gaunt in "Richard II." (ii. 1):

> "Small showers last long, but sudden storms are short."

---

[1] Polwhele's "Cornish Vocabulary."
[2] Cf. "Macbeth," iii. 4, "O, these flaws and starts."

Thus, in Norfolk, the peasantry say that "the faster the rain, the quicker the hold up," which is only a difference in words from the popular adage, "after a storm comes a calm."

Clouds. In days gone by, clouds floating before the wind, like a reek or vapor, were termed racking clouds. Hence in "3 Henry VI." (ii. 1), Richard speaks of:

> "Three glorious suns, each one a perfect sun;
> Not separated with the racking clouds."

This verb, though now obsolete, was formerly in common use; and in "King Edward III.," 1596, we read:

> "Like inconstant clouds,
> That, rack'd upon the carriage of the winds,
> Increase," etc.

At the present day one may often hear the phrase, the rack of the weather, in our agricultural districts; many, too, of the items of weather-lore noticed by Shakespeare being still firmly credited by our peasantry.

CHAPTER VI.

BIRDS.

IN the present chapter we have not only a striking proof of Shakespeare's minute acquaintance with natural history, but of his remarkable versatility as a writer. While displaying a most extensive knowledge of ornithology, he has further illustrated his subject by alluding to those numerous legends, popular sayings, and superstitions which have, in this and other countries, clustered round the feathered race. Indeed, the following pages are alone sufficient to show, if it were necessary, how fully he appreciated every branch of antiquarian lore ; and what a diligent student he must have been in the pursuit of that wide range of information, the possession of which has made him one of the most many-sided writers that the world has ever seen. The numerous incidental allusions, too, by Shakespeare, to the folk-lore of bygone days, while showing how deeply he must have read and gathered knowledge from every available source, serve as an additional proof of his retentive memory, and marvellous power of embellishing his ideas by the most apposite illustrations. Unfortunately, however, these have, hitherto, been frequently lost sight of through the reader's unacquaintance with that extensive field of folk-lore which was so well known to the poet. For the sake of easy reference, the birds with which the present chapter deals are arranged alphabetically.

Barnacle-Goose. There was a curious notion, very prevalent in former times, that this bird (*Anser bernicla*) was generated from the barnacle (*Lepas anatifera*), a shell-fish, growing on a flexible stem, and adhering to loose timber, bottoms of ships, etc., a metamorphosis to which Shakespeare alludes in "The Tempest" (iv. 1), where he makes Caliban say :

"we shall lose our time,
And all be turn'd to barnacles."

This vulgar error, no doubt, originated in mistaking the fleshy peduncle of the shell-fish for the neck of a goose, the shell for its head, and the tentacula for a tuft of feathers. These shell-fish, therefore, bearing, as seen out of the water, a resemblance to the goose's neck, were ignorantly, and without investigation, confounded with geese themselves. In France, the barnacle-goose may be eaten on fast days, by virtue of this old belief in its fishy origin.[1] Like other fictions this one had its variations,[2] for sometime the barnacles were supposed to grow on trees, and thence to drop into the sea, and become geese, as in Drayton's account of Furness ("Polyolb." 1622, song 27, l. 1190). As early as the 12th century this idea[3] was promulgated by Giraldus Cambrensis in his "Topographia Hiberniæ." Gerarde, who in the year 1597 published his "Herball, or Generall Historie of Plantes," narrates the following: "There are found in the north parts of Scotland, and the isles adjacent called Orcades, certain trees, whereon do grow certain shell-fishes, of a white color, tending to russet, wherein are contained little living creatures; which shells in time of maturity do open, and out of them grow those little living things which, falling into the water, do become fowls, whom we call barnacles, in the north of England brant geese, and in Lancashire tree geese; but the others that do fall upon the land perish, and do come to nothing. Thus much of the writings of others, and also from the mouths of people of those parts, which may very well accord with truth. But what our eyes have seen and hands have touched, we shall declare. There is a small island in Lancashire called the Pile of Foulders, wherein are found the broken pieces of old ships, some whereof have been cast thither by shipwreck, and also the trunks or bodies,

---

[1] See Harland and Wilkinson's "Lancashire Folk-Lore," 1867, pp. 116–121; "Notes and Queries," 1st series, vol. viii. p. 224; "Penny Cyclopædia," vol. vii. p. 206, article "Cirripeda."

Nares's "Glossary," 1872, vol. i. p. 56.

[3] See Harting's "Ornithology of Shakespeare," 1871, pp. 246–257.

with the branches, of old rotten trees, cast up there likewise, whereon is found a certain spume or froth, that in time breedeth into certain shells, in shape like those of the mussel, but sharper pointed, and of a whitish color; wherein is contained a thing in form like a lace of silk, one end whereof is fastened unto the inside of the shell, even as the fish of oysters and mussels are. The other end is made fast unto the belly of a rude mass or lump, which in time cometh to the shape and form of a bird; when it is perfectly formed the shell gapeth open, and the first thing that appeareth is the foresaid lace or string; next come the legs of the bird hanging out, and as it groweth greater it openeth the shell by degrees, till at length it is all come forth and hangeth only by the bill. In short space after it cometh to full maturity, and falleth into the sea, where it gathereth feathers and groweth to a fowl, bigger than a mallard, and lesser than a goose; having black legs and bill, or beak, and feathers black and white, spotted in such a manner as is our magpie, which the people of Lancashire call by no other name than a tree goose." An interesting cut of these birds so growing is given by Mr. Halliwell-Phillipps from a manuscript of the 14th century, who is of opinion that the barnacle mentioned by Caliban was the tree-goose. It is not to be supposed, however, that there were none who doubted this marvellous story, or who took steps to refute it. Belon, so long ago as 1551, says Mr. Harting,[1] and others after him, treated it with ridicule, and a refutation may be found in Willughby's " Ornithology," which was edited by Ray in 1678.[2] This vulgar error is mentioned by many of the old writers. Thus Bishop Hall, in his " Virgidemiarum " (lib. iv. sat. 2), says:

> " The Scottish barnacle, if I might choose,
> That of a worme doth waxe a winged goose."

---

[1] "Ornithology of Shakespeare," 1871, p. 252.

[2] See " Philosophical Transactions " for 1835; Darwin's "Monograph of the Cirrhipedia," published by the Ray Society; a paper by Sir J. Emerson Tennent in "Notes and Queries," 1st series, vol. viii. p. 223; Brand's "Popular Antiquities," 1849, vol. iii. pp. 361, 362; Douce's "Illustrations of Shakespeare," 1839, p. 14.

Butler, too, in his "Hudibras" (III. ii. l. 655), speaks of it; and Marston, in his "Malecontent" (1604), has the following: "Like your Scotch barnacle, now a block, instantly a worm, and presently a great goose."

Blackbird. This favorite is called, in the "Midsummer-Night's Dream" (iii. 1) an ousel (old French, *oisel*), a term still used in the neighborhood of Leeds:

> "The ousel cock, so black of hue,
> With orange-tawny bill."

In "2 Henry IV." (iii. 2) when Justice Shallow inquires of Justice Silence, "And how doth my cousin?" he is answered: "Alas, a black ousel,[1] cousin Shallow," a phrase which, no doubt, corresponded to our modern one, "a black sheep." In Spenser's "Epithalamium" (l. 82), the word occurs:

> "The ousel shrills, the ruddock warbles soft."

Buzzard. Mr. Staunton suggests that in the following passage of the "Taming of the Shrew" (ii. 1) a play is intended upon the words, and that in the second line "buzzard" means a beetle, from its peculiar buzzing noise:

> "*Pet.* O slow-wing'd turtle! shall a buzzard take thee?
> *Kath.* Ay, for a turtle, as he takes a buzzard."

The beetle was formerly called a buzzard; and in Staffordshire, a cockchafer is termed a hum-buz. In Northamptonshire we find a proverb, "I'm between a hawk and a buzzard," which means, "I don't know what to do, or how to act."[2]

Chaffinch. Some think that this bird is alluded to in the song in the "Midsummer-Night's Dream" (iii. 1), where the expression "finch" is used; the chaffinch having always

---

[1] See Yarrell's "History of British Birds," 2d edition, vol. i. p. 218; "Dialect of Leeds," 1862, p. 329. In "Hamlet" (iii. 2), some modern editions read "ouzle;" the old editions all have *weasel*, which is now adopted.

[2] Miss Baker's "Northamptonshire Glossary," 1854, vol. i. p. 94. See Nares's "Glossary," 1872, vol. i. p. 124; and "Richard III.," i. 1.

been a favorite cage-bird with the lower classes.[1]   In " Troilus
and Cressida " (v. 1) Thersites calls Patroclus a " finch-egg,"
which was evidently meant as a term of reproach.   Others,
again, consider the phrase as equivalent to coxcomb.

Chough.   In using this word Shakespeare probably, in
most cases, meant the jackdaw;[2] for in " A Midsummer-
Night's Dream " (iii. 2) he says:

> " russet-pated choughs, many in sort,
> Rising and cawing at the gun's report ;"

the term russet-pated being applicable to the jackdaw, but
not to the real chough.   In " 1 Henry IV." (v. 1), Prince Henry
calls Falstaff *chewet*—" Peace, chewet, peace "—in allusion,
no doubt, to the chough or jackdaw, for common birds have
always had a variety of names.[3]   Such an appellation would
be a proper reproach to Falstaff, for his meddling and im-
pertinent talk.   Steevens and Malone, however, finding that
chewets were little round pies made of minced meat, thought
that the Prince compared Falstaff, for his unseasonable chat-
tering, to a minced pie.   Cotgrave[4] describes the French
chouette as an owlet ; also, a " chough," which many consider to be the simple and satisfactory explanation of *chewet*.
Belon, in his " History of Birds " (Paris, 1855), speaks of the
chouette as the smallest kind of chough or crow.   Again, in
" 1 Henry IV." (ii. 2), in the amusing scene where Falstaff,
with the Prince and Poins, meet to rob the travellers at Gads-

[1] Harting's " Ornithology of Shakespeare," p. 144 ; Halliwell-Phillipps's " Handbook Index to Shakespeare," 1866, p. 187.   The term
finch, also, according to some, may mean either the bullfinch or goldfinch.

[2] See Yarrell's " History of British Birds," 2d edition, vol. ii. p. 58.

[3] Nares's " Glossary," vol. i. p. 156; Singer's " Shakespeare," 1875, vol.
v. p. 115 ; Dyce's " Glossary," 1876, p. 77.

[4] Mr. Dyce says that if Dr. Latham had been acquainted with the
article " Chouette," in Cotgrave, he would not probably have suggested
that Shakespeare meant here the lapwing or pewit.   Some consider
the magpie is meant.   See Halliwell-Phillipps's " Handbook Index to
Shakespeare," 1866, p. 83.   Professor Newton would read " russet-
patted," or " red-legged," thinking that Shakespeare meant the chough.

hill, Falstaff calls the victims "fat chuffs," probably, says Mr. Harting, who connects the word with chough, from their strutting about with much noise. Nares,[1] too, in his explanation of *chuff*, says, that some suppose it to be from chough, which is similarly pronounced, and means a kind of sea-bird, generally esteemed a stupid one. Various other meanings are given. Thus, Mr. Gifford[2] affirms that *chuff* is always used in a bad sense, and means " a coarse, unmannered clown, at once sordid and wealthy;" and Mr. Halliwell-Phillipps explains it as spoken in contempt for a fat person.[3] In Northamptonshire,[4] we find the word chuff used to denote a person in good condition, as in Clare's "Village Minstrel:"

> " His chuff cheeks dimpling in a fondling smile."

Shakespeare alludes to the practice of teaching choughs to talk, although from the following passages he does not appear to have esteemed their talking powers as of much value; for in "All's Well That Ends Well" (iv. 1), he says: "Choughs' language, gabble enough, and good enough." And in "The Tempest" (ii. 1), he represents Antonio as saying:

> " There be that can rule Naples
> As well as he that sleeps; lords that can prate
> As amply and unnecessarily
> As this Gonzalo; I myself could make
> A chough of as deep chat."

Shakespeare always refers to the jackdaw as the " daw."[5] The chough or jackdaw was one of the birds considered ominous by our forefathers, an allusion to which occurs in "Macbeth" (iii. 4):

---

[1] " Glossary," vol. i. p. 162; Singer's " Notes to Shakespeare," 1875, vol. v. p. 42.

[2] Massinger's Works, 1813, vol. i. p. 281.

[3] " Handbook Index to Shakespeare," 1866, p. 86.

[4] Miss Baker's " Northamptonshire Glossary," 1854, vol. i. p. 116.

[5] "Coriolanus," iv. 5; "Troilus and Cressida," i. 2; " Much Ado About Nothing," ii. 3; " Twelfth Night," iii. 4; " Love's Labour's Lost," v. 2, song; " 1 Henry VI." ii. 4.

"Augurs and understood relations have,
  By magot-pies and choughs and rooks brought forth
  The secret'st man of blood."

At the present day this bird is not without its folk-lore, and there is a Norwich rhyme to the following effect :[1]

"When three daws are seen on St. Peter's vane together,
  Then we're sure to have bad weather."

In the north of England,[2] too, the flight of jackdaws down the chimney is held to presage death.

Cock. The beautiful notion which represents the cock as crowing all night long on Christmas Eve, and by its vigilance dispelling every kind of malignant spirit [3] and evil influence is graphically mentioned in "Hamlet" (i. 1), where Marcellus, speaking of the ghost, says :

"It faded on the crowing of the cock.
  Some say, that ever 'gainst that season comes
  Wherein our Saviour's birth is celebrated,
  The bird of dawning singeth all night long :
  And then, they say, no spirit dares stir abroad ;
  The nights are wholesome ; then no planets strike,
  No fairy takes, nor witch hath power to charm,
  So hallow'd and so gracious is the time."

In short, there is a complete prostration of the powers of darkness ; and thus, for the time being, mankind is said to be released from the influence of all those evil forces which otherwise exert such sway. The notion that spirits fly at cock-crow is very ancient, and is mentioned by the Christian poet Prudentius, who flourished in the beginning of the fourth century. There is also a hymn, said to have been composed by St. Ambrose, and formerly used in the Salisbury Service, which so much resembles the following speech of Horatio (i. 1), that one might almost suppose Shakespeare had seen it :[4]

---

[1] Swainson's "Weather-Lore," 1873, p. 240.
[2] Henderson's "Folk-Lore of Northern Counties," 1879, p. 48.
[3] See Douce's "Illustrations of Shakespeare," p. 438.
[4] See Ibid.

> " The cock, that is the trumpet to the morn,
>   Doth with his lofty and shrill-sounding throat
>   Awake the god of day ; and, at his warning,
>   Whether in sea or fire, in earth or air,
>   The extravagant and erring spirit hies
>   To his confine."

This disappearance of spirits at cock-crow is further alluded to (i. 2) :[1]

> " the morning cock crew loud,
>   And at the sound it shrunk in haste away,
>   And vanished from our sight."

Blair, too, in his " Grave," has these graphic words:

> " the tale
>   Of horrid apparition, tall and ghastly,
>   That walks at dead of night, or takes his stand
>   O'er some new-open'd grave, and, strange to tell,
>   Evanishes at crowing of the cock."

This superstition has not entirely died out in England, and a correspondent of " Notes and Queries "[2] relates an amusing legend current in Devonshire : " Mr. N. was a squire who had been so unfortunate as to sell his soul to the devil, with the condition that after his funeral the fiend should take possession of his skin. He had also persuaded a neighbor to be present on the occasion of the flaying. On the death of Mr. N. this man went, in a state of great alarm, to the parson of the parish, and asked his advice. By him he was told to fulfil his engagement, but he must be sure and carry a cock into the church with him. On the night after the funeral the man proceeded to the church, armed with the cock, and, as an additional security, took up his position in the parson's pew. At twelve o'clock the devil arrived, opened the grave, took the corpse from the coffin, and flayed it. When the operation was concluded, he held the skin up before him and remarked, ' Well, 'twas not worth

---

[1] See Brand's " Pop. Antiq.," 1849, vol. ii. pp. 51–57 ; Hampson's " Medii Œvi Kalendarium," vol. i. p. 84.

[2] 1st series, vol. iii. p. 404.

coming for after all, for it is all full of holes!' As he said
this the cock crew, whereupon the fiend, turning round to
the man, exclaimed, 'If it had not been for the bird you
have got there under your arm, I would have your skin too!'
But, thanks to the cock, the man got home safe again."
Various origins have been assigned to this superstition,
which Hampson[1] regards as a misunderstood tradition of
some Sabæan fable. The cock, he adds, which seems by its
early voice to call forth the sun, was esteemed a sacred solar
bird; hence it was also sacred to Mercury, one of the personifications of the sun.

A very general amusement, up to the end of the last century, was cock-fighting, a diversion of which mention is occasionally made by Shakespeare, as in "Antony and Cleopatra (ii. 3):

> "His cocks do win the battle still of mine,
> When it is all to nought."

And again Hamlet says (v. 2):

> "O, I die, Horatio;
> The potent poison quite o'er-crows my spirit"—

meaning, the poison triumphs over him, as a cock over his
beaten antagonist. Formerly, cock-fighting entered into the
occupations of the old and young.[2] Schools had their cock-
fights. Travellers agreed with coachmen that they were to
wait a night if there was a cock-fight in any town through
which they passed. When country gentlemen had sat long
at table, and the conversation had turned upon the relative
merits of their several birds, a cock-fight often resulted, as
the birds in question were brought for the purpose into the
dining-room. Cock-fighting was practised on Shrove Tuesday to a great extent, and in the time of Henry VII. seems
to have been practised within the precincts of court. The
earliest mention of this pastime in England is by Fitzste-

---

[1] "Medii Œvi Kalendarium," vol. i. p. 85.
[2] Roberts's "Social History of Southern Counties of England," 1856,
p. 421; see "British Popular Customs," 1876, p. 65.

phens, in 1191. Happily, nowadays, cock-fighting is, by law, a misdemeanor, and punishable by penalty. One of the popular terms for a cock beaten in a fight was "a craven," to which we find a reference in the "Taming of the Shrew" (ii. 1):

> "No cock of mine; you crow too like a craven."

We may also compare the expression in "Henry V." (iv. 7): "He is a craven and a villain else." In the old appeal or wager of battle,[1] in our common law, we are told, on the authority of Lord Coke, that the party who confessed himself wrong, or refused to fight, was to pronounce the word *cravent*, and judgment was at once given against him. Singer[2] says the term may be satisfactorily traced from *crant, creant*, the old French word for an act of submission. It is so written in the old metrical romance of "Ywaine and Gawaine" (Ritson, i. 133):

> "Or yelde the til us als creant."

And in "Richard Cœur de Lion" (Weber, ii. 208):

> "On knees he fel down, and cryde, crêaunt."

It then became *cravant, cravent*, and at length *craven*.

In the time of Shakespeare the word *cock* was used as a vulgar corruption or purposed disguise of the name of God, an instance of which occurs in "Hamlet" (iv. 5): "By cock, they are to blame." This irreverent alteration of the sacred name is found at least a dozen times[3] in Heywood's "Edward the Fourth," where one passage is,

> "*Herald.* Sweare on this booke, King Lewis, so help you God,
> You mean no otherwise then you have said.
> *King Lewis.* So helpe me Cock as I dissemble not."

We find, too, other allusions to the sacred name, as in " cock's passion," " cock's body ;" as in " Taming of the Shrew " (iv.

---

[1] Nares's "Glossary," 1872, vol. i. p. 203.

[2] Singer's "Shakespeare," 1875, vol. ix. p. 256; Halliwell-Phillipps's "Handbook Index to Shakespeare," p. 112.

[3] Dyce's "Glossary to Shakespeare," p. 85.

1): "Cock's passion, silence!" A not uncommon oath, too, in Shakespeare's time was "Cock and pie"—*cock* referring to God, and *pie* being supposed to mean the service-book of the Romish Church; a meaning which, says Mr. Dyce, seems much more probable than Douce's[1] supposition that this oath was connected with the making of solemn vows by knights in the days of chivalry, during entertainments at which a roasted peacock was served up. It is used by Justice Shallow ("2 Henry IV.," v. 1): "By cock and pye, sir, you shall not away to-night." We may also compare the expression in the old play of "Soliman and Perseda" (1599): "By cock and pye and mousefoot." Mr. Harting[2] says the "Cock and Pye" (*i. e.*, magpie) was an ordinary ale-house sign, and may have thus become a subject for the vulgar to swear by.

The phrase, "Cock-a-hoop"[3]—which occurs in "Romeo and Juliet" (i. 5),

> "You'll make a mutiny among my guests!
> You will set cock-a-hoop! you'll be the man!"

—no doubt refers to a reckless person, who takes the cock or tap out of a cask, and lays it on the top or hoop of the barrel, thus letting all the contents of the cask run out. Formerly, a quart pot was called a hoop, being formed of staves bound together with hoops like barrels. There were generally three hoops to such a pot; hence, in "2 Henry VI." (iv. 2), one of Jack Cade's popular reformations was to increase their number: "the three-hooped pot shall have ten hoops; and I will make it felony to drink small beer." Some, however, consider the term Cock-a-hoop[4] refers to the boastful crowing of the cock.

In "King Lear" (iii. 2) Shakespeare speaks of the "cataracts and hurricanoes" as having

> "drenched our steeples, drowned the cocks!"

---

[1] "Illustrations of Shakespeare," 1839, p. 290.
[2] "Ornithology of Shakespeare," p. 171.
[3] It is also an ale-house sign.
[4] See Dyce's "Glossary to Shakespeare," p. 85.

Vanes on the tops of steeples were in days gone by made in the form of a cock—hence weathercocks—and put up, in papal times, to remind the clergy of watchfulness.[1] Apart, too, from symbolism, the large tail of the cock was well adapted to turn with the wind.[2]

Cormorant. The proverbial voracity of this bird[3] gave rise to a man of large appetite being likened to it, a sense in which Shakespeare employs the word, as in " Coriolanus " (i. 1): "the cormorant belly;" in " Love's Labour's Lost " (i. 1): "cormorant devouring Time ;" and in " Troilus and Cressida " (ii. 2): " this cormorant war." "Although," says Mr. Harting,[4] "Shakespeare mentions the cormorant in several of his plays, he has nowhere alluded to the sport of using these birds, when trained, for fishing ; a fact which is singular, since he often speaks of the then popular pastime of hawking, and he did not die until some years after James I. had made fishing with cormorants a fashionable amusement."

Crow. This has from the earliest times been reckoned a bird of bad omen ; and in " Julius Cæsar " (v. 1), Cassius, on the eve of battle, predicted a defeat, because, to use his own words :

> "crows and kites
> Fly o'er our heads and downward look on us,
> As we were sickly prey : their shadows seem
> A canopy most fatal, under which
> Our army lies, ready to give up the ghost."

Allusions to the same superstition occur in " Troilus and Cressida " (i. 2) ; " King John " (v. 2), etc. Vergil (" Bu-

---

[1] See " Book of Days," 1863, vol. i. p. 157.

[2] In " King Lear " (iv. 6), where Edgar says :

> " Yond tall anchoring bark,
> Diminish'd to her cock ; her cock, a buoy
> Almost too small for sight,"

the word " cock " is an abbreviation for cock-boat.

[3] For superstitions associated with this bird, see Brand's " Pop. Antiq.," 1849. vol. iii. p. 218.

[4] " Ornithology of Shakespeare," p. 260.

colic," i. 18) mentions the croaking of the crow as a bad omen :

> "Sæpe sinistra cava prædixit ab ilice cornix."

And Butler, in his "Hudibras" (part ii. canto 3), remarks :

> "Is it not ominous in all countries,
> When crows and ravens croak upon trees."

Even children, nowadays, regard with no friendly feelings this bird of ill-omen ;[1] and in the north of England there is a rhyme to the following effect :

> "Crow, crow, get out of my sight,
> Or else I'll eat thy liver and lights."

Among other allusions made by Shakespeare to the crow may be noticed the crow-keeper—a person employed to drive away crows from the fields. At present,[2] in all the midland counties, a boy set to drive away the birds is said to keep birds; hence, a stuffed figure, now called a *scarecrow*, was also called a crow-keeper, as in "King Lear" (iv. 6): "That fellow handles his bow like a crow-keeper." One of Tusser's directions for September is :

> "No sooner a-sowing, but out by-and-by,
> With mother or boy that alarum can cry:
> And let them be armed with a sling or a bow,
> To scare away pigeon, the rook, or the crow."

In "Romeo and Juliet" (i. 4) a scarecrow seems meant :

> "Bearing a Tartar's painted bow of lath,
> Scaring the ladies like a crow-keeper."

Among further references to this practice is that in "1 Henry VI." (i. 4), where Lord Talbot relates that, when a prisoner in France, he was publicly exhibited in the market-place :

> "Here, said they, is the terror of the French,
> The scarecrow that affrights our children so."[3]

---

[1] See "Folk-Lore Record," 1879, vol. i. p. 52 ; Henderson's "Folk-Lore of Northern Counties," 1879, pp. 25, 126, 277.

[2] Nares's "Glossary," vol. i. p. 208.

[3] Cf. "Henry IV.," iv. 2.

And once more, in " Measure for Measure " (ii. 1):

> " We must not make a scarecrow of the law,
> Setting it up to fear the birds of prey,
> And let it keep one shape, till custom make it
> Their perch and not their terror."

The phrase "to pluck a crow " is to complain good-naturedly, but reproachfully, and to threaten retaliation.[1] It occurs in " Comedy of Errors " (iii. 1): " We'll pluck a crow together." Sometimes the word *pull* is substituted for pluck, as in Butler's " Hudibras " (part ii. canto 2):

> " If not, resolve before we go
> That you and I must pull a crow."

The crow has been regarded as the emblem of darkness, which has not escaped the notice of Shakespeare, who, in " Pericles " (iv. introd.), speaking of the white dove, says:

> " With the dove of Paphos might the crow
> Vie feathers white." [2]

Cuckoo. Many superstitions have clustered round the cuckoo, and both in this country and abroad it is looked upon as a mysterious bird, being supposed to possess the gift of second-sight, a notion referred to in " Love's Labour's Lost " (v. 2):

> " Cuckoo, cuckoo :[3] O word of fear,
> Unpleasing to a married ear."

And again, in "A Midsummer-Night's Dream " (iii. 1), Bottom sings:

> " The plain-song cuckoo gray,
> Whose note full many a man doth mark,
> And dares not answer nay."

It is still a common idea that the cuckoo, if asked, will

---

[1] Miss Baker's " Northamptonshire Glossary," vol. ii. p. 161 ; Brand's " Pop. Antiq.," 1849, vol. iii. p. 393.

[2] Cf. " Romeo and Juliet," i. 5.

[3] " A cuckold being called from the cuckoo, the note of that bird was supposed to prognosticate that destiny."—Nares's " Glossary," vol. i. p. 212.

tell any one, by the repetition of its cries, how long he has to live. The country lasses in Sweden count the cuckoo's call to ascertain how many years they have to remain unmarried, but they generally shut their ears and run away on hearing it a few times.[1] Among the Germans the notes of the cuckoo, when heard in spring for the first time, are considered a good omen. Cæsarius (1222) tells us of a convertite who was about to become a monk, but changed his mind on hearing the cuckoo's call, and counting twenty-two repetitions of it. "Come," said he, "I have certainly twenty-two years still to live, and why should I mortify myself during all that time? I will go back to the world, enjoy its delights for twenty years, and devote the remaining two to penitence."[2] In England the peasantry salute the cuckoo with the following invocation:

> "Cuckoo, cherry-tree,
> Good bird, tell me,
> How many years have I to live"—

the allusion to the cherry-tree having probably originated in the popular fancy that before the cuckoo ceases its song it must eat three good meals of cherries. Pliny mentions the belief that when the cuckoo came to maturity it devoured the bird which had reared it, a superstition several times alluded to by Shakespeare. Thus, in "King Lear" (i. 4), the Fool remarks:

> "The hedge-sparrow fed the cuckoo so long,
> That it had its head bit off by its young."

Again, in "1 Henry IV." (v. 1), Worcester says:

> "And being fed by us you used us so
> As that ungentle gull, the cuckoo's bird,
> Useth the sparrow; did oppress our nest;
> Grew by our feeding to so great a bulk
> That even our love durst not come near your sight
> For fear of swallowing."

---

[1] Engel's "Musical Myths and Facts," 1876, vol. i. p. 9.
[2] See Kelly's "Indo-European Folk-Lore," 1863, p. 99; "English Folk-Lore," 1879, pp. 55–62.

Once more, the opinion that the cuckoo made no nest of its own, but laid its eggs in that of another bird, is mentioned in "Antony and Cleopatra" (ii. 6):

> "Thou dost o'er-count me oi my father's house;
> But, since the cuckoo builds not for himself,
> Remain in't as thou may'st."

It has been remarked,[1] however, in reference to the common idea that the young cuckoo ill-treats its foster-mother, that if we watch the movements of the two birds, when the younger is being fed, we cannot much wonder at this piece of folk-lore. When the cuckoo opens its great mouth, the diminutive nurse places her own head so far within its precincts that it has the exact appearance of a voluntary surrender to decapitation.

The notion[2] " which couples the name of the cuckoo with the character of the man whose wife is unfaithful to him appears to have been derived from the Romans, and is first found in the Middle Ages in France, and in the countries of which the modern language is derived from the Latin. But the ancients more correctly gave the name of the bird, not to the husband of the faithless wife, but to her paramour, who might justly be supposed to be acting the part of the cuckoo. They applied the name of the bird in whose nest the cuckoo's eggs were usually deposited—'carruca'—to the husband. It is not quite clear how, in the passage from classic to mediæval, the application of the term was transferred to the husband." In further allusion to this bird, we may quote the following from "All's Well That Ends Well" (i. 3):

> "For I the ballad will repeat,
>   Which men full true shall find,
> Your marriage comes by destiny,
>   Your cuckoo sings by kind."

The cuckoo has generally been regarded as the harbinger of spring, and, according to a Gloucester rhyme:

---

[1] See Mary Howitt's "Pictorial Calendar of the Seasons," p. 155; Knight's "Pictorial Shakespeare," vol. i. pp. 225, 226.

[2] Chambers's "Book of Days," vol. i. p. 531.

> "The cuckoo comes in April,
> Sings a song in May;
> Then in June another tune,
> And then she flies away."

Thus, in " 1 Henry IV." (iii. 2), the king, alluding to his pre-decessor, says:

> "So, when he had occasion to be seen,
> He was but as the cuckoo is in June,
> Heard, not regarded."

In "Love's Labour's Lost" (v. 2) spring is maintained by the cuckoo, in those charming sonnets descriptive of the beauties of the country at this season.

The word cuckoo has, from the earliest times, been used as a term of reproach;[1] and Plautus[2] has introduced it on more than one occasion. In this sense we find it quoted by Shakespeare in " 1 Henry IV." (ii. 4): "O' horseback, ye cuckoo." The term *cuckold*, too, which so frequently occurs throughout Shakespeare's plays, is generally derived from cuculus,[3] from the practice already alluded to of depositing its eggs in other birds' nests.

Domestic Fowl. In "The Tempest" (v. 1), the word chick is used as a term of endearment: "My Ariel; chick," etc.; and in "Macbeth" (iv. 3) Macduff speaks of his children as "all my pretty chickens." In "Coriolanus" (v. 3), hen is applied to a woman: "poor hen, fond of no second brood;" and in "Taming of the Shrew" (ii. 1), Petruchio says: "so Kate will be my hen;" and, once more, " 1 Henry IV." (iii. 3), Falstaff says, "How now, Dame Partlet the hen?" In "Othello" (i. 3) Iago applies the term "guinea-hen" to Desdemona, a cant phrase in Shakespeare's day for a fast woman.

Dove. Among the many beautiful allusions to this bird

---

[1] See Brand's "Pop. Antiq.," 1849, vol. ii. p. 201.

[2] "Asinaria," v. 1.

[3] Nares, in his "Glossary" (vol. i. p. 212), says: "Cuckold, perhaps, *quasi* cuckoo'd, *i. e.*, one served; *i. e.*, forced to bring up a brood that is not his own."

we may mention one in " Hamlet " (v. 1), where Shakespeare speaks of the dove only laying two eggs :[1]

> "as patient as the female dove
> When that her golden couplets are disclosed."

The young nestlings, when first disclosed, are only covered with a yellow down, and the mother rarely leaves the nest, in consequence of the tenderness of her young ; hence the dove has been made an emblem of patience.   In " 2 Henry IV." (iv. 1), it is spoken of as the symbol of peace :

> " The dove and very blessed spirit of peace."

Its love, too, is several times referred to, as in " Romeo and Juliet " (ii. 1), " Pronounce but — love and dove ;" and in " 1 Henry VI." (ii. 2), Burgundy says :

> " Like to a pair of loving turtle-doves,
> That could not live asunder, day or night."

This bird has also been regarded as the emblem of fidelity, as in the following graphic passage in " Troilus and Cressida " (iii. 2) :

> " As true as steel, as plantage to the moon,
> As sun to day, as turtle to her mate,
> As iron to adamant, as earth to the centre ;"

and in " Winter's Tale " (iv. 4), we read :

> " turtles pair,
> " That never mean to part."

Its modesty is alluded to in the " Taming of the Shrew " (ii. 1): " modest as the dove ;" and its innocence in " 2 Henry VI." (iii. 1) is mentioned, where King Henry says :

> " Our kinsman Gloster is as innocent
> From meaning treason to our royal person
> As is the sucking lamb or harmless dove :
> The duke is virtuous, mild and too well given
> To dream on evil, or to work my downfall."

The custom of giving a pair of doves or pigeons as a present

---

[1] Singer's " Shakespeare," 1875, vol. ix. p. 294.

or peace-offering is alluded to in " Titus Andronicus" (iv. 4), where the clown says, "God and Saint Stephen give you good den: I have brought you a letter and a couple of pigeons here;" and when Gobbo tried to find favor with Bassanio, in " Merchant of Venice" (ii. 2), he began by saying, "I have here a dish of doves, that I would bestow upon your worship." Shakespeare alludes in several places to the "doves of Venus," as in " Venus and Adonis:"

> " Thus weary of the world, away she [Venus] hies,
>   And yokes her silver doves; by whose swift aid
>   Their mistress, mounted, through the empty skies
>   In her light chariot quickly is conveyed;
>   Holding their course to Paphos, where their queen
>   Means to immure herself and not be seen;"

and in " A Midsummer-Night's Dream" (i. 1), where Hermia speaks of "the simplicity of Venus' doves." This will also explain, says Mr. Harting,[1] the reference to "the dove of Paphos," in " Pericles" (iv. Introd.). The towns of Old and New Paphos are situated on the southwest extremity of the coast of Cyprus. Old Paphos is the one generally referred to by the poets, being the peculiar seat of the worship of Venus, who was fabled to have been wafted thither after her birth amid the waves. The "dove of Paphos" may therefore be considered as synonymous with the "dove of Venus."

Mahomet, we are told, had a dove, which he used to feed with wheat out of his ear; when hungry, the dove lighted on his shoulder, and thrust its bill in to find its breakfast, Mahomet persuading the rude and simple Arabians that it was the Holy Ghost, that gave him advice.[2] Hence, in " 1 Henry VI." (i. 2), the question is asked:

> " Was Mahomet inspired with a dove?"

Duck. A barbarous pastime in Shakespeare's time was hunting a tame duck in the water with spaniels. For the

---

[1] "Ornithology of Shakespeare," pp. 190, 191.
[2] Sir W. Raleigh's "History of the World," bk. i. pt. i. ch. 6.

performance of this amusement [1] it was necessary to have recourse to a pond of water sufficiently extensive to give the duck plenty of room for making its escape from the dogs when closely pursued, which it did by diving as often as any of them came near it, hence the following allusion in " Henry V." (ii. 3):

> " And hold-fast is the only dog, my duck." [2]

" To swim like a duck " is a common proverb, which occurs in " The Tempest " (ii. 2), where Trinculo, in reply to Stephano's question how he escaped, says: " Swam ashore, man, like a duck; I can swim like a duck, I'll be sworn."

Eagle. From the earliest time this bird has been associated with numerous popular fancies and superstitions, many of which have not escaped the notice of Shakespeare. A notion of very great antiquity attributes to it the power of gazing at the sun undazzled, to which Spenser, in his " Hymn of Heavenly Beauty " refers:

> " And like the native brood of eagle's kind,
> On that bright sun of glory fix thine eyes."

In " Love's Labour's Lost " (iv. 3) Biron says of Rosaline :

> " What peremptory eagle-sighted eye
> Dares look upon the heaven of her brow,
> That is not blinded by her majesty?" [3]

And in " 3 Henry VI." (ii. 1) Richard says to his brother Edward :

> " Nay, if thou be that princely eagle's bird,
> Show thy descent by gazing 'gainst the sun."

The French naturalist, Lacepede, [4] has calculated that the clearness of vision in birds is nine times more extensive than

---

[1] Strutt's " Sports and Pastimes," 1876, p. 329.

[2] There is an allusion to the proverbial saying, " Brag is a good dog, but Hold-fast is a better."

[3] In the same scene we are told,

> " A lover's eyes will gaze an eagle blind."

Cf. " Romeo and Juliet," iii. 5 ; " Richard II.," iii. 3.

[4] Quoted by Harting, in " Ornithology of Shakespeare," p. 24.

that of the farthest-sighted man. The eagle, too, has always been proverbial for its great power of flight, and on this account has had assigned to it the sovereignty of the feathered race. Aristotle and Pliny both record the legend of the wren disputing for the crown, a tradition which is still found in Ireland :[1] " The birds all met together one day, and settled among themselves that whichever of them could fly highest was to be the king of them all. Well, just as they were starting, the little rogue of a wren perched itself on the eagle's tail. So they flew and flew ever so high, till the eagle was miles above all the rest, and could not fly another stroke, for he was so tired. Then says he, 'I'm the king of the birds,' says he; 'hurroo!' 'You lie,' says the wren, darting up a perch and a half above the big fellow. The eagle was so angry to think how he was outwitted by the wren, that when the latter was coming down he gave him a stroke of his wing, and from that day the wren has never been able to fly higher than a hawthorn bush." The swiftness of the eagle's flight is spoken of in " Timon of Athens," (i. 1):

> "an eagle flight, bold, and forth on,
> Leaving no tract behind."[2]

The great age, too, of the eagle is well known; and the words of the Psalmist are familiar to most readers:

> "His youth shall be renewed like the eagle's."

Apemantus, however, asks of Timon (" Timon of Athens," iv. 3):

> "will these moss'd trees,
> That have outlived the eagle, page thy heels,
> And skip when thou point'st out?"

Turbervile, in his " Booke of Falconrie," 1575, says that the great age of this bird has been ascertained from the circumstance of its always building its eyrie or nest in the same

---

[1] Kelly's " Indo-European Folk-Lore," pp. 75, 79.

[2] Cf. " Antony and Cleopatra," ii. 2 : " This was but as a fly by an eagle."

place. The Romans considered the eagle a bird of good omen, and its presence in time of battle was supposed to foretell victory. Thus, in " Julius Cæsar " (v. 1) we read :

> "Coming from Sardis, on our former ensign
> Two mighty eagles fell; and there they perch'd,
> Gorging and feeding from our soldiers' hands."

It was selected for the Roman legionary standard,[1] through being the king and most powerful of all birds. As a bird of good omen it is mentioned also in " Cymbeline " (i. 1):

> " I chose an eagle,
> And did avoid a puttock ;"

and in another scene (iv. 2) the Soothsayer relates how

> " Last night the very gods show'd me a vision,
> . . . . thus :—
> I saw Jove's bird, the Roman eagle, wing'd
> From the spungy south to this part of the west,
> There vanish'd in the sunbeams : which portends
> (Unless my sins abuse my divination),
> Success to the Roman host."

The conscious superiority[2] of the eagle is depicted by Tamora in " Titus Andronicus " (iv. 4):

> " The eagle suffers little birds to sing,
> And is not careful what they mean thereby,
> Knowing that with the shadow of his wing,
> He can at pleasure stint their melody."

Goose. This bird was the subject[3] of many quaint proverbial phrases often used in the old popular writers. Thus, a *tailor's goose* was a jocular name for his pressing-iron, probably from its being often roasting before the fire, an allusion to which occurs in " Macbeth" (ii. 3): " come in, tailor; here you may roast your goose." The " wild-goose chase," which is mentioned in " Romeo and Juliet " (ii. 4)—" Nay, if thy wits run the wild-goose chase, I have done "—was

---

[1] Josephus, " De Bello Judico," iii. 5.
[2] Harting's " Ornithology of Shakespeare," p. 33.
[3] Nares's " Glossary," vol. i. p. 378.

a kind of horse-race, which resembled the flight of wild geese. Two horses were started together, and whichever rider could get the lead, the other was obliged to follow him over whatever ground the foremost jockey chose to go. That horse which could distance the other won the race. This reckless sport is mentioned by Burton, in his "Anatomy of Melancholy," as a recreation much in vogue in his time among gentlemen. The term "Winchester goose" was a cant phrase for a certain venereal disease, because the stews in Southwark were under the jurisdiction of the Bishop of Winchester, to whom Gloster tauntingly applies the term in the following passage ("1 Henry VI.," i. 3):

> "Winchester goose! I cry—a rope! a rope!"

In "Troilus and Cressida" (v. 10) there is a further allusion:

> "Some galled goose of Winchester would hiss."

Ben Jonson [1] calls it:

> "the Winchestrian goose,
> Bred on the banke in time of Popery,
> When Venus there maintain'd the mystery."

"Plucking geese" was formerly a barbarous sport of boys ("Merry Wives of Windsor," v. 1), which consisted in stripping a living goose of its feathers.[2]

In "Coriolanus" (i. 4), the goose is spoken of as the emblem of cowardice. Marcius says:

> "You souls of geese,
> That bear the shapes of men, how have you run
> From slaves that apes would beat!"

Goldfinch. The Warwickshire name [3] for this bird is "Proud Tailor," to which, some commentators think, the words in "1 Henry IV." (iii. 1) refer:

> "*Lady P.* I will not sing.
> *Hotsp.* 'Tis the next way to turn tailor, or be red-breast teacher."

---

[1] "Execration against Vulcan," 1640, p. 37.
[2] Singer's "Notes," 1875, vol. i. p. 283.
[3] See "Archæologia," vol. iii. p. 33.

It has, therefore, been suggested that the passage should be read thus: "'Tis the next way to turn tailor, or red-breast teacher," *i. e.*, "to turn teacher of goldfinches or redbreasts." [1] Singer,[2] however, explains the words thus: "Tailors, like weavers, have ever been remarkable for their vocal skill. Percy is jocular in his mode of persuading his wife to sing; and this is a humorous turn which he gives to his argument, 'Come, sing.' 'I will not sing.' ''Tis the next [*i. e.*, the readiest, nearest] way to turn tailor, or redbreast teacher '— the meaning being, to sing is to put yourself upon a level with tailors and teachers of birds."

Gull. Shakespeare often uses this word as synonymous with fool. Thus in "Henry V." (iii. 6) he says:

> "Why, 'tis a gull, a fool."

The same play upon the word occurs in "Othello" (v. 2), and in "Timon of Athens" (ii. 1). In "Twelfth Night" (v. 1) Malvolio asks:

> "Why have you suffer'd me to be imprison'd,
> Kept in a dark house, visited by the priest,
> And made the most notorious geck and gull
> That e'er invention played on? tell me why."

It is also used to express a trick or imposition, as in "Much Ado About Nothing" (ii. 3): "I should think this a gull, but that the white-bearded fellow speaks it."[3] "Gull-catchers," or "gull-gropers," to which reference is made in "Twelfth Night" (ii. 5), where Fabian, on the entry of Maria, exclaims: "Here comes my noble gull-catcher," were the names by which sharpers[4] were known in Shakespeare's

---

[1] Nares's "Glossary," vol. ii. p. 693. Some think that the bullfinch is meant.

[2] Singer's "Notes," 1875, vol. v. p. 82; see Dyce's "Glossary," p. 433.

[3] Some doubt exists as to the derivation of *gull*. Nares says it is from the old French *guiller*. Tooke holds that gull, guile, wile, and guilt are all from the Anglo-Saxon "wiglian, gewiglian," that by which any one is deceived. Harting's "Ornithology of Shakespeare," p. 267.

[4] See D'Israeli's "Curiosities of Literature," vol. iii. p. 84.

time.[1] The "gull-catcher" was generally an old usurer, who lent money to a gallant at an ordinary, who had been unfortunate in play.[2] Decker devotes a chapter to this character in his "Lanthorne and Candle-light," 1612. According to him, "the gull-groper is commonly an old monymonger, who having travailed through all the follyes of the world in his youth, knowes them well, and shunnes them in his age, his whole felicitie being to fill his bags with golde and silver." The person so duped was termed a gull, and the trick also. In that disputed passage in "The Tempest" (ii. 2), where Caliban, addressing Trinculo, says:

> "sometimes I'll get thee
> Young scamels from the rock."

some think that the sea-mew, or sea-gull, is intended,[3] seamall, or sea-mell, being still a provincial name for this bird. Mr. Stevenson, in his "Birds of Norfolk" (vol. ii. p. 260), tells us that "the female bar-tailed godwit is called a 'scammell' by the gunners of Blakeney. But as this bird is not a rockbreeder,[4] it cannot be the one intended in the present passage, if we regard it as an accurate description from a naturalist's point of view." Holt says that "scam" is a limpet, and scamell probably a diminutive. Mr. Dyce[5] reads "scamels," i. e., the kestrel, stannel, or windhover, which breeds in rocky situations and high cliffs on our coasts. He also further observes that this accords well with the context "from the rock," and adds that staniel or stannyel occurs in "Twelfth Night" (ii. 5), where all the old editions exhibit the gross misprint "stallion."

Hawk. The diversion of catching game with hawks was very popular in Shakespeare's time,[6] and hence, as might be

---

[1] See Thornbury's "Shakespeare's England," vol. i. pp. 311–322.

[2] Nares's "Glossary," vol. i. p. 394.

[3] Harting's "Ornithology of Shakespeare," p. 269.

[4] Aldis Wright's "Notes to The Tempest, 1875, pp. 120, 121.

[5] See Dyce's "Shakespeare," vol. i. p. 245.

[6] See Strutt's "Sports and Pastimes," 1876, pp. 60–97, and "Book of Days," 1863, vol. ii. pp. 211–213; Smith's "Festivals, Games, and Amusements," 1831, p. 174.

expected, we find many scattered allusions to it throughout his plays. The training of a hawk for the field was an essential part of the education of a young Saxon nobleman; and the present of a well-trained hawk was a gift to be welcomed by a king. Edward the Confessor spent much of his leisure time in either hunting or hawking; and in the reign of Edward III. we read how the Bishop of Ely attended the service of the church at Bermondsey, Southwark, leaving his hawk in the cloister, which in the meantime was stolen—the bishop solemnly excommunicating the thieves. On one occasion Henry VIII. met with a serious accident when pursuing his hawk at Hitchin, in Hertfordshire. In jumping over a ditch his pole broke, and he fell headlong into the muddy water, whence he was with some difficulty rescued by one of his followers. Sir Thomas More, writing in the reign of Henry VIII., describing the state of manhood, makes a young man say:

> " Man-hod I am, therefore I me delyght
> To hunt and hawke, to nourish up and fede
> The greyhounde to the course, the hawke to th' flight,
> And to bestryde a good and lusty stede."

In noticing, then, Shakespeare's allusions to this sport, we have a good insight into its various features, and also gain a knowledge of the several terms associated with it. Thus frequent mention is made of the word " haggard "—a wild, untrained hawk—and in the following allegory (" Taming of the Shrew," iv. 1), where it occurs, much of the knowledge of falconry is comprised:

> " My falcon now is sharp, and passing empty;
> And, till she stoop, she must not be full-gorged,[1]
> For then she never looks upon her lure.
> Another way I have to man my haggard,
> To make her come, and know her keeper's call;
> That is, to watch her, as we watch these kites
> That bate, and beat, and will not be obedient.

---

[1] " A hawk full-fed was untractable, and refused the lure—the lure being a thing stuffed to look like the game the hawk was to pursue; its lure was to tempt him back after he had flown."

She eat no meat to-day, nor none shall eat;
Last night she slept not, nor to-night she shall not." [1]

Further allusions occur in " Twelfth Night" (iii. 1), where Viola says of the Clown:

"This fellow is wise enough to play the fool;
And to do that well craves a kind of wit:
He must observe their mood on whom he jests,
The quality of persons, and the time;
And, like the haggard, check at every feather
That comes before his eye."

In " Much Ado About Nothing" (iii. 1), Hero, speaking of Beatrice, says that:

"her spirits are as coy and wild
As haggards of the rock."

And Othello (iii. 3), mistrusting Desdemona, and likening her to a hawk, exclaims:

"if I do prove her haggard,—
I'd whistle her off." [2]

The word " check" alluded to above was a term in falconry applied to a hawk when she forsook her proper game and followed some other of inferior kind that crossed her in her flight [3]—being mentioned again in " Hamlet" (iv. 7), where the king says:

"If he be now return'd
As checking at his voyage." [4]

Another common expression used in falconry is " tower,"

---

[1] In the same play (iv. 2) Hortensio describes Bianca as "this proud disdainful haggard." See Dyce's "Glossary," p. 197; Cotgrave's "French and English Dictionary," sub. "Hagard;" and Latham's "Falconry," etc., 1658.

[2] " To whistle off," or dismiss by a whistle; a hawk seems to have been usually sent off in this way against the wind when sent in pursuit of prey.

[3] Dyce's "Glossary," p. 77; see "Twelfth Night," ii. 5.

[4] The use of the word is not quite the same here, because the voyage was Hamlet's "proper game," which he abandons. "Notes to Hamlet," Clark and Wright, 1876, p. 205.

applied to certain hawks, etc., which tower aloft, soar spirally to a height in the air, and thence swoop upon their prey. In "Macbeth" (ii. 4) we read of

> "A falcon, towering in her pride of place;"

in "2 Henry VI." (ii. 1) Suffolk says,

> "My lord protector's hawks do tower so well;"

and in "King John" (v. 2) the Bastard says,

> "And like an eagle o'er his aery[1] towers."

The word "quarry," which occurs several times in Shakespeare's plays, in some instances means the "game or prey sought." The etymology has, says Nares, been variously attempted, but with little success. It may, perhaps, originally have meant the square, or enclosure (*carrée*), into which the game was driven (as is still practised in other countries), and hence the application of it to the game there caught would be a natural extension of the term. Randle Holme, in his "Academy of Armory" (book ii. c. xi. p. 240), defines it as "the fowl which the hawk flyeth at, whether dead or alive." It was also equivalent to a heap of slaughtered game, as in the following passages. In "Coriolanus" (i. 1), Caius Marcius says:

> "I'd make a quarry
> With thousands of these quarter'd slaves."

In "Macbeth" (iv. 3)[2] we read "the quarry of these murder'd deer;" and in "Hamlet" (v. 2), "This quarry cries on havock."

Another term in falconry is "stoop," or "swoop," denot-

---

[1] See Dyce's "Glossary," p. 456; Harting's "Ornithology of Shakespeare," p. 39; Tuberville's "Booke of Falconrie," 1611, p. 53.

[2] Also in i. 2 we read:

> "And fortune, on his damned quarrel smiling,
> Show'd like a rebel's whore."

Some read "quarry;" see "Notes to Macbeth," Clark and Wright, p. 77. It denotes the square-headed bolt of a cross-bow; see Douce's "Illustrations," 1839, p. 227; Nares's "Glossary," vol. ii. p. 206.

ing the hawk's violent descent from a height upon its prey. In "Taming of the Shrew" (iv. 1) the expression occurs, "till she stoop, she must not be full-gorged." In "Henry V." (iv. 1), King Henry, speaking of the king, says, "though his affections are higher mounted than ours, yet, when they stoop, they stoop with the like wing." In "Macbeth" (iv. 3), too, Macduff, referring to the cruel murder of his children, exclaims, "What! . . . at one fell swoop?"[1] Webster, in the "White Devil,"[2] says:

> "If she [*i. e.*, Fortune] give aught, she deals it in small parcels,
> That she may take away all at one swoop."

Shakespeare gives many incidental allusions to the hawk's trappings. Thus, in "Lucrece" he says:

> "Harmless Lucretia, marking what he tells
> With trembling fear, as fowl hear falcon's bells."

And in "As You Like It" (iii. 3),[3] Touchstone says, "As the ox hath his bow, sir, the horse his curb, and the falcon her bells, so man hath his desires." The object of these bells was to lead the falconer to the hawk when in a wood or out of sight. In Heywood's play entitled "A Woman Killed with Kindness," 1617, is a hawking scene, containing a striking allusion to the hawk's bells. The dress of the hawk consisted of a close-fitting hood of leather or velvet, enriched with needlework, and surmounted with a tuft of colored feathers, for use as well as ornament, inasmuch as they assisted the hand in removing the hood when the birds for the hawk's attack came in sight. Thus in "Henry V." (iii. 7), the Constable of France, referring to the valor of the Dauphin, says, "'Tis a hooded valour; and when it appears, it will bate."[4] And again, in "Romeo and Juliet" (iii. 2), Juliet says:

---

[1] See Spenser's "Fairy Queen," book i. canto xi. l. 18:

> "Low stooping with unwieldy sway."

[2] Ed. Dyce, 1857, p. 5.   [3] See "3 Henry VI." i. 1.

[4] A quibble is perhaps intended between bate, the term of falconry, and abate, *i. e.*, fall off, dwindle. "Bate is a term in falconry, to flutter

> " Hood my unmann'd [1] blood, bating in my cheeks."

The " jesses " were two short straps of leather or silk, which were fastened to each leg of a hawk, to which was attached a swivel, from which depended the leash or strap which the falconer [2] twisted round his hand.　Othello (iii. 3) says:

> "Though that her jesses were my dear heart-strings."

We find several allusions to the training of hawks. [3]　They were usually trained by being kept from sleep, it having been customary for the falconers to sit up by turns and " watch " the hawk, and keep it from sleeping, sometimes for three successive nights.　Desdemona, in " Othello " (iii. 3), says:

> " my lord shall never rest;
> I'll watch him tame and talk him out of patience;
> His bed shall seem a school, his board a shrift;
> I'll intermingle everything he does
> With Cassio's suit."

So, in Cartwright's " Lady Errant " (ii. 2):

> " We'll keep you as they do hawks,
> Watching until you leave your wildness."

In " The Merry Wives of Windsor " (v. 5), where Page says,

> " Nay, do not fly: I think we have watch'd you now,"

the allusion is, says Staunton, to this method employed to tame or " reclaim " hawks.

---

the wings as preparing for flight, particularly at the sight of prey.　In ' 1 Henry IV.' (iv. 1):

> " ' All plumed like estridges, that with the wind
> Bated, like eagles having lately bathed.' "

-Nares's " Glossary," vol. i. p. 60.

[1] " Unmann'd " was applied to a hawk not tamed.

[2] See Singer's " Notes to Shakespeare," 1875, vol. x. p. 86; Nares's " Glossary," vol. i. p. 448.

[3] See passage in " Taming of the Shrew," iv. 1, already referred to, p. 122.

Again, in "Othello" (iii. 3),[1] Iago exclaims:

> "She that, so young, could give out such a seeming,
> To seel her father's eyes up close as oak ;"

in allusion to the practice of seeling a hawk, or sewing up her eyelids, by running a fine thread through them, in order to make her tractable and endure the hood of which we have already spoken.[2] King Henry ("2 Henry IV." iii. 1), in his soliloquy on sleep, says:

> "Wilt thou upon the high and giddy mast
> Seal up the ship-boy's eyes, and rock his brains
> In cradle of the rude imperious surge."

In Spenser's "Fairy Queen" (I. vii. 23), we read:

> "Mine eyes no more on vanity shall feed,
> But sealed up with death, shall have their deadly meed."

It was a common notion that if a dove was let loose with its eyes so closed it would fly straight upwards, continuing to mount till it fell down through mere exhaustion.[3]

In "Cymbeline" (iii. 4), Imogen, referring to Posthumus, says:

> "I grieve myself
> To think, when thou shalt be disedged by her
> That now thou tir'st on,"—

this passage containing two metaphorical expressions from falconry. A bird was said to be *disedged* when the keenness of its appetite was taken away by *tiring*, or feeding upon some tough or hard substance given to it for that purpose. In "3 Henry VI." (i. 1), the king says:

> "that hateful duke,
> Whose haughty spirit, winged with desire,
> Will cost my crown, and like an empty eagle
> Tire on the flesh of me and of my son."

---

[1] Also in same play, i. 3.

[2] Turbervile, in his "Booke of Falconrie," 1575, gives some curious directions as "how to seele a hawke ;" we may compare similar expressions in "Antony and Cleopatra," iii. 13; v. 2.

[3] Nares's "Glossary," vol. ii. pp. 777, 778; cf. Beaumont and Fletcher, "Philaster," v. 1.

In "Timon of Athens" (iii. 6), one of the lords says: "Upon that were my thoughts tiring, when we encountered."

In "Venus and Adonis," too, we find a further allusion:

"Even as an empty eagle, sharp by fast,
Tires with her beak on feathers, flesh, and bone," etc.

Among other allusions to the hawk may be mentioned one in "Measure for Measure" (iii. 1):

"This outward-sainted deputy,
Whose settled visage and deliberate word
Nips youth i' the head, and follies doth *emmew*,
As falcon doth the fowl"

— the word "emmew" signifying the place where hawks were shut up during the time they moulted. In "Romeo and Juliet" (iii. 4), Lady Capulet says of Juliet:

"To-night she's mew'd up to her heaviness;"

and in "Taming of the Shrew" (i. 1), Gremio, speaking of Bianca to Signor Baptista, says: "Why will you mew her?"

When the wing or tail feathers of a hawk were dropped, forced out, or broken, by any accident, it was usual to supply or repair as many as were deficient or damaged, an operation called "to imp[1] a hawk." Thus, in "Richard II." (ii. 1), Northumberland says:

"If, then, we shall shake off our slavish yoke,
Imp out our drooping country's broken wing."

So Massinger, in his "Renegado" (v. 8), makes Asambeg say:

"strive to imp
New feathers to the broken wings of time."

Hawking was sometimes called birding.[2] In the "Merry Wives of Windsor" (iii. 3) Master Page says: "I do invite you to-morrow morning to my house to breakfast; after,

---

[1] Imp, from Anglo-Saxon, *impan*, to graft. Turbervile has a whole chapter on "The way and manner how to ympe a hawke's feather, howsoever it be broken or bruised."

[2] Harting's "Ornithology of Shakspeare," p. 72.

we'll a-birding together, I have a fine hawk for the bush."
In the same play (iii. 5) Dame Quickly, speaking of Mistress
Ford, says: "Her husband goes this morning a-birding;"
and Mistress Ford says (iv. 2): "He's a-birding, sweet Sir
John." The word hawk, says Mr. Harting, is invariably
used by Shakespeare in its generic sense; and in only two
instances does he allude to a particular species. These are
the kestrel and sparrowhawk. In "Twelfth Night" (ii. 5)
Sir Toby Belch, speaking of Malvolio, as he finds the letter
which Maria has purposely dropped in his path, says:

> "And with what wing the staniel[1] checks at it"

—staniel being a corruption of stangdall, a name for the
kestrel hawk.[2] "Gouts" is the technical term for the spots
on some parts of the plumage of a hawk, and perhaps Shakespeare uses the word in allusion to a phrase in heraldry.
Macbeth (ii. 1), speaking of the dagger, says:

> "I see thee still,
> And on thy blade and dudgeon gouts of blood."

Heron. This bird was frequently flown at by falconers.
Shakespeare, in "Hamlet" (ii. 2), makes Hamlet say, "I am
but mad north-north-west; when the wind is southerly, I
know a hawk from a handsaw;" handsaw being a corruption of "heronshaw," or "hernsew," which is still used, in
the provincial dialects, for a heron. In Suffolk and Norfolk
it is pronounced "harnsa," from which to "handsaw" is but
a single step.[3] Shakespeare here alludes to a proverbial
saying, "He knows not a hawk from a handsaw."[4] Mr. J.
C. Heath[5] explains the passage thus: "The expression obviously refers to the sport of hawking. Most birds, espe-

---

[1] The reading of the folios here is stallion; but the word wing, and
the falconer's term *checks*, prove that the bird must be meant. See
Nares's "Glossary," vol. ii. p. 832.

[2] See kestrel and sparrowhawk.

[3] "Notes to Hamlet," Clark and Wright, 1876, p. 159.

[4] Ray's "Proverbs," 1768, p. 196.

[5] Quoted in "Notes to Hamlet," by Clark and Wright, p. 159; see
Nares's "Glossary," vol. i. p. 416.

cially one of heavy flight like the heron, when roused by the
falconer or his dog, would fly down or with the wind, in order to escape. When the wind is from the north the heron
flies towards the south, and the spectator may be dazzled
by the sun, and be unable to distinguish the hawk from the
heron. On the other hand, when the wind is southerly the
heron flies towards the north, and it and the pursuing hawk
are clearly seen by the sportsman, who then has his back to
the sun, and without difficulty knows the hawk from the
hernsew."

Jay. From its gay and gaudy plumage this bird has
been used for a loose woman, as " Merry Wives of Windsor" (iii. 3): " we'll teach him to know turtles from jays,"
i. e., to distinguish honest women from loose ones. Again,
in " Cymbeline " (iii. 4), Imogen says:

<blockquote>
" Some jay of Italy,
Whose mother was her painting,[1] hath betray'd him."
</blockquote>

Kestrel. A hawk of a base, unserviceable breed,[2] and
therefore used by Spenser, in his " Fairy Queen " (II. iii. 4),
to signify base:

<blockquote>
" Ne thought of honour ever did assay
　His baser breast, but in his kestrell kynd
　A pleasant veine of glory he did fynd."
</blockquote>

By some[3] it is derived from " coystril," a knave or peasant,
from being the hawk formerly used by persons of inferior
rank. Thus, in " Twelfth Night " (i. 3), we find " coystrill,"
and in " Pericles " (iv. 6) " coystrel." The name kestrel,
says Singer,[4] for an inferior kind of hawk, was evidently a
corruption of the French *quercelle* or *quercerelle*, and originally had no connection with coystril, though in later times

---

[1] That is, made by art: the creature not of nature, but of painting;
cf. " Taming of the Shrew," iv. 3 ; " The Tempest," ii. 2.

[2] Nares's " Glossary," vol. ii. p. 482.

[3] Harting's " Ornithology of Shakespeare," p. 74.

[4] " Notes," vol. iii. pp. 357, 358.

they may have been confounded. Holinshed[1] classes coi-
sterels with lackeys and women, the unwarlike attendants
on an army. The term was also given as a nickname to the
emissaries employed by the kings of England in their French
wars. Dyce[2] also considers kestrel distinct from coistrel.

Kingfisher. It was a common belief in days gone by that
during the days the halcyon or kingfisher was engaged in
hatching her eggs, the sea remained so calm that the sailor
might venture upon it without incurring risk of storm or
tempest; hence this period was called by Pliny and Aristotle "the halcyon days," to which allusion is made in " 1
Henry VI." (i. 2):

> "Expect Saint Martin's summer, halcyon days."

Dryden also refers to this notion:

> "Amidst our arms as quiet you shall be,
> As halcyons brooding on a winter's sea."

Another superstition connected with this bird occurs in
" King Lear " (ii. 2), where the Earl of Kent says:

> "turn their halcyon beaks
> With every gale and vary of their masters;"

the prevalent idea being that a dead kingfisher, suspended
from a cord, would always turn its beak in that direction
from whence the wind blew. Marlowe, in his " Jew of Malta " (i. 1), says:

> "But now how stands the wind?
> Into what corner peers my halcyon's bill?"

Occasionally one may still see this bird hung up in cot-
tages, a remnant, no doubt, of this old superstition.[3]

Kite. This bird was considered by the ancients to be unlucky. In " Julius Cæsar " (v. 1) Cassius says:

> "ravens, crows, and kites,
> Fly o'er our heads, and downward look on us."

---

[1] "Description of England," vol. i. p. 162.
[2] "Glossary to Shakespeare," p. 88.
[3] Sir Thomas Browne's " Vulgar Errors," bk. iii. chap. 10.

In "Cymbeline" (i. 2), too, Imogen says,

> "I chose an eagle,
> And did avoid a puttock,"

puttock, here, being a synonym sometimes applied to the kite.[1] Formerly the kite became a term of reproach from its ignoble habits. Thus, in "Antony and Cleopatra" (iii. 13), Antony exclaims, "you kite!" and King Lear (i. 4) says to Goneril, "Detested kite! thou liest." Its intractable disposition is alluded to in "Taming of the Shrew," by Petruchio (iv. 1). A curious peculiarity of this bird is noticed in "Winter's Tale" (iv. 3), where Autolycus says: "My traffic is sheets; when the kite builds, look to lesser linen"—meaning that his practice was to steal sheets; leaving the smaller linen to be carried away by the kites, who will occasionally carry it off to line their nests.[2] Mr. Dyce[3] quotes the following remarks of Mr. Peck on this passage: "Autolycus here gives us to understand that he is a thief of the first class. This he explains by an allusion to an odd vulgar notion. The common people, many of them, think that if any one can find a kite's nest when she hath young, before they are fledged, and sew up their back doors, so as they cannot mute, the mother-kite, in compassion to their distress, will steal lesser linen, as caps, cravats, ruffles, or any other such small matters as she can best fly with, from off the hedges where they are hanged to dry after washing, and carry them to her nest, and there leave them, if possible to move the pity of the first comer, to cut the thread and ease them of their misery."

Lapwing. Several interesting allusions are made by Shakespeare to this eccentric bird. It was a common notion that the young lapwings ran out of the shell with part of it sticking on their heads, in such haste were they to be hatched. Horatio ("Hamlet," v. 2) says of Osric: "This lapwing runs away with the shell on his head."

---

[1] Also to the buzzard, which see, p. 100.
[2] Singer's "Shakespeare," vol. iv. p. 67.
[3] "Glossary," p. 243.

It was, therefore, regarded as the symbol of a forward fellow. Webster,[1] in the " White Devil" (1857, p. 13), says:

> " forward lapwing!
> He flies with the shell on's head."

The lapwing, like the partridge, is also said to draw pursuers from her nest by fluttering along the ground in an opposite direction or by crying in other places. Thus, in the " Comedy of Errors " (iv. 2), Shakespeare says:

> " Far from her nest the lapwing cries away."

Again, in " Measure for Measure " (i. 4), Lucio exclaims:

> " though 'tis my familiar sin,
> With maids to seem the lapwing, and to jest,
> Tongue far from heart."

Once more, in " Much Ado About Nothing " (iii. 1), we read:

> " For look where Beatrice, like a lapwing, runs,
> Close by the ground, to hear our conference."

Several, too, of our older poets refer to this peculiarity. In Ben Jonson's " Underwoods " (lviii.) we are told:

> " Where he that knows will like a lapwing fly,
> Farre from the nest, and so himself belie."

Through thus alluring intruders from its nest, the lapwing became a symbol of insincerity; and hence originated the proverb, " The lapwing cries tongue from heart," or, " The lapwing cries most, farthest from her nest." [2]

Lark. Shakespeare has bequeathed to us many exquisite passages referring to the lark, full of the most sublime pathos and lofty conceptions. Most readers are doubtless acquainted with that superb song in " Cymbeline " (ii. 3), where this sweet songster is represented as singing " at heaven's gate;" and again, as the bird of dawn, it is described in " Venus and Adonis," thus:

---

[1] " Glossary," vol. ii. p. 495 ; see Yarrell's " History of British Birds," 2d edition, vol. ii. p. 482.

[2] Ray's " Proverbs," 1768, p. 199.

> "Lo, here the gentle lark, weary of rest,
> From his moist cabinet mounts up on high,
> And wakes the morning, from whose silver breast
> The sun ariseth in his majesty." [1]

In "Love's Labour's Lost" (v. 2, song) we have a graphic touch of pastoral life:

> "When shepherds pipe on oaten straws,
> And merry larks are ploughmen's clocks."

The words of Portia, too, in "Merchant of Venice" (v. 1), to sing "as sweetly as the lark," have long ago passed into a proverb.

It was formerly a current saying that the lark and toad changed eyes, to which Juliet refers in "Romeo and Juliet" (iii. 5):

> "Some say, the lark and loathed toad change eyes;"

Warburton says this popular fancy originated in the toad having very fine eyes, and the lark very ugly ones. This tradition was formerly expressed in a rustic rhyme:

> "to heav'n I'd fly,
> But that the toad beguil'd me of mine eye."

In "Henry VIII." (iii. 2) the Earl of Surrey, in denouncing Wolsey, alludes to a curious method of capturing larks, which was effected by small mirrors and red cloth. These, scaring the birds, made them crouch, while the fowler drew his nets over them:

> "let his grace go forward,
> And dare us with his cap, like larks."

In this case the cap was the scarlet hat of the cardinal, which it was intended to use as a piece of red cloth. The same idea occurs in Skelton's "Why Come Ye not to Court?" a satire on Wolsey:

> "The red hat with his lure
> Bringeth all things under cure."

---

[1] Cf. "Midsummer-Night's Dream" (iv. 1), "the morning lark;" "Romeo and Juliet" (iii. 5), "the lark, the herald of the morn."

The words " tirra-lirra " (" Winter's Tale," iv. 3) are a fanciful combination of sounds,[1] meant to imitate the lark's note ; borrowed, says Nares, from the French *tire-lire*. Browne, " British Pastorals " (bk. i. song 4), makes it " teeryleery." In one of the Coventry pageants there is the following old song sung by the shepherds at the birth of Christ, which contains the expression :

> "As I out rode this endenes night,
>   Of three joli sheppards I sawe a syght,
>   And all aboute there fold a stare shone bright,
>   They sang terli terlow,
>   So mereli the sheppards their pipes can blow."

In Scotland[2] and the north of England the peasantry say that if one is desirous of knowing what the lark says, he must lie down on his back in the field and listen, and he will then hear it say :

> "Up in the lift go we,
>   Tehee, tehee, tehee, tehee !
>   There's not a shoemaker on the earth
>   Can make a shoe to me, to me !
>   Why so, why so, why so ?
>   Because my heel is as long as my toe."

Magpie. It was formerly known as magot-pie, probably from the French *magot*, a monkey, because the bird chatters and plays droll tricks like a monkey. It has generally been regarded with superstitious awe as a mysterious bird,[3] and is thus alluded to in " Macbeth " (iii. 4):

> " Augurs and understood relations, have
>   By magot-pies, and choughs, and rooks, brought forth
>   The secret'st man of blood."

And again, in " 3 Henry VI." (v. 6), it is said :

> "chattering pies in dismal discords sung."

There are numerous rhymes[4] relating to the magpie, of

---

[1] Nares's " Glossary," vol. ii. p. 886 ; Douce's " Illustrations of Shakespeare," 1839, p. 217.

[2] Chambers's " Popular Rhymes of Scotland," 1870, p. 192.

[3] See " English Folk-Lore," p. 81.

[4] Henderson's " Folk-Lore of Northern Counties," p. 127.

which we subjoin, as a specimen, one prevalent in the north of England :

> "One is sorrow, two mirth,
> Three a wedding, four a birth,
> Five heaven, six hell,
> Seven the de'il's ain sell."

In Devonshire, in order to avert the ill-luck from seeing a magpie, the peasant spits over his right shoulder three times, and in Yorkshire various charms are in use. One is to raise the hat as a salutation, and then to sign the cross on the breast ; and another consists in making the same sign by crossing the thumbs. It is a common notion in Scotland that magpies flying near the windows of a house portend a speedy death to one of its inmates. The superstitions associated with the magpie are not confined to this country, for in Sweden[1] it is considered the witch's bird, belonging to the evil one and the other powers of night. In Denmark, when a magpie perches on a house it is regarded as a sign that strangers are coming.

Martin. The martin, or martlet, which is called in "Macbeth" (i. 6) the "guest of summer," as being a migratory bird, has been from the earliest times treated with superstitious respect—it being considered unlucky to molest or in any way injure its nest. Thus, in the "Merchant of Venice" (ii. 9), the Prince of Arragon says :

> "the martlet
> Builds in the weather, on the outward wall,
> Even in the force and road of casualty."

Forster[2] says that the circumstance of this bird's nest being built so close to the habitations of man indicates that it has long enjoyed freedom from molestation. There is a popular rhyme still current in the north of England :

> "The martin and the swallow
> Are God Almighty's bow and arrow."

---

[1] Thorpe's "Northern Mythology," vol. ii. p. 34 ; Brand's "Pop. Antiq.," 1849, pp. 215, 216 ; see also Harland and Wilkinson's "Lancashire Folk-Lore," 1867, pp. 143, 145.

[2] "Atmospherical Researches," 1823, p. 262.

Nightingale. The popular error that the nightingale sings with its breast impaled upon a thorn is noticed by Shakespeare, who makes Lucrece say:

> "And whiles against a thorn thou bear'st thy part
> To keep thy sharp woes waking."

In the " Passionate Pilgrim " (xxi.) there is an allusion:

> "Everything did banish moan,
> Save the nightingale alone.
> She, poor bird, as all forlorn,
> Lean'd her breast up-till a thorn,
> And there sung the dolefull'st ditty,
> That to hear it was great pity."

Beaumont and Fletcher, in " The Faithful Shepherdess " (v. 3), speak of

> "The nightingale among the thick-leaved spring,
> That sits alone in sorrow, and doth sing
> Whole nights away in mourning."

Sir Thomas Browne[1] asks " Whether the nightingale's sitting with her breast against a thorn be any more than that she placeth some prickles on the outside of her nest, or roosteth in thorny, prickly places, where serpents may least approach her?"[2]   In the " Zoologist" for 1862 the Rev. A. C. Smith mentions "the discovery, on two occasions, of a strong thorn projecting upwards in the centre of the nightingale's nest."   Another notion is that the nightingale never sings by day; and thus Portia, in " Merchant of Venice " (v. 1), says:

> "I think,
> The nightingale, if she should sing by day,
> When every goose is cackling, would be thought
> No better a musician than the wren."

Such, however, is not the case, for this bird often sings as sweetly in the day as at night-time.   There is an old superstition[3] that the nightingale sings all night, to keep itself

---

[1] Sir Thomas Browne's Works, 1852, vol. i. p. 378.
[2] See " Book of Days," vol. i. p. 515.
[3] Southey's " Commonplace Book," 5th series, 1851, p. 305.

awake, lest the glowworm should devour her.   The classical
fable[1] of the unhappy Philomela turned into a nightingale,
when her sister Progne was changed to a swallow, has doubtless given rise to this bird being spoken of as *she;* thus
Juliet tells Romeo (iii. 5):

> "It was the nightingale, and not the lark,
>   That pierc'd the fearful hollow of thine ear;
>   Nightly she sings on yon pomegranate tree;
>   Believe me, love, it was the nightingale."

Sometimes the nightingale is termed Philomel, as in " Midsummer-Night's Dream" (ii. 2, song):[2]

> "Philomel, with melody,
>   Sing in our sweet lullaby."

Osprey.   This bird,[3] also called the sea-eagle, besides having a destructive power of devouring fish, was supposed
formerly to have a fascinating influence, both which qualities
are alluded to in the following passage in "Coriolanus"
(iv. 7):

> "I think he'll be to Rome,
>   As is the osprey to the fish, who takes it
>   By sovereignty of nature."

Drayton, in his "Polyolbion" (song xxv.), mentions the
same fascinating power of the osprey:

> "The osprey, oft here seen, though seldom here it breeds,
>   Which over them the fish no sooner do espy,
>   But, betwixt him and them by an antipathy,
>   Turning their bellies up, as though their death they saw,
>   They at his pleasure lie, to stuff his gluttonous maw."

Ostrich.   The extraordinary digestion of this bird[4] is said

---

[1] Ovid's "Metamorphoses," bk. vi. ll. 455–676; "Titus Andronicus,"
iv. 1.
[2] Cf. "Lucrece," ll. 1079, 1127.
[3] See Yarrell's "History of British Birds," 1856, vol. i. p. 30; Nares's
"Glossary," vol. ii. p. 620; also Pennant's "British Zoology;" see
Peele's Play of the "Battle of Alcazar" (ii. 3), 1861, p. 28.
[4] Called *estridge* in "1 Henry IV." iv. 1.

to be shown by its swallowing iron and other hard substances.[1] In "2 Henry VI." (iv. 10), the rebel Cade says to Alexander Iden: "Ah, villain, thou wilt betray me, and get a thousand crowns of the king by carrying my head to him; but I'll make thee eat iron like an ostrich, and swallow my sword like a great pin, ere thou and I part." Cuvier,[2] speaking of this bird, says, "It is yet so voracious, and its senses of taste and smell are so obtuse, that it devours animal and mineral substances indiscriminately, until its enormous stomach is completely full. It swallows without any choice, and merely as it were to serve for ballast, wood, stones, grass, iron, copper, gold, lime, or, in fact, any other substance equally hard, indigestible, and deleterious." Sir Thomas Browne,[3] writing on this subject, says, "The ground of this conceit in its swallowing down fragments of iron, which men observing, by a forward illation, have therefore conceived it digesteth them, which is an inference not to be admitted, as being a fallacy of the consequent." In Loudon's "Magazine of Natural History" (No. 6, p. 32) we are told of an ostrich having been killed by swallowing glass.

Owl. The dread attached to this unfortunate bird is frequently spoken of by Shakespeare, who has alluded to several of the superstitions associated with it. At the outset, many of the epithets ascribed to it show the prejudice with which it was regarded—being in various places stigmatized as "the vile owl," in "Troilus and Cressida" (ii. 1); and the "obscure bird," in "Macbeth" (ii. 3), etc. From the earliest period it has been considered a bird of ill-omen, and Pliny tells us how, on one occasion, even Rome itself underwent a lustration, because one of them strayed into the Capitol. He represents it also as a funereal bird, a monster of the night, the very abomination of human kind. Vergil[4] describes its death-howl from the top of the temple by night, a circum-

---

[1] See Brand's "Pop. Antiq.," 1849, vol. iii. p. 365.
[2] "Animal Kingdom," 1829, vol. viii. p. 427.
[3] See Sir Thomas Browne's Works, 1852, vol. i. pp. 334–337.
[4] "Æneid," bk. iv. l. 462.

stance introduced as a precursor of Dido's death. Ovid,[1] too, constantly speaks of this bird's presence as an evil omen; and indeed the same notions respecting it may be found among the writings of most of the ancient poets. This superstitious awe in which the owl is held may be owing to its peculiar look, its occasional and uncertain appearance, its loud and dismal cry,[2] as well as to its being the bird of night.[3] It has generally been associated with calamities and deeds of darkness.[4] Thus, its weird shriek pierces the ear of Lady Macbeth (ii. 2), while the murder is being committed:

> "Hark!—Peace!
> It was the owl that shriek'd, the fatal bellman,
> Which gives the stern'st good night."

And when the murderer rushes in, exclaiming,

> "I have done the deed. Didst thou not hear a noise?"

she answers:

> "I heard the owl scream."

Its appearance at a birth has been said to foretell ill-luck to the infant, a superstition to which King Henry, in "3 Henry VI." (v. 6), addressing Gloster, refers:

> "The owl shriek'd at thy birth, an evil sign."

Its cries[5] have been supposed to presage death, and, to quote the words of the *Spectator*, "a screech-owl at midnight has alarmed a family more than a band of robbers." Thus, in "A Midsummer-Night's Dream" (v. 1), we are told how

> "the screech-owl, screeching loud,
> Puts the wretch that lies in woe
> In remembrance of a shroud;"

and in "1 Henry VI." (iv. 2), it is called the "ominous and

---

[1] "Metamorphoses," bk. v. l. 550; bk. vi. l. 432; bk. x. l. 453; bk. xv. l. 791.

[2] "2 Henry VI." iii. 2; iv. 1.　　[3] "Titus Andronicus," ii. 3.

[4] Cf. "Lucrece," l. 165; see Yarrell's "History of British Birds," vol. i. p. 122.

[5] See Brand's "Pop. Antiq.," 1849, vol. iii. p. 209.

fearful owl of death." Again, in " Richard III." (iv. 4), where Richard is exasperated by the bad news, he interrupts the third messenger by saying :

> "Out on ye, owls ! nothing but songs of death ?"

The owl by day is considered by some equally ominous, as in " 3 Henry VI." (v. 4) :

> "the owl by day,
> If he arise, is mock'd and wonder'd at."

And in " Julius Cæsar " (i. 3), Casca says :

> " And yesterday the bird of night did sit,
> Even at noon-day, upon the market-place,
> Hooting and shrieking. When these prodigies
> Do so conjointly meet, let not men say,
> ' These are their reasons,—they are natural ;'
> For, I believe, they are portentous things
> Unto the climate that they point upon."

Considering, however, the abhorrence with which the owl is generally regarded, it is not surprising that the " owlet's wing"[1] should form an ingredient of the caldron in which the witches in " Macbeth " (iv. 1) prepared their " charm of powerful trouble." The owl is, too, in all probability, represented by Shakespeare as a witch,[2] a companion of the fairies in their moonlight gambols. In " Comedy of Errors " (ii. 2), Dromio of Syracuse says :

> " This is the fairy land : O, spite of spites !
> We talk with goblins, owls, and elvish sprites.
> If we obey them not, this will ensue,
> They'll suck our breath, or pinch us black and blue !"

Singer, in his Notes on this passage (vol. ii. p. 28) says : " It has been asked, how should Shakespeare know that screech-owls were considered by the Romans as witches ?" Do these cavillers think that Shakespeare never looked into a book ?

---

[1] The spelling of the folios is " howlets." In Holland's translation of Pliny (chap. xvii. book x.), we read " of owlls or howlets." Cotgrave gives " Hulotte."

[2] Halliwell-Phillipps's, " Handbook Index," 1866, p. 354.

Take an extract from the Cambridge Latin Dictionary (1594, 8vo), probably the very book he used: "Strix, a *scritche owle;* an unluckie kind of bird (as they of olde time said) which sucked out the blood of infants lying in their cradles; a witch, that changeth the favour of children; an hagge or fairie." So in the "London Prodigal," a comedy, 1605: "Soul, I think I am sure crossed or witch'd with an owl." [1] In "The Tempest" (v. I) Shakespeare introduces Ariel as saying:

> "Where the bee sucks, there suck I,
> In a cowslip's bell I lie,
> There I couch when owls do cry."

Ariel,[2] who sucks honey for luxury in the cowslip's bell, retreats thither for quiet when owls are abroad and screeching. According to an old legend, the owl was originally a baker's daughter, to which allusion is made in "Hamlet" (iv. 5), where Ophelia exclaims: "They say the owl was a baker's daughter. Lord! we know what we are, but know not what we may be." Douce[3] says the following story was current among the Gloucestershire peasantry: "Our Saviour went into a baker's shop where they were baking, and asked for some bread to eat; the mistress of the shop immediately put a piece of dough into the oven to bake for him; but was reprimanded by her daughter, who, insisting that the piece of dough was too large, reduced it to a very small size; the dough, however, immediately began to swell, and presently became a most enormous size, whereupon the baker's daughter cried out, 'Heugh, heugh, heugh!' which owl-like noise probably induced our Saviour to transform her into that bird for her wickedness." Another version of the same story, as formerly known in Herefordshire, substitutes a fairy in the place of our Saviour. Similar legends are found on the Continent.[4]

---

[1] See Dyce's "Glossary," p. 302.
[2] See Singer's "Notes to The Tempest," 1875, vol. i. p. 82.
[3] See *Gentleman's Magazine*, November, 1804, pp. 1083, 1084. Grimm's "Deutsche Mythologie."
[4] See Dasent's "Tales of the Norse," 1859, p. 230.

Parrot. The "popinjay," in "I Henry IV." (i. 3), is another name for the parrot—from the Spanish *papagayo*—a term which occurs in Browne's "Pastorals" (ii. 65):

> "Or like the mixture nature dothe display
> Upon the quaint wings of the popinjay."

Its supposed restlessness before rain is referred to in "As You Like It" (iv. 1): "More clamorous than a parrot against rain." It was formerly customary to teach the parrot unlucky words, with which, when any one was offended, it was the standing joke of the wise owner to say, "Take heed, sir, my parrot prophesies"—an allusion to which custom we find in "Comedy of Errors" (iv. 4), where Dromio of Ephesus says: "prophesy like the parrot, *beware the rope's end.*" To this Butler hints, where, speaking of Ralpho's skill in augury, he says:[1]

> "Could tell what subtlest parrots mean,
> That speak and think contrary clean;
> What member 'tis of whom they talk,
> When they cry *rope,* and *walk, knave, walk.*"

The rewards given to parrots to encourage them to speak are mentioned in "Troilus and Cressida" (v. 2):[2] "the parrot will not do more for an almond." Hence, a proverb for the greatest temptation that could be put before a man seems to have been "An almond for a parrot." To "talk like a parrot" is a common proverb, a sense in which it occurs in "Othello" (ii. 3).

Peacock. This bird was as proverbially used for a proud, vain fool as the lapwing for a silly one. In this sense some would understand it in the much-disputed passage in "Hamlet" (iii. 2):

> "For thou dost know, O Damon dear,
> This realm dismantled was
> Of Jove himself; and now reigns here
> A very, very—peacock."[3]

---

[1] "Hudibras," pt. i. ch. i.

[2] In "Much Ado About Nothing" (i. 1), Benedick likens Beatrice to a "parrot-teacher," from her talkative powers.

[3] This is the reading adopted by Singer.

The third and fourth folios read *pajock*,[1] the other editions
have "paiock," "paiocke," or "pajocke," and in the later
quartos the word was changed to "paicock" and "pecock,"
whence Pope printed peacock.

Dyce says that in Scotland the peacock is called the pea-
jock.   Some have proposed to read *paddock*, and in the last
scene Hamlet bestows this opprobrious name upon the king.
It has been also suggested to read *puttock*, a kite.[2]   The peacock has also been regarded as the emblem of pride and ar-
rogance, as in " 1 Henry VI." (iii. 3):[3]

> " Let frantic Talbot triumph for a while,
>   And, like a peacock, sweep along his tail;
>   We'll pull his plumes, and take away his train."

Pelican.   There are several allusions by Shakespeare to
the pelican's piercing her own breast to feed her young.
Thus, in " Hamlet " (iv. 5), Laertes says:

> "To his good friends thus wide I'll ope my arms;
>   And like the kind life-rendering pelican,
>   Repast them with my blood."

And in " King Lear," where the young pelicans are represented as piercing their mother's breast to drink her blood,
an illustration of filial impiety (iii. 4), the king says:

> " Is it the fashion, that discarded fathers
>   Should have thus little mercy on their flesh?
>   Judicious punishment! 'Twas this flesh begot
>   Those pelican daughters."[4]

It is a common notion that the fable here alluded to is a
classical one, but this is an error.   Shakespeare, says Mr.
Harting, " was content to accept the story as he found it, and
to apply it metaphorically as the occasion required."   Mr.
Houghton, in an interesting letter to " Land and Water "[5]

---

[1] " Notes to Hamlet," Clark and Wright, 1876, pp. 179, 180.

[2] See Nares's "Glossary," vol. ii. p. 645; Singer's "Notes," vol. ix.
p. 228.   [3] Cf. " Troilus and Cressida," iii. 3.

[4] Cf. " Richard II." i. 1.

[5] Mr. Harting, in his " Ornithology of Shakespeare," quotes an interesting correspondence from " Land and Water " (1869), on the subject.

on this subject, remarks that the Egyptians believed in a bird feeding its young with its blood, and this bird is none other than the vulture. He goes on to say that the fable of the pelican doubtless originated in the Patristic annotations on the Scriptures. The ecclesiastical Fathers transferred the Egyptian story from the vulture to the pelican, but magnified the story a hundredfold, for the blood of the parent was not only supposed to serve as food for the young, but was also able to reanimate the dead offspring. Augustine, commenting on Psalm cii. 6—" I am like a pelican of the wilderness"—remarks: "These birds [male pelicans] are said to kill their offspring by blows of their beaks, and then to bewail their death for the space of three days. At length, however, it is said that the mother inflicts a severe wound on herself, pouring the flowing blood over the dead young ones, which instantly brings them to life." To the same effect write Eustathius, Isidorus, Epiphanius, and a host of other writers.[1]

According to another idea[2] pelicans are hatched dead, but the cock pelican then wounds his breast, and lets one drop of blood fall upon each, and this quickens them.

Pheasant. This bird is only once alluded to, in " Winter's Tale " (iv. 4), where the Clown jokingly says to the Shepherd, "Advocate's the court-word for a pheasant; say, you have none."

Phœnix. Many allusions are made to this fabulous bird, which is said to rise again from its own ashes. Thus, in " Henry VIII." (v. 4), Cranmer tells how

> "when
> The bird of wonder dies, the maiden phœnix,
> Her ashes new create another heir,
> As great in admiration as herself."

Again, in " 3 Henry VI." (i. 4), the Duke of York exclaims:

> " My ashes, as the phœnix, may bring forth
> A bird that will revenge upon you all."

---

[1] See Sir Thomas Browne's Works, 1852, vol. ii. pp. 1–4.
[2] See Brand's " Pop. Antiq.," 1849, vol. iii. pp. 366, 367.

Once more, in " 1 Henry VI." (iv. 7), Sir William Lucy, speaking of Talbot and those slain with him, predicts that

> " from their ashes shall be rear'd
> A phœnix that shall make all France afeard." [1]

Sir Thomas Browne [2] tells us that there is but one phœnix in the world, " which after many hundred years burns herself, and from the ashes thereof ariseth up another." From the very earliest times there have been countless traditions respecting this wonderful bird. Thus, its longevity has been estimated from three hundred to fifteen hundred years; and among the various localities assigned as its home are Ethiopia, Arabia, Egypt, and India. In " The Phœnix and Turtle," it is said,

> " Let the bird of loudest lay
> On the sole Arabian tree,
> Herald sad and trumpet be."

Pliny says of this bird, " Howbeit, I cannot tell what to make of him; and first of all, whether it be a tale or no, that there is never but one of them in the whole world, and the same not commonly seen." Malone [3] quotes from Lyly's " Euphues and his England " (p. 312, ed. Arber): " For as there is but one phœnix in the world, so is there but one tree in Arabia wherein she buyldeth;" and Florio's " New Worlde of Wordes " (1598), " Rasin, a tree in Arabia, whereof there is but one found, and upon it the phœnix sits."

Pigeon. As carriers, these birds have been used from a very early date, and the Castle of the Birds, at Bagdad, takes its name from the pigeon-post which the old monks of the convent established. The building has crumbled into ruins long ago by the lapse of time, but the bird messengers of Bagdad became celebrated as far westward as Greece, and were a regular commercial institution between the distant

---

[1] Cf. "The Tempest," iii. 3: "All's Well that Ends Well," i. 1; "Antony and Cleopatra," iii. 2; "Cymbeline," i. 6.

[2] Works, 1852, vol. i. pp. 277–284.

[3] See Aldis Wright's " Notes to The Tempest," 1875, p. 129.

parts of Asia Minor, Arabia, and the East.[1] In ancient Egypt, also, the carrier breed was brought to great perfection, and, between the cities of the Nile and the Red Sea, the old traders used to send word of their caravans to each other by letters written on silk, and tied under the wings of trained doves. In "Titus Andronicus" (iv. 3) Titus, on seeing a clown enter with two pigeons, says:

> "News, news from heaven! Marcus, the post is come.
> Sirrah, what tidings? have you any letters?"

From the same play we also learn that it was customary to give a pair of pigeons as a present. The Clown says to Saturninus (iv. 4), "I have brought you a letter and a couple of pigeons here."[2]

In "Romeo and Juliet" (i. 3) the dove is used synonymously for pigeon, where the nurse is represented as

> "Sitting in the sun under the dove-house wall."

Mr. Darwin, in his "Variation of Animals and Plants under Domestication" (vol. i. pp. 204, 205), has shown that from the very earliest times pigeons have been kept in a domesticated state. He says: "The earliest record of pigeons in a domesticated condition occurs in the fifth Egyptian dynasty, about 3000 B.C.; but Mr. Birch, of the British Museum, informs me that the pigeon appears in a bill of fare in the previous dynasty. Domestic pigeons are mentioned in Genesis, Leviticus, and Isaiah. Pliny informs us that the Romans gave immense prices for pigeons; 'nay, they are come to this pass that they can reckon up their pedigree and race.' In India, about the year 1600, pigeons were much valued by Akbar Khan; 20,000 birds were carried about with the court." In most countries, too, the breeding and taming of pigeons has been a favorite recreation. The constancy of the pigeon has been proverbial from time immemorial,

---

[1] *Daily Telegraph*, January 31, 1880; see Southey's "Commonplace Book," 1849, 2d series, p. 447.

[2] See *Dove*, pp. 114, 115.

allusions to which occur in " Winter's Tale " (iv. 3), and in " As You Like It " (iii. 3).

Quail. The quail was thought to be an amorous bird, and hence was metaphorically used to denote people of a loose character.[1] In this sense it is generally understood in " Troilus and Cressida " (v. 1): " Here's Agamemnon, an honest fellow enough, and one that loves quails." Mr. Harting,[2] however, thinks that the passage just quoted refers to the practice formerly prevalent of keeping quails, and making them fight like game-cocks. The context of the passage would seem to sanction the former meaning. Quail fighting[3] is spoken of in " Antony and Cleopatra " (ii. 3), where Antony, speaking of the superiority of Cæsar's fortunes to his own, says:

> " if we draw lots, he speeds ;
> His cocks do win the battle still of mine,
> When it is all to nought ; and his quails ever
> Beat mine, inhoop'd, at odds."

It appears that cocks as well as quails were sometimes made to fight within a broad hoop—hence the term *inhoop'd* —to keep them from quitting each other. Quail-fights were well known among the ancients, and especially at Athens.[4] Julius Pollux relates that a circle was made, in which the birds were placed, and he whose quail was driven out of this circle lost the stake, which was sometimes money, and occasionally the quails themselves. Another practice was to produce one of these birds, which being first smitten with the middle finger, a feather was then plucked from its head. If the quail bore this operation without flinching, his master gained the stake, but lost it if he ran away. Some doubt exists as to whether quail-fighting prevailed in the time of

---

[1] Nares's " Glossary," vol. ii. p. 704 ; Halliwell-Phillipps's " Handbook Index to Shakespeare," 1866, p. 398 ; Dyce's " Glossary," p. 345 ; Singer's " Shakespeare," vol. vii. p. 264.

[2] " Ornithology of Shakespeare," p. 218.

[3] Strutt's " Sports and Pastimes," 1876, pp. 19, 97, 677 ; Brand's " Pop. Antiq.," 1849, vol. ii. pp. 59, 60.

[4] Douce's " Illustrations of Shakespeare," 1839, p. 367.

Shakespeare. At the present day[1] the Sumatrans practise these quail combats, and this pastime is common in some parts of Italy, and also in China. Mr. Douce has given a curious print, from an elegant Chinese miniature painting, which represents some ladies engaged at this amusement, where the quails are actually inhooped.

Raven. Perhaps no bird is so universally unpopular as the raven, its hoarse croak, in most countries, being regarded as ominous. Hence, as might be expected, Shakespeare often refers to it, in order to make the scene he depicts all the more vivid and graphic. In "Titus Andronicus" (ii. 3), Tamora, describing "a barren detested vale," says:

> "The trees, though summer, yet forlorn and lean,
> O'ercome with moss and baleful mistletoe:
> Here never shines the sun; here nothing breeds,
> Unless the nightly owl or fatal raven."

And in "Julius Cæsar" (v. 1), Cassius tells us how ravens

> "Fly o'er our heads, and downward look on us,
> As we were sickly prey."[2]

It seems that the superstitious dread[3] attaching to this bird has chiefly arisen from its supposed longevity,[4] and its frequent mention and agency in Holy Writ. By the Romans it was consecrated to Apollo, and was believed to have a prophetic knowledge—a notion still very prevalent. Thus, its supposed faculty[5] of "smelling death" still renders its presence, or even its voice, ominous. Othello (iv. 1) exclaims,

> "O, it comes o'er my memory,
> As doth the raven o'er the infected house,
> Boding to all."

There is no doubt a reference here to the fanciful notion that it was a constant attendant on a house infected with

---

[1] Marsden's "History of Sumatra," 1811, p. 276.
[2] Cf. "2 Henry VI." iii. 2; "Troilus and Cressida," v. 2.
[3] See Brand's "Pop. Antiq.," 1849, vol. iii. pp. 211, 212.
[4] "English Folk-lore," 1878, p. 78.
[5] See Hunt's "Popular Romances of West of England," 1881, p. 380.

the plague.　Most readers, too, are familiar with that famous passage in " Macbeth " (i. 5) where Lady Macbeth, having heard of the king's intention to stay at the castle, exclaims,

> "the raven himself is hoarse
> That croaks the fatal entrance of Duncan
> Under my battlements.　Come, you spirits
> That tend on mortal thoughts, unsex me here,
> And fill me, from the crown to the toe, top-full
> Of direst cruelty !"

We may compare Spenser's language in the " Fairy Queen " (bk. ii. c. vii. l. 23):

> " After him owles and night ravens flew,
> The hateful messengers of heavy things,
> Of death and dolor telling sad tidings."

And once more the following passage from Drayton's " Barons' Wars " (bk. v. stanza 42) illustrates the same idea :

> " The ominous raven often he doth hear,
> Whose croaking him of following horror tells."

In " Much Ado About Nothing " (ii. 3), the " night-raven " is mentioned.　Benedick observes to himself: " I had as lief have heard the night-raven, come what plague could have come after it."　This inauspicious bird, according to Steevens, is the owl; but this conjecture is evidently wrong, " being at variance with sundry passages in our early writers, who make a distinction between it and the night-raven."[1]

Thus Johnson, in his " Seven Champions of Christendom " (part i.), speaks of " the dismal cry of night-ravens, . . . and the fearefull sound of schriek owles."　Cotgrave regarded the " night-crow " and the " night-raven " as synonymous; and Mr. Yarrell considered them only different names for the night-heron.[2]　In " 3 Henry VI." (v. 6) King Henry says:

> " The night-crow cried, aboding luckless time."

---

[1] Dyce's " Glossary," 1876, p. 288.

[2] See Harting's " Ornithology of Shakespeare," pp. 101, 102; Yarrell's " History of British Birds," vol. ii. p. 581.

Goldsmith, in his "Animated Nature," calls the bittern the night-raven, and says: "I remember, in the place where I was a boy, with what terror the bird's note affected the whole village; they consider it as the presage of some sad event, and generally found or made one to succeed it. If any person in the neighborhood died, they supposed it could not be otherwise, for the night-raven had foretold it; but if nobody happened to die, the death of a cow or a sheep gave completion to the prophecy."

According to an old belief the raven deserts its own young, to which Shakespeare alludes in " Titus Andronicus " (ii. 3):

> "Some say that ravens foster forlorn children,
> The whilst their own birds famish in their nests."

" It was supposed that when the raven," says Mr. Harting,[1] " saw its young ones newly hatched and covered with down, it conceived such an aversion that it forsook them, and did not return to the nest until a darker plumage had shown itself." To this belief the commentators consider the Psalmist refers, when he says, " He giveth to the beast his food, and to the young ravens which cry " (Psalm cxlvii. 9). We are told, too, in Job, " Who provideth for the raven his food? when his young ones cry unto God, they wander for lack of meat (xxxviii. 41). Shakespeare, in " As You Like It " (ii. 3), probably had the words of the Psalmist in his mind:

> "He that doth the ravens feed,
> Yea, providently caters for the sparrow."

The raven has from earliest times been symbolical of blackness, both in connection with color and character. In " Romeo and Juliet " (iii. 2), Juliet exclaims:

> "O serpent heart, hid with a flowering face!
> Did ever dragon keep so fair a cave?
> Beautiful tyrant! fiend angelical!
> Dove-feather'd raven!"[2]

Once more, ravens' feathers were formerly used by witches,

---

[1] " Ornithology of Shakespeare," p. 107.
[2] Cf. " Midsummer-Night's Dream," ii. 2; " Twelfth Night," v. 1.

from an old superstition that the wings of this bird carried
with them contagion wherever they went.   Hence, in " The
Tempest " (i. 2), Caliban says:

> " As wicked dew as e'er my mother brush'd
> With raven's feather from unwholesome fen
> Drop on you both !"

Robin Redbreast.   According to a pretty notion,[1] this little bird is said to cover with leaves any dead body it may
chance to find unburied ; a belief which probably, in a great
measure, originated in the well-known ballad of the " Children in the Wood," although it seems to have been known
previously.   Thus Singer quotes as follows from " Cornuco-
pia, or Divers Secrets," etc. (by Thomas Johnson, 1596):
" The robin redbreast, if he finds a man or woman dead, will
cover all his face with moss ; and some think that if the
body should remain unburied that he would cover the whole
body also."   In Dekker's " Villaines Discovered by Lanthorn
and Candlelight " (1616), quoted by Douce, it is said, " They
that cheere up a prisoner but with their sight, are robin redbreasts that bring strawes in their bills to cover a dead man
in extremitie."   Shakespeare, in a beautiful passage in "Cymbeline " (iv. 2), thus touchingly alludes to it, making Arviragus, when addressing the supposed dead body of Imogen,
say :

> " With fairest flowers,
> Whilst summer lasts, and I live here, Fidele,
> I'll sweeten thy sad grave : thou shalt not lack
> The flower that's like thy face, pale primrose, nor
> The azured harebell, like thy veins ; no, nor
> The leaf of eglantine, whom not to slander
> Out-sweeten'd not thy breath : the ruddock would,
> With charitable bill,—O bill, sore-shaming
> Those rich-left heirs, that let their fathers lie
> Without a monument !—bring thee all this ;
> Yea, and furr'd moss besides, when flowers are none
> To winter-ground thy corse "—

---

[1] " English Folk-Lore," pp. 62–64 ; Brand's " Pop. Antiq.," 1849, vol.
iii. p. 191 ; Singer's " Shakespeare," vol. x. p. 424 ; Douce's " Illustrations of Shakespeare," 1839, p. 380.

the "ruddock"[1] being one of the old names for the redbreast, which is nowadays found in some localities. John Webster, also, refers to the same idea in "The White Devil" (1857, ed. Dyce, p. 45):

> "Call for the robin redbreast and the wren
> Since o'er shady groves they hover,
> And with leaves and flowers do cover
> The friendless bodies of unburied men."

Drayton, too, in "The Owl," has the following lines:

> "Cov'ring with moss the dead's unclosed eye,
> The little redbreast teaching charitie."

Rook. As an ominous bird this is mentioned in "Macbeth" (iii. 4). Formerly the nobles of England prided themselves in having a rookery[2] in the neighborhood of their castles, because rooks were regarded as "fowls of good omen." On this account no one was permitted to kill them, under severe penalties. When rooks desert a rookery[3] it is said to foretell the downfall of the family on whose property it is. A Northumbrian saying informs us that the rooks left the rookery of Chipchase before the family of Reed left that place. There is also a notion that when rooks haunt a town or village "mortality is supposed to await its inhabitants, and if they feed in the street it shows that a storm is at hand."[4]

The expression "bully-rook," in "Merry Wives of Windsor" (i. 3), in Shakespeare's time, says Mr. Harting,[5] had the same meaning as "jolly dog" nowadays; but subsequently it became a term of reproach, meaning a cheating sharper. It has been suggested that the term derives its origin from

---

[1] Cf. Spenser's "Epithalamium," v. 8:

> "The thrush replies, the mavis descant plays,
> The ouzell shrills, the ruddock warbles soft."

[2] *Standard*, January 26, 1877.
[3] "English Folk-Lore," p. 76.
[4] Henderson's "Folk-Lore of Northern Counties," 1879, p. 122.
[5] "Ornithology of Shakespeare," p. 121.

the *rook* in the game of chess; but Douce [1] considers it very improbable that this noble game, "never the amusement of gamblers, should have been ransacked on this occasion."

Snipe. This bird was in Shakespeare's time proverbial for a foolish man. [2] In "Othello" (i. 3), Iago, speaking of Roderigo, says:

> "For I mine own gain'd knowledge should profane,
> If I would time expend with such a snipe,
> But for my sport and profit."

Sparrow. A popular name for the common sparrow was, and still is, Philip, perhaps from its note, "Phip, phip." Hence the allusion to a person named Philip, in "King John" (i. 1):

> *Gurney.* Good leave, good Philip.
> *Bastard.*   Philip?—sparrow!

Staunton says perhaps Catullus alludes to this expression in the following lines:

> "Sed circumsiliens, modo huc, modo illuc,
> Ad solam dominam usque pipilabat."

Skelton, in an elegy upon a sparrow, calls it "Phyllyp Sparowe;" and Gascoigne also writes "The praise of Philip Sparrow."

In "Measure for Measure" (iii. 2), Lucio, speaking of Angelo, the deputy-duke of Vienna, says: "Sparrows must not build in his house-eaves, because they are lecherous." [3]

Sparrow-hawk. A name formerly given to a young sparrow-hawk was eyas-musket, [4] a term we find in "Merry Wives

---

[1] "Illustrations of Shakespeare," 1839, p. 36; the term "bully-rook" occurs several times in Shadwell's "Sullen Lovers;" see Dyce's "Glossary," p. 58.

[2] In Northamptonshire the word denotes an icicle, from its resemblance to the long bill of the bird so-called.—Baker's "Northamptonshire Glossary," 1854, vol. ii. p. 260.

[3] See Nares's "Glossary," vol. ii. p. 653; Dyce's "Glossary," p. 320.

[4] Derived from the French *mouschet*, of the same meaning.

of Windsor" (iii. 3): " How now, my eyas-musket! what news with you?" It was thus metaphorically used as a jocular phrase for a small child. As the invention, too, of fire-arms took place[1] at a time when hawking was in high fashion, some of the new weapons were named after those birds, probably from the idea of their fetching their prey from on high. *Musket* has thus become the established name for one sort of gun. Some, however, assert that the musket was invented in the fifteenth century, and owes its name to its inventors.

Starling. This was one of the birds that was in days gone by trained to speak. In " 1 Henry IV." (i. 3), Hotspur says :

> " I'll have a starling shall be taught to speak
> Nothing but 'Mortimer,' and give it him,
> To keep his anger still in motion."

Pliny tells us how starlings were taught to utter both Latin and Greek words for the amusement of the young Cæsars ; and there are numerous instances on record of the clever sentences uttered by this amusing bird.

Swallow. This bird has generally been honored as the harbinger of spring, and Athenæus relates that the Rhodians had a solemn song to welcome it. Anacreon has a well-known ode. Shakespeare, in the " Winter's Tale" (iv. 3), alludes to the time of the swallow's appearance in the following passage :

> " daffodils,
> That come before the swallow dares, and take
> The winds of March with beauty."

And its departure is mentioned in " Timon of Athens" (iii. 6): " The swallow follows not summer more willing than we your lordship."

We may compare Tennyson's notice of the bird s approach and migration in " The May Queen :"

---

[1] Nares's " Glossary," vol. ii. p. 593 ; Douce's " Illustrations of Shakespeare," 1839, p. 46. Turbervile tells us " the first name and terme that they bestowe on a falcon is an eyesse, and this name doth laste as long as she is an eyrie and for that she is taken from the eyrie."

" And the swallow 'll come back again with summer o'er the wave."

It has been long considered lucky for the swallow to build its nest on the roof of a house, but just as unlucky for it to forsake a place which it has once tenanted. Shakespeare probably had this superstition in his mind when he represents Scarus as saying, in " Antony and Cleopatra" (iv. 12):

> " Swallows have built
> In Cleopatra's sails their nests: the augurers
> Say, they know not,—they cannot tell ;—look grimly,
> And dare not speak their knowledge."

Swan. According to a romantic notion, dating from antiquity, the swan is said to sing sweetly just before its death, many pretty allusions to which we find scattered here and there throughout Shakespeare's plays. In " Merchant of Venice" (iii. 2), Portia says:

> " he makes a swan-like end,
> Fading in music."

Emilia, too, in " Othello" (v. 2), just before she dies, exclaims:

> " I will play the swan,
> And die in music."

In " King John" (v. 7), Prince Henry, at his father's deathbed, thus pathetically speaks:

> " 'Tis strange that death should sing.
> I am the cygnet to this pale faint swan,
> Who chants a doleful hymn to his own death,
> And from the organ-pipe of frailty sings
> His soul and body to their lasting rest."

Again, in " Lucrece" (1611), we have these touching lines:

> " And now this pale swan in her watery nest,
> Begins the sad dirge of her certain ending."

And once more, in " The Phœnix and Turtle:"

> " Let the priest in surplice white,
> That defunctive music can,
> Be the death-divining swan,
> Lest the requiem lack his right."

This superstition, says Douce,[1] "was credited by Plato, Chrysippus, Aristotle, Euripides, Philostratus, Cicero, Seneca, and Martial. Pliny, Ælian, and Athenæus, among the ancients, and Sir Thomas More, among the moderns, treat this opinion as a vulgar error. Luther believed in it." This notion probably originated in the swan being identified with Orpheus. Sir Thomas Browne[2] says, we read that, "after his death, Orpheus, the musician, became a swan. Thus was it the bird of Apollo, the bird of music by the Greeks." Alluding to this piece of folk-lore, Carl Engel[3] remarks: "Although our common swan does not produce sounds which might account for this tradition, it is a well-known fact that the wild swan (*Cygnus ferus*), also called the 'whistling swan,' when on the wing emits a shrill tone, which, however harsh it may sound if heard near, produces a pleasant effect when, emanating from a large flock high in the air, it is heard in a variety of pitches of sound, increasing or diminishing in loudness according to the movement of the birds and to the current of the air." Colonel Hawker[4] says, "The only note which I ever heard the wild swan make, in winter, is his well-known 'whoop.'"[5]

Tassel-Gentle.[6] The male of the goshawk was so called on account of its tractable disposition, and the facility with which it was tamed. The word occurs in "Romeo and Juliet" (ii. 2):

> "O, for a falconer's voice
> To lure this tassel-gentle back again!"

Spenser, in his "Fairy Queen" (bk. iii. c. iv. l. 49), says:

> "Having far off espied a tassel-gent
> Which after her his nimble wings doth straine."[1]

---

[1] "Illustrations of Shakespeare," 1839, p. 161.

[2] Works, 1852, vol. i. p. 357.

[3] "Musical Myths and Facts," 1876, vol. i. p. 89.

[4] "Instructions to Young Sportsmen," 11th ed., p. 269.

[5] See Baring-Gould's "Curious Myths of the Middle Ages," 1877, p. 561; Thorpe's "Northern Mythology," 1852, vol. iii. pp. 302–328.

[6] Properly "tiercel gentle," French, *tiercelet*; cf. "Troilus and Cressida," iii. 2, "the falcon as the tercel."

This species of hawk was also commonly called a "falcon-gentle," on account of "her familiar, courteous disposition."[1]

Turkey. This bird, so popular with us at Christmas-tide, is mentioned in "1 Henry IV." (ii. 1), where the First Carrier says: "God's body! the turkeys in my pannier are quite starved." This, however, is an anachronism on the part of Shakespeare, as the turkey was unknown in this country until the reign of Henry VIII. According to a rhyme written in 1525, commemorating the introduction of this bird, we are told how:

> "Turkies, carps, hoppes, piccarell, and beere,
> Came into England all in one yeare."

The turkey is again mentioned by Shakespeare in "Twelfth Night" (ii. 5), where Fabian says of Malvolio: "Contemplation makes a rare turkey-cock of him: how he jets under his advanced plumes!"

Vulture. In several passages Shakespeare has most forcibly introduced this bird to deepen the beauty of some of his exquisite passages. Thus, in "King Lear" (ii. 4), when he is complaining of the unkindness of a daughter, he bitterly exclaims:

> "O Regan, she hath tied
> Sharp-tooth'd unkindness, like a vulture, here."

What, too, can be more graphic than the expression of Tamora in "Titus Andronicus" (v. 2):

> "I am Revenge, sent from the infernal kingdom,
> To ease the gnawing vulture of thy mind."

Equally forcible, too, are Pistol's words in "The Merry Wives of Windsor" (i. 3): "Let vultures gripe thy guts."

Johnson considers that "the vulture of sedition" in "2 Henry VI." (iv. 3) is in allusion to the tale of Prometheus, but of this there is a decided uncertainty.

Wagtail. In "King Lear" (ii. 2), Kent says, "Spare my

---

[1] "Gentleman's Recreation," p. 19, quoted in Nares's "Glossary," vol. ii. p. 867.

grey beard, you wagtail?" the word being used in an opprobrious sense, to signify an officious person.

Woodcock. In several passages this bird is used to denote
a fool or silly person; as in "Taming of the Shrew" (i. 2):
"O this woodcock! what an ass it is!" And again, in "Much
Ado About Nothing" (v. 1), where Claudio, alluding to the
plot against Benedick, says: "Shall I not find a woodcock
too?" In "Love's Labour's Lost" (iv. 3) Biron says:

> "O heavens, I have my wish!
> Dumain transformed: four woodcocks in a dish."

The woodcock has generally been proverbial as a foolish
bird—perhaps because it is easily caught in springes or nets.[1]
Thus the popular phrase "Springes to catch woodcocks"
meant arts to entrap simplicity,[2] as in "Hamlet" (i. 3):

> "Aye, springes to catch woodcocks."

A similar expression occurs in Beaumont and Fletcher's
"Loyal Subject" (iv. 4):

> "Go like a woodcock,
> And thrust your neck i' th' noose."

"It seems," says Nares, "that woodcocks are now grown
wiser by time, for we do not now hear of their being so easily
caught. If they were sometimes said to be without brains,
it was only founded on their character, certainly not on any
examination of the fact."[3] Formerly, one of the terms for
twilight[4] was "cock-shut time," because the net in which
cocks, *i. e.*, woodcocks, were shut in during the twilight, was
called a "cock-shut." It appears that a large net was
stretched across a glade, and so suspended upon poles as
to be easily drawn together. Thus, in "Richard III." (v. 3),
Ratcliff says:

---

[1] Dyce's "Glossary," p. 508.
[2] Nares's "Glossary," vol. ii. p. 971.
[3] See Willughby's "Ornithology," iii. section 1.
[4] Minsheu's "Guide into Tongues," ed. 1617.

> "Thomas the Earl of Surrey, and himself,
> Much about cock-shut time, from troop to troop,
> Went through the army, cheering up the soldiers."

In Ben Jonson's "Masque of Gypsies" we read:

> "Mistress, this is only spite;
> For you would not yesternight
> Kiss him in the cock-shut light."

Sometimes it was erroneously written "cock-shoot." "Come, come away then, a fine cock-shoot evening." In the "Two Noble Kinsmen" (iv. 1) we find the term "cock-light."

Wren. The diminutive character of this bird is noticed in "A Midsummer-Night's Dream" (iii. 1, song):

> "The wren with little quill."

In "Macbeth" (iv. 2), Lady Macbeth says:

> "the poor wren,
> The most diminutive of birds, will fight,
> Her young ones in her nest, against the owl."

Considering, too, that as many as sixteen young ones have been found in this little bird's nest, we can say with Grahame, in his poem on the birds of Scotland:

> "But now behold the greatest of this train
> Of miracles, stupendously minute;
> The numerous progeny, claimant for food
> Supplied by two small bills, and feeble wings
> Of narrow range, supplied—ay, duly fed—
> Fed in the dark, and yet not one forgot."

The epithet "poor," applied to the wren by Lady Macbeth, was certainly appropriate in days gone by, when we recollect how it was cruelly hunted in Ireland on St. Stephen's day— a practice which prevailed also in the Isle of Man.[1]

---

[1] See Yarrell's "History of British Birds," vol. ii. p. 178.

CHAPTER VII.

ANIMALS.

As in the case of the birds considered in the previous chapter, Shakespeare has also interwoven throughout his plays an immense deal of curious folk-lore connected with animals. Not only does he allude with the accuracy of a naturalist to the peculiarities and habits of certain animals, but so true to nature is he in his graphic descriptions of them that it is evident his knowledge was in a great measure acquired from his own observation. It is interesting, also, to note how carefully he has, here and there, worked into his narrative some old proverb or superstition, thereby adding a freshness to the picture which has, if possible, imbued it with an additional lustre. In speaking of the dog, he has introduced many an old hunting custom; and his references to the tears of the deer are full of sweet pathos, as, for instance, where Hamlet says (iii. 2), "Let the stricken deer go weep." It is not necessary, however, to add further illustrations, as these will be found in the following pages.

Ape. In addition to Shakespeare's mention of this animal as a common term of contempt, there are several other allusions to it. There is the well-known phrase, "to lead apes in hell," applied to old maids, mentioned in the "Taming of the Shrew" (ii. 1)—the meaning of this term not having been yet satisfactorily explained.[1] (It is further discussed in the chapter on Marriage.)

In "2 Henry IV." (ii. 4), the word is used as a term of endearment, "Alas, poor ape, how thou sweat'st."

Ass. Beyond the proverbial use of this much ill-treated animal to denote a silly, foolish person, Shakespeare has said

---

[1] See page 165.

little about it. In "Troilus and Cressida" (ii. 1), Thersites uses the word *assinego*, a Portuguese expression for a young ass, "Thou hast no more brain than I have in mine elbows; an assinego may tutor thee." It is used by Beaumont and Fletcher in the "Scornful Lady" (v. 4): "All this would be forsworn, and I again an assinego, as your sister left me."[1] Dyce[2] would spell the word "asinico," because it is so spelled in the old editions of Shakespeare, and is more in accordance with the Spanish word.[3] In "King Lear" (i. 4), the Fool alludes to Æsop's celebrated fable of the old man and his ass: "thou borest thine ass on thy back o'er the dirt."

Bat. The bat, immortalized by Shakespeare ("The Tempest," v. 1) as the "delicate Ariel's" steed—

"On the bat's back I do fly,"

—has generally been an object of superstitious dread, and proved to the poet and painter a fertile source of images of gloom and terror.[4] In Scotland[5] it is still connected with witchcraft, and if, while flying, it rise and then descend again earthwards, it is a sign that the witches' hour is come—the hour in which they are supposed to have power over every human being who is not specially shielded from their influence. Thus, in "Macbeth" (iv. 1) the "wool of bat" forms an ingredient in the witches' caldron. One of its popular names is "rere-mouse," which occurs in "A Midsummer-Night's Dream" (ii. 2), where Titania says:

"Some, war with rere-mice for their leathern wings,
   To make my small elves coats."

This term is equivalent to the Anglo-Saxon, *hrére-mús*, from *hreran*, to stir, agitate, and so the same as the old name

---

[1] Nares's "Glossary," vol. i. p. 38.

[2] "Glossary to Shakespeare," 1876, p. 20.

[3] "Asinico, a little ass," Connelly's "Spanish and English Dictionary," Madrid, 4to.

[4] "English Folk-Lore," p. 115; cf. "Macbeth," iii. 2.

[5] Henderson's "Folk-Lore of Northern Counties," 1879, pp. 125, 126.

" flitter-mouse." [1] The early copies spell the word *reremise*. [2]
It occurs in the Wicliffite version of Leviticus xi. 19, and
the plural in the form " reremees" or " rere-myis" is found in
Isaiah ii. 20.   At Polperro, Cornwall, [3] the village boys call it
" airy-mouse," and address it in the following rhyme :

> " Airy mouse, airy mouse! fly over my head,
> And you shall have a crust of bread ;
> And when I brew, and when I bake,
> You shall have a piece of my wedding-cake."

In Scotland [4] it is known as the Backe or Bakie bird.   An
immense deal of folk-lore has clustered round this curious
little animal. [5]

Bear.   According to an old idea, the bear brings forth unformed lumps of animated flesh, and then licks them into
shape—a vulgar error, referred to in " 3 Henry VI." (iii. 2),
where Gloster, bemoaning his deformity, says of his mother :

> " She did corrupt frail nature with some bribe,
>
> *   *   *   *   *   *
>
> To disproportion me in every part,
> Like to a chaos, or an unlick'd bear-whelp,
> That carries no impression like the dam."

This erroneous notion, however, was long ago confuted by
Sir Thomas Browne. [6]   Alexander Ross, in his " Arcana
Microcosmi," nevertheless affirms that bears bring forth their
young deformed and misshapen, by reason of the thick
membrane in which they are wrapped, that is covered over
with a mucous matter.   This, he says, the dam contracts in
the winter-time, by lying in hollow caves without motion, so

---

[1] It has been speciously derived from the English word *rear*, in the
sense of being able to raise itself in the air, but this is erroneous.
Nares's "Glossary," vol. ii. p. 726.

[2] Aldis Wright's " Notes to A Midsummer-Night's Dream, " 1877, p.
101.

[3] " Folk-Lore Record," 1879, p. 201.

[4] Jamieson's " Scottish Dictionary," 1879, vol. i. p. 106.

[5] See Brand's " Pop. Antiq.," 1849, vol. iii. p. 189; Harting's " Ornithology of Shakespeare," 1871, pp. 13, 14.

[6] " Vulgar Errors," 1852, vol. i. p. 247.

that to the eye the cub appears like an unformed lump. The above mucilage is afterwards licked away by the dam, and the membrane broken, whereby that which before seemed to be unformed appears now in its right shape. This, he contends, is all that the ancients meant.[1] Ovid (Metamorphoses, bk. xv. l. 379) thus describes this once popular fancy:

> " Nec catulus, partu quem reddidit ursa recenti,
> Sed male viva caro est : lambendo mater in artus
> Fingit, et in formam, quantam capit ipsa, reducit."

Bears, in days gone by, are reported to have been surprised by means of a mirror, which they would gaze on, affording their pursuers an opportunity of taking the surer aim. In " Julius Cæsar " (ii. 1), this practice is mentioned by Decius:

> "unicorns may be betray'd with trees,
> And bears with glasses."[2]

Batman, " On Bartholomæus " (1582), speaking of the bear, says, " And when he is taken he is made blinde with a bright basin, and bound with chaynes, and compelled to playe." This, however, says Mr. Aldis Wright,[3] probably refers to the actual blinding of the bear.

A favorite amusement with our ancestors was bear-baiting. As early as the reign of Henry II. the baiting of bears by dogs was a popular game in London,[4] while at a later period " a royal bear-ward " was an officer regularly attached to the royal household. In " 2 Henry VI." (v. 1), this personage is alluded to by Clifford, who says:

> " Are these thy bears ? We'll bait thy bears to death,
> And manacle the bear-ward in their chains,
> If thou dar'st bring them to the baiting place."

And again, in " Much Ado About Nothing " (ii. 1), Beatrice·

---

[1] See Bartholomæus, " De Proprietate Rerum," lib. xviii. c. 112; Aristotle, " History of Animals," lib. vi. c. 31 ; Pliny's " Natural History," lib. viii. c. 54.   [2] Steevens on this passage.

[3] "Notes on Julius Cæsar," 1878, p. 134.

[4] "Notices Illustrative of the Drama and other Popular Amusements," incidentally illustrating Shakespeare and his contemporaries, extracted from the MSS. of Leicester, by W. Kelly, 1865, p. 152.

says, " I will even take sixpence in earnest of the bear-ward, and lead his apes into hell." The synonymous term, " bear-herd," occurs in " Taming of the Shrew" (Ind. scene 2), where Sly speaks of himself as " by transmutation a bear-herd ;" and in " 2 Henry IV." (i. 2), Sir John Falstaff remarks how " true valor is turned bear-herd." Among the Harleian MSS.[1] is preserved the original warrant of Richard III. appointing John Brown to this office, and which recites " the diligent service he had done the king" as the ground for granting him the privilege of wandering about the country with his bears and apes, and receiving the " loving benevolence and favors of the people."[2] In the time of Queen Elizabeth bear-baiting was still a favorite pastime, being considered a fashionable entertainment for ladies of the highest rank.[3] James I. encouraged this sport. Nichols[4] informs us that on one occasion the king, accompanied by his court, took the queen, the Princess Elizabeth, and the two young princes to the Tower to witness a fight between a lion and a bear, and by the king's command the bear (which had killed a child that had been negligently left in the bear-house) was afterwards " baited to death upon a stage in the presence of many spectators." Popular, says Mr. Kelly, as bear-baiting was in the metropolis and at court, it was equally so among all classes of the people.[5] It is on record that at Congleton, in Cheshire, " the town-bear having died, the corporation in 1601 gave orders to sell their Bible, in order to purchase another, which was done, and the town no longer without a bear." This event is kept up in a popular rhyme :

> " Congleton rare, Congleton rare,
> Sold the Bible to pay for a bear."

---

[1] No. 433. The document is given at length in Collier's " Annals of the Stage," vol. i. p. 35, note.

[2] Kelly's " Notices of Leicester," p. 152.

[3] Wright's " Domestic Manners," p. 304.

[4] " Progresses and Processions," vol. ii. p. 259.

[5] About 1760 it was customary to have a bear baited at the election of the mayor. Corry, " History of Liverpool," 1810, p. 93.

The same legend attaches to Clifton, a village near Rugby:

> "Clifton-upon-Dunsmore, in Warwickshire,
> Sold the Church Bible to buy a bear."

In Pulleyn's "Etymological Compendium,"[1] we are told that "this cruel amusement is of African origin, and was introduced into Europe by the Romans. It is further alluded to by Shakespeare in "Twelfth Night" (i. 3), "dancing and bear-baiting;" and further on in the same play (ii. 5) Fabian says, "he brought me out o' favor with my lady about a bear-baiting here;" and Macbeth (v. 7) relates:

> "They have tied me to a stake; I cannot fly,
> But, bear-like, I must fight the course."[2]

And in "Julius Cæsar" (iv. 1), Octavius says:

> "we are at the stake,
> And bay'd about with many enemies."

Boar. It appears that in former times boar-hunting was a favorite recreation; many allusions to which we find in old writers. Indeed, in the Middle Ages, the destruction of a wild boar ranked among the deeds of chivalry,[3] and "won for a warrior almost as much renown as the slaying an enemy in the open field." So dangerous, too, was boar-hunting considered, that Shakespeare represents Venus as dissuading Adonis from the perilous practice:

> "'O, be advised! thou know'st not what it is,
> With javelin's point a churlish swine to gore,
>   Whose tushes never sheathed he whetteth still,
>   Like to a mortal butcher, bent to kill.
>
> *   *   *   *   *   *
>
> His brawny sides, with hairy bristles arm'd,
> Are better proof than thy spear's point can enter;
> His short thick neck cannot be easily harm'd;
> Being ireful, on the lion he will venture.'"

---

[1] Edited by M. A. Thoms, 1853, p. 170.

[2] For further information on this subject consult Strutt's "Sports and Pastimes," 1876; Kelly's "Notices of Leicester," pp. 152–159.

[3] Chambers's "Book of Days," 1864, vol. ii. pp. 518, 519.

Such hunting expeditions were generally fatal to some of the dogs, and occasionally to one or more of the hunters. An old tradition of Grimsby, in Lincolnshire,[1] asserts that every burgess, at his admission to the freedom of the borough, anciently presented to the mayor a boar's head, or an equivalent in money, when the animal could not be procured. The old seal of the mayor of Grimsby represents a boar hunt. The lord, too, of the adjacent manor of Bradley, was obliged by his tenure to keep a supply of these animals in his wood, for the entertainment of the mayor and burgesses.[2] A curious triennial custom called the "Rhyne Toll," is observed at Chetwode, a small village about five miles from Buckingham.[3] According to tradition, it originated in the destruction of an enormous wild boar—the terror of the surrounding county—by one of the lords of Chetwode; who, after fighting with it for four hours on a hot summer's day, eventually killed it:

> "Then Sir Ryalas he drawed his broad sword with might,
>   Wind well thy horn, good hunter;
> And he fairly cut the boar's head off quite,
>   For he was a jovial hunter."

As a reward, it is said, the king "granted to him and to his heirs forever, among other immunities and privileges, the full right to levy every year the Rhyne Toll." This is still kept up, and consists of a yearly tax on all cattle found within the manor of Chetwode between the 30th of October and the 7th of November, inclusive. In "Antony and Cleopatra" (iv. 13) Cleopatra alludes to the famous boar killed by Meleager,

> "the boar of Thessaly
> Was never so emboss'd."[4]

---

[1] Hampson's "Œvi Medii Kalendarium," vol. i. p. 96.
[2] See *Gentleman's Magazine*, vol. xcviii. pp. 401, 402.
[3] See "Book of Days," vol. ii. pp. 517–519.
[4] "Embossed" is a hunting term, properly applied to a deer when foaming at the mouth from fatigue, see p. 179; also Dyce's "Glossary to Shakespeare," p. 142; see Nares's "Glossary," vol. i. p. 275.

Bull. Once upon a time there was scarcely a town or village of any magnitude which had not its bull-ring.[1] Indeed, it was not until the year 1835 that baiting was finally put down by an act of Parliament, "forbidding the keeping of any house, pit, or other place for baiting or fighting any bull, bear, dog, or other animal;" and, after an existence of at least seven centuries, this ceased to rank among the amusements of the English people.[2] This sport is alluded to in "Merry Wives of Windsor" (v. 5), "Remember, Jove, thou wast a bull for thy Europa." We may, too, compare the expressions in "Troilus and Cressida" (v. 7), "Now, bull, now, dog! . . . The bull has the game."[3]

Cat. Few animals, in times past, have been more esteemed than the cat, or been honored with a wider folk-lore. Indeed, among the Egyptians this favored animal was held sacred to Isis, or the moon, and worshipped with great ceremony. In the mythology of all the Indo-European nations the cat holds a prominent place; and its connection with witches is well known. "The picture of a witch," says Mr. Henderson,[4] "is incomplete without her cat, by rights a black one." In "Macbeth" (iv. 1) the first witch says:

"Thrice the brinded cat hath mew'd"—

it being a common superstition that the form most generally assumed by the familiar spirits of witches was the cat. Thus, in another passage of the same play (i. 1), the first witch says: "I come, Graymalkin"—the word otherwise spelled Grimalkin,[5] meaning a gray cat. Numerous stories are on record of witches having disguised themselves as

[1] Wright's "Domestic Manners," p. 304; see Strutt's "Sports and Pastimes;" Smith's "Festivals, Games, and Amusements," 1831, pp. 192–229.

[2] "Book of Days," vol. ii. p. 59.

[3] Cf. "2 Henry IV." ii. 2, "the town-bull."

[4] "Folk-Lore of Northern Counties," p. 267; Brand's "Pop. Antiq.," 1849, vol. iii. p. 7.

[5] Malkin is a diminutive of "Mary;" "Maukin," the same word, is still used in Scotland for a hare. "Notes to Macbeth," by Clark and Wright, 1877, p. 75.

cats, in order to carry out their fiendish designs. A wood-man out working in the forest has his dinner every day stolen by a cat. Exasperated at the continued repetition of the theft, he lies in wait for the aggressor, and succeeds in cutting off her paw, when lo! on his return home he finds his wife minus a hand.[1] An honest Yorkshireman,[2] who bred pigs, often lost the young ones. On applying to a certain wise man of Stokesley, he was informed that they were bewitched by an old woman who lived near. The owner of the pigs, calling to mind that he had often seen a cat prowling about his yard, decided that this was the old woman in disguise. He watched for her, and, as soon as she made her appearance, flung at her a poker with all his might. The cat disappeared, and, curiously enough, the poor old woman in question that night fell and broke her leg. This was considered as conclusive that she was the witch that had simulated the form of a cat. This notion is very prevalent on the Continent. It is said that witch-cats have a great hankering after beer.[3] Witches are adepts in the art of brewing, and therefore fond of tasting what their neighbors brew. On these occasions they always masquerade as cats, and what they steal they consume on the spot. There was a countryman whose beer was all drunk up by night whenever he brewed, so that at last he resolved for once to sit up all night and watch. As he was standing by his brewing pan, a number of cats made their appearance, and calling to them, he said; "Come, puss, puss, come, warm you a bit." So in a ring they all sat round the fire as if to warm themselves. After a time, he asked them "if the water was hot." "Just on the boil," said they; and as he spoke he dipped his long-handled pail in the wort, and soused the whole company with it. They all vanished at once, but on the following day his wife had a terribly scalded face, and then he knew who it was that had always drunk his beer. This story is widely prevalent, and is current among the

---

[1] Sternberg's "Dialect and Folk-Lore of Northamptonshire," 1851, p. 148.
[2] Henderson's "Folk-Lore of Northern Counties," 1879, p. 206.
[3] Kelly's "Indo-European Folk-Lore," 1863, p. 238.

Flemish-speaking natives of Belgium.   Again, a North German tradition[1] tells us of a peasant who had three beautiful large cats.   A neighbor begged to have one of them, and obtained it.   To accustom it to the place, he shut it up in the loft.   At night, the cat, popping its head through the window, said, "What shall I bring to-night?"   "Thou shalt bring mice," answered the man.   The cat then set to work, and cast all it caught on the floor.   Next morning the place was so full of dead mice that it was hardly possible to open the door, and the man was employed the whole day in throwing them away by bushels.   At night the cat again asked, "What shall I bring to-night?"   "Thou shalt bring rye," answered the peasant.   The cat was now busily employed in shooting down rye, so that in the morning the door could not be opened.   The man then discovered that the cat was a witch, and carried it back to his neighbor. A similar tradition occurs in Scandinavian mythology.[2] Spranger[3] relates that a laborer, on one occasion, was attacked by three young ladies in the form of cats, and that they were wounded by him.   On the following day they were found bleeding in their beds.   In Vernon,[4] about the year 1566, "the witches and warlocks gathered in great multitudes under the shape of cats.   Four or five men were attacked in a lone place by a number of these beasts.   The men stood their ground, and succeeded in slaying one cat and wounding many others.   Next day a number of wounded women were found in the town, and they gave the judge an accurate account of all the circumstances connected with their wounding."   It is only natural, then, that Shakespeare, in his description of the witches in "Macbeth," should have associated them with the popular superstition which represents the cat as their agent—a notion that no doubt originated in the classic story of Galanthis being turned into a

---

[1] Thorpe's "Northern Mythology," 1851, vol. iii. p. 32.
[2] Ibid., vol. ii. p. 32; vol. iii. pp. 26–236.
[3] See Baring-Gould's "Book of Werewolves," 1869, p. 65.
[4] Ibid., p. 66.

cat, and becoming, through the compassion of Hecate, her priestess. From their supposed connection with witchcraft, cats were formerly often tormented by the ignorant vulgar. Thus it appears[1] that, in days gone by, they (occasionally fictitious ones) were hung up in baskets and shot at with arrows. In some counties, too, they were enclosed, with a quantity of soot, in wooden bottles suspended on a line, and he who could beat out the bottom of the bottle as he ran under it, and yet escape its contents, was the hero of the sport.[2] Shakespeare alludes to this practice in " Much Ado About Nothing" (i. 1), where Benedick says: " Hang me in a bottle like a cat, and shoot at me."

Percy, in his " Reliques of Ancient English Poetry " (1794, vol. i. p. 155), says: " It is still a diversion in Scotland to hang up a cat in a small cask or firkin, half filled with soot; and then a parcel of clowns on horseback try to beat out the ends of it, in order to show their dexterity in escaping before the contents fall upon them."

This practice was once kept up at Kelso, in Scotland, according to Ebenezer Lazarus, who, in his " Description of Kelso " (1789, p. 144), has given a graphic description of the whole ceremony. He says, " This is a sport which was common in the last century at Kelso on the Tweed. A large concourse of men, women, and children assembled in a field about half a mile from the town, and a cat having been put into a barrel stuffed full of soot, was suspended on a cross-beam between two high poles. A certain number of the whipmen, or husbandmen, who took part in this savage and unmanly amusement, then kept striking, as they rode to and fro on horseback, the barrel in which the unfortunate animal was confined, until at last, under the heavy blows of their clubs and mallets, it broke, and allowed the cat to drop. The victim was then seized and tortured to death." He justly stigmatizes it, saying:

---

[1] Dyce's "Glossary to Shakespeare," p. 70.

[2] See Brand's " Pop. Antiq.," 1849, vol. iii. p. 39; also Wright's " Essays on the Superstitions of the Middle Ages," 1846.

> " The cat in the barrel exhibits such a farce,
> That he who can relish it is worse than an ass."

Cats, from their great powers of resistance, are said to have nine lives;[1] hence Mercutio, in " Romeo and Juliet " (iii. 1), says: "Good king of cats, nothing but one of your nine lives." Ben Jonson, in " Every Man in His Humour " (iii. 2), makes Edward Knowell say to Bobadil, " 'Twas pity you had not ten; a cat's and your own." And in Gay's fable of the " Old Woman and her Cats," one of these animals is introduced, upbraiding the witch:

> " 'Tis infamy to serve a hag,
> Cats are thought imps, her broom a nag;
> And boys against our lives combine,
> Because 'tis said, your cats have nine."

In Marston's " Dutch Courtezan " we read:

> " Why, then, thou hast nine lives like a cat."

And in Dekker's " Strange Horse-Race " (1613): " When the grand Helcat had gotten these two furies with nine lives." This notion, it may be noted, is quite the reverse of the well-known saying, " Care will kill a cat," mentioned in " Much Ado About Nothing " (v. 1), where Claudio says: " What though care killed a cat."

For some undiscovered reason a cat was formerly called Tybert or Tybalt;[2] hence some of the insulting remarks of Mercutio, in " Romeo and Juliet " (iii. 1), who calls Tybalt " rat-catcher " and " king of cats." In the old romance of " Hystorye of Reynard the Foxe " (chap. vi.), we are told how " the king called for Sir Tibert, the cat, and said to him, Sir Tibert, you shall go to Reynard, and summon him the second time."[3] A popular term for a wild cat was " cat-o'-mountain," an expression[4] borrowed from the Spaniards, who call the wild cat " gato-montes." In the " Merry Wives

---

[1] See Brand's " Pop. Antiq.," vol. iii. p. 42.
[2] Dyce's " Glossary to Shakespeare," p. 466.
[3] From Tibert, Tib was also a common name for a cat.
[4] Douce's " Illustrations of Shakespeare," 1839, p. 41.

of Windsor " (ii. 2), Falstaff says of Pistol, " Your cat-a-moun-
tain looks."

The word cat was used as a term of contempt, as in " The
Tempest " (ii. 1) and "A Midsummer-Night's Dream " (iii. 2),
where Lysander says, " Hang off, thou cat." Once more,
too, in " Coriolanus " (iv. 2), we find it in the same sense :

> " 'Twas you incensed the rabble ;
> Cats, that can judge as fitly of his worth,
> As I can of those mysteries which heaven
> Will not have earth to know."

A gib, or a gib cat, is an old male cat [1]—gib being the contraction of Gilbert,[2] and is, says Nares, an expression exactly
analogous to that of jackass.[3] Tom-cat is now the usual
term. The word was certainly not bestowed upon a cat
early in life, as is evident from the melancholy character ascribed to it in Shakespeare's allusion in " 1 Henry IV." (i. 2) :
" I am as melancholy as a gib cat." Ray gives " as melancholy as a gib'd [a corruption of gib] cat." The term occurs
again in " Hamlet " (iii. 4). It is improperly applied to a
female by Beaumont and Fletcher, in the " Scornful Lady "
(v. 1) : " Bring out the cat-hounds ! I'll make you take a tree,
whore ; then with my tiller bring down your gib-ship, and
then have you cased and hung up in the warren."

Chameleon. This animal was popularly believed to feed
on air, a notion which Sir Thomas Browne[4] has carefully
discussed. He has assigned, among other grounds for this
vulgar opinion, its power of abstinence, and its faculty of
self-inflation. It lives on insects, which it catches by its
long, gluey tongue, and crushes between its jaws. It has
been ascertained by careful experiment that the chameleon
can live without eating for four months. It can inflate not
only its lungs, but its whole body, including even the feet

---

[1] Dyce's " Glossary," p. 183.

[2] A gibbe (an old male cat), Macou, Cotgrave's " French and Engiish
Dictionary."

[3] " Glossary," vol. i. p. 360.

[4] " Vulgar Errors," bk. iii. p. 21, 1852 ; bk. i. p. 321, *note.*

and tail. In allusion to this supposed characteristic, Shakespeare makes Hamlet say (iii. 2), "Of the chameleon's dish: I eat the air, promise-crammed; you cannot feed capons so;" and in the "Two Gentlemen of Verona" (ii. 1) Speed says: "Though the chameleon, Love, can feed on the air, I am one that am nourished by my victuals, and would fain have meat." There is, too, a popular notion that this animal undergoes frequent changes of color, according to that of the bodies near it. This, however, depends on the volition of the animal, or the state of its feelings, on its good or bad health, and is subordinate to climate, age, and sex.[1] In "3 Henry VI." (iii. 2) Gloster boasts:

> ".I can add colours to the chameleon,
> Change shapes, with Proteus, for advantages."

Cockatrice. This imaginary creature, also called a basilisk, has been the subject of extraordinary prejudice. It was absurdly said to proceed from the eggs of old cocks. It has been represented as having eight feet, a crown on the head, and a hooked and recurved beak.[2] Pliny asserts that the basilisk had a voice so terrible that it struck terror into all other species. Sir Thomas Browne,[3] however, distinguishes the cockatrice from the ancient basilisk. He says, "This of ours is generally described with legs, wings, a serpentine and winding tail, and a crest or comb somewhat like a cock. But the basilisk of elder times was a proper kind of serpent, not above three palms long, as some account; and different from other serpents by advancing his head and some white marks, or coronary spots upon the crown, as all authentic writers have delivered." No other animal, perhaps, has given rise to so many fabulous notions. Thus, it was supposed to have so deadly an eye as to kill by its very look, to which Shakespeare often alludes. In "Romeo and Juliet" (iii. 2), Juliet says:

---

[1] Ovid ("Metamorphoses," bk. xv. l. 411) speaks of its changes of color.

[2] Cuvier's "Animal Kingdom," 1831, vol. ix. p. 226.

[3] "Vulgar Errors," bk. iii. p. 7.

> "say thou but 'I,'
> And that bare vowel, 'I,' shall poison more
> Than the death-darting eye of cockatrice."

In " Richard III." (iv. 1) the Duchess exclaims :

> "O my accursed womb, the bed of death !
> A cockatrice hast thou hatch'd to the world,
> Whose unavoided eye is murderous !"

In " Lucrece " (l. 540) we read :

> " Here with a cockatrice' dead-killing eye
> He rouseth up himself, and makes a pause."

Once more,[1] in "Twelfth Night" (iii. 4), Sir Toby Belch affirms : " This will so fright them both that they will kill one another by the look, like cockatrices." It has also been affirmed that this animal could not exercise this faculty unless it first perceived the object of its vengeance ; if first seen, it died. Dryden has alluded to this superstition :

> "Mischiefs are like the cockatrice's eye,
> If they see first they kill, if seen, they die."

Cockatrice was a popular phrase for a loose woman, probably from the fascination of the eye.[2] It appears, too, that basilisk[3] was the name of a huge piece of ordnance carrying a ball of very great weight. In the following passage in " Henry V." (v. 2), there is no doubt a double allusion—to pieces of ordnance, and to the fabulous creature already described :

> "The fatal balls of murdering basilisks."

Colt. From its wild tricks the colt was formerly used to designate, according to Johnson, "a witless, heady, gay youngster." Portia mentions it with a quibble in "The Merchant of Venice" (i. 2), referring to the Neapolitan prince : " Ay, that's a colt, indeed." The term "to colt"

---

[1] See "Cymbeline," ii. 4 ; "Winter's Tale," i. 2.

[2] Nares's " Glossary," vol. i. p. 173.

[3] Dyce's " Glossary," p. 29 ; see " 1 Henry IV.," ii. 3, " of basilisks, of cannon, culverin."

meant to trick, or befool; as in the phrase in " 1 Henry IV."
(ii. 2): "What a plague mean ye to colt me thus?"   Mr.
Halliwell-Phillipps[1] explains the expression in " Henry
VIII." (i. 3), " Your colt's tooth is not cast yet," to denote
a love of youthful pleasure.   In "Cymbeline" (ii. 4) it is
used in a coarser sense: " She hath been colted by him."

Crocodile.   According to fabulous accounts the crocodile
was the most deceitful of animals; its tears being proverbially fallacious.   Thus Othello (iv. 1) says:

> " O devil, devil!
> If that the earth could teem with woman's tears,
> Each drop she falls would prove a crocodile.—
> Out of my sight!"

We may also compare the words of the queen in " 2 Henry
VI." (iii. 1):

> "Henry my lord is cold in great affairs,
>   Too full of foolish pity; and Gloster's show
>   Beguiles him, as the mournful crocodile
> With sorrow snares relenting passengers."

It is said that this treacherous animal weeps over a man's
head when it has devoured the body, and will then eat up
the head too.   In Bullokar's " Expositor," 1616, we read:
" Crocodile lachrymæ, crocodiles teares, do signify such
teares as are feigned, and spent only with intent to deceive
or do harm."   In Quarles's " Emblems " there is the following allusion:

> " O what a crocodilian world is this,
>   Compos'd of treachries and ensnaring wiles!
> She cloaths destruction in a formal kiss,
>   And lodges death in her deceitful smiles."

In the above passage from " Othello," Singer says there is,
no doubt, a reference to the doctrine of equivocal generation,
by which new animals were supposed to be producible by
new combinations of matter.[2]

---

[1] " Handbook Index to Shakespeare."
[2] Singer's " Shakespeare," 1875, vol. x. p. 118.

Deer. In " King Lear " (iii. 4) Edgar uses deer for wild animals in general :

> " But mice, and rats, and such small deer,
>   Have been Tom's food for seven long year."

Shakespeare frequently refers to the popular sport of hunting the deer ;[1] and by his apt allusions shows how thoroughly familiar he was with the various amusements of his day.[2] In " Winter's Tale " (i. 2) Leontes speaks of "the mort o' the deer:" certain notes played on the horn at the death of the deer, and requiring a deep-drawn breath.[3] It was anciently, too, one of the customs of the chase for all to stain their hands in the blood of the deer as a trophy. Thus, in " King John " (ii. 1), the English herald declares to the men of Angiers how

> " like a jolly troop of huntsmen, come
> Our lusty English, all with purpled hands,
> Dyed in the dying slaughter of their foes."

The practice is again alluded to in " Julius Cæsar " (iii. 1):

> " here thy hunters stand,
> Sign'd in thy spoil, and crimson'd in thy lethe."

Old Turbervile gives us the details of this custom : " Our order is, that the prince, or chief, if so please them, do alight, and take assay of the deer, with a sharp knife, the which is done in this manner—the deer being laid upon his back, the prince, chief, or such as they do appoint, comes to it, and the chief huntsman, kneeling if it be a prince, doth hold the deer by the forefoot, whilst the prince, or chief, do cut a slit drawn along the brisket of the deer."

In " Antony and Cleopatra " (v. 2), where Cæsar, speaking of Cleopatra's death, says:

---

[1] See Strutt's " Sports and Pastimes," 1876, pp. 66, 75, 79, 80, 113, 117.

[2] See " As You Like It," iv. 2 ; " All's Well That Ends Well," v. 2 ; " Macbeth," iv. 3 ; " 1 Henry IV.," v. 4 ; " 1 Henry VI.," iv. 2 ; " 2 Henry VI.," v. 2 ; " Titus Andronicus," iii. 1, etc.

[3] Singer's " Shakespeare," vol. viii. p. 421.

> "bravest at the last,
> She levell'd at our purposes, and, being royal,
> Took her own way"—

there is possibly an allusion to the *hart royal*, which had the privilege of roaming unmolested, and of taking its own way to its lair.

Shooting with the cross-bow at deer was an amusement of great ladies. Buildings with flat roofs, called stands, partly concealed by bushes, were erected in the parks for the purpose. Hence the following dialogue in " Love's Labour's Lost " (iv. 1):

> " *Princess.* Then forester, my friend, where is the bush
> That we must stand and play the murderer in?
> *Forester.* Hereby, upon the edge of yonder coppice;
> A stand where you may make the fairest shoot."

Among the hunting terms to which Shakespeare refers may be mentioned the following:

"To draw" meant to trace the steps of the game, as in " Comedy of Errors " (iv. 2):

> " A hound that runs counter, and yet draws dry-foot well."

The term "to run counter" was to mistake the course of the game, or to turn and pursue the backward trail."

The "recheat" denoted certain notes sounded on the horn, properly and more usually employed to recall the dogs from a wrong scent. It is used in " Much Ado About Nothing " (i. 1): " I will have a recheat winded in my forehead." We may compare Drayton's " Polyolbion " (xiii.):

> "Recheating with his horn, which then the hunter cheers."

The phrase " to recover the wind of me," used by Hamlet (iii. 2), is borrowed from hunting, and means to get the animal pursued to run with the wind, that it may not scent the toil or its pursuers. Again, when Falstaff, in " 2 Henry IV." (ii. 4), speaks of "fat rascals," he alludes to the phrase of the forest—" rascall," says Puttenham, " being properly the hunting term given to a young deer leane and out of season."

The phrase "a hunts-up" implied any song intended to arouse in the morning—even a love song—the name having been derived from a tune or song employed by early hunters.[1] The term occurs in "Romeo and Juliet" (iii. 5), where Juliet says to Romeo, speaking of the lark:

> "Since arm from arm that voice doth us affray,
> Hunting thee hence with hunts-up to the day."

In Drayton's "Polyolbion" (xiii.) it is used:

> "No sooner doth the earth her flowery bosom brave,
> At such time as the year brings on the pleasant spring,
> But hunts-up to the mórn the feather'd sylvans sing."

In Shakespeare's day it was customary to hunt as well after dinner as before, hence, in "Timon of Athens" (ii. 2), Timon says:

> "So soon as dinner's done, we'll forth again."

The word "embossed" was applied to a deer when foaming at the mouth from fatigue. In "Taming of the Shrew" (Ind. scene 1) we read: "the poor cur is embossed," and in "Antony and Cleopatra" (iv. 13):

> "the boar of Thessaly
> Was never so emboss'd."

It was usual to call a pack of hounds "a cry," from the French *meute de chiens.* The term is humorously applied to any troop or company of players, as by Hamlet (iii. 2), who speaks of "a fellowship in a cry of players." In "Coriolanus" (iv. 6) Menenius says,

> "You have made
> Good work, you and your cry."

Antony, in "Julius Cæsar" (iii. 1), alludes to the technical phrase to "let slip a dog," employed in hunting the hart. This consisted in releasing the hounds from the leash or *slip*

---

[1] Chappell's "Popular Music of the Olden Time," 2d ed. vol. i. p. 61; see Douce's "Illustrations of Shakespeare," p. 432; see, too, Nares's "Glossary," vol. i. p. 440.

of leather by which they were held in hand until it was judged proper to let them pursue the animal chased.[1] In " 1 Henry IV." (i. 3) Northumberland tells Hotspur:

> "Before the game's afoot, thou still let'st slip."

In " Taming of the Shrew " (v. 2) Tranio says:

> " O, sir, Lucentio slipp'd me like his greyhound,
> Which runs himself, and catches for his master."

A sportsman's saying, applied to hounds, occurs in " 2 Henry IV." (v. 3): " a' will not out; he is true bred," serving to expound Gadshill's expression, " such as can hold in," " 1 Henry IV." (ii. 1).

The severity of the game laws under our early monarchs was very stringent; and a clause in the " Forest Charter "[2] grants " to an archbishop, bishop, earl, or baron, when travelling through the royal forests, at the king's command, the privilege to kill one deer or two in the sight of the forester, if he was at hand; if not, they were commanded to cause a horn to be sounded, that it might not appear as if they had intended to steal the game." In " Merry Wives of Windsor " (v. 5), Falstaff, using the terms of the forest, alludes to the perquisites of the keeper. Thus he speaks of the " shoulders for the fellow of this walk," *i. e.*, the keeper.

Shakespeare has several pretty allusions to the tears of the deer, this animal being said to possess a very large secretion of tears. Thus Hamlet (iii. 2) says: "let the strucken deer go weep;" and in " As You Like It " (ii. 1) we read of the " sobbing deer," and in the same scene the first lord narrates how, at a certain spot,

> " a poor sequester'd stag
> That from the hunter's aim had ta'en a hurt
> Did come to languish; . . . .
> . . . . and the big round tears
> Coursed one another down his innocent nose
> In piteous chase."

---

[1] See Dyce's " Glossary," p. 401.
[2] See Strutt's " Sports and Pastimes," 1876, p. 65.

Bartholomæus[1] says, that "when the hart is arered, he fleethe to a ryver or ponde, and roreth cryeth and wepeth when he is take."[2] It appears that there were various superstitions connected with the tears of the deer. Batman[3] tells us that "when the hart is sick, and hath eaten many serpents for his recoverie, he is brought unto so great a heate that he hasteth to the water, and there covereth his body unto the very eares and eyes, at which time distilleth many tears from which the [Bezoar] stone is gendered."[4] Douce[5] quotes the following passage from the "Noble Art of Venerie," in which the hart thus addresses the hunter:

"O cruell, be content, to take in worth my tears,
  Which growe to gumme, and fall from me: content thee with my
        heares,
  Content thee with my hornes, which every year I new,
  Since all these three make medicines, some sickness to eschew.
  My tears congeal'd to gumme, by peeces from me fall,
  And thee preserve from pestilence, in pomander or ball.
  Such wholesome tears shedde I, when thou pursewest me so."

Dog. As the favorite of our domestic animals, the dog not unnaturally possesses an extensive history, besides entering largely into those superstitions which, more or less, are associated with every stage of human life. It is not surprising, therefore, that Shakespeare frequently speaks of the dog, making it the subject of many of his illustrations. Thus he has not omitted to mention the fatal significance of its howl, which is supposed either to foretell death or misfortune. In "2 Henry VI." (i. 4) he makes Bolingbroke say:

"The time when screech-owls cry, and ban-dogs howl,[6]
  And spirits walk, and ghosts break up their graves."

---

[1] "De Proprietate Rerum," lib. xviii. c. 30.

[2] Cf. Vergil's description of the wounded stag in "Æneid," bk. vii.

[3] Commentary on Bartholomæus's "De Proprietate Rerum."

[4] The drops which fall from their eyes are not tears from the lachrymal glands, but an oily secretion from the inner angle of the eye close to the nose.—Brewer's "Dictionary of Phrase and Fable," p. 217.

[5] "Illustrations of Shakespeare," p. 183.

[6] These dogs were kept for baiting bears, when that amusement was

And, again, in " 3 Henry VI." (v. 6), King Henry, speaking of Gloster, says:

> "The owl shriek'd at thy birth,—an evil sign;
> The night-crow cried, aboding luckless time;
> Dogs howl'd, and hideous tempests shook down trees."

The same superstition prevails in France and Germany,[1] and various charms are resorted to for averting the ill-conse-quences supposed to attach to this sign of ill-omen. Several of these, too, are practised in our own country. Thus, in Staffordshire, when a dog howls, the following advice is given: "Take off your shoe from the left foot, and spit upon the sole, place it on the ground bottom upwards, and your foot upon the place you sat upon, which will not only preserve you from harm, but stop the howling of the dog."[2] A similar remedy is recommended in Norfolk:[3] "Pull off your left shoe, and turn it, and it will quiet him. A dog won't howl three times after." We are indebted to antiq-uity for this superstition, some of the earliest writers refer-ring to it. Thus, Pausanias relates how, previous to the de-struction of the Messenians, the dogs pierced the air by rais-ing a louder barking than usual; and it is on record how, before the sedition in Rome, about the dictatorship of Pom-pey, there was an extraordinary howling of dogs. Vergil[4] ("Georgic," lib. i. l. 470), speaking of the Roman misfortunes, says:

> "Obscenæque canes, importunæque volucres
> Signa dabant."

Capitolinus narrates, too, how the dogs, by their howling, presaged the death of Maximinus. The idea which asso-ciates the dog's howl with the approach of death is probably

---

in vogue, and "from their terrific howling they are occasionally intro-duced to heighten the horror of the picture." Nares's "Glossary," vol. i. p. 50.

[1] See Kelly's "Indo-European Folk-Lore," p. 109.

[2] Henderson's "Folk-Lore of the Northern Counties," p. 48.

[3] See "English Folk-Lore," p. 101.

[4] See Hardwick's "Traditions, Superstitions, and Folk-Lore," p. 171.

derived from a conception in Aryan mythology, which represents a dog as summoning the departing soul. Indeed, as Mr. Fiske [1] remarks, "Throughout all Aryan mythology, the souls of the dead are supposed to ride on the night-wind, with their howling dogs, gathering into their throng the souls of those just dying as they pass by their houses."

Another popular superstition—in all probability derived from the Egyptians—refers to the setting and rising of Sirius, or the dog-star, as infusing madness into the canine race. Hence the name of the "dog-days" was given by the Romans to the period between the 3d of July and the 11th of August, to which Shakespeare alludes in "Henry VIII." (v. 3): "the dog-days now reign." We may, too, compare the words of Benvolio, in "Romeo and Juliet" (iii. 1):

"For now, these hot days, is the mad blood stirring."

It is obvious, however, that this superstition is utterly groundless, for not only does the star vary in its rising, but is later and later every year. The term "dog-day" is still a common phrase, and it is difficult to say whether it is from superstitious adherence to old custom, or from a belief in the injurious effect of heat upon dogs, that the magistrates, often unwisely, at this season of the year order them to be muzzled or tied up. It was the practice to put them to death; and Ben Jonson, in his "Bartholomew Fair," speaks of "the dog-killer" in this month of August. Lord Bacon, too, in his "Sylva Sylvarum," tells us that "it is a common experience that dogs know the dog-killer, when, as in times of infection, some petty fellow is sent out to kill them. Although they have never seen him before, yet they will all come forth and bark and fly at him."

A "curtal dog," to which allusion is made in "Merry Wives of Windsor" (ii. 1), by Pistol—

"Hope is a curtal dog in some affairs,"

denoted "originally the dog of an unqualified person, which, by the forest laws, must have its tail cut short, partly as a

---

[1] "Myths and Mythmakers," 1873, p. 36.

mark, and partly from a notion that the tail of a dog is necessary to him in running." In later usage, *curtail dog* means either a common dog, not meant for sport, or a dog that missed the game, which latter sense it has in the passage above.[1]

Dragon. As the type and embodiment of the spirit of evil, the dragon has been made the subject of an extensive legendary lore. The well-known myth of St. George and the Dragon," which may be regarded as a grand allegory representing the hideous and powerful monster against whom the Christian soldier is called to fight, has exercised a remarkable influence for good in times past, over half-instructed people. It has been truly remarked that "the dullest mind and hardest heart could not fail to learn from it something of the hatefulness of evil, the beauty of self-sacrifice, and the all-conquering might of truth." This graceful conception is alluded to by Shakespeare, in his "King John" (ii. 1), where, according to a long-established custom, it is made a subject for sign-painting:[2]

> "St. George, that swinged the dragon, and e'er since,
> Sits on his horseback at mine hostess' door,
> Teach us some fence!"

In ancient mythology the task of drawing the chariot of night was assigned to dragons, on account of their supposed watchfulness. In "Cymbeline" (ii. 2) Iachimo, addressing them, says:

> "Swift, swift, you dragons of the night, that dawning
> May bare the raven's eye!"[3]

Milton, in his "Il Penseroso," mentions the dragon yoke of night, and in his "Comus" (l. 130):

> "the dragon womb
> Of Stygian darkness."

---

[1] "Nares's Glossary," vol. i. p. 218.

[2] For the various versions of this myth consult Baring-Gould's "Curious Myths of the Middle Ages," 1877, pp. 266–316.

[3] Cf. "Troilus and Cressida," v. 8; "Midsummer-Night's Dream," iii. 2.

It may be noticed that the whole tribe of serpents sleep with their eyes open, and so appear to exert a constant watchfulness.[1]

In devising loathsome ingredients for the witches' mess, Shakespeare ("Macbeth," iv. 1) speaks of "the scale of dragon," alluding to the horror in which this mythical being was held. Referring, also, to the numerous legends associated with its dread form, he mentions "the spleen of fiery dragons" ("Richard III.," v. 3), "dragon's wings" ("1 Henry VI.," i. 1), and ("Pericles," i. 1), "death-like dragons." Mr. Conway[2] has admirably summed up the general views respecting this imaginary source of terror: "Nearly all the dragon forms, whatever their original types and their region, are represented in the conventional monster of the European stage, which meets the popular conception. The dragon is a masterpiece of the popular imagination, and it required many generations to give it artistic shape. Every Christmas he appears in some London pantomime, with aspect similar to that which he has worn for many ages. His body is partly green, with the memories of the sea and of slime, and partly brown or dark, with lingering shadow of storm clouds. The lightning flames still in his red eyes, and flashes from his fire-breathing mouth. The thunderbolt of Jove, the spear of Wodan, are in the barbed point of his tail. His huge wings—bat-like, spiked—sum up all the mythical life of extinct harpies and vampires. Spine of crocodile is on his neck, tail of the serpent, and all the jagged ridges of rocks and sharp thorns of jungles bristle around him, while the ice of glaciers and brassy glitter of sunstrokes are in his scales. He is ideal of all that is hard, obstructive, perilous, loathsome, horrible in nature; every detail of him has been seen through and vanquished by man, here or there, but in selection and combination they rise again as principles, and conspire to form one great generaliza-

---

[1] Singer's "Shakespeare," vol. x. p. 363.
[2] "Demonology and Devil-Lore," 1880, vol. i. p. 383.

tion of the forms of pain — the sum of every creature's worst."[1]

Elephant. According to a vulgar error, current in bygone times, the elephant was supposed to have no joints—a notion which is said to have been first recorded from tradition by Ctesias the Cnidian.[2] Sir Thomas Browne has entered largely into this superstition, arguing, from reason, anatomy, and general analogy with other animals, the absurdity of the error. In "Troilus and Cressida" (ii. 3), Ulysses says: "The elephant hath joints, but none for courtesy: his legs are legs for necessity, not for flexure." Steevens quotes from "The Dialogues of Creatures Moralized"—a curious specimen of our early natural history — the following: "the olefawnte that bowyth not the kneys." In the play of "All Fools," 1605, we read: "I hope you are no elephant—you have joints." In a note to Sir Thomas Browne's Works,[3] we are told, "it has long been the custom for the exhibitors of itinerant collections of wild animals, when showing the elephant, to mention the story of its having no joints, and its consequent inability to kneel; and they never fail to think it necessary to demonstrate its untruth by causing the animal to bend one of its fore-legs, and to kneel also."

In "Julius Cæsar" (ii. 1) the custom of seducing elephants into pitfalls, lightly covered with hurdles and turf, on which a proper bait to tempt them was exposed, is alluded to.[4] Decius speaks of elephants being betrayed "with holes."

Fox. It appears that the term fox was a common expression for the old English weapon, the broadsword of Jonson's days, as distinguished from the small (foreign) sword. The name was given from the circumstance that Andrea Ferrara adopted a fox as the blade-mark of his weapons—a practice, since his time, adopted by other foreign sword-cutlers. Swords with a running fox rudely engraved on

---

[1] The dragon formerly constituted a part of the morris-dance.
[2] Sir Thomas Browne's Works, 1852, vol. i. pp. 220–232.
[3] Edited by Simon Wilkin, 1852, vol. i. p. 226.
[4] See Pliny's "Natural History," bk. viii.

the blades are still occasionally to be met with in the old curiosity shops of London.[1]   Thus, in " Henry V." (iv. 4), Pistol says :

> " O Signieur Dew, thou diest on point of fox,
> Except, O signieur, thou do give to me
> Egregious ransom."

In Ben Jonson's " Bartholomew Fair " (ii. 6) the expression occurs : " What would you have, sister, of a fellow that knows nothing but a basket-hilt, and an old fox in it ?"

The tricks and artifices of a hunted fox were supposed to be very extraordinary ; hence Falstaff makes use of this expression in " 1 Henry IV." (iii. 3) : " No more truth in thee than in a drawn fox."

Goat.   It is curious that the harmless goat should have had an evil name, and been associated with devil-lore. Thus, there is a common superstition in England and Scotland that it is never seen for twenty-four hours together ; and that once in this space it pays a visit to the devil, in order to have its beard combed.   It was, formerly, too, a popular notion that the devil appeared frequently in the shape of a goat, which accounted for his horns and tail.   Sir Thomas Browne observes that the goat was the emblem of the sin-offering, and is the emblem of sinful men at the day of judgment.   This may, perhaps, account for Shakespeare's enumerating the "gall of goat" (" Macbeth," iv. 1) among the ingredients of the witches' caldron.   His object seems to have been to include the most distasteful and ill-omened things imaginable—a practice shared, indeed, by other poets contemporary with him.

Hare.   This was formerly esteemed a melancholy animal, and its flesh was supposed to engender melancholy in those who ate it.   This idea was not confined to our own country, but is mentioned by La Fontaine in one of his " Fables " (liv. ii. fab. 14) :

Staunton's " Shakespeare," 1864, vol. ii. p. 367 ; Nares's " Glossary," vol. i. p. 331.

> "Dans un profond ennui ce lievre se plongeoit,
> Cet animal est triste, et la crainte le rounge ;"

and later on he says: " Le melancolique animal."   Hence,
in " 1 Henry IV." (i. 2), Falstaff is told by Prince Henry
that he is as melancholy as a hare.   This notion was not
quite forgotten in Swift's time ; for in his " Polite Conversation," Lady Answerall, being asked to eat hare, replies : " No,
madam ; they say 'tis melancholy meat."   Mr. Staunton
quotes the following extract from Turbervile's book on
Hunting and Falconry : " The hare first taught us the use
of the hearbe called wyld succory, which is very excellent
for those which are disposed to be melancholicke.   She herself is one of the most melancholicke beasts that is, and to
heale her own infirmitie, she goeth commonly to sit under
that hearbe."

The old Greek epigram relating to the hare—

> " Strike ye my body, now that life is fled ;
> So hares insult the lion when he's dead,"

—is alluded to by the Bastard in " King John " (ii. 1) :

> " You are the hare of whom the proverb goes,
> Whose valour plucks dead lions by the beard."

A familiar expression among sportsmen for a hare is " Wat,"
so called, perhaps, from its long ears or wattles.   In " Venus
and Adonis " the term occurs :

> " By this, poor Wat, far off upon a hill,
> Stands on his hinder legs, with listening ear."

In Drayton's " Polyolbion " (xxiii.) we read :

> " The man whose vacant mind prepares him to the sport,
> The finder sendeth out, to seek out nimble Wat,
> Which crosseth in the field, each furlong, every flat,
> Till he this pretty beast upon the form hath found."

Hedgehog.   The urchin or hedgehog, like the toad, for its
solitariness, the ugliness of its appearance, and from a popular belief that it sucked or poisoned the udders of cows, was
adopted into the demonologic system ; and its shape was

sometimes supposed to be assumed by mischievous elves.[1]
Hence, in " The Tempest " (i. 2), Prospero says :

> " Urchins
> Shall, for that vast of night that they may work,
> All exercise on thee ;"

and later on in the same play (ii. 2) Caliban speaks of being
frighted with " urchin shows." In the witch scene in " Macbeth " (iv. 1) the hedgepig is represented as one of the
witches' familiars ; and in the " Midsummer-Night's Dream "
(ii. 2), in the incantation of the fairies, " thorny hedgehogs "
are exorcised. For the use of urchins in similar associations
we may quote " Merry Wives of Windsor " (iv. 4), " like urchins, ouphes, and fairies ;" and " Titus Andronicus " (ii. 3),
" ten thousand swelling toads, as many urchins."[2] In the
phrase still current, of " little urchin " for a child, the idea
of the fairy also remains. In various legends we find this
animal holding a prominent place. Thus, for example, it
was in the form of a hedgehog[3] that the devil is said to have
made his attempt to let the sea in through the Brighton
Downs, which was prevented by a light being brought,
though the seriousness of the scheme is still attested in the
Devil's Dyke. There is an ancient tradition that when the
devil had smuggled himself into Noah's Ark he tried to sink
it by boring a hole ; but this scheme was defeated, and the
human race saved, by the hedgehog stuffing himself into the
hole. In the Brighton story, as Mr. Conway points out, the
devil would appear to have remembered his former failure in
drowning people, and to have appropriated the form which
defeated him. In " Richard III." (i. 2), the hedgehog is used
as a term of reproach by Lady Anne, when addressing
Gloster.

Horse. Although Shakespeare's allusions to the horse are
most extensive, yet he has said little of the many widespread
superstitions, legends, and traditional tales that have been

---

[1] Singer's " Shakespeare," vol. ix. p. 75.
[2] See Wright's Notes to " The Tempest," 1875, p. 94.
[3] Conway's " Demonology and Devil-Lore," 1880, vol. i. p. 122.

associated from the earliest times with this brave and intel-
lectual animal.   Indeed, even nowadays, both in our own
country and abroad, many a fairy tale is told and credited
by the peasantry in which the horse occupies a prominent
place.   It seems to have been a common notion that, at
night-time, fairies in their nocturnal revels played various
pranks with horses, often entangling in a thousand knots
their hair—a superstition to which we referred in our chapter on Fairies, where Mercutio, in " Romeo and Juliet " (i. 4),
says:

> " This is that very Mab
> That plats the manes of horses in the night,
> And bakes the elf-locks in foul sluttish hairs,
> Which, once untangled, much misfortune bodes."

In " King Lear " (ii. 3), Edgar says :. " I'll . . . elf all my hair
in knots."

Mr. Hunt, in his " Popular Romances of the West of England " (1871, p. 87), tells us that, when a boy, he was on a
visit at a farmhouse near Fowey River, and well remembers
the farmer, with much sorrow, telling the party one morning
at breakfast, how " the piskie people had been riding Tom
again."   The mane was said to be knotted into fairy stirrups,
and the farmer said he had no doubt that at least twenty
small people had sat upon the horse's neck.   Warburton [1]
considers that this superstition may have originated from the
disease called " Plica Polonica."   Witches, too, have generally been supposed to harass the horse, using it in various
ways for their fiendish purposes.   Thus, there are numerous
local traditions in which the horse at night-time has been
ridden by the witches, and found in the morning in an almost prostrate condition, bathed in sweat.

It was a current notion that a horse-hair dropped into
corrupted water would soon become an animal.   The fact,
however, is that the hair moves like a living thing because
a number of animalculæ cling to it.[2]   This ancient vulgar
error is mentioned in " Antony and Cleopatra " (i. 2):

---

[1] Warburton on " Romeo and Juliet," i. 4.

[2] Dyce's " Glossary," p. 104.

> " much is breeding,
> Which, like the courser's hair, hath yet but life,
> And not a serpent's poison."

Steevens quotes from Churchyard's " Discourse of Rebell-
ion," 1570:

> " Hit is of kinde much worse than horses heare,
> That lyes in donge, where on vyle serpents brede."

Dr. Lister, in the " Philosophical Transactions," says that
these animated horse-hairs are real thread-worms. It was
asserted that these worms moved like serpents, and were
poisonous to swallow. Coleridge tells us it was a common
experiment with boys in Cumberland and Westmoreland to
lay a horse-hair in water, which, when removed after a time,
would twirl round the finger and sensibly compress it—having become the supporter of an immense number of small,
slimy water-lice.

A horse is said to have a " cloud in his face " when he
has a dark-colored spot in his forehead between his eyes.
This gives him a sour look, and, being supposed to indicate
an ill-temper, is generally considered a great blemish. This
notion is alluded to in " Antony and Cleopatra " (iii. 2),
where Agrippa, speaking of Cæsar, says:

> " He has a cloud in's face,"

whereupon Enobarbus adds:

> " He were the worse for that, were he a horse;
> So is he, being a man."

Burton, in his " Anatomy of Melancholy," uses the phrase
for the look of a woman: " Every lover admires his mistress,
though she be very deformed of herselfe—thin, leane, chitty
face, have clouds in her face," etc.

" To mose in the chine," a phrase we find in " Taming of
the Shrew " (iii. 2)—" Possessed with the glanders, and like
to mose in the chine "—refers to a disorder in horses, also
known as " mourning in the chine."

Alluding to the custom associated with horses, we may
note that a stalking-horse, or stale, was either a real or arti-

ficial one, under cover of which the fowler approached towards and shot at his game. It is alluded to in "As You
Like It" (v. 4) by the Duke, who says of Touchstone: "He
uses his folly like a stalking-horse, and under the presentation
of that he shoots his wit." In "Much Ado About Nothing"
(ii. 3), Claudio says: "Stalk on, stalk on; the fowl sits."[1] In
"Comedy of Errors" (ii. 1), Adriana says: "I am but his
stale," upon which Malone remarks: "Adriana undoubtedly
means to compare herself to a stalking-horse, behind whom
Antipholus shoots at such game as he selects." In "Taming of the Shrew," Katharina says to her father (i. 1):

> "is it your will
> To make a stale of me amongst these mates?"

which, says Singer, means "make an object of mockery."
So in "3 Henry VI." (iii. 3), Warwick says:

> "Had he none else to make a stale but me?"

That it was also a hunting term might be shown, adds
Dyce,[2] by quotations from various old writers. In the in-
ventories of the wardrobe belonging to King Henry VIII.
we frequently find the allowance of certain quantities of
stuff for the purpose of making "stalking-coats and stalking-
hose for the use of his majesty."[3]

Again, the forehorse of a team was generally gayly ornamented with tufts and ribbons and bells. Hence, in "All's
Well That Ends Well" (ii. 1), Bertram complains that, be-
dizened like one of these animals, he will have to squire
ladies at the court, instead of achieving honor in the wars—

> "I shall stay here the forehorse to a smock,
>   Creaking my shoes on the plain masonry,
>   Till honour be bought up, and no sword worn
>   But one to dance with."

A familiar name for a common horse was "Cut"—either
from its being docked or gelded—a name occasionally ap-

---

[1] See Douce's "Illustrations of Shakespeare," p. 106; Nares's "Glossary," vol. ii. p. 830.   [2] "Glossary," p. 412.
[3] See Strutt's "Sports and Pastimes," p. 48.

plied to a man as a term of contempt. In "Twelfth Night" (ii. 3), Sir Toby Belch says: "Send for money, knight; if thou hast her not i' the end, call me cut." In "1 Henry IV." (ii. 1), the first carrier says: "I prithee, Tom, beat Cut's saddle." We may compare, too, what Falstaff says further on in the same play (ii. 4): "I tell thee what, Hal, if I tell thee a lie, spit in my face, call me horse." Hence, *call me cut* is the same as *call me horse*—both expressions having been used.

In Shakespeare's day a *race* of horses was the term for what is now called a stud. So in "Macbeth" (ii. 4), Rosse says:

> "And Duncan's horses—a thing most strange and certain—
> Beauteous and swift, the minions of their race,
> Turn'd wild in nature."

The words "minions of their race," according to Steevens, mean the favorite horses on the race-ground.

Lion. The traditions and stories of the darker ages abounded with examples of the lion's generosity. "Upon the supposition that these acts of clemency were true, Troilus, in the passage below, reasons not improperly ('Troilus and Cressida,' v. 3) that to spare against reason, by mere instinct and pity, became rather a generous beast than a wise man:"[1]

> "Brother, you have a vice of mercy in you,
> Which better fits a lion than a man."

It is recorded by Pliny[2] that "the lion alone of all wild animals is gentle to those that humble themselves before him, and will not touch any such upon their submission, but spareth what creature soever lieth prostrate before him." Hence Spenser's Una, attended by a lion; and Perceval's lion, in "Morte d'Arthur" (bk. xiv. c. 6). Bartholomæus says the lion's "mercie is known by many and oft ensamples: for they spare them that lie on the ground." Shakespeare again alludes to this notion in "As You Like It" (iv. 3):

---

[1] Singer's "Shakespeare," 1875, vol. vii. p. 277.
[2] "Natural History," bk. viii. c. 19.

> " for 'tis
> The royal disposition of that beast
> To prey on nothing that doth seem as dead."

It was also supposed that the lion would not injure a royal prince. Hence, in " 1 Henry IV." (ii. 4) the Prince says: " You are lions too, you ran away upon instinct, you will not touch the true prince; no, fie!" The same notion is alluded to by Beaumont and Fletcher in " The Mad Lover" (iv. 5):

> " Fetch the Numidian lion I brought over;
> If she be sprung from royal blood, the lion
> He'll do you reverence, else—
>
>   *   *   *   *   *   *
>
> He'll tear her all to pieces."

According to some commentators there is an allusion in " 3 Henry VI." (i. 3) to the practice of confining lions and keeping them without food that they may devour criminals exposed to them:

> " So looks the pent-up lion o'er the wretch
> That trembles under his devouring paws."

Mole. The eyes of the mole are so extremely minute, and so perfectly hid in its hair, that our ancestors considered it blind—a vulgar error, to which reference is made by Caliban in " The Tempest" (iv. 1):

> " Pray you, tread softly, that the blind mole may not
> Hear a foot fall."

And again by Pericles (i. 1):

> " The blind mole casts
> Copp'd hills towards heaven."

Hence the expression " blind as a mole." Alexander Ross[1] absurdly speaks of the mole's eyes as only the " forms of eyes," given by nature " rather for ornament than for use; as wings are given to the ostrich, which never flies, and a long tail to the rat, which serves for no other purpose but to be catched sometimes by it." Sir Thomas Browne, how-

---

[1] " Arcana Microcosmi," p. 151.

ever, in his " Vulgar Errors " (bk. iii. c. xviii.),[1] has, with his
usual minuteness, disproved this idea, remarking " that they
have eyes in their head is manifested unto any that wants
them not in his own." A popular term for the mole was the
" moldwarp " or " mouldiwarp,"[2] so called from the Anglo-
Saxon, denoting turning the mould. Thus, in " 1 Henry IV."
(iii. 1) Hotspur says:

> "sometime he angers me
> With telling me of the moldwarp and the ant."

Mouse. This word was formerly used as a term of endearment, from either sex to the other. In this sense it is used
by Rosaline in " Love's Labour's Lost " (v. 2):

> " What's your dark meaning, mouse, of this light word ?"

and again in " Hamlet " (iii. 4).

Some doubt exists as to the exact meaning of " Mouse-
hunt," by Lady Capulet, in " Romeo and Juliet " (iv. 4):

> " Ay, you have been a mouse-hunt in your time,
> But I will watch you from such watching now."

According to some, the expression implies " a hunter of gay
women," mouse having been used in this signification.[3]
Others are of opinion that the stoat[4] is meant, the smallest
of the weasel tribe, and others again the polecat. Mr.
Staunton[5] tells us that the mouse-hunt is the marten, an
animal of the weasel tribe which prowls about for its prey at
night, and is applied to any one of rakish propensities.

Holinshed, in his " History of Scotland " (1577, p. 181),
quotes from the laws of Kenneth II., King of Scotland : " If
a sowe eate her pigges, let hyr be stoned to death and buried,
that no man eate of hyr fleshe." This offence is probably

---

[1] 1852, vol. i. pp. 312–315.

[2] See Nares's " Glossary," vol. ii. p. 577 ; Singer's " Shakespeare,"
vol. v. p. 77.

[3] Halliwell-Phillipps's " Handbook Index to Shakespeare," 1866,
p. 331.

[4] Forby's " Vocabulary of East Anglia," vol. ii. p. 222.

[5] See Staunton's " Shakespeare," vol. i. p. 278.

alluded to by Shakespeare in " Macbeth" (iv. 1), where the witch says :

> " Pour in sow's blood, that hath eaten
> Her nine farrow."

Polecat, or *Fitchew*. This animal is supposed to be very amorous; and hence its name, Mr. Steevens says, was often applied to ladies of easy or no virtue. In " Othello " (iv. 1) Cassio calls Bianca a " fitchew," and in " Troilus and Cressida " (v. 1) Thersites alludes to it.[1]

Porcupine. Another name for this animal was the porpentine, which spelling occurs in " Hamlet " (i. 5):

> "Like quills upon the fretful porpentine."

And again, in " 2 Henry VI." (iii. 1) York speaks of " a sharp-quill'd porpentine." Ajax, too, in " Troilus and Cressida " (ii. 1), applies the term to Thersites : " do not, porpentine." In the above passages, however, and elsewhere, the word has been altered by editors to porcupine. According to a popular error, the porcupine could dart his quills. They are easily detached, very sharp, and slightly barbed, and may easily stick to a person's legs, when he is not aware that he is near enough to touch them.[2]

Rabbit. In " 2 Henry IV." (ii. 2) this animal is used as a term of reproach, a sense in which it was known in Shakespeare's day. The phrase " cony-catch," which occurs in " Taming of the Shrew " (v. 1)—" Take heed, Signior Baptista, lest you be cony-catched in this business "—implied the act of deceiving or cheating a simple person—the cony or rabbit being considered a foolish animal.[3] It has been shown, from Dekker's " English Villanies," that the system of cheating was carried to a great length in the early part of the seventeenth century, that a collective society of sharpers was called " a warren," and their dupes " rabbit - suckers," *i. e.*, young rabbit or conies.[4] Shakespeare has once used the term to

---

[1] Cf. " King Lear," iv. 6.
[2] See Nares's " Glossary," vol. ii. p. 673.
[3] Ibid., vol. ii. p. 189.
[4] See D'Israeli's " Curiosities of Literature," vol. iii. p. 78.

express harmless roguery, in the "Taming of the Shrew" (iv. 1). When Grumio will not answer his fellow-servants, except in a jesting way, Curtis says to him: "Come, you are so full of cony-catching."

Rat. The fanciful idea that rats were commonly rhymed to death, in Ireland, is said to have arisen from some metrical charm or incantation, used there for that purpose, to which there are constant allusions in old writers. In the "Merchant of Venice" (iv. 1) Shylock says:

> "What if my house be troubled with a rat,
>   And I be pleased to give ten thousand ducats
>   To have it baned?"

And in "As You Like It" (iii. 2), Rosalind says: "I was never so be-rhymed since Pythagoras' time, that I was an Irish rat, which I can hardly remember." We find it mentioned by Ben Jonson in the "Poetaster" (v. 1):

> "Rhime them to death, as they do Irish rats,
>   In drumming tunes."

"The reference, however, is generally referred, in Ireland," says Mr. Mackay, "to the supposed potency of the verses pronounced by the professional rhymers of Ireland, which, according to popular superstition, could not only drive rats to destruction, but could absolutely turn a man's face to the back of his head."[1]

Sir W. Temple, in his "Essay on Poetry," seems to derive

---

[1] "The strange phrase and the superstition that arose out of it seem to have been produced by a mistranslation, by the English-speaking population of a considerable portion of Ireland, of two Celtic or Gaelic words, *ran*, to *roar*, to shriek, to bellow, to make a great noise on a wind instrument; and *rann*, to versify, to rhyme. It is well known that rats are scared by any great and persistent noise in the house which they infest. The Saxon English, as well as Saxon Irish, of Shakespeare's time, confounding *rann*, a rhyme, with *ran*, a *roar*, fell into the error which led to the English phrase as used by Shakespeare."—*Antiquarian Magazine and Bibliographer*, 1882, vol. ii. p. 9, "On Some Obscure Words and Celtic Phrases in Shakespeare," by Charles Mackay.

the idea from the Runic incantations, for, after speaking of them in various ways, he adds, "and the proverb of rhyming rats to death, came, I suppose, from the same root."

According to a superstitious notion of considerable antiquity, rats leaving a ship are considered indicative of misfortune to a vessel, probably from the same idea that crows will not build upon trees that are likely to fall. This idea is noticed by Shakespeare in "The Tempest" (i. 2), where Prospero, describing the vessel in which himself and daughter had been placed, with the view to their certain destruction at sea, says:

> "they hurried us aboard a bark,
> Bore us some leagues to sea; where they prepared
> A rotten carcass of a boat, not rigg'd,
> Nor tackle, sail, nor mast; the very rats
> Instinctively have quit it."

The *Shipping Gazette* of April, 1869, contained a communication entitled, "A Sailor's Notion about Rats," in which the following passage occurs: "It is a well-authenticated fact that rats have often been known to leave ships in the harbor previous to their being lost at sea. Some of those wiseacres who want to convince us against the evidence of our senses will call this superstition. As neither I have time, nor you space, to cavil with such at present, I shall leave them alone in their glory." The fact, however, as Mr. Hardwick has pointed out in his "Traditions, Superstitions, and Folk-lore" (1872, p. 251), that rats do sometimes migrate from one ship to another, or from one barn or corn-stack to another, from various causes, ought to be quite sufficient to explain such a superstition. Indeed, a story is told of a cunning Welsh captain who wanted to get rid of rats that infested his ship, then lying in the Mersey, at Liverpool. Having found out that there was a vessel laden with cheese in the basin, and getting alongside of her about dusk, he left all his hatches open, and waited till all the rats were in his neighbor's ship, and then moved off.

Snail. A common amusement among children consists in charming snails, in order to induce them to put out their

horns—a couplet, such as the following, being repeated on
the occasion:

> "Peer out, peer out, peer out of your hole,
> Or else I'll beat you as black as a coal."

In Scotland, it is regarded as a token of fine weather if the
snail obey the command and put out its horn:[1]

> "Snailie, snailie, shoot out your horn,
> And tell us if it will be a bonnie day the morn."

Shakespeare alludes to snail-charming in the "Merry
Wives of Windsor" (iv. 2), where Mrs. Page says of Mrs.
Ford's husband, he "so buffets himself on the forehead, crying, *Peer out! peer out!* that any madness I ever yet beheld
seemed but tameness, civility, and patience, to this his distemper he is in now." In "Comedy of Errors" (ii. 2), the
snail is used to denote a lazy person.

Tiger. It was an ancient belief that this animal roared
and raged most furiously in stormy and high winds—a piece
of folk-lore alluded to in "Troilus and Cressida" (i. 3), by
Nestor, who says:

> "The herd hath more annoyance by the breese
> Than by the tiger; but when the splitting wind
> Makes flexible the knees of knotted oaks,
> And flies fled under shade, why then, the thing of courage,
> As roused with rage, with rage doth sympathize."

Unicorn. In "Julius Cæsar" (ii. 1) Decius tells how "unicorns may be betray'd with trees," alluding to their traditionary mode of capture. They are reported to have been
taken by one who, running behind a tree, eluded the violent
push the animal was making at him, so that his horn spent
its force on the trunk, and stuck fast, detaining the animal
till he was despatched by the hunter.[2] In Topsell's "History
of Beasts" (1658, p. 557), we read of the unicorn: "He is an
enemy to the lions, wherefore, as soon as ever a lion seeth a

---

[1] See "English Folk-Lore," 1878, p. 120.
[2] See Brewer's "Dictionary of Phrase and Fable," p. 922.

unicorn, he runneth to a tree for succour, that so when the
unicorn maketh force at him, he may not only avoid his
horn, but also destroy him; for the unicorn, in the swiftness
of his course, runneth against the tree, wherein his sharp
horn sticketh fast, that when the lion seeth the unicorn fastened by the horn, without all danger he falleth upon him
and killeth him." With this passage we may compare the
following from Spenser's "Fairy Queen" (bk. ii. canto 5):

> "Like as a lyon, whose imperiall power
> A prowd rebellious unicorn defyes,
> T' avoide the rash assault and wrathful stowre
> Of his fiers foe, him to a tree applyes,
> And when him ronning in full course he spyes,
> He slips aside: the whiles that furious beast
> His precious horne, sought of his enimyes
> Strikes in the stocke, ne thence can be releast,
> But to the mighty victor yields a bounteous feast."

Weasel. To meet a weasel was formerly considered a bad
omen.[1] That may be a tacit allusion to this superstition in
"Lucrece" (l. 307):

> "Night-wandering weasels shriek to see him there;
> They fright him, yet he still pursues his fear."

It appears that weasels were kept in houses, instead of cats,
for the purpose of killing vermin. Phædrus notices this
their feline office in the first and fourth fables of his fourth
book. The supposed quarrelsomeness of this animal is
spoken of by Pisanio in "Cymbeline" (iii. 4), who tells
Imogen that she must be "as quarrelous as the weasel;"
and in "1 Henry IV." (ii. 3), Lady Percy says to Hotspur:

> "A weasel hath not such a deal of spleen
> As you are toss'd with."

This character of the weasel is not, however, generally
mentioned by naturalists.

---

[1] See Brand's "Pop. Antiq.," 1849, vol. iii. p, 283.

CHAPTER VIII.

PLANTS.

THAT Shakespeare possessed an extensive knowledge of the history and superstitions associated with flowers is evident, from even only a slight perusal of his plays. Apart from the extensive use which he has made of these lovely objects of nature for the purpose of embellishing, or adding pathos to, passages here and there, he has also, with a master hand, interwoven many a little legend or superstition, thereby infusing an additional force into his writings. Thus we know with what effect he has made use of the willow in "Othello," in that touching passage where Desdemona (iv. 3), anticipating her death, relates how her mother had a maid called Barbara:

> "She was in love; and he she lov'd prov'd mad,
> And did forsake her; she had a song of willow,
> An old thing 'twas, but it express'd her fortune,
> And she died singing it: that song, to-night,
> Will not go from my mind."

In a similar manner Shakespeare has frequently introduced flowers with a wonderful aptness, as in the case of poor Ophelia. Those, however, desirous of gaining a good insight into Shakespeare's knowledge of flowers, as illustrated by his plays, would do well to consult Mr. Ellacombe's exhaustive work on the "Plant-Lore of Shakespeare," a book to which we are much indebted in the following pages, as also to Mr. Biesly's "Shakespeare's Garden."

Aconite.[1] This plant, from the deadly virulence of its juice, which, Mr. Turner says, "is of all poysones the most

---

[1] *Aconitum napellus,* Wolf's-bane or Monk's-hood.

hastie poysone," is compared by Shakespeare to gunpowder, as in " 2 Henry IV." (iv. 4):

> " the united vessel of their blood,
> Mingled with venom of suggestion,
> As, force perforce, the age will pour it in,
> Shall never leak, though it do work as strong
> As aconitum, or rash gunpowder."

It is, too, probably alluded to in the following passage in " Romeo and Juliet " (v. 1), where Romeo says:

> " let me have
> A dram of poison ; such soon-speeding gear
> As will disperse itself through all the veins,
> That the life-weary taker may fall dead ;
> And that the trunk may be discharg'd of breath
> As violently, as hasty powder fir'd
> Doth hurry from the fatal cannon's womb."

According to Ovid, it derived its name from growing upon rock (Metamorphoses, bk. vii. l. 418):

> " Quæ, quia nascuntur, dura vivacia caute,
> Agrestes aconita vocant."

It is probably derived from the Greek ἀκόνιτος, " without a struggle," in allusion to the intensity of its poisonous qualities. Vergil[1] speaks of it, and tells us " how the aconite deceives the wretched gatherers, because often mistaken for some harmless plant.[2] The ancients fabled it as the invention of Hecate,[3] who caused the plant to spring from the foam of Cerberus, when Hercules dragged him from the gloomy regions of Pluto. Ovid pictures the stepdame as preparing a deadly potion of aconite (Metamorphoses, bk. i. l. 147):

> " Lurida terribiles miscent aconita novercæ."

In hunting, the ancients poisoned their arrows with this venomous plant, as " also when following their mortal brutal

---

[1] " Miseros fallunt aconita legentis " (Georgic, bk. ii. l. 152).
[2] See Ellacombe's " Plant-Lore of Shakespeare," 1878, pp. 7, 8.
[3] Dr. Prior's " Popular Names of British Plants," 1870, pp. 1, 2.

trade of slaughtering their fellow-creatures."[1] Numerous instances are on record of fatal results through persons eating this plant. In the "Philosophical Transactions" (1732, vol. xxxvii.) we read of a man who was poisoned in that year, by eating some of it in a salad, instead of celery. Dr. Turner mentions the case of some Frenchmen at Antwerp, who, eating the shoots of this plant for masterwort, all died, with the exception of two, in forty-eight hours. The aconitum is equally pernicious to animals.

Anemone. This favorite flower of early spring is probably alluded to in the following passage of "Venus and Adonis:"

> " By this, the boy that by her side lay kill'd
> Was melted like a vapour from her sight;
> And in his blood, that on the ground lay spill'd,
> A purple flower sprung up, chequer'd with white,
> Resembling well his pale cheeks, and the blood
> Which in round drops upon their whiteness stood."

According to Bion, it is said to have sprung from the tears that Venus wept over the body of Adonis:

> "Alas, the Paphian! fair Adonis slain!
> Tears plenteous as his blood she pours amain,
> But gentle flowers are born, and bloom around;
> From every drop that falls upon the ground
> Where streams his blood, there blushing springs the rose,
> And where a tear has dropp'd a wind-flower blows."

Other classical writers make the anemone to be the flower of Adonis. Mr. Ellacombe[2] says that although Shakespeare does not actually name the anemone, yet the evidence is in favor of this plant. The "purple color," he adds, is no objection, for purple in Shakespeare's time had a very wide signification, meaning almost any bright color, just as " purpureus " had in Latin.[3]

Apple. Although Shakespeare has so frequently introduced the apple into his plays, yet he has abstained from

---

[1] Phillips, " Flora Historica," 1829, vol. ii. pp. 122, 128.
[2] " Plant-Lore of Shakespeare," pp. 10, 11.
[3] Phillips, " Flora Historica," 1829, vol. i. p. 104.

alluding to the extensive folk-lore associated with this favorite fruit. Indeed, beyond mentioning some of the popular nicknames by which the apple was known in his day, little is said about it. The term apple was not originally confined to the fruit now so called, but was a generic name applied to any fruit, as we still speak of the love-apple, pine-apple, etc."[1] So when Shakespeare (Sonnet xciii.) makes mention of Eve's apple, he simply means that it was some fruit that grew in Eden:

> "How like Eve's apple doth thy beauty grow,
> If thy sweet virtue answer not thy show."

(*a*) The "apple-John," called in France *deux-années* or *deux-ans*, because it will keep two years, and considered to be in perfection when shrivelled and withered,[2] is evidently spoken of in "1 Henry IV." (iii. 3), where Falstaff says: "My skin hangs about me like an old lady's loose gown; I am withered like an old apple-John." In "2 Henry IV." (ii. 4) there is a further allusion:

1st Drawer. What the devil hast thou brought there? apple-Johns? thou know'st Sir John cannot endure an apple-John.

2d Drawer. Mass, thou sayest true. The prince once set a dish of apple-Johns before him, and told him there were five more Sir Johns, and, putting off his hat, said, 'I will now take my leave of these six dry, round, old, withered knights.'"

This apple, too, is well described by Phillips ("Cider," bk. i.):

> "Nor John Apple, whose wither'd rind, entrench'd
> By many a furrow, aptly represents
> Decrepit age."

In Ben Jonson's "Bartholomew Fair" (i. 1), where Little-wit encourages Quarlus to kiss his wife, he says: "she may call you an apple-John if you use this." Here apple-John[3]

---

[1] Ellacombe's "Plant-Lore of Shakespeare," p. 13.

[2] Dyce's "Glossary to Shakespeare," p. 15.

[3] See Nares's "Glossary," vol. ii. p. 29; probably synonymous with the term "apple-Squire," which formerly signified a pimp.

evidently means a procuring John, besides the allusion to the fruit so called.[1]

(b) The "bitter-sweet, or sweeting," to which Mercutio alludes in "Romeo and Juliet" (ii. 4): "Thy wit is a very bitter sweeting; it is a most sharp sauce;" was apparently a favorite apple, which furnished many allusions to poets. Gower, in his "Confessio Amantis" (1554, fol. 174), speaks of it:

> "For all such time of love is lore
> And like unto the *bitter swete*,
> For though it thinke a man first sweete,
> He shall well felen atte laste
> That it is sower, and maie not laste."

The name is "now given to an apple of no great value as a table fruit, but good as a cider apple, and for use in silk dyeing."[2]

(c) The "crab," roasted before the fire and put into ale, was a very favorite indulgence, especially at Christmas, in days gone by, and is referred to in the song of winter in "Love's Labour's Lost" (v. 2):

> "When roasted crabs hiss in the bowl
> Then nightly sings the staring owl."

The beverage thus formed was called "Lambs-wool," and generally consisted of ale, nutmeg, sugar, toast, and roasted crabs, or apples. It formed the ingredient of the wassail-bowl;[3] and also of the gossip's bowl[4] alluded to in "Midsummer-Night's Dream" (ii. 1), where Puck says:

> "And sometime lurk I in a gossip's bowl,
> In very likeness of a roasted crab,
> And when she drinks, against her lips I bob,
> And on her wither'd dewlap pour the ale."

---

[1] Forby, in his "Vocabulary of East Anglia," says of this apple, "we retain the name, but whether we mean the same variety of fruit which was so called in Shakespeare's time, it is not possible to ascertain."

[2] Ellacombe's "Plant-Lore of Shakespeare," p. 16; Dyce's "Glossary," p. 430; Nares's "Glossary," vol. i. p. 81; Coles's "Latin and English Dictionary." "A bitter-suete [apple]—Amari-mellum."

[3] See chapter xi., Customs connected with the Calendar.

[4] See chapter on Customs connected with Birth and Baptism.

In Peele's "Old Wives' Tale," it is said:

> "Lay a crab in the fire to roast for lamb's wool."[1]

And in Herrick's "Poems:"

> "Now crowne the bowle
> With gentle lamb's wooll,
> Add sugar, and nutmegs, and ginger."

(d) The "codling," spoken of by Malvolio in "Twelfth Night" (i. 5)—"Not yet old enough for a man, nor young enough for a boy; as a squash is before 'tis a peascod, or a codling when 'tis almost an apple"—is not the variety now so called, but was the popular term for an immature apple, such as would require cooking to be eaten, being derived from "coddle," to stew or boil lightly—hence it denoted a boiling apple, an apple for coddling or boiling.[2] Mr. Gifford[3] says that codling was used by our old writers for that early state of vegetation when the fruit, after shaking off the blossom, began to assume a globular and determinate form.

(e) The "leather-coat" was the apple generally known as "the golden russeting."[4]   Davy, in "2 Henry IV." (v. 3), says: "There is a dish of leather-coats for you."

(f) The "pippin" was formerly a common term for an apple, to which reference is made in "Hudibras Redivivus" (1705):

> "A goldsmith telling o'er his cash,
> A pipping-monger selling trash."

In Taylor's "Workes"[5] (1630) we read:

> "Lord, who would take him for a pippin squire,
> That's so bedaub'd with lace and rich attire?"

---

[1] Edited by Dyce, 1861, p. 446. Many fanciful derivations for this word have been thought of, but it was no doubt named from its smoothness and softness, resembling the wool of lambs.

[2] Dr. Prior's "Popular Names of British Plants," 1870, p. 50.

[3] Note on Jonson's Works, vol. iv. p. 24.

[4] Dyce's "Glossary," p. 242.

[5] Quoted by Nares's "Glossary," vol. ii. p. 662.

Mr. Ellacombe[1] says the word "pippin" denoted an apple raised from pips and not from grafts, and "is now, and probably was in Shakespeare's time, confined to the bright-colored long-keeping apples of which the golden pippin is the type." Justice Shallow, in "2 Henry IV." (v. 3), says: "Nay, you shall see my orchard, where, in an arbour, we will eat a last year's pippin of my own graffing."

(g) The "pomewater" was a species of apple evidently of a juicy nature, and hence of high esteem in Shakespeare's time; for in "Love's Labour's Lost" (iv. 2) Holofernes says: "The deer was, as you know, *sanguis*—in blood; ripe as the pomewater, who now hangeth like a jewel in the ear of *cœlo* —the sky, the welkin, the heaven; and anon falleth like a crab on the face of *terra*—the soil, the land, the earth."

Parkinson[2] tells us the "pomewater" is an excellent, good, and great whitish apple, full of sap or moisture, somewhat pleasant, sharp, but a little bitter withal; it will not last long, the winter's frost soon causing it to rot and perish.

It appears that apples and caraways were formerly always eaten together; and it is said that they are still served up on particular days at Trinity College, Cambridge. This practice is probably alluded to by Justice Shallow, in the much-disputed passage in "2 Henry IV." (v. 3), when he speaks of eating "a last year's pippin, . . . with a dish of carraways." The phrase, too, seems further explained by the following quotations from Cogan's "Haven of Health" (1599). After stating the virtues of the seed, and some of its uses, he says: "For the same purpose *careway seeds* are used to be made in comfits, and to be eaten with apples, and surely very good for that purpose, for all such things as breed wind would be eaten with other things that break wind." Again, in his chapter on Apples, he says: "Howbeit wee are wont to eat carrawaies or biskets, or some other kind of comfits, or seeds together with apples, thereby to breake winde ingendred by them, and surely this is a verie good way for students."

---

[1] "Plant-Lore of Shakespeare," p. 16.
[2] "Theatrum Botanicum," 1640.

Mr. Ellacombe,[1] however, considers that in "the dish of carraways," mentioned by Justice Shallow, neither caraway seeds, nor cakes made of caraways, are meant, but the caraway or caraway-russet apple. Most of the commentators are in favor of one of the former explanations. Mr. Dyce[2] reads caraways in the sense of comfits or confections made with caraway-seeds, and quotes from Shadwell's "Woman-Captain" the following: "The fruit, crab-apples, sweetings, and horse-plumbs; and for confections, a few carraways in a small sawcer, as if his worship's house had been a lousie inn."

Apricot. This word, which is spelled by Shakespeare "apricock," occurs in "Richard II." (iii. 4), where the gardener says:

> "Go, bind thou up yond dangling apricocks,
> Which, like unruly children, make their sire
> Stoop with oppression of their prodigal weight."

And in "A Midsummer-Night's Dream" (iii. 1) Titania gives directions:

> "Be kind and courteous to this gentleman,
>
> *   *   *   *   *
>
> Feed him with apricocks, and dewberries."

The spelling "apricock"[3] is derived from the Latin *præcox*, or *præcoquus;* and it was called "the precocious tree," because it flowered and fruited earlier than the peach. The term "apricock" is still in use in Northamptonshire.

Aspen. According to a mediæval legend, the perpetual motion of this tree dates from its having supplied the wood of the Cross, and that its leaves have trembled ever since at the recollection of their guilt. De Quincey, in his essay on "Modern Superstition," says that this belief is coextensive with Christendom. The following verses,[4] after telling how other trees were passed by in the choice of wood for the

---

[1] "Plant-Lore of Shakespeare," pp. 17, 37.

[2] "Glossary," pp. 65, 66.

[3] See "Notes and Queries," 2d series, bk. i. p. 420.

[4] See Henderson's "Folk-Lore of Northern Counties," 1879, pp. 151, 152.

Cross, describe the hewing down of the aspen, and the dragging of it from the forest to Calvary:

> " On the morrow stood she, trembling
>   At the awful weight she bore,
> When the sun in midnight blackness
>   Darkened on Judea's shore.
>
> " Still, when not a breeze is stirring,
>   When the mist sleeps on the hill,
> And all other trees are moveless,
>   Stands the aspen, trembling still."

The Germans, says Mr. Henderson, have a theory of their own, embodied in a little poem, which may be thus translated:

> " Once, as our Saviour walked with men below,
>   His path of mercy through a forest lay ;
> And mark how all the drooping branches show,
>   What homage best a silent tree may pay.
>
> " Only the aspen stands erect and free,
>   Scorning to join that voiceless worship pure ;
> But see ! He casts one look upon the tree,
>   Struck to the heart she trembles evermore !"

Another legend tells us [1] that the aspen was said to have been the tree on which Judas hanged himself after the betrayal of his Master, and ever since its leaves have trembled with shame. Shakespeare twice alludes to the trembling of the aspen. In "Titus Andronicus" (ii. 4) Marcus exclaims:

> " O, had the monster seen those lily hands
>   Tremble, like aspen leaves, upon a lute ;"

and in " 2 Henry IV." (ii. 4) the hostess says : " Feel, masters, how I shake. Yea, in very truth, do I, an 'twere an aspen leaf."

Bachelor's Buttons. This was a name given to several flowers, and perhaps in Shakespeare's time was more loosely applied to any flower in bud. It is now usually understood to be a *double variety* of ranunculus ; according to others,

---

[1] Napier's " Folk-Lore of West of Scotland," 1879, p. 124.

the *Lychnis sylvestris;* and in some counties it is applied to the *Scabiosa succisa.*[1] According to Gerarde, this plant was so called from the similitude of its flowers "to the jagged cloathe buttons, anciently worne in this kingdome." It was formerly supposed, by country people, to have some magical effect upon the fortunes of lovers. Hence it was customary for young people to carry its flowers in their pockets, judging of their good or bad success in proportion as these retained or lost their freshness. It is to this sort of divination that Shakespeare probably refers in "Merry Wives of Windsor" (iii. 2), where he makes the hostess say, "What say you to young Master Fenton? he capers, he dances, he has eyes of youth, he writes verses, he speaks holiday, he smells April and May; he will carry 't, he will carry 't; 'tis in his buttons; he will carry 't." Mr. Warter, in one of his notes in Southey's "Commonplace Book" (1851, 4th series, p. 244), says that this practice was common in his time, in Shropshire and Staffordshire. The term "to wear bachelor's buttons" seems to have grown into a phrase for being unmarried.[2]

Balm. From very early times the balm, or balsam, has been valued for its curative properties, and, as such, is alluded to in "Troilus and Cressida" (i. 1):

> "But, saying thus, instead of oil and balm,
> Thou lay'st in every gash that love hath given me
> The knife that made it."

In "3 Henry VI." (iv. 8) King Henry says:[3]

> "My pity hath been balm to heal their wounds."

Alcibiades, in "Timon of Athens" (iii. 5), says:

> "Is this the balsam, that the usuring senate
> Pours into captains' wounds? Banishment!"

Macbeth, too, in the well-known passage ii. 2, introduces it:

---

[1] Dr. Prior's "Popular Names of British Plants," p. 13.
[2] Nares's "Glossary," vol. i. p. 45.
[3] See "Richard III.," i. 2; "Timon of Athens," iii. 5.

"Sleep that knits up the ravell'd sleave of care,
The death of each day's life, sore labour's bath,
Balm of hurt minds, great nature's second course,
Chief nourisher in life's feast."

As the oil of consecration [1] it is spoken of by King Richard ("Richard II.," iii. 2):

"Not all the water in the rough rude sea
Can wash the balm from an anointed king."

And again, in "3 Henry VI." (iii. 1), King Henry, when in disguise, speaks thus:

"Thy place is fill'd, thy sceptre wrung from thee,
Thy balm wash'd off wherewith thou wast anointed:
No bending knee will call thee Cæsar now."

The origin of balsam, says Mr. Ellacombe,[2] "was for a long time a secret, but it is now known to have been the produce of several gum-bearing trees, especially the *Pistacia lentiscus* and the *Balsamodendron Gileadense*, and now, as then, the name is not strictly confined to the produce of any one plant."

Barley. The barley broth, of which the Constable, in "Henry V." (iii. 5), spoke so contemptuously as the food of English soldiers, was probably beer,[3] which long before the time of Henry was so celebrated that it gave its name to the plant (barley being simply the beer-plant):

"Can sodden water,
A drench for sur-rein'd jades, their barley broth,
Decoct their cold blood to such valiant heat?"

Bay-tree. The withering and death of this tree were reckoned a prognostic of evil, both in ancient and modern times, a notion[4] to which Shakespeare refers in "Richard II." (ii. 4):

"'Tis thought, the king is dead; we will not stay.
The bay-trees in our country are all wither'd"

---

[1] See "2 Henry IV.," iv. 5.
[2] "Plant-Lore of Shakespeare," p. 22.
[3] Ellacombe's "Plant-Lore of Shakespeare," p. 23.
[4] See Dyce's "Glossary," p. 32.

—having obtained it probably from Holinshed, who says: "In this yeare, in a manner throughout all the realme of Englande, old baie trees withered." Lupton, in his "Syxt Booke of Notable Things," mentions this as a bad omen: "Neyther falling-sickness, neyther devyll, wyll infest or hurt one in that place whereas a bay-tree is. The Romaynes call it the plant of the good angel." [1]

Camomile. It was formerly imagined that this plant grew the more luxuriantly for being frequently trodden or pressed down; a notion alluded to in "1 Henry IV." (ii. 4) by Falstaff: "For though the camomile, the more it is trodden on the faster it grows, yet youth, the more it is wasted, the sooner it wears." Nares [2] considers that the above was evidently written in ridicule of the following passage, in a book very fashionable in Shakespeare's day, Lyly's "Euphues," of which it is a parody: "Though the camomile, the more it is trodden and pressed down, the more it spreadeth; yet the violet, the oftener it is handled and touched, the sooner it withereth and decayeth," etc.

Clover. According to Johnson, the "honey-stalks" in the following passage ("Titus Andronicus," iv. 4) are "clover-flowers, which contain a sweet juice." It is not uncommon for cattle to overcharge themselves with clover, and die, hence the allusion by Tamora:

> "I will enchant the old Andronicus
> With words more sweet, and yet more dangerous,
> Than baits to fish, or honey-stalks to sheep."

Columbine. This was anciently termed "a thankless flower," and was also emblematical of forsaken lovers. It is somewhat doubtful to what Ophelia alludes in "Hamlet" (iv. 5), where she seems to address the king: "There's fennel for you, and columbines." Perhaps she regarded it as symbolical of ingratitude.

Crow-flowers. This name, which in Shakespeare's time

---

[1] See also Evelyn's "Sylva," 1776, p. 396.
[2] "Glossary," vol. i. p. 150; see Dyce's "Glossary," p. 63.

was applied to the " ragged robin," is now used for the but-
tercup. It was one of the flowers that poor Ophelia wove
into her garland (" Hamlet," iv. 7):

> " There with fantastic garlands did she come
> Of crow-flowers, nettles, daisies, and long purples."

Cuckoo-buds. Commentators are uncertain to what flower
Shakespeare refers in " Love's Labour's Lost " (v. 2):

> " When daisies pied and violets blue,
> And lady-smocks all silver-white,
> And cuckoo-buds of yellow hue
> Do paint the meadows with delight."

Mr. Miller, in his " Gardener's Dictionary," says that the
flower here alluded to is the *Ranunculus bulbosus;* but
Mr. Biesly, in his " Shakespeare's Garden," considers it to
be the *Ranunculus ficaria* (lesser celandine), or pile-wort, as
this flower appears earlier in spring, and is in bloom at the
same time as the other flowers named in the song. Mr.
Swinfen Jervis, however, in his " Dictionary of the Language
of Shakespeare " (1868), decides in favor of cowslips;[1] and
Dr. Prior suggests the buds of the crowfoot. At the present day the nickname cuckoo-bud is assigned to the meadow
cress (*Cardamine pratensis*).

Cuckoo-flowers. By this flower, Mr. Biesly[2] says, the ragged robin is meant, a well-known meadow and marsh plant,
with rose-colored flowers and deeply-cut, narrow segments.
It blossoms at the time the cuckoo comes, hence one of its
names. In " King Lear " (iv. 4) Cordelia narrates how

> " he was met even now
> As mad as the vex'd sea ; singing aloud ;
> Crown'd with rank fumiter, and furrow weeds,
> With burdocks, hemlock, nettles, cuckoo-flowers,
> Darnel, and all the idle weeds that grow
> In our sustaining corn."

Cypress. From the earliest times the cypress has had a

---

[1] See Nares's " Glossary," vol. i. p. 212.
[2] " Shakespeare's Garden," p. 143.

mournful history, being associated with funerals and church-yards, and as such is styled by Spenser " cypress funereal."

In Quarles's "Argalus and Parthenia" (1726, bk. iii.) a knight is introduced, whose

> " horse was black as jet,
> His furniture was round about beset
> With branches slipt from the sad cypress tree."

Formerly coffins were frequently made of cypress wood, a practice to which Shakespeare probably alludes in " Twelfth Night" (ii. 4), where the Clown says: "In sad cypress let me be laid." Some, however, prefer[1] understanding cypress to mean "a shroud of cyprus or cypress"—a fine, transparent stuff, similar to crape, either white or black, but more commonly the latter.[2] Douce[3] thinks that the expression "laid" seems more applicable to a coffin than to a shroud, and also adds that the shroud is afterwards expressly mentioned by itself.

Daffodil. The daffodil of Shakespeare is the wild daffodil which grows so abundantly in many parts of England. Perdita, in "Winter's Tale" (iv. 4), mentions a little piece of weather-lore, and tells us how

> "daffodils,
> That come before the swallow dares, and take
> The winds of March with beauty."

And Autolycus, in the same play (iv. 3), sings thus:

> "When daffodils begin to peer,—
> With, heigh! the doxy over the dale,
> Why, then comes in the sweet o' the year."

---

[1] See "Winter's Tale," iv. 4:

> "Lawn as white as driven snow;
> Cyprus black as e'er was crow."

Its transparency is alluded to in "Twelfth Night," iii. 1:

> "a cyprus, not a bosom,
> Hides my heart."

[2] See Dyce's "Glossary," 1872, p. 113.

[3] Douce's "Illustrations of Shakespeare," 1839, p. 56. See Mr. Gough's "Introduction to Sepulchral Monuments," p. lxvi.; also Nares's "Glossary," vol. i. p. 221.

Darnel. This plant, like the cockle, was used in Shakespeare's day to denote any hurtful weed. Newton,[1] in his "Herbal to the Bible," says that "under the name of cockle and darnel is comprehended all vicious, noisome, and unprofitable graine, encombring and hindering good corne." Thus Cordelia, in "King Lear" (iv. 4), says:

> "Darnel, and all the idle weeds that grow
> In our sustaining corn."

According to Gerarde, "darnel hurteth the eyes, and maketh them dim, if it happen either in corne for breade or drinke." Hence, it is said, originated the old proverb, "lolio victitare"—applied to such as were dim-sighted. Steevens considers that Pucelle, in the following passage from "1 Henry VI." (iii. 2), alludes to this property of the darnel—meaning to intimate that the corn she carried with her had produced the same effect on the guards of Rouen, otherwise they would have seen through her disguise and defeated her stratagem:

> "Good morrow, gallants! want ye corn for bread?
> I think the Duke of Burgundy will fast,
> Before he'll buy again at such a rate:
> 'Twas full of darnel: do you like the taste?"

Date. This fruit of the palm-tree was once a common ingredient in all kinds of pastry, and some other dishes, and often supplied a pun for comedy, as, for example, in "All's Well That Ends Well" (i. 1), where Parolles says: "Your date is better in your pie and your porridge, than in your cheek. And in "Troilus and Cressida" (i. 2): "Ay, a minced man; and then to be baked with no date in the pie; for then the man's date's out."

Ebony. The wood of this tree was regarded as the typical emblem of darkness; the tree itself, however, was unknown in this country in Shakespeare's time. It is mentioned in "Love's Labour's Lost" (iv. 3):

---

[1] See Dr. Prior's "Popular Names of British Plants," 1870, p. 63.

> "*King.* By heaven, thy love is black as ebony.
> *Biron.* Is ebony like her? O wood divine!
> A wife of such wood were felicity."

In the same play we read of " the ebon-coloured ink " (i. 1), and in " Venus and Adonis " (948) of " Death's ebon dart."

Elder. This plant, while surrounded by an extensive folk-lore, has from time immemorial possessed an evil reputation, and been regarded as one of bad omen. According to a popular tradition " Judas was hanged on an elder," a superstition mentioned by Biron in " Love's Labour's Lost " (v. 2); and also by Ben Jonson in " Every Man Out of His Humour " (iv. 4): " He shall be your Judas, and you shall be his elder-tree to hang on." In " Piers Plowman's Vision " (ll. 593–596) we are told how

> " Judas, he japed
> With jewen silver,
> And sithen on an eller
> Hanged hymselve."

So firmly rooted was this belief in days gone by that Sir John Mandeville tells us in his Travels, which he wrote in 1364, that he was actually shown the identical tree at Jerusalem, " And faste by is zit, the tree of Elder that Judas henge himself upon, for despeyr that he hadde when he solde and betrayed oure Lord." This tradition no doubt, in a great measure, helped to give it its bad fame, causing it to be spoken of as " the stinking elder." Shakespeare makes it an emblem of grief. In " Cymbeline " (iv. 2) Arviragus says:

> " Grow, patience!
> And let the stinking elder, grief, untwine
> His perishing root with the increasing vine!"

The dwarf elder[1] (*Sambucus ebulus*) is said only to grow where blood has been shed either in battle or in murder. The Welsh call it " Llysan gward gwyr," or "plant of the blood of man." Shakespeare, perhaps, had this piece of folk-lore in mind when he represents Bassianus, in " Titus

---

[1] " Flower-Lore," p. 35.

Andronicus" (ii. 4), as killed at a pit beneath an elder-tree:

> "This is the pit and this the elder tree."

Eringoes. These were formerly said to be strong provocatives, and as such are mentioned by Falstaff in "Merry Wives of Windsor" (v. 5): "Let the sky rain potatoes; let it thunder to the tune of Green Sleeves, hail kissing comfits, and snow eringoes." Mr. Ellacombe[1] thinks that in this passage the globe artichoke is meant, "which is a near ally of the eryngium, and was a favorite dish in Shakespeare's time."

Fennel. This was generally considered as an inflammatory herb; and to eat "conger and fennel" was "to eat two high and hot things together," which was an act of libertinism.[2] Thus in "2 Henry IV." (ii. 4) Falstaff says of Poins, he "eats conger and fennel." Mr. Beisly states[3] that fennel was used as a sauce with fish hard of digestion, being aromatic, and as the old writers term it, "hot in the third degree." One of the herbs distributed by poor Ophelia, in her distraction, is fennel, which she offers either as a cordial or as an emblem of flattery: "There's fennel for you, and columbines." Mr. Staunton, however, considers that fennel here signifies *lust*, while Mr. Beisly thinks its reputed property of clearing the sight is alluded to. It is more probable that it denotes flattery; especially as, in Shakespeare's time, it was regarded as emblematical of flattery. In this sense it is often quoted by old writers. In Greene's "Quip for an Upstart Courtier," we read, "Fennell I meane for flatterers." In "Phyala Lachrymarum"[4] we find:

> "Nor fennel-finkle bring for flattery,
> Begot of his, and fained courtesie."

Fern. According to a curious notion fern-seed was supposed to possess the power of rendering persons invisible.

---

[1] "Plant-Lore of Shakespeare," p. 66.
[2] Nares's "Glossary," vol. i. p. 302; Dyce's "Glossary," p. 159.
[3] "Shakspere's Garden," p. 158.
[4] Quoted in Nares's "Glossary," vol. i. p. 303.

Hence it was a most important object of superstition, being gathered mystically, especially on Midsummer Eve. It was believed at one time to have neither flower nor seed; the seed, which lay on the back of the leaf, being so small as to escape the detection of the hasty observer. On this account, probably, proceeding on the fantastic doctrine of signatures, our ancestors derived the notion that those who could obtain and wear this invisible seed would be themselves invisible; a belief which is referred to in " 1 Henry IV." (ii. 1):

> "*Gadshill.* We have the receipt of fern-seed, we walk invisible.
>
> *Chamberlain.* Nay, by my faith, I think you are more beholding to the night, than to fern-seed, for your walking invisible."

This superstition is mentioned by many old writers; a proof of its popularity in times past. It is alluded to in Beaumont and Fletcher's " Fair Maid of the Inn " (i. 1):

> "Did you think that you had Gyges' ring?
> Or the herb that gives invisibility?"

Again, in Ben Jonson's " New Inn " (i. 1):

> "I had
> No medicine, sir, to go invisible,
> No fern-seed in my pocket."

As recently as Addison's day, we are told in the *Tatler* (No. 240) that " it was impossible to walk the streets without having an advertisement thrust into your hand of a doctor who had arrived at the knowledge of the green and red dragon, and had discovered the female fern-seed." [1]

Fig. Formerly the term fig served as a common expression of contempt, and was used to denote a thing of the least importance. Hence the popular phrase, " not to care a fig for one;" a sense in which it is sometimes used by Shakespeare, who makes Pistol say, in " Merry Wives of Windsor " (i. 3), " a fico for the phrase!" and in " Henry V." (iii. 6) Pistol exclaims, " figo for thy friendship!" In " Othello " (i. 3) Iago says, " Virtue! a fig!"

The term " to give or make the fig," as an expression of

---

[1] See Brand's " Pop. Antiq.," 1849, vol. i. pp. 314–316.

insult, has for many ages been very prevalent among the nations of Europe, and, according to Douce,[1] was known to the Romans. It consists in thrusting the thumb between two of the closed fingers, or into the mouth, a practice, as some say,[2] in allusion to a contemptuous punishment inflicted on the Milanese, by the Emperor Frederic Barbarossa, in 1162, when he took their city. This, however, is altogether improbable, the real origin, no doubt, being a coarse representation of a disease, to which the name of *ficus* or fig has always been given.[3]

The "fig of Spain," spoken of in "Henry V." (iii. 6), may either allude to the poisoned fig employed in Spain as a secret way of destroying an obnoxious person, as in Webster's "White Devil:"[4]

> "I do look now for a Spanish fig, or an Italian salad, daily;"

and in Shirley's "Brothers:"[5]

> "I must poison him;
> One fig sends him to Erebus;"

or it may, as Mr. Dyce remarks,[6] simply denote contempt or insult in the sense already mentioned.

Flower-de-luce. The common purple iris which adorns our gardens is now generally agreed upon as the fleur-de-luce, a corruption of fleur de Louis—being spelled either fleur-de-lys or fleur-de-lis. It derives its name from Louis VII., King of France, who chose this flower as his heraldic emblem when setting forth on his crusade to the Holy Land. It had already been used by the other French kings, and by the emperors of Constantinople; but it is still a matter of

---

[1] "Illustrations of Shakespeare," pp. 302–308.

[2] See Nares's "Glossary," vol. i. p. 305.

[3] See Gifford's note on Jonson's Works, vol. i. p. 52; Dyce's "Glossary," p. 161; Du Cange's "Glossary;" Connelly's "Spanish and English Dictionary," 4to.

[4] Edited by Dyce, 1857, p. 30.

[5] Edited by Gifford and Dyce, vol. i. p. 231.

[6] "Glossary," p. 161.

dispute among antiquarians as to what it was originally intended to represent.   Some say a flower, some a toad, some
a halbert-head.   It is uncertain what plant is referred to by
Shakespeare when he alludes to the flower-de-luce in the
following passage[1] in " 2 Henry VI." (v. 1), where the Duke
of York says:

> " A sceptre shall it have,—have I a soul,—
>   On which I'll toss the flower-de-luce of France."

In " 1 Henry VI." (i. 2) Pucelle declares:

> " I am prepared ; here is my keen-edged sword,
>   Deck'd with five flower-de-luces on each side."

Some think the lily is meant, others the iris.   For the lily
theory, says Mr. Ellacombe,[2] " there are the facts that Shakespeare calls it one of the lilies, and that the other way of
spelling is fleur-de-lys."

Chaucer seems to connect it with the lily (" Canterbury
Tales," Prol. 238):

> " Her nekke was white as the flour-de-lis."

On the other hand, Spenser separates the lilies from the
flower-de-luces in his " Shepherd's Calendar ;" and Ben Jonson mentions " rich carnations, flower-de-luces, lilies."

The fleur-de-lis was not always confined to royalty as a
badge.   Thus, in the square of La Pucelle, in Rouen, there
is a statue of Jeanne D'Arc with fleurs-de-lis sculptured upon
it, and an inscription as follows:

> " The maiden's sword protects the royal crown ;
>   Beneath the maiden's sword the lilies safely blow."

St. Louis conferred upon the Chateaubriands the device
of a fleur-de-lis, and the motto, " Mon sang teint les bannièrs
de France."   When Edward III. claimed the crown of France,
in the year 1340, he quartered the ancient shield of France
with the lions of England.   It disappeared, however, from
the English shield in the first year of the present century.

---

[1] See " Winter's Tale," iv. 3 ; " Henry V.," v. 2 ; " 1 Henry VI.," i. 1.
[2] " Plant-Lore of Shakespeare," p. 73.

Gillyflower. This was the old name for the whole class of carnations, pinks, and sweet-williams, from the French *girofle*, which is itself corrupted from the Latin *caryophyllum*.[1] The streaked gillyflowers, says Mr. Beisly,[2] noticed by Perdita in " Winter's Tale " (iv. 4)—

> "the fairest flowers o' the season
> Are our carnations and streak'd gillyvors,
> Which some call nature's bastards "—

" are produced by the flowers of one kind being impregnated by the pollen of another kind, and this art (or law) in nature Shakespeare alludes to in the delicate language used by Perdita, as well as to the practice of increasing the plants by slips." Tusser, in his " Five Hundred Points of Good Husbandry," says :

> "The gilloflower also the skilful doe know,
> Doth look to be covered in frost and in snow."

Harebell. This flower, mentioned in "Cymbeline" (iv. 2), is no doubt another name for the wild hyacinth.

Arviragus says of Imogen :

> "thou shalt not lack
> The flower that's like thy face, pale primrose; nor
> The azured harebell, like thy veins."

Hemlock. In consequence of its bad and poisonous character, this plant was considered an appropriate ingredient for witches' broth. In " Macbeth " (iv. 1) we read of

> " Root of hemlock, digged i' the dark."

Its scientific name, *conium*, is from the Greek word meaning cone or top, whose whirling motion resembles the giddiness produced on the constitution by its poisonous juice. It is by most persons supposed to be the death-drink of the Greeks, and the one by which Socrates was put to death.

Herb of Grace or *Herb Grace*. A popular name in days gone by for rue. The origin of the term is uncertain. Most

---

[1] " Nares's Glossary," vol. i. p. 363.
[2] " Shakespeare's Garden," p. 82; see Dyce's " Glossary," p. 184.

probably it arose from the extreme bitterness of the plant, which, as it had always borne the name *rue* (to be sorry for anything), was not unnaturally associated with repentance. It was, therefore, the herb of repentance,[1] " and this was soon changed into ' herb of grace,' repentance being the chief sign of grace." The expression is several times used by Shakespeare. In " Richard II." (iii. 4) the gardener narrates:

> " Here did she fall a tear ; here, in this place
> I'll set a bank of rue, sour herb of grace :
> Rue, even for ruth, here shortly shall be seen,
> In the remembrance of a weeping queen."

In " Hamlet " (iv. 5), Ophelia, when addressing the queen, says, " There's rue for you ; and here's some for me : we may call it herb-grace o' Sundays : O, you must wear your rue with a difference." [2]

Malone observes that there is no ground for supposing that rue was called " herb of grace " from its being used in exorcisms in churches on Sunday, a notion entertained by Jeremy Taylor, who says, referring to the *Flagellum Dæmonum*, " First, they (the Romish exorcisers) are to try the devil by holy water, incense, sulphur, rue, which from thence, as we suppose, came to be called ' herb of grace.' " [3] Rue was also a common subject of puns, from being the same word which signified sorrow or pity (see " Richard II.," iii. 4, cited above).

Holy Thistle. The Carduus Benedictus, called also " blessed thistle," was so named, like other plants which bear the specific name of " blessed," from its supposed power of counteracting the effect of poison.[4] Cogan, in his " Haven of

---

[1] Ellacombe's " Plant-Lore of Shakespeare," p. 204; Prior's " Popular Names of British Plants," 1870, p. 111.

[2] Cf. " All's Well that Ends Well," iv. 5 ; " Antony and Cleopatra," iv. 2 ; " Romeo and Juliet," ii. 3, where Friar Laurence says :

> " In man as well as herbs, grace and rude will."

[3] " A Dissuasive from Popery," pt. i. chap. ii. sec. 9 ; see Dyce's " Glossary," p. 371.

[4] Nares's " Glossary," vol. i. p. 464.

Health," 1595, says, " This herbe may worthily be called *Benedictus*, or *Omnimorbia*, that is, a salve for every sore, not known to physitians of old time, but lately revealed by the special providence of Almighty God." It is alluded to in " Much Ado About Nothing " (iii. 4):

Margaret. Get you some of this distilled Carduus Benedictus, and lay it to your heart; it is the only thing for a qualm.

Hero. There thou prickest her with a thistle.

Beatrice. Benedictus! why Benedictus? you have some moral in this Benedictus.

Margaret. Moral? no, by my troth, I have no moral meaning: I meant, plain holy-thistle."

Insane Root. There is much doubt as to what plant is meant by Banquo in " Macbeth " (i. 3):

" have we eaten on the insane root
That takes the reason prisoner?"

The origin of this passage is probably to be found in North's " Plutarch," 1579 (" Life of Antony," p. 990), where mention is made of a plant which " made them out of their wits." Several plants have been suggested—the hemlock, belladonna, mandrake, henbane, etc. Douce supports the last, and cites the following passage:[1] " Henbane . . . is called insana, mad, for the use thereof is perillous; for if it be eate or dronke, it breedeth madness, or slow lykenesse of sleepe." Nares[2] quotes from Ben Jonson (" Sejanus," iii. 2), in support of hemlock:

" well, read my charms,
And may they lay that hold upon thy senses
As thou hadst snufft up hemlock."

Ivy. It was formerly the general custom in England, as it is still in France and the Netherlands, to hang a bush of ivy at the door of a vintner.[3] Hence the allusion in " As

---

[1] Batman's " Upon Bartholomæus de Proprietate Rerum," lib. xvii. chap. 87.

[2] " Glossary," vol. i. p. 465.

[3] See Hotten's " History of Sign Boards."

You Like It" (v. 4, Epilogue), where Rosalind wittily remarks: "If it be true that good wine needs no bush, 'tis true
that a good play needs no epilogue." This custom is often
referred to by our old writers, as, for instance, in Nash's
"Summer's Last Will and Testament," 1600:

> "Green ivy bushes at the vintner's doors."

And in the "Rival Friends," 1632:

> "'Tis like the ivy bush unto a tavern."

This plant was no doubt chosen from its being sacred to
Bacchus. The practice was observed at statute hirings,
wakes, etc., by people who sold ale at no other time. The
manner, says Mr. Singer,[1] in which they were decorated appears from a passage in Florio's "Italian Dictionary," in
voce tremola, "Gold foile, or thin leaves of gold or silver,
namely, thinne plate, as our vintners adorn their bushes
with." We may compare the old sign of "An owl in an ivy
bush," which perhaps denoted the union of wisdom or prudence with conviviality, with the phrase "be merry and
wise."

Kecksies. These are the dry, hollow stalks of hemlock.
In "Henry V." (v. 2) Burgundy makes use of the word:

> "and nothing teems,
> But hateful docks, rough thistles, kecksies, burs,
> Losing both beauty and utility."

It has been suggested[2] that kecksies may be a mistaken
form of the plural kex; and that kex may have been formed
from keck, something so dry that the eater would keck at it,
or be unable to swallow it. The word is probably derived
from the Welsh "cecys," which is applied to several plants of
the umbelliferous kind. Dr. Prior,[3] however, says that kecksies is from an old English word keek, or kike, retained in
the northern counties in the sense of "peep" or "spy."

---

[1] "Shakespeare," vol. iii. p. 112.
[2] See Nares's "Glossary," vol. ii. p. 482.
[3] "Popular Names of British Plants," 1879, p. 128.

Knotgrass.[1] The allusion to this plant in "A Midsummer-Night's Dream" (iii. 2)—

> "Get you gone, you dwarf!
> You minimus, of hindering knot-grass made;
> You bead, you acorn!"—

refers to its supposed power of hindering the growth of any child or animal, when taken in an infusion, a notion alluded to by Beaumont and Fletcher ("Coxcombe," ii. 2):

> "We want a boy extremely for this function,
> Kept under for a year with milk and knot-grass."

In "The Knight of the Burning Pestle" (ii. 2) we read: "The child's a fatherless child, and say they should put him into a strait pair of gaskins, 'twere worse than knot-grass; he would never grow after it."

Lady-smocks. This plant is so called from the resemblance of its white flowers to little smocks hung out to dry ("Love's Labour's Lost," v. 2), as they used to be at that season of the year especially

> "When daisies pied, and violets blue,
>   And lady-smocks all silver white,
> And cuckoo-buds of yellow hue,
>   Do paint the meadows with delight,
> *   *   *   *   *
> When shepherds pipe on oaten straws,
> *   *   *   *   *
> And maidens bleach their summer smocks."

According to another explanation, the lady-smock is a corruption of "Our Lady's Smock," so called from its first flowering about Lady-tide. This plant has also been called cuckoo-flower, because, as Gerarde says, "it flowers in April and May, when the cuckoo doth begin to sing her pleasant notes without stammering."

Laurel. From the very earliest times this classical plant has been regarded as symbolical of victory, and used for crowns. In "Titus Andronicus" (i. 1) Titus says:

> "Cometh Andronicus, bound with laurel boughs."

---

[1] *Polygonum aviculare.*

And in " Antony and Cleopatra" (i. 3) the latter exclaims :

> " upon your sword
> Sit laurelled victory." [1]

Leek. The first of March is observed by the Welsh in honor of St. David, their patron saint, when, as a sign of their patriotism, they wear a leek. Much doubt exists as to the origin of this custom. According to the Welsh, it is because St. David ordered his Britons to place leeks in their caps, that they might be distinguished in fight from their Saxon foes. Shakespeare, in " Henry V." (iv. 7), alludes to the custom when referring to the battle of Cressy. Fluellen says, " If your majesties is remembered of it, the Welshmen did good service in a garden where leeks did grow, wearing leeks in their Monmouth caps, which your majesty know to this hour is an honourable badge of the service ; and I do believe your majesty takes no scorn to wear the leek upon Saint Tavy's day." [2] Dr. Owen Pughe [3] supposes the custom arose from the practice of every farmer contributing his leek to the common repast when they met at the Cymmortha, an association by which they reciprocated assistance in ploughing the land. Anyhow, the subject is one involved in complete uncertainty, and the various explanations given are purely conjectural (see p. 303).

Lily. Although so many pretty legends and romantic superstitions have clustered round this sweet and favorite flower, yet they have escaped the notice of Shakespeare, who, while attaching to it the choicest epithets, has simply made it the type of elegance and beauty, and the symbol of purity and whiteness.

Long Purples. This plant, mentioned by Shakespeare in " Hamlet " (iv. 7) as forming part of the nosegay of poor Ophelia, is generally considered to be the early purple orchis (*Orchis mascula*), which blossoms in April or May. It grows

---

[1] See " 3 Henry VI.," iv. 6; "Troilus and Cressida," i. 3.

[2] See " Henry V.," iv. 1.

[3] " Cambrian Biography," 1803, p. 86; see Brand's " Pop. Antiq.," 1849, vol. i. pp. 102–108.

in meadows and pastures, and is about ten inches high.
Tennyson ("A Dirge") uses the name:

> " Round thee blow, self-pleached deep,
> Bramble roses, faint and pale,
> And long purples of the dale."

Another term applied by Shakespeare to this flower was
"Dead Men's Fingers," from the pale color and hand-like
shape of the palmate tubers:

> "Our cold maids do dead men's fingers call them."

In "Flowers from Stratford-on-Avon," it is said, "there
can be no doubt that the wild arum is the plant alluded to
by Shakespeare," but there seems no authority for this statement.

Love-in-Idleness, or, with more accuracy, *Love-in-Idle*,[1] is
one of the many nicknames of the pansy or heart's-ease—a
term said to be still in use in Warwickshire. It occurs in
"Midsummer-Night's Dream" (ii. 1),[2] where Oberon says:

> "Yet mark'd I where the bolt of Cupid fell:
> It fell upon a little western flower,
> Before milk-white, now purple with love's wound,
> And maidens call it love-in-idleness."

The phrase literally signifies love in vain, or to no purpose,
as Taylor alludes to it in the following couplet:

> "When passions are let loose without a bridle,
> Then precious time is turned to *love and idle*."

That flowers, and pansies especially, were used as love-
philters,[3] or for the object of casting a spell over people, in
Shakespeare's day, is shown in the passage already quoted,

---

[1] See Dr. Prior's "Popular Names of British Plants," 1870, p. 139.
[2] Cf. "Taming of the Shrew," i. 1.
[3] Cf. what Egeus says (i. 1) when speaking of Lysander:

> "This man hath bewitch'd the bosom of my child;
> Thou, thou Lysander, thou hast given her rhymes
> And interchanged love-tokens with my child."

where Puck and Oberon amuse themselves at Titania's expense. Again, a further reference occurs (iv. 1), where the fairy king removes the spell:

> " But first I will release the fairy queen.
>   Be as thou wast wont to be:
>   See as thou wast wont to see:
>   Dian's bud [1] o'er Cupid's flower [2]
>   Hath such force and blessed power.
> Now, my Titania; wake you, my sweet queen."

" It has been suggested," says Mr. Aldis Wright,[3] " that the device employed by Oberon to enchant Titania by anointing her eyelids with the juice of a flower, may have been borrowed by Shakespeare from the Spanish romance of ' Diana' by George of Montemayor. But apart from the difficulty which arises from the fact that no English translation of this romance is known before that published by Young in 1598, there is no necessity to suppose that Shakespeare was indebted to any one for what must have been a familiar element in all incantations at a time when a belief in witch-craft was common." Percy (" Reliques," vol. iii. bk. 2) quotes a receipt by the celebrated astrologer, Dr. Dee, for " an ungent to anoynt under the eyelids, and upon the eyelids eveninge and morninge, but especially when you call," that is, upon the fairies. It consisted of a decoction of various flowers.

Mandragora or *Mandrake*. No plant, perhaps, has had, at different times, a greater share of folk-lore attributed to it than the mandrake; partly owing, probably, to the fancied resemblance of its root to the human figure, and the accidental circumstance of *man* being the first syllable of the word. An inferior degree of animal life was assigned to it; and it was commonly supposed that, when torn from the ground, it uttered groans of so pernicious a character, that

---

[1] Dian's bud is the bud of the *Agnus castus*, or chaste tree. " The virtue this herbe is, that he will kepe man and woman chaste." " Macer's Herbal," 1527.

[2] Cupid's flower, another name for the pansy.

[3] Notes to " A Midsummer-Night's Dream," 1877.   Preface, p. xx.

the person who committed the violence either went mad or died. In " 2 Henry VI." (iii. 2) Suffolk says:

> " Would curses kill, as doth the mandrake's groan,
> I would invent," etc.

And Juliet (" Romeo and Juliet," iv. 3) speaks of

> " shrieks like mandrakes' torn out of the earth,
> That living mortals, hearing them, run mad."

To escape this danger, it was recommended to tie one end of a string to the plant and the other to a dog, upon whom the fatal groan would discharge its whole malignity. The ancients, it appears, were equally superstitious with regard to this mysterious plant, and Columella, in his directions for the site of gardens, says they may be formed where

> " the mandrake's flowers
> Produce, whose root shows half a man, whose juice
> With madness strikes."

Pliny [1] informs us that those who dug up this plant paid particular attention to stand so that the wind was at their back ; and, before they began to dig, they made three circles round the plant with the point of the sword, and then, proceeding to the west, commenced digging it up. It seems to have been well known as an opiate in the time of Shakespeare, who makes Iago say in " Othello " (iii. 3):

> " Not poppy, nor mandragora,
> Nor all the drowsy syrups of the world,
> Shall ever medicine thee to that sweet sleep
> Which thou ow'dst yesterday."

In " Antony and Cleopatra " (i. 5), the queen pathetically says :

> " Give me to drink mandragora.
> *Char.*   Why, madam ?
> *Cleo.*   That I might sleep out this great gap of time,
> My Antony is away."

Lyte, in his translation of " Dodoens " (1578), p. 438, tells

---

[1] " Natural History," bk. xxv. chap. 94.

us that "the leaves and fruit be also dangerous, for they cause deadly sleepe, and peevish drowsiness, like opium." It was sometimes regarded as an emblem of incontinence, as in "2 Henry IV." (iii. 2): "yet lecherous as a monkey, and the whores called him—mandrake." A very diminutive figure was, too, often compared to a mandrake. In "2 Henry IV." (i. 2), Falstaff says: "Thou whoreson mandrake, thou art fitter to be worn in my cap, than to wait at my heels." Tracing back the history of this plant into far-distant times, it is generally believed that it is the same as that which the ancient Hebrews called Dudain.[1] That these people held it in the highest esteem in the days of Jacob is evident from its having been found by Reuben, who carried the plant to his mother; and the inducement which tempted Leah to part with it proves the value then set upon this celebrated plant. According to a curious superstition, this plant was thought to possess the properties of making childless wives become mothers, and hence, some suppose, Rachel became so desirous of possessing the mandrakes which Reuben had found. Among the many other items of folk-lore associated with the mandrake, there is one which informs us that "it is perpetually watched over by Satan, and if it be pulled up at certain holy times, and with certain invocations, the evil spirit will appear to do the bidding of the practitioner."[2] In comparatively recent times, quacks and impostors counterfeited with the root briony figures resembling parts of the human body, which were sold to the credulous as endued with specific virtues.[3] The Germans, too, equally superstitious, formed little idols of the roots of the mandrake, which were regularly dressed every day, and consulted as oracles—their repute being such that they were manufactured in great numbers, and sold in cases. They were, also, imported into this country during the time of Henry VIII., it

[1] Phillips's "Flora Historica," 1829, vol. i. pp. 324, 325; see Smith's "Dictionary of the Bible," 1869, vol. ii. p. 1777.

[2] "Mystic Trees and Flowers," by M. D. Conway; *Fraser's Magazine*, 1870, vol. ii. p. 705.

[3] Singer's "Shakespeare," 1875, vol. v. p. 153.

being pretended that they would, with the assistance of some mystic words, increase whatever money was placed near them. In order, too, to enhance the value of these so-called miracle-workers, it was said that the roots of this plant were produced from the flesh of criminals which fell from the gibbet, and that it only grew in such a situation.[1]

Marigold. This flower was a great favorite with our old writers, from a curious notion that it always opened or shut its flowers at the sun's bidding; in allusion to which Perdita remarks, in "Winter's Tale" (iv. 3):

> "The marigold, that goes to bed wi' the sun,
> And with him rises weeping."

It was also said, but erroneously, to turn its flowers to the sun, a quality attributed to the sunflower (*Helianthus annuus*), and thus described by Moore:

> "The sunflower turns on her god when he sets
> The same look which she turn'd when he rose."

A popular name for the marigold was "mary-bud," mention of which we find in "Cymbeline" (ii. 3):

> "winking Mary-buds begin
> To ope their golden eyes."

Medlar. This fruit, which Shakespeare describes as only fit to be eaten when rotten, is applied by Lucio to a woman of loose character, as in "Measure for Measure" (iv. 3): "they would else have married me to the rotten medlar."

Chaucer, in the "Reeve's Prologue," applies the same name to it:

> "That ilke fruit is ever lenger the wers,
> Till it be roten in mullok, or in stre.
> We olde men, I drede, so faren we,
> Till we be roten can we not be ripe."

Mistletoe. This plant, which, from the earliest times, has been an object of interest to naturalists, on account of its curious growth, deriving its subsistence entirely from the

---

[1] See Sir Thomas Browne's "Vulgar Errors," 1852, vol. ii. p. 6.

branch to which it annexes itself, has been the subject of widespread superstition.   In " Titus Andronicus " (ii. 3), Tamora describes it in the graphic passage below as the " baleful mistletoe," an epithet which, as Mr. Douce observes, is extremely appropriate, either conformably to an ancient, but erroneous, opinion, that the berries of the mistletoe were poisonous, or on account of the use made of this plant by the Druids during their detestable human sacrifices.[1]

> "*Demetrius.* How now, dear sovereign, and our gracious mother,
> Why doth your highness look so pale and wan ?
>   *Tamora.* Have I not reason, think you, to look pale ?
> These two have 'tic'd me hither to this place :—
> A barren detested vale, you see, it is ;
> The trees, though summer, yet forlorn and lean,
> O'ercome with moss and baleful mistletoe :
> Here never shines the sun ; here nothing breeds,
> Unless the nightly owl, or fatal raven."

Mushroom.   Besides his notice of the mushroom in the following passages, Shakespeare alludes to the fairy rings[2] which are formed by fungi, though, as Mr. Ellacombe[3] points out, he probably knew little of this.   In " The Tempest " (v. 1), Prospero says of the fairies :

> " you demi-puppets, that
> By moonshine do the green-sour ringlets make,
> Whereof the ewe not bites ; and you, whose pastime
> Is to make midnight mushrooms ;"

the allusion in this passage being to the superstition that sheep will not eat the grass that grows on fairy rings.

Mustard.   Tewksbury mustard, to which reference is made in " 2 Henry IV." (ii. 4), where Falstaff speaks of " wit as thick as Tewksbury mustard," was formerly very famous. Shakespeare speaks only of its thickness, but others have celebrated its pungency.   Coles, writing in 1657, says : " In Gloucestershire, about Teuxbury, they grind mustard and

---

[1] " Illustrations of Shakespeare," p. 386.

[2] See page 15.

[3] " Plant-Lore of Shakespeare," p. 131.

make it into balls, which are brought to London, and other remote places, as being the best that the world affords."

Narcissus. The old legend attached to this flower is mentioned by Emilia in " The Two Noble Kinsmen" (ii. 1):

> " That was a fair boy certain, but a fool,
>   To love himself; were there not maids enough ?"

Nutmeg. A gilt nutmeg was formerly a common gift at Christmas and on other festive occasions, a notice of which occurs in "Love's Labour's Lost" (v. 2), in the following dialogue :[1]

> " *Armado.* ' The armipotent Mars, of lances the almighty,
> Gave Hector a gift,—'
> *Dumain.* A gilt nutmeg."

Oak. A crown of oak was considered by the Romans worthy of the highest emulation of statesmen and warriors. To him who had saved the life of a Roman soldier was given a crown of oak-leaves; one, indeed, which was accounted more honorable than any other. In "Coriolanus" (ii. 1), Volumnia says: "he comes the third time home with the oaken garland." And again (i. 3): "To a cruel war I sent him ; from whence he returned, his brows bound with oak." Montesquieu, indeed, said that it was with two or three hundred crowns of oak that Rome conquered the world. Although so much historical and legendary lore have clustered round the oak, yet scarcely any mention is made of this by Shakespeare. The legend of Herne the Hunter, which seems to have been current at Windsor, is several times alluded to, as, for instance, in " Merry Wives of Windsor " (iv. 4):

> " *Mrs. Page.* There is an old tale goes, that Herne the hunter,
> Sometime a keeper here in Windsor forest,
> Doth all the winter time, at still midnight,
> Walk round about an oak, with great ragg'd horns.
> *   *   *   *   *   *   *
> *Page.* . . . there want not many, that do fear
> In deep of night to walk by this Herne's oak."

Herne's Oak, so long an object of much curiosity and en-

---

[1] Nares's "Glossary," vol. ii. p. 612.

thusiasm, is now no more. According to one theory, the old tree was blown down August 31, 1863; and a young oak was planted by her Majesty, September 12, 1863, to mark the spot where Herne's Oak stood.[1] Mr. Halliwell-Phillipps, however, tells us, "the general opinion is that it was accidentally destroyed in the year 1796, through an order of George III. to the bailiff Robinson, that all the unsightly trees in the vicinity of the castle should be removed; an opinion confirmed by a well-established fact, that a person named Grantham, who contracted with the bailiff for the removal of the trees, fell into disgrace with the king for having included the oak in his gatherings."[2]

Olive. This plant, ever famous from its association with the return of the dove to the ark, has been considered typical of peace. It was as an emblem of peace that a garland of olive was given to Judith when she restored peace to the Israelites by the death of Holofernes (Judith, xv. 13). It was equally honored by Greeks and Romans. It is, too, in this sense that Shakespeare speaks of it when he makes Viola, in "Twelfth Night" (i. 5), say: "I bring no overture of war, no taxation of homage; I hold the olive in my hand, my words are as full of peace as matter." In Sonnet CVII. occurs the well-known line:[3]

> "And peace proclaims olives of endless age."

Palm. As the symbol of victory, this was carried before the conqueror in triumphal processions. Its classical use is noticed by Shakespeare in "Coriolanus" (v. 3). Volumnia says:[4]

> "And bear the palm, for having bravely shed
> Thy wife and children's blood."

---

[1] See "Windsor Guide," p. 5.

[2] See "Notes and Queries," 3d series, vol. xii. p. 160.

[3] See also "3 Henry VI.," iv. 6; "Timon of Athens," v. 4; "Antony and Cleopatra," iv. 6; "2 Henry IV.," iv. 4.

[4] See "As You Like It," iii. 2; "Timon of Athens," v. 1; cf. "Henry VIII.," iv. 2.

In " Julius Cæsar " (i. 2), Cassius exclaims:

> " Ye gods, it doth amaze me,
> A man of such a feeble temper should
> So get the start of the majestic world,
> And bear the palm alone."

Pilgrims were formerly called "palmers," from the staff or bough of palm they were wont to carry. So, in " All's Well That Ends Well " (iii. 5), Helena asks:

> " Where do the palmers lodge, I do beseech you ?"

Pear. In his few notices of the pear Shakespeare only mentions two by name, the warden and the poperin; the former was chiefly used for roasting or baking, and is mentioned by the clown in the " Winter's Tale " (iv. 3):

> " I must have saffron, to colour the warden pies."

Hence Ben Jonson makes a pun upon Church-warden pies. According to some antiquarians, the name warden is from the Anglo-Saxon *wearden*, to preserve, as it keeps for a long time; but it is more probable that the word had its origin from the horticultural skill of the Cistercian monks of Wardon Abbey, in Bedfordshire, founded in the 12th century. Three warden pears appeared on the armorial bearings of the abbey.[1] It is noticeable that the warden pies of Shakespeare's day, colored with saffron, have been replaced by stewed pears colored with cochineal.

The poperin pear was probably introduced from Flanders by the antiquary Leland, who was made rector of Popering by Henry VIII. It is alluded to by Mercutio in " Romeo and Juliet " (ii. 1), where he wishes that Romeo were "a poperin pear." In the old dramas there is much attempt at wit on this pear.

Peas. A practice called " peascod wooing " was formerly a common mode of divination in love affairs. The cook, when shelling green peas, would, if she chanced to find a pod having nine, lay it on the lintel of the kitchen-door, and

---

[1] See " Archæological Journal," vol. v. p. 301.

the first man who entered was supposed to be her future husband. Another way of divination by peascod consisted in the lover selecting one growing on the stem, snatching it away quickly, and if the good omen of the peas remaining in the husk were preserved, in then presenting it to the lady of his choice. Touchstone, in "As You Like It" (ii. 4), alludes to this piece of popular suggestion: "I remember the wooing of a peascod[1] instead of her." Gay, who has carefully chronicled many a custom of his time, says, in his "Fourth Pastoral:"

> "As peascods once I pluck'd, I chanc'd to see,
> One that was closely fill'd with three times three,
> Which when I cropp'd I safely home convey'd,
> And o'er my door the spell in secret laid."

We may quote, as a further illustration, the following stanza from Browne's "Pastorals" (bk. ii. song 3):

> "The peascod greene, oft with no little toyle,
> He'd seek for in the fattest, fertil'st soile,
> And rende it from the stalke to bring it to her,
> And in her bosom for acceptance wooe her."[2]

Plantain. The leaves of this plant were carefully valued by our forefathers for their supposed efficacy in healing wounds, etc. It was also considered as a preventive of poison; and to this supposed virtue we find an allusion in "Romeo and Juliet" (i. 2):

> "*Benvolio.* Take thou some new infection to thy eye,
> And the rank poison of the old will die.
> *Romeo.* Your plantain leaf is excellent for that.
> *Benvolio.*   For what, I pray thee?
> *Romeo.* For your broken shin."[3]

In the "Two Noble Kinsmen" (i. 2) Palamon says:

> "These poor slight sores
> Need not a plantain."

---

[1] The cod was what we now call the pod.
[2] See Brand's "Pop. Antiq.," 1849, vol. ii. p. 99.
[3] See "Love's Labour's Lost," iii. 1.

Poppy. The plant referred to by Shakespeare in "Othello" (iii. 3) is the opium poppy, well known in his day for its deadly qualities. It is described by Spenser in the "Fairy Queen" (ii. 7, 52) as the "dead-sleeping poppy," and Drayton ("Nymphidia," v.) enumerates it among the flowers that procure "deadly sleeping."

Potato. It is curious enough, says Nares,[1] to find that excellent root, which now forms a regular portion of the daily nutriment of every individual, and is the chief or entire support of multitudes in Ireland, spoken of continually as having some powerful effect upon the human frame, in exciting the desires and passions; yet this is the case in all the writings contemporary with Shakespeare. Thus Falstaff, in "Merry Wives of Windsor" (v. 5), says: "Let the sky rain potatoes; let it thunder to the tune of 'Green Sleeves,' hail kissing comfits," etc. In "Troilus and Cressida" (v. 2), Thersites adds: "How the devil luxury, with his fat rump and potato finger, tickles these together."[2] It appears, too, that the medical writers of the times countenanced this fancy. Mr. Ellacombe[3] observes that the above passages are of peculiar interest, inasmuch as they contain almost the earliest notice of potatoes after their introduction into England.

Primrose. Although the early primrose has always been such a popular and favorite flower, yet it seems to have been associated with sadness,[4] or even worse than sadness; for, in the following passages, the "primrose paths" and "primrose way" are meant to be suggestive of sinful pleasures. Thus, in "Hamlet" (i. 3), Ophelia says:

> "like a puff'd and reckless libertine,
> Himself the primrose path of dalliance treads,
> And recks not his own rede."

---

[1] "Glossary," vol. ii. p. 677.
[2] See Beaumont and Fletcher, "Elder Brother," iv. 4; Massinger, "New Way to Pay Old Debts," ii. 2; Ben Jonson, "Cynthia's Revels," ii. 1, etc.
[3] "Plant-Lore of Shakespeare," p. 173.
[4] Ibid., p. 179.

And in "Macbeth" (ii. 3), the Porter declares: "I had thought to have let in some of all professions, that go the primrose way to the everlasting bonfire." Curious to say, too, Shakespeare's only epithets for this fair flower are, "pale," "faint," "that die unmarried." Nearly all the poets of that time spoke of it in the same strain, with the exception of Ben Jonson and the two Fletchers.

Reed. Among the uses to which the reed was formerly applied were the thatching of houses and the making of shepherds' pipes. The former is alluded to in the "Tempest" (v. 1):

> "His tears run down his beard, like winter's drops
> From eaves of reeds;"

and the latter in "Merchant of Venice" (iii. 4), where Portia speaks of "a reed voice." It has generally been regarded as the emblem of weakness, as in "Antony and Cleopatra" (ii. 7): "a reed that will do me no service."

Rose. As might be expected, the rose is the flower most frequently mentioned by Shakespeare, a symbol, in many cases, of all that is fair and lovely. Thus, for instance, in "Hamlet" (iii. 4), Hamlet says:

> "Such an act . . . takes off the rose
> From the fair forehead of an innocent love,
> And sets a blister there."

And Ophelia (iii. 1) describes Hamlet as,

> "The expectancy and rose of the fair state."

In days gone by the rose entered largely into the customs and superstitions of most nations, and even nowadays there is an extensive folk-lore associated with it.

It appears that, in Shakespeare's time, one of the fashions of the day was the wearing of enormous roses on the shoes, of which full-length portraits afford striking examples.[1] Hamlet (iii. 2) speaks of "two Provincial roses on my razed shoes;" meaning, no doubt, rosettes of ribbon in the shape of roses of Provins or Provence. Douce favors the former, Warton

---

[1] Singer's "Shakespeare," 1875, vol. ix. p. 227.

the latter locality. In either case, it was a large rose. The Provence, or damask rose, was probably the better known. Gerarde, in his " Herbal," says that the damask rose is called by some *Rosa Provincialis*.[1] Mr. Fairholt[2] quotes, from " Friar Bacon's Prophecy" (1604), the following, in allusion to this fashion :

> " When roses in the gardens grew,
>   And not in ribbons on a shoe :
>   Now ribbon roses take such place
>   That garden roses want their grace."

Again, in " King John " (i. 1), where the Bastard alludes to the three-farthing silver pieces of Queen Elizabeth, which were extremely thin, and had the profile of the sovereign, with a rose on the back of her head, there doubtless is a fuller reference to the court fashion of sticking roses in the ear :[3]

> " my face so thin,
> That in mine ear I durst not stick a rose,
> Lest men should say, ' Look, where three-farthings goes.' "

Shakespeare also mentions the use of the rose in rose-cakes and rose-water, the former in " Romeo and Juliet " (v. 1), where Romeo speaks of " old cakes of roses," the latter in " Taming of the Shrew " (Induction, 1) :

> " Let one attend him with a silver basin
> Full of rose-water and bestrew'd with flowers."

Referring to its historical lore, we may mention its famous connection with the Wars of the Roses. In the fatal dispute in the Temple Gardens, Somerset, on the part of Lancaster, says (" 1 Henry VI." ii. 4) :

> " Let him that is no coward, nor no flatterer,
>   But dare maintain the party of the truth,
>   Pluck a red rose from off this thorn with me."

---

[1] " Notes to Hamlet," Clark and Wright, 1876, p. 179.

[2] " Costume in England," p. 238. At p. 579 the author gives several instances of the extravagances to which this fashion led.

[3] Some gallants had their ears bored, and wore their mistresses' silken shoe-strings in them. See Singer's " Notes," vol. iv. p. 257.

Warwick, on the part of York, replies:

> "I love no colours, and, without all colour
> Of base insinuating flattery,
> I pluck this white rose with Plantagenet."

The trailing white dog-rose is commonly considered to have been the one chosen by the House of York. A writer, however, in the *Quarterly Review* (vol. cxiv.) has shown that the white rose has a very ancient interest for Englishmen, as, long before the brawl in the Temple Gardens, the flower had been connected with one of the most ancient names of our island. The elder Pliny, in discussing the etymology of the word Albion, suggests that the land may have been so named from the white roses which abounded in it. The York and Lancaster rose, with its pale striped flowers, is a variety of the French rose known as *Rosa Gallica*. It became famous when the two emblematical roses, in the persons of Henry VII. and Elizabeth of York, at last brought peace and happiness to the country which had been so long divided by internal warfare. The canker-rose referred to by Shakespeare is the wild dog-rose, a name occasionally applied to the common red poppy.

Rosemary. This plant was formerly in very high esteem, and was devoted to various uses. It was supposed to strengthen the memory; hence it was regarded as a symbol of remembrance, and on this account was often given to friends. Thus, in " Hamlet " (iv. 5), where Ophelia seems to be addressing Laertes, she says: " There's rosemary, that's for remembrance." In the " Winter's Tale " (iv. 4) rosemary and rue are beautifully put together:

> "For you there's rosemary and rue; these keep
> Seeming and savour all the winter long:
> Grace and remembrance be to you both,
> And welcome to our shearing !"

Besides being used at weddings, it was also in request at funerals, probably for its odor, and as a token of remembrance of the deceased. Thus the Friar, in " Romeo and Juliet " (iv. 5), says:

> "Dry up your tears, and stick your rosemary
> On this fair corse."

This practice is thus touchingly alluded to by Gay, in his " Pastorals:"

> " To shew their love, the neighbours far and near
> Followed, with wistful look, the damsel's bier:
> Sprigg'd rosemary the lads and lasses bore,
> While dismally the parson walk'd before."

Rosemary, too, was one of the evergreens with which dishes were anciently garnished during the season of Christmas, an allusion to which occurs in " Pericles " (iv. 6): " Marry, come up, my dish of chastity with rosemary and bays."

Rush. Before the introduction of carpets, the floors of churches and houses were strewed with rushes, a custom to which Shakespeare makes several allusions. In " Taming of the Shrew " (iv. 1), Grumio asks: " Is supper ready, the house trimmed, rushes strewed, cobwebs swept?" and Glendower, in " 1 Henry IV." (iii. 1), says:

> " She bids you on the wanton rushes lay you down,
> And rest your gentle head upon her lap."

At the coronation of Henry V. (" 2 Henry IV.," v. 5), when the procession is coming, the grooms cry, " More rushes! more rushes!" which seems to have been the usual cry for rushes to be scattered on a pavement or a platform when a procession was approaching.[1]   Again, in " Richard II." (i. 3), the custom is further alluded to by John of Gaunt, who speaks of " the presence strew'd," referring to the presence-chamber.   So, too, in " Cymbeline " (ii. 2), Iachimo soliloquizes:

> "Tarquin thus
> Did softly press the rushes, ere he waken'd
> The chastity he wounded."

And in " Romeo and Juliet " (i. 4), Romeo says:

> " Let wantons, light of heart,
> Tickle the senseless rushes with their heels;"

---

[1] Dyce's " Glossary," p. 373.

an expression which Middleton has borrowed in his "Blunt Master Constable," 1602:

> "Bid him, whose heart no sorrow feels,
> Tickle the rushes with his wanton heels,
> I have too much lead at mine."

In the "Two Noble Kinsmen" (ii. 1) the Gaoler's Daughter is represented carrying "strewings" for the two prisoners' chamber.

Rush-bearings were a sort of rural festival, when the parishioners brought rushes to strew the church.[1]

The "rush-ring" appears to have been a kind of token for plighting of troth among rustic lovers. It was afterwards vilely used, however, for mock-marriages, as appears from one of the Constitutions of Salisbury. In "All's Well that Ends Well" (ii. 2) there seems a covert allusion to the rush-ring: "As Tib's rush for Tom's fore-finger." Spenser, in the "Shepherd's Kalendar," speaks of

> "The knotted rush-rings and gilt Rosemarie."

Du Breul, in his "Antiquities of Paris,"[2] mentions the rush-ring as "a kind of espousal used in France by such persons as meant to live together in a state of concubinage; but in England it was scarcely ever practised except by designing men, for the purpose of corrupting those young women to whom they pretended love."

The "rush candle," which, in times past, was found in nearly every house, and served as a night-light for the rich and candle for the poor, is mentioned in "Taming of the Shrew" (iv. 5):

> "be it moon, or sun, or what you please:
> An if you please to call it a rush candle,
> Henceforth, I vow, it shall be so for me."

Saffron. In the following passage ("All's Well that Ends

---

[1] See Brand's "Pop. Antiq.," 1849, vol. ii. pp. 13, 14.

[2] Douce's "Illustrations of Shakespeare," 1839, p. 194.

Well," iv. 5) there seems to be an allusion[1] by Lafeu to the fashionable and fantastic custom of wearing yellow, and to that of coloring paste with saffron : " No, no, no, your son was misled with a snipt-taffeta fellow there, whose villanous saffron would have made all the unbaked and doughy youth of a nation in his colour."

Spear-grass. This plant—perhaps the common reed—is noticed in " 1 Henry IV." (ii. 4) as used for tickling the nose and making it bleed. In Lupton's " Notable Things " it is mentioned as part of a medical recipe : " Whoever is tormented with sciatica or the hip-gout, let them take an herb called spear-grass, and stamp it, and lay a little thereof upon the grief." Mr. Ellacombe[2] thinks that the plant alluded to is the common couch-grass (*Triticum repens*), which is still known in the eastern counties as spear-grass.

Stover. This word, which is often found in the writings of Shakespeare's day, denotes fodder and provision of all sorts for cattle. In Cambridgeshire stover signifies hay made of coarse, rank grass, such as even cows will not eat while it is green. In " The Tempest " (iv. 1), Iris says :

> " Thy turfy mountains, where live nibbling sheep,
>   And flat meads thatch'd with stover, them to keep."

According to Steevens, stover was used as a thatch for cart-lodges and other buildings that required but cheap coverings.

Strawberry. Shakespeare's mention of the strawberry in connection with the nettle, in " Henry V." (i. 1),

> " The strawberry grows underneath the nettle,
>   And wholesome berries thrive and ripen best
>   Neighbour'd by fruit of baser quality,"

deserves, says Mr. Ellacombe, a passing note. " It was the common opinion in his day that plants were affected by the neighborhood of other plants to such an extent that they imbibed each others virtues and faults. Thus sweet flowers

---

[1] Dyce's " Glossary," p. 381.
[2] " Plant-Lore of Shakespeare," p. 319.

were planted near fruit-trees with the idea of improving the flavor of the fruit, and evil-smelling trees, like the elder, were carefully cleared away from fruit-trees, lest they should be tainted. But the strawberry was supposed to be an exception to the rule, and was said to thrive in the midst of 'evil communications, without being corrupted.'"

Thorns. The popular tradition, which represents the marks on the moon[1] to be that of a man carrying a thorn-bush on his head, is alluded to in "Midsummer-Night's Dream" v. 1), in the Prologue:

> "This man, with lanthorn, dog, and bush of thorn,
> Presenteth Moonshine."

Little else is mentioned by Shakespeare with regard to thorns, save that they are generally used by him as the emblems of desolation and trouble.

Violets. An old superstition is alluded to by Shakespeare when he makes Laertes wish that violets may spring from the grave of Ophelia ("Hamlet," v. 1):

> "Lay her i' the earth:
> And from her fair and unpolluted flesh
> May violets spring!"

an idea which occurs in Persius's "Satires" (i. 39):

> "E tumulo fortunataque favilla
> Nascentur violæ."

The violet has generally been associated with early death. This, Mr. Ellacombe considers,[2] "may have arisen from a sort of pity for flowers that were only allowed to see the opening year, and were cut off before the first beauty of summer had come, and so were looked upon as apt emblems of those who enjoyed the bright springtide of life, and no more." Thus, the violet is one of the flowers which Marina carries to hang "as a carpet on the grave" in "Pericles" (iv. 1):

---

[1] See p. 68.
[2] "Plant-Lore of Shakespeare," p. 248.

> "the yellows, blues,
> The purple violets, and marigolds,
> Shall, as a carpet, hang upon thy grave,
> While summer days do last."

Again, in that exquisite passage in the "Winter's Tale" (iv. 4), where Perdita enumerates the flowers of spring, she speaks of,

> "violets, dim,
> But sweeter than the lids of Juno's eyes,
> Or Cytherea's breath;"

upon which Mr. Singer[1] thus comments: "The eyes of Juno were as remarkable as those of Pallas, and

> 'Of a beauty never yet
> Equalled in height of tincture.'"

The beauties of Greece and other Asiatic nations tinged their eyes of an obscure violet color, by means of some unguent, which was doubtless perfumed, like those for the hair, etc., mentioned by Athenæus.

Willow. From time immemorial the willow has been regarded as the symbol of sadness. Hence it was customary for those who were forsaken in love to wear willow garlands, a practice to which Shakespeare makes several allusions. In "Othello" (iv. 3), Desdemona, anticipating her death, says:

> "My mother had a maid call'd Barbara;
> She was in love; and he she lov'd prov'd mad,
> And did forsake her: she had a song of—Willow;
> An old thing 'twas, but it express'd her fortune,
> And she died singing it: that song, to-night,
> Will not go from my mind."

The following is the song:[2]

---

[1] "Shakespeare," vol. iv. p. 76.

[2] "The old ballad on which Shakespeare formed this song is given in Percy's 'Reliques of Ancient Poetry' (1794, vol. i. p. 208), from a copy in the Pepysian collection. A different version of it may be seen in Chappell's 'Popular Music of the Olden Time' (2d edition, vol. i. p. 207). The original ditty is the lamentation of a lover for the inconstancy of his mistress."—Dyce's "Shakespeare," vol. vii. p. 450.

> "The poor soul sat sighing by a sycamore tree,
>   Sing all a green willow;
> Her hand on her bosom, her head on her knee,
>   Sing willow, willow, willow:
> The fresh streams ran by her, and murmur'd her moans,
>   Sing willow, willow, willow;
> Her salt tears fell from her, and soften'd the stones,
>   Sing willow, willow, willow:
> Sing all a green willow must be my garland."

And further on Emilia says (v. 2):

> "I will play the swan,
> And die in music.—[*Singing*] 'Willow, willow, willow.'"

And, again, Lorenzo, in "Merchant of Venice" (v. 1), narrates:

> "In such a night
> Stood Dido, with a willow in her hand,
> Upon the wild sea-banks."

It was, too, in reference to this custom that Shakespeare, in "Hamlet" (iv. 7), represented poor Ophelia hanging her flowers on the "willow aslant a brook." "This tree," says Douce,[1] "might have been chosen as the symbol of sadness from the cxxxvii. Psalm (verse 2): 'We hanged our harps upon the willows;' or else from a coincidence between the *weeping*-willow and falling tears." Another reason has been assigned. The *Agnus castus* was supposed to promote chastity, and "the willow being of a much like nature," says Swan, in his "Speculum Mundi" (1635), "it is yet a custom that he which is deprived of his love must wear a willow garland." Bona, the sister of the King of France, on receiving news of Edward the Fourth's marriage with Elizabeth Grey, exclaimed,

> "in hope he'll prove a widower shortly,
> I'll wear the willow garland for his sake."

Wormwood. The use of this plant in weaning infants is alluded to in "Romeo and Juliet" (i. 3), by Juliet's nurse, in the following passage:

---

[1] Illustrations of Shakespeare," p. 105.

"For I had then laid wormwood to my dug,

*   *   *   *   *

When it did taste the wormwood on the nipple
Of my dug, and felt it bitter, pretty fool."

Yew. This tree, styled by Shakespeare "the dismal yew" (Titus Andronicus," ii. 3), apart from the many superstitions associated with it, has been very frequently planted in churchyards, besides being used at funerals. Paris, in "Romeo and Juliet" (v. 3), says:

"Under yond yew-trees lay thee all along,
Holding thine ear close to the hollow ground;
So shall no foot upon the churchyard tread,
Being loose, unfirm, with digging up of graves,
But thou shalt hear it."

Although various reasons have been assigned for planting the yew-tree in churchyards, it seems probable that the practice had a superstitious origin. As witches were supposed to exercise a powerful influence over the winds, they were believed occasionally to exert their formidable power against religious edifices. Thus Macbeth says (iv. 1):

"Though you untie the winds, and let them fight
Against the churches."

To counteract, therefore, this imaginary danger, our ancestors may have planted the yew-tree in their churchyards, not only on account of its vitality as an evergreen, but as connected in some way, in heathen times, with the influence of evil powers.[1] In a statute made in the latter part of Edward I.'s reign, to prevent rectors from cutting down trees in churchyards, we find the following: "Verum arbores ipsæ, propter ventorum impetus ne ecclesiis noceant, sœpe plantantur."[2]

The custom of sticking yew in the shroud is alluded to in the following song in "Twelfth Night" (ii. 4):

---

[1] Douce's "Illustrations of Shakespeare," p. 244.
[2] See Brand's "Pop. Antiq.," 1849, vol. ii. pp. 255–266.

> "My shroud of white, stuck all with yew,
> O, prepare it!
> My part of death, no one so true
> Did share it."

Through being reckoned poisonous, it is introduced in "Macbeth" (iv. 1) in connection with the witches:

> "Gall of goat, and slips of yew,
> Sliver'd in the moon's eclipse."

"How much the splitting or tearing off of the slip had to do with magic we learn from a piece of Slavonic folklore. It is unlucky to use for a beam a branch or a tree broken by the wind. The devil, or storm-spirit, claims it as his own, and, were it used, the evil spirit would haunt the house. It is a broken branch the witches choose; a sliver'd slip the woodman will have none of."[1]

Its epithet, "double-fatal" ("Richard II.," iii. 2), no doubt refers to the poisonous quality of the leaves, and on account of its wood being employed for instruments of death. Sir Stephen Scroop, when telling Richard of Bolingbroke's revolt, declares that

> "Thy very beadsmen learn to bend their bows
> Of double-fatal yew against thy state."

It has been suggested that the poison intended by the Ghost in "Hamlet" (i. 5), when he speaks of the "juice of cursed hebenon," is that of the yew, and is the same as Marlowe's "juice of hebon" ("Jew of Malta," iii. 4). The yew is called hebon by Spenser and by other writers of Shakespeare's age; and, in its various forms of eben, eiben, hiben, etc., this tree is so named in no less than five different European languages. From medical authorities, both of ancient and modern times, it would seem that the juice of the yew is a rapidly fatal poison; next, that the symptoms attendant upon yew-poisoning correspond, in a very remarkable manner, with those which follow the bites of poisonous snakes; and, lastly, that no other poison but the yew pro-

---

[1] "Notes and Queries," 5th series, vol. xii. p. 468.

duces the "lazar-like" ulcerations on the body upon which Shakespeare, in this passage, lays so much stress.[1]

Among the other explanations of this passage is the well-known one which identifies "hebenon" with henbane. Mr. Beisly suggests that nightshade may be meant, while Nares considers that ebony is meant.[2]

From certain ancient statutes it appears that every Englishman, while archery was practised, was obliged to keep in his house either a bow of yew or some other wood.[3]

---

[1] Extract of a paper read by Rev. W. A. Harrison, New Shakespeare Society, 12th May, 1882.

[2] See Douce's "Illustrations of Shakespeare;" Nares's "Glossary," vol. i. p. 412; Beisly's "Shakespeare's Garden," p. 4.

[3] Singer's "Shakespeare," vol. iv. p. 427. See a paper in the "Antiquary" (1882, vol. vi. p. 13), by Mr. George Black, on the yew in Shakespearian folk-lore.

CHAPTER IX.

INSECTS AND REPTILES.

As Dr. Johnson has truly remarked, Shakespeare is "the poet of nature," for "his attention was not confined to the actions of men; he was an exact surveyor of the inanimate world; his descriptions have always some peculiarity, gathered by contemplating things as they really exist. Whether life or nature be his subject, Shakespeare shows plainly that he has seen with his own eyes." So, too, he was in the habit of taking minute observation of the popular notions relating to natural history, so many of which he has introduced into his plays, using them to no small advantage. In numerous cases, also, the peculiarities of certain natural objects have furnished the poet with many excellent metaphors. Thus, in "Richard II." (ii. 3), Bolingbroke speaks of "the caterpillars of the commonwealth;" and in "2 Henry VI." (iii. 1) the Duke of York's reflection on the destruction of his hopes is,

> "Thus are my blossoms blasted in the bud,
> And caterpillars eat my leaves away,"

their destructive powers being familiar.

Ant. An ancient name for the ant is "pismire," probably a Danish word, from *paid* and *myre*, signifying such ants as live in hillocks. In "1 Henry IV." (i. 3) Hotspur says:

> "Why, look you, I am whipp'd and scourg'd with rods,
> Nettled, and stung with pismires, when I hear
> Of this vile politician, Bolingbroke."

Blue-bottle. This well-known insect has often been used as a term of reproach. Thus, in "2 Henry IV." (v. 4), it furnishes an epithet applied by the abusive tongue of Doll Tearsheet to the beadle who had her in custody. She re-

viles him as a " blue-bottle rogue," a term, says Mr. Patterson,[1] " evidently suggested by the similarity of the colors
of his costume to that of the insect."

Bots. Our ancestors imagined that poverty or improper
food engendered these worms, or that they were the offspring of putrefaction. In " 1 Henry IV." (ii. 1), one of
the carriers says: " Peas and beans are as dank here as a
dog, and that is the next way to give poor jades the bots."
And one of the misfortunes of the miserable nag of Petruchio (" Taming of the Shrew," iii. 2), is that he is so " be-
gnawn with the bots."

Cricket. The presence of crickets in a house has generally been regarded as a good omen, and said to prognosticate cheerfulness and plenty. Thus, Poins, in answer to
the Prince's question in " 1 Henry IV." (ii. 4), " Shall we be
merry?" replies, " As merry as crickets." By many of our
poets the cricket has been connected with cheerfulness and
mirth. Thus, in Milton, " Il Penseroso " desires to be

> " Far from all resort of mirth,
> Save the cricket on the hearth."

It has not always, however, been regarded in the same
light, for Gay, in his " Pastoral Dirge," among the rural
prognostications of death, gives the following :

> " And shrilling crickets in the chimney cry'd."

And in Dryden's " Œdipus " occurs the subjoined :

> " Owls, ravens, crickets, seem the watch of death."

Lady Macbeth, also (" Macbeth," ii. 2), in replying to the
question of her husband after the murder of Duncan, says :

> " I heard the owl scream, and the crickets cry."

In " Cymbeline " (ii. 2), also, when Iachimo, at midnight,
commences his survey of the chamber where Imogen lies
sleeping, his first words refer to the chirping of crickets,

---

[1] " Insects Mentioned by Shakespeare," 1841, p. 181.

rendered all the more audible by the repose which at that
moment prevailed throughout the palace:

> "The crickets sing, and man's o'er-labour'd sense
> Repairs itself by rest."

Gilbert White, in his "History of Selborne" (1853, p. 174),
remarks that "it is the housewife's barometer, foretelling
her when it will rain; and is prognostic, sometimes, she
thinks, of ill or good luck, of the death of a near relation, or
the approach of an absent lover. By being the constant
companion of her solitary home, it naturally becomes the
object of her superstition." [1]

Its supposed keen sense of hearing is referred to in the
"Winter's Tale" (ii. 1) by Mamillius, who, on being asked
by Hermione to tell a tale, replies:

> "I will tell it softly;
> Yond crickets shall not hear it."

Frog. In the "Two Noble Kinsmen" (iii. 4), the Gaoler's
Daughter says:

> "Would I could find a fine frog! he would tell me
> News from all parts o' the world; then would I make
> A carack of a cockle-shell, and sail
> By east and north-east to the King of Pigmies,
> For he tells fortunes rarely."

In days gone by frogs were extensively used for the purpose of divination.

Gad-fly. A common name for this fly is the "brize" or
"breese," [2] an allusion to which occurs in "Troilus and Cressida" (i. 3), where Nestor, speaking of the sufferings which
cattle endure from this insect, says:

> "The herd hath more annoyance by the breese
> Than by the tiger."

And in "Antony and Cleopatra" (iii. 10) Shakespeare

---

[1] See Brand's "Pop. Antiq.," 1849, vol. iii. pp. 190, 191.
[2] See Patterson's "Insects Mentioned by Shakespeare," 1841, pp.
104, 105.

makes the excited Scarus draw a comparison between the effect which this insect produces on a herd of cattle and the abruptness and sudden frenzy of Cleopatra's retreat from the naval conflict:

> "Yon ribaudred nag of Egypt,
> Whom leprosy o'ertake! i' the midst o' the fight,
> When vantage like a pair of twins appear'd,
> Both as the same, or rather ours the elder,—
> The breese upon her, like a cow in June,—
> Hoists sails, and flies."

It is said that the terror this insect causes in cattle proceeds solely from the alarm occasioned by " a peculiar sound it emits while hovering for the purpose of oviposition."[1]

Lady-bird. This is used in " Romeo and Juliet " (i. 3) as a term of endearment. Lady Capulet having inquired after her daughter Juliet, the Nurse replies:

> "I bade her come. What, lamb! What, lady-bird!
> God forbid! Where's this girl? What, Juliet!"

Mr. Staunton regards this passage as an exquisite touch of nature. " The old nurse," he says, " in her fond garrulity, uses 'lady-bird' as a term of endearment; but, recollecting its application to a female of loose manners, checks herself— 'God forbid!' her darling should prove such a one." Mr. Dyce,[2] however, considers this explanation incorrect, and gives the subjoined note: " The nurse says that she has already bid Juliet come; she then calls out, 'What, lamb! What, lady-bird!' and Juliet not yet making her appearance, she exclaims, 'God forbid! Where's this girl?' The words 'God forbid' being properly an ellipsis of 'God forbid that any accident should keep her away,' but used here merely as an expression of impatience."

Lizard. It was a common superstition in the time of Shakespeare that lizards were venomous, a notion which probably originated in their singular form. Hence the liz-

---

[1] " Linnæan Transactions," vol. xv. p. 407 ; cf. Virgil's " Georgics," iii. l. 148.

[2] " Glossary," 1876, p. 238.

ard's leg was thought a suitable ingredient for the witches'
caldron in "Macbeth" (iv. 1). Suffolk, in "2 Henry VI."
(iii. 2), refers to this idea:

> "Their chiefest prospect murdering basilisks!
> Their softest touch as smart as lizards' stings.

Again, in "3 Henry VI." (ii. 2), Queen Margaret speaks of

> "venom toads, or lizards' dreadful stings."

In "Troilus and Cressida" (v. 1) it is classed with the toad
and owl.

Moth. This term, as Mr. Patterson remarks in his "Insects Mentioned by Shakespeare" (1841, p. 164), does not
awaken many pleasing associations. In the minds of most
people it stands for an insect either contemptible from its
size and inertness, or positively obnoxious from its attacks
on many articles of clothing. Thus Shakespeare, he says,
employs the expression "moth" to denote something trifling
or extremely minute. And in "King John" (iv. 1) we have
the touching appeal of Prince Arthur to Hubert, in which,
for mote, he would substitute moth:

> "*Arthur.* Is there no remedy?
> *Hubert.*   None, but to lose your eyes.
> *Arthur.* O heaven!—that there were but a mote in yours,
> A grain, a dust, a gnat, a wandering hair,
> Any annoyance in that precious sense!
> Then, feeling what small things are boisterous there,
> Your vile intent must needs seem horrible."

See also "Henry V." (iv. 1). In these two passages, however, the correct reading is probably "mote."[1]

Serpent. A term used by our old writers to signify a serpent was "a worm," which is still found in the north of
England in the same sense. It is used several times by
Shakespeare; as, for instance, in "Measure for Measure"
(iii. 1), where the Duke, addressing Claudio, says:

---

[1] Nares's "Glossary," vol. ii. p. 973.

> " Thou'rt by no means valiant ;
> For thou dost fear the soft and tender fork
> Of a poor worm."

This passage also illustrates an error very prevalent in days gone by, that the forked tongue of the serpent tribe was their instrument of offence, without any thought of the teeth or fangs, which are its real weapons.[1] Again, the " blind-worm " or " slow-worm "—a little snake with very small eyes, falsely supposed to be venomous—is spoken of in " A Midsummer-Night's Dream " (ii. 2), in that charming passage where the fairies are represented as singing to their queen, Titania :

> " You spotted snakes, with double tongue,
>   Thorny hedgehogs, be not seen ;
> Newts, and blind-worms, do no wrong,
>   Come not near our fairy queen."

In " Macbeth " (iv. 1), among the ingredients of the witches' caldron are

> " Adder's fork, and blind-worm's sting."

To quote a further allusion, Shakespeare, in " Timon of Athens " (iv. 3), speaks of

> " The gilded newt and eyeless venom'd worm."

Massinger employs the same term in his " Parliament of Love " (iv. 2) :

> " The sad father
> That sees his son stung by a snake to death,
> May, with more justice, stay his vengeful hand,
> And let the worm escape, than you vouchsafe him
> A minute to repent." [2]

There was an old notion that the serpent caused death

---

[1] Cf. " Macbeth " (iii. 4) :

> " There the grown serpent lies : the worm, that's fled,
> Hath nature that in time will venom breed."

[2] Worm is used for serpent or viper, in the Geneva version of the New Testament, in Acts xxvii. 4, 5.

without pain, a popular fancy which Shakespeare has introduced in his "Antony and Cleopatra" (v. 2):

> "Hast thou the pretty worm of Nilus there,
>   That kills and pains not?"

The term "worm" was also occasionally used to signify a
"poor creature," as also was the word "snake." Thus, in
the "Taming of the Shrew" (v. 2), Katharina says:

> "Come, come, you froward and unable worms!
>   My mind hath been as big as one of yours,
>   My heart as great, my reason, haply, more."

So, in "As You Like It" (iv. 3), Rosalind uses "snake" in
the sense of reproach: "Well, go your way to her, for I see
love hath made thee a tame snake."

The serpent, as the emblem of ingratitude, is alluded to
by King Lear (ii. 4), who, referring to his daughter, says
how she

> "struck me with her tongue,
>   Most serpent-like, upon the very heart:—
>   All the stor'd vengeances of heaven fall
>   On her ingrateful top!"

According to a popular belief, still credited, a poisonous
bite could be cured by the blood of the viper which darted
the poison. Thus, in "Richard II." (i. 1), Mowbray says:

> "I am disgrac'd, impeach'd, and baffled here,
>   Pierc'd to the soul with slander's venom'd spear,
>   The which no balm can cure, but his heart-blood
>   Which breath'd this poison."

In Cornwall it is still believed that the dead body of a
serpent, bruised on the wound it has occasioned, is an infal-
lible remedy for its bite.[1] Hence has originated the following rhyme:

> "The beauteous adder hath a sting,
>   Yet bears a balsam too."

---

[1] See Hunt's "Popular Romances of the West of England," 1871,
p. 415; and Brand's "Pop. Antiq.," 1849, vol. iii. p. 270.

The old notion that the snake, in casting off its slough, or skin, annually, is supposed to regain new vigor and fresh youth, is alluded to by King Henry ("Henry V.," iv. 1), who speaks of "casted slough and fresh legerity"—legerity meaning lightness, nimbleness. In "Twelfth Night" (ii. 5), in the letter which Malvolio finds, there is this passage: "to inure thyself to what thou art like to be, cast thy humble slough and appear fresh." One of the most useful miracles which St. Patrick is reported to have performed was his driving the venomous reptiles out of Ireland, and forbidding them to return. This tradition is probably alluded to by King Richard ("Richard II.," ii. 1):

> "Now for our Irish wars:
> We must supplant those rough rug-headed kerns,
> Which live like venom, where no venom else,
> But only they, hath privilege to live."

The way, we are told, by which the saint performed this astounding feat of his supernatural power was by means of a drum. Even spiders, too, runs the legend, were included in this summary process of excommunicating the serpent race. One of the customs, therefore, observed on St. Patrick's day, is visiting Croagh Patrick. This sacred hill is situated in the county of Mayo, and is said to have been the spot chosen by St. Patrick for banishing the serpents and other noxious animals into the sea.

In "Julius Cæsar" (ii. 1), where Brutus says,

> "It is the bright day that brings forth the adder;
> And that craves wary walking,"

we may compare the popular adage,

> "March wind
> Wakes the ether (*i. e.*, adder) and blooms the whin."[1]

Spider. This little creature, which, in daily life, is seldom noticed except for its cobweb, the presence of which in a house generally betokens neglect, has, however, an interest-

---

[1] Denham's "Weather Proverbs," 1842.

ing history, being the subject of many a curious legend and quaint superstition. Thus, it has not escaped the all-pervading eye of Shakespeare, who has given us many curious scraps of folk-lore concerning it. In days gone by the web of the common house-spider was much in request for stopping the effusion of blood; and hence Bottom, in addressing one of his fairy attendants in " A Midsummer-Night's Dream " (iii. 1), says : " I shall desire you of more acquaintance, good Master Cobweb : if I cut my finger, I shall make bold with you."

Its medicinal virtues, however, do not end here, for, in Sussex[1] it is used in cases of jaundice, many an old doctress prescribing " a live spider rolled up in butter." It is stated, too, that the web is narcotic, and has been administered internally in certain cases of fever, with success.[2] As a remedy for ague it has been considered most efficacious. Some years ago a lady in the south of Ireland was celebrated far and near for her cure of this disorder. Her remedy was a large house-spider taken alive, enveloped in treacle or preserve. Of course, the parties were carefully kept in ignorance of what the wonderful remedy was.[3]

According to a universal belief, spiders were formerly considered highly venomous, in allusion to which notion King Richard II. (iii. 2), in saluting the " dear earth " on which he stands, after " late tossing on the breaking seas," accosts it thus :

> " Feed not thy sovereign's foe, my gentle earth,
> Nor with thy sweets comfort his ravenous sense ;
> But let thy spiders, that suck up thy venom,
> And heavy-gaited toads, lie in their way,
> Doing annoyance to the treacherous feet,
> Which with usurping steps do trample thee."

Again, Leontes, in the " Winter's Tale " (ii. 1), remarks :

> " There may be in the cup
> A spider steep'd."

---

[1] " Folk-Lore Record," 1878, vol. i. p. 45.

[2] See Brand's " Pop. Antiq.," vol. iii. pp. 223, 287, 381.

[3] See article on " Spider-Lore," in *Graphic*, November 13, 1880.

In "Cymbeline" (iv. 2) and "Richard III." (i. 2) Shakespeare classes it with adders and toads; and in the latter play (i. 3), when Queen Margaret is hurling imprecations on her enemies, she is turned from her encounter with Gloster by a remark made by Queen Elizabeth; and while a pitying spirit seems for a minute to supplant her rage, she addresses her successor in these words:

> " Poor painted queen, vain flourish of my fortune!
> Why strew'st thou sugar on that bottled spider,
> Whose deadly web ensnareth thee about?"

In another part of the same play (iv. 4) the epithet "bottled" is again applied in a similar manner by Queen Elizabeth:

> "That bottled spider, that foul bunch-back'd toad!"

Ritson, on these two passages, has the following remarks on the term, bottled spider: "A large, bloated, glossy spider, supposed to contain venom proportionate to its size."

The origin of the silvery threads of gossamer which are so frequently seen extending from bush to bush was formerly unknown. Spenser, for instance, speaks of them as "scorched dew;" and Thomson, in his "Autumn," mentions "the filmy threads of dew evaporate;" which probably, says Mr. Patterson,[1] refers to the same object. The gossamer is now, however, known to be the production of a minute spider. It is twice mentioned by Shakespeare, but not in connection with the little being from which it originates. One of the passages is in "Romeo and Juliet" (ii. 6):

> " A lover may bestride the gossamer
> That idles in the wanton summer air,
> And yet not fall; so light is vanity."

The other occurs in "King Lear" (iv. 6), where Edgar accosts his father, after his supposed leap from that

> "cliff, whose high and bending head
> Looks fearfully in the confined deep."

---

[1] "Insects Mentioned by Shakespeare," 1841, p. 220.

He says:

> " Hadst thou been aught but gossamer, feathers, air,
>   So many fathom down precipitating,
>   Thou'dst shiver'd like an egg."

In each case it is expressive of extreme lightness. Nares, in his " Glossary " (vol. i. p. 378), considers that the term "gossamer " originally came from the French *gossampine*, the cotton-tree, and is equivalent to cotton-wool. He says that it also means any light, downy matter, such as the flying seeds of thistles and other plants, and, in poetry, is not unfrequently used to denote the long, floating cobwebs seen in fine weather. In the above passage from " King Lear " he thinks it has the original sense, and in the one from " Romeo and Juliet " probably the last. Some are of opinion that the word is derived from *goss*, the gorse or furze.[1] In Germany the popular belief attributes the manufacture of the gossamer to the dwarfs and elves. Of King Oberon, it may be remembered, we are told,

> " A rich mantle he did wear,
>   Made of tinsel gossamer,
>   Bestarred over with a few
>   Diamond drops of morning dew."

Hogg, too, introduces it as a vehicle fit for the fairy bands, which he describes as

> " sailing 'mid the golden air
> In skiffs of yielding gossamer."

Toad. Among the vulgar errors of Shakespeare's day was the belief that the head of the toad contained a stone possessing great medicinal virtues. In " As You Like It," (ii. 1), the Duke says:

> " Sweet are the uses of adversity ;
>   Which, like the toad, ugly and venomous,
>   Wears yet a precious jewel in his head."

---

[1] See Croker's " Fairy Legends and Traditions of the South of Ireland," edited by T. Wright, 1862, p. 215.

Lupton, in his "One Thousand Notable Things," says that "a toad-stone, called *Crepaudina*, touching any part envenomed by the bite of a rat, wasp, spider, or other venomous beast, ceases the pain and swelling thereof." In the Londesborough Collection is a silver ring of the fifteenth century, in which one of these stones is set.[1]

It was also generally believed that the toad was highly venomous—a notion to which there are constant allusions in Shakespeare's plays; as, for example, in the above passage, where it is spoken of as "ugly and venomous." In "Richard III." (i. 2), Lady Anne says to Gloster:

> "Never hung poison on a fouler toad."

And, in another scene (i. 3), Queen Margaret speaks of "this pois'nous bunch-back'd toad."

Once more, in "Titus Andronicus" (iv. 2), the Nurse describes Queen Tamora's babe as being "as loathsome as a toad." There is doubtless some truth in this belief, as the following quotation from Mr. Frank Buckland's "Curiosities of Natural History" seems to show: "Toads are generally reported to be poisonous; and this is perfectly true to a certain extent. Like the lizards, they have glands in their skin which secrete a white, highly acid fluid, and just behind the head are seen two eminences like split beans; if these be pressed, this acid fluid will come out—only let the operator mind that it does not get into his eyes, for it generally comes out with a jet. There are also other glands dispersed through the skin. A dog will never take a toad in his mouth, and the reason is that this glandular secretion burns his tongue and lips. It is also poisonous to the human subject. Mr. Blick, surgeon, of Islip, Oxfordshire,[2] tells me that a man once made a wager, when half drunk, in a village public-house, that he would bite a toad's head off; he did so, but in a few hours his lips, tongue, and throat began to swell in a

---

[1] See Brand's "Pop. Antiq.," vol. ii. pp. 50–55; Douce's "Illustrations of Shakespeare," pp. 181–183.

[2] See "Notes and Queries," 6th series, vol. v. pp. 32, 173; also, Gilbert White's "Natural History of Selborne," letter xvii.

most alarming way, and he was dangerously ill for some time."

Owing to the supposed highly venomous character of the toad, "superstition," says Pennant,[1] "gave it preternatural powers, and made it a principal ingredient in the incantations of nocturnal hags." Thus, in Macbeth " (iv. 1), the witch says:

> " Toad that under cold stone,
> Days and nights has thirty-one
> Swelter'd venom sleeping got,
> Boil thou first i' the charmed pot."

Pennant adds that this was intended "for a design of the first consideration, that of raising and bringing before the eyes of Macbeth a hateful second-sight of the prosperity of Banquo's line. This shows the mighty power attributed to this animal by the dealers in the magic art."

The evil spirit, too, has been likened by one of our master bards to the toad, as a semblance of all that is devilish and disgusting (" Paradise Lost," iv. 800):

> " Him they found,
> Squat like a toad, close at the ear of Eve,
> Assaying with all his devilish art to reach
> The organs of her fancy."

In " Macbeth " (i. 1), the paddock or toad is made the name of a familiar spirit:

> " Paddock[2] calls.—Anon !"

Wasp. So easily, we are told,[3] is the wrathful temperament of this insect aroused, that extreme irascibility can scarcely be better expressed than by the term "waspish." It is in this sense that Shakespeare has applied the epithet, " her waspish-headed son," in the " Tempest " (iv. 1), where we are told that Cupid is resolved to be a boy outright. Again, in " As You Like It " (iv. 3), Silvius says:

---

[1] "Zoology," 1766, vol. iii. p. 15.
[2] Cf. " Hamlet," iii. 4 ; here paddock is used for a toad.
[3] Patterson's " Insects Mentioned by Shakespeare," 1841, p. 137.

> " I know not the contents; but, as I guess
> By the stern brow and waspish action
> Which she did use as she was writing of it,
> It bears an angry tenor."

Again, in the "Taming of the Shrew" (ii. 1), Petruchio addresses his intended spouse in language not highly complimentary:

> "*Pet.* Come, come, you wasp; i' faith, you are too angry.
> *Kath.* If I be waspish, best beware my sting.
> *Pet.* My remedy is, then, to pluck it out."

In the celebrated scene in " Julius Cæsar " (iv. 3), in which the reconciliation between Brutus and Cassius is effected, the word is used in a similar sense:

> " I'll use you for my mirth, yea, for my laughter,
> When you are waspish." [1]

Water-Fly. This little insect, which, on a sunny day, may be seen almost on every pool, dimpling the glassy surface of the water, is used as a term of reproach by Shakespeare. Thus, Hamlet (v. 2), speaking of Osric, asks Horatio, " Dost know this water-fly?" In " Troilus and Cressida " (v. 1), Thersites exclaims : " Ah, how the poor world is pestered with such water-flies, diminutives of nature." Johnson says it is the proper emblem of a busy trifler, because it skips up and down upon the surface of the water without any apparent purpose.

---

[1] Cf. " Titus Andronicus," ii. 3 ; " Henry VIII.," iii. 3.

CHAPTER X.

FOLK-MEDICINE.

WITHOUT discussing the extent of Shakespeare's technical medical knowledge, the following pages will suffice to show that he was fully acquainted with many of the popular notions prevalent in his day respecting certain diseases and their cures. These, no doubt, he collected partly from the literature of the period, with which he was so fully conversant, besides gathering a good deal of information on the subject from daily observation. Anyhow, he has bequeathed to us some interesting particulars relating to the folk-medicine of bygone times, which is of value, in so far as it helps to illustrate the history of medicine in past years. In Shakespeare's day the condition of medical science was very unlike that at the present day. As Mr. Goadby, in his "England of Shakespeare" (1881, p. 104), remarks, "the man of science was always more or less of an alchemist, and the students of medicine were usually extensive dealers in charms and philtres." If a man wanted bleeding he went to a barber-surgeon, and when he required medicine he consulted an apothecary; the shop of the latter being well described by Romeo (v. 1):

> "And in his needy shop a tortoise hung,
> An alligator stuff'd, and other skins
> Of ill-shap'd fishes; and about his shelves
> A beggarly account of empty boxes,
> Green earthen pots, bladders and musty seeds,
> Remnants of pack-thread and old cakes of roses,
> Were thinly scattered, to make up a show."

Such a man was as ready "to sell love-philtres to a maiden as narcotics to a friar."

Bleeding. Various remedies were in use in Shakespeare's

day to stop bleeding. Thus, a key, on account of the cold-ness of the metal of which it is composed, was often em-ployed; hence the term "key-cold" became proverbial, and is referred to by many old writers. In " Richard III." (i. 2), Lady Anne, speaking of the corpse of King Henry the Sixth, says

> " Poor key-cold figure of a holy king."

In the " Rape of Lucrece " (l. 1774) the same expression is used:

> "And then in key-cold Lucrece' bleeding stream
> He falls, and bathes the pale fear in his face."

In Beaumont and Fletcher's " Wild Goose Chase " (iv. 3) we read: "For till they be key-cold dead, there's no trust-ing of 'em."[1]

Another common remedy was the one alluded to in " King Lear " (iii. 7), where one of the servants says:

> " I'll fetch some flax, and whites of eggs,
> To apply to his bleeding face."

This passage has been thought to be parodied in Ben Jon-son's play, "The Case is Altered " (ii. 4): " Go, get a white of an egg and a little flax, and close the breach of the head; it is the most conducible thing that can be." Mr. Gifford, however, has shown the incorrectness of this assertion, point-ing out that Jonson's play was written in 1599, some years before " King Lear " appeared, while the allusion is "to a method of cure common in Jonson's time to every barber-surgeon and old woman in the kingdom."[2]

Cobwebs are still used to stanch the bleeding from small wounds, and Bottom's words seem to refer to this remedy of domestic surgery: "I shall desire you of more acquaint-ance, good Master Cobweb; if I cut my finger, I shall make bold with you."

---

[1] See Nares's " Glossary," vol. ii. p. 482 ; also, Brand's " Pop. Antiq.," 1849, vol. iii. p. 311 ; Henderson's " Folk-Lore of Northern Counties," 1879, pp. 168, 169.

[2] Aldis Wright's " Notes to King Lear," 1877, p. 179.

Anciently, says Mr. Singer, "a superstitious belief was annexed to the accident of bleeding at the nose;" hence, in the "Merchant of Venice" (ii. 5), Launcelot says: "It was not for nothing that my nose fell a-bleeding on Black Monday last." In days gone by, it was customary with our forefathers to be bled periodically, in spring and in autumn, in allusion to which custom King Richard refers ("Richard II.," i. 1), when he says to his uncle:

> "Our doctors say this is no month to bleed."

Hence the almanacs of the time generally gave particular seasons as the most beneficial for bleeding. The forty-seventh aphorism of Hippocrates (sect. 6) is, that "persons who are benefited by venesection or purging should be bled or purged in the spring."

Blindness. The exact meaning of the term "sand-blind," which occurs in the "Merchant of Venice" (ii. 2), is somewhat obscure:

> "*Launcelot.* O heavens, this is my true-begotten father! who, being more than sand-blind, high gravel blind, knows me not.
>   *   *   *   *   *   *   *   *
> *Gobbo.* Alack, sir, I am sand-blind, I know you not."

It probably means very dim-sighted,[1] and in Nares's "Glossary"[2] it is thus explained: "Having an imperfect sight, as if there was sand in the eye." The expression is used by Beaumont and Fletcher in "Love's Cure" (ii. 1): "Why, signors, and my honest neighbours, will you impute that as a neglect of my friends, which is an imperfection in me? I have been *sand-blind* from my infancy." The term was probably one in vulgar use.[3]

Blister. In the following passage of "Timon of Athens" (v. 1), Timon appears to refer to the old superstition that a lie produces a blister on the tongue, though, in the malice

---

[1] Dyce's "Glossary," p. 381 ; cf. the word "Berlué, pur-blinded, made sand-blind," Cotgrave's "Fr. and Eng. Dict."

[2] Vol. ii. p. 765.

[3] Bucknill's "Medical Knowledge of Shakespeare," p. 93.

of his rage, he imprecates the minor punishment on truth, and the old surgery of cauterization on falsehood:[1]

> "Thou sun, that comfort'st, burn!—Speak, and be hang'd;
> For each true word, a blister! and each false
> Be as a caut'rizing to the root o' the tongue,
> Consuming it with speaking!"

We may also compare the passage in "Winter's Tale" (ii. 2), where Paulina declares:

> "If I prove honey-mouth'd, let my tongue blister,
> And never to my red-look'd anger be
> The trumpet any more."[2]

Bone-ache. This was a nickname, in bygone years, for the *Lues venerea*, an allusion to which we find in "Troilus and Cressida" (ii. 3), where Thersites speaks of "the bone-ache" as "the curse dependent on those that war for a placket." Another name for this disease was the "brenning or burning," a notice of which we find in "King Lear" (iv. 6).

Bruise. A favorite remedy in days past for bruises was parmaceti, a corruption of spermaceti, in allusion to which Hotspur, in "1 Henry IV." (i. 3), speaks of it as "the sovereign'st thing on earth for an inward bruise." So, too, in Sir T. Overbury's "Characters," 1616 ["An Ordinarie Fencer"]: "His wounds are seldom skin-deepe; for an *inward bruise*, lambstones and sweetbreads are his only spermaceti." A well-known plant called the "Shepherd's Purse" has been popularly nicknamed the "Poor Man's Parmacetti," being a joke on the Latin word *bursa*, a purse, which, to a poor man, is always the best remedy for his bruises.[3] In "Romeo and Juliet" (i. 2), a plantain-leaf is pronounced to be an excellent cure "for your broken shin." Plantain-water was a remedy in common use with the old surgeons.[4]

---

[1] Bucknill's "Medical Knowledge of Shakespeare," p. 258.

[2] Cf., too, "Love's Labour's Lost" (v. 2):

> "A blister on his sweet tongue, with my heart,
> That put Armado's page out of his part."

[3] Dr. Prior's "Popular Names of British Plants," 1870, p. 185.

[4] "The Medical Knowledge of Shakespeare," 1860, p. 78.

Bubukle. According to Johnson, this denoted "a red pimple." Nares says it is "a corrupt word for a carbuncle, or something like;" and Mr. Halliwell-Phillipps, in his " Dictionary of Archaic and Provincial Words," defines it as a botch or imposthume. It occurs in "Henry V." (iii. 6), where Fluellen describes Bardolph's face as "all bubukles."

Burn. The notion of one heat driving out another gave rise to the old-fashioned custom of placing a burned part near the fire to drive out the fire—a practice, says Dr. Bucknill,[1] certainly not without benefit, acting on the same principle as the application of turpentine and other stimulants to recent burns. This was one of the many instances of the ancient homœopathic doctrine, that what hurts will also cure.[2] Thus, in " King John " (iii. 1), Pandulph speaks of it:

> "And falsehood falsehood cures; as fire cools fire
> Within the scorched veins of one new burn'd."

Again, in the " Two Gentlemen of Verona " (ii. 4), Proteus tells how:

> "Even as one heat another heat expels,
> Or as one nail by strength drives out another,
> So the remembrance of my former love
> Is by a newer object quite forgotten."

We may also compare the words of Mowbray in " Richard II." (i. 1), where a similar idea is contained:

> "I am disgrac'd, impeach'd, and baffled here;
> Pierc'd to the soul with slander's venom'd spear,
> The which no balm can cure, but his heart-blood
> Which breath'd this poison."

Once more, in " Romeo and Juliet " (i. 2), Benvolio relates how

> "one fire burns out another's burning,
> One pain is lessen'd by another's anguish;
> Turn giddy, and be holp by backward turning;
> One desperate grief cures with another's languish."

Cataract. One of the popular names for this disease of the

---

[1] "The Medical Knowledge of Shakespeare," 1860, p. 65.
[2] See Tylor's " Primitive Culture," vol. i. p. 761.

eye was the "web and the pin." Markham, in his "Cheap and Good Husbandry" (bk. i. chap. 37), thus describes it in horses: "But for the wart, pearle, pin, or web, which are evils grown in or upon the eye, to take them off, take the juyce of the herb betin and wash the eye therewith, it will weare the spots away." Florio ("Ital. Dict.") gives the following: "Cataratta is a dimnesse of sight occasioned by humores hardened in the eies, called a cataract or a pin and a web." Shakespeare uses the term in the "Winter's Tale" (i. 2), where Leontes speaks of

> "all eyes blind
> With the pin and web, but theirs;"

and in "King Lear" (iii. 4), alluding to "the foul fiend Flibbertigibbet," says, "he gives the web and the pin."[1] Acerbi, in his "Travels" (vol. ii. p. 290), has given the Lapland method of cure for this disease. In a fragment of an old medical treatise it is thus described: "Another sykenes ther byth of *yezen; on a webbe*, a nother a wem, that hydyth the myddel of the yezen; and this hes to maners, other whilys he is white and thynne, and other whilys he is thykke, as whenne the obtalmye ne is noght clene yhelyd up, bote the rote abydyth stylle. Other whilys the webbe is noght white but rede, other blake."[2] In the Statute of the 34 and 35 of Henry VIII. a pin and web in the eye is recited among the "customable diseases," which honest persons, not being surgeons, might treat with herbs, roots, and waters, with the knowledge of whose nature God had endowed them.

Chilblains. These are probably alluded to by the Fool in "King Lear" (i. 5): "If a man's brains were in's heels, were't not in danger of kibes?" Hamlet, too, says (v. 1): "the age is grown so picked, that the toe of the peasant comes so near the heel of the courtier, he galls his kibe."

Deformity. It was an old prejudice, which is not quite ex-

---

[1] See Nares's "Glossary," vol. ii. pp. 660, 661; Dyce's "Glossary," p. 322.

[2] Quoted in Singer's "Shakespeare."

tinct, that those who are defective or deformed are marked by nature as prone to mischief. Thus, in " Richard III." (i. 3), Margaret says of Richard, Duke of Gloster:

> " Thou elvish-mark'd, abortive, rooting hog !
> Thou that was seal'd in thy nativity
> The slave of nature, and the son of hell."

She calls him *hog*, in allusion to his cognizance, which was a boar. A popular expression in Shakespeare's day for a deformed person was a " stigmatic." It denoted any one who had been *stigmatized*, or burned with an iron, as an ignominious punishment, and hence was employed to represent a person on whom nature has set a mark of deformity. Thus, in " 3 Henry VI." (ii. 2), Queen Margaret says:

> " But thou art neither like thy sire, nor dam ;
> But like a foul misshapen stigmatic
> Mark'd by the destinies to be avoided,
> As venom toads, or lizards' dreadful stings."

Again, in " 2 Henry VI." (v. 1), young Clifford says to Richard :

> " Foul stigmatic, that's more than thou canst tell."

We may note, too, how, in " A Midsummer-Night's Dream " (v. 1), mothers' marks and congenital forms are deprecated by Oberon from the issue of the happy lovers :

> " And the blots of Nature's hand
> Shall not in their issue stand ;
> Never mole, hare-lip, nor scar,
> Nor mark prodigious, such as are
> Despised in nativity,
> Shall upon their children be." [1]

Indeed, constant allusions are to be met with in our old writers relating to this subject, showing how strong were the feelings of our forefathers on the point. But, to give one further instance of this superstition given by Shakespeare, we may quote the words of King John (iv. 2), with refer-

---

[1] Cf. " King John " (iii. 1), where Constance gives a catalogue of congenital defects.

ence to Hubert and his supposed murder of Prince Arthur:

> "A fellow by the hand of Nature mark'd,
> Quoted, and sign'd, to do a deed of shame,
> This murder had not come into my mind."

This adaptation of the mind to the deformity of the body concurs, too, with Bacon's theory: "Deformed persons are commonly even with nature; for, as nature hath done ill by them, so do they by nature, being void of natural affection, and so they have their revenge on nature."

Drowning. The old superstition[1] of its being dangerous to save a person from drowning is supposed, says Mr. Halliwell-Phillipps, to be alluded to in "Twelfth Night." It was owing to the belief that the person saved would, sooner or later, injure the man who saved him. Thus, in Sir Walter Scott's "Pirate," Bryce, the pedler, warns the hero not to attempt to resuscitate an inanimate form which the waves had washed ashore on the mainland of Shetland. "'Are you mad,' exclaimed the pedler, 'you that have lived sae lang in Zetland, to risk the saving of a drowning man? Wot ye not if ye bring him to life again he will do you some capital injury?'"

Epilepsy. A popular name for this terrible malady was the "falling-sickness," because, when attacked with one of these fits, the patient falls suddenly to the ground. In "Julius Cæsar" (i. 2) it is thus mentioned in the following dialogue:

> "*Cassius.* But, soft, I pray you: what, did Cæsar swoon?
>
> *Casca.* He fell down in the market-place, and foamed at mouth, and was speechless.
>
> *Brutus.* 'Tis very like; he hath the falling-sickness.
>
> *Cassius.* No, Cæsar hath it not; but you, and I,
> And honest Casca, we have the falling-sickness."

Fistula. At the present day a fistula means an abscess external to the rectum, but in Shakespeare's day it was used

---

[1] "Handbook Index to Shakespeare," p. 150. See "Notes and Queries" for superstitions connected with drowning, 5th series, vol. ix. pp. 111, 218, 478, 516; vol. x. pp. 38, 276; vol. xi. pp. 119, 278.

in a more general signification for a burrowing abscess in any situation.[1] The play of " All's Well that Ends Well" has a special interest, because, as Dr. Bucknill says, its very plot may be said to be medical. " The orphan daughter of a physician cures the king of a fistula by means of a secret remedy left to her as a great treasure by her father. The royal reward is the choice of a husband among the nobles of the court, and 'thereby hangs the tale.' " The story is taken from the tale of Gilletta of Narbonne, in the " Decameron " of Boccaccio. It came to Shakespeare through the medium of Painter's " Palace of Pleasure," and is to be found in the first volume, which was printed as early as 1566.[2] The story is thus introduced by Shakespeare in the following dialogue (i. 1), where the Countess of Rousillon is represented as inquiring:

" What hope is there of his majesty's amendment?

Laf. He hath abandoned his physicians, madam; under whose practices he hath persecuted time with hope; and finds no other advantage in the process but only the losing of hope by time.

Count. This young gentlewoman had a father—O, that ' had!' how sad a passage 'tis!—whose skill was almost as great as his honesty; had it stretched so far, would have made nature immortal, and death should have play for lack of work. Would, for the king's sake, he were living! I think it would be the death of the king's disease.

Laf. How called you the man you speak of, madam?

Count. He was famous, sir, in his profession, and it was his great right to be so; Gerard de Narbon.

Laf. He was excellent, indeed, madam; the king very lately spoke of him admiringly and mourningly; he was skilful enough to have lived still, if knowledge could be set up against mortality.

Ber. What is it, my good lord, the king languishes of?

Laf. A fistula, my lord."

The account given of Helena's secret remedy and the king's reason for rejecting it give, says Dr. Bucknill, an excellent idea of the state of opinion with regard to the practice of physic in Shakespeare's time."

Fit. Formerly the term " rapture " was synonymous with

---

[1] Dr. Bucknill's " Medical Knowledge of Shakespeare," p. 95.

[2] Singer's " Shakespeare," vol. iii. p. 225.

a fit or trance. The word is used by Brutus in "Coriolanus" (ii. 1):

> "your prattling nurse
> Into a rapture lets her baby cry
> While she chats him."

Steevens quotes from the "Hospital for London's Follies" (1602), where Gossip Luce says: "Your darling will weep itself into a rapture, if you take not good heed."[1]

Gold. It was a long-prevailing opinion that a solution of gold had great medicinal virtues, and that the incorruptibility of the metal might be communicated to a body impregnated with it. Thus, in "2 Henry IV." (iv. 4), Prince Henry, in the course of his address to his father, says:

> "Coming to look on you, thinking you dead,
> And dead almost, my liege, to think you were,
> I spake unto this crown, as having sense,
> And thus upbraided it: 'The care on thee depending
> Hath fed upon the body of my father;
> Therefore, thou, best of gold, art worst of gold;
> Other, less fine in carat, is more precious,
> Preserving life in medicine potable.'"

Potable gold was one of the panaceas of ancient quacks. In John Wight's translation of the "Secretes of Alexis" is a receipt "to dissolve and reducte golde into a potable licour, which conserveth the youth and healthe of a man, and will heale every disease that is thought incurable, in the space of seven daies at the furthest." The receipt, however, is a highly complicated one, the gold being acted upon by juice of lemons, honey, common salt, and *aqua vitæ*, and distillation frequently repeated from a "urinall of glass"—as the oftener it is distilled the better it is. "Thus doyng," it is said, "ye shall have a right naturall, and perfecte potable golde, whereof somewhat taken alone every monthe once or twice, or at least with the said licour, whereof we have spoken in the second chapter of this boke, is very excellent to preserve a man's youthe and healthe, and to heale in a

---

[1] See Singer's "Shakespeare," vol. vii. p. 347.

fewe daies any disease rooted in a man, and thought incurable. The said golde will also be good and profitable for diverse other operations and effectes: as good wittes and diligent searchers of the secretes of nature may easily judge." A further allusion to gold as a medicine is probably made in " All's Well that Ends Well " (v. 3), where the King says to Bertram:

> " Plutus himself,
> That knows the tinct and multiplying medicine,
> Hath not in nature's mystery more science,
> Than I have in this ring."

Chaucer, too, in his sarcastic excuse for the doctor's avarice, refers to this old belief:

> " And yet he was but esy of despence:
> He kept that he wan in the pestilence.
> For gold in physic is a cordial;
> Therefore he loved it in special."

Once more, in Sir Kenelm Digby's " Receipts " (1674), we are told that the gold is to be calcined with three salts, ground with sulphur, burned in a reverberatory furnace with sulphur twelve times, then digested with spirit of wine " which will be tincted very yellow, of which, few drops for a dose in a fit vehicle hath wrought great effects." The term " grand liquor " is also used by Shakespeare for the *aurum potabile* of the alchemist, as in " Tempest " (v. 1):

> " Where should they
> Find this grand liquor that hath gilded them ?"

Good Year. This is evidently a corruption of *goujère*, a disease derived from the French *gouge*, a common camp-follower, and probably alludes to the *Morbus Gallicus*. Thus, in " King Lear " (v. 3), we read:

> " The good-years shall devour them, flesh and fell,
> Ere they shall make us weep."

With the corruption, however, of the spelling, the word lost in time its real meaning, and it is, consequently, found in passages where a sense opposite to the true one is intended.[1] It was often used in exclamations, as in "Merry Wives of Windsor" (i. 4): "We must give folks leave to prate: what, the good-jear!" In "Troilus and Cressida" (v. 1), Thersites, by the "rotten diseases of the south," probably meant the *Morbus Gallicus*.

Handkerchief. It was formerly a common practice in England for those who were sick to wear a kerchief on their heads, and still continues at the present day among the common people in many places. Thus, in "Julius Cæsar" (ii. 1), we find the following allusion:

> "O, what a time have you chose out, brave Caius,
> To wear a kerchief! Would you were not sick!"

"If," says Fuller, "this county [Cheshire] hath bred no writers in that faculty [physic], the wonder is the less, if it be true what I read, that if any here be sick, they make him a posset and tye a kerchief on his head, and if that will not mend him, then God be merciful to him."[2]

Hysteria. This disorder, which, in Shakespeare's day, we are told, was known as "the mother," or *Hysterica passio*, was not considered peculiar to women only. It is probable that, when the poet wrote the following lines in "King Lear" (ii. 4), where he makes the king say,

> "O, how this mother swells up toward my heart!
> *Hysterica passio!* down, thou climbing sorrow,
> Thy element's below!—Where is this daughter?"

he had in view the subjoined passages from Harsnet's "Declaration of Popish Impostures" (1603), a work which, it has been suggested,[3] "he may have consulted in order to furnish out his character of Tom of Bedlam with demoniacal gibberish." The first occurs at p. 25: "Ma. Maynie had a spice of the *hysterica passio*, as it seems, from his youth; hee

---

[1] Wright's "Notes to King Lear" (1877), p. 196.
[2] "Worthies of England" (1662), p. 180.
[3] Singer's "Shakespeare," pp. 384, 385; Wright's "Notes to King Lear," pp. 154, 155.

himselfe termes it the moother (as you may see in his con-
fessione)." Master Richard Mainy, who was persuaded by
the priests that he was possessed of the devil, deposes as
follows (p. 263): " The disease I speake of was a spice of the
mother, wherewith I had been troubled (as is before mentioned) before my going into Fraunce. Whether I doe rightly terme it the *mother* or no I know not." Dr. Jordan, in
1603, published " A Briefe Discourse of a Disease called the
Suffocation of the Mother."

Infection. According to an old but erroneous belief, infection communicated to another left the infector free; in
allusion to which Timon (" Timon of Athens,"iv. 3) says:

> " I will not kiss thee; then the rot returns
> To thine own lips again."

Among other notions prevalent in days gone by was the
general contagiousness of disease, to which an allusion seems
to be made in " A Midsummer-Night's Dream " (i. 1), where
Helena says:

> "Sickness is catching: O, were favour so,
> Yours would I catch, fair Hermia, ere I go."

Malone considers that Shakespeare, in the following passage in "Venus and Adonis," alludes to a practice of his day,
when it was customary, in time of the plague, to strew the
rooms of every house with rue and other strong-smelling
herbs, to prevent infection:

> " Long may they kiss each other, for this cure!
> O, never let their crimson liveries wear!
> And as they last, their verdure still endure,
> To drive infection from the dangerous year!"

Again, the contagiousness of pestilence is thus alluded to by
Beatrice in " Much Ado About Nothing " (i. 1): " O Lord, he
will hang upon him like a disease: he is sooner caught than
the pestilence, and the taker runs presently mad." The belief, too, that the poison of pestilence dwells in the air, is
spoken of in " Timon of Athens " (iv. 3):

> "When Jove
> Will o'er some high-viced city hang his poison
> In the sick air."

And, again, in " Richard II." (i. 3):

> "Devouring pestilence hangs in our air."

It is alluded to, also, in " Twelfth Night " (i. 1), where the Duke says:

> " O, when mine eyes did see Olivia first,
> Methought she purged the air of pestilence."

While on this subject, we may quote the following dialogue from the same play (ii. 3), which, as Dr. Bucknill[1] remarks, " involves the idea that contagion is bound up with something appealing to the sense of smell, a mellifluous voice being miscalled contagious; unless one could apply one organ to the functions of another, and thus admit contagion, not through its usual portal, the nose:"

> " *Sir Andrew.* A mellifluous voice, as I am true knight.
> *Sir Toby.* A contagious breath.
> *Sir Andrew.* Very sweet and contagious, i' faith.
> *Sir Toby.* To hear by the nose, it is dulcet in contagion."

Insanity. That is a common idea that the symptoms of madness are increased by the full moon. Shakespeare mentions this popular fallacy in " Othello " (v. 2), where he tells us that the moon makes men insane when she comes nearer the earth than she was wont.[2]

Music as a cure for madness is, perhaps, referred to in " King Lear" (iv. 7), where the physician of the king says: " Louder the music there."[3] Mr. Singer, however, has this note: "Shakespeare considered soft music favorable to sleep. Lear, we may suppose, had been thus composed to rest; and now the physician desires louder music to be played, for the purpose of waking him."

---

[1] " Medical Knowledge of Shakespeare," p. 121.

[2] See p. 73.

[3] Halliwell-Phillipps's " Handbook Index to Shakespeare" (1866), p. 333.

So, in " Richard II." (v. 5), the king says:

> " This music mads me ; let it sound no more ;
> For though it have holp madmen to their wits,
> In me, it seems, it will make wise men mad."

The power of music as a medical agency has been recognized from the earliest times, and in mental cases has often been highly efficacious.[1] Referring to music as inducing sleep, we may quote the touching passage in " 2 Henry IV." (iv. 5), where the king says :

> " Let there be no noise made, my gentle friends ;
> Unless some dull and favourable hand
> Will whisper music to my weary spirit.
> *Warwick.* Call for the music in the other room."

Ariel, in " The Tempest " (ii. 1), enters playing *solemn music* to produce this effect.

A mad-house seems formerly to have been designated a " dark house." Hence, in " Twelfth Night " (iii. 4), the reason for putting Malvolio into a dark room was, to make him believe that he was mad. In the following act (iv. 2) he says : " Good Sir Topas, do not think I am mad ; they have laid me here in hideous darkness ;" and further on (v. 1) he asks, ·

> " Why have you suffer'd me to be imprison'd,
> Kept in a dark house ?"

In " As You Like It " (iii. 2), Rosalind says that " Love is merely a madness, and . . . deserves as well a dark-house and a whip as madmen do."

The expression " horn-mad," *i. e.*, quite mad, occurs in the " Comedy of Errors " (ii. 1) : " Why, mistress, sure my master is horn-mad." And, again, in " Merry Wives of Windsor " (i. 4), Mistress Quickly says, " If he had found the young man, he would have been horn-mad."

Madness in cattle was supposed to arise from a distemper

---

[1] " A Book of Musical Anecdote," by F. Crowest (1878), vol. ii. pp. 251, 252.

in the internal substance of their horns, and furious or mad cattle had their horns bound with straw.

King's Evil. This was a common name in years gone by for scrofula, because the sovereigns of England were supposed to possess the power of curing it, "without other medicine, save only by handling and prayer." This custom of "touching for the king's evil" is alluded to in "Macbeth" (iv. 3), where the following dialogue is introduced:

> "*Malcolm.*   Comes the king forth, I pray you?
> *Doctor.* Ay, sir; there are a crew of wretched souls
> That stay his cure; their malady convinces
> The great assay of art; but, at his touch—
> Such sanctity hath heaven given his hand——
> They presently amend.
> *Malcolm.*   I thank you, doctor.
> *Macduff.* What's the disease he means?
> *Malcolm.*   'Tis call'd the evil:
> A most miraculous work in this good king;
> Which often, since my here-remain in England,
> I have seen him do. How he solicits heaven,
> Himself best knows: but strangely-visited people,
> All swoln and ulcerous, pitiful to the eye,
> The mere despair of surgery, he cures;
> Hanging a golden stamp about their necks,
> Put on with holy prayers: and 'tis spoken,
> To the succeeding royalty he leaves
> The healing benediction. With this strange virtue
> He hath a heavenly gift of prophecy;
> And sundry blessings hang about his throne,
> That speak him full of grace."

This reference, which has nothing to do with the progress of the drama, is introduced, obviously, in compliment to King James, who fancied himself endowed with the Confessor's powers.[1] The poet found authority for the passage in Holinshed (vol. i. p. 279): "As hath bin thought, he was enspired with the gift of prophecie, and also to haue hadde the gift of healing infirmities and diseases. Namely,

---

[1] See Beckett's "Free and Impartial Enquiry into the Antiquity and Efficacy of Touching for the King's Evil," 1722.

he vsed to help those that were vexed with the disease, commonly called the kyngs euill, and left that vertue as it were a portion of inheritance vnto his successors the kyngs of this realme." Edward's miraculous powers were believed in, we are told, by his contemporaries, or at least soon after his death, and were expressly recognized by Pope Alexander III., who canonized him. In Plot's "Oxfordshire" (chap. x. sec. 125) there is an account, accompanied with a drawing, of the touch-piece supposed to have been given by this monarch. James I.'s practice of touching for the evil is frequently mentioned in Nichols's "Progresses." Charles I., when at York, touched seventy persons in one day. Indeed, few are aware to what an extent this superstition once prevailed. In the course of twenty years, between 1660 and 1682, no less than 92,107 persons were touched for this disease. The first English monarch who refused to touch for the king's evil was William III., but the practice was resumed by Queen Anne, who officially announced, in the *London Gazette*, March 12, 1712, her royal intention to receive patients afflicted with the malady in question. It was probably about that time that Johnson was touched by her majesty, upon the recommendation of the celebrated physician Sir John Floyer, of Lichfield. King George I. put an end to this practice, which is said to have originated with Edward the Confessor, in 1058.[1] The custom was also observed by French kings; and on Easter Sunday, 1686, Louis XIV. is said to have touched 1600 persons.

Lethargy. This is frequently confounded by medical men of former times, and by Shakespeare himself, with apoplexy. The term occurs in the list of diseases quoted by Thersites in "Troilus and Cressida" (v. 1).[2]

Leprosy. This was, in years gone by, used to denote the *lues venerea*, as in "Antony and Cleopatra" (iii. 8):

---

[1] See "Notes and Queries," 1861, 2d series, vol. xi. p. 71; Burns's "History of Parish Registers," 1862, pp. 179, 180; Pettigrew's "Superstitions Connected with Medicine and Surgery," 1844, pp. 117–154.

[2] Bucknill's "Medical Knowledge of Shakespeare," p. 235.

> " Yon ribaudred nag of Egypt,—
> Whom leprosy o'ertake !
> *   *   *   *
> Hoists sails and flies."

Leech. The old medical term for a leech is a "blood-sucker," and a knot would be an appropriate term for a number of clustering leeches. So, in " Richard III." (iii. 3), Grey, being led to the block, says of Richard's minions :

> "A knot you are of damned blood-suckers."

In " 2 Henry VI." (iii. 2) mention is made by Warwick of the " blood-sucker of sleeping men," which, says Dr. Bucknill, appears to mean the vampire-bat.

Measles. This word originally signified leprosy, although in modern times used for a very different disorder. Its derivation is the old French word *meseau,* or *mesel,* a leper. Thus, Cotgrave has " Meseau, a meselled, scurvy, leaporous, lazarous person." Distempered or scurvied hogs are still said to be measled. It is in this sense that it is used in " Coriolanus " (iii. 1) :

> " As for my country I have shed my blood,
>   Not fearing outward force, so shall my lungs
>   Coin words till their decay, against those measles,
>   Which we disdain should tetter us, yet sought
>   The very way to catch them."

Pleurisy. This denotes a plethora, or redundancy of blood, and was so used, probably, from an erroneous idea that the word was derived from *plus pluris.* It is employed by Shakespeare in " Hamlet " (iv. 7) :

> " For goodness, growing to a plurisy,
>   Dies in his own too-much."

In the " Two Noble Kinsmen " (v. 1) there is a similar phrase :

> "that heal'st with blood
>   The earth when it is sick, and cur'st the world
>   O' the plurisy of people.

The word is frequently used by writers contemporary with Shakespeare. Thus, for instance, Massinger, in " The Picture " (iv. 2), says :

> " A plurisy of ill blood you must let out
> By labour."

Mummy. This was a preparation for magical purposes, made from dead bodies, and was used as a medicine both long before and long after Shakespeare's day. Its virtues seem to have been chiefly imaginary, and even the traffic in it fraudulent.[1] The preparation of mummy is said to have been first brought into use in medicine by a Jewish physician, who wrote that flesh thus embalmed was good for the cure of divers diseases, and particularly bruises, to prevent the blood's gathering and coagulating. It has, however, long been known that no use whatever can be derived from it in medicine, and " that all which is sold in the shops, whether brought from Venice or Lyons, or even directly from the Levant by Alexandria, is factitious, the work of certain Jews, who counterfeit it by drying carcasses in ovens, after having prepared them with powder of myrrh, caballine aloes, Jewish pitch, and other coarse or unwholesome drugs."[2] Shakespeare speaks of this preparation. Thus Othello (iii. 4), referring to the handkerchief which he had given to Desdemona, relates how:

> " it was dyed in mummy which the skilful
> Conserv'd of maidens' hearts."

And, in " Macbeth " (iv. 1), the " witches' mummy " forms one of the ingredients of the boiling caldron. Webster, in " The White Devil " (1857, p. 5), speaks of it:

> " Your followers
> Have swallow'd you like mummia, and, being sick,
> With such unnatural and horrid physic,
> Vomit you up i' the kennel."

Sir Thomas Browne, in his interesting " Fragment on Mummies," tells us that Francis I. always carried mummy[3] with

---

[1] See Pettigrew's " History of Mummies," 1834; also Gannal, " Traité d'Embaumement," 1838.

[2] Rees's " Encyclopædia," 1829, vol. xxiv.

[3] Mr. Halliwell-Phillipps, in his " Handbook Index to Shakespeare," 1866, p. 332, calls it a balsamic liquid.

him as a panacea against all disorders. Some used it for epilepsy, some for gout, some used it as a styptic. He further adds: "The common opinion of the virtues of mummy bred great consumption thereof, and princes and great men contended for this strange panacea, wherein Jews dealt largely, manufacturing mummies from dead carcasses, and giving them the names of kings, while specifics were compounded from crosses and gibbets leavings."

Nightmare. There are various charms practised, in this and other countries, for the prevention of nightmare, many of which are exceedingly quaint. In days gone by it appears that St. Vitalis, whose name has been corrupted into St. Withold, was invoked; and, by way of illustration, Theobald quotes from the old play of "King John"[1] the following:

"Sweet S. Withold, of thy lenitie, defend us from extremitie."

Shakespeare, alluding to the nightmare, in his "King Lear" (iii. 4), refers to the same saint, and gives us a curious old charm:

"Saint Withold footed thrice the old [wold];
He met the night-mare, and her nine-fold;
Bid her alight
And her troth plight,
And, aroint thee, witch, aroint thee!"

For what purpose, as Mr. Singer[2] has pointed out, the incubus is enjoined to "plight her troth," will appear from a charm against the nightmare, in Reginald Scot's "Discovery of Witchcraft," which occurs, with slight variation, in Fletcher's "Monsieur Thomas" (iv. 6):

"St. George, St. George, our lady's knight,
He walks by day, so does he by night,
And when he had her found,
He her beat and her bound,
Until to him her troth she plight,
She would not stir from him that night."

[1] "Six Old Plays," ed. Nichols, p. 256, quoted by Mr. Aldis Wright, in his "Notes to King Lear," 1877, p. 170.
[2] "Shakespeare," vol. ix. p. 413.

Paralysis. An old term for chronic paralysis was "cold palsies," which is used by Thersites in "Troilus and Cressida" (v. 1).[1]

Philosopher's Stone. This was supposed, by its touch, to convert base metal into gold. It is noticed by Shakespeare in "Antony and Cleopatra" (i. 5):

> "*Alexas.* Sovereign of Egypt, hail!
>   *Cleopatra.* How much unlike art thou Mark Antony!
> Yet, coming from him, that great medicine hath
> With his tinct gilded thee."

The alchemists call the matter, whatever it may be, says Johnson, by which they perform transmutation, a medicine. Thus, Chapman, in his "Shadow of Night" (1594): "O, then, thou *great elixir* of all treasures;" on which passage he has the following note: "The philosopher's stone, or *philosophica medicina*, is called the *great elixir*." Another reference occurs in "Timon of Athens" (ii. 2), where the Fool, in reply to the question of Varro's Servant, "What is a whoremaster, fool?" answers, "A fool in good clothes, and something like thee. 'Tis a spirit: sometime 't appears like a lord; sometime like a lawyer; sometime like a philosopher, with two stones moe than's artificial one," etc.; a passage which Johnson explains as meaning "more than the philosopher's stone," or twice the value of a philosopher's stone; though, as Farmer observes, "Gower has a chapter, in his 'Confessio Amantis,' of the three stones that philosophers made." Singer,[2] in his note on the philosopher's stone, says that Sir Thomas Smith was one of those who lost considerable sums in seeking of it. Sir Richard Steele was one of the last eminent men who entertained hopes of being successful in this pursuit. His laboratory was at Poplar.[3]

Pimple. In the Midland Counties, a common name for a pimple, which, by rubbing, is made to smart, or *rubbed to*

---

[1] Bucknill's "Medical Knowledge of Shakespeare," p. 235.

[2] "Shakespeare," 1875, vol. iii. p. 284.

[3] See Pettigrew's "Medical Superstitions," pp. 13, 14.

sense, is "a quat." The word occurs in "Othello" (v. 1), where Roderigo is so called by Iago:

> "I have rubb'd this young quat almost to the sense,
> And he grows angry."

—Roderigo being called a quat by the same mode of speech as a low fellow is now called a *scab*. It occurs in Langham's "Garden of Health," p. 153: "The leaves [of coleworts] laid to by themselves, or bruised with barley meale, are good for the inflammations, and soft swellings, burnings, impostumes, and cholerick sores or quats," etc.

Plague. "Tokens," or "God's tokens," were the terms for those spots on the body which denoted the infection of the plague. In "Love's Labour's Lost" (v. 2), Biron says:

> "For the Lord's tokens on you do I see;"

and in "Antony and Cleopatra" (iii. 10) there is another allusion:

> "*Enobarbus.*　　　　　How appears the fight?
> *Scarus.* On our side like the token'd pestilence,
> Where death is sure."

In "Troilus and Cressida" (ii. 3), Ulysses says of Achilles:

> "He is so plaguy proud that the death tokens of it
> Cry—'No recovery.'"

King Lear, too, it would seem, compares Goneril (ii. 4) to these fatal signs, when he calls her "a plague sore." When the *tokens* had appeared on any of the inhabitants, the house was shut up, and "Lord have mercy upon us" written or printed upon the door. Hence Biron, in "Love's Labour's Lost" (v. 2), says:

> "Write, 'Lord have mercy on us,' on those three;
> They are infected, in their hearts it lies;
> They have the plague, and caught it of your eyes."

The "red pestilence," referred to by Volumnia in "Coriolanus" (iv. 1), probably alludes to the cutaneous eruptions common in the plague:

> " Now the red pestilence strike all trades in Rome,
> And occupations perish !"

In " The Tempest " (i. 2), Caliban says to Prospero, " The red plague rid you."

Poison. According to a vulgar error prevalent in days gone by, poison was supposed to swell the body, an allusion to which occurs in " Julius Cæsar " (iv. 3), where, in the quarrel between Brutus and Cassius, the former declares :

> " You shall digest the venom of your spleen,
> Though it do split you."

We may also compare the following passage in " 2 Henry IV." (iv. 4), where the king says :

> " Learn this, Thomas,
> And thou shalt prove a shelter to thy friends ;
> A hoop of gold to bind thy brothers in,
> That the united vessel of their blood,
> Mingled with venom of suggestion—
> As, force perforce, the age will pour it in—
> Shall never leak, though it do work as strong
> As aconitum, or rash gunpowder."

In " King John," Hubert, when describing the effect of the poison upon the monk (v. 6), narrates how his " bowels suddenly burst out." This passage also contains a reference to the popular custom prevalent in the olden days, of great persons having their food tasted by those who were supposed to have made themselves acquainted with its wholesomeness. This practice, however, could not always afford security when the taster was ready to sacrifice his own life, as in the present case : [1]

> " *Hubert.* The king, I fear, is poison'd by a monk :
> I left him almost speechless. . . .
> *Bastard.* How did he take it ? who did taste to him ?
> *Hubert.* A monk, I tell you ; a resolved villain."

The natives of Africa have been supposed to be possessed of the secret how to temper poisons with such art as not

---

[1] Bucknill's " Medical Knowledge of Shakespeare," p. 136.

to operate till several years after they were administered. Their drugs were then as certain in their effect as subtle in their preparation.[1] Thus, in " The Tempest " (iii. 3), Gonzalo says:

> " All three of them are desperate : their great guilt,
> Like poison given to work a great time after,
> Now 'gins to bite the spirits."

The belief in slow poisoning was general in bygone times, although no better founded on fact, remarks Dr. Bucknill,[2] than the notion that persons burst with poison, or that narcotics could, like an alarum clock, be set for a certain number of hours.   So, in " Cymbeline " (v. 5), Cornelius relates to the king the queen's confession:

> " She did confess, she had
> For you a mortal mineral; which, being took,
> Should by the minute feed on life, and, lingering,
> By inches waste you."

Pomander.   This was either a composition of various perfumes wrought in the shape of a ball or other form, and worn in the pocket or hung about the neck, and even sometimes suspended to the wrist; or a case for containing such a mixture of perfumes.   It was used as an amulet against the plague or other infections, as well as for an article of luxury. There is an allusion to its use in the "Winter's Tale" (iv. 3), by Autolycus, who enumerates it among all his trumpery that he had sold.   The following recipe for making a pomander we find in an old play:[3] " Your only way to make a pomander is this: take an ounce of the purest garden mould, cleans'd and steep'd seven days in change of motherless rose-water.   Then take the best labdanum, benjoin, with storaxes, ambergris, civet, and musk.   Incorporate them together, and work them into what form you please.   This, if your breath be not too valiant, will make you smell as sweet as any lady's dog."

---

[1] Singer's " Shakespeare," vol. i. p. 65.
[2] " Medical Knowledge of Shakespeare," p. 226.
[3] Quoted in Nares's " Glossary," vol. ii. p. 671.

Rheumatism. In Shakespeare's day this was used in a far wider sense than nowadays, including, in addition to what is now understood by the term, distillations from the head, catarrhs, etc. Malone quotes from the "Sidney Memorials" (vol. i. p. 94), where the health of Sir Henry Sidney is described: "He hath verie much distempored divers parts of his bodie; as namelie, his heade, his stomack, &c., and thereby is always subject to distillacions, coughes, and other rumatick diseases." Among the many superstitions relating to the moon,[1] one is mentioned in "A Midsummer-Night's Dream" (ii. 1), where Titania tells how the moon,

> "Pale in her anger, washes all the air,
> That rheumatic diseases do abound."

The word "rheumatic" was also formerly used in the sense of choleric or peevish, as in "2 Henry IV." (ii. 4), where the Hostess says: "You two never meet but you fall to some discord: you are both, in good troth, as rheumatic as two dry toasts." Again, in "Henry V." (ii. 3), the Hostess says of Falstaff: "A' did in some sort, indeed, handle women; but then he was rheumatic,[2] and talked of the whore of Babylon."

Serpigo. This appears to have been a term extensively used by old medical authors for any creeping skin disease, being especially applied to that known as the *herpes circinatus.* The expression occurs in "Measure for Measure" (iii. 1), being coupled by the Duke with "the gout" and the "rheum." In "Troilus and Cressida" (ii. 3), Thersites says: "Now, the dry serpigo on the subject."

Sickness. Sickness of stomach, which the slightest disgust is apt to provoke, is still expressed by the term "queasy;" hence the word denoted *delicate, unsettled;* as in "King Lear" (ii. 1), where it is used by Edmund:

> "I have one thing, of a queasy question,
> Which I must act."

---

[1] See p. 74.

[2] Malone suggests that the hostess may mean "then he was lunatic."

So Ben Jonson employs it in " Sejanus" (i. 1):

> " These times are rather queasy to be touched."

Sigh. It was a prevalent notion that sighs impair the strength and wear out the animal powers. Thus, in " 2 Henry VI." (iii. 2), Queen Margaret speaks of "blood-drinking sighs." We may, too, compare the words of Oberon in "A Midsummer-Night's Dream " (iii. 2), who refers to " sighs of love, that cost the fresh blood dear." In " 3 Henry VI." (iv. 4), Queen Elizabeth says :

> "for this I draw in many a tear,
> And stop the rising of blood-sucking sighs."

Once more, in " Hamlet " (iv. 7), the King mentions the " spendthrift sigh, that hurts by easing." Fenton, in his " Tragical Discourses" (1579), alludes to this notion in the following words : " Your scorching sighes that have already drayned your body of his wholesome humoures."

It was also an ancient belief that sorrow consumed the blood and shortened life. Hence Romeo tells Juliet (iii. 5):

> "And trust me, love, in my eye so do you :
> Dry sorrow drinks our blood."

Small-pox. Such a terrible plague was this disease in the days of our ancestors, that its name was used as an imprecation. Thus, in " Love's Labour's Lost " (v. 2), the Princess says : " A pox of that jest."

Saliva. The color of the spittle was, with the medical men of olden times, an important point of diagnosis. Thus, in " 2 Henry IV." (i. 2), Falstaff exclaims against fighting on a hot day, and wishes he may "never spit white again," should it so happen.[1]

Sterility. The charm against sterility referred to by Cæsar in " Julius Cæsar" (i. 2) is copied from Plutarch, who, in his description of the festival Lupercalia, tells us how "noble young men run naked through the city, striking in sport

---

[1] Bucknill's " Medical Knowledge of Shakespeare," p. 150.

whom they meet in the way with leather thongs," which blows were commonly believed to have the wonderful effect attributed to them by Cæsar:

> " The barren, touched in this holy chase,
>   Shake off their sterile curse."

Suicide.   Cominius, in " Coriolanus " (i. 9), arguing against Marcius's overstrained modesty, refers to the manner in which suicide was thought preventable in olden times:

> " If 'gainst yourself you be incens'd, we'll put you,
>   Like one that means his proper harm, in manacles,
>   Then reason safely with you."

Toothache.   It was formerly a common superstition—and one, too, not confined to our own country—that toothache was caused by a little worm, having the form of an eel, which gradually gnawed a hole in the tooth.   In " Much Ado About Nothing " (iii. 2), Shakespeare speaks of this curious belief:

> " *Don Pedro.* What! sigh for the toothache?
>   *Leonato.* Where is but a humour, or a worm."

This notion was, some years ago, prevalent in Derbyshire,[1] where there was an odd way of extracting, as it was thought, the worm.   A small quantity of a mixture, consisting of dry and powdered herbs, was placed in some small vessel, into which a live coal from the fire was dropped.   The patient then held his or her open mouth over the vessel, and inhaled the smoke as long as it could be borne.   The cup was then taken away, and in its place a glass of water was put before the patient.   Into this glass the person breathed hard for a few moments, when it was supposed the grub or worm could be seen in the water.   In Orkney, too, toothache goes by the name of " the worm," and, as a remedy, the following charm, called " wormy lines," is written on a piece of paper, and worn as an amulet, by the person affected, in some part of his dress:

---

[1] See " English Folk-Lore," p. 156.

> " Peter sat on a marble stone weeping;
>   Christ came past, and said, ' What aileth thee, Peter?'
>   ' O my Lord, my God, my tooth doth ache.'
>   ' Arise, O Peter! go thy way; thy tooth shall ache no more.' "

This notion is still current in Germany, and is mentioned by Thorpe, in his "Northern Mythology" (vol. iii. p. 167), who quotes a North German incantation, beginning,

> " Pear tree, I complain to thee;
>   Three worms sting me."

It is found, too, even in China and New Zealand,[1] the following charm being used in the latter country:

> " An eel, a spiny back
>   True indeed, indeed: true in sooth, in sooth.
>   You must eat the head
>   Of said spiny back."

A writer in the *Athenæum* (Jan. 28, 1860), speaking of the Rev. R. H. Cobbold's "Pictures of the Chinese, Drawn by Themselves," says: "The first portrait is that of a quack doctress, who pretends to cure toothache by extracting a maggot—the cause of the disorder. This is done—or, rather, pretended to be done—by simply placing a bright steel pin on the part affected, and tapping the pin with a piece of wood. Mr. Cobbold compares the operation to procuring worms for fishing by working a spade backwards and forwards in the ground. He and a friend submitted to the process, but in a very short time compelled the doctress to desist, by the excessive precautions they took against imposition." We may further note that John of Gatisden, one of the oldest medical authors, attributes decay of the teeth to "a humour or a worm." In his "Rosa Anglica"[2] he says: "Si vermes sint in dentibus, ℞ semen porri, seu lusquiami contere et misce cum cera, pone super carbones, et fumus recipiatur per embotum, quoniam sanat. Solum etiam semen lusquiami valet coctum in aqua calida, supra

---

[1] See Shortland's "Traditions and Superstitions of the New-Zealanders," 1856, p. 131.

[2] Liber Secundus—"De Febribus," p. 923, ed. 1595.

quam aquam patiens palatum apertum si tenuerit, cadent
vermes evidenter vel in illam aquam, vel in aliam quæ ibi
fuerit ibi posita.   De myrrha et aloe ponantur in dentem,
ubi est vermis : semen caulis, et absinthium, per se vermes
interficit."

Tub-fast.   In years past "the discipline of sweating in a
heated tub for a considerable time, accompanied with strict
abstinence, was thought necessary for the cure of venereal
taint."[1]   Thus, in "Timon of Athens" (iv. 3), Timon says
to Timandra :

> " Be a whore still ! they love thee not that use thee ;
> Give them diseases, leaving with thee their lust.
> Make use of thy salt hours : season the slaves
> For tubs and baths : bring down rose-cheeked youth
> To the tub-fast, and the diet."

As beef, too, was usually salted down in a tub, the one
process was jocularly compared to the other.   So, in "Measure for Measure" (iii. 2), Pompey, when asked by Lucio
about his mistress, replies, "Troth, sir, she hath eaten up
all her beef, and she is herself in the tub."   Again, in "Henry V." (ii. 1), Pistol speaks of "the powdering-tub of infamy."

Vinegar.   In Shakespeare's day this seems to have been
termed " eisel " (from A. S. *aisel*), being esteemed highly
efficacious in preventing the communication of the plague
and other contagious diseases.   In this sense it has been
used by Shakespeare in Sonnet cxi. :

> "like a willing patient, I will drink
> Potions of eisel, 'gainst my strong infection."

In a MS. Herbal in the library of Trinity College, Cambridge, occurs "acetorum, an[ce] vynegre or aysel."   The
word occurs again in "Hamlet" (v. 1), where Laertes is
challenged by Hamlet :

> "Woo't drink up eisel ? eat a crocodile ?"

The word woo't, in the northern counties, is the common
contraction of *wouldst thou*, which is the reading of the old

---

[1] Nares's " Glossary," vol. ii. p. 906.

copies. In former years it was the fashion with gallants to do some extravagant feat, as a proof of their love, in honor of their mistresses, and, among others, the swallowing of some nauseous potion was one of the most frequent. Hence, in the above passage, some bitter potion is evidently meant, which it was a penance to drink. Some are of opinion that *wormwood* is alluded to; and Mr. Singer thinks it probable that "the propoma called absinthites, a nauseously bitter medicament then much in use, may have been in the poet's mind, to drink up a quantity of which would be an extreme pass of amorous demonstration." It has been suggested by a correspondent of "Notes and Queries,"[1] that the reference in this passage from "Hamlet" is to a Lake Esyl, which figures in Scandinavian legends. Messrs. Wright and Clark, however, in their "Notes to Hamlet" (1876, p. 218), say that they have consulted Mr. Magnusson on this point, and he writes as follows: "No such lake as Esyl is known to Norse mythology and folk-lore." Steevens supposes it to be the river Yssell.[2]

Water-casting. The fanciful notion of recognizing diseases by the mere inspection of the urine was denounced years ago, by an old statute of the College of Physicians, as belonging to tricksters and impostors, and any member of the college was forbidden to give advice by this so-called "water-casting" without he also saw the patient. The statute of the college runs as follows: "Statuimus, et ordinamus, ut nemo, sive socius, sive candidatus, sive permissus consilii quidquam impertiat veteratoriis, et impostoribus, super urinarum nuda inspectione, nisi simul ad ægrum vocetur, ut ibidem, pro re natû, idonea medicamenta ab honesto aliquo pharmacopoea componenda præscribat." An allusion to this vulgar error occurs in the "Two Gentlemen of Verona" (ii. 1), where, after Speed has given to Valentine his amusing description of a lover, in which, among other signs, are "to walk alone, like one that had the pestilence,"

---

[1] See 4th series, vol. x. pp. 108, 150, 229, 282, 356.
[2] See Dyce's "Shakespeare," vol. vii. p. 239.

and "to fast, like one that takes diet," the following quibble takes place upon the within and the without of the symptoms:

> "*Valentine.* Are all these things perceived in me?
>
> *Speed.* They are all perceived without ye.
>
> *Valentine.* Without me? they cannot.
>
> *Speed.* Without you? nay, that's certain; for, without you were so simple, none else would: but you are so without these follies, that these follies are within you, and shine through you like the water in an urinal, that not an eye that sees you but is a physician to comment on your malady."

This singular pretence, says Dr. Bucknill,[1] is "alleged to have arisen, like the barber surgery, from the ecclesiastical interdicts upon the medical vocations of the clergy. Priests and monks, being unable to visit their former patients, are said first to have resorted to the expedient of divining the malady, and directing the treatment upon simple inspection of the urine. However this may be, the practice is of very ancient date." Numerous references to this piece of medical quackery occur in many of our old writers, most of whom condemn it in very strong terms. Thus Forestus, in his "Medical Politics," speaks of it as being, in his opinion, a practice altogether evil, and expresses an earnest desire that medical men would combine to repress it. Shakespeare gives a further allusion to it in the passage where he makes Macbeth (v. 3) say:

> "If thou couldst, doctor, cast
> The water of my land, find her disease,
> And purge it to a sound and pristine health,
> I would applaud thee to the very echo."

And in "2 Henry IV" (i. 2) Falstaff asks the page, "What says the doctor to my water?" and, once more, in "Twelfth Night" (iii. 4), Fabian, alluding to Malvolio, says, "Carry his water to the wise woman."

---

[1] "The Medical Knowledge of Shakespeare," 1860, pp. 1–64.

It seems probable, too, that, in the "Merry Wives of Windsor" (ii. 3), the term "mock-water," employed by the host to the French Dr. Caius, refers to the mockery of judging of diseases by the water or urine—"mock-water," in this passage, being equivalent to "you pretending water-doctor!"

CHAPTER XI.

CUSTOMS CONNECTED WITH THE CALENDAR.

In years gone by the anniversaries connected with the calendar were kept up with an amount of enthusiasm and merry-making quite unknown at the present day. Thus, for instance, Shakespeare tells us, with regard to the May-day observance, that it was looked forward to so eagerly as to render it impossible to make the people sleep on this festive occasion. During the present century the popular celebrations of the festivals have been gradually on the decline, and nearly every year marks the disuse of some local custom. Shakespeare has not omitted to give a good many scattered allusions to the old superstitions and popular usages associated with the festivals of the year, some of which still survive in our midst.

Alluding to the revels, there can be no doubt that Shakespeare was indebted to the revel-books for some of his plots. Thus, in "The Tempest" (iv. 1), Prospero remarks to Ferdinand and Miranda, after Iris, Ceres, and Juno have appeared, and the dance of the nymphs is over:

> "You do look, my son, in a mov'd sort,
> As if you were dismay'd; be cheerful, sir.
> Our revels now are ended. These our actors,
> As I foretold you, were all spirits, and
> Are melted into air, into thin air:
> And, like the baseless fabric of this vision,
> The cloud-capp'd towers, the gorgeous palaces,
> The solemn temples, the great globe itself,
> Yea, all which it inherit, shall dissolve,
> And, like this insubstantial pageant faded,
> Leave not a rack behind."

It has been inferred that Shakespeare was present at Kenilworth, in 1575, when Elizabeth was so grandly entertained there. Lakes and seas are represented in the masque. Triton, in the likeness of a mermaid, came towards the queen, says George Gascoigne, and " Arion appeared, sitting on a dolphin's back." In the dialogue in " A Midsummer-Night's Dream," between Oberon and Puck (ii. 1), there seems a direct allusion to this event:

> " *Oberon.* My gentle Puck, come hither. Thou remember'st
> Since once I sat upon a promontory,
> And heard a mermaid on a dolphin's back
> Uttering such dulcet and harmonious breath,
> That the rude sea grew civil at her song,
> And certain stars shot madly from their spheres,
> To hear the sea-maid's music.
> *Puck.*   I remember."

Then, too, there were the " Children of the Revels," a company who performed at Blackfriars Theatre. In " Hamlet " (ii. 2), Shakespeare alludes to these " children-players."[1] Rosencrantz says, in the conversation preceding the entry of the players, in reply to Hamlet's inquiry whether the actors have suffered through the result of the late inhibition, evidently referring to the plague, " Nay, their endeavour keeps in the wonted pace; but there is, sir, an aery of children, little eyases, that cry out on the top of question, and are most tyrannically clapped for 't; these are now the fashion; and so berattle the common stages—so they call them—that many wearing rapiers are afraid of goose-quills, and dare scarce come thither."

Twelfth-Day. There can be no doubt that the title of Shakespeare's play, " Twelfth Night," took its origin in the festivities associated with this festival. The season has, from time immemorial, been one of merriment, " the more decided from being the proper close of the festivities of Christmas, when games of chance were traditionally rife, and the sport of sudden and casual elevation gave the tone of the time. Of like tone is the play, and to this,"[2] says Mr.

---

[1] "The England of Shakespeare," E. Goadby, 1881, p. 153.
[2] "Critical Essays on the Plays of Shakespeare," 1875, p. 145; see Singer's " Shakespeare," vol. iii. pp. 347, 348.

Lloyd, "it apparently owes its title." The play, it appears, was probably originally acted at the barristers' feast at the Middle Temple, on February 2, 1601–2, as Manningham tells us in his "Diary" (Camden Society, 1868, ed. J. Bruce, p. 18). It is worthy of note that the festive doings of the Inns of Court, in days gone by, at Christmas-tide were conducted on the most extravagant scale.[1] In addition to the merry disports of the Lord of Misrule, there were various revels. The Christmas masque at Gray's Inn, in 1594, was on a magnificent scale.

St. Valentine's Day (Feb. 14). Whatever may be the historical origin of this festival, whether heathen or Christian, there can be no doubt of its antiquity. According to an old tradition, to which Chaucer refers, birds choose their mates on this day; and hence, in "A Midsummer-Night's Dream" (iv. 1), Theseus asks:

> "Good morrow, friends. St. Valentine is past:
> Begin these wood-birds but to couple now?"

From this notion, it has been suggested, arose the once popular practice of choosing valentines, and also the common belief that the first two single persons who meet in the morning of St. Valentine's day have a great chance of becoming wed to each other. This superstition is alluded to in Ophelia's song in "Hamlet" (iv. 5):

> "To-morrow is Saint Valentine's day,
>   All in the morning betime,
>   And I a maid at your window,
>   To be your valentine."

There seems every probability that St. Valentine's day, with its many customs, has come down to us from the Romans, but was fathered upon St. Valentine in the earlier ages of the Church in order to Christianize it.[2] In France St. Valentine's was a movable feast, celebrated on the first

---

[1] See "British Popular Customs," p. 473.
[2] "Notes and Queries," 6th series, vol. i. p. 129.

Sunday in Lent, which was called the *jour des brandons*, because the boys carried about lighted torches on that day.

Shrove-Tuesday. This day was formerly devoted to feasting and merriment of every kind, but whence originated the custom of eating pancakes is still a matter of uncertainty. The practice is alluded to in "All's Well that Ends Well" (ii. 2), where the clown speaks of "a pancake for Shrove-Tuesday."[1] In "Pericles" (ii. 1) they are termed "flap-jacks," a term used by Taylor, the Water-Poet, in his "Jack-a-Lent Workes" (1630, vol. i. p. 115): "Until at last by the skill of the cooke it is transformed into the form of a flap-jack, which in our translation is called a pancake." Shrove-tide was, in times gone by, a season of such mirth that *shroving*, or *to shrove*, signified to be merry. Hence, in "2 Henry IV." (v. 3), Justice Silence says:

> "Be merry, be merry, my wife has all;
> For women are shrews, both short and tall;
> 'Tis merry in hall, when beards wag all,
>   And welcome merry shrove-tide.
> Be merry, be merry."

It was a holiday and a day of license for apprentices, laboring persons, and others.[2]

Lent. This season was at one time marked by a custom now fallen into disuse. A figure, made up of straw and cast-off clothes, was drawn or carried through the streets amid much noise and merriment; after which it was either burned, shot at, or thrown down a chimney. This image was called a "Jack-a-Lent," and was, according to some, intended to represent Judas Iscariot. It occurs twice in the "Merry Wives of Windsor;" once merely as a jocular appellation (iii. 3), where Mrs. Page says to Robin, "You little Jack-a-Lent, have you been true to us?" and once (v. 5) as a butt,

---

[1] Cf. "As You Like It" (i. 2). Touchstone alludes to a "certain knight, that swore by his honour they were good pancakes."

[2] See Hone's "Every Day Book," 1836, vol. i. p. 258; "Book of Days," vol. i. p. 239; see, also, Dekker's "Seven Deadly Sins," 1606, p. 35; "British Popular Customs," pp. 62–91.

or object of satire and attack, Falstaff remarking, " How wit may be made a Jack-a-Lent, when 'tis upon ill employment !" It is alluded to by Ben Jonson in his " Tale of a Tub " (iv. 2):

> " Thou cam'st but half a thing into the world,
> And wast made up of patches, parings, shreds ;
> Thou, that when last thou wert put out of service,
> Travell'd to Hamstead Heath on an Ash Wednesday,
> Where thou didst stand six weeks the Jack of Lent,
> For boys to hurl three throws a penny at thee,
> To make thee a purse."

Elderton, in a ballad called " Lenton Stuff," in a MS. in the Ashmolean Museum, thus concludes his account of Lent :[1]

> "When Jakke a' Lent comes justlynge in,
> With the hedpeece of a herynge,
> And saythe, repent yowe of yower syn,
> For shame, syrs, leve yowre swerynge :
> And to Palme Sonday doethe he ryde,
> With sprots and herryngs by his syde,
> And makes an end of Lenton tyde !"[2]

In the reign of Elizabeth butchers were strictly enjoined not to sell fleshmeat in Lent, not with a religious view, but for the double purpose[3] of diminishing the consumption of fleshmeat during that period, and so making it more plentiful during the rest of the year, and of encouraging the fisheries and augmenting the number of seamen. Butchers, however, who had an interest at court frequently obtained a dispensation to kill a certain number of beasts a week during Lent ; of which indulgence the wants of invalids, who could not subsist without animal food, was made the pretence. It is to this practice that Cade refers in " 2 Henry VI." (iv. 3), where he tells Dick, the butcher of Ashford : " Therefore, thus will I reward thee,—the Lent shall be as

---

[1] " Notes and Queries," 1st series, vol. xii. p. 297.

[2] See Nares's " Glossary," vol. i. p. 443 ; Brand's " Pop. Antiq.," 1849, vol. i. p. 101. Taylor, the Water-Poet, has a tract entitled " *Jack-a-Lent*, his Beginning and Entertainment, with the mad Prankes of Gentlemen-Usher, Shrove Tuesday."

[3] Singer's " Shakespeare," vol. vi. p. 219.

long again as it is; and thou shalt have a license to kill for a hundred lacking one."

In " 2 Henry IV." (ii. 4), Falstaff mentions an indictment against Hostess Quickly, " for suffering flesh to be eaten in thy house, contrary to the law; for the which I think thou wilt howl." Whereupon she replies, "All victuallers do so: what's a joint of mutton or two in a whole Lent?"

The sparing fare in olden days, during Lent, is indirectly referred to by Rosencrantz in " Hamlet" (ii. 2): " To think, my lord, if you delight not in man, what lenten entertainment the players shall receive." We may compare, too, Maria's words in " Twelfth Night " (i. 5), where she speaks of a good lenten answer, *i. e.*, short.

By a scrap of proverbial rhyme quoted by Mercutio in " Romeo and Juliet " (ii. 4), and the speech introducing it, it appears that a stale hare might be used to make a pie in Lent; he says:

" No hare, sir: unless a hare, sir, in a lenten pie, that is something stale and hoar ere it be spent.

> An old hare hoar,
> And an old hare hoar,
> Is very good meat in Lent," etc.

Scambling days. The days so called were Mondays and Saturdays in Lent, when no regular meals were provided, and our great families scambled. There may possibly be an indirect allusion to this custom in " Henry V." (v. 2), where Shakespeare makes King Henry say: " If ever thou beest mine, Kate, as I have a saving faith within me tells me thou shalt, I get thee with scambling." In the old household book of the fifth Earl of Northumberland there is a particular section appointing the order of service for these days, and so regulating the licentious contentions of them. We may, also, compare another passage in the same play (i. 1), where the Archbishop of Canterbury speaks of " the scambling and unquiet time."

Good Friday. Beyond the bare allusion to this day, Shakespeare makes no reference to the many observances formerly associated with it. In "King John" (i. 1) he makes Philip the Bastard say to Lady Faulconbridge :

> " Madam, I was not old Sir Robert's son :
> Sir Robert might have eat his part in me
> Upon Good Friday, and ne'er broke his fast."

And, in " 1 Henry IV." (i. 2), Poins inquires : " Jack, how agrees the devil and thee about thy soul, that thou soldest him on Good Friday last, for a cup of Madeira and a cold capon's leg ?"

Easter. According to a popular superstition, it is considered unlucky to omit wearing new clothes on Easter Day, to which Shakespeare no doubt alludes in " Romeo and Juliet " (iii. 1), when he makes Mercutio ask Benvolio whether he did "not fall out with a tailor for wearing his new doublet before Easter." In East Yorkshire, on Easter Eve, young folks go to the nearest market-town to buy some new article of dress or personal adornment to wear for the first time on Easter Day, as otherwise they believe that birds—notably rooks or " crakes "—will spoil their clothes.[1] In " Poor Robin's Almanac " we are told :

> " At Easter let your clothes be new,
> Or else be sure you will it rue."

Some think that the custom of " clacking " at Easter—which is not quite obsolete in some counties—is incidentally alluded to in " Measure for Measure " (iii. 2) by Lucio : "his use was, to put a ducat in her clack-dish."[2] The clack or clap dish was a wooden dish with a movable cover, formerly carried by beggars, which they clacked and clattered to show that it was empty. In this they received the alms. Lepers and other paupers deemed infectious originally used it, that the sound might give warning not to approach too near, and alms be given without touching the person.

A popular name for Easter Monday was Black Monday,

---

[1] " Notes and Queries," 4th series, vol. v. p. 595

[2] See Singer's " Shakespeare," vol. i. p. 362 ; Nares's " Glossary," vol. i. p. 164 ; Brand's " Pop. Antiq.," 1849, vol. iii. p. 94.

so called, says Stow, because "in the 34th of Edward III. (1360), the 14th of April, and the morrow after Easter Day, King Edward, with his host, lay before the city of Paris; which day was full dark of mist and hail, and so bitter cold, that many men died on their horses' backs with the cold. Wherefore unto this day it hath been call'd the Blacke Monday." Thus, in the "Merchant of Venice" (ii. 5), Launcelot says, "it was not for nothing that my nose fell a-bleeding on Black Monday last at six o'clock i' the morning."

St. David's Day (March 1). This day is observed by the Welsh in honor of St. David, their patron saint, when, as a sign of their patriotism, they wear a leek. Much doubt exists as to the origin of this custom. According to the Welsh, it is because St. David ordered his Britons to place leeks in their caps, that they might be distinguished from their Saxon foes. Shakespeare introduces the custom into his play of "Henry V." (iv. 7), where Fluellen, addressing the monarch, says:

"Your grandfather of famous memory, an't please your majesty, and your great uncle Edward the Plack Prince of Wales, as I have read in the chronicles, fought a most prave pattle here in France.

K. Henry. They did, Fluellen.

Flu. Your majesty says very true: if your majesties is remembered of it, the Welshmen did goot service in a garden where leeks did grow, wearing leeks in their Monmouth caps; which, your majesty know, to this hour is an honourable padge of the service; and I do pelieve, your majesty takes no scorn to wear the leek upon Saint Tavy's day."

It has been justly pointed out, however, that this allusion by Fluellen to the Welsh having worn the leek in battle under the Black Prince is not, as some writers suppose, wholly decisive of its having originated in the fields of Cressy, but rather shows that when Shakespeare wrote Welshmen wore leeks.[1] In the same play, too (iv. 1), the well-remembered Fluellen's enforcement of Pistol to eat

---

[1] See Hone's "Every Day Book," vol. i. p. 318; "British Popular Customs," pp. 110–113.

the leek he had ridiculed further establishes the wearing as a usage. Pistol says:

> "Tell him I'll knock his leek about his pate
> Upon Saint Davy's day."

In days gone by this day was observed by royalty; and in 1695 we read how William III. wore a leek on St. David's Day, "presented to him by his sergeant, Porter, who hath as perquisites all the wearing apparel his majestie had on that day, even to his sword." It appears that formerly, among other customs, a Welshman was burned in effigy upon "St. Tavy's Day," an allusion to which occurs in "Poor Robin's Almanack" for 1757:

> "But it would make a stranger laugh,
> To see th' English hang poor Taff:
> A pair of breeches and a coat,
> Hat, shoes, and stockings, and what not,
> Are stuffed with hay, to represent
> The Cambrian hero thereby meant."

St. Patrick's Day (March 17). Shakespeare, in "Hamlet" (i. 5), makes the Danish prince swear by St. Patrick, on which Warburton remarks that the whole northern world had their learning from Ireland.[1] As Mr. Singer[2] observes, however, it is more probable that the poet seized the first popular imprecation that came to his mind, without regarding whether it suited the country or character of the person to whom he gave it. Some, again, have supposed that there is a reference here to St. Patrick's purgatory, but this does not seem probable.

St. George's Day (April 23). St. George, the guardian saint of England, is often alluded to by Shakespeare. His festival, which was formerly celebrated by feasts of cities and corporations, is now almost passed over without notice. Thus, Bedford, in "1 Henry VI." (i. 1), speaks of keeping "our great Saint George's feast withal." "God and St. George" was once a common battle-cry, several references

---

[1] St. Patrick rids Ireland of snakes; see p. 257.
[2] Singer's "Shakespeare," 1870, vol. ix. p. 168.

to which occur in Shakespeare's plays. Thus, in "Henry V." (iii. 1), the king says to his soldiers:[1]

> "Cry, God for Harry, England, and Saint George."

Again, in "1 Henry VI." (iv. 2), Talbot says:

> "God and Saint George, Talbot and England's right,
> Prosper our colours in this dangerous fight!"

The following injunction, from an old act of war, concerning the use of St. George's name in onsets, is curious: "Item, that all souldiers entering into battaile, assault, skirmish, or other faction of armes, shall have for their common crye and word, *St. George, forward*, or, *Upon them, St. George*, whereby the souldier is much comforted, and the enemie dismaied, by calling to minde the ancient valour of England, with which that name has so often been victorious."[2]

The combat of this saint on horseback with a dragon has been very long established as a subject for sign-painting. In "King John" (ii. 1) Philip says:

> "Saint George, that swing'd the dragon, and e'er since
> Sits on his horseback at mine hostess' door."

It is still a very favorite sign. In London alone[3] there are said to be no less than sixty-six public-houses and taverns with the sign of St. George and the Dragon, not counting beer-houses and coffee-houses.

May Day. The festival of May day has, from the earliest times, been most popular in this country, on account of its association with the joyous season of spring. It was formerly celebrated with far greater enthusiasm than nowadays, for Bourne tells us how the young people were in the habit of rising a little after midnight and walking to some neighboring wood, accompanied with music and the blowing of horns, where they broke down branches from the

---

[1] Cf. "Henry V.," v. 2; "3 Henry VI.," ii. 1, 2; "Taming of the Shrew," ii. 1; "Richard II.," i. 3.

[2] Cited by Warton in a note on "Richard III.," v. 3.

[3] Hotten's "History of Sign-boards," 1866, 3d ed., p. 287.

trees, which, decorated with nosegays and garlands of flowers, were brought home soon after sunrise, and placed at
their doors and windows. Shakespeare, alluding to this
practice, informs us how eagerly it was looked forward to,
and that it was impossible to make the people sleep on May
morning. Thus, in " Henry VIII." (v. 4), it is said :

> " Pray, sir, be patient : 'tis as much impossible—
> Unless we sweep 'em from the door with cannons—
> To scatter 'em, as 'tis to make 'em sleep
> On May-day morning."

Again, in " A Midsummer-Night's Dream " (i. 1), Lysander, speaking of these May-day observances, says to Hermia :

> " If thou lov'st me, then,
> Steal forth thy father's house to-morrow night ;
> And in the wood, a league without the town,
> Where I did meet thee once with Helena,
> To do observance to a morn of May,
> There will I stay for thee."

And Theseus says (iv. 1) :

> " No doubt they rose up early to observe
> The rite of May." [1]

In the " Two Noble Kinsmen " (ii. 3), one of the four countrymen asks : " Do we all hold against the Maying ?"

In Chaucer's " Court of Love " we read that early on
May day " Fourth goth al the Court, both most and lest, to
fetche the flowris fresh and blome." In the reign of Henry
VIII. it is on record that the heads of the corporation of
London went out into the high grounds of Kent to gather
the May, and were met on Shooter's Hill by the king and
his queen, Katherine of Arragon, as they were coming from
the palace of Greenwich. Until within a comparatively recent period, this custom still lingered in some of the counties. Thus, at Newcastle-upon-Tyne, the following doggerel
was sung :

---

[1] Cf. " Twelfth Night " (iii. 4) : " More matter for a May morning."

> "Rise up, maidens, fie for shame!
> For I've been four long miles from hame,
> I've been gathering my garlands gay,
> Rise up, fair maidens, and take in your May."

Many of the ballads sung nowadays, in country places, by the village children, on May morning, as they carry their garlands from door to door, undoubtedly refer to the old practice of going a-Maying, although fallen into disuse.

In olden times nearly every village had its May-pole, around which, decorated with wreaths of flowers, ribbons, and flags, our merry ancestors danced from morning till night. The earliest representation of an English May-pole is that published in the "Variorum Shakespeare," and depicted on a window at Betley, in Staffordshire, then the property of Mr. Tollet, and which he was disposed to think as old as the time of Henry VIII. The pole is planted in a mound of earth, and has affixed to it St. George's red-cross banner and a white pennon or streamer with a forked end. The shaft of the pole is painted in a diagonal line of black colors upon a yellow ground, a characteristic decoration of all these ancient May-poles, as alluded to by Shakespeare in "A Midsummer-Night's Dream" (iii. 2), where it gives point to Hermia's allusion to her rival Helena as "a painted May-pole."[1] The popularity of the May-pole in former centuries is shown by the fact that one of our London parishes, St. Andrew Undershaft, derives its name from the May-pole which overhung its steeple, a reference to which we find made by Geoffrey Chaucer, who, speaking of a vain boaster, says:

> "Right well aloft, and high ye bear your head,
> As ye would bear the great shaft of Cornhill."

London, indeed, had several May-poles, one of which stood in Basing Lane, near St. Paul's Cathedral. It was a large fir pole, forty feet high and fifteen inches in diameter, and fabled

---

[1] "Book of Days," vol. i. p. 575; see "British Popular Customs," pp. 228–230, 249.

to be the justing staff of Gerard the Giant. Only a few, however, of the old May-poles remain scattered here and there throughout the country. One still supports a weather-cock in the churchyard at Pendleton, Manchester; and in Derbyshire, a few years ago, several were to be seen standing on some of the village greens. The rhymes made use of as the people danced round the May-pole varied according to the locality, and oftentimes combined a curious mixture of the jocose and sacred.

Another feature of the May-day festivities was the morris-dance, the principal characters of which generally were Robin Hood, Maid Marian, Scarlet, Stokesley, Little John, the Hobby-horse, the Bavian or Fool, Tom the Piper, with his pipe and tabor. The number of characters varied much at different times and places. In "All's Well that Ends Well" (ii. 2), the clown says: "As fit as ten groats is for the hand of an attorney . . . a morris for May-day."[1]

In " 2 Henry VI." (iii. 1) the Duke of York says of Cade:

> " I have seen
> Him caper upright, like a wild Morisco,
> Shaking the bloody darts, as he his bells."

In the " Two Noble Kinsmen" (iii. 5) Gerrold, the school-master, thus describes to King Theseus the morris-dance:

> " If you but favour, our country pastime made is.
> We are a few of those collected here,
> That ruder tongues distinguish villagers;
> And, to say verity and not to fable,
> We are a merry rout, or else a rable,
> Or company, or, by a figure, choris,
> That 'fore thy dignity will dance a morris.
> And I, that am the rectifier of all,
> By title *Pædagogus*, that let fall
> The birch upon the breeches of the small ones,
> And humble with a ferula the tall ones,
> Do here present this machine, or this frame:
> And, dainty duke, whose doughty dismal fame,

---

[1] See Brand's " Pop. Antiq.," vol. i. pp. 247–270; " Book of Days," vol. i. pp. 630–633.

From Dis to Dædalus, from post to pillar,
Is blown abroad, help me, thy poor well willer,
And, with thy twinkling eyes, look right and straight
Upon this mighty *morr*—of mickle weight—
Is—now comes in, which being glu'd together
Makes *morris*, and the cause that we came hether,
The body of our sport, of no small study.
I first appear, though rude, and raw, and muddy,
To speak, before thy noble grace, this tenner ;
At whose great feet I offer up my penner:
The next, the Lord of May and Lady bright,
The chambermaid and serving-man, by night
That seek out silent hanging: then mine host
And his fat spouse, that welcomes to their cost
The galled traveller, and with a beck'ning,
Inform the tapster to inflame the reck'ning:
Then the beast-eating clown, and next the fool,
The bavian, with long tail and eke long tool ;
Cum multis aliis that make a dance :
Say 'Ay,' and all shall presently advance."

Among the scattered allusions to the characters of this dance may be noticed that in " 1 Henry IV." (iii. 3): "and for womanhood, Maid Marian may be the deputy's wife of the ward to thee"—the allusion being to "the degraded Maid Marian of the later morris-dance, more male than female."[1]

The "hobby-horse," another personage of the morris-dance on May day, was occasionally omitted, and appears to have given rise to a popular ballad, a line of which is given by "Hamlet" (iii. 2):

"For, O, for, O, the hobby-horse is forgot."

This is quoted again in "Love's Labour's Lost" (iii. 1). The hobby-horse was formed by a pasteboard horse's head, and a light frame made of wicker-work to join the hinder parts. This was fastened round the body of a man, and covered with a foot-cloth which nearly reached the ground, and concealed the legs of the performer, who displayed his antic

---

[1] Nares's "Glossary," vol. ii. p. 550.

equestrian skill, and performed various juggling tricks, to the amusement of the bystanders. In Sir Walter Scott's "Monastery" there is a spirited description of the hobby-horse.

The term "hobby-horse" was applied to a loose woman, and in the "Winter's Tale" (i. 2) it is so used by Leontes, who says to Camillo:

> "Then say
> My wife's a hobby-horse; deserves a name
> As rank as any flax-wench, that puts to
> Before her troth-plight."

In "Othello" (iv. 1), Bianca, speaking of Desdemona's handkerchief, says to Cassio: "This is some minx's token, and I must take out the work! There, give it your hobby-horse." It seems also to have denoted a silly fellow, as in "Much Ado About Nothing" (iii. 2), where it is so used by Benedick.

Another character was Friar Tuck, the chaplain of Robin Hood, and as such is noticed in the "Two Gentlemen of Verona" (iv. 1), where one of the outlaws swears:

> "By the bare scalp of Robin Hood's fat friar."

He is also represented by Tollet as a Franciscan friar in the full clerical tonsure, for, as he adds, "When the parish priests were inhibited by the diocesan to assist in the May games, the Franciscans might give attendance, as being exempted from episcopal jurisdiction."[1]

It was no uncommon occurrence for metrical interludes of a comic species, and founded on the achievements of the outlaw Robin Hood, to be performed after the morris, on the May-pole green. Mr. Drake thinks that these interludes are alluded to in "Twelfth Night" (iii. 4), where Fabian exclaims, on the approach of Sir Andrew Aguecheek with his challenge, "More matter for a May morning."

Whitsuntide. Apart from its observance as a religious festival, Whitsuntide was, in times past, celebrated with much ceremony. In the Catholic times of England it was

---

[1] See Drake's "Shakespeare and his Times," 1817, vol. i. p. 163.

usual to dramatize the descent of the Holy Ghost, which this festival commemorates — a custom which we find alluded to in Barnaby Googe's translation of *Naogeorgus* :

> "On Whit-Sunday white pigeons tame in strings from heaven flie,
> And one that framed is of wood still hangeth in the skie,
> Thou seest how they with idols play, and teach the people too :
> None otherwise than little girls with puppets used to do."

This custom appears to have been carried to an extravagant height in Spain, for Mr. Fosbroke [1] tells us that the gift of the Holy Ghost was represented by "thunder from engines which did much damage." Water, oak leaves, burning torches, wafers, and cakes were thrown down from the church roof; pigeons and small birds, with cakes tied to their legs, were let loose ; and a long censer was swung up and down. In our own country, many costly pageants were exhibited at this season. Thus, at Chester, the Whitsun Mysteries were acted during the Monday, Tuesday, and Wednesday in Whitsun week. The performers were carried from one place to another by means of a scaffold—a huge and ponderous machine mounted on wheels, gayly decorated with flags, and divided into two compartments—the upper of which formed the stage, and the lower, defended from vulgar curiosity by coarse canvas draperies, answered the purposes of a green-room. To each craft in the city a separate mystery was allotted. Thus, the drapers exhibited the "Creation," the tanners took the "Fall of Lucifer," the water-carriers of the Dee acted the "Deluge," etc. The production, too, of these pageants was extremely costly ; indeed, each one has been set down at fifteen or twenty pounds sterling. An allusion to this custom is made in the "Two Gentlemen of Verona" (iv. 4), where Julia says :

> "At Pentecost,
> When all our pageants of delight were play'd,
> Our youth got me to play the woman's part,
> And I was trimm'd in Madam Julia's gown."

The morris-dance, too, was formerly a common accom-

---

[1] "Encyclopædia of Antiquities," 1843, vol. ii. p. 653.

paniment to the Whitsun ales, a practice which is still kept up in many parts of the country. In " Henry V." (ii. 4), the Dauphin thus alludes to it:

> " I say, 'tis meet we all go forth,
> To view the sick and feeble parts of France:
> And let us do it with no show of fear;
> No, with no more than if we heard that England
> Were busied with a Whitsun morris-dance."

And once more, in the " Winter's Tale " (iv. 4), Perdita says to Florizel:

> " Methinks I play as I have seen them do
> In Whitsun pastorals."

A custom formerly kept up in connection with Whitsun-tide was the " Whitsun ale." Ale was so prevalent a drink among us in olden times as to become a part of the name of various festal meetings, as Leet ale, Lamb ale, Bride ale (bridal), and, as we see, Whitsun ale. Thus our ancestors were in the habit of holding parochial meetings every Whitsuntide, usually in some barn near the church, consisting of a kind of picnic, as each parishioner brought what victuals he could spare. The ale, which had been brewed pretty strong for the occasion, was sold by the churchwardens, and from its profits a fund arose for the repair of the church.[1] These meetings are referred to by Shakespeare in " Pericles " (i. 1):

> " It hath been sung at festivals,
> On ember-eves and holy-ales."

In the " Two Gentlemen of Verona " (ii. 5), when Launce tells Speed, " thou hast not so much charity in thee as to go to the ale with a Christian," these words have been explained to mean the rural festival so named, though, as Mr. Dyce remarks (" Glossary," p. 10), the previous words of Launce, " go with me to the ale-house," show this explanation to be wrong.

---

[1] See " British Popular Customs," p. 278; Brand's " Pop. Antiq.," 1849, vol. i. p. 276.

In the old miracle-plays performed at this and other seasons Herod was a favorite personage, and was generally represented as a tyrant of a very overbearing, violent character. Thus Hamlet says (iii. 2): "O, it offends me to the soul, to hear a robustious periwig-pated fellow tear a passion to tatters, to very rags, to split the ears of the groundlings; who, for the most part, are capable of nothing but inexplicable dumb-shows and noise: I would have such a fellow whipped for o'er-doing Termagant; it out-herods Herod." On this account Alexas mentions him as the most daring character when he tells Cleopatra ("Antony and Cleopatra," iii. 3):

> "Good majesty,
> Herod of Jewry dare not look upon you
> But when you are well pleas'd."

In the "Merry Wives of Windsor" (ii. 1), Mrs. Page speaks of him in the same signification: "What a Herod of Jewry is this!"

Mr. Dyce, in his "Glossary" (p. 207), has this note: "If the reader wishes to know what a swaggering, uproarious tyrant Herod was represented to be in those old dramatic performances, let him turn to 'Magnus Herodes' in 'The Towneley Mysteries,' p. 140, ed. Surtees Society; to 'King Herod' in the 'Coventry Mysteries,' p. 188, ed. Shakespeare Society; and to 'The Slaughter of the Innocents' in 'The Chester Plays,' vol. i. p. 172, ed. Shakespeare Society."

Like Herod, Termagant[1] was a hectoring tyrant of the miracle-plays, and as such is mentioned by Hamlet in the passage quoted above. Hence, in course of time, the word was used as an adjective, in the sense of violent, as in "1 Henry IV." (v. 4), "that hot termagant Scot." Hall mentions him in his first satire:

> "Nor fright the reader with the Pagan vaunt
> Of mighty Mahound and great Termagaunt."

---

[1] According to the crusaders and the old romance writers a Saracen deity. See Singer's "Shakespeare," vol. ix. p. 214.

While speaking of the old mysteries or miracle-plays we may also here refer to the "moralities," a class of religious plays in which allegorical personifications of the virtues and vices were introduced as *dramatis personæ*. These personages at first only took part in the play along with the Scriptural or legendary characters, but afterwards entirely superseded them. They continued in fashion till the time of Queen Elizabeth. Several allusions are given by Shakespeare to these moral plays. Thus, in "Twelfth Night" (iv. 1), the clown sings:

> " I am gone, sir,
>   And anon, sir,
> I'll be with you again
>   In a trice,
>   Like to the old Vice,
> Your need to sustain ;
>
> Who, with dagger of lath,
> In his rage and his wrath,
>   Cries, Ah, ha ! to the devil," etc.

Again, in " 1 Henry IV." (ii. 4), Prince Henry speaks of " that reverend Vice, that grey Iniquity :" and in " 2 Henry IV." (iii. 2), Falstaff says, " now is this Vice's dagger become a squire."

Again, further allusions occur in " Richard III." (iii. 1). Gloster says:

> " Thus, like the formal Vice, Iniquity,
>   I moralize two meanings in one word."

And once more, Hamlet (iii. 4), speaks of " a Vice of kings," " a king of shreds and patches."

According to Nares, " Vice " had the name sometimes of one vice, sometimes of another, but most commonly of *Iniquity*, or Vice itself. He was grotesquely dressed in a cap with ass's ears, a long coat, and a dagger of lath. One of his chief employments was to make sport with the devil, leaping on his back, and belaboring him with his dagger of lath, till he made him roar. The devil, however, always carried him off in the end. He was, in short, the buffoon of the morality, and was succeeded in his office by the clown, whom we see in Shakespeare and others.[1]

Again, there may be a further allusion to the moralities in " King Lear" (ii. 2), where Kent says to Oswald, " take Vanity, the puppet's, part, against the royalty of her father."

Then, too, there were the " pageants "—shows which were usually performed in the highways of our towns, and assimilated in some degree to the miracle-plays, but were of a more mixed character, being partly drawn from profane history. According to Strutt, they were more frequent in London, being required at stated periods, such as the setting of the Midsummer Watch, and the Lord Mayor's Show.[2]   Among the allusions to these shows given by Shakespeare, we may quote one in " Richard III." (iv. 4), where Queen Margaret speaks of

> "The flattering index of a direful pageant"

—the pageants displayed on public occasions being generally preceded by a brief account of the order in which the characters were to walk.   These indexes were distributed among the spectators, that they might understand the meaning of such allegorical representations as were usually exhibited. In the " Merchant of Venice" (i. 1), Salarino calls argosies " the pageants of the sea," in allusion, says Douce,[3] " to those enormous machines, in the shapes of castles, dragons, ships, giants, etc., that were drawn about the streets in the ancient shows or pageants, and which often constituted the most important part of them."   Again, in " As You Like It" (iii. 4), Corin says:

> " If you will see a pageant truly play'd,
>   Between the pale complexion of true love
>   And the red glow of scorn and proud disdain,
>   Go hence a little, and I shall conduct you,
>   If you will mark it."

---

[1] See Dyce's " Glossary," p. 482.

[2] " Sports and Pastimes," 1876, pp. 25–28; see Warton's " History of English Poetry," vol. ii. p. 202.

[3] " Illustrations of Shakespeare," p. 154.

And in " Antony and Cleopatra " (iv. 14), Antony speaks of
" black vesper's pageants."

The nine worthies, originally comprising Joshua, David,
Judas Maccabæus, Hector, Alexander, Julius Cæsar, Arthur,
Charlemagne, and Godfrey of Bouillon, appear from a very
early period to have been introduced occasionally in the
shows and pageants of our ancestors. Thus, in " Love's
Labour's Lost " (v. 2), the pageant of the nine worthies is
introduced. As Shakespeare, however, introduces Hercules
and Pompey among his presence of worthies, we may infer
that the characters were sometimes varied to suit the circumstances of the period, or the taste of the auditory. A
MS. preserved in the library of Trinity College, Dublin,
mentions the " Six Worthies " having been played before
the Lord Deputy Sussex in 1557.[1]

Another feature of the Whitsun merrymakings were the
Cotswold games, which were generally on the Thursday in
Whitsun week, in the vicinity of Chipping Campden. They
were instituted by an attorney of Burton-on-the-Heath, in
Warwickshire, named Robert Dover, and, like the Olympic
games of the ancients, consisted of most kinds of manly
sports, such as wrestling, leaping, pitching the bar, handling
the pike, dancing, and hunting. Ben Jonson, Drayton, and
other poets of that age wrote verses on this festivity, which,
in 1636, were collected into one volume, and published under the name of " Annalia Dubrensia."[2] In the " Merry
Wives of Windsor " (i. 1), Slender asks Page, " How does
your fallow greyhound, sir? I heard say, he was outrun on
Cotsall." And in " 2 Henry IV."[3] (iii. 2), Shallow, by distinguishing Will Squele as " a Cotswold man," meant to imply
that he was well versed in manly exercises, and consequently
of a daring spirit and athletic constitution. A sheep was
jocularly called a " Cotsold," or " Cotswold lion," from the
extensive pastures in that part of Gloucestershire.

---

[1] Staunton's " Shakespeare," 1864, vol. i. pp. 147, 148.

[2] See " Book of Days," vol. i. p. 712.

[3] See Singer's " Shakespeare," vol. v. p. 206.

While speaking of Whitsuntide festivities, we may refer to the " roasted Manningtree ox with the pudding in his belly," to which Prince Henry alludes in " 1 Henry IV." (ii. 4). It appears that Manningtree, in Essex, formerly enjoyed the privilege of fairs, by the tenure of exhibiting a certain number of Stage Plays yearly. There were, also, great festivities there, and much good eating, at Whitsun ales and other times. Hence, it seems that roasting an ox whole was not uncommon on such occasions. The pudding spoken of by Prince Henry often accompanied the ox, as we find in a ballad written in 1658:[1]

> " Just so the people stare
> At an ox in the fair
> Roasted whole with a pudding in 's belly."

Sheep-shearing Time commences as soon as the warm weather is so far settled that the sheep may, without danger, lay aside their winter clothing; the following tokens being laid down by Dyer, in his " Fleece " (bk. i), to mark out the proper time:[2]

> " If verdant elder spreads
> Her silver flowers; if humble daisies yield
> To yellow crowfoot and luxuriant grass
> Gay shearing-time approaches."

Our ancestors, who took advantage of every natural holiday, to keep it long and gladly, celebrated the time of sheep-shearing by a feast exclusively rural. Drayton,[3] the countryman of Shakespeare, has graphically described this festive scene, the Vale of Evesham being the locality of the sheep-shearing which he has pictured so pleasantly:

> " The shepherd king,
> Whose flock hath chanc'd that year the earliest lamb to bring,

---

[1] See Nichol's " Collection of Poems," 1780, vol. iii. p. 204.

[2] See Knight's " Life of Shakespeare," 1845, p. 71 ; Howitt's " Pictorial Calendar of the Seasons," 1854, pp. 254–267.

[3] " Polyolbion," song 14; see Brand's " Pop. Antiq.," 1849, vol. ii. p. 34; Timbs's " A Garland for the Year," pp. 74, 75.

> In his gay baldric sits at his low, grassy board,
> **With flawns,** curds, clouted cream, and country dainties stored;
> And whilst the bag-pipe **plays, each lusty,** jocund swain
> Quaffs syllabubs in cans, to all upon the plain,
> And to their country girls, whose nosegays they do wear;
> Some roundelays do sing; the rest the burthen bear."

In the "Winter's Tale," one of the most delicious scenes (iv. 4) is that of the sheep-shearing, in which we have the more poetical "shepherd-queen." Mr. Furnivall,[1] in his introduction to this play, justly remarks: "How happily it brings Shakespeare before us, mixing with his Stratford neighbors at their sheep-shearing and country sports, enjoying the vagabond pedler's gammon and talk, delighting in the sweet Warwickshire maidens, and buying them 'fairings,' telling goblin stories to the boys, 'There was a man dwelt in a churchyard,' opening his heart afresh to all the innocent mirth, and the beauty of nature around him." The expense attaching to these festivities appears to have afforded matter of complaint. Thus, the clown asks, "What am I to buy for our sheep-shearing feast?" and then proceeds to enumerate various things which he will have to purchase. In Tusser's "Five Hundred Points of Husbandry" this festival is described under "The Ploughman's Feast-days:"

> "Wife, make us a dinner, spare flesh neither corne,
> Make wafers and cakes, for our sheep must be shorne;
> At sheepe-shearing, neighbours none other things crave,
> But good cheere and welcome like neighbours to have."

Midsummer Eve appears to have been regarded as a period when the imagination ran riot, and many a curious superstition was associated with this season. Thus, people gathered on this night the rose, St. John's wort, vervain, trefoil, and rue, all of which were supposed to have magical properties. They set the orpine in clay upon pieces of slate or potsherd in their houses, calling it a "Midsummer man." As the stalk was found next morning to incline to

---

[1] Introduction to the "Leopold Shakespeare," p. xci.

the right or left, the anxious maiden knew whether her lover would prove true to her or not. Young men sought, also, for pieces of coal, but, in reality, certain hard, black, dead roots, often found under the living mugwort, designing to place these under their pillows, that they might dream of themselves.[1] It was also supposed that any person fasting on Midsummer-eve, and sitting in the church-porch, would at midnight see the spirits of those persons of that parish who would die that year come and knock at the church-door, in the order and succession in which they would die. Midsummer was formerly thought to be a season productive of madness. Thus, Malvolio's strange conduct is described by Olivia in " Twelfth Night " (iii. 4) as " A very midsummer madness." And, hence, " A Midsummer-Night's Dream " is no inappropriate title for " the series of wild incongruities of which the play consists."[2] The Low-Dutch have a proverb that, when men have passed a troublesome night, and could not sleep, "they have passed St. John Baptist's night " —that is, they have not taken any sleep, but watched all night. Heywood seems to allude to a similar notion when he says:

> " As mad as a March hare : where madness compares,
> Are not midsummer hares as mad as March hares ?"

A proverbial phrase, too, to signify that a person was mad, was, " 'Tis midsummer moon with you "—hot weather being supposed to affect the brain.

Dog-days. A popular superstition—in all probability derived from the Egyptians—referred to the rising and setting of Sirius, or the Dog-star, as infusing madness into the canine race. Consequently, the name of " Dog-days " was given by the Romans to the period between the 3d of July and 11th of August, to which Shakespeare alludes in " Henry VIII." (v. 3), " the dog-days now reign." It is obvious that the

---

[1] " Book of Days," vol. i. p. 816; see Brand's " Pop. Antiq.," vol. i. p. 314 ; Soane's " Book of the Months."
[2] See Brand's " Pop. Antiq.," 1849, vol. i. pp. 336, 337.

notion is utterly groundless, for not only does the star vary in its rising, but is later and later every year. According to the Roman belief, "at the rising of the Dog-star the seas boil, the wines ferment in the cellars, and standing waters are set in motion; the dogs, also, go mad, and the sturgeon is blasted." The term Dog-days is still a common phrase, and it is difficult to say whether it is from superstitious adherence to old custom or from a belief of the injurious effect of heat upon the canine race that the magistrates, often unwisely, at this season of the year order them to be muzzled or tied up.

Lammas-day (August 1). According to some antiquarians, Lammas is a corruption of loaf-mass, as our ancestors made an offering of bread from new wheat on this day. Others derive it from lamb-mass, because the tenants who held lands under the Cathedral Church of York were bound by their tenure to bring a live lamb into the church at high mass.[1] It appears to have been a popular day in times past, and is mentioned in the following dialogue in "Romeo and Juliet" (i. 3), where the Nurse inquires:

> "How long is it now
> To Lammas-tide?
> *Lady Capulet.* A fortnight, and odd days.
> *Nurse.* Even or odd, of all days in the year,
> Come Lammas-eve at night, shall she be fourteen?"

In Neale's "Essays on Liturgiology" (2d. ed., p. 526), the Welsh equivalent for Lammas-day is given as "dydd degwm wyn," lamb-tithing day.

St. Charity (August 1). This saint is found in the Martyrology on the 1st of August: "Romæ passio Sanctaram Virginum Fidei, Spei, et Charitatis, quæ sub Hadriano principe martyriæ coronam adeptæ sunt."[2] She is alluded to by Ophelia, in her song in "Hamlet" (iv. 5):

---

[1] See "British Popular Customs," pp. 347–351.
[2] Douglas's "Criterion," p. 68, cited by Ritson; see Douce's "Illustrations of Shakespeare," p. 475.

> "By Gis,[1] and by Saint Charity,
> Alack, and fie for shame!" etc.

In the " Faire Maide of Bristowe " (1605) we find a similar allusion:

> "Now, by Saint Charity, if I were judge,
> A halter were the least should hamper him."

St. Bartholomew's Day (August 24). The anniversary of this festival was formerly signalized by the holding of the great Smithfield Fair, the only real fair held within the city of London. One of the chief attractions of Bartholomew Fair were roasted pigs. They were sold "piping hot, in booths and on stalls, and ostentatiously displayed to excite the appetite of passengers." Hence, a "Bartholomew pig" became a popular subject of allusion. Falstaff, in "2 Henry IV." (ii. 4), in coaxing ridicule of his enormous figure, is playfully called, by his favorite Doll: "Thou whoreson little tidy Bartholomew boar-pig." Dr. Johnson, however, thought that paste pigs were meant in this passage; but this is improbable, as the true Bartholomew pigs were real roasted pigs, as may be seen from Ben Jonson's play of "Bartholomew Fair" (i. 6), where Ursula, the pig-woman, is an important personage.[2] Gay, too, speaks of the pig-dressers: "Like Bartholomew Fair pig-dressers, who look like the dams, as well as the cooks, of what they roasted." A further allusion to this season is found in "Henry V." (v. 2), where Burgundy tells how "maids, well-summered and warm kept, are like flies at Bartholomew-tide, blind, though they have their eyes; and then they will endure handling, which before would not abide looking on."

Harvest Home. The ceremonies which graced the ingathering of the harvest in bygone times have gradually disappeared, and at the present day only remnants of the old

---

[1] This is, perhaps, a corrupt abbreviation of "By Jesus." Some would read "By Cis," and understand by it "St. Cicely."

[2] See Nares's "Glossary," vol. i. p. 57; Morley's "Memoirs of Bartholomew Fair," 1859.

usages which once prevailed are still preserved. Shakespeare, who has chronicled so many of our old customs, and seems to have had a special delight in illustrating his writings with these characteristics of our social life, has given several interesting allusions to the observances which, in his day, graced the harvest-field. Thus, in Warwickshire, the laborers, at their harvest-home, appointed a judge to try misdemeanors committed during harvest, and those who were sentenced to punishment were placed on a bench and beaten with a pair of boots. Hence the ceremony was called "giving them the boots." It has been suggested that this custom is alluded to in the "Two Gentlemen of Verona" (i. 1), where Shakespeare makes Proteus, parrying Valentine's raillery, say, "nay, give me not the boots."

In Northamptonshire, when any one misconducted himself in the field during harvest, he was subjected to a mock-trial at the harvest-home feast, and condemned to be booted, a description of which we find in the introduction to Clare's "Village Minstrel:" "A long form is placed in the kitchen, upon which the boys who have worked well sit, as a terror and disgrace to the rest, in a bent posture, with their hands laid on each other's backs, forming a bridge for the 'hogs' (as the truant boys are called) to pass over; while a strong chap stands on each side with a boot-legging, soundly strapping them as they scuffle over the bridge, which is done as fast as their ingenuity can carry them." Some, however, think the allusion in the "Two Gentlemen of Verona" is to the diabolical torture of the boot. Not a great while before this play was written, it had been inflicted, says Douce,[1] in the presence of King James, on one Dr. Fian, a supposed wizard, who was charged with raising the storms that the king encountered in his return from Denmark. The unfortunate man was afterwards burned. This horrible torture, we are told,[2] consisted in the leg and knee of the criminal

---

[1] "Illustrations of Shakespeare," p. 21.

[2] Dyce's "Glossary," p. 47; Douce has given a representation of this instrument of torture from Millœus's "Praxis Criminis Persequendi," Paris, 1541.

being enclosed within a tight iron boot or case, wedges of iron being then driven in with a mallet between the knee and the iron boot. Sir Walter Scott, in " Old Mortality," has given a description of Macbriar undergoing this punishment. At a later period " the boot " signified, according to Nares,[1] an instrument for tightening the leg or hand, and was used as a cure for the gout, and called a " bootikins." The phrase "to give the boots" seems to have been a proverbial expression, signifying " Don't make a laughing-stock of me ; don't play upon me."

In the " Merchant of Venice " (v. 1), where Lorenzo says:

> "Come, ho! and wake Diana with a hymn :
> With sweetest touches pierce your mistress' ear,
> And draw her home with music,"

we have, doubtless, an allusion to the " Hock Cart " of the old harvest-home. This was the cart which carried the last corn away from the harvest-field,[2] and was generally profusely decorated, and accompanied by music, old and young shouting at the top of their voices a doggerel after the following fashion :

> " We have ploughed, we have sowed,
> We have reaped, we have mowed,
> We have brought home every load,
> Hip, hip, hip! harvest home."[3]

In " Poor Robin's Almanack " for August, 1676, we read :

> " Hoacky is brought home with hallowing,
> Boys with plumb-cake the cart following."

Holyrood Day (September 14). This festival,[4] called also

---

[1] " Glossary," vol. i. p. 95.
[2] Cf. " 1 Henry IV." (i. 3) :

> " His chin, new reap'd,
> Show'd like a stubble-land at harvest-home."

[3] See Brand's " Pop. Antiq.," 1849, vol. ii. pp. 16–33.
[4] See " British Popular Customs," pp. 372, 373. In Lincolnshire this day is called " Hally-Loo Day."

Holy-Cross Day, was instituted by the Romish Church, on account of the recovery of a large piece of the supposed cross by the Emperor Heraclius, after it had been taken away, on the plundering of Jerusalem, by Chosroes, king of Persia. Among the customs associated with this day was one of going a-nutting, alluded to in the old play of " Grim, the Collier of Croydon " (ii. 1):

> " To-morrow is Holy-rood day,
>   When all a-nutting take their way."

Shakespeare mentions this festival in " 1 Henry IV." (i. 1), where he represents the Earl of Westmoreland relating how,

> " On Holy-rood day, the gallant Hotspur there,
>   Young Harry Percy and brave Archibald,
>   That ever-valiant and approved Scot,
>   At Holmedon met."

St. Lambert's Day (September 17). This saint, whose original name was Landebert, but contracted into Lambert, was a native of Maestricht, in the seventh century, and was assassinated early in the eighth.[1] His festival is alluded to in " Richard II." (i. 1), where the king says:

> " Be ready, as your lives shall answer it,
>   At Coventry, upon Saint Lambert's day."

Michaelmas (September 29). In the " Merry Wives of Windsor " (i. 1), this festival is alluded to by Simple, who, in answer to Slender, whether he had " the Book of riddles " about him, replies: " Why, did you not lend it to Alice Shortcake upon All-hallowmas last, a fortnight afore Michaelmas,"—this doubtless being an intended blunder.

In " 1 Henry IV." (ii. 4), Francis says: " Let me see— about Michaelmas next I shall be."

St. Etheldreda, or *Audry*, commemorated in the Romish Calendar on the 23d of June, but in the English Calendar on the 17th of October, was daughter of Annas, King of the East Angles. She founded the convent and church of Ely,

---

[1] See Butler's " Lives of the Saints."

on the spot where the cathedral was subsequently erected. Formerly, at Ely, a fair was annually held, called in her memory St. Audry's Fair, at which much cheap lace was sold to the poorer classes, which at first went by the name of St. Audry's lace, but in time was corrupted into "tawdry lace." Shakespeare makes an allusion to this lace in the "Winter's Tale" (iv. 4), where Mopsa says: "Come, you promised me a tawdry lace, and a pair of sweet gloves;" although in his time the expression rather meant a rustic necklace.[1] An old English historian makes St. Audry die of a swelling in her throat, which she considered as a particular judgment for having been in her youth addicted to wearing fine necklaces.[2]

St. Crispin's Day (October 25) has for centuries been a red-letter day in the calendar of the shoemakers, being the festival of their patron saint. According to tradition, the brothers Crispin and Crispinian, natives of Rome, having become converted to Christianity, travelled to Soissons, in France, in order to preach the gospel. Being desirous, however, of rendering themselves independent, they earned their daily bread by making shoes, with which, it is said, they furnished the poor, at an extremely low price. When the governor of the town discovered that they maintained the Christian faith, and also tried to make proselytes of the inhabitants, he ordered them to be beheaded. From this time the shoemakers have chosen them for their tutelary saints. Shakespeare has perpetuated the memory of this festival by the speech which he has given to Henry V. (iv. 3), before the battle of Agincourt:

> "This day is call'd the feast of Crispian:
> He that outlives this day, and comes safe home,
> Will stand a tip-toe when this day is nam'd,
> And rouse him at the name of Crispian.
> He that shall live this day, and see old age,
> Will yearly on the vigil feast his neighbours,
> And say, 'To-morrow is Saint Crispian.'"

---

[1] See Nares's "Glossary," vol. ii. p. 868 ; Brady's "Clavis Calendaria.'
[2] Nich. Harpsfield, "Hist. Eccl. Anglicana," p. 86.

St. Dennis has been adopted as the patron saint of France (October 9), in the same manner as the English have chosen St. George. The guardianship of the two countries is thus expressed in the chorus to the old ballad:

> " St. George he was for England,
>   St. Denis was for France,
>   Singing, Honi soit qui mal y pense."

King Henry (" Henry V.," v. 2) says to Princess Katherine: " Shall not thou and I, between Saint Dennis and Saint George, compound a boy, half French, half English," etc. In " 1 Henry VI." (iii. 2), Charles says:

> " Saint Dennis bless this happy stratagem,
>   And once again we'll sleep secure in Rouen."

Hallowmas (November 1) is one of the names for the feast of All-hallows, that is, All-Saints. Shakespeare alludes to a custom relative to this day, some traces of which are still to be found in Staffordshire, Cheshire, and other counties. The poor people go from parish to parish *a-souling*, as they term it, that is, begging, in a certain lamentable tone, for soul-cakes, at the same time singing a song which they call the souler's song. This practice is, no doubt, a remnant of the Popish ceremony of praying for departed souls, especially those of friends, on the ensuing day, November 2, the feast of All-Souls.[1] The following is a specimen of the doggerel sung on these occasions:

> " Soul! soul! for a soul-cake;
>   Pray, good mistress, for a soul-cake.
>   One for Peter, and two for Paul,
>   Three for them who made us all.
>
> Soul! soul! for an apple or two;
>   If you've got no apples, pears will do.
>   Up with your kettle, and down with your pan,
>   Give me a good big one, and I'll be gone.
>   Soul! soul! for a soul-cake, etc.
>
> An apple, a pear, a plum, or a cherry,
>   Is a very good thing to make us merry."

---

[1] See " British Popular Customs," p. 404.

In the "Two Gentlemen of Verona" (ii. 1), Speed thus speaks of this practice: "To watch, like one that fears robbing; to speak puling,[1] like a beggar at Hallowmas."

The season of Hallowmas, having been frequently mild, has been, from time immemorial, proverbially called "All-hallown summer," *i. e.*, late summer. Thus, in "1 Henry IV." (i. 2), Prince Henry, likening Falstaff, with his old age and young passions, to this November summer, addresses him: "Farewell, thou latter spring! Farewell, All-hallown summer."[2] In some parts of Germany there is a proverb, "All-Saints' Day brings the second summer;" and in Sweden there is often about this time a continuance of warm, still weather, which is called "the All-Saints' rest."

There is another reference to this festival in "Richard II." (v. 1), where the king says of his wife:

> "She came adorned hither like sweet May,
> Sent back like Hallowmas or short'st of day."

All-Souls' Day (November 2)—which is set apart by the Roman Catholic Church for a solemn service for the repose of the dead—was formerly observed in this country, and among the many customs celebrated in its honor were ringing the passing bell, making soul-cakes, blessing beans, etc.[3] In "Richard III." (v. 1), Buckingham, when led to execution, says:

"This is All-Souls' day, fellows, is it not?
   Sheriff. It is, my lord.
   Buckingham. Why, then, All-Souls' day is my body's doomsday."

Lord-Mayor's Day (November 9). A custom which was in days gone by observed at the inauguration dinner was that of the Lord Mayor's fool leaping, clothes and all, into a large bowl of custard. It is alluded to in "All's Well that Ends Well" (ii. 5), by Lafeu: "You have made shift to run into 't, boots and spurs and all, like him that leaped into the cus-

---

[1] Puling, or singing small, as Bailey explains the word.
[2] See Swainson's "Weather-Lore," 1873, pp. 141–143.
[3] See "British Popular Customs," p. 409.

tard." Ben Jonson, in his " Devil's an Ass " (i. 1), thus refers
to it :

> " He may, perchance, in tail of a sheriff's dinner,
>   Skip with a rime o' the table, from new nothing,
>   And take his almain leap into a custard,
>   Shall make my lady mayoress and her sisters,
>   Laugh all their hoods over their shoulders."

St. Martin's Day (November 11). The mild weather
about this time has given rise to numerous proverbs ; one
of the well-known ones being " St. Martin's little summer,"
an allusion to which we find in " 1 Henry VI." (i. 2), where
Joan of Arc says:

> " Expect Saint Martin's summer, halcyon days."

which Johnson paraphrases thus: " Expect prosperity after
misfortune, like fair weather at Martlemas, after winter has
begun." As an illustration, too, of this passage, we may
quote from the *Times*, October 6, 1864 : " It was one of those
rare but lovely exceptions to a cold season, called in the
Mediterranean St. Martin's summer."

A corruption of Martinmas is Martlemas. Falstaff is jocularly so called by Poins, in " 2 Henry IV." (ii. 2), as being in
the decline, as the year is at this season : " And how doth
the martlemas, your master?"

This was the customary time for hanging up provisions to
dry, which had been salted for winter use.

St. Nicholas (December 6). This saint was deemed the
patron of children in general, but more particularly of all
schoolboys, among whom his festival used to be a very great
holiday. Various reasons have been assigned for his having
been chosen as the patron of children—either because the
legend makes him to have been a bishop while yet a boy,
or from his having restored three young scholars to life who
had been cruelly murdered,[1] or, again, on account of his early

---

[1] See Douce's " Illustrations of Shakespeare," p. 25 ; " The Church
of Our Fathers," by D. Rock, 1853, vol. iii. p. 215 ; *Gent. Mag.*, 1777,
vol. xliii. p. 158 ; see Nares's " Glossary," vol. ii. pp. 601, 602 ; Brady's
" Clavis Calendaria."

abstinence when a boy. In the " Two Gentlemen of Verona "
(iii. 1) he is alluded to in this capacity :

> "*Speed.* Come, fool, come ; try me in thy paper.
> *Launce.* There ; and Saint Nicholas be thy speed."

Nicholas's clerks was, and still is, a cant term for highway-
men and robbers ; but though the expression is very common, its origin is a matter of uncertainty. In " 1 Henry IV."
(ii. 1) it is thus alluded to :

> "*Gadshill.* Sirrah, if they meet not with Saint Nicholas' clerks, I'll
> give thee this neck.
> *Chamberlain.* No, I'll none of it : I pr'thee, keep that for the hang-
> man : for I know thou worshippest Saint Nicholas as truly as a man
> of falsehood may."

Christmas. Among the observances associated with this
season, to which Shakespeare alludes, we may mention the
Christmas Carol, a reference to which is probably made in
" A Midsummer-Night's Dream " (ii. 1), by Titania :

> "No night is now with hymn or carol blest."

Hamlet (ii. 2) quotes two lines from a popular ballad, entitled the " Song of Jephthah's Daughter," and adds : " The
first row of the pious chanson will show you more." [1]
In days gone by, the custom of carol-singing was most
popular, and Warton, in his " History of English Poetry,"
notices a license granted in 1562 to John Tysdale for printing " Certayne goodly carowles to be songe to the glory of
God ;" and again " Crestenmas Carowles auctorisshed by
my lord of London." [2]
In the " Taming of the Shrew " (Ind., sc. 2), Sly asks
whether " a comonty [3] is not a Christmas gambold." Formerly the sports and merry-makings at this season were on
a most extensive scale, being presided over by the Lord of

---

[1] Drake's " Shakespeare and his Times," vol. i. p. 198.
[2] See Sandy's " Christmastide, its History, Festivities, and Carols ;"
also *Athenæum*, Dec. 20, 1856.
[3] His blunder for comedy.

Misrule.¹ Again, in "Love's Labour's Lost" (v. 2), Biron speaks of "a Christmas comedy."

As we have noticed, too, in our chapter on Plants, a gilt nutmeg was formerly a common gift at Christmas, and on other festive occasions, to which an allusion is probably made in the same scene. Formerly, at this season, the head of the house assembled his family around a bowl of spiced ale, from which he drank their healths, then passed it to the rest, that they might drink too. The word that passed among them was the ancient Saxon phrase *wass hael, i. e.*, to your health. Hence this came to be recognized as the was-sail or wassel bowl; and was the accompaniment to festivity of every kind throughout the year. Thus Hamlet (i. 4) says:

> "The king doth wake to-night, and takes his rouse,
> Keeps wassail."

And in "Love's Labour's Lost" (v. 2), Biron speaks of:

> "wakes and wassails, meetings, markets, fairs."

In "Macbeth" (i. 7), it is used by Lady Macbeth in the sense of intemperance, who, speaking of Duncan's two chamberlains, says:

> "Will I with wine and wassail so convince,
> That memory, the warder of the brain,
> Shall be a fume, and the receipt of reason
> A limbeck only."

In "Antony and Cleopatra" (i. 4), Cæsar advises Antony to live more temperately, and to leave his "lascivious wassails."³

In the same way, a "wassail candle" denoted a large candle lighted up at a festival, a reference to which occurs in "2 Henry IV." (i. 2):

---

¹ See "British Popular Customs," 1876, pp. 459, 463; Nares's "Glossary," vol. ii. p. 943; "Antiquarian Repertory," vol. i. p. 218.

² This was a deep draught to the health of any one, in which it was customary to empty the glass or vessel.

³ See Douce's "Illustrations of Shakespeare," 1839, pp. 441–449.

"*Chief-Justice.* You are as a candle, the better part burnt out.
  Falstaff. A wassail candle, my lord ; all tallow."

A custom which formerly prevailed at Christmas, and has not yet died out, was for mummers to go from house to house, attired in grotesque attire, performing all kinds of odd antics.[1] Their performances, however, were not confined to this season. Thus, in " Coriolanus " (ii. 1) Menenius speaks of making " faces like mummers."

Cakes and Ale. It was formerly customary on holidays and saints' days to make cakes in honor of the day. In " Twelfth Night " (ii. 3), Sir Toby says : " Dost thou think, because thou art virtuous, there shall be no more cakes and ale ?" To which the Clown replies : " Yes, by Saint Anne ; and ginger shall be hot i' the mouth too."

Wakes. In days gone by, the church wake was an important institution, and was made the occasion for a thorough holiday. Each church, when consecrated, was dedicated to a saint, and on the anniversary of that day was kept the wake. In many places there was a second wake on the birthday of the saint. At such seasons, the floor of the church was strewed with rushes and flowers, and in the churchyard tents were erected, to supply cakes and ale for the use of the merrymakers on the following day, which was kept as a holiday. They are still kept up in many parishes, but in a very different manner.[2] In " King Lear " (iii. 6), Edgar says : " Come, march to wakes and fairs, and market towns." We may also compare " Love's Labour's Lost " (v. 2) and " Winter's Tale " (iv. 2). In " Hamlet " (i. 4) it is used in the sense of revel.

---

[1] See " British Popular Customs," pp. 461, 469, 478, 480.
[2] See Brand's " Pop. Antiq.," 1849, vol. i. pp. 1–15.

CHAPTER XII.

BIRTH AND BAPTISM.

As every period of human life has its peculiar rites and ceremonies, its customs and superstitions, so has that ever all-eventful hour which heralds the birth of a fresh actor upon the world's great stage. From the cradle to the grave, through all the successive epochs of man's existence, we find a series of traditional beliefs and popular notions, which have been handed down to us from the far-distant past. Although, indeed, these have lost much of their meaning in the lapse of years, yet in many cases they are survivals of primitive culture, and embody the conceptions of the ancestors of the human race. Many of these have been recorded by Shakespeare, who, acting upon the great principle of presenting his audience with matters familiar to them, has given numerous illustrations of the manners and superstitions of his own country, as they existed in his day. Thus, in " Richard III." (iii. 1), when he represents the Duke of Gloster saying,

> " So wise so young, they say, do never live long,"

he alludes to the old superstition, still deeply rooted in the minds of the lower orders, that a clever child never lives long. In Bright's " Treatise of Melancholy " (1586, p. 52), we read : " I have knowne children languishing of the splene, obstructed and altered in temper, talke with gravity and wisdom surpassing those tender years, and their judgments carrying a marvellous imitation of the wisdome of the ancient, having after a sort attained that by disease, which others have by course of yeares ; whereof I take it the proverb ariseth, that ' they be of shorte life who are of wit so pregnant.' " There are sundry superstitious notions relating to the teething of children prevalent in our own and other countries. In "3 Henry VI." (v. 6), the Duke of Gloster, alluding to the peculiarities connected with his birth, relates how

> "The midwife wonder'd; and the women cried
> 'O, Jesus bless us, he is born with teeth!'
> And so I was; which plainly signified
> That I should snarl, and bite, and play the dog."

It is still believed, for instance, in many places, that if a child's first tooth appears in the upper jaw it is an omen of its dying in infancy; and when the teeth come early it is regarded as an indication that there will soon be another baby. In Sussex there is a dislike to throwing away the cast teeth of children, from a notion that, should they be found and gnawed by any animal, the child's new tooth would be exactly like the animal's that had bitten the old one. In Durham, when the first teeth come out the cavities must be filled with salt, and each tooth burned, while the following words are repeated:

> "Fire, fire, burn bone,
> God send me my tooth again."

In the above passage, then, Shakespeare simply makes the Duke of Gloster refer to that extensive folk-lore associated with human birth, showing how careful an observer he was in noticing the whims and oddities of his countrymen.

Again, one of the foremost dangers supposed to hover round the new-born infant was the propensity of witches and fairies to steal the most beautiful and well-favored children, and to leave in their places such as were ugly and stupid. These were usually called "changelings." Shakespeare alludes to this notion in "A Midsummer-Night's Dream" (ii. 1), where Puck says:

> "Because that she, as her attendant, hath
> A lovely boy, stol'n from an Indian king;
> She never had so sweet a changeling."

And further on, in the same scene, Oberon says:

> " I do but beg a little changeling boy,
>   To be my henchman."

As a fairy is, in each case, the speaker, the changeling in this case denotes the child taken by them. So, too, in the " Winter's Tale " (iii. 3), in the passage where the Shepherd relates : " it was told me, I should be rich by the fairies ; this is some changeling :—open't." As the child here found was a beautiful one, the changeling must naturally mean the child stolen by the fairies, especially as the gold left with it is conjectured to be fairy gold. The usual signification, however, of the term *changeling* is thus marked by Spenser (" Fairy Queen," I. x. 65) :

> " From thence a faery thee unweeting reft,
>   There as thou slepst in tender swadling band,
>   And her base elfin brood there for thee left :
>   Such men do chaungelings call, so chaunged by faeries theft."

Occasionally fairies played pranks with new-born children by exchanging them. To this notion King Henry refers (" 1 Henry IV." i. 1) when, speaking of Hotspur compared with his own profligate son, he exclaims :

> " O that it could be prov'd
>   That some night-tripping fairy had exchang'd
>   In cradle-clothes our children where they lay,
>   And call'd mine Percy, his Plantagenet !"

To induce the fairies to restore the stolen child, it was customary in Ireland either to put the one supposed of being a changeling on a hot shovel, or to torment it in some other way. It seems that, in Denmark, the mother heats the oven, and places the changeling on the peel, pretending to put it in, or whips it severely with a rod, or throws it into the water. In the Western Isles of Scotland idiots are supposed to be the fairies' changelings, and, in order to regain the lost child, parents have recourse to the following device. They place the changeling on the beach, below high-water mark, when the tide is out, and pay no heed to its screams, believing that the fairies, rather than suffer their offspring to be drowned by the rising water, will convey it away, and restore the child they had stolen. The sign that this has been done is the cessation of the child's screaming. The most effectual preservative, however, against fairy influence, is supposed to be baptism; and hence, among the superstitious, this rite is performed as soon as possible.

A form of superstition very common in days gone by was the supposed influence of the " Evil eye," being designated by the terms "o'erlooked," "forelooked," or "eye-bitten," certain persons being thought to possess the power of inflicting injury by merely looking on those whom they wished to harm. Even the new-born child was not exempt from this danger, and various charms were practised to avert it. In the " Merry Wives of Windsor " (v. 5), Pistol says of Falstaff:

> " Vile worm, thou wast o'erlook'd, even in thy birth."

This piece of folk-lore may be traced back to the time of the Romans, and, in the late Professor Conington's translation of the " Satires of Persius," it is thus spoken of: " Look here! a grandmother or a superstitious aunt has taken baby from his cradle, and is charming his forehead against mischief by the joint action of her middle-finger and her purifying spittle; for she knows right well how to check the evil eye."[1] Is is again alluded to in the " Merchant of Venice " (iii. 2), where Portia, expressing to Bassanio her feelings of regard, declares:

> " Beshrew your eyes,
> They have o'erlook'd me, and divided me;
> One half of me is yours, the other half yours;"

and in " Titus Andronicus " (ii. 1), Aaron speaks of Tamora as:

> " faster bound to Aaron's charming eyes
> Than is Prometheus tied to Caucasus."

This superstition, however, is not yet obsolete, but lingers on in many country places.

---

[1] See Douce's " Illustrations of Shakespeare," p. 383; Brand's " Pop. Antiq.," 1849, vol. iii. pp. 44–46, 326.

We may also compare a similar phrase made use of by Cleopatra ("Antony and Cleopatra," iii. 7), in answer to Enobarbus:

> "Thou hast forspoke my being in these wars,"

the word *forespeak* having anciently had the meaning of charm or bewitch, like *forbid* in "Macbeth" (i. 3):

> "He shall live a man forbid."[1]

Among the numerous customs associated with the birth of a child may be mentioned the practice of giving presents at the announcement of this important event. In "Henry VIII." (v. 1), on the old lady's making known to the king the happy tidings of the birth of a princess, he says to Lovell:

> "Give her an hundred marks. I'll to the queen."

The old lady, however, resents what she considers a paltry sum:

> "An hundred marks! By this light, I'll ha' more.
> An ordinary groom is for such payment.
> I will have more, or scold it out of him."

It was an ancient custom—one which is not quite out of use—for the sponsors at christenings to offer silver or gilt spoons as a present to the child. These were called "apostle spoons," because the extremity of the handle was formed into the figure of one or other of the apostles. Such as were opulent and generous gave the whole twelve; those who were moderately rich or liberal escaped at the expense of the four evangelists, or even sometimes contented themselves with presenting one spoon only, which exhibited the figure of any saint, in honor of whom the child received its name. In "Henry VIII." (v. 2) it is in allusion to this custom that, when Cranmer professes to be unworthy of being a sponsor to the young princess, Shakespeare makes the king reply:

---

[1] See Napier's "Folk-Lore of West of Scotland," 1879, pp. 34–40; Keightley's "Fairy Mythology;" Brand's "Pop. Antiq.," 1849, vol. iii. pp. 73, 74.

"Come, come, my lord, you'd spare your spoons."

A story is related of Shakespeare promising spoons to one of Ben Jonson's children, in a collection of anecdotes entitled "Merry Passages and Jests," compiled by Sir Nicholas L'Estrange (MSS. Harl. 6395): "Shakespeare was godfather to one of Ben Jonson's children, and after the christ'ning, being in a deepe study, Jonson came to cheere him up, and ask't him why he was so melancholy. 'No faith, Ben (says he), not I; but I have been considering a great while what should be the fittest gift for me to bestow upon my godchild, and I have resolv'd at last.' 'I pr'y thee, what?' sayes he. 'I' faith, Ben, I'le e'en give him a douzen good Latin spoones, and thou shalt translate them.'" "Shakespeare," says Mr. Thoms,[1] "willing to show his wit, if not his wealth, gave a dozen spoons, not of silver, but of latten, a name formerly used to signify a mixed metal resembling brass, as being the most appropriate gift to the child of a father so learned." In Middleton's "Chaste Maid of Cheapside," 1620:

"2 *Gossip.* What has he given her? What is it, gossip?
3 *Gossip.* A fair, high-standing cup, and two great 'postle spoons, one of them gilt."

And Beaumont and Fletcher, in the "Noble Gentleman" (v. 1):

"I'll be a gossip, Beaufort,
I have an odd apostle spoon."

The gossip's feast, held in honor of those who were associated in the festivities of a christening, was a very ancient English custom, and is frequently mentioned by dramatists of the Elizabethan age. The term gossip or godsip, a Saxon word signifying *cognata ex parte dei*, or godmother, is well defined by Richard Verstegan, in his "Restitution of Decayed Intelligence." He says: "Our Christian ancestors, understanding a spiritual affinity to grow between the parents and such as undertooke for the child at baptism, called

---

[1] "Anecdotes and Traditions," 1839, p. 3.

each other by the name of *godsib*, which is as much as to say that they were *sib* together, that is, of *kin* together through God. And the childe, in like manner, called such his god-fathers or godmothers."

As might be expected, it is often alluded to by Shakespeare. Thus, in the "Comedy of Errors" (v. 1), we read :

> "*Abbess.* Thirty-three years have I but gone in travail
> Of you, my sons : and till this present hour
> My heavy burthen ne'er delivered.
> The duke, my husband, and my children both,
> And you the calendars of their nativity,
> Go to a gossip's feast, and go with me ;
> After so long grief, such festivity !
> *Duke.* With all my heart I'll gossip at this feast."

And again, in "A Midsummer-Night's Dream" (ii. 1), the mischievous Puck says :

> "sometime lurk I in a gossip's bowl,
> In very likeness of a roasted crab ;
> And, when she drinks, against her lips I bob,
> And on her wither'd dewlap pour the ale."

And, once more, we find Capulet, in "Romeo and Juliet" (iii. 5), saying to the Nurse :

> "Peace, you mumbling fool !
> Utter your gravity o'er a gossip's bowl ;
> For here we need it not."

Referring to entertainments at christenings, we find the following in the "Batchelor's Banquet," 1603 (attributed to Dekker) : "What cost and trouble it will be to have all things fine against the Christening Day ; what store of sugar, biskets, comphets, and caraways, marmalet, and marchpane, with all kinds of sweet-suckers and superfluous banqueting stuff, with a hundred other odd and needless trifles, which at that time must fill the pockets of dainty dames," by which it appears the ladies not only ate what they pleased, but pocketed likewise. Upon this and the falling-off of the custom of giving "apostle spoons" at the christening, we read in "Shipman's Gossip," 1666 :

> " Especially since gossips now
>   Eat more at christenings than bestow.
>   Formerly when they us'd to troul
>   Gilt bowls of sack, they gave the bowl ;
>   Two spoons at least ; an use ill kept ;
>   'Tis well now if our own be left."

Strype tells us that, in 1559, the son of Sir Thomas Chamberlayne was baptized at St. Benet's Church, Paul's Wharf, when " the Church was hung with cloth of arras, and after the christening were brought wafers, comfits, and divers banqueting dishes, and hypocras and ·Muscadine wine, to entertain the guests."

In " Henry VIII." (v. 4), the Porter says : " Do you look for ale and cakes here, you rude rascals ?"

A term formerly in use for the name given at baptism was " Christendom," an allusion to which we find in " All's Well that Ends Well " (i. 1), where Helena says :

> " with a world
>   Of pretty, fond, adoptious christendoms
>   That blinking Cupid gossips,"

the meaning evidently being, a number of pretty, fond, adopted appellations or Christian names to which blind Cupid stands godfather.   The expression is often used for baptism by old writers ; and Singer [1] quotes from " King John " (iv. 1):

> " By my christendom,
>   So I were out of prison, and kept sheep,
>   I should be as merry as the day is long."

Steevens observes that, in the Puritanical times, it was usual to christen children with the names of moral and religious virtues—a practice to which allusion seems to be made in " The Tempest " (ii. 1) by Antonio :

> " Temperance was a delicate wench."

So Taylor, the Water-Poet, in his description of a strumpet, says :

---

[1] " Shakespeare," 1875, vol. iv. p. 314.

"Though bad they be, they will not bate an ace,
   To be call'd Prudence, Temperance, Faith, or Grace."

In days gone by a "chrisom" or "christom child" was one who had recently been baptized, and died within the month of birth, the term having originated in the "face-cloth, or piece of linen, put upon the head of a child newly baptized." The word was formed from the chrism, that is, the anointing, which formed a part of baptism before the Reformation. Thus, in "Henry V." (ii. 3), the hostess, Mrs. Quickly, means "chrisom child" in the following passage, where she speaks of Falstaff's death: "'A made a finer end, and went away an it had been any christom child." In a beautiful passage of Bishop Taylor's "Holy Dying" (chap. i. sec. 2), this custom is thus spoken of: "Every morning creeps out of a dark cloud, leaving behind it an ignorance and silence deep as midnight, and undiscerned as are the phantoms that made a chrisom child to smile." Referring to the use of the chrisom-cloth in connection with baptism, it appears that, after the usual immersion in water, the priest made a cross on the child's head with oil, after which the chrisom was put on, the priest asking at the same time the infant's name, and saying, "Receive this white, pure, and holy vestment, which thou shalt wear before the tribunal of our Lord Jesus Christ, that thou mayest inherit eternal life. Amen." It was to be worn seven days; but after the Reformation, however, the use of oil was omitted, and the chrisom was worn by the child till the mother's churching, when it was returned to the church. If the child died before the churching, it was buried in the chrisom, and hence it may be that the child itself was called a chrisom or chrisomer.[1] Thus, it will be seen that Dame Quickly simply compares the manner of Falstaff's death to that of a young infant. In registers and bills of mortality we find infants alluded to under the term "Chrisoms." Burn, in his "His-

---

[1] Douce's "Illustrations of Shakespeare," 1859, pp. 299, 300; Nares's "Glossary," vol. i. p. 160; see Brand's "Pop. Antiq.," 1849, vol. ii. pp. 84, 85.

tory of Parish Registers" (1862, p. 127), gives the sub-joined entry from a register of Westminster Abbey: "The Princess Ann's child a chrissome, bu. in ye vault, Oct. 22, 1687."

In Graunt's "Bills of Mortality," cited in Johnson's Dictionary, we read: "When the convulsions were but few, the number of chrisoms and infants was greater." The "bearing-cloth" was the mantle which generally covered the child when it was carried to the font. It is noticed in the "Winter's Tale" (iii. 3), by the Shepherd, who, on the discovery of Perdita, says to the Clown: "Here's a sight for thee; look thee, a bearing-cloth for a squire's child! Look thee here; take up, take up, boy; open't." In Stow's "Chronicle" (1631, p. 1039), we are told that about this time it was not customary "for godfathers and godmothers generally to give plate at the baptisme of children, but only to give 'christening shirts,' with little bands and cuffs, wrought either with silk or blue thread. The best of them, for chief persons, were edged with a small lace of black silk and gold, the highest price of which, for great men's children, was seldom above a noble, and the common sort, two, three, or four, and six shillings a piece."

CHAPTER XIII.

MARRIAGE.

THE style of courtship which prevailed in Shakespeare's time, and the numerous customs associated with the marriage ceremony, may be accurately drawn from the many allusions interspersed through his plays. From these, it would seem that the mode of love-making was much the same among all classes, often lacking that polish and refined expression which are distinguishing characteristics nowadays. As Mr. Drake remarks,[1] the amatory dialogues of Hamlet, Hotspur, and Henry V. are not more refined than those which occur between Master Fenton and Anne Page, in the "Merry Wives of Windsor," between Lorenzo and Jessica, in the "Merchant of Venice," and between Orlando and Rosalind, in "As You Like It." These last, which may be considered as instances taken from the middle class of life, together with a few drawn from the lower rank of rural manners, such as the courtship of Touchstone and Audrey, and of Silvius and Phœbe, in "As You Like It," are good illustrations of this subject, although it must be added that, in point of fancy, sentiment, and simplicity, the most pleasing love-scenes in Shakespeare are those of Romeo and Juliet and of Florizel and Perdita.

The ancient ceremony of betrothing seems still to have been in full use in Shakespeare's day. Indeed, he gives us several interesting passages upon the subject of troth-plight. Thus, in "Measure for Measure" (iii. 1), we learn that the unhappiness of the poor, dejected Mariana was caused by a violation of the troth-plight:

---

[1] "Shakespeare and His Times," 1817, vol. i. p. 220.

"*Duke.* She should this Angelo have married; was affianced to her by oath, and the nuptial appointed: between which time of the contract, and limit of the solemnity, her brother Frederick was wrecked at sea, having in that perished vessel the dowry of his sister. But mark how heavily this befell to the poor gentlewoman: there she lost a noble and renowned brother, in his love toward her ever most kind and natural; with him, the portion and sinew of her fortune, her marriage-dowry; with both, her combinate husband, this well-seeming Angelo.

Isabella. Can this be so? Did Angelo so leave her?

Duke. Left her in her tears, and dried not one of them with his comfort; swallowed his vows whole, pretending in her discoveries of dishonour; in few, bestowed her on her own lamentation, which she yet wears for his sake; and he, a marble to her tears, is washed with them, but relents not."

It is evident that Angelo and Mariana were bound by oath; the nuptial was appointed; there was a prescribed time between the contract and the performance of the solemnity of the Church. The lady, however, having lost her dowry, the contract was violated by her "combinate" or affianced husband—the oath, no doubt, having been tendered by a minister of the Church, in the presence of witnesses. In "Twelfth Night" (iv. 3) we have a minute description of such a ceremonial; for, when Olivia is hastily espoused to Sebastian, she says:

> "Now go with me and with this holy man
> Into the chantry by: there, before him,
> And underneath that consecrated roof,
> Plight me the full assurance of your faith;
> That my most jealous and too doubtful soul
> May live at peace. He shall conceal it,
> Whiles you are willing it shall come to note;
> What time we will our celebration keep
> According to my birth."

This, then, was a private ceremony before a single witness, who would conceal it till the proper period of the public ceremonial. Olivia, fancying that she has thus espoused the page, repeatedly calls him "husband;" and, being rejected, she summons the priest to declare (v. 1):

> "what thou dost know
> Hath newly pass'd between this youth and me."

The priest answers:

> "A contract of eternal bond of love,
> Confirm'd by mutual joinder of your hands,
> Attested by the holy close of lips,
> Strengthen'd by interchangement of your rings;
> And all the ceremony of this compact
> Seal'd in my function, by my testimony:
> Since when, my watch hath told me, toward my grave
> I have travell'd but two hours."

Again, in the "Winter's Tale" (iv. 4), which contains many a perfect picture of real rustic life, it appears that, occasionally, the troth-plight was exchanged without the presence of a priest; but that witnesses were essential to the ceremony:

> "*Florizel.* . . . O, hear me breathe my life
> Before this ancient sir, who, it should seem,
> Hath sometime lov'd: I take thy hand, this hand,
> As soft as dove's down and as white as it,
> Or Ethiopian's tooth, or the fann'd snow, that's bolted
> By the northern blasts twice o'er.
> *Polixenes.* What follows this?—
> How prettily the young swain seems to wash
> The hand, was fair before!—I have put you out:—
> But, to your protestation; let me hear
> What you profess.
> *Florizel.* Do, and be witness to 't.
> *Polixenes.* And this my neighbour too?
> *Florizel.* And he, and more
> Than he, and men; the earth, the heavens, and all;
> That, were I crown'd the most imperial monarch,
> Thereof most worthy; were I the fairest youth
> That ever made eye swerve; had force and knowledge
> More than was ever man's, I would not prize them
> Without her love; for her employ them all;
> Commend them, and condemn them, to her service,
> Or to their own perdition.
> *Polixenes.* Fairly offer'd.
> *Camillo.* This shows a sound affection.

> *Shepherd.*   But, my daughter,
> Say you the like to him?
>   *Perdita.*   I cannot speak
> So well, nothing so well; no, nor mean better:
> By the pattern of mine own thoughts I cut out
> The purity of his.
>   *Shepherd.*   Take hands, a bargain!
> And, friends unknown, you shall bear witness to't:
> I give my daughter to him, and will make
> Her portion equal his.[1]
>   *Florizel.*   O, that must be
> I' the virtue of your daughter: one being dead,
> I shall have more than you can dream of yet;
> Enough then for your wonder.   But, come on,
> Contract us 'fore these witnesses.
>   *Shepherd.*   Come, your hand;
> And, daughter, yours."

To the argument of Polixenes, that the father of Florizel ought to know of his proceeding, the young man answers:

> "Come, come, he must not.
> Mark our contract."

And then the father, discovering himself, exclaims:

> "Mark your divorce, young sir."

Here, then, as Mr. Knight remarks,[2] in the publicity of a

---

[1] On entering into any contract, or plighting of troth, the clapping of the hands together set the seal, as in the "Winter's Tale" (i. 2), where Leontes says:

> "Ere I could make thee open thy white hand,
> And clap thyself my love; then didst thou utter
> *I am yours forever.*"

So, too, in "The Tempest" (iii. 1):

> "*Miranda.*   My husband, then?
> *Ferdinand.* Ay, with a heart as willing
> As bondage e'er of freedom: here's my hand.
> *Miranda.* And mine, with my heart in't."

And in the old play of "Ram Alley," by Barry (1611), we read, "Come, clap hands, a match."   The custom is not yet disused in common life.

[2] "The Stratford Shakespeare," 1854, vol. i. p. 70.

village festival, the hand of the loved one is solemnly taken by her lover, who breathes his love before the ancient stranger who is accidentally present. The stranger is called to be a witness to the protestation, and so is the neighbor who has come with him. The maiden is called upon by her father to speak, and then the old man adds:

> "Take hands, a bargain!"

The friends are to bear witness to it:

> "I give my daughter to him, and will make
> Her portion equal his."

The impatient lover then again exclaims:

> "Contract us 'fore these witnesses."

The shepherd takes the hands of the youth and the maiden. Again the lover exclaims:

> "Mark our contract."

The ceremony is left incomplete, for the princely father discovers himself with:

> "Mark your divorce, young sir."

It appears, therefore, that espousals before witnesses were considered as constituting a valid marriage, if followed up within a limited time by the marriage of the Church. However much the Reformed Church might have endeavored to abrogate this practice, it was unquestionably the ancient habit of the people.[1] It was derived from the Roman law, and still prevails in the Lutheran Church.

Besides exchanging kisses,[2] accompanied with vows of everlasting affection, and whispering lovers' reassurances of fidelity, it was customary to interchange rings. In Shakespeare's plays, however, espousals are made with and without

---

[1] Knight's "Stratford Shakespeare," p. 73.
[2] Cf. "King John" (ii. 2):

> "*King Philip.*   Young princes, close your hands.
> *Austria.* And your lips too; for, I am well assured,
> That I did so, when I was first assured."

the use of the ring.   Thus, in the case of Ferdinand and
Miranda, we read of their joining hands only (" Tempest,"
iii. 1):

> " *Ferdinand.* Ay, with a heart as willing
> As bondage e'er of freedom ; here's my hand.
>   *Miranda.* And mine, with my heart in't ; and now farewell,
> Till half an hour hence."

In the passage already quoted from " Twelfth Night " (v. 1)
there seems to have been a mutual interchange of rings.

Some, indeed, considered that a betrothal was not complete unless each spouse gave the other a circlet.   Lady
Anne, in " Richard III." (i. 2), is made to share in this mis-
conception :

> " *Gloster.* Vouchsafe to wear this ring.
>   *Anne.* To take, is not to give.
>   *Gloster.* Look, how my ring encompasseth thy finger,
> Even so thy breast encloseth my poor heart :
> Wear both of them, for both of them are thine."

In " Two Gentlemen of Verona " (ii. 2) we read :

> " *Julia.* Keep this remembrance for thy Julia's sake (*giving a ring*).
>   *Proteus.* Why, then, we'll make exchange ; here, take you this.
>   *Julia.* And seal the bargain with a holy kiss."

A joint, or gimmal, ring was anciently a common token
among lovers, an allusion to which is made by Emilia, in
" Othello " (iv. 3): " I would not do such a thing for a joint-
ring."   Their nature will be best understood by a passage in
Dryden's " Don Sebastian " (1690, act v.) :

> " A curious artist wrought them,
> With joints so close, as not to be perceiv'd ;
> Yet are they both each other's counterpart,
>   .   .   .   .   and in the midst,
> A heart, divided in two halves, was plac'd."

They were generally made of two or three hoops, so chased
and engraved that, when fastened together by a single rivet,
the whole three formed one design, the usual device being
a hand.   When an engagement was contracted, the ring was

taken apart, each spouse taking a division, and the third one
being presented to the principal witness of the contract.[1]
Hence such a ring was known as a " Sponsalium Annulis,"
to which Herrick thus refers:

> " Thou sent'st me a true-love knot, but I
> Returned a ring of jimmals, to imply
> Thy love hath one knot, mine a triple tye."

The term is used by the Duke of Anjou, in " 1 Henry VI."
(i. 2):

> " I think, by some odd gimmors or device,
> Their arms are set like clocks, still to strike on;
> Else ne'er could they hold out so as they do."

Again, in " Henry V." (iv. 2), Grandpré tells how,

> " in their pale dull mouths the gimmal bit
> Lies foul with chew'd grass, still and motionless."

Most readers of the " Merchant of Venice" remember
the mirthful use which Shakespeare makes of lovers' rings.
Portia says (iii. 2), when giving her wealth and self to Bassanio:

> " I give them with this ring;
> Which when you part from, lose, or give away,
> Let it presage the ruin of your love."

The last act, too, gives several particulars about lovers' rings,
which, in Elizabethan England,[2] often had posies engraved
on them, and were worn by men on the left hand. Gratiano, for example, says:

> " About a hoop of gold, a paltry ring
> That she did give me; whose posy was
> For all the world like cutlers' poetry
> Upon a knife, ' Love me and leave me not.' "

Again Bassanio exclaims:

> " Why, I were best to cut my left hand off,
> And swear I lost the ring defending it."

---

[1] See Nares's " Glossary," vol. ii. p. 363; " Archæologia," vol. xiv.
p. 7; Jones's " Finger Ring Lore," 1877, pp. 313–318.
[2] See Jeaffreson's " Brides and Bridals," 1873, vol. i. pp. 77, 78.

In "Taming of the Shrew" Shakespeare gives numerous allusions to the customs of his day connected with courtship and marriage. Indeed, in the second act (sc. 2) we have a perfect betrothal scene:

> "*Petruchio*. Give me thy hand, Kate: I will unto Venice,
> To buy apparel 'gainst the wedding-day.—
> Provide the feast, father, and bid the guests;
> I will be sure my Katharine shall be fine.
> *Baptista*. I know not what to say: but give me your hands;
> God send you joy, Petruchio! 'tis a match.
> *Gremio. Tranio*. Amen, say we; we will be witnesses.
> *Petruchio*. Father, and wife, and gentlemen, adieu;
> I will to Venice; Sunday comes apace.
> We will have rings, and things, and fine array;
> And, kiss me, Kate, we will be married o' Sunday."

Although Katharina is only his spouse, and Baptista not yet his father-in-law, Petruchio, in accordance with fashion, calls her "wife" and him "father." The spouses of old times used to term one another "husband" and "wife," for, as they argued, they were as good as husband and wife.

Formerly there was a kind of betrothal or marriage contract prevalent among the low orders called "hand-fasting," or "hand-festing," said to have been much in use among the Danes, and which is mentioned by Ray in his "Glossary of Northumbrian Words." It simply means hand-fastening or binding. In "Cymbeline" (i. 5) the phrase is used in its secondary sense by the Queen, who, speaking of Pisanio, declares that he is

> "A sly and constant knave,
> Not to be shak'd; the agent for his master,
> And the remembrancer of her, to hold
> The hand-fast to her lord."

In the "Christian State of Matrimony," 1543, we find the following illustration of this custom: "Yet in this thing almost must I warn every reasonable and honest person to beware that in the contracting of marriage they dissemble not, nor set forth any lie. Every man, likewise, must esteem the person to whom he is 'handfasted' none otherwise than for his own spouse; though as yet it be not done in the church, nor in the street. After the handfasting and making of the contract, the church-going and wedding should not be deferred too long." The author then goes on to rebuke a custom "that at the handfasting there is made a great feast and superfluous banquet." Sir John Sinclair, in the "Statistical Account of Scotland" (1794, vol. xii. p. 615), tells us that at a fair annually held at Eskdalemuir, Dumfriesshire, "it was the custom for the unmarried persons of both sexes to choose a companion according to their liking, with whom they were to live till that time next year. This was called 'handfasting,' or hand-in-fist. If they were pleased with each other at that time then they continued together for life; if not, they separated, and were free to make another choice as at the first."

Shakespeare has given us numerous illustrations of the marriage customs of our forefathers, many of which are interesting as relics of the past, owing to their having long ago fallen into disuse. The fashion of introducing a bowl of wine into the church at a wedding, which is alluded to in the "Taming of the Shrew" (iii. 2), to be drunk by the bride and bridegroom and persons present, immediately after the marriage ceremony, is very ancient. Gremio relates how Petruchio

> "stamp'd and swore,
> As if the vicar meant to cozen him.
> But after many ceremonies done,
> He calls for wine :—'A health !' quoth he, as if
> He had been aboard, carousing to his mates
> After a storm :—quaff'd off the muscadel,
> And threw the sops [1] all in the sexton's face ;
> Having no other reason
> But that his beard grew thin and hungerly,
> And seem'd to ask him sops as he was drinking."

It existed even among our Gothic ancestors, and is mentioned in the ordinances of the household of Henry VII., "For the Marriage of a Princess :—' Then pottes of ipocrice

---

[1] Sops in wine.

to be ready, and to be put into cupps with soppe, and to be borne to the estates, and to take a soppe and drinke.'" It was also practised at the magnificent marriage of Queen Mary and Philip, in Winchester Cathedral, and at the marriage of the Elector Palatine to the daughter of James I., in 1612–13. Indeed, it appears to have been the practice at most marriages. In Jonson's "Magnetic Lady" it is called a "knitting cup;" in Middleton's "No Wit like a Woman's," the "contracting cup." In Robert Armin's comedy of "The History of the Two Maids of More Clacke," 1609, the play begins with:

> "*Enter a maid strewing flowers, and a serving-man perfuming the door.*
> *Maid.* Strew, strew.
> *Man.* The muscadine stays for the bride at church:
> The priest and Hymen's ceremonies tend
> To make them man and wife."

Again, in Beaumont and Fletcher's "Scornful Lady" (i. 1), the custom is referred to:[1]

> "If my wedding-smock were on,
> Were the gloves bought and given, the license come,
> Were the rosemary branches dipp'd, and all
> The hippocras and cakes eat and drunk off."

We find it enjoined in the Hereford missal. By the Sarum missal it is directed that the sops immersed in this wine, as well as the liquor itself, and the cup that contained it, should be blessed by the priest. The beverage used on this occasion was to be drunk by the bride and bridegroom and the rest of the company.

The nuptial kiss in the church was anciently part of the marriage ceremony, as appears from a rubric in one of the Salisbury missals. In the "Taming of the Shrew," Shakespeare has made an excellent use of this custom, where he relates how Petruchio (iii. 2)

> "took the bride about the neck
> And kiss'd her lips with such a clamorous smack
> That, at the parting, all the church did echo."

---

[1] See "Brand's Pop. Antiq.," 1849, vol. ii. pp. 136, 139.

Again, in " Richard II." (v. 1), where the Duke of Nor-thumberland announces to the king that he is to be sent to Pomfret, and his wife to be banished to France, the king exclaims :

> " Doubly divorc'd!—Bad men, ye violate
> A twofold marriage,—'twixt my crown and me,
> And then, betwixt me and my married wife.—
> Let me unkiss the oath 'twixt thee and me ;
> And yet not so, for with a kiss 'twas made."

Marston, too, in his " Insatiate Countess," mentions it :

> " The kisse thou gav'st me in the church, here take."

The practice is still kept up among the poor; and Brand[1] says it is " still customary among persons of middling rank as well as the vulgar, in most parts of England, for the young men present at the marriage ceremony to salute the bride, one by one, the moment it is concluded."

Music was the universal accompaniment of weddings in olden times.[2] The allusions to wedding music that may be found in the works of Shakespeare, Ben Jonson, and other Elizabethan dramatists, testify, as Mr. Jeaffreson points out, that, in the opinion of their contemporaries, a wedding without the braying of trumpets and beating of drums and clash-ing of cymbals was a poor affair. In " As You Like It " (v. 4), Hymen says:

> " Whiles a wedlock-hymn we sing."

And in " Romeo and Juliet " (iv. 5), Capulet says :

> " Our wedding cheer, to a sad burial feast;
> Our solemn hymns to sullen dirges change."

It seems to have been customary for the bride at her wedding to wear her hair unbraided and hanging loose over her shoulders. There may be an allusion to this custom in " King John " (iii. 1), where Constance says :

---

[1] " Pop. Antiq.," vol. ii. p. 140.
[2] " Brides and Bridals," 1873, vol. i. p. 252.

> "O Lewis, stand fast! the devil tempts thee here
> In likeness of a new untrimmed bride."

At the celebration of her marriage with the Palatine, Elizabeth Stuart wore " her hair dishevelled and hanging down her shoulders." Heywood speaks of this practice in the following graphic words:

> "At length the blushing bride comes, with her hair
> Dishevelled 'bout her shoulders."

It has been suggested that the bride's veil, which of late years has become one of the most conspicuous features of her costume, may be nothing more than a milliner's substitute, which in old time concealed not a few of the bride's personal attractions, and covered her face when she knelt at the altar. Mr. Jeafferson [1] thinks it may be ascribed to the Hebrew ceremony; or has come from the East, where veils have been worn from time immemorial. Some, again, connect it with the yellow veil which was worn by the Roman brides. Strange, too, as it may appear, it is nevertheless certain that knives and daggers were formerly part of the customary accoutrements of brides. Thus, Shakespeare, in the old quarto, 1597, makes Juliet wear a knife at the friar's cell, and when she is about to take the potion. This custom, however, is easily accounted for, when we consider that women anciently wore a knife suspended from their girdle. Many allusions to this practice occur in old writers.[2] In Dekker's "Match Me in London," 1631, a bride says to her jealous husband:

> "See, at my girdle hang my wedding knives!
> With those dispatch me."

In the "Witch of Edmonton," 1658, Somerton says:

> "But see, the bridegroom and bride come; the new
> Pair of Sheffield knives fitted both to one sheath."

Among other wedding customs alluded to by Shakespeare

---

[1] "Brides and Bridals," vol. i. p. 177.
[2] See Brand's "Pop. Antiq.," 1849, vol. ii. pp. 131–133.

we may mention one referred to in " Taming of the Shrew "
(ii. 1), where Katharina, speaking of Bianca, says to her father:

> " She is your treasure, she must have a husband :
> I must dance bare-foot on her wedding-day,
> And, for your love to her, lead apes in hell,"

it being a popular notion that unless the elder sisters danced
barefoot at the marriage of a younger one, they would in-
evitably become old maids, and be condemned " to lead
apes in hell." The expression " to lead apes in hell," applied above to old maids, has given rise to much discussion,
and the phrase has not yet been satisfactorily explained.
Steevens suggests that it might be considered an act of
posthumous retribution for women who refused to bear children to be condemned to the care of apes in leading-strings
after death. Malone says that " to lead apes " was in
Shakespeare's time one of the employments of a bear-ward,
who often carried about one of these animals with his bear.
Nares explains the expression by reference to the word ape
as denoting a fool, it probably meaning that those coquettes
who made fools of men, and led them about without real
intention of marriage, would have them still to lead against
their will hereafter. In " Much Ado About Nothing " (ii. 1),
Beatrice says: "therefore I will even take sixpence in earnest of the bear-ward, and lead his apes into hell." Douce [1]
tells us that homicides and adulterers were in ancient times
compelled, by way of punishment, to lead an ape by the
neck, with their mouths affixed in a very unseemly manner
to the animal's tail.

In accordance with an old custom, the bride, on the wed-
ding-night, had to dance with every guest, and play the
amiable, however much against her own wishes. In " Henry
VIII." (v. 2), there seems to be an allusion to this practice,
where the king says:

> " I had thought,
> They had parted so much honesty among them,
> At least, good manners, as not thus to suffer
> A man of his place, and so near our favour,
> To dance attendance on their lordships' pleasures."

---

[1] " Illustrations of Shakespeare," p. 203.

In the "Christian State of Matrimony" (1543) we read thus: "Then must the poor bryde kepe foote with a dauncers, and refuse none, how scabbed, foule, droncken, rude, and shameless soever he be."

As in our own time, so, too, formerly, flowers entered largely into the marriage festivities. Most readers will at once call to mind that touching scene in "Romeo and Juliet" (iv. 5), where Capulet says, referring to Juliet's supposed untimely death:

> "Our bridal flowers serve for a buried corse."

It seems, too, in days gone by to have been customary to deck the bridal bed with flowers, various allusions to which are given by Shakespeare. Thus, in "Hamlet" (v. 1), the queen, speaking of poor Ophelia, says:

> "I hop'd thou should'st have been my Hamlet's wife;
> I thought thy bride-bed to have deck'd, sweet maid."

In "The Tempest" (iv. 1) we may compare the words of Prospero, who, alluding to the marriage of his daughter Miranda with Ferdinand, by way of warning, cautions them lest

> "barren hate,
> Sour-ey'd disdain and discord shall bestrew
> The union of your bed with weeds so loathly
> That you shall hate it both."

In the Papal times no new-married couple could go to bed together till the bridal-bed had been blessed—this being considered one of the most important of the marriage ceremonies. "On the evening of the wedding-day," says Mr. Jeaffreson,[1] "when the married couple sat in state in the bridal-bed, before the exclusion of the guests, who assembled to commend them yet again to Heaven's keeping, one or more priests, attended by acolytes swinging to and fro lighted censers, appeared in the crowded chamber to bless the couch, its occupants, and the truckle-bed, and fumigate

---

[1] "Brides and Bridals," vol. i. p. 98; see Brand's "Pop. Antiq.," vol. ii. p. 175.

the room with hallowing incense." In "A Midsummer-Night's Dream" (v. 1), Oberon says:

> " Now, until the break of day,
> Through this house each fairy stray.
> To the best bride-bed will we,
> Which by us shall blessed be ;
> And the issue there create
> Ever shall be fortunate."

Steevens, in illustration of this custom, quotes from Chaucer's " The Merchant's Tale " (ed. Tyrwhitt), line 9693 :

> " And when the bed was with the preest yblessed."

The formula for this curious ceremony is thus given in the Manual for the use of Salisbury: " Nocte vero sequente cum sponsus et sponsa ad lectum pervenerint, accedat sacerdos et benedicat thalamum, dicens. Benedic, Domine, thalamum istum et omnes habitantes in eo ; ut in tua pace consistant, et in tua voluntate permaneant : et in tuo amore vivant et senescant et multiplicentur in longitudine dierum. Per Dominum.—Item benedictio super lectum. Benedic, Domine, hoc cubiculum, respice, quinon dormis neque dormitas. Qui custodis Israel, custodi famulos tuos in hoc lecto quiescentes ab omnibus fantasmaticis demonum illusionibus. Custodi eos vigilantes ut in preceptis tuis meditentur dormientes, et te per soporem sentiant ; ut hic et ubique depensionis tuæ muniantur auxilio. Per Dominum.—Deinde fiat benedictio super eos in lecto tantum cum oremus. Benedicat Deus corpora vestra et animas vestras ; et det super eos benedictionem sicut benedixit Abraham, Isaac, et Jacob, Amen. His peractis aspergat eos aqua benedicta, et sic discedat et dimittat eos in pace." [1]

In the French romance of Melusine, the bishop who marries her to Raymondin blesses the nuptial-bed. The ceremony is there presented in a very ancient cut, of which Douce has given a copy. The good prelate is sprinkling the parties with holy water. It appears that, occasionally,

---

[1] See Douce's " Illustrations of Shakespeare," pp. 123, 124.

during the benediction, the married couple only sat on the bed; but they generally received a portion of the consecrated bread and wine. It is recorded in France, that, on frequent occasions, the priest was improperly detained till midnight, while the wedding guests rioted in the luxuries of the table, and made use of language that was extremely offensive to the clergy. It was therefore ordained, in the year 1577, that the ceremony of blessing the nuptial-bed should for the future be performed in the day-time, or at least before supper, and in the presence of the bride and bridegroom, and of their nearest relations only.

On the morning after the celebration of the marriage, it was formerly customary for friends to serenade a newly married couple, or to greet them with a morning song to bid them good-morrow. In "Othello" (iii. 1) this custom is referred to by Cassio, who, speaking of Othello and Desdemona, says to the musicians:

> "Masters, play here; I will content your pains:
> Something that's brief; and bid, 'Good morrow, general.'"

According to Cotgrave, the morning-song to a newly married woman was called the "hunt's up." It has been suggested that this may be alluded to by Juliet (iii. 5), who, when urging Romeo to make his escape, tells him:

> "Some say the lark and loathed toad change eyes;
> O, now I would they had chang'd voices too!
> Since arm from arm that voice doth us affray,
> Hunting thee hence with hunt's-up to the day.
> O, now be gone."

In olden times torches were used at weddings—a practice, indeed, dating as far back as the time of the Romans. From the following lines in Herrick's "Hesperides," it has been suggested that the custom once existed in this country:

> "*Upon a maid that dyed the day she was marryed.*
> "That morne which saw me made a bride,
> The ev'ning witnest that I dy'd.
> Those holy lights, wherewith they guide
> Unto the bed the bashful bride,

> Serv'd but as tapers for to burne
> And light my reliques to their urne.
> This epitaph which here you see,
> Supply'd the Epithalamie."[1]

Shakespeare alludes to this custom in " 1 Henry VI." (iii. 2), where Joan of Arc, thrusting out a burning torch on the top of the tower at Rouen, exclaims:

> "Behold, this is the happy wedding torch,
> That joineth Rouen unto her countrymen."

In " The Tempest," too (iv. 1), Iris says:

> "no bed-right shall be paid
> Till Hymen's torch be lighted."

According to a Roman marriage custom, the bride, on her entry into her husband's house, was prohibited from treading over his threshold, and lest she should even so much as touch it, she was always lifted over it. Shakespeare seems inadvertently to have overlooked this usage in " Coriolanus " (iv. 5), where he represents Aufidius as saying:

> "I lov'd the maid I married; never man
> Sigh'd truer breath; but that I see thee here,
> Thou noble thing! more dances my rapt heart,
> Than when I first my wedded mistress saw
> Bestride my threshold."

Lucan in his " Pharsalia " (lib. ii. l. 359), says:

> "Translata vetuit contingere limina planta."

Once more, Sunday appears to have been a popular day for marriages; the brides of the Elizabethan dramas being usually represented as married on Sundays. In the " Taming of the Shrew " (ii. 1), Petruchio, after telling his future father-in-law " that upon Sunday is the wedding-day," and laughing at Katharina's petulant exclamation, " I'll see thee hanged on Sunday first," says:

> "Father, and wife, and gentlemen, adieu;
> .I will to Venice; Sunday comes apace:—
> We will have rings, and things, and fine array;
> And, kiss me, Kate, we will be married o' Sunday."

---

[1] See Brand's " Pop. Antiq.," 1849, vol. ii. p. 159.

Thus Mr. Jeaffreson, speaking of this custom in his "Brides and Bridals," rightly remarks: "A fashionable wedding, celebrated on the Lord's Day in London, or any part of England, would nowadays be denounced by religious people of all Christian parties. But in our feudal times, and long after the Reformation, Sunday was of all days of the week the favorite one for marriages. Long after the theatres had been closed on Sundays, the day of rest was the chief day for weddings with Londoners of every social class."

Love-charms have from the earliest times been much in request among the credulous, anxious to gain an insight into their matrimonial prospects.[1] In the "Merchant of Venice" (v. 1), we have an allusion to the practice of kneeling and praying at wayside crosses for a happy marriage, in the passage where Stephano tells how his mistress

> "doth stray about
> By holy crosses, where she kneels and prays
> For happy wedlock hours."

The use of love-potions by a despairing lover, to secure the affections of another, was a superstitious practice much resorted to in olden times.[2] This mode of enchantment, too, was formerly often employed in our own country, and Gay, in his "Shepherd's Week," relates how Hobnelia was guilty of this questionable practice:

> "As I was wont, I trudged, last market-day,
> To town with new-laid eggs, preserved in hay.
> I made my market long before 'twas night;
> My purse grew heavy, and my basket light.
> Straight to the 'pothecary's shop I went,
> And in love-powder all my money spent.
> Behap what will, next Sunday after prayers,
> When to the ale-house Lubberkin repairs,
> These golden flies into his mug I'll throw,
> And soon the swain with fervent love shall glow."

---

[1] See "Merry Wives of Windsor," iv. 2.
[2] See Potter's "Antiquities of Greece;" Brand's "Pop. Antiq.," vol. iii. p. 306.

In the " Character of a Quack Astrologer," 1673, quoted by Brand, we are told how " he trappans a young heiress to run away with a footman, by persuading a young girl 'tis her destiny ; and sells the old and ugly philtres and love-powder to procure them sweethearts." Shakespeare has represented Othello as accused of winning Desdemona " by conjuration and mighty magic." Thus Brabantio (i. 2) says:

> " thou hast practised on her with foul charms ;
> Abus'd her delicate youth with drugs, or minerals,
> That weaken motion."

And in the following scene he further repeats the same charge against Othello:

> " She is abus'd, stol'n from me, and corrupted
>   By spells and medicines bought of mountebanks ;
>   For nature so preposterously to err,
>   Being not deficient, blind, or lame of sense,
>   Sans witchcraft could not."

Othello, however, in proving that he had won Desdemona only by honorable means, addressing the Duke, replies:

> " by your gracious patience,
> I will a round unvarnish'd tale deliver
> Of my whole course of love ; what drugs, what charms,
> What conjuration, and what mighty magic,—
> For such proceeding I am charg'd withal,—
> I won his daughter."

It may have escaped the poet's notice that, by the Venetian law, the giving love-potions was held highly criminal, as appears in the code " Della Promission del Malefico," cap. xvii., " Del Maleficii et Herbarie."

A further allusion to this practice occurs in " A Midsummer-Night's Dream " (ii. 1), where Puck and Oberon amuse themselves at Titania's expense.[1]

An expression common in Shakespeare's day for any one born out of wedlock is mentioned by the Bastard in " King John " (i. 1):

> " In at the window, or else o'er the hatch."

---

[1] See page 227.

The old saying also that " Hanging and wiving go by destiny " is quoted by Nerissa in the " Merchant of Venice " (ii. 9). In " Much Ado About Nothing " (ii. 1), Don Pedro makes use of an old popular phrase in asking Claudio : "When mean you to go to church ?" referring to his marriage.

A solemn and even melancholy air was often affected by the beaux of Queen Elizabeth's time, as a refined mark of gentility, a most sad and pathetic allusion to which custom is made by Arthur in " King John " (iv. 1):

> " Methinks, nobody should be sad but I :
> Yet, I remember, when I was in France,
> Young gentlemen would be as sad as night,
> Only for wantonness." [1]

There are frequent references to this fashion in our old writers. Thus, in Ben Jonson's " Every Man in His Humor " (i. 3), we read : " Why, I do think of it ; and I will be more proud, and melancholy, and gentlemanlike than I have been, I'll insure you."

---

[1] See Nares's " Glossary," vol. ii. p. 563.

CHAPTER XIV.

DEATH AND BURIAL.

FROM a very early period there has been a belief in the existence of a power of prophecy at that period which precedes death. It took its origin in the assumed fact that the soul becomes divine in the same ratio as its connection with the body is loosened. It has been urged in support of this theory that at the hour of death the soul is, as it were, on the confines of two worlds, and may possibly at the same moment possess a power which is both prospective and retrospective. Shakespeare, in " Richard II." (ii. 1), makes the dying Gaunt exclaim, alluding to his nephew, the young and self-willed king:

> "Methinks I am a prophet new inspir'd,
> And thus, expiring, do foretell of him."

Again, the brave Percy, in " 1 Henry IV." (v. 4), when in the agonies of death, expresses the same idea:

> " O, I could prophesy,
> But that the earthy and cold hand of death
> Lies on my tongue."

We may also compare what Nerissa says of Portia's father in " Merchant of Venice " (i. 2), " Your father was ever virtuous; and holy men, at their death, have good inspirations."

Curious to say, this notion may be traced up to the time of Homer. Thus Patroclus prophesies the death of Hector (" Iliad," π. 852): " You yourself are not destined to live long, for even now death is drawing nigh unto you, and a violent fate awaits you—about to be slain in fight by the hands of Achilles." Aristotle tells us that the soul, when on the point of death, foretells things about to happen. Others have sought for the foundation of this belief in the 49th chapter of Genesis: "And Jacob called unto his sons, and said, Gather yourselves together, that I may tell you that which shall befall you in the last days.... And when Jacob had made an end of commanding his sons, he gathered up his feet into the bed, and yielded up the ghost, and was gathered unto his people." Whether, however, we accept this origin or not, at any rate it is very certain that the notion in question has existed from the earliest times, being alluded to also by Socrates, Xenophon, and Diodorus Siculus. It still lingers on in Lancashire and other parts of England.

Among other omens of death may be mentioned high spirits, which have been supposed to presage impending death. Thus, in "Romeo and Juliet" (v. 3), Romeo exclaims:

> "How oft, when men are at the point of death,
> Have they been merry! which their keepers call
> A lightning before death."

This idea is noticed by Ray, who inserts it as a proverb, "It's a lightening before death;" and adds this note: "This is generally observed of sick persons, that a little before they die their pains leave them, and their understanding and memory return to them—as a candle just before it goes out gives a great blaze." It was also a superstitious notion that unusual mirth was a forerunner of adversity. Thus, in the last act of "Romeo and Juliet" (sc. 1), Romeo comes on, saying:

> "If I may trust the flattering truth of sleep,
> My dreams presage some joyful news at hand:
> My bosom's lord sits lightly in his throne;
> And all this day an unaccustom'd spirit
> Lifts me above the ground with cheerful thoughts."

Immediately, however, a messenger enters to announce Juliet's death.

In "Richard III." (iii. 2), Hastings is represented as rising in the morning in unusually high spirits. Stanley says:

> "The lords at Pomfret, when they rode from London,
> Were jocund, and suppos'd their state was sure,

And they, indeed, had no cause to mistrust;
But yet, you see, how soon the day o'ercast."

This idea, it may be noted, runs throughout the whole scene. Before dinner-time, Hastings was beheaded.

Once more, in " 2 Henry IV." (iv. 2), the same notion is alluded to in the following dialogue:

"*Westmoreland.* Health to my lord and gentle cousin, Mowbray.
Mowbray. You wish me health in very happy season;
For I am, on the sudden, something ill.
Archbishop. Against ill chances men are ever merry;
But heaviness foreruns the good event.
Westmoreland. Therefore be merry, coz; since sudden sorrow
Serves to say thus, ' Some good thing comes to-morrow.'
Archbishop. Believe me, I am passing light in spirit.
Mowbray. So much the worse, if your own rule be true."

Tytler, in his " History of Scotland," thus speaks of the death of King James I.: " On this fatal evening (Feb. 20, 1437), the revels of the court were kept up to a late hour. The prince himself appears to have been in unusually gay and cheerful spirits. He even jested, if we may believe the contemporary manuscript, about a prophecy which had declared that a king that year should be slain." Shelley strongly entertained this superstition: " During all the time he spent in Leghorn, he was in brilliant spirits, to him a sure prognostic of coming evil."

Again, it is a very common opinion that death announces its approach by certain mysterious noises, a notion, indeed, which may be traced up to the time of the Romans, who believed that the genius of death announced his approach by some supernatural warning. In " Troilus and Cressida " (iv. 4), Troilus says:

"Hark! you are call'd : some say, the Genius so
Cries ' Come !' to him that instantly must die."

This superstition was frequently made use of by writers of bygone times, and often served to embellish, with touching pathos, their poetic sentiment. Thus Flatman, in some pretty lines, has embodied this thought:

> " My soul, just now about to take her flight,
>   Into the regions of eternal night,
>   Methinks I hear some gentle spirit say,
>   Be not fearful, come away."

Pope speaks in the same strain :

> " Hark ! they whisper, angels say,
>   Sister spirit, come away."

Shakespeare, too, further alludes to this idea in "Macbeth" (ii. 3), where, it may be remembered, Lennox graphically describes how, on the awful night in which Duncan is so basely murdered :.

> " Our chimneys were blown down ; and, as they say,
>   Lamentings heard i' the air; strange screams of death ;
>   And prophesying, with accents terrible,
>   Of dire combustion, and confus'd events,
>   New hatch'd to the woful time."

As in Shakespeare's day, so, too, at the present time, there is perhaps no superstition so deeply rooted in the minds of many people as the belief in what are popularly termed " death-warnings." Modern folk-lore holds either that a knocking or rumbling in the floor is an omen of a death about to happen, or that dying persons themselves announce their dissolution to their friends in such strange sounds.[1] Many families are supposed to have particular warnings, such as the appearance of a bird, the figure of a tall woman, etc. Such, moreover, are not confined to our own country, but in a variety of forms are found on the Continent. According to another belief, it was generally supposed that when a man was on his death-bed the devil or his agents tried to seize his soul, if it should happen that he died without receiving the sacrament of the Eucharist, or without confessing his sins. Hence, in " 2 Henry VI." (iii. 3), the king says :

> " O, beat away the busy meddling fiend
>   That lays strong siege unto this wretch's soul,
>   And from his bosom purge this black despair."

---

[1] Tylor's " Primitive Culture," 1873, vol. i. p. 145.

In the old Office books of the Church, these "busy meddling fiends" are often represented with great anxiety besieging the dying man; but on the approach of the priest and his attendants, they are shown to display symptoms of despair at their impending discomfiture. Douce[1] quotes from an ancient manuscript book of devotion, written in the reign of Henry VI., the following prayer to St. George: "Judge for me whan the moste hedyous and damnable dragons of helle shall be redy to take my poore soule and engloute it in to theyr infernall belyes."

Some think that the "passing-bell," which was formerly tolled for a person who was dying, was intended to drive away the evil spirit that might be hovering about to seize the soul of the deceased. Its object, however, was probably to bespeak the prayers of the faithful, and to serve as a solemn warning to the living. Shakespeare has given several touching allusions to it. Thus, in Sonnet lxxi. he says:

> "No longer mourn for me when I am dead,
> Than you shall hear the surly sullen bell
> Give warning to the world that I am fled
> From this vile world."

In "2 Henry IV." (i. 1), Northumberland speaks in the same strain:

> "Yet the first bringer of unwelcome news
> Hath but a losing office: and his tongue
> Sounds ever after as a sullen bell,
> Remember'd knolling a departing friend."

We may quote a further allusion in "Venus and Adonis" (l. 701):

> "And now his grief may be compared well
> To one sore sick that hears the passing-bell."

In a statute passed during the reign of Henry VIII., it is ordered "that clarks are to ring no more than the passing bell for poare people, nor less for an honest householder, and he be a citizen; nor for children, maydes, journeymen,

---

[1] "Illustrations of Shakespeare," 1829, pp. 324–326.

apprentices, day-labourers, or any other poare person." In
1662, the Bishop of Worcester[1] asks, in his visitation charge:
" Doth the parish clerk or sexton take care to admonish the
living, by tolling of a passing-bell, of any that are dying,
thereby to meditate of their own deaths, and to commend
the other's weak condition to the mercy of God?" It was,
also, called the " soul-bell," upon which Bishop Hall remarks:
" We call it the soul-bell because it signifies the departure
of the soul, not because it helps the passage of the soul."
Ray, in his " Collection of Proverbs," has the following
couplet:

> " When thou dost hear a toll or knell
> Then think upon thy passing-bell."

It was formerly customary to draw away the pillow from
under the heads of dying persons, so as to accelerate their
departure — an allusion to which we find in " Timon of
Athens " (iv. 3), where Timon says:

> " Pluck stout men's pillows from below their heads."

This, no doubt, originated in the notion that a person cannot die happily on a bed made of pigeons' feathers. Grose
says: " It is impossible for a person to die whilst resting on
a pillow stuffed with the feathers of a dove; but that he
will struggle with death in the most exquisite torture. The
pillows of dying persons are therefore frequently taken away
when they appear in great agonies, lest they may have pigeon's feathers in them." Indeed, in Lancashire, this practice is carried to such an extent that some will not allow
dying persons to lie on a feather bed, because they hold that
it very much increases their pain and suffering, and actually
retards their departure.[2]

The departure of the human soul from this world, and its
journey to its untried future, have become interwoven with

---

[1] " Annals of Worcester," 1845.

[2] Harland and Wilkinson's " Lancashire Folk-Lore," 1869, p. 268 ; see
" English Folk-Lore," 1878, pp. 99, 100; also " Notes and Queries," 1st
series, vol. iv. p. 133.

an extensive network of superstitions, varying more or less in every country and tribe. Shakespeare has alluded to the numerous destinations of the disembodied spirit, enumerating the many ideas prevalent in his time on the subject. In " Measure for Measure " (iii. 1), Claudio thus speaks:

> " Ay, but to die, and go we know not where;
> To lie in cold obstruction and to rot ;
> This sensible warm motion to become
> A kneaded clod ; and the delighted spirit
> To bathe in fiery floods, or to reside
> In thrilling region of thick-ribbed ice ;
> To be imprison'd in the viewless winds,
> And blown with restless violence round about
> The pendent world." [1]

We may compare also the powerful language of Othello (v. 2):

> " This look of thine will hurl my soul from heaven,
> And fiends will snatch at it.   Cold, cold, my girl !
> Even like thy chastity.—
> O cursed, cursed slave !   Whip me, ye devils,
> From the possession of this heavenly sight !
> Blow me about in winds ! roast me in sulphur !
> Wash me in steep-down gulfs of liquid fire !
> O Desdemona ! Desdemona ! dead !"

Douce [2] says that in the former passage it is difficult to decide whether Shakespeare is alluding to the pains of hell or purgatory. Both passages are obscure, and have given rise to much criticism. It seems probable, however, that while partly referring to the notions of the time, relating to departed souls, Shakespeare has in a great measure incorporated the ideas of what he had read in books of Catholic divinity. The passages quoted above remind us of the legend of St. Patrick's purgatory, where mention is made of a lake of ice and snow into which persons were plunged up to their necks; and of the description of hell given in the " Shepherd's Calendar:"

---

[1] Cf. Milton's " Paradise Lost," v. 595–683.
[2] See " Illustrations of Shakespeare," 1839. pp. 82, 83.

"a great froste in a water rounes
And after a bytter wynde comes
Which gothe through the soules with eyre;
Fends with pokes pulle theyr flesshe ysondre,
They fight and curse, and eche on other wonder."

We cannot here enter, however, into the mass of mystic details respecting "the soul's dread journey[1] by caverns and rocky paths and weary plains, over steep and slippery mountains, by frail bank or giddy bridge, across gulfs or rushing rivers, abiding the fierce onset of the soul-destroyer or the doom of the stern guardian of the other world." Few subjects, indeed, have afforded greater scope for the imagination than the hereafter of the human soul, and hence, as might be expected, numerous myths have been invented in most countries to account for its mysterious departure in the hour of death, from the world of living men to its unseen, unknown home in the distant land of spirits.

Shakespeare several times uses the word "limbo" in a general signification for hell, as in "Titus Andronicus" (iii. 1):

"As far from help as limbo is from bliss."

And in "All's Well that Ends Well" (v. 3), Parolles says: "for, indeed, he was mad for her, and talked of Satan, and of limbo, and of furies, and I know not what." In "Henry VIII." (v. 4), "in Limbo Patrum" is jocularly put for a prison; and, again, in "Comedy of Errors" (iv. 2), "he's in Tartar limbo." "According to the schoolmen, *Limbus Patrum* was the place, bordering on hell, where the souls of the patriarchs and saints of the Old Testament remained till the death of Christ, who, descending into hell, set them free."[2]

One of the punishments invented of old for the covetous and avaricious, in hell, was to have melted gold poured down their throats, to which allusion is made by Flaminius, in "Timon of Athens" (iii. 1), who, denouncing Lucullus

---

[1] Tylor's "Primitive Culture," vol. ii. p. 46.
[2] Dyce's "Glossary," p. 246.

for his mean insincerity towards his friend Timon, exclaims, on rejecting the bribe offered him to tell his master that he had not seen him:

> " May these add to the number that may scald thee!
> Let molten coin be thy damnation."

In the " Shepherd's Calendar," Lazarus declares himself to have seen covetous men and women in hell dipped in caldrons of molten lead.   Malone quotes the following from an old black-letter ballad of " The Dead Man's Song:"

> " Ladles full of melted gold
> Were poured down their throats."

Crassus was so punished by the Parthians.[1]

There is possibly a further allusion to this imaginary punishment in " Antony and Cleopatra " (ii. 5), where Cleopatra says to the messenger:

> " But, sirrah, mark, we use
> To say, the dead are well: bring it to that,
> The gold I give thee will I melt, and pour
> Down thy ill-uttering throat."

According to a well-known superstition among sailors, it is considered highly unlucky to keep a corpse on board, in case of a death at sea.   Thus, in Pericles " (iii. 1), this piece of folk-lore is alluded to:

" 1 *Sailor.* Sir, your queen must overboard; the sea works high, the wind is loud, and will not lie till the ship be cleared of the dead.

Pericles. That's your superstition.

1 *Sailor.* Pardon us, sir; with us at sea it hath been still observed; and we are strong in custom.   Therefore briefly yield her; for she must overboard straight."

It was also a popular opinion that death is delayed until the ebb of the tide—a superstition to which Mrs. Quickly refers in " Henry V." (ii. 3); speaking of Falstaff's death, she says: " 'A made a finer end, and went away, an it had

---

[1] Singer's " Shakespeare," 1875, vol. viii. p. 291.

been any christom child; 'a parted even just between twelve and one, even at the turning o' the tide." Hence, in cases of sickness, many pretended that they could foretell the hour of the soul's departure. It may be remembered how Mr. Peggotty explained to David Copperfield, by poor Barkis's bedside, that "people can't die along the coast except when the tide's pretty nigh out. They can't be born unless it's pretty nigh in—not properly born till flood. He's a-going out with the tide—he's a-going out with the tide. It's ebb at half arter three, slack-water half an hour. If he lives till it turns he'll hold his own till past the flood, and go out with the next tide." Mr. Henderson[1] quotes from the parish register of Heslidon, near Hartlepool, the subjoined extracts of old date, in which the state of the tide at the time of death is mentioned:

"The xi^th daye of Maye, A.D. 1595, at vi. of ye clocke in the morninge, being full water, Mr. Henrye Mitford, of Hoolam, died at Newcastel, and was buried the xvi^th daie, being Sondaie, at evening prayer, the hired preacher maid ye sermon."

"The xvii^th daie of Maie, at xii. of ye clock at noon, being lowe water, Mrs. Barbara Mitford died, and was buried the xviii^th daie of Maie, at ix. of the clocke. Mr. Holsworth maid ye sermon."

According to Mr. Henderson, this belief is common along the east coast of England, from Northumberland to Kent. It has been suggested that there may be "some slight foundation for this belief in the change of temperature which undoubtedly takes place on the change of tide, and which may act on the flickering spark of life, extinguishing it as the ebbing sea recedes."

We may compare, too, the following passage in "2 Henry IV." (iv. 4), where Clarence, speaking of the approaching death of the king, says:

"The river hath thrice flow'd, no ebb between;
And the old folk, time's doting chronicles,

---

[1] "Folk-Lore of Northern Counties," 1880, p. 58.

> Say it did so a little time before
> That our great grandsire, Edward, sick'd and died."

This was an historical fact, having happened on October 12, 1411.

The prayers of the Church, which are used for the recovery of the sick, were, in the olden time, also supposed to have a morbific influence, to which Gloster attributes the death of the king in " 1 Henry VI." (i. 1):

> "The church! where is it? Had not churchmen pray'd,
> His thread of life had not so soon decay'd."

Once more, the custom of closing the eyes at the moment of death is touchingly referred to in " Antony and Cleopatra" (v. 2), where Charmian may be supposed to close Cleopatra's eyes:

> " Downy windows, close ;
> And golden Phœbus never be beheld
> Of eyes again so royal."

Passing on from that solemn moment in human life when the soul takes its flight from the fragile tenement of clay that contained it during its earthly existence, we find that, even among the lowest savages, there has generally been a certain respect paid to the dead body; and, consequently, various superstitious rites have, from time to time, been associated with its burial, which has been so appropriately termed "the last act." While occasionally speaking of death, Shakespeare has not only pictured its solemnity in the most powerful and glowing language, but, as opportunity allowed, given us a slight insight into those customs that formerly prevailed in connection with the committal of the body to its final resting-place in the grave. At the present day, when there is an ever-growing tendency to discard and forget, as irrational and foolish, the customs of bygone years, it is interesting to find chronicled, for all future time, in the immortal pages of our illustrious poet, those superstitious rites and social usages which may be said to have been most intimately identified with the age to which they belonged. One custom, perhaps, that will always re-

tain its old hold among us—so long as we continue to bury
the remains of our departed ones—is the scattering of flowers on their graves ; a practice, indeed, which may be traced
up to pagan times.   It is frequently mentioned by Shakespeare in some of his superb passages ; as, for instance, in
"Cymbeline" (iv. 2), where Arviragus says :

> "With fairest flowers,
> Whilst summer lasts, and I live here, Fidele,
> I'll sweeten thy sad grave : thou shalt not lack
> The flower that's like thy face, pale primrose, nor
> The azur'd hare-bell, like thy veins ; no, nor
> The leaf of eglantine, whom not to slander,
> Out-sweeten'd not thy breath.
> *   *   *   *   *   *   *
> Yea, and furr'd moss besides, when flowers are none,
> To winter-ground thy corse."

In "Hamlet" (iv. 5), the poor, bewildered Ophelia sings :

> "Larded with sweet flowers ;
> Which bewept to the grave did go
> With true-love showers."

Then, further on (v. 1), there is the affecting flower-strewing
scene, where the Queen, standing over the grave of Ophelia,
bids her a long farewell :

> "Sweets to the sweet : farewell !
> I hop'd thou should'st have been my Hamlet's wife ;
> I thought thy bride-bed to have deck'd, sweet maid,
> And not have strew'd thy grave."

In "Romeo and Juliet" (iv. 5), Capulet says :

> "Our bridal flowers serve for a buried corse."

And further on (v. 3) the Page says :

> "He came with flowers to strew his lady's grave."[1]

Once more, in "Pericles" (iv. 1), Marina is introduced, entering with a basket of flowers, uttering these sad words :

---

[1] Cf. "Winter's Tale," iv. 4.

> " No, I will rob Tellus of her weed,
>   To strew thy green with flowers; the yellows, blues,
>   The purple violets, and marigolds,
>   Shall, as a carpet, hang upon thy grave,
>   While summer days do last."

Flowers, which so soon droop and wither, are, indeed, sweet emblems of that brief life which is the portion of mankind in this world, while, at the same time, their exquisite beauty is a further type of the glory that awaits the redeemed hereafter, when, like fair flowers, they shall burst forth in unspeakable grandeur on the resurrection morn. There is a pretty custom observed in South Wales on Palm Sunday, of spreading fresh flowers upon the graves of friends and relatives, the day being called Flowering Sunday.

The practice of decorating the corpse is mentioned by many old writers. In " Romeo and Juliet " (iv. 5), Friar Laurence says:

> " Dry up your tears, and stick your rosemary
>   On this fair corse; and, as the custom is,
>   In all her best array bear her to church."

Queen Katharine, in " Henry VIII." (iv. 2), directs:

> " When I am dead, good wench,
>   Let me be us'd with honour: strew me over
>   With maiden flowers."

It was formerly customary, in various parts of England, to have a garland of flowers and sweet herbs carried before a maiden's coffin, and afterwards to suspend it in the church. In allusion to this practice, the Priest, in " Hamlet " (v. 1), says:

> " Yet here she is allow'd her virgin crants,
>   Her maiden strewments, and the bringing home
>   Of bell and burial."

—crants[1] meaning garlands. It may be noted that no other

---

[1] The word in German is *kranz*, in other Teutonic dialects *krants*, *krans*, and *crance*—the latter being Lowland Scotch—and having *cransies* for plural. Clark and Wright's " Hamlet," 1876, p. 216.

instance has been found of this word in English. These garlands are thus described by Gay:

> "To her sweet mem'ry flow'ry garlands strung,
> On her now empty seat aloft were hung."

Nichols, in his "History of Lancashire" (vol. ii. pt. i. p. 382), speaking of Waltham, in Framland Hundred, says: "In this church, under every arch, a garland is suspended, one of which is customarily placed there whenever any young unmarried woman dies." Brand[1] tells us he saw in the churches of Wolsingham and Stanhope, in the county of Durham, specimens of these garlands; the form of a woman's glove, cut in white paper, being hung in the centre of each of them.

The funerals of knights and persons of rank were, in Shakespeare's day, performed with great ceremony and ostentation. Sir John Hawkins observes that "the sword, the helmet, the gauntlets, spurs, and tabard are still hung over the grave of every knight." In "Hamlet" (iv. 5), Laertes speaks of this custom:

> "His means of death, his obscure burial,—
> No trophy, sword, nor hatchment, o'er his bones,
> No noble rite, nor formal ostentation,—
> Cry to be heard, as 'twere from heaven to earth,
> That I must call't in question."

Again, in "2 Henry VI." (iv. 10), Iden says:

> "Is't Cade that I have slain, that monstrous traitor?
> Sword, I will hallow thee for this thy deed,
> And hang thee o'er my tomb when I am dead."

The custom of bearing the dead body in its ordinary habiliments, and with the face uncovered—a practice referred to in "Romeo and Juliet" (iv. 1)—appears to have been peculiar to Italy:

> "Then, as the manner of our country is,
> In thy best robes uncover'd on the bier,

---

[1] "Pop. Antiq." vol. ii. p. 303.

> Thou shalt be borne to that same ancient vault
> Where all the kindred of the Capulets lie."

In Coryat's "Crudities" (1776, vol. ii. p. 27) the practice is thus described: "The burials are so strange, both in Venice and all other cities, towns, and parishes of Italy, that they differ not only from England, but from all other nations whatever in Christendom. For they carry the corse to church with the face, hands, and feet all naked, and wearing the same apparel that the person wore lately before he died, or that which he craved to be buried in; which apparel is interred together with the body."[1] Singer[2] says that Shakespeare no doubt had seen this custom particularly described in the "Tragicall History of Romeus and Juliet:"

> " Another use there is, that, whosoever dies,
> Borne to the church, with open face, upon the bier he lies,
> In wonted weed attir'd, not wrapt in winding sheet."

He alludes to it again in Ophelia's song, in "Hamlet" (iv. 5):

> "They bore him barefac'd on the bier."

It was, in bygone times, customary to bury the Danish kings in their armor; hence the remark of Hamlet (i. 4), when addressing the Ghost:

> " What may this mean,
> That thou, dead corse, again, in complete steel,
> Revisit'st thus the glimpses of the moon,
> Making night hideous ?"

Shakespeare was probably guilty of an anachronism in "Coriolanus" (v. 6) when he makes one of the lords say:

> " Bear from hence his body,
> And mourn you for him: let him be regarded
> As the most noble corse that ever herald
> Did follow to his urn,"

the allusion being to the public funeral of English princes,

---

[1] See Staunton's "Shakespeare," 1864, vol. i. p. 305.

[2] "Shakespeare," 1875, vol. ix. pp. 209, 210.

at the conclusion of which a herald proclaimed the style of the deceased.

We may compare what Queen Katharine says in "Henry VIII." (iv. 2):

> "After my death I wish no other herald,
> No other speaker of my living actions,
> To keep my honour from corruption,
> But such an honest chronicler as Griffith."

It seems to have been the fashion, as far back as the thirteenth century, to ornament the tombs of eminent persons with figures and inscriptions on plates of brass; hence, in "Love's Labour's Lost" (i. 1), the King says:

> "Let fame, that all hunt after in their lives,
> Live register'd upon our brazen tombs."

In "Much Ado About Nothing" (v. 1), Leonato, speaking of his daughter's death, says:

> "Hang her an epitaph upon her tomb,
> And sing it to her bones: sing it to-night."

And also in a previous scene (iv. 1) this graceful custom is noticed:

> "Maintain a mourning ostentation,
> And on your family's old monument
> Hang mournful epitaphs."

It was also the custom, in years gone by, on the death of an eminent person, for his friends to compose short laudatory verses, epitaphs, etc., and to affix them to the hearse or grave with pins, wax, paste, etc. Thus, in "Henry V." (i. 2), King Henry declares:

> "Either our history shall with full mouth
> Speak freely of our acts, or else our grave,
> Like Turkish mute, shall have a tongueless mouth,
> Not worshipp'd with a waxen epitaph,"

meaning, says Gifford, "I will either have my full history recorded with glory, or lie in an undisturbed grave; not merely without an inscription sculptured in stone, but un-worshipped, unhonoured, even by a waxen epitaph."[1]

We may also compare what Lucius says in "Titus Andronicus" (i. 1):

> "There lie thy bones, sweet Mutius, with thy friends,
> Till we with trophies do adorn thy tomb!"

The custom was still general when Shakespeare lived; many fine and interesting examples existing in the old Cathedral of St. Paul's, and other churches of London, down to the time of the great fire, in the form of pensil-tables of wood and metal, painted or engraved with poetical memorials, suspended against the columns and walls.

"Feasts of the Dead," which have prevailed in this and other countries from the earliest times, are, according to some antiquarians, supposed to have been borrowed from the *cœna feralis* of the Romans—an offering, consisting of milk, honey, wine, olives, and strewed flowers, to the ghost of the deceased. In a variety of forms this custom has prevailed among most nations—the idea being that the spirits of the dead feed on the viands set before them; hence the rite in question embraced the notion of a sacrifice. In Christian times, however, these funeral offerings have passed into commemorative banquets, under which form they still exist among us. In allusion to these feasts, Hamlet (i. 2), speaking of his mother's marriage, says:

> "The funeral bak'd meats
> Did coldly furnish forth the marriage tables."

Again, in "Romeo and Juliet" (iv. 5), Capulet narrates how:

> "All things that we ordained festival,
> Turn from their office to black funeral:
> Our instruments, to melancholy bells;
> Our wedding cheer, to a sad burial feast."

Mr. Tylor,[2] in discussing the origin of funeral feasts, and

---

[1] Notes on "Jonson's Works," vol. ix. p. 58.
[2] "Primitive Culture," vol. ii. p. 43.

in tracing their origin back to the savage and barbaric times
of the institution of feast of departed souls, says we may find
a lingering survival of this old rite in the doles of bread and
drink given to the poor at funerals, and " soul-mass cakes,"
which peasant girls beg for at farmhouses, with the traditional formula,

> " Soul, soul, for a soul cake,
> Pray you, mistress, a soul cake."[1]

In the North of England the funeral feast is called an
" arval," and the loaves that are sometimes distributed
among the poor are termed " arval bread."

Among other funeral customs mentioned by Shakespeare,
may be mentioned his allusion to the burial service. Originally, before the reign of Edward VI., it was the practice for
the priest to throw earth on the body in the form of a cross,
and then to sprinkle it with holy water. Thus, in the
" Winter's Tale " (iv. 4), the Shepherd says:

> " Some hangman must put on my shroud, and lay me
> Where no priest shovels in dust,"

implying, " I must be buried as a common malefactor, out
of the pale of consecrated ground, and without the usual
rites of the dead "—a whimsical anachronism, as Mr. Douce[2]
points out, when it is considered that the old Shepherd was
a pagan, a worshipper of Jupiter and Apollo.

In " Antony and Cleopatra " (i. 3), we find an allusion to
the lachrymatory vials filled with tears which the Romans
were in the habit of placing in the tomb of a departed friend.
Cleopatra sorrowfully exclaims:

> " O most false love !
> Where be the sacred vials thou shouldst fill
> With sorrowful water ? Now I see, I see,
> In Fulvia's death, how mine receiv'd shall be."

---

[1] See " British Popular Customs," p. 404; Brand's " Pop. Antiq.,"
1849, vol. ii. pp. 237, 246; Douce's " Illustrations of Shakespeare," 1839,
p. 439.

[2] See Douce's " Illustrations of Shakespeare," 1839, p. 222.

This is another interesting instance of Shakespeare's knowledge of the manners of distant ages, showing how varied and extensive his knowledge was, and his skill in applying it whenever occasion required.

The winding or shrouding sheet, in which the body was wrapped previous to its burial, is alluded to in "Hamlet" (v. 1), in the song of the clown:

> "A pick-axe, and a spade, a spade,
> For and a shrouding sheet:
> O, a pit of clay for to be made
> For such a guest is meet."

Again, in "A Midsummer-Night's Dream" (v. 1), Puck says:

> "the screech-owl, screeching loud,
> Puts the wretch that lies in woe
> In remembrance of a shroud."

Ophelia speaks of the shroud as white as the mountain snow ("Hamlet," iv. 5). The following song, too, in "Twelfth Night" (ii. 4), mentions the custom of sticking yew in the shroud:

> "Come away, come away, death,
> And in sad cypress let me be laid;
> Fly away, fly away, breath:
> I am slain by a fair cruel maid.
> My shroud of white, stuck all with yew,
> O prepare it!
> My part of death, no one so true
> Did share it!"

To quote two further illustrations, Desdemona ("Othello," iv. 2) says to Emilia: "Lay on my bed my wedding-sheets," and when in the following scene Emilia answers:

> "I have laid those sheets you bade me on the bed,"

Desdemona adds:

> "If I do die before thee, pr'thee, shroud me
> In one of those same sheets"

—a wish, indeed, which her cruel fate so speedily caused to be realized. And in "3 Henry VI." (i. 1) we have King Henry's powerful words:

> "Think'st thou, that I will leave my kingly throne,
> Wherein my grandsire and my father sat?
> No: first shall war unpeople this my realm;
> Ay, and their colours,—often borne in France,
> And now in England, to our heart's great sorrow,—
> Shall be my winding-sheet."

The custom, still prevalent, of carrying the dead to the grave with music—a practice which existed in the primitive church—to denote that they have ended their spiritual warfare, and are become conquerors, formerly existed very generally in this country.[1] In "Cymbeline" (iv. 2), Arviragus says:

> "And let us, Polydore, though now our voices
> Have got the mannish crack, sing him to the ground,
> As once our mother; use like note and words,
> Save that Euriphile must be Fidele."

The tolling of bells at funerals is referred to in "Hamlet" (v. 1), where the priest says of Ophelia:

> "she is allow'd her virgin crants,
> Her maiden strewments, and the bringing home
> Of bell and burial."

It has been a current opinion for centuries that places of burial are haunted with spectres and apparitions—a notion, indeed, that prevailed as far back as the times of heathenism. Ovid speaks of ghosts coming out of their sepulchres and wandering about; and Vergil, quoting the popular opinion of his time, tells us how Moeris could call the ghosts out of their sepulchres ("Bucol." viii. 98):

> "Moerim, sæpe animas imis excire sepulchris,
> Atque satas alio vidi traducere messis."

---

[1] See Brand's "Pop. Antiq.," 1849, vol. ii. pp. 267–270.

Indeed, the idea of the ghost remaining near the corpse is of world-wide prevalence; and as Mr. Tylor[1] points out, "through all the changes of religious thought from first to last, in the course of human history, the hovering ghosts of the dead make the midnight burial-ground a place where men's flesh creeps with terror." In "A Midsummer-Night's Dream" (v. 1), Puck declares:

> "Now it is the time of night,
>   That the graves, all gaping wide,
>　Every one lets forth his sprite,
>   In the church-way paths to glide."

In the same play, too (iii. 2), Puck, speaking of "Aurora's harbinger," says:

> "At whose approach, ghosts, wandering here and there,
> Troop home to churchyards: damned spirits all,
> That in cross-ways and floods have burial,
> Already to their wormy beds are gone;
> For fear lest day should look their shames upon."

In this passage two curious superstitions are described; the ghosts of self-murderers, who are buried in cross-roads, and of those who have been drowned at sea, being said to wander for a hundred years, owing to the rites of sepulture having never been properly bestowed on their bodies.

We may further compare Hamlet's words (iii. 2):

> "'Tis now the very witching time of night,
> When churchyards yawn, and hell itself breathes out
> Contagion to this world."

From the earliest period much importance has been attached to the position of the grave, the popular direction being from east to west, that from north to south being regarded as not only dishonorable, but unlucky. Thus, in "Cymbeline" (iv. 2), Guiderius, when arranging about the apparently dead body of Imogen, disguised in man's apparel, says:

> "Nay, Cadwal, we must lay his head to the east;
> My father had a reason for't."

---

[1] "Primitive Culture," vol. ii. p. 30.

Indeed, the famous antiquary Hearne had such precise views in this matter that he left orders for his grave to be made straight by a compass, due east and west. This custom was practised by the ancient Greeks, and thus, as Mr. Tylor points out,[1] it is not to late and isolated fancy, but to the carrying on of ancient and widespread solar ideas, that we trace the well-known legend that the body of Christ was laid with the head towards the west, thus looking eastward, and the Christian usage of digging graves east and west, which prevailed through mediæval times, and is not yet forgotten. The rule of laying the head to the west, and its meaning that the dead shall rise looking towards the east, are perfectly stated in the following passage from an ecclesiastical treatise of the 16th century:[2] " Debet autem quis sic sepeliri ut capite ad occidentem posito, pedes dirigat ad Orientem, in quo quasi ipsa positione orat: et innuit quod promptus est, ut de occasu festinet ad ortum: de mundo ad seculum."[3]

Within old monuments and receptacles for the dead perpetual lamps were supposed to be lighted up, an allusion to which is made by Pericles (iii. 1), who, deploring the untimely death of Thaisa at sea, and the superstitious demand made by the sailors that her corpse should be thrown overboard, says:

" Nor have I time
To give thee hallow'd to thy grave, but straight
Must cast thee, scarcely coffin'd, in the ooze ;
Where, for a monument upon thy bones,
And aye-remaining lamps, the belching whale
And humming water must o'erwhelm thy corpse,
Lying with simple shells."

---

[1] " Primitive Culture," 1873, vol. ii. p. 423.

[2] Durandus, " De Officio Mortuorum," lib. vii. chap. 35–39.

[3] Dr. Johnson thought the words of the clown in " Hamlet" (v. 1), " make her grave straight," meant, " make her grave from east to west, in a direct line parallel to the church." This interpretation seems improbable, as the word straight in the sense of immediately occurs frequently in Shakespeare's plays.

Again, in " Troilus and Cressida" (iii. 2), we find a further reference in the words of Troilus:

> " O, that I thought it could be in a woman,
> To feed for aye her lamp and flames of love."

Pope, too, in his " Eloisa to Abelard," has a similar allusion (l. 261, 262):

> " Ah, hopeless lasting flames, like those that burn
> To light the dead, and warm th' unfruitful urn !"

D'Israeli, in his " Curiosities of Literature," thus explains this superstition: " It has happened frequently that inquisitive men, examining with a flambeau ancient sepulchres which have just been opened, the fat and gross vapors engendered by the corruption of dead bodies kindled as the flambeau approached them, to the great astonishment of the spectators, who frequently cried out ' A miracle !' This sudden inflammation, although very natural, has given room to believe that these flames proceeded from *perpetual lamps*, which some have thought were placed in the tombs of the ancients, and which, they said, were extinguished at the moment that these tombs opened, and were penetrated by the exterior air." Mr. Dennis, however, in his " Cities and Cemeteries of Etruria" (1878, vol. ii. p. 404), says that the use of sepulchral lamps by the ancients is well known, and gave rise to the above superstition. Sometimes lamps were kept burning in sepulchres long after the interment, as in the case of the Ephesian widow described by Petronius (" Satyr," c. 13), who replaced the lamp placed in her husband's tomb.

A common expression formerly applied to the dead occurs in the " Winter's Tale " (v. 1), where Dion asks:

> " What were more holy,
> Than to rejoice the former queen is well ?"

So in " Antony and Cleopatra " (ii. 5):

"*Messenger.* First, madam, he is well.
    Cleopatra.   Why, there's more gold.
But, sirrah, mark, we use
To say, the dead are well."[1]

Lastly, commentators have differed as to the meaning of the words of Julia in the "Two Gentlemen of Verona" (i. 2):

"I see you have a month's mind to them."

Douce says she refers to the mind or remembrance days of our popish ancestors; persons in their wills having often directed that in a month, or at some other specific time, some solemn office, as a mass or a dirge, should be performed for the repose of their souls. Thus Ray quotes a proverb: "To have a month's mind to a thing," and mentions the above custom. For a further and not improbable solution of this difficulty, the reader may consult Dyce's "Glossary" (p. 277).

---

[1] See Malone's note, Variorum edition, xiv. 400.

CHAPTER XV.

RINGS AND PRECIOUS STONES.

FROM a very early period, rings and precious stones have held a prominent place in the traditionary lore, customs, and superstitions of most nations. Thus, rings have been supposed "to protect from evil fascinations of every kind, against the evil eye, the influence of demons, and dangers of every possible character; though it was not simply in the rings themselves that the supposed virtues existed, but in the materials of which they were composed — in some particular precious stones that were set in them as charms or talismans, in some device or inscription on the stone, or some magical letters engraved on the circumference of the ring."[1] Rings, too, in days gone by, had a symbolical importance. Thus, it was anciently the custom for every monarch to have a ring, the temporary possession of which invested the holder with the same authority as the owner himself could exercise. Thus, in " Henry VIII." (v. 1), we have the king's ring given to Cranmer, and presented by him (sc. 2), as a security against the machinations of Gardiner and others of the council, who were plotting to destroy him. Thus the king says :

> " If entreaties
> Will render you no remedy, this ring
> Deliver them, and your appeal to us
> There make before them."

This custom, too, was not confined to royalty, for in " Richard II." (ii. 2), the Duke of York gives this order to his servant :

---

[1] Jones's " Finger-Ring Lore," 1877, p. 91.

> " Sirrah, get thee to Plashy, to my sister Gloster ;
> Bid her send me presently a thousand pound :—
> Hold, take my ring."

There is an interesting relic of the same custom still kept up at Winchester College.[1] When the captain of the school petitions the head-master for a holiday, and obtains it, he receives from him a ring, in token of the indulgence granted, which he wears during the holiday, and returns to the head-master when it is over. The inscription upon the ring was, formerly, " Potentiam fero, geroque." It is now " Commendat rarior usus " (Juvenal, " Sat." xi. 208).

Token Rings date from very early times. Edward I., in 1297, presented Margaret, his fourth daughter, with a golden pyx, in which he deposited a ring, as a token of his unfailing love.

In " Richard III." (i. 2) when Gloster brings his hasty wooing to a conclusion, he gives the Lady Anne a ring, saying :

> " Look, how my ring encompasseth thy finger,
> Even so thy breast encloseth my poor heart ;
> Wear both of them, for both of them are thine."

In " Cymbeline " (i. 1) Imogen gives Posthumus a ring when they part, and he presents her with a bracelet in exchange :

> " Look here, love ;
> This diamond was my mother's ; take it, heart ;
> But keep it till you woo another wife,
> When Imogen is dead.
>   *Posthumus.* How ! how ! another ?—
> You gentle gods, give me but this I have,
> And sear up my embracements from a next
> With bonds of death ! Remain, remain thou here,
>   (*Putting on the ring*)
> While sense can keep it on."

Yet he afterwards gives it up to Iachimo (ii. 4)—upon a false representation—to test his wife's honor :

---

[1] Wordsworth's " Shakespeare and the Bible," 1880, p. 283.

> " Here, take this too;
> It is a basilisk unto mine eye,
> Kills me to look on't."

The exchange of rings, a solemn mode of private contract between lovers, we have already referred to in the chapter on Marriage, a practice alluded to in the " Two Gentlemen of Verona " (ii. 2), where Julia gives Proteus a ring, saying :

> " Keep this remembrance for thy Julia's sake ;"

and he replies :

> " Why, then we'll make exchange : here, take you this."

Death's-head rings. Rings engraved with skulls and skeletons were not necessarily mourning rings, but were also worn by persons who affected gravity ; and, curious to say, by the procuresses of Elizabeth's time. Biron, in " Love's Labour's Lost " (v. 2), refers to " a death's face in a ring ;" and we may quote Falstaff's words in " 2 Henry IV." (ii. 4): " Peace, good Doll ! do not speak like a death's head ; do not bid me remember mine end." We may compare the following from " The Chances " (i. 5), by Beaumont and Fletcher :

> " As they keep deaths' heads in rings,
> To cry ' memento ' to me."

According to Mr. Fairholt, " the skull and skeleton decorations for rings first came into favor and fashion at the obsequious court of France, when Diana of Poictiers became the mistress of Henry II. At that time she was a widow, and in mourning, so black and white became fashionable colors ; jewels were formed like funeral memorials; golden ornaments, shaped like coffins, holding enamelled skeletons, hung from the neck; watches, made to fit in little silver skulls, were attached to the waists of the denizens of a court that alternately indulged in profanity or piety, but who mourned for show."[1]

Posy-rings were formerly much used, it having been cus-

---

[1] See Jones's " Finger-Ring Lore," 1877, p. 372.

tomary to inscribe a motto or " posy " within the hoop of
the betrothal ring. Thus, in the " Merchant of Venice "
(v. 1), Gratiano, when asked by Portia the reason of his
quarrel with Nerissa, answers:

> " About a hoop of gold, a paltry ring
> That she did give me; whose posy was
> For all the world like cutlers' poetry
> Upon a knife, ' Love me, and leave me not.' "

In " As You Like It " (iii. 2), Jaques tells Orlando, " You
are full of pretty answers. Have you not been acquainted
with goldsmiths' wives, and conned them out of rings?"
Again, " Hamlet " (iii. 2) asks:

> " Is this a prologue, or the posy of a ring?"

Many of our old writers allude to the posy-rings. Thus Herrick, in his " Hesperides," says:

> " What posies for our wedding rings,
> What gloves we'll give, and ribbonings."

Henry VIII. gave Anne of Cleves a ring with the following
posy: " God send me well to kepe;" a most unpropitious
alliance, as the king expressed his dislike to her soon after
the marriage.

Thumb-rings. These were generally broad gold rings
worn on the thumb by important personages. Thus Falstaff (" 1 Henry IV." ii. 4) bragged that, in his earlier years,
he had been so slender in figure as to " creep into an alderman's thumb-ring;" and a ring thus worn—probably as
more conspicuous—appears to have been considered as appropriate to the customary attire of a civic dignitary at a
much later period. A character in the Lord Mayor's Show,
in 1664, is described as " habited like a grave citizen—gold
girdle, and gloves hung thereon, rings on his fingers, and a
seal ring on his thumb." [1] Chaucer, in his " Squire's Tale,"
says of the rider of the brazen horse who advanced into the

---

[1] See Jones's " Finger-Ring Lore," 1877, p. 88.

hall, Cambuscan, that "upon his thumb he had of gold a ring." In "Romeo and Juliet" (i. 4), Mercutio speaks of the

> "agate stone
> On the forefinger of an alderman."

It has been suggested that Shakespeare, in the following passage, alludes to the annual celebration, at Venice, of the wedding of the Doge with the Adriatic, when he makes Othello say (i. 2):

> "But that I love the gentle Desdemona,
> I would not my unhoused free condition
> Put into circumscription and confine
> For the sea's worth."

This custom, it is said, was instituted by Pope Alexander III., who gave the Doge a gold ring from his own finger, in token of the victory by the Venetian fleet, at Istria, over Frederick Barbarossa, in defence of the Pope's quarrel. When his holiness gave the ring, he desired the Doge to throw a similar ring into the sea every year on Ascension Day, in commemoration of the event.

Agate. This stone was frequently cut to represent the human form, and was occasionally worn in the hat by gallants. In "2 Henry IV." (i. 2) Falstaff says: "I was never manned with an agate till now"—meaning, according to Johnson, "had an agate for my man," was waited on by an agate.

Carbuncle. The supernatural lustre of this gem[1] is supposed to be described in "Titus Andronicus" (ii. 3), where, speaking of the ring on the finger of Bassianus, Martius says:

> "Upon his bloody finger he doth wear
> A precious ring, that lightens all the hole,
> Which, like a taper in some monument,
> Doth shine upon the dead man's earthy cheeks,
> And shows the ragged entrails of the pit."

In Drayton's "Muses' Elysium" ("Nymphal," ix.) it is thus eulogized:

---

[1] See Sir Thomas Browne's "Vulgar Errors."

> " That admired mighty stone,
> The carbuncle that's named,
> Which from it such a flaming light
> And radiancy ejecteth,
> That in the very darkest night
> The eye to it directeth."

Milton, speaking of the cobra, says:

> " His head
> Crested aloof, and carbuncle his eyes."

John Norton,[1] an alchemist in the reign of Edward IV., wrote a poem entitled the " Ordinal," or a manual of the chemical art. One of his projects, we are told, was a bridge of gold over the Thames, crowned with pinnacles of gold, which, being studded with carbuncles, would diffuse a blaze of light in the dark. Among the other references to it given by Shakespeare may be mentioned one in " Henry VIII." (ii. 3), where the Princess Elizabeth is spoken of as

> "a gem
> To lighten all this isle."

And Hamlet (ii. 2) uses the phrase, " With eyes like carbuncles."

Chrysolite. This stone was supposed to possess peculiar virtues, and, according to Simon Maiolus, in his " Dierum Caniculares " (1615–19), Thetel the Jew, who wrote a book, " De Sculpturiis," mentions one naturally in the form of a woman, which was potent against fascination of all kinds. " Othello " (v. 2) thus alludes to this stone in reference to his wife:

> " Nay, had she been true,
> If heaven would make me such another world
> Of one entire and perfect chrysolite,
> I'd not have sold her for it."

Pearls. The Eastern custom of powdering sovereigns at their coronation with gold-dust and seed-pearl is alluded to in " Antony and Cleopatra "[2] (ii. 5):

---

[1] Jones's " Precious Stones," 1880, p. 62.
[2] See Singer's " Shakespeare," vol. x. p. 213.

> "I'll set thee in a shower of gold, and hail
> Rich pearls upon thee."

So Milton (" Paradise Lost," ii. 4):

> "The gorgeous East, with liberal hand,
> Showers on her kings barbaric pearl and gold."

Again, to swallow a pearl in a draught seems to have been common to royal and mercantile prodigality. In "Hamlet" (v. 2) the King says:

> "The king shall drink to Hamlet's better breath;
> And in the cup an union[1] shall he throw."

Further on Hamlet himself asks, tauntingly:

> "Here, thou incestuous, murderous, damned Dane,
> Drink off this potion. Is thy union here?"

Malone, as an illustration of this custom, quotes from the second part of Heywood's "If You Know Not Me You Know Nobody:"

> "Here sixteen thousand pound at one clap goes
> Instead of sugar. Gresham drinks this pearl
> Unto the queen, his mistress."

In former times powdered pearls were considered invaluable for stomach complaints; and Rondeletius tells us that they were supposed to possess an exhilarating quality; " Uniones quæ a conchis, et valde cordiales sunt."

Much mystery was, in bygone days, thought to hang over the origin of pearls, and, according to the poetic Orientals,[2] "Every year, on the sixteenth day of the month Nisan, the pearl oysters rise to the sea and open their shells, in order to receive the rain which falls at that time, and the drops thus caught become pearls." Thus, in "Richard III." (iv. 4) the king says:

> "The liquid drops of tears that you have shed
> Shall come again, transform'd to orient pearl,

---

[1] A union is a precious pearl, remarkable for its size.
[2] See Jones's " History and Mystery of Precious Stones," p. 116.

> Advantaging their loan with interest
> Of ten times double gain of happiness."

Moore, in one of his Melodies, notices this pretty notion:

> "And precious the tear as that rain from the sky
> Which turns into pearls as it falls in the sea."

Turquoise. This stone was probably more esteemed for its secret virtues than from any commercial value; the turquoise, turkise, or turkey-stone, having from a remote period been supposed to possess talismanic properties. Thus, in the "Merchant of Venice" (iii. 1), Shylock says: "It was my turquoise; I had it of Leah when I was a bachelor: I would not have given it for a wilderness of monkeys." Mr. Dyce[1] says that Shylock valued his turquoise, "not only as being the gift of Leah, but on account of the imaginary virtues ascribed to it; which was supposed to become pale or to brighten according as the health of the wearer was bad or good." Thus, Ben Jonson, in "Sejanus" (i. 1), alludes to its wonderful properties:

> "And true as turkoise in the dear lord's ring,
> Look well or ill with him."

Fenton, in his "Certain Secret Wonders of Nature" (1569), thus describes it: "The turkeys doth move when there is any evil prepared to him that weareth it." There were numerous other magical properties ascribed to the turquoise. Thus, it was supposed to lose its color entirely at the death of its owner, but to recover it when placed upon the finger of a new and healthy possessor. It was also said that whoever wore a turquoise, so that either it or its setting touched the skin, might fall from any height, the stone attracting to itself the whole force of the blow. With the Germans, the turquoise is still the gem appropriated to the ring, the "gage d'amour," presented by the lover on the acceptance of his suit, the permanence of its color being believed to depend upon the constancy of his affection.[2]

---

[1] "Glossary," p. 465.
[2] See C. W. King on "Precious Stones," 1867, p. 267.

CHAPTER XVI.

SPORTS AND PASTIMES.

VERY many of the old sports and pastimes in popular use in Shakespeare's day have long ago not only been laid aside, but, in the course of years, have become entirely forgotten. This is to be regretted, as a great number of these capital diversions were admirably suited both for in and out of doors, the simplicity which marked them being one of their distinguishing charms. That Shakespeare, too, took an interest in these good old sources of recreation, may be gathered from the frequent reference which he has made to them; his mention of some childish game even serving occasionally as an illustration in a passage characterized by its force and vigor.

Archery. In Shakespeare's day this was a very popular diversion, and the " Knights of Prince Arthur's Round Table " was a society of archers instituted by Henry VIII., and encouraged in the reign of Elizabeth.[1] Fitzstephen, who wrote in the reign of Henry II., notices it among the summer pastimes of the London youth; and the repeated statutes, from the thirteenth to the sixteenth century, enforcing the use of the bow, generally ordered the leisure time upon holidays to be passed in its exercise.[2] Shakespeare seems to have been intimately acquainted with the numerous terms connected with archery, many of which we find scattered throughout his plays. Thus, in " Love's Labour's Lost " (iv. 1), Maria uses the expression, " Wide o' the bow hand," a term which signified a good deal to the left of the mark.

---

[1] See Drake's " Skakespeare and His Times," vol. ii. pp. 178–181.

[2] Brand's " Pop. Antiq.," 1870, vol. ii. p. 290.

The "clout" was the nail or pin of the target, and "from the passages," says Dyce,[1] "which I happen to recollect in our early writers, I should say that the clout, or pin, stood in the centre of the inner circle of the butts, which circle, being painted white, was called the white; that, to 'hit the white' was a considerable feat, but that to 'hit or cleave the clout or pin' was a much greater one, though, no doubt, the expressions were occasionally used to signify the same thing, viz., to hit the mark." In "Love's Labour's Lost" (iv. 1), Costard says of Boyet:

"Indeed, a' must shoot nearer, or he'll ne'er hit the clout;"

and, in "2 Henry IV." (iii. 2), Shallow says of old Double: "He would have clapped i' the clout at twelve score"—that is, he would have hit the clout at twelve-score yards. And "King Lear" (iv. 6) employs the phrase "i' the clout, i' the clout: hewgh!"

In "Romeo and Juliet" (ii. 4), where Mercutio relates how Romeo is "shot thorough the ear with a love-song; the very pin of his heart cleft with the blind bow-boy's butt-shaft," the metaphor, of course, is from archery.

The term "loose" was the technical one for the discharging of an arrow, and occurs in "Love's Labour's Lost" (v. 2).

According to Capell,[2] the words of Bottom, in "A Midsummer-Night's Dream" (i. 2), "hold, or cut bow-strings," were a proverbial phrase, and alluded to archery. "When a party was made at butts, assurance of meeting was given in the words of that phrase, the sense of the person using them being that he would 'hold' or keep promise, or they might 'cut his bow-strings,' demolish him for an archer." Whether, adds Dyce, "this be the true explanation of the phrase, I am unable to determine."

All hid, all hid. Biron, in "Love's Labour's Lost" (iv. 3), no doubt means the game well-known as hide-and-seek, "All hid, all hid; an old infant play." The following note, however, in Cotgrave's "French and English Dictionary," has been adduced to show that he may possibly mean blind-

---

[1] "Glossary," p. 84.   [2] "Glossary," p. 210.

man's-buff: "Clignemasset.　The childish play called Hod-man-blind [*i.e.*, blind-man's-buff], Harrie-racket, or Are you all hid."

Backgammon.　The old name for this game was "Tables," as in "Love's Labour's Lost" (v. 2):

> " This is the ape of form, monsieur the nice
>   That, when he plays at tables, chides the dice."

An interesting history of this game will be found in Strutt's "Sports and Pastimes" (1876, pp. 419–421).

Barley-break.　This game, called also the "Last Couple in Hell," which is alluded to in the "Two Noble Kinsmen," (iv. 3), was played by six people, three of each sex, who were coupled by lot.[1]　A piece of ground was then chosen, and divided into three compartments, of which the middle one was called hell.　It was the object of the couple condemned to this division to catch the others, who advanced from the two extremities; in which case a change of situation took place, and hell was filled by the couple who were excluded by preoccupation from the other places.　This catching, however, was not so easy, as, by the rules of the game, the middle couple were not to separate before they had suc-ceeded, while the others might break hands whenever they found themselves hard pressed.　When all had been taken in turn, the last couple were said "to be in hell," and the game ended.

The game was frequently mentioned by old writers, and appears to have been very popular.　From Herrick's Poems, it is seen that the couples in their confinement occasionally solaced themselves by kisses:

> "*Barley-break ; or, Last in Hell.*
> " We two are last in hell; what may we fear,
>   To be tormented, or kept pris'ners here?
>   Alas, if kissing be of plagues the worst,
>   We'll wish in hell we had been last and first."

In Scotland it was called barla - breikis, and was, says

---

[1] From Gifford's Note on Massinger's Works, 1813, vol. i. p. 104.

Jamieson, "generally played by young people in a corn-yard, hence its name, barla-bracks, about the stacks."[1] The term "hell," says Nares,[2] "was indiscreet, and must have produced many profane allusions, besides familiarizing what ought always to preserve its due effect of awe upon the mind." Both its names are alluded to in the following passage in Shirley's "Bird in a Cage:"

> "Shall's to barlibreak?
> I was in hell last; 'tis little less to be in a petticoat sometimes."

Base. This was a rustic game, known also as "Prison base" or "Prison bars." It is mentioned in "Cymbeline" (v. 3) by Posthumus:

> "Lads more like to run
> The country base, than to commit such slaughter."

And in "Two Gentlemen of Verona" (i. 2) by Lucetta:

> "Indeed, I bid the base for Proteus."[3]

The success of this pastime depended upon the agility of the candidates, and their skill in running. Early in the reign of Edward III. it is spoken of as a childish amusement, and was prohibited to be played in the avenues of the palace at Westminster during the session of Parliament, because of the interruption it occasioned to the members and others in passing to and fro as their business required. It was also played by men, and especially in Cheshire and other adjoining counties, where it seems to have been in high repute among all classes. Strutt thus describes the game:[4] "The performance of this pastime requires two parties of equal number, each of them having a base or home to themselves, at the distance of about twenty or thirty yards. The players then on either side, taking hold of hands, extend themselves in length, and opposite to each other, as far as they conveniently can, always remembering that one of them must touch the base. When any one of

---

[1] See Jamieson's "Scottish Dictionary," 1879, vol. i. p. 122.
[2] "Glossary," vol. i. p. 57.   [3] Ibid. vol. i. p. 58.
[4] "Sports and Pastimes," 1876, p. 143.

them quits the hand of his fellow and runs into the field,
which is called giving the chase, he is immediately followed
by one of his opponents. He is again followed by a second
from the former side, and he by a second opponent, and so
on alternately until as many are out as choose to run, every
one pursuing the man he first followed, and no other; and
if he overtake him near enough to touch him, his party
claims one towards their game, and both return home.
They then run forth again and again in like manner until
the number is completed that decides the victory. This
number is optional, and rarely exceeds twenty."

The phrase to "bid the base," means to run fast, chal-
lenging another to pursue. It occurs again in "Venus and
Adonis:"

> "To bid the wind a base he now prepares."

In Spenser's "Fairy Queen" (bk. v. canto 8), we read:

> "So ran they all as they had been at base,
> They being chased that did others chase."

Bat-fowling. This sport, which is noticed in "The Tempest" (ii. 1) by Sebastian, was common in days gone by. It
is minutely described in Markham's "Hunger's Prevention"
(1600), which is quoted by Dyce.[1] The term "bat-fowling,"
however, had another signification, says Mr. Harting,[2] in
Shakespeare's day, and it may have been in this secondary
sense that it is used in "The Tempest," being a slang word
for a particular mode of cheating. Bat-fowling was practised about dusk, when the rogue pretended to have
dropped a ring or a jewel at the door of some well-fur-

---

[1] "Glossary," pp. 29, 30.

[2] See Harting's "Ornithology of Shakespeare," p. 156; Strutt's
"Sports and Pastimes," 1876, p. 98. A simple mode of bat-fowling,
by means of a large clap-net and a lantern, and called bird-batting, is
alluded to in Fielding's "Joseph Andrews" (bk. ii. chap. x.). Drake
thinks that it is to a stratagem of this kind Shakespeare alludes when
he paints Buckingham exclaiming ("Henry VIII." i. 1):

> "The net has fall'n upon me; I shall perish
> Under device and practice."

nished shop, and, going in, asked the apprentice of the house to light his candle to look for it. After some peering about the bat-fowler would drop the candle as if by accident. "Now, I pray you, good young man," he would say, "do so much as light the candle again." While the boy was away the rogue plundered the shop, and having stolen everything he could find stole himself away.

Billiards. Shakespeare is guilty of an anachronism in "Antony and Cleopatra" (ii. 5), where he makes Cleopatra say: "Let's to billiards"—the game being unknown to the ancients. The modern manner of playing at billiards differs from that formerly in use. At the commencement of the last century,[1] the billiard-table was square, having only three pockets for the balls to run in, situated on one of the sides— that is, at each corner, and the third between them. About the middle of the table a small arch of iron was placed, and at a little distance from it an upright cone called a king. At certain periods of the game it was necessary for the balls to be driven through the one and round the other, without knocking either of them down, which was not easily effected, because they were not fastened to the table.

Bone-ace. This old game, popularly called "One-and-Thirty," is alluded to by Grumio in "Taming of the Shrew" (i. 2): "Well, was it fit for a servant to use his master so; being, perhaps, for aught I see, two-and-thirty—a pip out."[2] It was very like the French game of "Vingt-un," only a longer reckoning. Strutt[3] says that "perhaps Bone-ace is the same as the game called Ace of Hearts, prohibited with all lotteries by cards and dice, An. 12 Geor. II., Cap. 38, sect. 2." It is mentioned in Massinger's "Fatal Dowry" (ii. 2): "You think, because you served my lady's mother, [you] are thirty-two years old, which is a pip out, you know."

The phrase "to be two-and-thirty," a pip out, was an old cant term applied to a person who was intoxicated.

Bo-peep. This nursery amusement, which consisted in

---

[1] Strutt's "Sports and Pastimes," 1876, p. 396.

[2] A pip is a spot upon a card.

[3] "Sports and Pastimes," 1876, p. 436.

peeping from behind something, and crying "Bo!" is referred to by the Fool in "King Lear" (i. 4): "That such a king should play bo-peep." In Sherwood's Dictionary it is defined, "Jeu d'enfant; ou (plustost) des nourrices aux petits enfans; se cachans le visage et puis se monstrant." Minsheu's derivation of bo-peep, from the noise which chickens make when they come out of the shell, is, says Douce,[1] more whimsical than just.

Bowls. Frequent allusions occur to this game, which seems to have been a popular pastime in olden times. The small ball, now called the jack, at which the players aim, was sometimes termed the "mistress." In "Troilus and Cressida" (iii. 2), Pandarus says: "So, so; rub[2] on, and kiss the mistress." A bowl that kisses the jack, or mistress, is in the most advantageous position; hence "to kiss the jack" served to denote a state of great advantage. Thus, in "Cymbeline" (ii. 1), Cloten exclaims, "Was there ever man had such luck! when I kissed the jack, upon an up-cast to be hit away! I had a hundred pound on't." There is another allusion to this game, according to Staunton, in "King John" (ii. 1): "on the outward eye of fickle France"—the aperture on one side which contains the bias or weight that inclines the bowl in running from a direct course, being sometimes called the eye.

A further reference to this game occurs in the following dialogue in "Richard II." (iii. 4):

> "*Queen.* What sport shall we devise here in this garden,
> To drive away the heavy thought of care?
>   1 *Lady.* Madam, we'll play at bowls.
>   *Queen.* 'Twill make me think the world is full of rubs,
> And that my fortune runs against the bias"

—the *bias*, as stated above, being a weight inserted in one side of a bowl, in order to give it a particular inclination in

---

[1] "Illustrations of Shakespeare," p. 405.

[2] Rub is still a term at the game, expressive of the movement of the balls. Cf. "King Lear" (ii. 2), and "Love's Labour's Lost" (iv. 1), where Boyet, speaking of the game, says: "I fear too much rubbing."

bowling. "To run against the bias," therefore, became a proverb. Thus, to quote another instance, in the "Taming of the Shrew" (iv. 5) Petruchio says:

> "Well, forward, forward! thus the bowl should run,
> And not unluckily against the bias."

And in "Troilus and Cressida" (iv. 5), the term "bias-cheek" is used to denote a cheek swelling out like the bias of a bowl.[1]

Cards. Some of the old terms connected with card-playing are curious, a few of which are alluded to by Shakespeare. Thus, in "King Lear" (v. 1), Edmund says:

> "And hardly shall I carry out my side,"

alluding to the card table, where to carry out a side meant to carry out the game with your partner successfully. So, "to set up a side" was to become partners in the game; "to pull or pluck down a side" was to lose it.[2]

A lurch at cards denoted an easy victory. So, in "Coriolanus" (ii. 2), Cominius says: "he lurch'd all swords of the garland," meaning, as Malone says, that Coriolanus gained from all other warriors the wreath of victory, with ease, and incontestable superiority.

A pack of cards was formerly termed "a deck of cards," as in "3 Henry VI." (v. 1):

> "The king was slily finger'd from the deck."

Again, "to vie" was also a term at cards, and meant particularly to increase the stakes, and generally to challenge any one to a contention, bet, wager, etc. So, Cleopatra (v. 2), says:

> "nature wants stuff
> To vie strange forms with fancy."

Cherry-pit. This consisted in throwing cherry stones into a little hole—a game, says Nares, still practised with dumps

---

[1] Halliwell-Phillipps' "Handbook Index to Shakespeare," p. 43.
[2] Staunton's "Shakespeare," vol. iii. p. 592.

or money.'[1] In "Twelfth Night" (iii. 4), Sir Toby alludes to it: "What, man! 'tis not for gravity to play at cherry-pit with Satan." Nash, in his "Pierce Pennilesse," speaking of the disfigurement of ladies' faces by painting, says: "You may play at cherry-pit in the dint of their cheeks."

Chess. As might be expected, several allusions occur in Shakespeare's plays to this popular game. In "The Tempest" (v. 1), Ferdinand and Miranda are represented playing at it; and in "King John" (ii. 1), Elinor says:

"That thou mayst be a queen, and check the world!"

In the "Taming of the Shrew" (i. 1), Katharina asks:

"I pray you, sir, is it your will
To make a stale[2] of me amongst these mates?"

alluding, as Douce[3] suggests, to the chess term of *stale-mate*, which is used when the game is ended by the king being alone and unchecked, and then forced into a situation from which he is unable to move without going into check. This is a dishonorable termination to the adversary, who thereby loses the game. Thus, in Bacon's Twelfth Essay: "They stand still like a stale at chess, where it is no mate, but yet the game cannot stir."

Dice. Among the notices of this game, may be quoted that in "Henry V." (iv. prologue):

"The confident and over-lusty French
Do the low-rated English play at dice."

Edgar, in "King Lear" (iii. 4), says: "Wine loved I deeply, dice dearly." Pistol, in "Merry Wives of Windsor" (i. 3), gives a double allusion:

"Let vultures gripe thy guts!—for gourd and fullam holds,
And high and low beguiles the rich and poor."

"Gourds" were false dice, with a secret cavity scooped out

---

[1] See Brand's "Pop. Antiq.," vol. ii. p. 409.

[2] She means, "Do you intend to make a mockery of me among these companions?"

[3] "Illustrations of Shakspeare," p. 20.

like a gourd. " Fullams " were also false dice, " loaded with metal on one side, so as better to produce high throws, or to turn up low numbers, as was required, and were hence named 'high men' or 'low men,' also 'high fullams' and 'low fullams.' "[1] It has been suggested that dice were termed *fullams* either because Fulham was the resort of sharpers, or because they were principally manufactured there.

Dun is in the mire. This is a Christmas sport, which Gifford[2] describes as follows : " A log of wood is brought into the midst of the room ; this is *Dun* (the cart-horse), and a cry is raised that he is stuck in the mire. Two of the company advance, either with or without ropes, to draw him out. After repeated attempts, they find themselves unable to do it, and call for more assistance. The game continues till all the company take part in it, when Dun is extricated. Much merriment is occasioned from the awkward efforts of the rustics to lift the log, and from sundry arch contrivances to let the ends of it fall on one another's toes. Thus, in " Romeo and Juliet " (i. 4), Mercutio says :

> " If thou art dun, we'll draw thee from the mire."

Beaumont and Fletcher, also, in the " Woman Hater " (iv. 3), allude to this game :

> " Dun's in the mire, get out again how he can."

Fast and Loose. This was a cheating game, much practised in Shakespeare's day, whereby gypsies and other vagrants beguiled the common people of their money ; and hence was very often to be seen at fairs. Its other name was " pricking at the belt or girdle ;" and it is thus described by Sir J. Hawkins : " A leathern belt was made up into a number of intricate folds, and placed edgewise upon a table. One of the folds was made to resemble the middle of the girdle, so that whoever could thrust a skewer into it would think he held it fast to the table ; whereas, when he has so done, the person with whom he plays may take hold of both

---

[1] Gifford's note on Jonson's Works, vol. ii. p. 3.
[2] Ibid., vol. vii. p. 283.

ends, and draw it away." In "Antony and Cleopatra" (iv. 12), Antony says:

> "Like a right gypsy, hath, at fast and loose,
> Beguil'd me to the very heart of loss."

The drift of this game seems to have been to encourage wagers whether the belt was fast or loose, which the juggler could easily make it at his option. It is constantly alluded to by old writers, and is thus described in Drayton's "Mooncalf:"

> "He like a gypsy oftentimes would go,
> All kinds of gibberish he hath learn'd to know,
> And with a stick, a short string, and a noose,
> Would show the people tricks at fast and loose."

Fencing. In years gone by, there were three degrees in fencing, a master's, a provost's, and a scholar's.[1] To each of these a prize was played, with various weapons, in some open place or square. In "Titus Andronicus" (i. 1), this practice is alluded to by Saturninus:

> "So, Bassianus, you have play'd your prize."

In the "Merry Wives of Windsor" (i. 1), Slender says: "I bruised my shin th' other day with playing at sword and dagger with a master of fence," *i. e.*, with one who had taken his master's degree in the science.

Among the numerous allusions to fencing quoted by Shakespeare may be mentioned the following: "Venue or veney" was a fencing term, meaning an attack or hit. It is used in the "Merry Wives of Windsor" (i. 1), by Slender, who relates how he bruised his shin "with playing at sword and dagger with a master of fence; three veneys for a dish of stewed prunes." It is used metaphorically in "Love's Labour's Lost" (v. 1), for a brisk attack, by Armado: "A sweet touch, a quick venue of wit! snip, snap, quick and home!"[2] The Italian term "Stoccado" or "Stoccata," ab-

---

[1] See Douce's "Illustrations of Shakespeare," p. 35.
[2] See Nares's "Glossary," vol. ii. p. 919.

breviated also into "Stock," seems to have had a similar signification. In "Romeo and Juliet" (iii. 1), Mercutio, drawing his sword, says:

> "Alla stoccata carries it away."

In the "Merry Wives of Windsor" (ii. 1), it is used by Shallow: "In these times you stand on distance, your passes, stoccadoes, and I know not what." Again, "Montant," an abbreviation of Montanto, denoted an upright blow or thrust, and occurs also in the "Merry Wives of Windsor" (ii. 3), where the Host tells Caius that he, with the others, has come —"to see thee pass thy punto, thy stock, thy reverse, thy distance, thy montant." Hence, in "Much Ado About Nothing" (i. 1), Beatrice jocularly calls Benedick "Signior Montanto," meaning to imply that he was a great fencer. Of the other old fencing terms quoted in the passage above, it appears that "passado" implied a pass or motion forwards. It occurs in "Romeo and Juliet" (ii. 4), where Mercutio speaks of the "immortal passado! the punto reverso!" Again, in "Love's Labour's Lost" (i. 2), Armado says of Cupid that "The passado he respects not, the duello he regards not." The "punto reverso" was a backhanded thrust or stroke, and the term "distance" was the space between the antagonists.

Shakespeare has also alluded to other fencing terms, such as the "foin," a thrust, which is used by the Host in the "Merry Wives of Windsor" (iii. 2), and in "Much Ado About Nothing" (v. 1), where Antonio says, in his heated conversation with Leonato:

> "Sir boy, I'll whip you from your foining fence;
> Nay, as I am a gentleman, I will."

The term "traverse" denoted a posture of opposition, and is used by the Host in the "Merry Wives of Windsor" (ii. 3). A "bout," too, is another fencing term, to which the King refers in "Hamlet" (iv. 7):

> "When in your motion you are hot and dry—
> As make your bouts more violent to that end."

Filliping the Toad. This is a common and cruel diversion of boys. They lay a board, two or three feet long, at right angles over a transverse piece two or three inches thick, then, placing the toad at one end of the board, the other end is struck by a bat or large stick, which throws the poor toad forty or fifty feet perpendicularly from the earth; and the fall generally kills it. In " 2 Henry IV." (i. 2), Falstaff says: " If I do, fillip me with a three-man beetle." [1]

Flap - dragon. [2] This pastime was much in use in days gone by. A small combustible body was set on fire, and put afloat in a glass of liquor. The courage of the toper was tried in the attempt to toss off the glass in such a manner as to prevent the flap-dragon doing mischief—raisins in hot brandy being the usual flap-dragons. Shakespeare several times mentions this custom, as in " Love's Labour's Lost" (v. 1) where Costard says: " Thou art easier swallowed than a flap-dragon." And in " 2 Henry IV." (ii. 4), he makes Falstaff say: " and drinks off candles' ends for flap-dragons." [3]

It appears that formerly gallants used to vie with each other in drinking off flap-dragons to the health of their mistresses—which were sometimes even candles' ends, swimming in brandy or other strong spirits, whence, when on fire, they were snatched by the mouth and swallowed; [4] an allusion to which occurs in the passage above. As candles' ends made the most formidable flap-dragon, the greatest merit was ascribed to the heroism of swallowing them. Ben Jonson, in " The Masque of the Moon " (1838, p. 616, ed. Gifford), says: " But none that will hang themselves for love, or eat candles' ends, etc., as the sublunary lovers do."

---

[1] A three-man beetle is a heavy implement, with three handles, used in driving piles, etc., which required three men to lift it.

[2] A correspondent of " Notes and Queries," 2d series, vol. vii. p. 277, suggests as a derivation the German *schnapps*, spirit, and *drache*, dragon, and that it is equivalent to spirit-fire.

[3] Cf. " Winter's Tale" (iii. 3): " But to make an end of the ship,—to see how the sea flap-dragoned it."

[4] See Nares's " Glossary," vol. i. p. 131.

Football. An allusion to this once highly popular game occurs in " Comedy of Errors " (ii. 1). Dromio of Ephesus asks :

> " Am I so round with you as you with me,
> That like a football you do spurn me thus ?
>   *   *   *   *   *   *   *
> If I last in this service, you must case me in leather."

In " King Lear " (i. 4), Kent calls Oswald "a base football player."

According to Strutt,[1] it does not appear among the popular exercises before the reign of Edward III.; and then, in 1349, it was prohibited by a public edict because it impeded the progress of archery. The danger, however, attending this pastime occasioned James I. to say: " From this Court I debarre all rough and violent exercises, as the football, meeter for laming than making able the users thereof."

Occasionally the rustic boys made use of a blown bladder, without the covering of leather, by way of a football, putting beans and horse-beans inside, which made a rattling noise as it was kicked about. Barclay, in his " Ship of Fools " (1508) thus graphically describes it :

> " Howe in the winter, when men kill the fat swine,
> They get the bladder and blow it great and thin,
> With many beans or peason put within :
> It ratleth, soundeth, and shineth clere and fayre,
> While it is thrown and caste up in the ayre,
> Eche one contendeth and hath a great delite
> With foote and with hande the bladder for to smite ;
> If it fall to grounde, they lifte it up agayne,
> This wise to labour they count it for no payne."

Shrovetide was the great season for football matches;[2] and at a comparatively recent period it was played in Derby, Nottingham, Kingston-upon-Thames, etc.

---

[1] " Sports and Pastimes," pp. 168, 169.
[2] See " British Popular Customs," 1876, pp. 78, 83, 87, 401.

Gleek. According to Drake,[1] this game is alluded to twice by Shakespeare—in " A Midsummer-Night's Dream" (iii. 1):

> " Nay, I can gleek upon occasion."

And in " Romeo and Juliet" (iv. 5):

> " 1 *Musician.* What will you give us?
> *Peter.* No money, on my faith, but the gleek."

Douce, however, considers that the word *gleek* was simply used to express a stronger sort of joke, a scoffing; and that the phrase " to give the gleek" merely denoted to pass a jest upon, or to make a person appear ridiculous.

Handy-dandy. A very old game among children. A child hides something in his hand, and makes his playfellow guess in which hand it is. If the latter guess rightly, he wins the article, if wrongly, he loses an equivalent.[2] Sometimes, says Mr. Halliwell-Phillipps, " the game is played by a sort of sleight-of-hand, changing the article rapidly from one hand into the other, so that the looker-on is often deceived, and induced to name the hand into which it is apparently thrown." This is what Shakespeare alludes to by " change places" in " King Lear" (iv. 6): " see how yond justice rails upon yond simple thief. Hark, in thine ear: change places; and, handy-dandy, which is the justice, which is the thief?"[3]

Hide-fox and all after. A children's game, considered by many to be identical with hide-and-seek. It is mentioned by Hamlet (iv. 2). Some commentators think that the term " kid-fox," in " Much Ado About Nothing" (ii. 3), may have been a technical term in the game of " hide-fox." Some editions have printed it " hid-fox." Claudio says:

> " O, very well, my lord: the music ended,
> We'll fit the kid-fox with a pennyworth."

Hoodman-blind. The childish sport now called blindman's buff was known by various names, such as hood-wink,

---

[1] "Shakespeare and his Times," vol. ii. p. 170; see Douce's "Illustrations of Shakspeare," pp. 118, 435.

[2] Dyce's "Glossary," p. 199.

[3] See Brand's "Pop. Antiq.," 1849, vol. ii. p. 420.

blind-hob, etc. It was termed "hoodman-blind," because the players formerly were blinded with their hoods,[1] and under this designation it is mentioned by Hamlet (iii. 4):

> "What devil was't
> That thus hath cozen'd you at hoodman-blind?"

In Scotland this game was called "belly-blind;" and Gay, in his "Shepherd's Week" (i. 96), says, concerning it:

> "As once I play'd at blindman's buff, it hapt
> About my eyes the towel thick was wrapt,
> I miss'd the swains, and seiz'd on Blouzelind.
> True speaks that ancient proverb, 'Love is blind.'"

The term "hoodman" occurs in "All's Well that Ends Well" (iv. 3). The First Lord says: "Hoodman comes!" and no doubt there is an allusion to the game in the same play (iii. 6), "we will bind and hoodwink him;" and in "Macbeth" (iv. 3) Macduff says: "the time you may so hoodwink." There may also have been a reference to falconry— the hawks being hooded in the intervals of sport. Thus, in Latham's "Falconry" (1615), "to hood" is the term used for the blinding, "to unhood" for the unblinding.

Horse-racing. That this diversion was in Shakespeare's day occasionally practised in the spirit of the modern turf is evident from "Cymbeline" (iii. 2):

> "I have heard of riding wagers,
> Where horses have been nimbler than the sands
> That run i' the clock's behalf."

Burton,[2] too, who wrote at the close of the Shakespearian era, mentions the ruinous consequences of this recreation: "Horse races are desports of great men, and good in themselves, though many gentlemen by such means gallop quite out of their fortunes."

Leap-frog. One boy stoops down with his hands upon

---

[1] See Strutt's "Sports and Pastimes," pp. 499, 500; Brand's "Pop. Antiq.," 1849, vol. ii. pp. 397, 398.

[2] "Anatomy of Melancholy;" Drake's "Shakespeare and His Times," vol. ii. p. 298.

his knees, and others leap over him, every one of them running forward and stooping in his turn. It is mentioned by Shakespeare in " Henry V." (v. 2), where he makes the king say, "If I could win a lady at leap-frog, or by vaulting into my saddle with my armour on my back, . . . I should quickly leap into a wife." Ben Jonson, in his comedy of " Bartholomew Fair," speaks of " a leappe frogge chance note."

Laugh-and-lie-down (more properly laugh-and-lay-down) was a game at cards, to which there is an allusion in the " Two Noble Kinsmen " (ii. 1):

> " *Emilia.*   I could laugh now.
> *Waiting-woman.* I could lie down, I'm sure."

Loggat. The game so called resembles bowls, but with notable differences.[1] First, it is played, not on a green, but on a floor strewed with ashes. The jack is a wheel of *lignum vitæ*, or other hard wood, nine inches in diameter, and three or four inches thick. The loggat, made of apple-wood, is a truncated cone, twenty - six or twenty - seven inches in length, tapering from a girth of eight and a half to nine inches at one end to three and a half or four inches at the other. Each player has three loggats, which he throws, holding lightly the thin end. The object is to lie as near the jack as possible. Hamlet speaks of this game (v. 1): " Did these bones cost no more the breeding, but to play at loggats with 'em?" comparing, perhaps, the skull to the jack at which the bones were thrown. In Ben Jonson's " Tale of a Tub " (iv. 5) we read:

> " Now are they tossing of his legs and arms,
>   Like loggets at a pear-tree."

Sir Thomas Hanmer makes the game the same as nine-pins or skittles. He says: " It is one of the unlawful games enumerated in the Thirty-third statute of Henry VIII.;[2] it is the same which is now called kittle-pins, in which the boys

---

[1] Clark and Wright's " Notes to Hamlet," 1876, pp. 212, 213.
[2] See Strutt's " Sports and Pastimes," p. 365; Nares's " Glossary," vol. ii. p. 522.

often make use of bones instead of wooden pins, throwing at them with another bone instead of bowling."

Marbles. It has been suggested that there is an allusion to this pastime in " Measure for Measure " (i. 3):

> " Believe not that the dribbling dart of love
> Can pierce a complete bosom."

—dribbling being a term used in the game of marbles for shooting slowly along the ground, in contradistinction to *plumping*, which is elevating the hand so that the marble does not touch the ground till it reaches the object of its aim.[1] According to others, a dribbler was a term in archery expressive of contempt.[2]

Muss. This was a phrase for a scramble, when any small objects were thrown down, to be taken by those who could seize them. In "Antony and Cleopatra" (iii. 13), Antony says:

> " Like boys unto a muss, kings would start forth."

The word is used by Dryden, in the Prologue to the " Widow Ranter:"

> " Bauble and cap no sooner are thrown down
> But there's a muss of more than half the town."

Nine-Men's-Morris. This rustic game, which is still extant in some parts of England, was sometimes called " the nine men's merrils," from *merelles*, or *mereaux*, an ancient French word for the jettons or counters with which it was played.[3] The other term, *morris*, is probably a corruption suggested by the sort of dance which, in the progress of the game, the counters performed. Some consider[4] that it was identical with the game known as " Nine-holes,"[5] mentioned by Herrick in his " Hesperides:"

---

[1] Baker's " Northamptonshire Glossary," 1854, vol. i. p. 198.
[2] See Dyce's "Glossary," p. 134.
[3] Douce's " Illustrations of Shakespeare," p. 144.
[4] See Nares's " Glossary," vol. ii. p. 605.
[5] See Strutt's " Sports and Pastimes," 1876, pp. 368, 369.

> "Raspe playes at nine-holes, and 'tis known he gets
> Many a tester by his game, and bets."

Cotgrave speaks of " Le jeu des merelles," the boyish game called "merills," or "five pennie morris," played here most commonly with stones, but in France with pawns or men made on purpose, and termed "merelles." It was also called "peg morris," as is evidenced by Clare, who, in his "Rural Muse," speaking of the shepherd boy, says:

> "Oft we may track his haunts, where he hath been
> To spend the leisure which his toils bestow,
> By nine-peg morris nicked upon the green."

The game is fully described by James, in the "Variorum Shakespeare," as follows: "In that part of Warwickshire where Shakespeare was educated, and the neighbouring parts of Northamptonshire, the shepherds and other boys dig up the turf with their knives to represent a sort of imperfect chessboard. It consists of a square, sometimes only a foot diameter, sometimes three or four yards. Within this is another square, every side of which is parallel to the external square; and these squares are joined by lines drawn from each corner of both squares, and the middle of each line. One party or player has wooden pegs, the other stones, which they move in such a manner as to take up each other's men, as they are called, and the area of the inner square is called the pound, in which the men taken up are impounded. These figures are, by the country people, called *nine-men's-morris*, or *merrils;* and are so called because each party has nine men. These figures are always cut upon the green turf or leys, as they are called, or upon the grass at the end of ploughed lands, and in rainy seasons never fail to be choked up with mud." This verifies the allusion made by Shakespeare in "A Midsummer-Night's Dream" (ii. 1):

> "The nine men's morris is fill'd up with mud;
> And the quaint mazes in the wanton green,
> For lack of tread are undistinguishable."

This game was also transferred to a board, and continues a

fireside recreation of the agricultural laborer. It is often called by the name of " Mill," or " Shepherd's Mill." [1]

Noddy. Some doubt exists as to what game at cards was signified by this term. It has been suggested that cribbage is meant. Mr. Singer thinks it bore some resemblance to the more recent game of " Beat the Knave out of Doors," which is mentioned together with " Ruff and new coat " in Heywood's play of " A Woman Killed with Kindness." The game is probably alluded to in " Troilus and Cressida" (i. 2), in the following dialogue :

> "*Pandarus.* When comes Troilus?—I'll show you Troilus anon: if he see me, you shall see him nod at me.
> *Cressida.* Will he give you the nod?
> *Pandarus.* You shall see.
> *Cressida.* If he do, the rich shall have more." [2]

The term " noddy " was also applied to a fool, because, says Minsheu, he nods when he should speak. In this sense it occurs in " Two Gentlemen of Verona " (i. 1) :

> "*Speed.* You mistook, sir : I say, she did nod ; and you ask me, if she did nod ; and I say, ' Ay.'
> *Proteus.* And that set together is noddy."

Novem Quinque. A game of dice, so called from its principal throws being five and nine. It is alluded to in " Love's Labour's Lost " (v. 2) by Biron, who speaks of it simply as " novem."

Parish-top. Formerly a top was kept for public exercise in a parish—a custom to which the old writers often refer. Thus, in " Twelfth Night " (i. 3), Sir Toby Belch says : " He's a coward, and a coystril, that will not drink to my niece till his brains turn o' the toe like a parish-top." On which passage Mr. Steevens says : " A large top was kept in every village, to be whipped in frosty weather, that the peasants might be kept warm by exercise, and out of mischief while they could not work." Beaumont and Fletcher, in " Thierry and Theodoret " (ii. 3), speak of the practice :

---

[1] See Brand's "Pop. Antiq.," 1849, vol. ii. pp. 429, 432.
[2] See Nares's "Glossary," vol. ii. p. 606.

" I'll hazard
My life upon it, that a body of twelve
Should scourge him hither like a parish top,
And make him dance before you."

And in their "Night Walker" (i. 3) they mention the
"town-top." Evelyn, enumerating the uses of willow-wood,
speaks of "great town-topps." Mr. Knight[1] remarks that
the custom which existed in the time of Elizabeth, and
probably long before, of a large top being provided for the
amusement of the peasants in frosty weather, presents a
curious illustration of the mitigating influences of social
kindness in an age of penal legislation.

Primero. In Shakespeare's time this was a very fashionable game at cards, and hence is frequently alluded to by
him. It was known under the various designations of *Pri-*
mero, Prime, and *Primavista ;* and, according to Strutt,[2] has
been reckoned among the most ancient games of cards
known to have been played in England. Shakespeare
speaks of Henry VIII. (v. 1) playing at primero with the
Duke of Suffolk, and makes Falstaff exclaim, in "Merry
Wives of Windsor" (iv. 5), "I never prospered since I for-
swore myself at primero." That it was the court game is
shown in a very curious picture described by Mr. Barrington,
in the "Archæologia" (vol. viii. p. 132), which represents
Lord Burleigh playing at this pastime with three other noblemen. Primero continued to be the most fashionable
game throughout the reigns of Henry VIII., Edward VI.,
Mary, Elizabeth, and James I.[3] In the Earl of Northumberland's letters about the Gunpowder-plot we find that
Josceline Percy was playing at primero on Sunday, when
his uncle, the conspirator, called on him at Essex House;
and in the Sydney Papers there is an account of a quarrel
between Lord Southampton and one Ambrose Willoughby,
on account of the former persisting to play at primero in

---

[1] "Pictorial Shakespeare," vol. ii. p. 145.

[2] "Sports and Pastimes."

[3] Smith's "Festivals, Games, and Amusements," 1831, p. 320.

the presence-chamber after the queen had retired to rest. The manner of playing was thus: Each player had four cards dealt to him one by one; the seven was the highest card in point of number that he could avail himself of, which counted for twenty-one; the six counted for sixteen, the five for fifteen, and the ace for the same; but the two, the three, and the four for their respective points only.

There may be further allusions to this game in " Taming of the Shrew " (ii. 1), where Tranio says:

> " A vengeance on your crafty, wither'd hide!
> Yet I have faced it with a card of ten "

—the phrase " to face it with a card of ten " being derived, as some suggest, possibly from primero, wherein the standing boldly on a ten was often successful. " To face " meant, as it still does, to attack by impudence of face. In " 1 Henry VI." (v. 3) Suffolk speaks of a "cooling card," which Nares considers is borrowed from primero—a card so decisive as to cool the courage of the adversary. Gifford objects to this explanation, and says a " cooling-card " is, literally, a *bolus*. There can be no doubt, however, that, metaphorically, the term was used to denote something which damped or overwhelmed the hopes of an expectant. Thus, in Fletcher's " Island Princess " (i. 3), Piniero says:

> " These hot youths
> I fear will find a cooling-card."

Push-pin was a foolish sport, consisting in nothing more than pushing one pin across another. Biron, in " Love's Labour's Lost " (iv. 3), speaks of Nestor playing " at push-pin with the boys."

Quintain. This was a figure set up for tilters to run at, in mock resemblance of a tournament, and is alluded to in " As You Like It " (i. 2) by Orlando, who says:

> " My better parts
> Are all thrown down, and that which here stands up
> Is but a quintain, a mere lifeless block."

It cannot be better or more minutely described than in the

words of Mr. Strutt:[1] "Tilting or combating at the quintain is a military exercise of high antiquity, and antecedent, I doubt not, to the jousts and tournaments. The quintain originally was nothing more than the trunk of a tree or post set up for the practice of the tyros in chivalry. Afterwards a staff or spear was fixed in the earth, and a shield being hung upon it, was the mark to strike at. The dexterity of the performer consisted in smiting the shield in such a manner as to break the ligatures and bear it to the ground. In process of time this diversion was improved, and instead of a staff and the shield, the resemblance of a human figure carved in wood was introduced. To render the appearance of this figure more formidable, it was generally made in the likeness of a Turk or a Saracen, armed at all points, bearing a shield upon his left arm, and brandishing a club or a sabre with his right. The quintain thus fashioned was placed upon a pivot, and so contrived as to move round with facility. In running at this figure, it was necessary for the horseman to direct his lance with great adroitness, and make his stroke upon the forehead between the eyes, or upon the nose; for if he struck wide of those parts, especially upon the shield, the quintain turned about with much velocity, and, in case he was not exceedingly careful, would give him a severe blow upon the back with the wooden sabre held in the right hand, which was considered as highly disgraceful to the performer, while it excited the laughter and ridicule of the spectators."[2] In Ben Jonson's "Underwoods" it is thus humorously mentioned:

> "Go, Captain Stub, lead on, and show
> What horse you come on, by the blow
> You give Sir Quintain, and the cuff
> You 'scape o' the sandbags counterbuff."

Quoits. This game derived its origin, according to Strutt,[3] from the ancient discus, and with us, at the present day, it

---

[1] "Sports and Pastimes," 1876, p. 182.
[2] See Nares's "Glossary," vol. ii. p. 713.
[3] "Sports and Pastimes," p. 141.

is a circular plate of iron perforated in the middle, not always of one size, but larger or smaller, to suit the strength or conveniency of the several candidates. It is referred to in "2 Henry IV." (ii. 4), by Falstaff, who assigns as one of the reasons why Prince Henry loves Poins: "Because their legs are both of a bigness, and 'a plays at quoits well."

Formerly, in the country, the rustics, not having the round perforated quoits to play with, used horse-shoes; and in many places the quoit itself, to this day, is called a shoe.

Running for the ring. This, according to Staunton, was the name of a sport, a ring having been one of the prizes formerly given in wrestling and running matches. Thus, in the "Taming of the Shrew" (i. 1), Hortensio says: "He that runs fastest gets the ring."

Running the figure of eight. Steevens says that this game is alluded to by Shakespeare in "A Midsummer-Night's Dream" (ii. 1), where Titania speaks of the "quaint mazes in the wanton green." Mr. Halliwell-Phillipps, in referring to this passage, says: "Several mazes of the kind here alluded to are still preserved, having been kept up from time immemorial. On the top of Catherine Hill, Winchester, the usual play-place of the school, was a very perplexed and winding path, running in a very small space over a great deal of ground, called a "miz-maze." The senior boys obliged the juniors to tread it, to prevent the figure from being lost, and I believe it is still retained."[1]

See-Saw. Another name for this childish sport is that given by Falstaff in "2 Henry IV." (ii. 4), where he calls it "riding the wild mare." Gay thus describes this well-known game:

> "Across the fallen oak the plank I laid,
> And myself pois'd against the tott'ring maid;
> High leap'd the plank, adown Buxonia fell."

Shove-Groat. The object of this game was to shake or push pieces of money on a board to reach certain marks. It is alluded to in "2 Henry IV." (ii. 4), where Falstaff says:

[1] See Milner's "History of Winchester," vol. ii. p. 155.

" Quoit him down, Bardolph, like a shove-groat shilling ;"
or, in other words, Bardolph was to quoit Pistol down-stairs
as quickly as the smooth shilling—the shove-groat—flies
along the board.   In a statute of 33 Henry VIII., shove-
groat is called a new game, and was probably originally
played with the silver groat.   The broad shilling of Edward
VI. came afterwards to be used in this game, which was, no
doubt, the same as shovel-board, with the exception that the
latter was on a larger scale.   Master Slender, in the " Merry Wives of Windsor " (i. 1), had his pocket picked of " two
Edward shovel-boards, that cost me two shilling and two
pence a-piece."   Mr. Halliwell-Phillipps, in describing the
game in his " Archaic Dictionary," says that " a shilling or
other smooth coin was placed on the extreme edge of the
shovel-board, and propelled towards a mark by a smart
stroke with the palm of the hand.   It is mentioned under
various names, according to the coin employed, as shove-
groat,[1] etc.   The game of shove-halfpenny is mentioned in
the *Times* of April 25, 1845, as then played by the lower
orders.   According to Strutt, it " was analogous to the modern pastime called Justice Jervis, or Jarvis, which is confined
to common pot-houses."

Snowballs.   These are alluded to in " Pericles " (iv. 6),
and in the " Merry Wives of Windsor " (iii. 5).

Span-counter.   In this boyish game one throws a counter,
or piece of money, which the other wins, if he can throw another so as to hit it, or lie within a span of it.   In " 2 Henry
VI." (iv. 2), Cade says : " Tell the king from me, that, for his
father's sake, Henry the Fifth, in whose time boys went to
span-counter for French crowns, I am content he shall reign."
It is called in France " tapper ;" and in Swift's time was
played with farthings, as he calls it " span-farthing."[2]

---

[1] According to Douce, " Illustrations of Shakespeare" (1839, p. 280),
it was known as " slide-groat," " slide-board," " slide-thrift," and " slip-
thrift."   See Strutt's " Sports and Pastimes," 1876, pp. 16, 394, 398 ;
Nares's " Glossary," vol. ii. p. 791 ; Brand's " Pop. Antiq.," 1849, vol. ii.
p. 441.

[2] See Strutt's " Sports and Pastimes," 1876, p. 491.

Stool-ball. This game, alluded to in the "Two Noble Kinsmen" (v. 2), was formerly popular among young women, and occasionally was played by persons of both sexes indiscriminately, as the following lines, from a song written by Durfey for his play of " Don Quixote," acted at Dorset Gardens, in 1694, show :[1]

> " Down in a vale on a summer's day,
>   All the lads and lasses met to be merry ;
>   A match for kisses at stool-ball to play,
>   And for cakes, and ale, and sider, and perry.
> *Chorus*—Come all, great, small, short, tall, away to stool-ball."

Strutt informs us that this game, as played in the north, " consists in simply setting a stool upon the ground, and one of the players takes his place before it, while his antagonist, standing at a distance, tosses a ball with the intention of striking the stool ; and this is the business of the former to prevent by beating it away with the hand, reckoning one to the game for every stroke of the ball ; if, on the contrary, it should be missed by the hand and touch the stool, the players change places. The conqueror is he who strikes the ball most times before it touches the stool."

Tennis. According to a story told by the old annalists, one of the most interesting historical events in connection with this game happened when Henry V. was meditating war against France. " The Dolphin," says Hall in his " Chronicle," " thynkyng King Henry to be given still to such plaies and lyght folies as he exercised and used before the tyme that he was exalted to the Croune, sent to hym a tunne of tennis balles to plaie with, as who saied that he had better skill of tennis than of warre." On the foundation of this incident, as told by Holinshed, Shakespeare has constructed his fine scene of the French Ambassadors' audience in " Henry V." (i. 2). As soon as the first Ambassador has given the Dauphin's message and insulting gift, the English king speaks thus :

---

[1] Quoted by Strutt, " Sports and Pastimes," p. 166.

> "We are glad the Dauphin is so pleasant with us ;
> His present and your pains we thank you for :
> When we have match'd our rackets to these balls,
> We will, in France, by God's grace, play a set
> Shall strike his father's crown into the hazard.
> Tell him, he hath made a match with such a wrangler
> That all the courts of France will be disturb'd
> With chases."

In " Hamlet " (ii. 1), Polonius speaks of this pastime, and alludes to " falling out at tennis." In the sixteenth century tennis-courts were common in England, and the establishment of such places was countenanced by the example of royalty. It is evident that Henry VII. was a tennis-player. In a MS. register of his expenditures, made in the thirteenth year of his reign, this entry occurs: " Item, for the king's loss at tennis, twelvepence ; for the loss of balls, threepence." Stow, in his " Survey of London," tells us that among the additions that King Henry VIII. made to Whitehall, were " divers fair tennis-courts, bowling-allies, and a cock-pit." Charles II. frequently diverted himself with playing at tennis, and had a particular kind of dress made for that purpose. Pericles, when he is shipwrecked and cast upon the coast of Pentapolis, addresses himself and the three fishermen whom he chances to meet thus (" Pericles," ii. 1):

> " A man whom both the waters and the wind,
> In that vast tennis-court, have made the ball
> For them to play upon, entreats you pity him."

In " Much Ado About Nothing " (iii. 2), Claudio, referring to Benedick, says: " the old ornament of his cheek hath already stuffed tennis-balls;"[1] and in " Henry V." (iii. 7), the Dauphin says his horse " bounds from the earth as if his entrails were hairs." Again, " bandy " was originally a term at tennis, to which Juliet refers in " Romeo and Juliet " (ii. 5), when speaking of her Nurse:

---

[1] In " Love's Labour's Lost " (v. 2), the Princess speaks of " a set of wit well play'd ;" upon which Mr. Singer (" Shakespeare," vol. ii. p. 263) adds that " a set is a term at tennis for a game."

> "Had she affections, and warm youthful blood,
> She'd be as swift in motion as a ball;
> My words would bandy her to my sweet love,
> And his to me."

Also, King Lear (i. 4) says to Oswald: "Do you bandy looks with me, you rascal?"

Tick-tack. This was a sort of backgammon, and is alluded to by Lucio in "Measure for Measure" (i. 2) who, referring to Claudio's unpleasant predicament, says: "I would be sorry should be thus foolishly lost at a game of tick-tack." In Weaver's "Lusty Juventus," Hipocrisye, seeing Lusty Juventus kiss Abhominable Lyuing, says:

> "What a hurly burly is here!
> Smicke smacke, and all thys gere!
> You well [will] to *tycke take*, I fere,
> If thou had tyme."[1]

"Jouer au tric-trac" is used, too, in France in a wanton sense.

Tray-trip. This was probably a game at cards, played with dice as well as with cards, the success in which chiefly depended upon the throwing of treys. Thus, in a satire called "Machivell's Dog" (1617):

> "But, leaving cardes, let's go to dice a while,
> To passage, treitrippe, hazarde, or mumchance."

In "Twelfth Night" (ii. 5), Sir Toby Belch asks: "Shall I play my freedom at tray-trip, and become thy bond-slave?" It may be remembered, too, that in "The Scornful Lady" of Beaumont and Fletcher (ii. 1), the Chaplain complains that the Butler had broken his head, and being asked the reason, says, for

> "Reproving him at tra-trip, sir, for swearing."

Some are of opinion that it resembled the game of hopscotch, or Scotch-hop; but this, says Nares,[2] "seems to rest merely upon unauthorized conjecture."

---

[1] Quoted by Dyce's "Glossary," p. 449; see Brand's "Pop. Antiq.," 1849, vol. ii. p. 445.   [2] "Glossary," vol. ii. p. 896.

Troll-my-dame. The game of Troll-madam, still familiar as Bagatelle, was borrowed from the French (*Trou-madame*). One of its names was Pigeon-holes, because played on a board, at one end of which were a number of arches, like pigeon-holes, into which small balls had to be bowled. In "Winter's Tale" (iv. 2), it is mentioned by Autolycus, who, in answer to the Clown, says that the manner of fellow that robbed him was one that he had "known to go about with troll-my-dames." Cotgrave declares it as "the game called Trunkes, or the Hole."

Trump. This was probably the *triumfo* of the Italians, and the *triomphe* of the French — being perhaps of equal antiquity in England with *primero.* At the latter end of the sixteenth century it was very common among the inferior classes. There is, no doubt, a particular allusion to this game in "Antony and Cleopatra" (iv. 14), where Antony says :

> "the queen—
> Whose heart I thought I had, for she had mine;
> Which, whilst it was mine, had annex'd unto't
> A million more, now lost—she, Eros, has
> Pack'd cards with Cæsar, and false-play'd my glory
> Unto an enemy's triumph."

The poet meant to say, that Cleopatra, by collusion, played the great game they were engaged in falsely, so as to sacrifice Antony's fame to that of his enemy. There is an equivoque between *trump* and *triumph.* The game in question bore a very strong resemblance to our modern whist—the only points of dissimilarity being that more or less than four persons might play at trump; that all the cards were not dealt out; and that the dealer had the privilege of discarding some, and taking others in from the stock. In Eliot's "Fruits for the French," 1593, it is called "a very common ale-house game in England."

Wrestling. Of the many allusions that are given by Shakespeare to this pastime, we may quote the phrase "to catch on the hip," made use of by Shylock in the "Merchant of Venice" (i. 3), who, speaking of Antonio, says,

> "If I can catch him once upon the hip,
> I will feed fat the ancient grudge I bear him"

—the meaning being, "to have at an entire advantage."[1] The expression occurs again in "Othello" (ii. 1), where Iago says:

> "I'll have our Michael Cassio on the hip."

Nares,[2] however, considers the phrase was derived from hunting; because, "when the animal pursued is seized upon the hip, it is finally disabled from flight."

In "As You Like It" (ii. 3), where Adam speaks of the "bonny priser of the humorous duke," Singer considers that a *priser* was the phrase for a wrestler, a *prise* being a term in that sport for a grappling or hold taken."

---

[1] Dyce's "Glossary," p. 208.   [2] "Glossary," vol. i. p. 421.

CHAPTER XVII.

DANCES.

WE are indebted to Shakespeare for having bequeathed to us many interesting allusions to some of the old dances in use in his day, but which have long ago passed into oblivion. As will be seen, these were of a very diverse character, but, as has been remarked, were well suited to the merry doings of our forefathers; and although in some cases they justly merited censure for their extravagant nature, yet the greater part of these sources of diversion were harmless. Indeed, no more pleasing picture can be imagined than that of a rustic sheep-shearing gathering in the olden times, when, the work over, the peasantry joined together in some simple dance, each one vieing with his neighbor to perform his part with as much grace as possible.

Antic. This was a grotesque dance. In " Macbeth " (iv. 1), the witch, perceiving how Macbeth is affected by the horrible apparitions which he has seen, says to her sisters :

> "Come, sisters, cheer we up his sprites.
> And show the best of our delights.
> I'll charm the air to give a sound,
> While you perform your antic round."

To quote another instance, Armado, in " Love's Labour's Lost " (v. 1), says :

> " We will have, if this fadge not, an antique."

Bergomask Dance. According to Sir Thomas Hanmer, this was a dance after the manner of the peasants of Bergomasco, a county in Italy belonging to the Venetians. All the buffoons in Italy affected to imitate the ridiculous jargon of that people, and from thence it became customary to mimic also their manner of dancing. In " A Midsummer-Night's

Dream" (v. 1), Bottom asks Theseus whether he would like "to hear a Bergomask dance," between two of their company.

Brawl. This was a kind of dance. It appears that several persons united hands in a circle, and gave one another continual shakes, the steps changing with the tune. With this dance balls were usually opened.[1] Kissing was occasionally introduced. In "Love's Labour's Lost" (iii. 1), Moth asks his master: "Will you win your love with a French brawl."

Canary. This was the name of a sprightly dance, the music to which consisted of two strains with eight bars in each; an allusion to which is made by Moth in "Love's Labour's Lost" (iii. 1), who speaks of jigging off a tune at the tongue's end, and canarying to it with the feet. And in "All's Well that End's Well" (ii. 1), Lafeu tells the king that he has seen a medicine

> "that's able to breathe life into a stone,
> Quicken a rock, and make you dance canary
> With spritely fire and motion."

This dance is said to have originated in the Canary Islands, an opinion, however, which has, says Dyce, been disputed.[2]

Cinque-pace. This was so named from its steps being regulated by the number five:

> "Five was the number of the music's feet,
> Which still the dance did with five paces meet."[3]

In "Much Ado About Nothing" (ii. 1), Shakespeare makes Beatrice make a quibble upon the term; for after comparing wooing, wedding, and repenting to a Scotch jig, a measure,

---

[1] Douce's "Illustrations of Shakespeare," p. 134.

[2] See Chappell's "Popular Music of the Olden Time," 2d edition, vol. i. p. 368; Dyce's "Glossary," vol. i. p. 63.

[3] Quoted by Nares from Sir John Davies on "Dancing." Mr. Dyce, "Glossary," p. 81, says that Nares wrongly confounded this with the "gallard."

and a cinque-pace, she says: "then comes repentance, and, with his bad legs, falls into the cinque-pace faster and faster, till he sink into his grave." A further reference occurs in "Twelfth Night" (i. 3), by Sir Toby Belch, who calls it a "sink-a-pace."

Coranto. An allusion to this dance, which appears to have been of a very lively and rapid character, is made in "Henry V." (iii. 5), where the Duke of Bourbon describes it as the "swift coranto;" and in "All's Well that Ends Well" (ii. 3) Lafeu refers to it. A further notice of it occurs in "Twelfth Night" (i. 3), in the passage where Sir Toby Belch speaks of "coming home in a coranto."

Fading. Malone quotes a passage from "Sportive Wit," 1666, which implies that this was a rustic dance:

> " The courtiers scorn us country clowns,
>   We country clowns do scorn the court;
> We can be as merry upon the downs
>   As you at midnight with all your sport,
> With a *fading*, with a *fading*."

It would appear, also, from a letter appended to Boswell's edition of Malone, that it was an Irish dance, and that it was practised, upon rejoicing occasions, as recently as 1803, the date of the letter:

" This dance is still practised on rejoicing occasions in many parts of Ireland; a king and queen are chosen from amongst the young persons who are the best dancers; the queen carries a garland composed of two hoops placed at right angles, and fastened to a handle; the hoops are covered with flowers and ribbons; you have seen it, I dare say, with the May-maids. Frequently in the course of the dance the king and queen lift up their joined hands as high as they can, she still holding the garland in the other. The most remote couple from the king and queen first pass under; all the rest of the line linked together follow in succession. When the last has passed, the king and queen suddenly face about and front their companions; this is often repeated during the dance, and the various undulations are pretty enough, resembling the movements of a serpent. The dancers on the first of

May visit such newly wedded pairs of a certain rank as have been married since last May-day in the neighborhood, who commonly bestow on them a stuffed ball richly decked with gold and silver lace, and accompanied with a present in money, to regale themselves after the dance. This dance is practised when the bonfires are lighted up, the queen hailing the return of summer in a popular Irish song beginning:

> 'We lead on summer—see! she follows in our train.'"

In the "Winter's Tale" (iv. 4), Shakespeare seems to allude to this dance where he makes the servant, speaking of the pedler, say: "he has the prettiest love songs for maids; so without bawdry, which is strange; with such delicate burdens of 'dildos' and 'fadings.'" Some commentators,[1] however, consider that only the song is meant.

Hay. Douce[2] says this dance was borrowed by us from the French, and is classed among the "brawls" in Thoinot Arbeau's "Orchesographie" (1588). In "Love's Labour's Lost" (v. 1), Dull says: "I will play on tabor to the Worthies, and let them dance their hay."

Jig. Besides meaning a merry, sprightly dance, a jig also implied a coarse sort of comic entertainment, in which sense it is probably used by Hamlet (ii. 2): "He's for a jig or a tale of bawdry." "It seems," says Mr. Collier,[3] "to have been a ludicrous composition in rhyme, sung, or said, by the clown, and accompanied by dancing and playing upon the pipe and tabor,"[4] an instance of which perhaps occurs in the Clown's song at the close of "Twelfth Night:"

> "When that I was and a little tiny boy."

---

[1] See Knight's "Pictorial Shakespeare," vol. ii. p. 375; Dyce's "Glossary," 1836, p. 152; "British Popular Customs," 1876, pp. 276, 277. See also Chappell's "Popular Music of the Olden Time," 2d edition, vol. i. p. 235; Nares's "Glossary," vol. i. p. 292.

[2] "Illustrations of Shakespeare," p. 146.

[3] "History of English Dramatic Poetry," vol. iii. p. 380; see Dyce's "Glossary," p. 229; Nares's "Glossary," vol. i. p. 450; Singer's "Shakespeare," vol. ix. pp. 198, 219.

[4] "Hamlet:" iii. 2: "your only jig-maker."

Fletcher, in the Prologue to the "Fair Maid of the Inn," says :

> "A jig should be clapt at, and every rhyme
> Praised and applauded by a clamorous chime."

Among the allusions to this dance we may quote one in "Much Ado About Nothing" (ii. 1), where Beatrice compares wooing to a Scotch jig; and another in "Twelfth Night" (i. 3), where Sir Toby Belch says, his "very walk should be a jig."

Lavolta. According to Florio, the lavolta is a kind of turning French dance, in which the man turns the woman round several times, and then assists her in making a high spring or *cabriole.* It is thus described by Sir John Davies:

> "Yet is there one the most delightful kind,
>   A loftie jumping, or a leaping round,
> Where arme in arme two dauncers are entwined,
>   And whirle themselves, with strict embracements bound ;
> And still their feet an anapest do sound,
>   An anapest is all their musicks song,
> Whose first two feet are short, and third is long."

Douce,[1] however, considers it to be of Italian origin, and says, "It passed from Italy into Provence and the rest of France, and thence into England." Scot, too, in his "Discovery of Witchcraft," thus speaks of it : "He saith, that these night-walking, or rather night-dancing, witches, brought out of Italie into France that dance which is called *la Volta*." Shakespeare, in his "Henry V." (iii. 5), makes the Duke of Bourbon allude to it :

> "They bid us to the English dancing-schools,
> And teach lavoltas high, and swift corantos."

Again, in "Troilus and Cressida" (iv. 4), Troilus says:

> "I cannot sing,
> Nor heel the high lavolt."

---

[1] "Illustrations of Shakespeare," p. 301 ; see Nares's "Glossary," vol. ii. p. 498.

Light o' Love. This was an old dance tune, and was a proverbial expression for levity, especially in love matters.[1] In "Much Ado About Nothing" (iii. 4), Margaret says: "Clap's into 'Light o' love;' that goes without a burden; do you sing it, and I'll dance it;" to which Beatrice answers: "Yea, light o' love, with your heels."

In "Two Gentlemen of Verona" (i. 2), it is alluded to:

> "*Julia.* Best sing it to the tune of 'Light o' love.'
> *Lucetta.* It is too heavy for so light a tune."

In the "Two Noble Kinsmen" (v. 2), we read:

> "He'll dance the morris twenty mile an hour,
> And gallops to the tune of 'Light o' love.'"

And in Beaumont and Fletcher's "Chances" (i. 3), Frederic says: "Sure he has encounter'd some light-o'-love or other."

Pavan. This was a grave and majestic dance, in which the gentlemen wore their caps, swords, and mantles, and the ladies their long robes and trains. The dancers stepped round the room and then crossed in the middle, trailing their garments on the ground, "the motion whereof," says Sir J. Hawkins, "resembled that of a peacock's tail." It is alluded to in "Twelfth Night" (v. 1) by Sir Toby: "A passy-measures pavin," although the reading of this passage is uncertain, the editors of the "Globe" edition substituting *panyn.*

It has been conjectured that the "passy-measure galliard," and the "passy-measure pavan" were only two different measures of the same dance, from the Italian *passamezzo.*[2]

Roundel. This was also called the "round," a dance of a circular kind, and is probably referred to by Titania in "A Midsummer-Night's Dream" (ii. 2), where she says to her train:[3]

> "Come now, a roundel and a fairy song."

---

[1] Nares's "Glossary," vol. ii. p. 510.

[2] See Dyce, vol. iii. p. 412, *note* 121.

[3] Roundel also meant a song. Mr. Dyce considers the dance is here meant.

Ben Jonson, in the " Tale of a Tub," [1] seems to call the rings, which such fairy dances are supposed to make, *roundels*.

> " I'll have no roundels, I, in the queen's paths."

Satyrs' Dance. A dance of satyrs was a not uncommon entertainment in Shakespeare's day, or even at an earlier period.[2] It was not confined to England, and has been rendered memorable by the fearful accident with which it was accompanied at the Court of France in 1392, a graphic description of which has been recorded by Froissart. In the " Winter's Tale " (iv. 4), the satyrs' dance is alluded to by the Servant, who says: " Master, there is three carters, three shepherds, three neat-herds, three swine-herds, that have made themselves all men of hair; they call themselves Saltiers: and they have a dance which the wenches say is a gallimaufry of gambols, because they are not in't." In a book of songs composed by Thomas Ravenscroft and others, in the time of Shakespeare, we find one [3] called the "Satyres' daunce." It is for four voices, and is as follows:

> " Round a round, a rounda, keepe your ring
>   To the glorious sunne we sing.
> Hoe, hoe !
>
> He that weares the flaming rayes,
> And the imperiall crowne of bayes,
> Him with shoutes and songs we praise.
> Hoe, hoe !
>
> That in his bountee would vouchsafe to grace
> The humble sylvanes and their shaggy race."

Sword-dance. In olden times there were several kinds of sword-dances, most of which afforded opportunities for the display of skill. In " Antony and Cleopatra " (iii. 11),

---

[1] See Singer's " Shakespeare," vol. ii. p. 333.

[2] See Knight's " Pictorial Shakespeare," vol. ii. p. 384; Singer's " Shakespeare," vol. iv. p. 85; Boswell's " Shakespeare," vol. xiv. p. 371.

[3] See Douce's " Illustrations of Shakespeare," p. 222.

there seems to be an allusion to this custom, where Antony, speaking of Cæsar, says :[1]

> " he, at Philippi, kept
> His sword e'en like a dancer."

And in " All's Well that Ends Well " (ii. 1), where Bertram, lamenting that he is kept from the wars, adds:

> " I shall stay here the forehorse to a smock,
> Creaking my shoes on the plain masonry,
> Till honour be bought up, and no sword worn
> But one to dance with."

In " Titus Andronicus " (ii. 1), too, Demetrius says to Chiron :

> " Why, boy, although our mother, unadvis'd
> Gave you a dancing-rapier by your side."

Tread a Measure, to which the King refers in " Love's Labour's Lost " (v. 2), when he tells Boyet to tell Rosaline

> " we have measur'd many miles,
> To tread a measure with her on this grass,"

was a grave solemn dance, with slow and measured steps, like the minuet. As it was of so solemn a nature, it was performed[2] at public entertainments in the Inns of Court, and it was " not unusual, nor thought inconsistent, for the first characters in the law to bear a part in treading a measure."

Trip and Go was the name of a favorite morris-dance, and appears, says Mr. Chappell, in his " Popular Music of the Olden Times," etc. (2d edition, vol. i. p. 131), to have become a proverbial expression. It is used in " Love's Labour's Lost " (iv. 2).

Up-spring. From the following passage, in Chapman's

---

[1] See Strutt's " Sports and Pastimes," 1876, pp. 300, 301 ; Douce's " Illustrations of Shakespeare," p. 193.

[2] Singer's " Shakespeare," vol. ii. p. 269; Sir Christopher Hatton was famous for it.

" Alphonsus, Emperor of Germany," it would seem that this was a German dance :

> " We Germans have no changes in our dances ;
> An almain and an up-spring, that is all."

Karl Elze,[1] who, a few years ago, reprinted Chapman's " Alphonsus " at Leipsic, says that the word " up-spring " " is the ' Hüpfauf,' the last and wildest dance at the old German merry-makings. No epithet could there be more appropriate to this drunken dance than Shakespeare's *swaggering*" in " Hamlet " (i. 4) :

> " The king doth wake to-night, and takes his rouse,
> Keeps wassail, and the swaggering up-spring reels."

---

[1] Quoted in Dyce's " Glossary," p. 476.

CHAPTER XVIII.

PUNISHMENTS.

SHAKESPEARE has not omitted to notice many of the punishments which were in use in years gone by; the scattered allusions to these being interesting in so far as they serve to illustrate the domestic manners and customs of our forefathers. Happily, however, these cruel tortures, which darken the pages of history, have long ago passed into oblivion; and at the present day it is difficult to believe that such barbarous practices could ever have been tolerated in any civilized country. The horrible punishment of " boiling to death," is mentioned in " Twelfth Night " (ii. 5), where Fabian says: " If I lose a scruple of this sport, let me be boiled to death with melancholy." In " Winter's Tale " (iii. 2), Paulina inquires:

> " What studied torments, tyrant, hast for me?
> What wheels? racks? fires? What flaying? boiling
> In leads or oils? What old or newer torture
> Must I receive?"

There seems to be an indirect allusion to this punishment in " The Two Noble Kinsmen " (iv. 3), where the Gaoler's Daughter in her madness speaks of those who " are mad, or hang, or drown themselves, being put into a caldron of lead and usurer's grease, and there boiling like a gammon of bacon that will never be enough."

The practice of holding burning basins before the eyes of captives, to destroy their eyesight, is probably alluded to by Macbeth (iv. 1), in the passage where the apparitions are presented to him by the witches:

> " Thou art too like the spirit of Banquo; down!
> Thy crown does sear mine eyeballs." [1]

---

[1] Halliwell-Phillipps's " Index to Shakespeare," p. 36.

In "Antony and Cleopatra" (ii. 4), soaking in brine as a punishment is referred to by Cleopatra, who says to the messenger:

> "Thou shalt be whipp'd with wire, and stew'd in brine,
>   Smarting in lingering pickle."

Drowning by the tide, a method of punishing criminals, is probably noticed in "The Tempest" (i. 1), by Antonio:

> "We are merely cheated of our lives by drunkards.
> This wide-chapp'd rascal—would thou might'st lie drowning
> The washing of ten tides!"

Baffle. This was formerly a punishment of infamy inflicted on recreant knights, one part of which consisted in hanging them up by the heels, to which Falstaff probably refers in " 1 Henry IV." (i. 2), where he says to the prince, "call me villain, and baffle me." And, further on (ii. 4): "if thou dost it half so gravely, so majestically, both in word and matter, hang me up by the heels for a rabbit-sucker, or a poulter's hare."[1] In "2 Henry IV." (i. 2), the Chief Justice tells Falstaff that "to punish him by the heels would amend the attention of his ears." And in "All's Well that Ends Well" (iv. 3), where the lord relates how Parolles has "sat in the stocks all night," Bertram says: "his heels have deserved it, in usurping his spurs so long."

Spenser, in his "Fairy Queen" (vi. 7), thus describes this mode of punishment:

> "And after all, for greater infamie
>   He by the heels him hung upon a tree,
>   And baffl'd so, that all which passed by
>   The picture of his punishment might see."

The appropriate term, too, for chopping off the spurs of a knight when he was to be degraded, was "hack"—a custom to which, it has been suggested, Mrs. Page alludes in the

---

[1] See Nares's "Glossary," vol. i. p. 46.

" Merry Wives of Windsor " (ii. 1):[1] " What?—Sir Alice
Ford! These knights will hack, and so thou shouldst not
alter the article of thy gentry." [2]

Mr. Dyce,[3] however, says the most probable meaning of
this obscure passage is, that there is an allusion to the extravagant number of knights created by King James, and
that *hack* is equivalent to " become cheap or vulgar."

It appears, too, that in days gone by the arms, etc., of
traitors and rebels might be defaced. Thus, in " Richard
II." (ii. 3), Berkeley tells Bolingbroke:

> " Mistake me not, my lord ; 'tis not my meaning
> To raze one title of your honour out."

Upon which passage we may quote from Camden's " Remains " (1605, p. 186): " How the names of them, which for
capital crimes against majestie, were erased out of the public
records, tables, and registers, or forbidden to be borne by
their posteritie, when their memory was damned, I could
show at large." In the following act (iii. 1) Bolingbroke
further relates how his enemies had:

> " Dispark'd my parks, and fell'd my forest woods,
> From mine own windows torn my household coat,
> Raz'd out my impress, leaving me no sign."

Bilboes. These were a kind of stocks or fetters used at
sea to confine prisoners, of which Hamlet speaks to Horatio
(v. 2):

> " Sir, in my heart there was a kind of fighting,
> That would not let me sleep : methought I lay
> Worse than the mutines in the bilboes."

This punishment is thus described by Steevens: " The *bilboes* is a bar of iron with fetters annexed to it, by which
mutinous or disorderly sailors were anciently linked together. The word is derived from Bilboa, a place in Spain where

---

[1] Mr. Halliwell-Phillipps, in his " Handbook Index to the Works of
Shakespeare" (1866, p. 231), suggests this meaning.

[2] See Nares's " Glossary," vol. i. p. 397.

[3] Dyce's " Glossary," p. 197.

instruments of steel were fabricated in the utmost perfection. To understand Shakespeare's allusion completely, it should be known that, as these fetters connect the legs of the offenders very close together, their attempts to rest must be as fruitless as those of Hamlet, in whose mind 'there was a kind of fighting that would not let him sleep.' Every motion of one must disturb his partner in confinement. The *bilboes* are still shown in the Tower of London, among the other spoils of the Spanish Armada." [1]

Brand.—The branding of criminals is indirectly alluded to in " 2 Henry VI." (v. 2), by Young Clifford, who calls the Duke of Richmond a " foul stigmatick," which properly meant " a person who had been branded with a hot iron for some crime, one notably defamed for naughtiness." The practice was abolished by law in the year 1822.

The practice, too, of making persons convicted of perjury wear papers, while undergoing punishment, descriptive of their offence, is spoken of in " Love's Labour's Lost " (iv. 3), where Biron says of Longaville :

> " Why, he comes in like a perjure, wearing papers."

Holinshed relates how Wolsey " so punished a perjure with open punishment and open paper-wearing that in his time it was disused."

Breech. This old term to whip or punish as a school-boy is noticed in the " Taming of the Shrew " (iii. 1) :

> " I am no breeching scholar in the schools ;
> I'll not be tied to hours nor 'pointed times "

—breeching being equivalent to " liable to be whipped."

In " Merry Wives of Windsor " (iv. 1), Sir Hugh Evans tells the boy page : " If you forget your ' quies,' your ' quæs,' and your ' quods,' you must be preeches " (breeched).

Crown. A burning crown, as the punishment of regi-

---

[1] Bilbo was also a rapier or sword ; thus, in " Merry Wives of Windsor " (iii. 5), Falstaff says to Ford : " I suffered the pangs of three several deaths ; first, an intolerable fright, to be detected . . . next, to be compassed, like a good bilbo . . . hilt to point," etc.

cides or other criminals, is probably alluded to by Anne in
" Richard III." (iv. 1):

> " O, would to God that the inclusive verge
> Of golden metal, that must round my brow,
> Were red-hot steel, to sear me to the brain !"

Mr. Singer,[1] in a note on this passage, quotes from Chettle's " Tragedy of Hoffman " (1631), where this punishment
is introduced:

> "Fix on thy master's head my burning crown."

And again:

> " Was adjudg'd
> To have his head sear'd with a burning crown."

The Earl of Athol, who was executed for the murder of
James I. of Scotland, was, before his death, crowned with a
hot iron. In some of the monkish accounts of a place of
future torments, a burning crown is appropriated to those
who deprived any lawful monarch of his kingdom.

Pillory. This old mode of punishment is referred to by
Launce in the " Two Gentlemen of Verona " (iv. 4), where
he speaks of having " stood on the pillory." In " Taming
of the Shrew " (ii. 1), Hortensio, when he tells Baptista how
he had been struck by Katharina because " I did but tell her
she mistook her frets," adds:

> "she struck me on the head,
> And through the instrument my pate made way;
> And there I stood amazed for a while,
> As on a pillory, looking through the lute."

It has been suggested that there may be an allusion to
the pillory in " Measure for Measure " (v. 1), where Lucio
says to the duke, disguised in his friar's hood: " you must
be hooded, must you? show your knave's visage, with a
pox to you! show your sheep-biting face, and be hanged
an hour !" The alleged crime was not capital, and suspen-

---

[1] "Shakespeare," vol. vi. p. 485; see " Boswell's Life of Johnson,"
vol. ii. p. 6.

sion in the pillory for an hour was all that the speaker intended."[1]

Press. Several allusions occur to this species of torture, applied to contumacious felons. It was also, says Malone, "formerly inflicted on those persons who, being indicted, refused to plead. In consequence of their silence, they were pressed to death by a heavy weight laid upon the stomach." In "Much Ado About Nothing" (iii. 1), Hero says of Beatrice:

> "she would laugh me
> Out of myself, press me to death with wit."

In "Richard II." (iii. 4) the Queen exclaims:

> "O, I am press'd to death, through want of speaking!"

And in "Measure for Measure" (v. 1), Lucio tells the Duke that, "Marrying a punk, my lord, is pressing to death, whipping, and hanging."

In the "Perfect Account of the Daily Intelligence" (April 16th, 1651), we find it recorded: "Mond., April 14th. This Session, at the Old Bailey, were four men pressed to death that were all in one robbery, and, out of obstinacy and contempt of the Court, stood mute, and refused to plead." This punishment was not abolished until by statute 12 George III. c. 20.

Rack. According to Mr. Blackstone, this "was utterly unknown to the law of England; though once, when the Dukes of Exeter and Suffolk, and other ministers of Henry VI., had laid a design to introduce the civil law into this kingdom as a rule of government, for the beginning thereof they erected a rack of torture, which was called, in derision, the Duke of Exeter's daughter; and still remains in the Tower of London, where it was occasionally used as an engine of state, not of law, more than once in the reign of Queen Elizabeth. But when, upon the assassination of Vil-

---

[1] Nares's "Glossary," vol. ii. p. 661 ; see Douce's "Illustrations of Shakespeare," 1839, pp. 90, 91, 109; Brand's "Pop. Antiq.," vol. iii. p. 111.

liers, Duke of Buckingham, it was proposed, in the Privy
Council, to put the assassin to the rack, in order to discover
his accomplices, the judges (being consulted) declared unan-
imously, to their own honor and the honor of the English
law, that no such proceeding was allowable by the law of
England." Mr. Hallam observes that, though the English
law never recognized the use of torture, yet there were
many instances of its employment in the reign of Elizabeth
and James; and, among others, in the case of the Gunpowder Plot. He further adds, in the latter part of the reign
of Elizabeth "the rack seldom stood idle in the Tower."
Of the many allusions to this torture may be mentioned Sebastian's word in " Twelfth Night " (v. 1):

> "Antonio! O my dear Antonio!
>   How have the hours rack'd and tortured me,
>   Since I have lost thee."

In " Measure for Measure " (v. 1), Escalus orders the " un-
reverend and unhallow'd friar " (the Duke disguised) to be
taken to the rack:

> "Take him hence; to the rack with him!—We'll touse you
>   Joint by joint."

The engine, which sometimes meant the rack, is spoken
of in " King Lear " (i. 4):

> "Which, like an engine, wrench'd my frame of nature
>   From the fix'd place."[1]

So, in Beaumont and Fletcher's " Night Walker " (iv. 5):

> "Their souls shot through with adders, torn on engines."

Once more, in " Measure for Measure " (ii. 1), where Escalus
tells how

> " Some run from brakes of ice, and answer none "

---

[1] It also meant a warlike engine, as in "Coriolanus," v. 4: "When
he walks, he moves like an engine, and the ground shrinks before his
treading;" so, also, in "Troilus and Cressida," ii. 3.

—a passage which Mr. Dyce would thus read:

"Some run from brakes of vice."

It has been suggested that there is an allusion to "engines of torture," although, owing to the many significations of the word "brake," its meaning here has been much disputed.[1]

Stocks. This old-fashioned mode of punishment is the subject of frequent allusion by Shakespeare. Thus, Launce, in the "Two Gentlemen of Verona" (iv. 4), says: "I have sat in the stocks for puddings he hath stolen." In "All's Well that Ends Well" (iv. 3), Bertram says: "Come, bring forth this counterfeit module, has deceived me, like a double-meaning prophesier." Whereupon one of the French lords adds: "Bring him forth: has sat i' the stocks all night, poor gallant knave." Volumnia says of Coriolanus (v. 3):

> "There's no man in the world
> More bound to's mother; yet here he lets me prate
> Like one i' the stocks."

Again, in the "Comedy of Errors" (iii. 1), Luce speaks of "a pair of stocks in the town," and in "King Lear" (ii. 2), Cornwall, referring to Kent, says:

> "Fetch forth the stocks!—
> You stubborn ancient knave."

It would seem that formerly, in great houses, as in some colleges, there were movable stocks for the correction of the servants. Putting a person in the stocks, too, was an exhibition familiar to the ancient stage. In "Hick Scorner,"[2] printed in the reign of Henry VIII., Pity is placed in the stocks, and left there until he is freed "by Perseverance and Contemplacyon."

Strappado. This was a military punishment, by which the unfortunate sufferer was cruelly tortured in the follow-

---

[1] See Dyce's "Glossary," p. 49; Halliwell-Phillipps's "Handbook Index to Shakespeare," p. 56; Nares's "Glossary," vol. i. p. 104.

[2] It is reprinted in Hawkins's "English Drama," 1773.

ing way: a rope being fastened under his arms, he was drawn up by a pulley to the top of a high beam, and then suddenly let down with a jerk. The result usually was a dislocation of the shoulder-blade. In " 1 Henry IV." (ii. 4), it is referred to by Falstaff, who tells Poins: "were I at the strappado, or all the racks in the world, I would not tell you on compulsion." At Paris, says Douce,[1] "there was a spot called *l'estrapade*, in the Faubourg St. Jacques, where soldiers received this punishment. The machine, whence the place took its name, remained fixed like a perpetual gallows." The term is probably derived from the Italian *strappare*, to pull or draw with violence.

Toss in a Sieve. This punishment, according to Cotgrave, was inflicted " on such as committed gross absurdities." In " 1 Henry VI." (i. 3), Gloster says to the Bishop of Winchester:

> " I'll canvass thee in thy broad cardinal's hat,
> If thou proceed in this thy insolence."

It is alluded to in Davenant's " Cruel Brother " (1630):

> " I'll sift and winow him in an old hat."

Wheel. The punishment of the wheel was not known at Rome, but we read of Mettius Tuffetius being torn asunder by *quadrigæ* driven in opposite directions. As Shakespeare, remarks Malone, " has coupled this species of punishment with another that certainly was unknown to ancient Rome, it is highly probable that he was not apprised of the story of Mettius Tuffetius, and that in this, as in various other instances, the practice of his own times was in his thoughts, for in 1594 John Chastel had been thus executed in France for attempting to assassinate Henry IV."

Coriolanus (iii. 2) says:

> " Let them pull all about mine ears, present me
> Death on the wheel, or at wild horses' heels."

Whipping. Three centuries ago this mode of punishment was carried to a cruel extent. By an act passed in the 2d year

---

[1] " Illustrations of Shakespeare," pp. 263, 264; see Dyce's " Glossary," p. 423.

of Henry VIII., vagrants were to be carried to some market-town, or other place, and there tied to the end of a cart, naked, and beaten with whips throughout such market-town, or other place, till the body should be bloody by reason of such whipping." The punishment was afterwards slightly mitigated, for, by a statute passed in 39th of Elizabeth's reign, vagrants " were only to be stripped naked from the middle upwards, and whipped till the body should be bloody." The stocks were often so constructed as to serve both for stocks and whipping-posts.[1] Among the numerous references to this punishment by Shakespeare, we may quote " 2 Henry IV." (v. 4), where the beadle says of Hostess Quickly: "The constables have delivered her over to me, and she shall have whipping-cheer enough, I warrant her." In the " Taming of the Shrew " (i. 1), Gremio says, speaking of Katharina, " I had as lief take her dowry with this condition,—to be whipped at the high-cross every morning," in allusion to what Hortensio had just said : " why, man, there be good fellows in the world, an a man could light on them, would take her with all faults, and money enough." In " 2 Henry VI." (ii. 1), Gloster orders Simpcox and his wife to

> " be whipped through every market-town,
> Till they come to Berwick, from whence they came."

Wisp. This was a punishment for a scold.[2] It appears that " a wisp, or small twist of straw or hay, was often applied as a mark of opprobrium to an immodest woman, a scold, or similar offender ; even, therefore, the showing it to a woman, was considered a grievous affront." In " 3 Henry VI." (ii. 2) Edward says of Queen Margaret :

> " A wisp of straw were worth a thousand crowns,
> To make this shameless callat [3] know herself."

---

[1] See " Book of Days," vol. i. pp. 598, 599.

[2] Nares's " Glossary," vol. ii. p. 965.

[3] " Callat," an immodest woman, also applied to a scold.   Cf. " Winter's Tale," ii. 3 :

> " A callat
> Of boundless tongue, who late hath beat her husband,
> And now baits me."

A wisp, adds Nares, seems to have been the badge of the
scolding woman in the ceremony of Skimmington;[1] an allusion to which is given in a " Dialogue between John and
Jone, striving who shall wear the breeches," in the " Pleasures of Poetry," cited by Malone:

> " Good, gentle Jone, with-holde thy handes,
>   This once let me entreat thee,
> And make me promise never more,
>   That thou shalt mind to beat me .
> For fear thou wear the wispe, good wife,
>   And make our neighbours ride."

In Nash's " Pierce Pennilesse " (1593) there is also an amusing allusion to it: " Why, thou errant butter-whore, thou
cotquean and scrattop of scolds, wilt thou never leave afflict-
ing a dead carcasse? continually read the rhetorick lecture
of Ramme-alley? a wispe, a wispe, you kitchen-stuffe wrang-
ler."

---

[1] Skimmington was a burlesque ceremony in ridicule of a man beaten
by his wife,   See Brand's " Pop. Antiq.," vol. ii. pp. 191, 192.

CHAPTER XIX.

PROVERBS.

In the present chapter are collected together the chief proverbs either quoted or alluded to by Shakespeare. Many of these are familiar to most readers, but have gained an additional interest by reason of their connection with the poet's writings. At the same time, it may be noted that very many of Shakespeare's pithy sayings have, since his day, passed into proverbs, and have taken their place in this class of literature. It is curious to notice, as Mrs. Cowden-Clarke remarks,[1] how "Shakespeare has paraphrased some of our commonest proverbs in his own choice and elegant diction." Thus, "Make hay while the sun shines" becomes

> "The sun shines hot; and if we use delay,
> Cold biting winter mars our hoped-for hay,"

a statement which applies to numerous other proverbial sayings.

"A black man is a jewel in a fair woman's eyes." In the "Two Gentlemen of Verona" (v. 2), the following passage is an amusing illustration of the above:

> "*Thurio.* What says she to my face?
> *Proteus.* She says it is a fair one.
> *Thurio.* Nay then, the wanton lies; my face is black.
> *Proteus.* But pearls are fair; and the old saying is,
> Black men are pearls in beauteous ladies' eyes."

In "Titus Andronicus" (v. 1) there is a further allusion to this proverb, where Lucius says of Aaron,

> "This is the pearl that pleas'd your empress' eye."

---

[1] "Shakespeare Proverbs," 1858.

"A beggar marries a wife and lice." So in "King Lear" (iii. 2), Song:

> "The cod-piece that will house,
> Before the head has any,
> The head and he shall louse;
> So beggars marry many."

Thus it is also said: "A beggar payeth a benefit with a louse."

"A cunning knave needs no broker." This old proverb is quoted by Hume, in "2 Henry VI." (i. 2):

> "A crafty knave does need no broker."

"A curst cur must be tied short." With this proverb we may compare what Sir Toby says in "Twelfth Night" (iii. 2), to Sir Andrew: "Go, write it in a martial hand; be curst and brief."

"A drop hollows the stone," or "many drops pierce the stone." We may compare "3 Henry VI." (iii. 2), "much rain wears the marble," and also the messenger's words (ii. 1), when he relates how "the noble Duke of York was slain:"

> "Environed he was with many foes;
> And stood against them, as the hope of Troy
> Against the Greeks, that would have enter'd Troy.
> But Hercules himself must yield to odds;
> And many strokes, though with a little axe,
> Hew down and fell the hardest-timber'd oak.

"A finger in every pie." So, in "Henry VIII." (i. 1), Buckingham says of Wolsey:

> "no man's pie is freed
> From his ambitious finger."

To the same purport is the following proverb:[1] "He had a finger in the pie when he burnt his nail off."

"A fool's bolt is soon shot." Quoted by Duke of Orleans in "Henry V." (iii. 7). With this we may compare the French: "De fol juge breve sentence."[2]

---

[1] Bohn's "Handbook of Proverbs," p. 159,

[2] Ibid. p. 94.

"A friend at court is as good as a penny in the purse."
So, in "2 Henry IV." (v. 1), Shallow says: "a friend i' the
court is better than a penny in purse." The French equivalent of this saying is: "Bon fait avoir ami en cour, car le
procès en est plus court."

"A little pot's soon hot." Grumio, in "Taming of the
Shrew" (iv. 1), uses this familiar proverb: "were not I a
little pot, and soon hot, my very lips might freeze to my
teeth," etc.

"A pox of the devil" ("Henry V.," iii. 7).

"A smoky chimney and a scolding wife are two bad companions." There are various versions of this proverb. Ray
gives the following: "Smoke, raining into the house, and a
scolding wife, will make a man run out of doors."

Hotspur, in "1 Henry IV." (iii. 1), says of Glendower:

> "O, he's as tedious
> As a tired horse, a railing wife;
> Worse than a smoky house."

"A snake lies hidden in the grass." This, as Mr. Green[1]
remarks, is no unfrequent proverb, and the idea is often
made use of by Shakespeare. Thus, in "2 Henry VI." (iii. 1),
Margaret declares to the attendant nobles:

> "Henry my lord is cold in great affairs,
> Too full of foolish pity: and Gloster's show
> Beguiles him, as the mournful crocodile
> With sorrow snares relenting passengers,
> Or as the snake, roll'd in a flowering bank,
> With shining checker'd slough, doth sting a child,
> That for the beauty thinks it excellent."

Lady Macbeth (i. 5) tells her husband:

> "look like the innocent flower,
> But be the serpent under't."

Juliet ("Romeo and Juliet," iii. 2) speaks of:

> "Serpent heart, hid with a flowering face."

---

[1] "Shakespeare and the Emblem Writers," 1870, p. 341.

"A staff is quickly found to beat a dog." Other versions of this proverb are: "It is easy to find a stick to beat a dog;" "It is easy to find a stone to throw at a dog."[1] So, in "2 Henry VI." (iii. 1), Gloster says:

> "I shall not want false witness to condemn me,
> Nor store of treasons to augment my guilt;
> The ancient proverb will be well effected,—
> A staff is quickly found to beat a dog."

"A wise man may live anywhere." In "Richard II." (i. 3), John of Gaunt says:

> "All places that the eye of heaven visits,
> Are to a wise man ports and happy havens."

"A woman conceals what she does not know." Hence Hotspur says to his wife, in "1 Henry IV." (ii. 3):

> Constant you are,
> But yet a woman: and for secrecy,
> No lady closer; for I well believe
> Thou wilt not utter what thou dost not know,—
> And so far will I trust thee, gentle Kate."

"All men are not alike" ("Much Ado About Nothing," iii. 5).[2]

"All's Well that Ends Well."

"As lean as a rake." So in "Coriolanus" (i. 1), one of the citizens says: "Let us revenge this with our pikes, ere we become rakes." So Spenser, in his "Fairy Queen" (bk. ii. can. 11):

> "His body leane and meagre as a rake."

This proverb is found in Chaucer's "Canterbury Tales" (i. 289):

> "Al so lene was his hors as is a rake."

"As thin as a whipping-post" is another proverb of the same kind.

---

[1] See Kelly's "Proverbs of All Nations," 1870, p. 157.

[2] Halliwell-Phillipps's "Handbook Index to Shakespeare," p. 390, under Proverbs.

"As mad as a March hare" ("The Two Noble Kinsmen," iii. 5). We may compare the expression "hare-brained:" "1 Henry IV." (v. 2).

"As sound as a bell." So in "Much Ado about Nothing" (iii. 2), Don Pedro says of Benedick: "He hath a heart as sound as a bell."

"As the bell clinketh, so the fool thinketh." This proverb is indirectly alluded to in "Much Ado About Nothing" (iii. 2), in the previous passage, where Don Pedro says of Benedick that "He hath a heart as sound as a bell, and his tongue is the clapper; for what his heart thinks, his tongue speaks."

Another form of the same proverb is: "As the fool thinks, the bell tinks." [1]

"As true as steel." This popular adage is quoted in "Troilus and Cressida" (iii. 2):

> "As true as steel, as plantage to the moon."

We may also compare the proverb: "As true as the dial to the sun."

"At hand, quoth pick-purse" ("1 Henry IV.," ii. 1). This proverbial saying arose, says Malone, from the pickpurse always seizing the prey nearest him.

"Ay, tell me that and unyoke" ("Hamlet," v. 1). This was a common adage for giving over or ceasing to do a thing; a metaphor derived from the unyoking of oxen at the end of their labor.

"Baccare, quoth Mortimer to his sow." With this Mr. Halliwell-Phillipps compares Gremio's words in the "Taming of the Shrew" (ii. 1):

> "Saving your tale, Petruchio, I pray,
> Let us, that are poor petitioners, speak too:
> Baccare! you are marvellous forward."

Mr. Dyce ("Glossary," p. 23) says the word signifies "go back," and cites one of John Heywood's epigrams upon it:

---

[1] See Kelly's "Proverbs of All Nations," p. 91.

> " Backare, quoth Mortimer to his sow ;
> Went that sowe backe at that bidding, trow you."

" Barnes are blessings " (" All's Well that Ends Well," i. 3).

" Base is the slave that pays " (" Henry V.," ii. 1).[1]

" Bastards are born lucky." This proverb is alluded to in " King John " (i. 1), by the Bastard, who says :

> " Brother, adieu ; good fortune come to thee !
> For thou wast got i' the way of honesty."

Philip wishes his brother good fortune, because Robert was not a bastard.

" Beggars mounted run their horses to death."[2]   Quoted by York in " 3 Henry VI." (i. 4). We may also compare the proverb : " Set a beggar on horseback, he'll ride to the devil."

" Begone when the sport is at the best." Mr. Halliwell-Phillipps quotes Benvolio's words in " Romeo and Juliet " (i. 5):

> " Away, be gone ; the sport is at the best."

To the same effect are Romeo's words (i. 4):

> " The game was ne'er so fair, and I am done."

" Be off while your shoes are good." This popular phrase, still in use, seems alluded to by Katharina in " Taming of the Shrew " (iii. 2), who says to Petruchio :

> " You may be jogging whiles your boots are green."

" Better a witty fool, than a foolish wit." Quoted by the clown in " Twelfth Night " (i. 5).

" Better fed than taught." This old saying may be alluded to in " All's Well that Ends Well " (ii. 2) by the clown, " I will show myself highly fed and lowly taught ;" and again (ii. 4) by Parolles :

> " A good knave, i' faith, and well fed."

" Blessing of your heart, you brew good ale." Quoted by

---

[1] Halliwell-Phillipps's " Handbook Index to Shakespeare," p. 391.
[2] See Bohn's " Handbook of Proverbs," p. 326.

Launce as a proverb in the "Two Gentlemen of Verona" (iii. 1).

"Blush like a black dog." This saying is referred to in "Titus Andronicus" (v. 1):

> "1 *Goth.*   What, canst thou say all this, and never blush?
> *Aaron.*   Ay, like a black dog, as the saying is."

"Bought and sold" ("Troilus and Cressida," ii. 1). A proverbial phrase applied to any one entrapped or made a victim by treachery or mismanagement. It is found again in the "Comedy of Errors" (iii. 1); in "King John" (v. 4); and in "Richard III." (v. 3).

"Bring your hand to the buttery-bar, and let it drink" ("Twelfth Night," i. 3). Mr. Dyce quotes the following explanation of this passage, although he does not answer for its correctness: "This is a proverbial phrase among forward abigails, to ask at once for a kiss and a present. Sir Andrew's slowness of comprehension in this particular gave her a just suspicion, at once, of his frigidity and avarice." The buttery-bar means the place in palaces and in great houses whence provisions were dispensed; and it is still to be seen in most of our colleges.

"Brag's a good dog, but Hold-fast is a better." This proverb is alluded to in "Henry V." (ii. 3), by Pistol:

> "Hold-fast is the only dog, my duck."[1]

"Bush natural, more hair than wit." Ray's Proverbs. So in "Two Gentlemen of Verona" (iii. 1), it is said, "She hath more hair than wit."

"By chance but not by truth"[2] ("King John," i. 1).

"Care will kill a cat; yet there's no living without it." So in "Much Ado About Nothing" (v. 1), Claudio says to Don Pedro: "What though care killed a cat, thou hast mettle enough in thee to kill care."

"Come cut and long-tail" ("Merry Wives of Windsor,"

---

[1] See Bohn's "Handbook of Proverbs," p. 333; Kelly's "Proverbs of all Nations," 1870, p. 173.

[2] Halliwell-Phillipps's "Handbook Index to Shakespeare," p. 391.

(iii. 4). This proverb means, "Let any come that may, good or bad;" and was, no doubt, says Staunton, originally applied to dogs or horses."

"Comparisons are odious." So, in "Much Ado About Nothing" (iii. 5), Dogberry tells Verges: "Comparisons are odorous."

"Confess and be hanged." This well-known proverb is probably alluded to in the "Merchant of Venice" (iii. 2):

> "*Bassanio*. Promise me life, and I'll confess the truth.
> *Portia*. Well then, confess, and live."

We may also refer to what Othello says (iv. 1): "To confess, and be hanged for his labour; first, to be hanged, and then to confess. I tremble at it."

In "Timon of Athens" (i. 2), Apemantus says: "Ho, ho, confess'd it! hang'd it, have you not?"

"Cry him, and have him." So Rosalind says, in "As You Like It" (i. 3), "If I could cry 'hem' and have him."

"Cry you mercy, I took you for a joint-stool" ("King Lear," iii. 6). It is given by Ray in his "Proverbs" (1768); see also "Taming of the Shrew" (ii. 1).

"Cucullus non facit monachum." So in "Henry VIII." (iii. 1), Queen Katherine says:

> "All hoods make not monks."

Chaucer thus alludes to this proverb:

> "Habite ne maketh monk ne feere;
> But a clean life and devotion
> Maketh gode men of religion."

"Dead as a door-nail." So, in "2 Henry VI." (iv. 10), Cade says to Iden: "I have eat no meat these five days; yet, come thou and thy five men, and if I do not leave you all as dead as a door-nail, I pray God I may never eat grass more."

We may compare the term, "dead as a herring," which Caius uses in the "Merry Wives of Windsor" (ii. 3), "By gar, de herring is no dead, so as I vill kill him."

"Death will have his day" ("Richard II.," iii. 2).

"Delays are dangerous." In "1 Henry VI." (iii. 2), Reignier says:

> "Defer no time, delays have dangerous ends."

"Diluculo surgere," etc. ("Twelfth Night," ii. 3).

"Dogs must eat." This, with several other proverbs, is quoted by Agrippa in "Coriolanus" (i. 1).

"Dun's the mouse" ("Romeo and Juliet," i. 4). This was a proverbial saying, of which no satisfactory explanation has yet been given. Nares thinks it was "frequently employed with no other intent than that of quibbling on the word *done*." Ray has, "as dun as a mouse." Mercutio says: "Tut, dun's the mouse, the constable's own word."

"Empty vessels give the greatest sound." Quoted in "Henry V." (iv. 4).

"Every dog hath his day, and every man his hour." This old adage seems alluded to by Hamlet (v. 1) :[1]

> "The cat will mew, and dog will have his day."

"Every man at forty is either a fool or a physician."[2] This popular proverb is probably referred to in "Merry Wives of Windsor" (iii. 4), by Mistress Quickly, who tells Fenton how she had recommended him as a suitor for Mr. Page's daughter instead of Doctor Caius: "This is my doing, now: 'Nay,' said I, 'will you cast away your child on a fool, and a physician? look on Master Fenton:'—this is my doing."

"Familiarity breeds contempt." So, in the "Merry Wives of Windsor" (i. 1), Slender says: "I hope, upon familiarity will grow more contempt."

"Fast bind, fast find." In "Merchant of Venice" (ii. 5), Shylock says:

> "Well, Jessica, go in :
> Perhaps I will return immediately :

---

[1] Bohn's "Handbook of Proverbs," p. 86.

[2] Ray gives another form : "Every man is either a fool or a physician after thirty years of age;" see Bohn's "Handbook of Proverbs," 1857, p. 27.

> Do as I bid you; shut doors after you;
> Fast bind, fast find;
> A proverb never stale in thrifty mind."

"Finis coronat opus." A translation of this Latin proverb is given by Helena in "All's Well that Ends Well" (iv. 4):

> "Still the fine's the crown."

In "2 Henry VI." (v. 2), also, Clifford's expiring words are: "La fin couronne les œuvres." We still have the expression *to crown*, in the sense of *to finish* or *make perfect*. Mr. Douce [1] remarks that "*coronidem imponere* is a metaphor well known to the ancients, and supposed to have originated from the practice of finishing buildings by placing a crown at the top as an ornament; and for this reason the words *crown*, *top*, and *head* are become synonymous in most languages. There is reason for believing that the ancients placed a crescent at the beginning, and a crown, or some ornament that resembled it, at the end of their books." In "Troilus and Cressida" (iv. 5), Hector says:

> "The fall of every Phrygian stone will cost
> A drop of Grecian blood: the end crowns all;
> And that old common arbitrator, Time,
> Will one day end it."

Prince Henry ("2 Henry IV.," ii. 2), in reply to Poins, gives another turn to the proverb: "By this hand, thou think'st me as far in the devil's book as thou and Falstaff, for obduracy and persistency: let the end try the man." [2]

"Fly pride, says the peacock." This is quoted by Dromio of Syracuse, in "The Comedy of Errors" (iv. 3). [3]

"Friends may meet, but mountains never greet." This is ironically alluded to in "As You Like It" (iii. 2), by Celia: "It is a hard matter for friends to meet; but mountains may be removed with earthquakes, and so encounter."

---

[1] "Illustrations of Shakespeare," p. 199.

[2] See Green's "Shakespeare and the Emblem Writers," 1870, pp. 319, 323.

[3] Halliwell-Phillipps's "Handbook Index to Shakespeare," p. 391.

"Give the devil his due." In "Henry V." (iii. 7) it is quoted by the Duke of Orleans.

"God sends fools fortune." It is to this version of the Latin adage, "Fortuna favet fatuis" ("Fortune favors fools"), that Touchstone alludes in his reply to Jaques, in "As You Like It" (ii. 7):

> "'No, sir,' quoth he,
> 'Call me not fool till heaven hath sent me fortune.'"

Under different forms, the same proverb is found on the Continent. The Spanish say, "The mother of God appears to fools;" and the German one is this, "Fortune and women are fond of fools."[1]

"God sends not corn for the rich only." This is quoted by Marcius in "Coriolanus" (i. 1).

"Good goose, do not bite." This proverb is used in "Romeo and Juliet" (ii. 4):

> "*Mercutio.* I will bite thee by the ear for that jest.
> *Romeo.* Nay, good goose, bite not."

"Good liquor will make a cat speak." So, in the "Tempest" (ii. 2), Stephano says: "Come on your ways: open your mouth; here is that which will give language to you, cat; open your mouth."

"Good wine needs no bush." This old proverb, which is quoted by Shakespeare in "As You Like It" (v. 4, "Epilogue")—"If it be true that good wine needs no bush, 'tis true that a good play needs no epilogue"—refers to the custom of hanging up a bunch of twigs, or a wisp of hay, at a roadside inn, as a sign that drink may be had within. This practice, "which still lingers in the cider-making counties of the west of England, and prevails more generally in France, is derived from the Romans, among whom a bunch of ivy was used as the sign of a wine-shop." They were also in the habit of saying, "Vendible wine needs no ivy hung up." The Spanish have a proverb, "Good wine needs no crier."[2]

---

[1] Kelly's "Proverbs of All Nations," 1872, p. 52.

[2] Ibid., 1870, pp. 175, 176.

"Greatest clerks not the wisest men." Mr. Halliwell-Phillipps, in his "Handbook Index to Shakespeare" (p. 391), quotes the following passage in "Twelfth Night" (iv. 2), where Maria tells the clown to personate Sir Topas, the curate: "I am not tall enough to become the function well, nor lean enough to be thought a good student; but to be said an honest man and a good housekeeper goes as fairly as to say a careful man and a great scholar."

"Happy man be his dole" ("Taming of the Shrew," i. 1; "1 Henry IV.," ii. 2). Ray has it, "Happy man, happy dole;" or, "Happy man by his dole."

"Happy the bride on whom the sun shines." Mr. Halliwell-Phillipps, in his "Handbook Index to Shakespeare" (p. 392), quotes, as an illustration of this popular proverb, the following passage in "Twelfth Night" (iv. 3), where Olivia and Sebastian, having made "a contract of eternal bond of love," the former says:

> "and heavens so shine,
> That they may fairly note this act of mine!"

"Happy the child whose father went to the devil."[1] So, in "3 Henry VI." (ii. 2), King Henry asks, interrogatively:

> "And happy always was it for that son,
> Whose father, for his hoarding, went to hell?"

The Portuguese say, "Alas for the son whose father goes to heaven."

"Hares pull dead lions by the beard." In "King John" (ii. 1), the Bastard says to Austria:

> "You are the hare of whom the proverb goes,
> Whose valour plucks dead lions by the beard."

"Have is have, however men do catch." Quoted by the Bastard in "King John" (i. 1).

"Heaven's above all." In "Richard II." (iii. 3) York tells Bolingbroke:

---

[1] See Bohn's "Handbook of Proverbs," p. 100; Kelly's "Proverbs of All Nations," p. 187.

> "Take not, good cousin, further than you should,
> Lest you mistake: the heavens are o'er our heads."

So, too, in "Othello" (ii. 3), Cassio says: "Heaven's above all."[1]

"He is a poor cook who cannot lick his own fingers." Under a variety of forms, this proverb is found in different countries. The Italians say, "He who manages other people's wealth does not go supperless to bed." The Dutch, too, say, "All officers are greasy," that is, something sticks to them.[2] In "Romeo and Juliet" (iv. 2) the saying is thus alluded to:

> "*Capulet*. Sirrah, go hire me twenty cunning cooks.
> 2 *Servant*. You shall have none ill, sir; for I'll try if they can lick their fingers.
> *Capulet*. How canst thou try them so?
> 2 *Servant*. Marry, sir, 'tis an ill cook that cannot lick his own fingers: therefore he that cannot lick his fingers goes not with me."

"He's mad, that trusts in the tameness of a wolf, a horse's health, a boy's love, or a whore's oath" ("King Lear," iii. 6).[3]

"Heroum filii noxæ." It is a common notion that a father above the common rate of men has usually a son below it. Hence, in "The Tempest" (i. 2), Shakespeare probably alludes to this Latin proverb:

> "My trust,
> Like a good parent, did beget of him
> A falsehood, in its contrary as great
> As my trust was."

"He knows not a hawk from a handsaw." Hamlet says (ii. 2): "When the wind is southerly, I know a hawk from a handsaw."

"He may hang himself in his own garters." So, Falstaff ("1 Henry IV." ii. 2) says: "Go, hang thyself in thine own heir-apparent garters."

---

[1] Halliwell-Phillipps's "Handbook Index to Shakespeare," p. 392.
[2] See Kelly's "Proverbs of All Nations," 1870, pp. 196, 197.
[3] Halliwell-Phillipps's "Handbook Index to Shakespeare," p. 392.

"He that is born to be hanged will never be drowned."
In "The Tempest" (i. 1), Gonzalo says of the Boatswain:
"I have great comfort from this fellow: methinks he hath
no drowning mark upon him; his complexion is perfect
gallows. Stand fast, good Fate, to his hanging! make the
rope of his destiny our cable, for our own doth little advantage! If he be not born to be hanged, our case is miserable."
The Italians say, "He that is to die by the gallows may
dance on the river."

"He that dies pays all debts" ("The Tempest," iii. 2).

"He who eats with the devil hath need of a long spoon."
This is referred to by Stephano, in "The Tempest" (ii. 2):
"This is a devil, and no monster: I will leave him; I have
no long spoon." Again, in the "Comedy of Errors" (iv. 3),
Dromio of Syracuse says: "He must have a long spoon that
must eat with the devil."

The old adage, which tells how

> "He that will not when he may,
> When he will he shall have nay,"

is quoted in "Antony and Cleopatra" (ii. 7) by Menas:

> "Who seeks, and will not take, when once 'tis offer'd,
> Shall never find it more."

"Hold hook and line" ("2 Henry IV.," ii. 4). This,
says Dyce, is a sort of cant proverbial expression, which
sometimes occurs in our early writers ("Glossary," p. 210).

"Hold, or cut bow-strings"[1] ("A Midsummer-Night's
Dream," i. 2).

"Honest as the skin between his brows" ("Much Ado
About Nothing," iii. 5).[2]

"Hunger will break through stone-walls." This is quoted
by Marcius in "Coriolanus" (i. 1), who, in reply to Agrippa's
question, "What says the other troop?" replies:

> "They are dissolved: hang 'em!
> They said they were an-hungry; sigh'd forth proverbs,—
> That hunger broke stone-walls," etc.

---

[1] See page 394.   [2] "Handbook Index to Shakespeare," p. 392.

According to an old Suffolk proverb,[1] "Hunger will break through stone-walls, or anything, except Suffolk cheese."

"I scorn that with my heels" ("Much Ado About Nothing," iii. 4). A not uncommon proverbial expression. It is again referred to, in the "Merchant of Venice" (ii. 2), by Launcelot: "do not run; scorn running with thy heels." Dyce thinks it is alluded to in "Venus and Adonis:"

> "Beating his kind embracements with her heels."

"If you are wise, keep yourself warm." This proverb is probably alluded to in the "Taming of the Shrew" (ii. 1):

> "*Petruchio.* Am I not wise?
> *Katharina.*   Yes; keep you warm."

So, in "Much Ado About Nothing" (i. 1): "that if he have wit enough to keep himself warm."

"I fear no colours" ("Twelfth Night," i. 5).

"Ill-gotten goods never prosper." This proverb is referred to by King Henry ("3 Henry VI.," ii. 2):

> "Clifford, tell me, didst thou never hear
> That things ill got had ever bad success?"

"Illotis manibus tractare sacra." Falstaff, in "1 Henry IV." (iii. 3), says: "Rob me the exchequer the first thing thou dost, and do it with unwashed hands too."

"Ill will never said well." This is quoted by Duke of Orleans in "Henry V." (iii. 7).

"In at the window, or else o'er the hatch" ("King John," i. 1). Applied to illegitimate children. Staunton has this note: "Woe worth the time that ever a gave suck to a child that came in at the window!" ("The Family of Love," 1608). So, also, in "The Witches of Lancashire," by Heywood and Broome, 1634: "It appears you came in at the window." "I would not have you think I scorn my grannam's cat to leap over the hatch."

"It is a foul bird which defiles its own nest." This seems

---

[1] Bohn's "Handbook of Proverbs," 1857, p. 409.

alluded to in " As You Like It " (iv. 1), where Celia says to Rosalind : " You have simply misused our sex in your love-prate : we must have your doublet and hose plucked over your head, and show the world what the bird hath done to her own nest."

" It is a poor dog that is not worth the whistling." So Goneril, in " King Lear " (iv. 2): " I have been worth the whistle."

" It is a wise child that knows its own father." In the " Merchant of Venice " (ii. 2), Launcelot has the converse of this : " It is a wise father that knows his own child."

" It is an ill wind that blows nobody good." So, in " 3 Henry VI." (ii. 5), we read :

> " Ill blows the wind that profits nobody."

And, in " 2 Henry IV." (v. 3), when Falstaff asks Pistol " What wind blew you hither?" the latter replies : " Not the ill wind which blows no man to good."

" It is easy to steal a shive from a cut loaf." In " Titus Andronicus " (ii. 1), Demetrius refers to this proverb. Ray has, " 'Tis safe taking a shive out of a cut loaf."

" It's a dear collop that's cut out of my own flesh." Mr. Halliwell-Phillipps thinks there may be possibly an allusion to this proverb in " 1 Henry VI." (v. 4), where the Shepherd says of La Pucelle :

> " God knows, thou art a collop of my flesh."

" I will make a shaft or a bolt of it." In the " Merry Wives of Windsor " (iii. 4) this proverb is used by Slender.[1] Ray gives " to make a bolt or a shaft of a thing." This is equivalent to, " I will either make a good or a bad thing of it ; I will take the risk."

" It is like a barber's chair " ("All's Well that Ends Well," ii. 2).

---

[1] A shaft is an arrow for the longbow, a bolt is for the crossbow. Kelly's " Proverbs of All Nations," p. 155.

The following passage, in " A Midsummer-Night's Dream "
(iii. 2):

> " Jack shall have Jill ;
> Nought shall go ill ;
> The man shall have his mare again,
> And all shall be well,"

refers to the popular proverb of olden times, says Staunton,
signifying " all ended happily." So, too, Biron says, in
"Love's Labour's Lost " (v. 2):

> " Our wooing doth not end like an old play ;
> Jack hath not Jill."

It occurs in Skelton's poem " Magnyfycence " (Dyce, ed. i.
p. 234): " Jack shall have Gyl;" and in Heywood's " Dialogue " (Sig. F. 3, 1598):

> "Come, chat at hame, all is well, Jack shall have Gill."

" Kindness will creep where it cannot go." Thus, in the
" Two Gentlemen of Verona " (iv. 2), Proteus tells Thurio how

> " love
> Will creep in service where it cannot go."

There is a Scotch proverb, " Kindness will creep whar it
mauna gang."

" Let the world slide " (" Taming of the Shrew," Induction, sc. i.).

" Let them laugh that win." Othello says (iv. 1):

> " So, so, so, so :—they laugh that win."

On the other hand, the French say, " Marchand qui perd ne
peut rire."

" Like will to like, as the devil said to the collier." With
this we may compare the following passage in " Twelfth
Night " (iii. 4): " What, man ! 'tis not for gravity to play at
cherry - pit with Satan : hang him, foul collier !"— collier
having been, in Shakespeare's day, a term of the highest
reproach.

" Losers have leave to talk." Titus Andronicus (iii. 1)
says:

> "Then give me leave, for losers will have leave
> To ease their stomachs with their bitter tongues."

"Maids say nay, and take." So Julia, in the "Two Gentlemen of Verona" (i. 2), says:

> "Since maids, in modesty, say 'No' to that
> Which they would have the profferer construe 'Ay.'"

In "The Passionate Pilgrim" we read:

> "Have you not heard it said full oft,
> A woman's nay doth stand for nought?"

"Make hay while the sun shines." King Edward, in "3 Henry VI." (iv. 8), alludes to this proverb:

> "The sun shines hot; and, if we use delay,
> Cold, biting winter mars our hop'd-for hay."

The above proverb is peculiar to England, and, as Trench remarks, could have its birth only under such variable skies as ours.

"Many talk of Robin Hood that never shot in his bow." So, in "2 Henry IV." (iii. 2), Justice Shallow, says Falstaff, "talks as familiarly of John o' Gaunt as if he had been sworn brother to him; and I'll be sworn a' never saw him but once in the Tilt-yard,—and then he burst his head, for crowding among the marshal's men."

"Marriage and hanging go by destiny." This proverb is the popular creed respecting marriage, and, under a variety of forms, is found in different countries. Thus, in "Merchant of Venice" (ii. 9), Nerissa says:

> "The ancient saying is no heresy,—
> Hanging and wiving goes by destiny."

Again, in "All's Well that Ends Well" (i. 3), the Clown says:

> "For I the ballad will repeat,
> Which men full true shall find;
> Your marriage comes by destiny,
> Your cuckoo sings by kind."

---

[1] "But now consider the old proverbe to be true, yt saieth that marriage is destinie."—Hall's "Chronicles."

We may compare the well-known proverb, "Marriages are made in heaven," and the French version, "Les mariages sont écrits dans le ciel."

"Marriage as bad as hanging." In "Twelfth Night" (i. 5), the Clown says: "Many a good hanging prevents a bad marriage."

"Marry trap" ("Merry Wives of Windsor," i. 1). This, says Nares, "is apparently a kind of proverbial exclamation, as much as to say, 'By Mary, you are caught.'"

"Meat was made for mouths." Quoted in "Coriolanus" (i. 1).

"Misfortunes seldom come alone." This proverb is beautifully alluded to by the King in "Hamlet" (iv. 5):

> "When sorrows come, they come not single spies,
>   But in battalions."

The French say:[1] "Malheur ne vient jamais seul."

"More hair than wit" ("Two Gentlemen of Verona," iii. 2). A well-known old English proverb.

"Mortuo leoni et lepores insultant." This proverb is alluded to by the Bastard in "King John" (ii. 1), who says to the Archduke of Austria:

> "You are the hare of whom the proverb goes,
>   Whose valour plucks dead lions by the beard."

"Much water goes by the mill the miller knows not of." This adage is quoted in "Titus Andronicus" (ii. 1), by Demetrius:

> "more water glideth by the mill
> Than wots the miller of."

"My cake is dough" ("Taming of the Shrew," v. 1). An obsolete proverb, repeated on the loss of hope or expectation: the allusion being to the old-fashioned way of baking cakes at the embers, when it may have been occasionally the case for a cake to be burned on one side and dough on the other. In a former scene (i. 1) Gremio says: "our

---

[1] See Bohn's "Handbook of Proverbs," p. 116.

cake's dough on both sides." Staunton quotes from " The Case is Altered," 1609:

> "Steward, your cake is dough, as well as mine."

" Murder will out." So, in the " Merchant of Venice" (ii. 2), Launcelot says: " Murder cannot be hid long,—a man's son may; but, in the end, truth will out."

" Near or far off, well won is still well shot " (" King John," i. 1).

" Needs must when the devil drives." In " All's Well that Ends Well" (i. 3), the Clown tells the Countess: " I am driven on by the flesh; and he must needs go, that the devil drives."

" Neither fish, nor flesh, nor good red herring."[1] Falstaff says of the Hostess in " 1 Henry IV." (iii. 3): " Why, she's neither fish nor flesh; a man knows not where to have her."

" One nail drives out another." In " Romeo and Juliet" (i. 2), Benvolio says:

> "Tut, man, one fire burns out another's burning,
>   One pain is lessen'd by another's anguish;
> Turn giddy, and be holp by backward turning;
>   One desperate grief cures with another's languish:
> Take thou some new infection to thy eye,
> And the rank poison of the old will die."

The allusion, of course, is to homœopathy. The Italians say, " Poison quells poison."

" Old men are twice children;" or, as they say in Scotland, " Auld men are twice bairns." We may compare the Greek Δὶς παῖδες οἱ γέροντες. The proverb occurs in " Hamlet" (ii. 2): " An old man is twice a child."

" Out of God's blessing into the warm sun." So Kent says in " King Lear" (ii. 2):

> "Good king, that must approve the common saw,—
> Thou out of heaven's benediction com'st
> To the warm sun."

---

[1] See Bohn's " Handbook of Proverbs," pp. 160, 251.

" Patience perforce is a medicine for a mad dog." This proverb is probably alluded to by Tybalt in " Romeo and Juliet" (i. 5):

> " Patience perforce with wilful choler meeting,
> Makes my flesh tremble in their different greeting."

And again, in " Richard III." (i. 1):

> " *Gloster.* Meantime, have patience.
> *Clarence.* I must perforce: farewell."

" Pitch and Pay " (" Henry V.," ii. 3). This is a proverbial expression equivalent to " Pay down at once." [1] It probably originated from pitching goods in a market, and paying immediately for their standing. Tusser, in his " Description of Norwich," calls it:

> " A city trim,
> Where strangers well may seem to dwell,
> That pitch and pay, or keep their day."

" Pitchers have ears." Baptista quotes this proverb in the " Taming of the Shrew " (iv. 4):

> " Pitchers have ears, and I have many servants."

According to another old proverb: " Small pitchers have great ears."

" Poor and proud! fy, fy." Olivia, in " Twelfth Night " (iii. 1), says:

> " O world, how apt the poor are to be proud !"

" Praise in departing " (" The Tempest," iii. 3). The meaning is: " Do not praise your entertainment too soon, lest you should have reason to retract your commendation." Staunton quotes from " The Paradise of Dainty Devises," 1596:

> " A good beginning oft we see, but seldome standing at one stay.
> For few do like the meane degree, then praise at parting some men say."

" Pray God, my girdle break " [2] (" 1 Henry IV.," iii. 3).

---

[1] See Dyce's " Glossary," p. 323.
[2] Halliwell-Phillipps's " Handbook Index to Shakespeare," p. 393.

" Put your finger in the fire and say it was your fortune."
An excellent illustration of this proverb is given by Edmund
in " King Lear" (i. 2): " This is the excellent foppery of
the world, that, when we are sick in fortune, we make guilty
of our disasters, the sun, the moon, and the stars: as if we
were villains on necessity; fools, by heavenly compulsion;
knaves, thieves, and treachers, by spherical predominance;
drunkards, liars, and adulterers, by an enforced obedience of
planetary influence; and all that we are evil in, by a divine
thrusting on: an admirable evasion," etc.

" Respice finem, respice furem." It has been suggested
that Shakespeare (" Comedy of Errors," iv. 4) may have met
with these words in a popular pamphlet of his time, by
George Buchanan, entitled " Chamæleon Redivivus; or, Na-
thaniel's Character Reversed"—a satire against the Laird
of Lidingstone, 1570, which concludes with the following
words, " Respice finem, respice furem."

" Seldom comes the better." In " Richard III." (ii. 3),
one of the citizens says:

> " Ill news, by'r lady; seldom comes the better:
> I fear, I fear, 'twill prove a troublous world "

—a proverbial saying of great antiquity. Mr. Douce[1] cites
an account of its origin from a MS. collection of stories in
Latin, compiled about the time of Henry III.

" Service is no inheritance." So, in " All's Well that Ends
Well" (i. 3), the Clown says: " Service is no heritage."

" Sit thee down, sorrow " (" Love's Labour's Lost," i. 1).

" Sit at the stern." A proverbial phrase meaning to have
the management of public affairs. So, in " 1 Henry VI."
(i. 1), Winchester says:

> " The king from Eltham I intend to steal,
> And sit at chiefest stern of public weal."

" She has the mends in her own hands." This proverbial
phrase is of frequent occurrence in our old writers, and probably signifies, " It is her own fault;" or, " The remedy lies

---

[1] " Illustrations of Shakespeare," p. 333.

with herself." It is used by Pandarus in "Troilus and Cressida" (i. 1). Burton, in his "Anatomy of Melancholy," writes: "And if men will be jealous in such cases, the mends is in their own hands, they must thank themselves."

"Small herbs have grace, great weeds do grow apace" ("Richard III.," ii. 4).

"So wise so young, do ne'er live long" ("Richard III.," iii. 1).[1]

"So like you, 'tis the worse." This is quoted as an old proverb by Paulina in the "Winter's Tale" (ii. 3).

"Something about, a little from the right" ("King John," i. 1).

"Sowed cockle, reap no corn" ("Love's Labour's Lost," iv. 3).

"Speak by the card" ("Hamlet," v. 1). A merchant's expression, equivalent to "be as precise as a map or book." The card is the document in writing containing the agreement made between a merchant and the captain of a vessel. Sometimes the owner binds himself, ship, tackle, and furniture, for due performance, and the captain is bound to declare the cargo committed to him in good condition. Hence, "to speak by the card" is to speak according to the indentures or written instructions.

"Still swine eat all the draff" ("Merry Wives of Windsor," iv. 2). Ray gives: "The still sow eats up all the draught."

"Still waters run deep." So in "2 Henry VI." (iii. 1), Suffolk says:

"Smooth runs the water where the brook is deep."

"Strike sail." A proverbial phrase to acknowledge one's self beaten. In "3 Henry VI." (iii. 3), it occurs:

"now Margaret
Must strike her sail and learn awhile to serve,
Where kings command."

---

[1] See page 332.

When a ship, in fight, or on meeting another ship, lets down her topsails at least half-mast high, she is said to strike, that is, to submit or pay respect to the other.[1]

" Strike while the iron is hot."   Poins probably alludes to this proverb in " 2 Henry IV." (ii. 4): " My lord, he will drive you out of your revenge, and turn all to a merriment, if you take not the heat."

Again, in " King Lear " (i. 1), Goneril adds : " We must do something, and i' the heat."

" Take all, pay all " (" Merry Wives of Windsor," ii. 2). Ray gives another version of this proverb : " Take all, and pay the baker."

" Tell the truth and·shame the devil."   In " 1 Henry IV." (iii. 1), Hotspur tells Glendower:

> " I can teach thee, coz, to shame the devil
> By telling truth : tell truth, and shame the devil."

" That was laid on with a trowel."[2]   This proverb, which is quoted by Ray, is used by Celia in " As You Like It " (i. 2).   Thus we say, when any one bespatters another with gross flattery, that he lays it on with a trowel.

" The cat loves fish, but she's loath to wet her feet."   It is to this proverb that Lady Macbeth alludes when she up-braids her husband for his irresolution (" Macbeth," i. 7):

> " Letting ' I dare not' wait upon 'I would,'
> Like the poor cat i' the adage."

There are various forms of this proverb.   Thus, according to the rhyme :

> " Fain would the cat fish eat,
> But she's loath to wet her feet."

The French version is " Le chat aime le poisson mais il n'aime pas à meuiller la patte " — so that it would seem Shakespeare borrowed from the French.

[1] Brewer's " Dictionary of Phrase and Fable," p. 860.
[2] Ray's " Proverbs " (Bohn's Edition), 1857, p. 76.

"The devil rides on a fiddlestick" (" 1 Henry IV.," ii. 4).

"The galled jade will wince." So Hamlet says (iii. 2), "let the galled jade wince, our withers are unwrung."

"The grace o' God is gear enough." This is the Scotch form of the proverb which Launcelot Gobbo speaks of as being well parted between Bassanio and Shylock, in the "Merchant of Venice" (ii. 2): "The old proverb is very well parted between my master Shylock and you, sir; you have the grace of God, sir, and he hath enough."

"The Mayor of Northampton opens oysters with his dagger." This proverb is alluded to by Pistol in "Merry Wives of Windsor" (ii. 2), when he says:

> "Why, then the world's mine oyster,
> Which I with sword will open."

Northampton being some eighty miles from the sea, oysters were so stale before they reached the town (before railroads, or even coaches, were known), that the "Mayor would be loath to bring them near his nose."

"The more haste the worse speed." In "Romeo and Juliet" (ii. 6), Friar Laurence says:

> "These violent delights have violent ends
> And in their triumph die; like fire and powder,
> Which, as they kiss, consume: the sweetest honey
> Is loathsome in his own deliciousness,
> And in the taste confounds the appetite:
> Therefore, love moderately; long love doth so;
> Too swift arrives as tardy as too slow."

The proverb thus alluded to seems to be derived from the Latin adage, "Festinatio tarda est." It defeats its own purpose by the blunders and imperfect work it occasions.[1] Hence the French say: "He that goes too hastily along often stumbles on a fair road."

"There is flattery in friendship"—used by the Constable of France in "Henry V." (iii. 7); the usual form of this proverb being: "There is falsehood in friendship."

---

[1] Kelly's "Proverbs of All Nations," p. 80.

"There was but one way" ("Henry V.," ii. 3). "This,"
says Dyce, "is a kind of proverbial expression for death."
("Glossary," p. 494.)

"The weakest goes to the wall." This is quoted by
Gregory in "Romeo and Juliet" (i. 1), whereupon Sampson
adds: "Women, being the weaker vessels, are ever thrust
to the wall: therefore, I will push Montague's men from the
wall, and thrust his maids to the wall."

"There went but a pair of shears between them" ("Measure for Measure," i. 2). That is, "We are both of the same
piece."

"The world goes on wheels." This proverbial expression
occurs in "Antony and Cleopatra" (ii. 7); and Taylor, the
Water-Poet, has made it the subject of one of his pamphlets:
"The worlde runnes on wheeles, or, oddes betwixt carts and
coaches."

"Three women and a goose make a market." This proverb is alluded to in "Love's Labour's Lost" (iii. 1):

> "thus came your argument in;
> Then the boy's fat *l'envoy*, the goose that you bought;
> And he ended the market."

The following lines in "1 Henry VI." (i. 6),

> "Thy promises are like Adonis' gardens
> That one day bloom'd, and fruitful were the next,"

allude to the *Adonis horti*, which were nothing but portable
earthen pots, with some lettuce or fennel growing in them.
On his yearly festival every woman carried one of them in
honor of Adonis, because Venus had once laid him in a lettuce bed. The next day they were thrown away. The
proverb seems to have been used always in a bad sense, for
things which make a fair show for a few days and then
wither away. The Dauphin is here made to apply it as an
encomium. There is a good account of it in Erasmus's
"Adagia;" but the idea may have been taken from the
"Fairy Queen," bk. iii. cant. 6, st. 42 (Singer's "Shakespeare," 1875, vol. vi. p. 32).

"To clip the anvil of my sword." "This expression, in

'Coriolanus' (iv. 5) is very difficult to be explained," says Mr. Green, " unless we regard it as a proverb, denoting the breaking of the weapon and the laying aside of enmity. Aufidius makes use of it in his welcome to the banished Coriolanus."

> "here I clip
> The anvil of my sword ; and do contest
> As hotly and as nobly with thy love,
> As ever in ambitious strength I did
> Contend against thy valour."

" To have a month's mind to a thing." Ray's " Proverbs." So, in the " Two Gentlemen of Verona " (i. 2), Julia says :

> " I see you have a month's mind to them."[1]

" 'Tis merry in hall when beards wag all."[2] This is quoted by Silence in " 2 Henry IV." (v. 3):

> " Be merry, be merry, my wife has all ;
> For women are shrews, both short and tall ;
> 'Tis merry in hall when beards wag all,
>   And welcome merry shrove-tide.
>   Be merry, be merry."

" To have one in the wind." This is one of Camden's proverbial sentences. In " All's Well that Ends Well " (iii. 6), Bertram says :

> " I spoke with her but once,
> And found her wondrous cold ; but I sent to her,
> By this same coxcomb that we have i' the wind,
> Tokens and letters which she did re-send."

" To hold a candle to the devil "—that is, " to aid or countenance that which is wrong." Thus, in the " Merchant of Venice " (ii. 6), Jessica says :

> " What, must I hold a candle to my shames?"

—the allusion being to the practice of the Roman Catholics who burn candles before the image of a favorite saint, carry them in funeral processions, and place them on their altars.

---

[1] See page 385.   [2] See Bohn's " Handbook of Proverbs," p. 115.

"To the dark house" ("All's Well that Ends Well," ii. 3). A house which is the seat of gloom and discontent.

"Truth should be silent." Enobarbus, in "Antony and Cleopatra" (ii. 2), says: "That truth should be silent I had almost forgot."

"To take mine ease in mine inn." A proverbial phrase used by Falstaff in " 1 Henry IV." (iii. 3), implying, says Mr. Drake, "a degree of comfort which has always been the peculiar attribute of an English house of public entertainment."[1]

"Twice away says stay" ("Twelfth Night," v. 1). Malone thinks this proverb is alluded to by the Clown: "conclusions to be as kisses, if your four negatives make your two affirmatives, why, then, the worse for my friends and the better for my foes;" and quotes Marlowe's "Last Dominion," where the Queen says to the Moor:

> "Come, let's kisse.
> *Moor.*   Away, away.
> *Queen.* No, no, sayes I, and twice away sayes stay."

"Trust not a horse's heel." In "King Lear" (iii. 6) the Fool says, "he's mad that trusts a horse's health." Malone would read "heels."

"Two may keep counsel, putting one away." So Aaron, in "Titus Andronicus" (iv. 2), says:

> "Two may keep counsel, when the third's away."

"Ungirt, unblest." Falstaff alludes to the old adage, in " 1 Henry IV." (iii. 3). "I pray God my girdle break." Malone quotes from an ancient ballad:

> "Ungirt, unblest, the proverbe sayes;
>   And they to prove it right,
> Have got a fashion now adayes,
>   That's odious to the sight;
> Like Frenchmen, all on points they stand,
>   No girdles now they wear."

---

[1] "Shakespeare and his Times," vol. i. p. 216.

"Walls have ears." So, in "A Midsummer-Night's Dream" (v. 1), Thisbe is made to say:

> "O wall, full often hast thou heard my moans,
> For parting my fair Pyramus and me."

"Wedding and ill-wintering tame both man and beast." Thus, in "Taming of the Shrew" (iv. 1), Grumio says: "Winter tames man, woman, and beast; for it hath tamed my old master, and my new mistress, and myself." We may also compare the Spanish adage: "You will marry and grow tame."

"We steal as in a castle" ("1 Henry IV.," ii. 1). This, says Steevens, was once a proverbial phrase.

"What can't be cured must be endured." With this popular adage may be compared the following: "Past cure is still past care," in "Love's Labour's Lost" (v. 2). So in "Richard II." (ii. 3), the Duke of York says:

> "Things past redress are now with me past care."

Again, in "Macbeth" (iii. 2) Lady Macbeth says:

> "Things without all remedy
> Should be without regard: what's done is done."

"What's mine is yours, and what is yours is mine" ("Measure for Measure," v. 1).

"When things come to the worst they'll mend." The truth of this popular adage is thus exemplified by Pandulph in "King John" (iii. 4):

> "Before the curing of a strong disease,
> Even in the instant of repair and health,
> The fit is strongest; evils that take leave,
> On their departure most of all show evil."

Of course it is equivalent to the proverb, "When the night's darkest the day's nearest."

"When? can you tell?" ("Comedy of Errors," iii. 1). This proverbial query, often met with in old writers, and perhaps alluded to just before in this scene, when Dromio of Syracuse says: "Right, sir; I'll tell you when, an you'll tell me wherefore;" occurs again in " 1 Henry IV." (ii. 1): "Ay, when? canst tell?"

"When two men ride the same horse one must ride behind." So in " Much Ado About Nothing " (iii. 5) Dogberry says: "An two men ride of a horse, one must ride behind."[1] With this may be compared the Spanish adage, " He who rides behind does not saddle when he will."

"While the grass grows, the steed starves." This is alluded to by Hamlet (iii. 2): "Ay, sir, but 'while the grass grows,' the proverb is something musty." See Dyce's " Glossary," p. 499.

"Who dares not stir by day must walk by night " (" King John," i. 1).

"Who goes to Westminster for a wife, to St. Paul's for a man, and to Smithfield for a horse, may meet with a queane, a knave, and a jade." This proverb, often quoted by old writers, is alluded to in " 2 Henry IV." (i. 2):

" *Falstaff.* Where's Bardolph?

Page. He's gone into Smithfield to buy your worship a horse.

Falstaff. I bought him in Paul's, and he'll buy me a horse in Smithfield : an I could get me but a wife in the stews, I were manned, horsed, and wived."

"Wit, whither wilt?" This was a proverbial expression not unfrequent in Shakespeare's day. It is used by Orlando in " As You Like It " (iv. 1): "A man that had a wife with such a wit, he might say—' Wit, whither wilt?' "

"Will you take eggs for money?" This was a proverbial phrase, quoted by Leontes in the " Winter's Tale " (i. 2), for putting up with an affront, or being cajoled or imposed upon.

"Words are but wind, but blows unkind." In "Comedy of Errors " (iii. 1), Dromio of Ephesus uses the first part of this popular adage.

"Worth a Jew's eye." Launcelot, in the " Merchant of Venice" (ii. 5), says:

" There will come a Christian by,
Will be worth a Jewess' eye."

---

[1] See Kelly's " Proverbs of All Nations," p. 49.

According to tradition, the proverb arose from the custom of torturing Jews to extort money from them.　It is simply, however, a corruption of the Italian *gióia* (a jewel).

"You'll never be burned for a witch." This proverb, which was applied to a silly person, is probably referred to in "Antony and Cleopatra" (i. 2) by Charmian, when he says to the soothsayer:

> "Out, fool; I forgive thee for a witch."

"Young ravens must have food" ("Merry Wives of Windsor," i. 3).[1]　Ray has "Small birds must have meat."

---

[1] "Handbook Index to Shakespeare," p. 395.

CHAPTER XX.

THE HUMAN BODY.

It would be difficult to enumerate the manifold forms of superstition which have, in most countries, in the course of past centuries, clustered round the human body. Many of these, too, may still be found scattered, here and there, throughout our own country, one of the most deep-rooted being palmistry, several allusions to which are made by Shakespeare.

According to a popular belief current in years past, a trembling of the body was supposed to be an indication of demoniacal possession. Thus, in the "Comedy of Errors" (iv. 4), the Courtezan says of Antipholus of Ephesus:

> "Mark how he trembles in his ecstasy!"

and Pinch adds:

> "I charge thee, Satan, hous'd within this man,
> To yield possession to my holy prayers,
> And to thy state of darkness hie thee straight;
> I conjure thee by all the saints in heaven!"

In "The Tempest" (ii. 2), Caliban says to Stephano, "Thou dost me yet but little hurt; thou wilt anon, I know it by thy trembling."

It was formerly supposed that our bodies consisted of the four elements—fire, air, earth, and water, and that all diseases arose from derangement in the due proportion of these elements. Thus, in Antony's eulogium on Brutus, in "Julius Cæsar" (v. 5), this theory is alluded to:

> "His life was gentle, and the elements
> So mix'd in him, that Nature might stand up,
> And say to all the world, 'This was a man!'"

In " Twelfth Night " (ii. 3) it is also noticed:

" *Sir Toby.* Do not our lives consist of the four elements?

Sir Andrew. 'Faith, so they say; but, I think, it rather consists of eating and drinking.

Sir Toby. Thou art a scholar; let us therefore eat and drink. Marian, I say!—a stoop of wine!"

In "Antony and Cleopatra" (v. 2), Shakespeare makes the latter say:

> " I am fire, and air, my other elements
> I give to baser life."

This theory is the subject, too, of Sonnets xliv. and xlv., and is set forth at large in its connection with physic in Sir Philip Sidney's " Arcadia:"

> " O elements, by whose (men say) contention,
> Our bodies be in living power maintained,
> Was this man's death the fruit of your dissension?
> O physic's power, which (some say) hath restrained
> Approach of death, alas, thou keepest meagerly,
> When once one is for Atropos distrained.
> Great be physicians' brags, but aide is beggarly
> When rooted moisture fails, or groweth drie;
> They leave off all, and say, death comes too eagerly.
> They are but words therefore that men doe buy
> Of any, since God Esculapius ceased."

This notion was substantially adopted by Galen, and embraced by the physicians of the olden times.[1]

Blood. In old phraseology this word was popularly used for disposition or temperament. In " Timon of Athens " (iv. 2), Flavius says:

> " Strange, unusual blood,
> When man's worst sin is, he does too much good!"

In the opening passage of " Cymbeline " it occurs in the same sense:

> " You do not meet a man but frowns: our bloods
> No more obey the heavens, than our courtiers
> Still seem as does the king,"

---

[1] See Bucknill's " Medical Knowledge of Shakespeare," p. 120.

the meaning evidently being that "our dispositions no longer obey the influences of heaven; they are courtiers, and still seem to resemble the disposition the king is in."

Again, in "Much Ado About Nothing" (ii. 3): "wisdom and blood combating in so tender a body, we have ten proofs to one, that blood hath the victory."

Once more, in "King Lear" (iv. 2), the Duke of Albany says to Goneril:

> "Were't my fitness
> To let these hands obey my blood,
> They are apt enough to dislocate and tear
> Thy flesh and bones."

Again, the phrase "to be in blood" was a term of the chase, meaning, to be in good condition, to be vigorous. In "1 Henry VI." (iv. 2), Talbot exclaims:

> "If we be English deer, be, then, in blood;
> Not rascal-like, to fall down with a pinch"

—the expression being put in opposition to "rascal," which was the term for the deer when lean and out of condition. In "Love's Labour's Lost" (iv. 2), Holofernes says: "The deer was, as you know, *sanguis*,—in blood."

The notion that the blood may be thickened by emotional influences is mentioned by Polixenes in the "Winter's Tale" (i. 2), where he speaks of "thoughts that would thick my blood." In King John's temptation of Hubert to murder Arthur (iii. 3), it is thus referred to:

> "Or if that surly spirit, melancholy,
> Had bak'd thy blood and made it heavy, thick,
> Which else runs tickling up and down the veins."

Red blood was considered a traditionary sign of courage. Hence, in the "Merchant of Venice" (ii. 1), the Prince of Morocco, when addressing himself to Portia, and urging his claims for her hand, says:

> "Bring me the fairest creature northward born,
> Where Phoebus' fire scarce thaws the icicles,

> And let us make incision for your love,[1]
> To prove whose blood is reddest, his or mine."

Again, in the same play, cowards are said to " have livers as white as milk," and an effeminate man is termed a " milk-sop." Macbeth, too (v. 3), calls one of his frighted soldiers a " lily-liver'd boy." And in " King Lear" (ii. 2), the Earl of Kent makes use of the same phrase. In illustration of this notion Mr. Douce[2] quotes from Bartholomew Glantville, who says: " Reed clothes have been layed upon deed men in remembrance of theyr hardynes and boldnes, whyle they were in theyr bloudde."

The absence of blood in the liver as the supposed property of a coward, originated, says Dr. Bucknill,[3] in the old theory of the circulation of the blood, which explains Sir Toby's remarks on his dupe, in " Twelfth Night" (iii. 2): " For Andrew, if he were opened, and you find so much blood in his liver as will clog the foot of a flea, I'll eat the rest of the anatomy."

We may quote here a notion referred to in " Lucrece" (1744-50), that, ever since the sad death of Lucrece, corrupted blood has watery particles:

> " About the mourning and congealed face
> Of that black blood a watery rigol goes,
> Which seems to weep upon the tainted place :
> And ever since, as pitying Lucrece' woes,
> Corrupted blood some watery token shows ;
>   And blood untainted still doth red abide,
>   Blushing at that which is so putrefied."

Brain. By old anatomists the brain was divided into

---

[1] Mr. Singer, in a note on this passage, says, " It was customary, in the East, for lovers to testify the violence of their passion by cutting themselves in the sight of their mistresses ; and the fashion seems to have been adopted here as a mark of gallantry in Shakespeare's time, when young men frequently stabbed their arms with daggers, and, mingling the blood with wine, drank it off to the healths of their mistresses."—Vol. ii. p. 417.

[2] " Illustrations of Shakspeare," 1839, p. 156.

[3] " Medical Knowledge of Shakespeare," p. 124.

three ventricles, in the hindermost of which they placed the memory. That this division was not unknown to Shakespeare is apparent from "Love's Labour's Lost" (iv. 2), where Holofernes says: "A foolish extravagant spirit, full of forms, figures, shapes, objects, ideas, apprehensions, motions, revolutions: these are begot in the ventricle of memory." Again, Lady Macbeth (i. 7), speaking of Duncan's two chamberlains, says:

> "Will I with wine and wassail so convince,
> That memory, the warder of the brain,
> Shall be a fume, and the receipt of reason
> A limbeck only."

The "third ventricle is the cerebellum, by which the brain is connected with the spinal marrow and the rest of the body; the memory is posted in the cerebellum, like a warder or sentinel, to warn the reason against attack. Thus, when the memory is converted by intoxication into a mere fume,' then it fills the brain itself—the receipt or receptacle of reason, which thus becomes like an alembic, or cap of a still." [2]

A popular nickname, in former times, for the skull, was "brain-pan;" to which Cade, in "2 Henry VI." (iv. 10) refers: "many a time, but for a sallet, my brain-pan had been cleft with a brown bill." The phrase "to beat out the brains" is used by Shakespeare metaphorically in the sense of defeat or destroy; just as nowadays we popularly speak of knocking a scheme on the head. In "Measure for Measure" (v. 1), the Duke, addressing Isabella, tells her:

> "O most kind maid,
> It was the swift celerity of his death,
> Which I did think with slower foot came on,
> That brain'd my purpose."

The expression "to bear a brain," which is used by the Nurse in "Romeo and Juliet" (i. 3),

---

[1] Cf. "Tempest," v. 1 :

> "the ignorant fumes that mantle
> Their clearer reason."

[2] Clark and Wright's "Notes to Macbeth," 1877, p. 101.

"Nay, I do bear a brain,"

denoted "much mental capacity either of attention, ingenuity, or remembrance."[1]   Thus, in Marston's "Dutch Courtezan" (1605), we read:

"My silly husband, alas! knows nothing of it, 'tis
I that must beare a braine for all."

The notion of the brain as the seat of the soul is mentioned by Prince Henry, who, referring to King John (v. 7), says:

"his pure brain,
Which some suppose the soul's frail dwelling-house,
Doth, by the idle comments that it makes,
Foretell the ending of mortality."

Ear.   According to a well-known superstition, much credited in days gone by, and still extensively believed, a tingling of the right ear is considered lucky, being supposed to denote that a friend is speaking well of one, whereas a tingling of the left is said to imply the opposite.   This notion, however, varies in different localities, as in some places it is the tingling of the left ear which denotes the friend, and the tingling of the right ear the enemy.   In "Much Ado About Nothing" (iii. 1), Beatrice asks Ursula and Hero, who had been talking of her:

"What fire is in mine ears?"

the reference, no doubt, being to this popular fancy.   Sir Thomas Browne[2] ascribes the idea to the belief in guardian angels, who touch the right or left ear according as the conversation is favorable or not to the person.

In Shakespeare's day it was customary for young gallants to wear a long lock of hair dangling by the ear, known as a "love-lock."   Hence, in "Much Ado About Nothing" (iii. 3), the Watch identifies one of his delinquents: "I know him; a' wears a lock."[3]

---

[1] Singer's "Shakespeare," vol. viii. p. 123.
[2] "Vulgar Errors," book v. chap. 23 (Bohn's edition, 1852, vol. ii. p. 82).
[3] Prynne attacked the fashion in his "Unloveliness of Love-locks."

Again, further on (v. 1), Dogberry gives another allusion to this practice: " He wears a key in his ear, and a lock hanging by it."

An expression of endearment current in years gone by was " to bite the ear." In " Romeo and Juliet " (ii. 4), Mercutio says:

> " I will bite thee by the ear for that jest,"

a passage which is explained in Nares (" Glossary," vol. i. p. 81) by the following one from Ben Jonson's " Alchemist " (ii. 3):

> " *Mammon.* Th' hast witch'd me, rogue ; take, go.
> *Face.* Your jack, and all, sir.
> *Mammon.* Slave, I could bite thine ear. . . . Away, thou dost not care for me !"

Gifford, in his notes on Jonson's " Works " (vol. ii. p. 184), says the odd mode of expressing pleasure by biting the ear seems " to be taken from the practice of animals, who, in a playful mood, bite each other's ears."

While speaking of the ear, it may be noted that the so-called want of ear for music has been regarded as a sign of an austere disposition. Thus Cæsar says of Cassius (" Julius Cæsar," i. 2):

> " He hears no music :
> Seldom he smiles."

There is, too, the well-known passage in the " Merchant of Venice " (v. 1):

> " The man that hath no music in himself,
>   Nor is not mov'd with concord of sweet sounds,
>   Is fit for treasons, stratagems, and spoils."

According to the Italian proverb : " Whom God loves not, that man loves not music." [1]

Elbow. According to a popular belief, the itching of the elbow denoted an approaching change of some kind or other.[2] Thus, in " 1 Henry IV." (v. 1), the king speaks of

---

[1] See Douce's " Illustrations of Shakespeare," pp. 165, 166.
[2] Ibid. p. 273.

> " Fickle changelings, and poor discontents,
> Which gape, and rub the elbow, at the news
> Of hurlyburly innovation."

With this idea we may compare similar ones connected with other parts of the body. Thus, in " Macbeth " (iv. 1), one of the witches exclaims :

> " By the pricking of my thumbs,
> Something wicked this way comes."

Again, in " Troilus and Cressida " (ii. 1), Ajax says : " My fingers itch,"[1] and an itching palm was said to be an indication that the person would shortly receive money. Hence, it denoted a hand ready to receive bribes. Thus, in " Julius Cæsar " (iv. 3), Brutus says to Cassius :

> " Let me tell you, Cassius, you yourself
> Are much condemn'd to have an itching palm ;
> To sell and mart your offices for gold
> To undeservers."

So, in " Merry Wives of Windsor " (ii. 3), Shallow says : " If I see a sword out, my finger itches to make one."

Again, in " Othello " (iv. 3), poor Desdemona says to Emilia :

> " Mine eyes do itch ;
> Doth that bode weeping ?"

Grose alludes to this superstition, and says : " When the right eye itches, the party affected will shortly cry ; if the left, they will laugh." The itching of the eye, as an omen, is spoken of by Theocritus, who says :

> " My right eye itches now, and I will see my love."

Eyes. A good deal of curious folk-lore has, at one time or another, clustered round the eye ; and the well-known superstition known as the " evil eye " has already been described in the chapter on Birth and Baptism. Blueness above the eye was, in days gone by, considered a sign of love, and as such is alluded to by Rosalind in " As You Like

---

[1] See " Romeo and Juliet " (iii. 5), where Capulet says, " My fingers itch," denoting anxiety.

It" (iii. 2), where she enumerates the marks of love to Orlando: "A lean cheek, which you have not ; a blue eye, and sunken, which you have not."

The term "baby in the eye" was sportively applied by our forefathers to the miniature reflection of himself which a person may see in the pupil of another's eye. In "Timon of Athens" (i. 2), one of the lords says:

> "Joy had the like conception in our eyes,
> And, at that instant, like a babe sprung up,"

an allusion probably being made to this whimsical notion. It is often referred to by old writers, as, for instance, by Drayton, in his "Ideas :"

> "But O, see, see ! we need enquire no further,
> Upon your lips the scarlet drops are found,
> And, in your eye, the boy that did the murder." [1]

We may compare the expression, "to look babies in the eyes," a common amusement of lovers in days gone by. In Beaumont and Fletcher's "Loyal Subject" (iii. 2), Theodore asks:

> "Can ye look babies, sisters,
> In the young gallants' eyes, and twirl their band-strings ?"

And once more, to quote from Massinger's "Renegado" (ii. 4), where Donusa says:

> "When a young lady wrings you by the hand, thus,
> Or with an amorous touch presses your foot ;
> Looks babies in your eyes, plays with your locks," etc.

Another old term for the eyes was "crystal," which is used by Pistol to his wife, Mrs. Quickly, in "Henry V." (ii. 3):

> "Therefore, *caveto* be thy counsellor.
> Go, clear thy crystals ;"

that is, dry thine eyes.

In "Romeo and Juliet" (i. 2), the phrase is employed by Benvolio:

> "Tut ! you saw her fair, none else being by,
> Herself pois'd with herself in either eye :

---

[1] See Nares's "Glossary," vol. i. p. 44.

> But in that crystal scales let there be weigh'd
> Your lady's love against some other maid."

It also occurs in Beaumont and Fletcher's "Double Marriage" (v. 3), where Juliana exclaims:

> "Sleep you, sweet glasses!
> An everlasting slumber crown those crystals."

The expression "wall-eyed" denotes, says Dyce ("Glossary," p. 486), "eyes with a white or pale-gray iris—glaring-eyed." It is used by Lucius in "Titus Andronicus" (v. 1):

> "Say, wall-ey'd slave, whither wouldst thou convey
> This growing image of thy fiend-like face?"

In "King John" (iv. 3), Salisbury speaks of "wall-eyed wrath."

Brockett, in his "Glossary of North Country Words," says: "In those parts of the north with which I am best acquainted, persons are said to be *wall-eyed* when the white of the eye is very large and to one side; on the borders 'sic folks' are considered lucky. The term is also occasionally applied to horses with similar eyes, though its wider general acceptation seems to be when the iris of the eye is white, or of a very pale color. A *wall-eyed* horse sees perfectly well."

Face. A common expression "to play the hypocrite," or feign, was "to face." So, in "1 Henry VI." (v. 3), Suffolk declares how:

> "Fair Margaret knows
> That Suffolk doth not flatter, face, or feign."

Hence the name of one of the characters in Ben Jonson's "Alchemist." So, in the "Taming of the Shrew" (ii. 1):

> "Yet I have faced it with a card of ten."

The phrase, also, "to face me down," implied insisting upon anything in opposition. So, in the "Comedy of Errors" (iii. 1), Antipholus of Ephesus says:

> "But here's a villain that would face me down
> He met me on the mart."

Feet. Stumbling has from the earliest period been considered ominous.[1]   Thus, Cicero mentions it among the superstitions of his day; and numerous instances of this unlucky act have been handed down from bygone times. We are told by Ovid how Myrrha, on her way to Cinyra's chamber, stumbled thrice, but was not deterred by the omen from an unnatural and fatal crime; and Tibullus (lib. I., eleg. iii. 20), refers to it:

> "O! quoties ingressus iter, mihi tristia dixi,
> Offensum in porta signa dedisse pedem."

This superstition is alluded to by Shakespeare, who, in " 3 Henry VI." (iv. 7), makes Gloster say:

> " For many men that stumble at the threshold
> Are well foretold that danger lurks within."

In " Richard III." (iii. 4), Hastings relates:[2]

> "Three times to-day my foot-cloth horse did stumble,
> And started when he look'd upon the Tower,
> As loath to bear me to the slaughter-house."

In the same way, stumbling at a grave has been regarded as equally unlucky; and in " Romeo and Juliet " (v. 3), Friar Laurence says:

> " how oft to-night
> Have my old feet stumbled at graves."

Hair.   From time immemorial there has been a strong antipathy to red hair, which originated, according to some antiquarians, in a tradition that Judas had hair of this color. One reason, it may be, why the dislike to it arose, was that this color was considered ugly and unfashionable, and on

---

[1] See Brand's " Pop. Antiq.," 1849, vol. iii. p. 249; Jones's " Credulities Past and Present," pp. 529–531 ; " Notes and Queries," 5th series, vol. viii. p. 201.

[2] The following is from Holinshed, who copies Sir Thomas More : " In riding toward the Tower the same morning in which he (Hastings) was beheaded his horse twice or thrice stumbled with him, almost to the falling; which thing, albeit each man wot well daily happeneth to them to whome no such mischance is toward ; yet hath it beene of an olde rite and custome observed as a token oftentimes notablie forego-ing some great misfortune."

this account a person with red hair would soon be regarded with contempt. It has been conjectured, too, that the odium took its rise from the aversion to the red-haired Danes. In "As You Like It" (iii. 4), Rosalind, when speaking of Orlando, refers to this notion:[1] "His very hair is of the dissembling colour," whereupon Ceila replies: "Something browner than Judas's."

Yellow hair, too, was in years gone by regarded with ill-favor, and esteemed a deformity. In ancient pictures and tapestries both Cain and Judas are represented with yellow beards, in allusion to which Simple, in the "Merry Wives of Windsor" (i. 4), when interrogated, says of his master: "He hath but a little wee face, with a little yellow beard—a Cain-coloured beard."[2]

In speaking of beards, it may be noted that formerly they gave rise to various customs. Thus, in Shakespeare's day, dyeing beards was a fashionable custom, and so Bottom, in "A Midsummer-Night's Dream" (i. 2), is perplexed as to what beard he should wear when acting before the duke. He says: "I will discharge it in either your straw-colour beard, your orange-tawny beard, your purple-in-grain beard, or your French-crown-colour beard, your perfect yellow."[3]

To mutilate a beard in any way was considered an irreparable outrage, a practice to which Hamlet refers (ii. 2):

> "Who calls me villain? breaks my pate across?
> Plucks off my beard, and blows it in my face?"

And in "King Lear" (iii. 7), Gloster exclaims:

> "By the kind gods, 'tis most ignobly done
> To pluck me by the beard."

Stroking the beard before a person spoke was preparatory to favor. Hence in "Troilus and Cressida" (i. 3), Ulysses,

---

[1] See Nares's "Glossary," vol. i. p. 127; Dyce's "Glossary," pp. 61, 230.

[2] The quartos of 1602 read "a kane-coloured beard."

[3] See Jaques's Description of the Seven Ages in "As You Like It," (ii. 6).

when describing how Achilles asks Patroclus to imitate certain of their chiefs, represents him as saying:

> " 'Now play me Nestor; hem, and stroke thy beard,
>   As he, being drest to some oration.' "

Again, the phrase "to beard" meant to oppose face to face in a hostile manner. Thus, in " 1 Henry IV." (iv. 1), Douglas declares:

> "No man so potent breathes upon the ground,
>   But I will beard him."

And in " 1 Henry VI." (i. 3), the Bishop of Winchester says to Gloster:

> "Do what thou dar'st; I'll beard thee to thy face."

It seems also to have been customary to swear by the beard, an allusion to which is made by Touchstone in "As You Like It " (i. 2): "stroke your chins, and swear by your beards that I am a knave."

We may also compare what Nestor says in "Troilus and Cressida (iv. 5):

> " By this white beard, I'd fight with thee to-morrow."

Our ancestors paid great attention to the shape of their beards, certain cuts being appropriated to certain professions and ranks. In "Henry V." (iii. 6), Gower speaks of "a beard of the general's cut." As Mr. Staunton remarks, " Not the least odd among the fantastic fashions of our forefathers was the custom of distinguishing certain professions and classes by the cut of the beard; thus we hear, *inter alia*, of the bishop's beard, the judge's beard, the soldier's beard, the citizen's beard, and even the clown's beard." Randle Holme tells us, " The broad or cathedral beard [is] so-called because bishops or gown-men of the church anciently did wear such beards." By the military man, the cut adopted was known as the stiletto or spade. The beard of the citizen was usually worn round, as Mrs. Quickly describes it in

"Merry Wives of Windsor" (i. 4), "like a glover's paring-knife." The clown's beard was left bushy or untrimmed. Malone quotes from an old ballad entitled "Le Prince d' Amour," 1660:

> "Next the clown doth out-rush
> With the beard of the bush."

According to an old superstition, much hair on the head has been supposed to indicate an absence of intellect, a notion referred to by Antipholus of Syracuse, in the "Comedy of Errors" (ii. 2): "there's many a man hath more hair than wit." In the "Two Gentlemen of Verona" (iii. 1), the same proverbial sentence is mentioned by Speed. Malone quotes the following lines upon Suckling's "Aglaura," as an illustration of this saying:[1]

> "This great voluminous pamphlet may be said
> To be like one that hath more hair than head;
> More excrement than body: trees which sprout
> With broadest leaves have still the smallest fruit."

Steevens gives an example from "Florio:" "A tisty-tosty wag-feather, more haire than wit."

Excessive fear has been said to cause the hair to stand on end; an instance of which Shakespeare records in "Hamlet" (iii. 4), in that celebrated passage where the Queen, being at a loss to understand her son's strange appearance during his conversation with the Ghost, which is invisible to her, says:

> "And, as the sleeping soldiers in the alarm,
> Your bedded hair, like life in excrements,
> Starts up, and stands on end."

A further instance occurs in "The Tempest" (i. 2), where Ariel, describing the shipwreck, graphically relates how

> "All, but mariners,
> Plunged in the foaming brine, and quit the vessel,
> Then all a-fire with me: the king's son, Ferdinand,

---

[1] "Parnassus Biceps," 1656.

> With hair up-staring—then like reeds, not hair—
> Was the first man that leap'd."

Again, Macbeth says (i. 3):

> "why do I yield to that suggestion
> Whose horrid image doth unfix my hair?"

And further on he says (v. 5):

> "The time has been, my senses would have cool'd
> To hear a night-shriek; and my fell of hair
> Would at a dismal treatise rouse, and stir
> As life were in't."

In "2 Henry VI." (iii. 2) it is referred to by Suffolk as a sign of madness:

> "My hair be fix'd on end, as one distract."

And, once more, in "Richard III." (i. 3), Hastings declares:

> "My hair doth stand on end to hear her curses."

Another popular notion mentioned by Shakespeare is, that sudden fright or great sorrow will cause the hair to turn white. In "1 Henry IV." (ii. 4), Falstaff, in his speech to Prince Henry, tells him: "thy father's beard is turned white with the news."

Among the many instances recorded to establish the truth of this idea, it is said that the hair and beard of the Duke of Brunswick whitened in twenty-four hours upon his hearing that his father had been mortally wounded in the battle of Auerstadt. Marie Antoinette, the unfortunate queen of Louis XVI., found her hair suddenly changed by her troubles; and a similar change happened to Charles I., when he attempted to escape from Carisbrooke Castle. Mr. Timbs, in his "Doctors and Patients" (1876, p. 201), says that "chemists have discovered that hair contains an oil, a mucous substance, iron, oxide of manganese, phosphate and carbonate of iron, flint, and a large proportion of sulphur. White hair contains also phosphate of magnesia, and its oil is nearly colourless. When hair becomes suddenly white from terror, it is probably owing to the sulphur absorbing the oil, as in the operation of whitening woollen cloths."

Hair was formerly used metaphorically for the color, complexion, or nature of a thing. In " 1 Henry IV." (iv. 1), Worcester says:

> " I would your father had been here,
> The quality and hair of our attempt
> Brooks no division."

In Beaumont and Fletcher's " Nice Valour " it is so used:

> " A lady of my hair cannot want pitying."

Hands. Various superstitions have, at different times, clustered round the hand. Thus, in palmistry, a moist one is said to denote an amorous constitution. In " Othello " (iii. 4) we have the following allusion to this popular notion:

> " *Othello.* Give me your hand. This hand is moist, my lady.
> *Desdemona.* It yet has felt no age, nor known no sorrow.
> *Othello.* This argues fruitfulness, and liberal heart."

Again, in " Antony and Cleopatra " (i. 2), Iras says: " There's a palm presages chastity;" whereupon Charmian adds: " If an oily palm be not a fruitful prognostication, I cannot scratch mine ear." And, in the " Comedy of Errors " (iii. 2), Dromio of Syracuse speaks of barrenness as " hard in the palm of the hand."

A dry hand, however, has been supposed to denote age and debility. In " 2 Henry IV." (i. 2) the Lord Chief Justice enumerates this among the characteristics of such a constitution.[1]

In the " Merchant of Venice " (ii. 2), Launcelot, referring to the language of palmistry, calls the hand " the table," meaning thereby the whole collection of lines on the skin within the hand: " Well, if any man in Italy have a fairer table, which doth offer to swear upon a book, I shall have good fortune." He then alludes to one of the lines in the hand, known as the " line of life:" " Go to, here's a simple line of life."

---

[1] See Brand's " Pop. Antiq.," 1849, vol. iii. p. 179.

In the " Two Noble Kinsmen " (iii. 5) palmistry is further mentioned:

> " *Gaoler's Daughter.* Give me your hand.
> *Gerrold.*   Why?
> *Gaoler's Daughter.* I can tell your fortune."

It was once supposed that little worms were bred in the fingers of idle servants. To this notion Mercutio refers in "Romeo and Juliet " (i. 4), where, in his description of Queen Mab, he says:

> " Her waggoner, a small grey-coated gnat,
> Not half so big as a round little worm
> Prick'd from the lazy finger of a maid."

This notion is alluded to by John Banister, a famous surgeon in Shakespeare's day, in his " Compendious Chyrurgerie " (1585, p. 465): " We commonly call them worms, which many women, sitting in the sunshine, can cunningly picke out with needles, and are most common in the handes."

A popular term formerly in use for the nails on the ten fingers was the "ten commandments," which, says Nares,[1] " doubtless led to the swearing by them, as by the real commandments." Thus, in " 2 Henry VI." (i. 3), the Duchess of Gloster says to the queen:

> " Could I come near your beauty with my nails
> I'd set my ten commandments in your face."

In the same way the fingers were also called the "ten bones," as a little further on in the same play, where Peter swears " by these ten bones."

The phrase " of his hands " was equivalent to " of his inches, or of his size, a hand being the measure of four inches." So, in the " Merry Wives of Windsor " (i. 4), Simple says: " Ay, forsooth : but he is as tall a man of his hands as any is between this and his head," " the expression being used probably for the sake of a jocular equivocation in the word tall, which meant either bold or high."[2]

Again, in the " Winter's Tale " (v. 2), the Clown tells the

---

[1] " Glossary," vol. ii. p. 871.   [2] Ibid. vol. i, p. 402.

Shepherd: "I'll swear to the prince, thou art a tall fellow of thy hands, and that thou wilt not be drunk; but I know thou art no tall fellow of thy hands, and that thou wilt be drunk; but I'll swear it, and I would thou wouldst be a tall fellow of thy hands."

A proverbial phrase for being tall from necessity was " to blow the nail." In " 3 Henry VI." (ii. 5) the king says:

> " When dying clouds contend with growing light,
> What time the shepherd, blowing of his nails,
> Can neither call it perfect day, nor night."

It occurs in the song at the end of " Love's Labour's Lost:"

> " And Dick the shepherd blows his nail."

" To bite the thumb" at a person implied an insult; hence, in " Romeo and Juliet " (i. 1), Sampson says: " I will bite my thumb at them; which is a disgrace to them, if they bear it."

The thumb, in this action, we are told, " represented a fig, and the whole was equivalent to a *fig* for you."[1] Decker, in his " Dead Term " (1608), speaking of the various groups that daily frequented St. Paul's Church, says: " What swearing is there, what shouldering, what justling, what jeering, what byting of thumbs, to beget quarrels?"

Hare-lip. A cleft lip, so called from its supposed resemblance to the upper lip of a hare. It was popularly believed to be the mischievous act of an elf or malicious fairy. So, in "King Lear" (iii. 4), Edgar says of Gloster: " This is the foul fiend Flibbertigibbet: he ... squints the eye, and makes the hare-lip." In " A Midsummer-Night's Dream " (v. 2), Oberon, in blessing the bridal-bed of Theseus and Hippolyta, says:

> " Never mole, hare-lip, nor scar,
> *　　*　　*　　*　　*
> Shall upon their children be."

The expression " hang the lip " meant to drop the lip in sullenness or contempt. Thus, in " Troilus and Cressida " (iii. 1), Helen explains why her brother Troilus is not abroad

---

[1] See page 218.

by saying: "He hangs the lip at something." We may compare, too, the words in "1 Henry IV." (ii. 4): "a foolish hanging of thy nether lip."

Head. According to the old writers on physiognomy, a round head denoted foolishness, a notion to which reference is made in "Antony and Cleopatra" (iii. 3), in the following dialogue, where Cleopatra, inquiring about Octavia, says to the Messenger:

> "Bear'st thou her face in mind? Is't long, or round?
> *Messenger.* Round, even to faultiness.
> *Cleopatra.* For the most part, too, they are foolish that are so."

In Hill's "Pleasant History," etc. (1613), we read: "The head very round, to be forgetful and foolish." Again: "The head long, to be prudent and wary."

Heart. The term "broken heart," as commonly applied to death from excessive grief, is not a vulgar error, but may arise from violent muscular exertion or strong mental emotions. In "Macbeth" (iv. 3), Malcolm says:

> "The grief, that does not speak,
> Whispers the o'er-fraught heart, and bids it break."

We may compare, too, Queen Margaret's words to Buckingham, in "Richard III." (i. 3), where she prophesies how Gloster

> "Shall split thy very heart with sorrow."

Mr. Timbs, in his "Mysteries of Life, Death, and Futurity" (1861, p. 149), has given the following note on the subject: "This affection was, it is believed, first described by Harvey; but since his day several cases have been observed. Morgagni has recorded a few examples: among them, that of George II., who died suddenly of this disease in 1760; and, what is very curious, Morgagni himself fell a victim to the same malady. Dr. Elliotson, in his Lumleyan Lectures on Diseases of the Heart, in 1839, stated that he had only seen one instance; but in the 'Cyclopædia of Practical Medicine' Dr. Townsend gives a table of twenty-five cases, collected from various authors."

In olden times the heart was esteemed the seat of the understanding. Hence, in " Coriolanus" (i. 1), the Citizen speaks of " the counsellor heart." With the ancients, also, the heart was considered the seat of courage, to which Shakespeare refers in " Julius Cæsar" (ii. 2):

> " *Servant.* Plucking the entrails of an offering forth,
> They could not find a heart within the beast.
> *Cæsar.* The gods do this in shame of cowardice:
> Cæsar should be a beast without a heart,
> If he should stay at home to-day for fear."

Liver. By a popular notion, the liver was anciently supposed to be the seat of love, a superstition to which Shakespeare frequently alludes. Thus, in " Love's Labour's Lost" (iv. 3), Biron, after listening to Longaville's sonnet, remarks:

> " This is the liver vein, which makes flesh a deity,
> A green goose, a goddess; pure, pure idolatry."

In " Much Ado About Nothing" (iv. 1), Friar Francis says:

> " If ever love had interest in his liver."

Again, in " As You Like It " (iii. 2), Rosalind, professing to be able to cure love, which, he says, is " merely a madness," says to Orlando, " will I take upon me to wash your liver as clean as a sound sheep's heart, that there shall not be one spot of love in't." In " Twelfth Night " (ii. 4), the Duke, speaking of women's love, says:

> " Their love may be call'd appetite,
> No motion of the liver, but the palate," etc.

And Fabian (ii. 5), alluding to Olivia's supposed letter to Malvolio, says: " This wins him, liver and all."

Once more, in " Merry Wives of Windsor " (ii. 1), Pistol alludes to the liver as being the inspirer of amorous passions, for, speaking of Falstaff, he refers to his loving Ford's wife " with liver burning hot." [1] Douce says, " there is some

---

[1] Cf. " Antony and Cleopatra" (i. 2):

> " *Soothsayer.* You shall be more beloving, than belov'd.
> *Charmian.* I had rather heat my liver with drinking."

reason for thinking that this superstition was borrowed from the Arabian physicians, or at least adopted by them; for, in the Turkish tales, an amorous tailor is made to address his wife by the titles of 'thou corner of my liver, and soul of my love;' and, in another place, the King of Syria, who had sustained a temporary privation of his mistress, is said to have had 'his liver, which had been burnt up by the loss of her, cooled and refreshed at the sight of her.'"[1] According to an old Latin distich:

"Cor sapit, pulmo loquitur, fel commoret iras
Splen ridere facit, cogit amare jecur."

Bartholomæus, in his "De Proprietatibus Rerum" (lib. v. 39), informs us that "the liver is the place of voluptuousness and lyking of the flesh."

Moles. These have, from time immemorial, been regarded as ominous, and special attention has been paid by the superstitious to their position on the body.[2] In "A Midsummer-Night's Dream" (v. I), a mole on a child is spoken of by Oberon as a bad omen, who, speaking of the three couples who had lately been married, says:

"And the blots of Nature's hand
Shall not in their issue stand;
Never mole, hare-lip, nor scar,
Nor mark prodigious, such as are
Despised in nativity,
Shall upon their children be."

Iachimo ("Cymbeline," ii. 2) represents Imogen as having

"On her left breast
A mole cinque-spotted, like the crimson drops
I' the bottom of a cowslip."

And we may also compare the words of Cymbeline (v. 5):

"Guiderius had
Upon his neck a mole, a sanguine star;
It was a mark of wonder."

---

[1] "Illustrations of Shakespeare," 1839, pp. 38, 39.
[2] See Brand's "Pop. Antiq.," 1849, vol. iii. pp. 252-255.

Spleen. This was once supposed to be the cause of laughter, a notion probably referred to by Isabella in " Measure for Measure " (ii. 2), where, telling how the angels weep over the follies of men, she adds:

> "who, with our spleens,
> Would all themselves laugh mortal."

In " Taming of the Shrew " (Induction, sc. i.), the Lord says:

> " haply my presence
> May well abate the over-merry spleen,
> Which otherwise would grow into extremes."

And Maria says to Sir Toby, in " Twelfth Night " (iii. 2): " If you desire the spleen, and will laugh yourselves into stitches, follow me."

Wits. With our early writers, the five senses were usually called the " five wits." So, in " Much Ado About Nothing " (i. 1), Beatrice says: " In our last conflict four of his five wits went halting off, and now is the whole man governed with one." In Sonnet cxli., Shakespeare makes a distinction between wits and senses:

> " But my five wits, nor my five senses can
> Dissuade one foolish heart from serving thee."

The five wits, says Staunton, are " common wit, imagination, fantasy, estimation, memory." Johnson says, the " wits seem to have been reckoned five, by analogy to the five senses, or the five inlets of ideas." In " King Lear " (iii. 4) we find the expression, " Bless thy five wits."

According to a curious fancy, eating beef was supposed to impair the intellect, to which notion Shakespeare has several allusions. Thus, in " Twelfth Night " (i. 3), Sir Andrew says: " Methinks sometimes I have no more wit than a Christian, or an ordinary man has: but I am a great eater of beef, and I believe that does harm to my wit." In " Troilus and Cressida " (ii. 1), Thersites says to Ajax: " The plague of Greece upon thee, thou mongrel beef-witted lord!"

CHAPTER XXI.

FISHES.

ALTHOUGH it has been suggested that Shakespeare found but little recreation in fishing,[1] rather considering, as he makes Ursula say, in "Much Ado About Nothing" (iii. 1):

> "The pleasant'st angling is to see the fish
> Cut with her golden oars the silver stream,
> And greedily devour the treacherous bait,"

and that it would be difficult to illustrate a work on angling with quotations from his writings, the Rev. H. N. Ellacombe, in his interesting papers[2] on "Shakespeare as an Angler," has not only shown the strong probability that he was a lover of this sport, but further adds, that " he may be claimed as the first English poet that wrote of angling with any freedom; and there can be little doubt that he would not have done so if the subject had not been very familiar to him —so familiar, that he could scarcely write without dropping the little hints and unconscious expressions which prove that the subject was not only familiar, but full of pleasant memories to him." His allusions, however, to the folk-lore associated with fishes are very few; but the two or three popular notions and proverbial sayings which he has quoted in connection with them help to embellish this part of our subject.

Carp. This fish was, proverbially, the most cunning of fishes, and so "Polonius's comparison of his own worldly-wise deceit to the craft required for catching a carp" is most apt ("Hamlet," ii. 1):[3]

---

[1] See Harting's "Ornithology of Shakespeare," 1871, p. 3.
[2] "The Antiquary," 1881, vol. iv. p. 193.   [3] Ibid.

> "See you now;
>   Your bait of falsehood takes this carp of truth."

This notion is founded on fact, the brain of the carp being six times as large as the average brain of other fishes.

Cockle. The badge of a pilgrim was, formerly, a cockle-shell, which was worn usually in the front of the hat. "The habit," we are told,[1] "being sacred, this served as a protection, and therefore was often assumed as a disguise." The *escalop* was sometimes used, and either of them was considered as an emblem of the pilgrim's intention to go beyond the sea. Thus, in Ophelia's ballad ("Hamlet," iv. 5, song), the lover is to be known:

> "By his cockle hat and staff,
>   And his sandal shoon."

In Peele's "Old Wives' Tale," 1595, we read, "I will give thee a palmer's staff of ivory, and a scallop-shell of beaten gold." Nares, too, quotes from Green's "Never Too Late" an account of the pilgrim's dress:

> "A hat of straw, like to a swain,
>   Shelter for the sun and rain,
>   With a scallop-shell before."

Cuttle. A foul-mouthed fellow was so called, says Mr. Halliwell-Phillipps,[2] because this fish is said to throw out of its mouth, upon certain occasions, an inky and black juice that fouls the water; and, as an illustration of its use in this sense, he quotes Doll Tearsheet's words to Pistol, "2 Henry IV." ii. 4: "By this wine, I'll thrust my knife in your mouldy chaps, an you play the saucy cuttle with me." Dyce says that the context would seem to imply that the term is equivalent to "culter, swaggerer, bully."[3]

Gudgeon. This being the bait for many of the larger fish, "to swallow a gudgeon" was sometimes used for to be caught or deceived. More commonly, however, the allusion

---

[1] Nares's "Glossary," vol. i. p. 175.

[2] "Handbook Index to the Works of Shakespeare," 1866, p. 119.

[3] See a note in Dyce's "Glossary," p. 112.

is to the ease with which the gudgeon itself is caught, as in the " Merchant of Venice " (i. 1), where Gratiano says :

> " But fish not, with this melancholy bait,
> For this fool-gudgeon."

Gurnet. The phrase " soused gurnet " was formerly a well-known term of reproach, in allusion to which Falstaff, in " 1 Henry IV." (iv. 2), says, " If I be not ashamed of my soldiers, I am a soused gurnet." The gurnet, of which there are several species, was probably thought a very coarse and vulgar dish when soused or pickled.

Loach. A small fish, known also as " the groundling." The allusion to it by one of the carriers, in " 1 Henry IV." (ii. 1), who says, " Your chamber-lie breeds fleas like a loach," has much puzzled the commentators. It appears, however, from a passage in Holland's translation of Pliny's " Natural History " (bk. ix. c. xlvii.), that anciently fishes were supposed to be infested with fleas : " Last of all some fishes there be which of themselves are given to breed fleas and lice ; among which the chalcis, a kind of turgot, is one." Malone suggests that the passage may mean, " breeds fleas as fast as a loach breeds loaches ;" this fish being reckoned a peculiarly prolific one. It seems probable, however, that the carrier alludes to one of those fanciful notions which make up a great part of natural history among the common people.[1] At the present day there is a fisherman's fancy on the Norfolk coast that fish and fleas come together. " Lawk, sir !" said an old fellow, near Cromer, to a correspondent of " Notes and Queries " (Oct. 7th, 1865), " times is as you may look in my flannel-shirt, and scarce see a flea, and then there ain't but a very few herrin's ; but times that'll be right alive with 'em, and then there's sartin to be a sight o' fish."

Mr. Houghton, writing in the *Academy* (May 27th, 1882), thinks that in the above passage the small river loach (*Cobitis barbatula*) is the fish intended. He says, " At certain times of the year, chiefly during the summer months,

---

[1] Nares's " Glossary," vol. ii. p. 518.

almost all fresh-water fish are liable to be infested with some kind of Epizoa. There are two kinds of parasitic creatures which are most commonly seen on various fish caught in the rivers and ponds of this country; and these are the *Argulus foliaceus*, a crustacean, and the *Piscicola piscium*, a small, cylindrical kind of leech."

Mermaids. From the earliest ages mermaids have had a legendary existence—the sirens of the ancients evidently belonging to the same remarkable family. The orthodox mermaid is half woman, half fish, the fishy half being sometimes depicted as *doubly*-tailed. Shakespeare frequently makes his characters talk about mermaids, as in the "Comedy of Errors" (iii. 2), where Antipholus of Syracuse says:

> "O, train me not, sweet mermaid, with thy note,
>   To drown me in thy sister's flood of tears;
> Sing, siren, for thyself, and I will dote:
>   Spread o'er the silver waves thy golden hairs,
>   And as a bed I'll take them and there lie,
>   And, in that glorious supposition, think
> He gains by death, that hath such means to die."

And, again, further on, he adds:

> "I'll stop mine ears against the mermaid's song."

Staunton considers that in these passages the allusion is obviously to the long-current opinion that the siren, or mermaid, decoyed mortals to destruction by the witchery of her songs. This superstition has been charmingly illustrated by Leyden, in his poem, "The Mermaid" (see Scott's "Minstrelsy of the Scottish Border," vol. iv. p. 294):

> "Thus, all to soothe the chieftain's woe,
>   Far from the maid he loved so dear,
> The song arose, so soft and slow,
>   He seem'd her parting sigh to hear.
>
> *   *   *   *   *   *   *
>
> That sea-maid's form of pearly light
>   Was whiter than the downy spray,
> And round her bosom, heaving bright,
>   Her glossy, yellow ringlets play.

Borne on a foaming, crested wave,
  She reached amain the bounding prow,
Then, clasping fast the chieftain brave,
  She, plunging, sought the deep below."

This tradition gave rise to a curious custom in the Isle of Man, which, in Waldron's time, was observed on the 24th of December, though afterwards on St. Stephen's Day. It is said that, once upon a time, a fairy of uncommon beauty exerted such undue influence over the male population that she induced, by the enchantment of her sweet voice, numbers to follow her footsteps, till, by degrees, she led them into the sea, where they perished. This barbarous exercise of power had continued for a great length of time, till it was apprehended that the island would be exhausted of its defenders. Fortunately, however, a knight-errant sprang up, who discovered a means of counteracting the charms used by this siren—even laying a plot for her destruction, which she only escaped by taking the form of a wren. Although she evaded instant annihilation, a spell was cast upon her, by which she was condemned, on every succeeding New Year's Day, to reanimate the same form, with the definite sentence that she must ultimately perish by human hand. Hence, on the specified anniversary, every effort was made to extirpate the fairy; and the poor wrens were pursued, pelted, fired at, and destroyed without mercy, their feathers being preserved as a charm against shipwreck for one year. At the present day there is no particular time for pursuing the wren; it is captured by boys alone, who keep up the old custom chiefly for amusement. On St. Stephen's Day, a band of boys go from door to door with a wren suspended by the legs. in the centre of two hoops crossing each other at right angles, decorated with evergreens and ribbons, singing lines called "Hunt the Wren."[1]

In "A Midsummer-Night's Dream" (ii. 1), Oberon speaks of hearing "a mermaid on a dolphin's back;" and in

---

[1] See "British Popular Customs," pp. 494, 495.

"Hamlet," the Queen, referring to Ophelia's death, says
(iv. 7):

> "Her clothes spread wide;
> And, mermaid-like, awhile they bore her up."

In two other passages Shakespeare alludes to this legendary creature. Thus, in "3 Henry VI." (iii. 2) Gloster boasts
that he will "drown more sailors than the mermaid shall,"
and in "Antony and Cleopatra" (ii. 2), Enobarbus relates
how

> "Her gentlewomen, like the Nereides,
> So many mermaids, tended her i' the eyes,
> And made their bends adornings: at the helm
> A seeming mermaid steers."

In all these cases Shakespeare,[1] as was his wont, made his
characters say what they were likely to think, in their several positions and periods of life. It has been suggested,[2]
however, that the idea of the mermaid, in some of the passages just quoted, seems more applicable to the siren, especially in "A Midsummer-Night's Dream," where the "mermaid on a dolphin's back" could not easily have been so
placed, had she had a fish-like tail instead of legs.

Notices of mermaids are scattered abundantly in books
of bygone times. Mermen and mermaids, men of the sea,
and women of the sea, having been as "stoutly believed in
as the great sea-serpent, and on very much the same kind
of evidence." Holinshed gives a detailed account of a merman caught at Orford, in Suffolk, in the reign of King John.
He was kept alive on raw meal and fish for six months, but
at last "gledde secretelye to the sea, and was neuer after
seene nor heard off." Even in modern times we are told
how, every now and then, a mermaid has made her appearance. Thus, in the *Gentleman's Magazine* (Jan., 1747), we
read: "It is reported from the north of Scotland that some
time this month a sea creature, known by the name of mermaid, which has the shape of a human body from the trunk

---

[1] See "Book of Days," vol. ii. pp. 612–614.

[2] Nares's "Glossary," vol. ii. p. 565; see Brand's "Pop. Antiq.," 1849,
vol. iii. pp. 411–414.

upwards, but below is wholly fish, was carried some miles up the water of Dévron." In 1824 a mermaid or merman made its appearance, when, as the papers of that day inform us, "upwards of 150 distinguished fashionables" went to see it.

The "Mermaid" was a famous tavern, situated in Bread Street.[1] As early as the fifteenth century, we are told it was one of the haunts of the pleasure-seeking Sir John Howard, whose trusty steward records, anno 1464: "Paid for wyn at the Mermayd in Bred Street, for my mastyr and Syr Nicholas Latimer, xd. ob." In 1603 Sir Walter Raleigh established a Literary Club in this house, among its members being Shakespeare, Ben Jonson, Beaumont and Fletcher, Selden, Carew, Martin, Donne, etc. It is often alluded to by Beaumont and Fletcher.

Minnow. This little fish, from its insignificant character, is used by "Coriolanus" (iii. 1) as a term of contempt: "Hear you this Triton of the minnows?" and, again, in "Love's Labour's Lost" (i. 1), it occurs: "'that base minnow of thy mirth.'"

Pike. An old name for this fish was *luce.* In the "Merry Wives of Windsor" (i. 1) we are told that "The luce is the fresh fish." There can be no doubt, too, that there is in this passage an allusion to the armorial bearings of Shakespeare's old enemy, Sir Thomas Lucy. Among the various instances of the use of this term we may quote Isaac Walton, who says: "The mighty luce or pike is taken to be the tyrant, as the salmon is the king, of the fresh waters." Stow, in his "Survey of London," describes a procession of the Fishmongers' Company in 1298, as having horses painted like *sea-luce*: "Then four salmons of silver on foure horses, and after them sixe and fortie armed knightes riding on horses made like *luces of the sea*.

Porpoise. According to sailors, the playing of porpoises round a ship is a certain prognostic of a violent gale of wind; hence the allusion in "Pericles" (ii. 1), where one of the

---

[1] "History of Sign-boards," 1866, p. 226.

fishermen says, speaking of the storm: "Nay, master, said not I as much, when I saw the porpus, how he bounced and tumbled?" Thus, too, in the "Canterbury Guests, or a Bargain Broken," by Ravenscroft, we read: "My heart begins to leap and play, like a porpice before a storm." And a further reference occurs in Wilsford's "Nature's Secrets:" "Porpoises, or sea-hogs, when observed to sport and chase one another about ships, expect then some stormy weather."

Sea-monster. The reference in "King Lear" (i. 4), to the "sea-monster"—

> "Ingratitude, thou marble-hearted fiend,
> More hideous, when thou show'st thee in a child,
> Than the sea-monster!"—

is generally supposed to be the hippopotamus, which, according to Upton, was the hieroglyphical symbol of impiety and ingratitude.[1] Sandys[2] gives a picture said to be portrayed in the porch of the temple of Minerva, at Sais, in which is the figure of a river-horse, denoting "murder, impudence, violence, and injustice; for they say that he killeth his sire and ravisheth his own dam." His account is, no doubt, taken from Plutarch's "Isis and Osiris;" and Shakespeare may have read it in Holland's translation (p. 1300), but why he should call the river-horse a "sea-monster" is not very clear. It is more likely, however, that the whale is meant.[3]

---

[1] Wright's "Notes to King Lear," 1877, p. 133.

[2] "Travels," 1673, p. 105.

[3] Cf. "King Lear," iv. 2; "Troilus and Cressida," v. 5; "All's Well that End's Well," iv. 3.

CHAPTER XXII.

ALMANACS. In Shakespeare's day these were published under this title: "An Almanack and Prognostication made for the year of our Lord God, 1595." So, in the "Winter's Tale" (iv. 3), Autolycus says: "the hottest day prognostication proclaims;" that is, the hottest day foretold in the almanac. In Sonnet xiv. the prognostications in almanacs are also noticed:

> "Not from the stars do I my judgment pluck;
> And yet methinks I have astronomy,
> But not to tell of good or evil luck,
> Of plagues, of dearths, or season's quality;
> Nor can I fortune to brief minutes tell,
> Pointing to each his thunder, rain, and wind:
> Or say with princes if it shall go well,
> By oft predict that I in heaven find."

In "Antony and Cleopatra" (i. 2) Enobarbus says: "They are greater storms and tempests than almanacs can report;" and in "2 Henry IV." (ii. 4), Prince Henry says: "Saturn and Venus this year in conjunction! what says the almanac to that?"

Amulets. A belief in the efficacy of an amulet or charm to ward off diseases and to avert contagion has prevailed from a very early period. The use of amulets was common among the Greeks and Romans, whose amulets were principally formed of gems, crowns of pearls, necklaces of coral, shells, etc. The amulet of modern times has been of the most varied kinds; objects being selected either from the animal, vegetable, or mineral kingdom, pieces of old rags or garments, scraps of writing in legible or illegible characters, in fact, of anything to which any superstitious property has been considered to belong.[1] This form of superstition is noticed in " 1 Henry VI." (v. 3), in the scene laid at Angiers, where La Pucelle exclaims :

> " The regent conquers, and the Frenchmen fly.
> Now help, ye charming spells and periapts "

—periapts being charms which were worn as preservatives against diseases or mischief. Thus Cotgrave[2] explains the word as " a medicine hanged about any part of the bodie."

Ceremonies. These, says Malone, were " omens or signs deduced from sacrifices or other ceremonial rites." Thus, in " Julius Cæsar " (ii. 1), Cassius says of Cæsar, that—

> " he is superstitious grown of late,
> Quite from the main opinion he held once
> Of fantasy, of dreams, and ceremonies."

And in the next scene Calpurnia adds :

> " Cæsar, I never stood on ceremonies,
> Yet now they fright me."

Charms. These, as Mr. Pettigrew[3] has pointed out, differ little from amulets, the difference consisting in the manner in which they are used rather than in their nature. Thus, whereas the amulet was to be suspended on the person when employed, the charm was not necessarily subjected to such a method of application. In days gone by, and even at the present day, in country districts, so universal has been the use of this source of supposed magical power that there is scarcely a disease for which a charm has not been given. It is not only to diseases of body and mind that the superstitious practice has been directed ; having been in popular request to avert evil, and to counteract supposed malignant influences. As might be expected, Shakespeare

---

[1] Pettigrew's " Medical Superstitions," p. 48.

[2] " French and English Dictionary ;" see Dyce's " Glossary to Shakespeare," p. 316 ; Nares describes it as " a bandage, tied on for magical purposes, from περιάπτω ;" see Brand's " Pop. Antiq.," 1849, vol. iii. pp. 324–326 ; Douce's " Illustrations of Shakespeare," 1839, pp. 305–307.

[3] " Medical Superstitions," p. 55.

has given various allusions to this usage, as, for example, in
"Cymbeline" (v. 3), where Posthumus says:

> "To day, how many would have given their honours
> To have sav'd their carcases! took heel to do't,
> And yet died too! I, in mine own woe charm'd,
> Could not find death where I did hear him groan,
> Nor feel him where he struck"

—this passage referring to the notion of certain charms being powerful enough to keep men unhurt in battle.

Othello (iii. 4), speaking of the handkerchief which he had
given to Desdemona, relates:

> "That handkerchief
> Did an Egyptian to my mother give;
> She was a charmer, and could almost read
> The thoughts of people."

And in the same play (i. 1), Brabantio asks:

> "Is there not charms,
> By which the property of youth and maidhood
> May be abus'd?"

Again, in "Much Ado About Nothing" (iii. 2), Benedick,
who is represented as having the toothache, after listening
to the banter of his comrades, replies: "Yet is this no charm
for the toothache."

Perfect silence seems to have been regarded as indispen-
sable for the success of any charm; and Pliny informs us
that "favete linguis" was the usual exclamation employed
on such an occasion. From this circumstance it has been
suggested that the well-known phrase "to charm a tongue"
may have originated. Thus we have the following dialogue
in "Othello" (v. 2):

> "*Iago.*   Go to, charm your tongue.
> *Emilia.* I will not charm my tongue; I am bound to speak."

Thus, on the appearance, amid thunder, of the first apparition to Macbeth, after the witches have performed certain
charms (iv. 1), Shakespeare introduces the following dialogue:

" *Macbeth.* Tell me, thou unknown power—
    First Witch.   He knows thy thought :
Hear his speech, but say thou nought."

Again, in " The Tempest " (iv. 1), Prospero says :

" hush, and be mute,
Or else our spell is marr'd."

Metrical Charms.   There was a superstition long prevalent
that life might be taken away by metrical charms.[1]   Reginald
Scot, in his " Discovery of Witchcraft " (1584), says : " The
Irishmen addict themselves, etc. ; yea, they will not sticke
to affirme that they can *rime* a man to death."   In " 1 Henry
VI." (i. 1), the Duke of Exeter, referring to the lamented
death of Henry V., says :

"Shall we think the subtle-witted French
Conjurers and sorcerers, that, afraid of him,
By magic verses have contrived his end ?"

These " magic verses," to which the death of Henry V. is
here attributed, were not required to be uttered in his presence ; their deadly energy existing solely in the words of
the imprecation and the malevolence of the reciter, which
were supposed to render them effectual at any distance.

Again, the alphabet was called the Christ-cross-row ; either
because a cross was prefixed to the alphabet in the old
primers, or, more probably, from a superstitious custom of
writing the alphabet in the form of a cross by way of a charm.
In " Richard III." (i. 1), Clarence relates how King Edward—

" Hearkens after prophecies and dreams ;
And from the cross-row plucks the letter G."

Dreams.   These, considered as prognostics of good or evil,
are frequently introduced by Shakespeare.   In " Troilus and
Cressida " (v. 3), Andromache exclaims :

" My dreams will, sure, prove ominous to the day."

While Romeo (" Romeo and Juliet," v. 1) declares :

" My dreams presage some joyful news at hand."

---

[1] See, under *Rat,* a similar superstition noticed.

It is chiefly as precursors of misfortune that the poet has availed himself of their supposed influence as omens of future fate. Thus, there are few passages in his dramas more terrific than the dreams of Richard III. and Clarence; the latter especially, as Mr. Drake says,[1] "is replete with the most fearful imagery, and makes the blood run chill with horror."

Dreaming of certain things has generally been supposed to be ominous either of good or ill luck;[2] and at the present day the credulous pay oftentimes no small attention to their dreams, should these happen to have referred to what they consider unlucky things. In the same way Shylock, in the "Merchant of Venice" (ii. 5), is a victim to much superstitious dread:

> "Jessica, my girl,
> Look to my house. I am right loath to go:
> There is some ill a brewing towards my rest,
> For I did dream of money-bags to-night."

In "Julius Cæsar," dreaming of banquet is supposed to presage misfortune.

It was also supposed that malicious spirits took advantage of sleep to torment their victims;[3] hence Macbeth (ii. 1) exclaims:

> "Merciful powers,
> Restrain in me the cursed thoughts that nature
> Gives way to in repose!"[4]

Duels. The death of the vanquished person was always considered a certain evidence of his guilt. Thus, in "2 Henry VI." (ii. 3), King Henry, speaking of the death of Horner in the duel with Peter, says:[5]

> "Go, take hence that traitor from our sight;
> For, by his death, we do perceive his guilt:
> And God in justice hath reveal'd to us

---

[1] "Shakespeare and his Times," p. 355.
[2] See Brand's "Pop. Antiq.," 1849, vol. iii. pp. 127–141.
[3] See p. 283.
[4] See Malone's "Variorum Shakespeare," 1821, vol. ii. p. 90.
[5] See Singer's "Shakespeare," vol. vi. p. 167.

> The truth and innocence of this poor fellow,
> Which he had thought to have murder'd wrongfully.—
> Come, fellow, follow us for thy reward."

We may also compare what Arcite says to Palamon in the "Two Noble Kinsmen" (iii. 6):

> "If I fall, curse me, and say I was a coward;
> For none but such dare die in these just trials."

Among the customs connected with duelling, it appears that, according to an old law, knights were to fight with the lance and the sword, as those of inferior rank fought with an ebon staff or baton, to the farther end of which was fixed a bag crammed hard with sand.[1] Thus Shakespeare, in " 2 Henry VI." (ii. 3), represents Horner entering "bearing his staff with a sand-bag fastened to it." Butler, in his " Hudibras," alludes to this custom:

> "Engag'd with money-bags, as bold
> As men with sand-bags did of old."

Steevens adds that "a passage in St. Chrysostom very clearly proves the great antiquity of this practice."

Fortune-tellers. A common method of fortune-tellers, in pretending to tell future events, was by means of a beryl or glass. In an extract from the " Penal Laws against Witches," it is said, " they do answer either by voice, or else set before their eyes, in glasses, chrystal stones, etc., the pictures or images of the persons or things sought for." It is to this kind of juggling prophecy that Angelo, in " Measure for Measure " (ii. 2), refers, when he tells how the law—

> "like a prophet,
> Looks in a glass, that shows what future evils,
> Either new, or by remissness new-conceiv'd."

Again, Macbeth (iv. 1), when " a show of eight kings " is presented to him, exclaims, after witnessing the seventh:

> "I'll see no more:—
> And yet the eighth appears, who bears a glass,
> Which shows me many more."

---

[1] See Nares's " Glossary," vol. ii. p. 765.

Spenser[1] has given a circumstantial account of the glass which Merlin made for King Ryence. A mirror of the same kind was presented to Cambuscan, in the " Squier's Tale " of Chaucer; and we are also told how " a certain philosopher did the like to Pompey, the which showed him in a glass the order of his enemies' march."[2] Brand, in his " Popular Antiquities,"[3] gives several interesting accounts of this method of fortune-telling; and quotes the following from Vallancey's " Collectanea de Rebus Hibernicis:" " In the Highlands of Scotland, a large chrystal, of a figure somewhat oval, was kept by the priests to work charms by; water poured upon it at this day is given to cattle against diseases; these stones are now preserved by the oldest and most superstitious in the country; they were once common in Ireland."

Further allusions to fortune-tellers occur in " Comedy of Errors " (v. 1), and " Merry Wives of Windsor " (iv. 2).

It appears, too, that the trade of fortune-telling was, in Shakespeare's day, as now, exercised by the wandering hordes of gypsies. In " Antony and Cleopatra " (iv. 12), the Roman complains that Cleopatra—

> " Like a right gipsy, hath, at fast and loose,
> Beguil'd me to the very heart of loss."

Giants. The belief in giants and other monsters was much credited in olden times, and, " among the legends of nearly every race or tribe, few are more universal than those relating to giants or men of colossal size and superhuman power."[4] That such stories were current in Shakespeare's day, is attested by the fact that the poet makes Othello (i. 3), in his eloquent defence before the Senate of Venice, when explaining his method of courtship, allude to—

---

[1] " Fairy Queen," bk. iii. c. 2; see Singer's " Shakespeare," vol. ix. p. 82.

[2] Boisteau's " Theatrum Mundi," translated by John Alday (1574).

[3] 1849, vol. iii. pp. 60, 61.

[4] See Hardwick's " Traditions, Superstitions, and Folk-Lore," 1872, pp. 197, 224.

"the Cannibals that each other eat,
The Anthropophagi, and men whose heads
Do grow beneath their shoulders."

In "The Tempest" (iii. 3), Gonzalo relates how—

"When we were boys,
Who would believe that there were mountaineers
Dew-lapp'd like bulls, whose throats had hanging at 'em
Wallets of flesh? or that there were such men,
Whose heads stood in their breasts?"

And after the appearance of Prospero's magic repast, Sebastian says:

"Now I will believe
That there are unicorns; that in Arabia
There is one tree, the phœnix' throne; one phœnix
At this hour reigning there."

Among the numerous references to giants by Shakespeare, we may quote the following. In "2 Henry VI." (ii. 3), Horner says: "Peter, have at thee with a downright blow [as Bevis of Southampton fell upon Ascapart]."[1]

Ascapart, according to the legend, was "ful thyrty fote longe," and was conquered by Sir Bevis of Southampton.

In "Cymbeline" (iii. 3), Belarius says:

"the gates of monarchs
Are arch'd so high, that giants may jet through
And keep their impious turbans on, without
Good morrow to the sun."

In the "Merry Wives of Windsor" (ii. 1), Mrs. Page says: "I had rather be a giantess, and lie under Mount Pelion."[2]

Lucky Days. From the most remote period certain days have been supposed to be just as lucky as others are the reverse, a notion which is not confined to any one country. In Shakespeare's day great attention was paid to this superstitious fancy, which is probably alluded to in the "Winter's

---

[1] The addition in brackets is rejected by the editors of the Globe edition.

[2] Cf. "Measure for Measure," ii. 2, iii. 1; "Much Ado About Nothing," v. 1; "Love's Labour's Lost," iii. 1.

Tale " (iii. 3), where the Shepherd says to the Clown, " 'Tis
a lucky day, boy ; and we'll do good deeds on't."

In " King John " (iii. 1) Constance exclaims :

> "What hath this day deserv'd ? what hath it done,
> That it in golden letters should be set
> Among the high tides in the calendar ?
> Nay, rather turn this day out of the week,
> This day of shame, oppression, perjury :
> Or, if it must stand still, let wives with child
> Pray that their burthens may not fall this day,
> Lest that their hopes prodigiously be cross'd :
> But on this day let seamen fear no wreck ;
> No bargains break that are not this day made :
> This day, all things begun come to ill end,
> Yea, faith itself to hollow falsehood change !"

Again, Macbeth (iv. 1) says :

> " Let this pernicious hour
> Stand aye accursed in the calendar !"

In the old almanacs the days supposed to be favorable or
unfavorable are enumerated, allusion to which occurs in
Webster's " Duchess of Malfy," 1623 :

> " By the almanack, I think,
> To choose good days and shun the critical."

At the present day this superstition still retains its hold
on the popular mind, and in the transactions of life exerts
an important influence.[1]

Magic. The system of magic, which holds such a prominent place in " The Tempest," was formerly an article in the
popular creed, and as such is frequently noticed by the writers of Shakespeare's time. Thus, in describing Prospero,
Shakespeare has given him several of the adjuncts, besides
the costume, of the popular magician, much virtue being
inherent in his very garments. So Prospero, when addressing his daughter (i. 2), says :

---

[1] See Brand's " Pop. Antiq.," 1879, vol. i. pp. 44–51 ; Jones's " Credulities Past and Present," pp. 493–507 ; Hampson's " Œvi Medii Kalendarium," vol. i. p. 210 ; see an article on " Day Fatality " in John Aubrey's " Miscellanies."

> " Lend thy hand,
> And pluck my magic garment from me.—So ;
> Lie there, my art."

A similar importance is assigned to his staff, for he tells
Ferdinand (i. 2) :

> ˙ " I can here disarm thee with this stick,
> And make thy weapon drop."

And when he abjures the practice of magic, one of the
requisites is " to break his staff," and to (v. 1)

> " Bury it certain fathoms in the earth."

The more immediate instruments of power were books,
by means of which spells were usually performed. Hence,
in the old romances, the sorcerer is always furnished with a
book, by reading certain parts of which he is enabled to
summon to his aid what demons or spirits he has occasion
to employ. When he is deprived of his book his power
ceases. Malone quotes, in illustration of this notion, Caliban's words in " The Tempest " (iii. 2) :

> " Remember,
> First to possess his books ; for without them
> He's but a sot, as I am, nor hath not
> One spirit to command."

Prospero, too, declares (iii. 1) :

> " I'll to my book ;
> For yet, ere supper time, must I perform
> Much business appertaining."

And on his relinquishing his art he says that :

> " Deeper than did ever plummet sound
> I'll drown my book."

Those who practise nocturnal sorcery are styled, in
" Troilus and Cressida " (iv. 2), " venomous wights."

Merlin's Prophecies. In Shakespeare's day there was an
extensive belief in strange and absurd prophecies, which
were eagerly caught up and repeated by one person to another. This form of superstition is alluded to in " 1 Henry

IV." (iii. 1), where, after Owen Glendower has been descant-
ing on the " omens and portents dire " which heralded his
nativity, and Hotspur's unbelieving and taunting replies to
the chieftain's assertions, the poet makes Hotspur, on Mortimer's saying,

> " Fie, cousin Percy! how you cross my father!"

thus reply:

> " I cannot choose: sometime he angers me,
> With telling me of the moldwarp and the ant,
> Of the dreamer Merlin and his prophecies;
> And of a dragon and a finless fish."

In " King Lear " (iii. 2) the Fool says:

> " I'll speak a prophecy ere I go:
> When priests are more in word than matter;
> When brewers mar their malt with water;
> When nobles are their tailors' tutors;
> No heretics burn'd, but wenches' suitors;
> When every case in law is right;
> No squire in debt, nor no poor knight;
> When slanders do not live in tongues:
> Nor cutpurses come not to throngs;
> When usurers tell their gold i' the field;
> And bawds and whores do churches build;—
> Then shall the realm of Albion
> Come to great confusion:
> Then comes the time, who lives to see't,
> That going shall be us'd with feet.
> This prophecy Merlin shall make; for I live before his time."

This witty satire was probably against the prophecies
attributed to Merlin, which were then prevalent among the
people.[1]

Formerly, too, prophecies of apparent impossibilities were
common in Scotland; such as the removal of one place to
another. So in " Macbeth " (iv. 1), the apparition says:

> " Macbeth shall never vanquish'd be, until
> Great Birnam wood to high Dunsinane hill
> Shall come against him."

---

[1] See Kelly's " Notices Illustrative of the Drama and Other Amusements at Leicester," 1865, pp. 116, 118.

Portents and Prodigies.   In years gone the belief in supernatural occurrences was a common article of faith ; and our
ancestors made use of every opportunity to prove the truth
of this superstitious belief.   The most usual monitions of
this kind were, "lamentings heard in the air ; shakings and
tremblings of the earth ; sudden gloom at noon-day ; the
appearance of meteors ; the shooting of stars ; eclipses of
the sun and moon ; the moon of a bloody hue ; the shriek-
ing of owls ; the croaking of ravens ; the shrilling of crickets ; night-howlings of dogs ; the death-watch ; the chatter-
ing of pies ; wild neighing of horses ; blood dropping from
the nose ; winding-sheets ; strange and fearful noises, etc.,"
many of which Shakespeare has used, introducing them as
the precursors of murder, sudden death, disasters, and superhuman events.[1]   Thus in " Richard II." (ii. 4), the following
prodigies are selected as the forerunners of the death or fall
of kings :

> "'Tis thought, the king is dead : we will not stay.
>   The bay-trees in our country are all wither'd,
>   And meteors fright the fixed stars of heaven ;
>   The pale-fac'd moon looks bloody on the earth,
>   And lean-look'd prophets whisper fearful change ;
>   Rich men look sad, and ruffians dance and leap,
>   The one in fear to lose what they enjoy,
>   The other to enjoy by rage and war :
>   These signs forerun the death or fall of kings."

Previous to the assassination of Julius Cæsar, we are told, in
" Hamlet " (i. 1), how :

> " In the most high and palmy state of Rome,
>   A little ere the mightiest Julius fell,
>   The graves stood tenantless, and the sheeted dead
>   Did squeak and gibber in the Roman streets ;
>   As stars with trains of fire and dews of blood,
>   Disasters in the sun ; and the moist star,
>   Upon whose influence Neptune's empire stands,
>   Was sick almost to doomsday with eclipse."

More appalling still are the circumstances which preceded

---

[1] Drake's " Shakespeare and his Times," p. 352.

and accompanied the murder of Duncan (" Macbeth," ii. 3).
We may also compare the omens which marked the births
of Owen Glendower and Richard III. Indeed, the supposed
sympathy of the elements with human joy or sorrow or
suffering is evidently a very ancient superstition; and this
presumed sensitiveness, not only of the elements, but of
animated nature, to the perpetration of deeds of darkness
and blood by perverted nature, has in all ages been extensively believed. It is again beautifully illustrated in the
lines where Shakespeare makes Lenox, on the morning following the murder of Duncan by his host (" Macbeth," ii. 3),
give the following narrative:

> " The night has been unruly; where we lay,
>   Our chimneys were blown down; and, as they say,
>   Lamentings heard i' the air; strange screams of death;
>   And prophesying with accents terrible
>   Of dire combustion, and confus'd events,
>   New hatch'd to the woeful time: the obscure bird
>   Clamour'd the livelong night: some say, the earth
>   Was feverous and did shake."

This idea is further illustrated in the dialogue which follows,
between Ross and an old man:

> " *Old Man.* Threescore and ten I can remember well:
> Within the volume of which time I have seen
> Hours dreadful, and things strange: but this sore night
> Hath trifled former knowings.
>   *Ross.*   Ah, good father,
> Thou seest, the heavens, as troubled with man's act,
> Threaten his bloody stage: by the clock, 'tis day,
> And yet dark night strangles the travelling lamp:
> Is't night's predominance, or the day's shame,
> That darkness does the face of earth entomb,
> When living light should kiss it?"

Supernatural Authority of Kings. The belief in the supernatural authority of monarchs is but a remnant of the long-
supposed " divine right " of kings to govern, which resulted
from a conviction that they could trace their pedigrees back

to the deities themselves.[1] Thus Shakespeare even puts into the mouth of the murderer and usurper Claudius, King of Denmark, the following sentence:

> "Let him go, Gertrude: do not fear our person:
> There's such divinity doth hedge a king,
> That treason can but peep to what it would,
> Acts little of his will."

This notion is by no means confined to either civilized or semi-civilized nations. It is, says Mr. Hardwick, "a universal feeling among savage tribes." The ignorant serf of Russia believed, and, indeed, yet believes, that if the deity were to die the emperor would succeed to his power and authority.

Sympathetic Indications. According to a very old tradition the wounds of a murdered person were supposed to bleed afresh at the approach or touch of the murderer. This effect, though impossible, remarks Nares,[2] except it were by miracle, was firmly believed, and almost universally, for a very long period. Poets, therefore, were fully justified in their use of it. Thus Shakespeare, in "Richard III." (i. 2) makes Lady Anne, speaking of Richard, Duke of Gloster, say:

> "O, gentlemen, see, see! dead Henry's wounds
> Open their congeal'd mouths, and bleed afresh!—
> Blush, blush, thou lump of foul deformity;
> For 'tis thy presence that exhales this blood
> From cold and empty veins, where no blood dwells;
> Thy deed, inhuman and unnatural,
> Provokes this deluge most unnatural."

Stow alludes to this circumstance in his "Annals" (p. 424). He says the king's body "was brought to St. Paul's in an open coffin, barefaced, where he bled; thence he was carried to the Blackfriars, and there bled." Matthew Paris also states that after Henry II.'s death his son Richard came to view the body—"Quo superveniente, confestim erupit sanguis ex naribus regis mortui; ac si indignaretur spiritus in adventu ejus, qui ejusdem mortis causa esse

---

[1] "Traditions, Superstitions, and Folk-Lore," p. 81.
[2] "Glossary," vol. ii. p. 974.

credebatur, ut videretur sanguis clamare ad Deum."[1] In the "Athenian Oracle" (i. 106), this supposed phenomenon is thus accounted for: "The blood is congealed in the body for two or three days, and then becomes liquid again, in its tendency to corruption. The air being heated by many persons coming about the body, is the same thing to it as motion is. 'Tis observed that dead bodies will bleed in a concourse of people, when murderers are absent, as well as present, yet legislators have thought fit to authorize it, and use this trial as an argument, at least to frighten, though 'tis no conclusive one to condemn them." Among other allusions to this superstition may be mentioned one by King James in his "Dæmonology," where we read: "In a secret murder, if the dead carkasse be at any time thereafter handled by the murderer, it will gush out of blood, as if the blood were crying to heaven for revenge of the murderer." It is spoken of also in a note to chapter v. of the "Fair Maid of Perth," that this bleeding of a corpse was urged as an evidence of guilt in the High Court of Justiciary at Edinburgh as late as the year 1668. An interesting survival of this curious notion exists in Durham, where, says Mr. Henderson,[2] "touching of the corpse by those who come to look at it is still expected by the poor on the part of those who come to their house while a dead body is lying in it, in token that they wished no ill to the departed, and were in peace and amity with him."

We may also compare the following passage, where Macbeth (iii. 4), speaking of the Ghost, says:

> "It will have blood; they say, blood will have blood:
> Stones have been known to move, and trees to speak;
> Augurs and understood relations have
> By magot-pies and choughs and rooks brought forth
> The secret'st man of blood."

Shakespeare perhaps alludes to some story in which the stones covering the corpse of a murdered man were said to

---

[1] See Brand's "Pop. Antiq.," 1849, vol. iii. pp. 229–231.
[2] Folk-Lore of Northern Counties," 1849, p. 57.

have moved of themselves, and so revealed the secret. The idea of trees speaking probably refers to the story of the tree which revealed to Æneas the murder of Polydorus (Verg., "Æneid," iii. 22, 599). Indeed, in days gone by, this superstition was carried to such an extent that we are told, in D'Israeli's "Curiosities of Literature," "by the side of the bier, if the slightest change was observable in the eyes, the mouth, feet, or hands of the corpse, the murderer was conjectured to be present, and many an innocent spectator must have suffered death. This practice forms a rich picture in the imagination of our old writers; and their histories and ballads are labored into pathos by dwelling on this phenomenon."

CHAPTER XXIII.

MISCELLANEOUS CUSTOMS, ETC.

Badge of Poverty. In the reign of William III., those who received parish relief had to wear a badge. It was the letter P, with the initial of the parish to which they belonged, in red or blue cloth, on the shoulder of the right sleeve. In " 2 Henry VI." (v. 1) Clifford says :

> " Might I but know thee by thy household badge."

Bedfellow. A proof of the simplicity of manners in olden times is evidenced by the fact that it was customary for men, even of the highest rank, to sleep together. In " Henry V." (ii. 2) Exeter says :

> " Nay, but the man that was his bedfellow,
> Whom he hath dull'd and cloy'd with gracious favours."

" This unseemly custom," says Malone, " continued common till the middle of the last century, if not later." Beaumont and Fletcher, in the " Coxcomb " (i. 1), thus refer to it :

> " Must we, that have so long time been as one,
> Seen cities, countries, kingdoms, and their wonders,
> Been bedfellows, and in our various journey
> Mixt all our observations."

In the same way, letters from noblemen to each other often began with the appellation *bedfellow.*[1]

Curfew Bell, which is generally supposed to be of Norman origin, is still rung in some of our old country villages, although it has long lost its significance. It seems to have been as important to ghosts as to living men, it being their signal for walking, a license which apparently lasted till the first cock. Fairies, too, and other spirits, were un-

---

[1] Nares's " Glossary," vol. i. p. 68.

der the same regulations; and hence Prospero, in "The Tempest" (v. 1), says of his elves that they

> "rejoice
> To hear the solemn curfew."

In "King Lear" (iii. 4) we find the fiend Flibbertigibbet obeying the same rule, for Edgar says: "This is the foul fiend Flibbertigibbet; he begins at curfew, and walks till the first cock."

In "Measure for Measure" (iv. 2) we find another allusion:

> "*Duke.* The best and wholesom'st spirits of the night
> Envelope you, good provost! Who call'd here of late?
> *Provost.* None, since the curfew rung."

And, once more, in "Romeo and Juliet" (iv. 4), Capulet says:

> "Come, stir, stir, stir! the second cock hath crow'd,
> The curfew bell hath rung, 'tis three o'clock."[1]

Sacring Bell. This was a bell which rang for processions and other holy ceremonies.[2] It is mentioned in "Henry VIII." (iii. 2), by the Earl of Surrey:

> "I'll startle you
> Worse than the sacring bell."

It is rung in the Romish Church to give notice that the "Host" is approaching, and is now called "Sanctus bell," from the words "Sanctus, Sanctus, Sanctus Dominus Deus Sabaoth," pronounced by the priest.

On the graphic passage where Macbeth (ii. 1) says:

> "The bell invites me.
> Hear it not, Duncan; for it is a knell
> That summons thee to heaven or to hell"—

Malone has this note: "Thus Raleigh, speaking of love, in England's 'Helicon' (1600):

> "'It is perhaps that sauncing bell
> That toules all into heaven or hell.'

---

[1] See Brand's "Pop. Antiq.," 1849, vol. iii. pp. 220–225; also, Harland and Wilkinson's "Lancashire Folk-Lore," 1867, p. 44.

[2] Dyce's "Glossary," p. 379.

Sauncing being probably a mistake for sacring or saint's bell, originally, perhaps, written saintis bell." In "Hudibras" we find:

> " The old saintis bell that rings all in."

Carpet-knights. These were knights dubbed at court by mere favor, and not on the field of battle, for their military exploits. In "Twelfth Night" (iii. 4), Sir Toby defines one of them thus: "He is knight, dubbed with unhatched rapier, and on carpet consideration."

A "trencher knight" was probably synonymous, as in "Love's Labour's Lost" (v. 2):

> "Some mumble-news, some trencher-knight, some Dick."

These carpet-knights were sometimes called " knights of the green cloth." [1]

Chair Days. Days of old age and infirmity. So, in "2 Henry VI." (v. 2), young Clifford, on seeing his dead father, says:

> " Wast thou ordain'd, dear father,
> To lose thy youth in peace, and to achieve .
> The silver livery of advised age,
> And, in thy reverence, and thy chair-days, thus
> To die in ruffian battle ?"

Chivalry. The expression " sworn brothers," which Shakespeare several times employs, refers to the " fratres jurati," who, in the days of chivalry, mutually bound themselves by oath to share each other's fortune. Thus, Falstaff says of Shallow, in "2 Henry IV." (iii. 2): "He talks as familiarly of John o' Gaunt as if he had been sworn brother to him." In "Henry V." (ii. 1), Bardolph says: "we'll be all three sworn brothers to France." In course of time it was used in a laxer sense, to denote intimacy, as in "Much Ado About Nothing" (i. 1), where Beatrice says of Benedick, that " He hath every month a new sworn brother." [2]

According to the laws of chivalry, a person of superior

---

[1] See Douce's "Illustrations of Shakespeare," pp. 65, 66.

[2] We may compare, too, what Coriolanus says (ii. 3): "I will, sir, flatter my sworn brother, the people."

birth might not be challenged by an inferior; or, if challenged, might refuse combat, a reference to which seems to be made by Cleopatra ("Antony and Cleopatra," ii. 4):

> "I will not hurt him.—
> These hands do lack nobility, that they strike
> A meaner than myself."

Again, in "Troilus and Cressida" (v. 4), the same practice is alluded to by Hector, who asks Thersites:

> "What art thou, Greek? art thou for Hector's match?
> Art thou of blood and honour?"

Singer quotes from "Melville's Memoirs" (1735, p. 165): "The Laird of Grange offered to fight Bothwell, who answered that he was not his equal. The like answer made he to Tullibardine. Then my Lord Lindsay offered to fight him, which he could not well refuse; but his heart failed him, and he grew cold on the business."

Clubs. According to Malone, it was once a common custom, on the breaking-out of a fray, to call out "Clubs, clubs!" to part the combatants. Thus, in "1 Henry VI." (i. 3), the Mayor declares:

> "I'll call for clubs, if you will not away."

In "Titus Andronicus" (ii. 1), Aaron says:

> "Clubs, clubs! these lovers will not keep the peace."

"Clubs," too, "was originally the popular cry to call forth the London apprentices, who employed their clubs for the preservation of the public peace. Sometimes, however, they used those weapons to raise a disturbance, as they are described doing in the following passage in "Henry VIII." (v. 4): "I miss'd the meteor once, and hit that woman; who cried out 'Clubs!' when I might see from far some forty truncheoners draw to her succour, which were the hope o' the Strand, where she was quartered."[1]

Color-Lore. Green eyes have been praised by poets of

---

[1] Cf. "Romeo and Juliet," i. 1; "As You Like It," v. 2.

nearly every land,[1] and, according to Armado, in "Love's Labour's Lost" (i. 2), "Green, indeed, is the colour of lovers."

In "A Midsummer-Night's Dream" (v. 1), Thisbe laments:

> "Lovers, make moan:
> His eyes were green as leeks."

The Nurse, in her description of Romeo's rival ("Romeo and Juliet," iii. 5), says:

> "An eagle, madam,
> Hath not so green, so quick, so fair an eye
> As Paris hath."

In the "Two Noble Kinsmen" (v. 1), Emilia, praying to Diana, says:

> "O vouchsafe,
> With that thy rare green eye—which never yet
> Beheld thing maculate—look on thy virgin."

The words of Armado have been variously explained as alluding to green eyes—Spanish writers being peculiarly enthusiastic in this praise—to the willow worn by unsuccessful lovers, and to their melancholy.[2] It has also been suggested that, as green is the color most suggestive of freshness and spring-time, it may have been considered the most appropriate lover's badge. At the same time, however, it is curious that, as green has been regarded as an ominous color, it should be connected with lovers, for, as an old couplet remarks:

> "Those dressed in blue
> Have lovers true;
> In green and white,
> Forsaken quite."[4]

In "Merchant of Venice" (iii. 2), "green-eyed jealousy," and in "Othello" (iii. 3), its equivalent, "green-eyed monster," are expressions used by Shakespeare.

Yellow is an epithet often, too, applied to jealousy, by the

---

[1] See Singer's "Shakespeare," vol. viii. p. 204.
[2] See Douce's "Illustrations of Shakespeare," p. 133.
[3] See an article by Mr. Black, in *Antiquary*, 1881, vol. iii.
[4] See Henderson's "Folk-Lore of the Northern Counties," pp. 34, 35.

old writers.   In the " Merry Wives of Windsor " (i. 3), Nym
says he will possess Ford " with yellowness."   In " Much
Ado About Nothing " (ii. 1), Beatrice describes the Count as
" civil as an orange, and something of that jealous complexion."   In " Twelfth Night " (ii. 4), Viola tells the Duke how
her father's daughter loved a man, but never told her love:

> " She pin'd in thought,
> And with a green and yellow melancholy
> She sat like patience on a monument."

Dinner Customs.   In days gone by there was but one
salt-cellar on the table, which was a large piece of plate,
generally much ornamented.   The tables being long, the
salt was commonly placed about the middle, and served as
a kind of boundary to the different quality of the guests
invited.   Those of distinction were ranked above ; the space
below being assigned to the dependants, inferior relations
of the master of the house, etc.[1]   Shakespeare would seem
to allude to this custom in the " Winter's Tale " (i. 2), where
Leontes says :

> " lower messes,
> Perchance, are to this business purblind ?"

Upon which passage Steevens adds, " Leontes comprehends
inferiority of understanding in the idea of inferiority of
rank."   Ben Jonson, speaking of the characteristics of an
insolent coxcomb, remarks : " His fashion is not to take
knowledge of him that is beneath him in clothes.   He never
drinks below the salt."

Ordinary.   This was a public dinner, where each paid his
share, an allusion to which custom is made by Enobarbus,
in " Antony and Cleopatra " (ii. 2), who, speaking of Antony,
says :

> " Being barber'd ten times o'er, goes to the feast,
> And, for his ordinary, pays his heart
> For what his eyes eat only."

---

[1] Gifford's note on " Massinger's Works," 1813, vol. i. p. 170; see
Dyce's " Glossary to Shakespeare," pp. 269, 380.

Again, in "All's Well that Ends Well" (ii. 3), Lafeu says: "I did think thee, for two ordinaries, to be a pretty wise fellow; thou didst make tolerable vent of thy travel."

The "ordinary" also denoted the lounging-place of the men of the town, and the fantastic gallants who herded together. They were, says the author of "Curiosities of Literature" (vol. iii. p. 82), "the exchange for news, the echoing-places for all sorts of town talk; there they might hear of the last new play and poem, and the last fresh widow sighing for some knight to make her a lady; these resorts were attended also to save charges of housekeeping."

Drinking Customs. Shakespeare has given several allusions to the old customs associated with drinking, which have always varied in different countries. At the present day many of the drinking customs still observed are very curious, especially those kept up at the universities and inns-of-court.

Alms-drink was a phrase in use, says Warburton, among good fellows, to signify that liquor of another's share which his companion drank to ease him. So, in "Antony and Cleopatra" (ii. 7), one of the servants says of Lepidus: "They have made him drink alms-drink."

By-drinkings. This was a phrase for drinkings between meals, and is used by the Hostess in "1 Henry IV." (iii. 3), who says to Falstaff: "You owe money here besides, Sir John, for your diet, and by-drinkings."

Hooped Pots. In olden times drinking-pots were made with hoops, so that, when two or more drank from the same tankard, no one should drink more than his share. There were generally three hoops to the pots: hence, in "2 Henry VI." (iv. 2), Cade says: "The three-hooped pot shall have ten hoops." In Nash's "Pierce Pennilesse" we read: "I believe hoopes on quart pots were invented that every man should take his hoope, and no more."

The phrases "to do a man right" and "to do him reason" were, in years gone by, the common expressions in pledging healths; he who drank a bumper expected that a bumper should be drunk to his toast. To this practice

alludes the scrap of a song which Silence sings in " 2 Henry
IV." (v. 3):

> "Do me right,
> And dub me knight:
> Samingo."

He who drank, too, a bumper on his knee to the health
of his mistress was dubbed a knight for the evening.   The
word Samingo is either a corruption of, or an intended blunder for, San Domingo, but why this saint should be the patron of topers is uncertain.

Rouse.   According to Gifford,[1] a *rouse* was a large glass in
which a health was given, the drinking of which, by the rest
of the company, formed a carouse.   Hamlet (i. 4) says:

> "The king doth wake to-night, and takes his rouse."

The word occurs again in the following act (1), where Polonius uses the phrase " o'ertook in's rouse;" and in the sense
of a bumper, or glass of liquor, in " Othello " (ii. 3), " they
have given me a rouse already."

Sheer Ale.   This term, which is used in the " Taming of
the Shrew " (Induction, sc. 2), by Sly—" Ask Marian Hacket,
the fat ale-wife of Wincot, if she know me not: if she say I
am not fourteen pence on the score for sheer ale "—according to some expositors, means " ale alone, nothing but ale,"
rather than " unmixed ale."

Sneak-cup.   This phrase, which is used by Falstaff in
" 1 Henry IV." (iii. 3)—" the prince is a Jack, a sneak-cup "
—was used to denote one who balked his glass.

Earnest Money.   It was, in olden times, customary to rat-
ify an agreement by a bent coin.   In " Henry VIII." (ii. 3),
the old lady remarks:

> " 'Tis strange: a three-pence bow'd would hire me,
> Old as I am, to queen it."

There were, however, no threepences so early as the reign
of Henry VIII.

---

[1] See Dyce, vol. iv. p. 395.

Exclamations. "Charity, for the Lord's sake!" was the form of ejaculatory supplication used by imprisoned debtors to the passers-by. So, in Davies's "Epigrams" (1611):

> "Good, gentle writers, 'for the Lord's sake, for the Lord's sake,'
> Like Ludgate prisoner, lo, I, begging, make
> My mone."

In "Measure for Measure" (iv. 3), the phrase is alluded to by Pompey: "all great doers in our trade, and are now 'for the Lord's sake.'"

"Cry Budget." A watchword. Thus Slender says to Shallow, in the "Merry Wives of Windsor" (v. 2): "We have a nay-word, how to know one another: I come to her in white, and cry 'mum;' she cries 'budget;' and by that we know one another."

"God save the mark." "Romeo and Juliet" (iii. 2). This exclamation has hitherto baffled the research of every commentator. It occurs again in "1 Henry IV." (i. 3); and in the "Merchant of Venice" (ii. 2) and in "Othello" (i. 1), we have "God bless the mark." In the quarto, 1597, instead of "God save the mark" in the first passage quoted, we have "God save the sample," an expression equally obscure.[1]

Halidom. This exclamation was used, says Minsheu,[2] by old countrymen, by manner of swearing. In "Two Gentlemen of Verona" (iv. 2), the Hostess says: "By my halidom, I was fast asleep;" the probable derivation being *holy*, with the termination *dome*.

Hall! Hall! An exclamation formerly used, to make a clear space in a crowd, for any particular purpose, was "*A hall, a hall.*" So, in "Romeo and Juliet" (i. 5), Capulet says:

> "Come, musicians, play.—
> A hall, a hall! give room! and foot it, girls."

Hay. This is equivalent to "you have it," an exclamation in fencing, when a thrust or hit is received by the antagonist.

---

[1] Staunton's "Shakespeare," vol. i. p. 257.
[2] "Guide into Tongues," 1607.

In " Romeo and Juliet" (ii. 4), Mercutio speaks of " the punto reverso ! the hay !"

Hold. To cry *hold !* when persons were fighting, was an authoritative way of separating them, according to the old military law. So Macbeth, in his struggle with Macduff, says:

> " And damn'd be he that first cries, ' Hold, enough !' "

We may compare Lady Macbeth's words (i. 5):

> " Nor heaven peep through the blanket of the dark,
> To cry, ' Hold, hold !' "

" I' the name of me." A vulgar exclamation formerly in use. So in the " Winter's Tale" (iv. 2) it is used by the Clown.

" *O ho, O ho !*" This savage exclamation was, says Steevens, constantly appropriated by the writers of our ancient mysteries and moralities to the devil. In " The Tempest" (i. 2), Caliban, when rebuked by Prospero for seeking " to violate the honor of my child," replies :

> " O ho, O ho ! would it had been done !
> Thou didst prevent me ; I had peopled else
> This isle with Calibans."

Push. An exclamation equivalent to *pish.*[1] It is used by Leonato in " Much Ado About Nothing" (v. 1):

> " And made a push at chance and sufferance ;"

and again, in " Timon of Athens" (iii. 6), where one of the lords says : " Push ! did you see my cap ?"

Rivo was an exclamation often used in Bacchanalian revels, but its origin is uncertain. It occurs in " 1 Henry IV." (ii. 4) : " ' Rivo !' says the drunkard." Gifford suggests that it is " corrupted, perhaps, from the Spanish *rio*, which is figuratively used for a large quantity of liquor," a derivation, however, which Mr. Dyce does not think probable.

---

[1] See Dyce's " Glossary," p. 343.

Sneck-up. This was an exclamation of contempt, equivalent to "go and hang yourself."[1] It is used by Sir Toby in "Twelfth Night" (ii. 3), in reply to Malvolio's rebuke: "We did keep time, sir, in our catches. Sneck up!"

So-ho. This is the cry of sportsmen when the hare is found in her seat.

Spy. "I spy" is the usual exclamation at a well-known childish game called "Hie spy, hie!"[2]

Tailor. Johnson explains the following words of Puck in "A Midsummer-Night's Dream" (ii. 1) thus:

> "The wisest aunt, telling the saddest tale,
>   Sometime for three-foot stool mistaketh me;
>   Then slip I from her bum, down topples she,
>   And 'tailor' cries, and falls into a cough."

"The custom of crying tailor at a sudden fall backwards, I think I remember to have observed. He that slips beside his chair, falls as a tailor squats upon his board." Mr. Dyce,[3] however, adds, "it may be doubted if this explains the text."

Tilly-vally. An exclamation of contempt, the etymology of which is uncertain. According to Douce it is a hunting phrase borrowed from the French. Singer says it is equivalent to *fiddle-faddle.* It occurs in "Twelfth Night" (ii. 3), being used by Sir Toby: "Am not I consanguineous? am I not of her blood? Tilly-vally, lady!"

In "2 Henry IV." (ii. 4), the Hostess corrupts it to *tilly-fally:* "Tilly-fally, Sir John, ne'er tell me: your ancient swaggerer comes not in my doors."

As a further illustration of the use of this word, Singer quotes a conversation between Sir Thomas More and his wife, given in Roper's Life: "Is not this house, quoth he, as nigh heaven as my own? To whom she, after her accustomed homely fashion, not liking such talk, answered, Tylle-valle, Tylle-valle."

Westward, ho. This was one of the exclamations of the

---

[1] Dyce's "Glossary," p. 402.   [2] Ibid., vol. vi. p. 45.   [3] Ibid., p. 43.

watermen who plied on the Thames, and is used by Viola in
" Twelfth Night " (iii. 1). Dyce[1] quotes from Peel's " Edward I." to illustrate the use of this word:

" *Queen Elinor.* Ay, good woman, conduct me to the court,
That there I may bewail my sinful life,
And call to God to save my wretched soul.
                                [*A cry of 'Westward, ho!'*
Woman, what noise is this I hear?
    Potter's Wife. An like your grace, it is the watermen that call for
passengers to go westward now."

Dekker took the exclamation " Westward, ho!" for the
title of a comedy; and Jonson, Chapman, and Marston
adopted that of " Eastward, ho!" for one jointly written by
them a few years afterwards.

Fools. Mr. Douce, in his essay " On the Clowns and Fools
of Shakespeare," has made a ninefold division of English
fools, according to quality or place of employment, as the
domestic fool, the city or corporation fool, the tavern fool,
the fool of the mysteries and moralities. The last is generally called the " vice," and is the original of the stage
clowns so common among the dramatists of the time of
Elizabeth, and who embody so much of the wit of Shakespeare.

A very palpable distinction is that which distinguishes
between such creatures as were chosen to excite to laughter
from some deformity of mind or body, and such as were
chosen for a certain alertness of mind and power of repartee
—or, briefly, butts and wits. The dress of the regular court
fool of the middle ages was not altogether a rigid uniform,
but seems to have changed from time to time. The head
was shaved, the coat was motley, and the breeches tight, with,
generally, one leg different in color from the other. The
head was covered with a garment resembling a monk's cowl,
which fell over the breast and shoulders, and often bore asses'
ears, and was crested with a coxcomb, while bells hung from
various parts of the attire. The fool's bauble was a short

---

[1] " Glossary," p. 497; see Nares's " Glossary," vol. ii. p. 952.

staff bearing a ridiculous head, to which was sometimes attached an inflated bladder, by which sham castigations were inflicted; a long petticoat was also occasionally worn, but seems to have belonged rather to the idiots than the wits. The fool's business was to amuse his master, to excite his laughter by sharp contrast, to prevent the over-oppression of state affairs, and, in harmony with a well-known physiological precept, by his liveliness at meals to assist his lord's digestion.[1]

The custom of shaving and nicking the head of a fool is very old. There is a penalty of ten shillings, in one of Alfred's Ecclesiastical Laws, if one opprobriously shave a common man like a fool; and Malone cites a passage from "The Choice of Change," etc., by S. R. Gent, 4to, 1598— "Three things used by monks, which provoke other men to laugh at their follies: 1. They are shaven and notched on the head like fooles."

In the "Comedy of Errors" (v. 1), the servant says:

> "My master preaches patience to him, and the while
> His man with scissors nicks him like a fool."

Forfeits. In order to enforce some kind of regularity in barbers' shops, which were once places of great resort for the idle, certain laws were usually made, the breaking of which was to be punished by forfeits. Rules of this kind, however, were as often laughed at as obeyed. So, in "Measure for Measure" (v. 1):

> "laws for all faults,
> But faults so countenanc'd, that the strong statutes
> Stand like the forfeits in a barber's shop,
> As much in mock as mark."

Gambling. It was once customary for a person when going abroad "to put out" a sum of money on condition of receiving good interest for it on his return home; if he never returned the deposit was forfeited. Hence such a one was

---

[1] "Encyclopædia Britannica," 1879, vol. ix. p. 366; see Doran's "History of Court Fools," 1858.

called "a putter-out." It is to this practice that reference is made in the following passage ("The Tempest," iii. 3):

> "or that there were such men
> Whose heads stood in their breasts? which now we find
> Each putter-out of five for one will bring us
> Good warrant of."

Malone quotes from Moryson's "Itinerary" (1617, pt. i. p. 198): "This custom of giving out money upon these adventures was first used in court and noblemen;" a practice which "banker-outs, stage-players, and men of base condition had drawn into contempt," by undertaking journeys merely for gain upon their return. In Ben Jonson's "Every Man Out of His Humour" (ii. 3) the custom is thus alluded to: "I do intend, this year of jubilee coming on, to travel; and because I will not altogether go upon expence, I am determined to put forth some five thousand pound, to be paid me *five for one*, upon the return of my wife, myself, and my dog, from the Turk's court at Constantinople. If all, or either of us, miscarry in the journey, 'tis gone; if we be successful, why then there will be five and twenty thousand pound to entertain time with."

Garters. It was the regular amorous etiquette in the reign of Elizabeth,[1] "for a man, professing himself deeply in love, to assume certain outward marks of negligence in his dress, as if too much occupied by his passion to attend to such trifles, or driven by despondency to a forgetfulness of all outward appearance." His "garters, in particular, were not to be tied up." In "As You Like It" (iii. 2), this custom is described by Rosalind, who tells Orlando: "There is none of my uncle's marks upon you; he taught me how to know a man in love; .... your hose should be ungarter'd, your bonnet unbanded, your sleeve unbuttoned, your shoe untied, and every thing about you demonstrating a careless desolation." Another fashion which seems to have been common among the beaux of Queen Elizabeth's reign, was that of

---

[1] Nares's "Glossary," vol. i. p. 350.

wearing garters across about the knees, an allusion to which we find in "Twelfth Night" (ii. 5), in the letter which Malvolio reads: "Remember who commended thy yellow stockings, and wished to see thee ever cross-gartered." Douce quotes from the old comedy of "The Two Angrie Women of Abingdon" (1599), where a servingman is thus described:

> "Hee's a fine neate fellow,
> A spruce slave, I warrant ye, he'ele have
> His cruell garters crosse about the knee."

In days gone by, when garters were worn in sight, the upper classes wore very expensive ones, but the lower orders worsted galloon ones. Prince Henry calls Poins ("1 Henry IV.," ii. 4) a "caddis garter," meaning a man of mean rank.

Gaudy Days. Feast-days in the colleges of our universities are so called, as they were formerly at the inns-of-court. In "Antony and Cleopatra" (iii. 13), Antony says:

> "come,
> Let's have one other gaudy night: call to me
> All my sad captains; fill our bowls once more;
> Let's mock the midnight bell."

They were so called, says Blount, "from *gaudium*, because, to say truth, they are days of joy, as bringing good cheer to the hungry students."

Glove. As an article of dress the glove held a conspicuous place in many of our old customs and ceremonies. Thus, it was often worn in the hat as a favor, and as a mark to be challenged by an enemy, as is illustrated by the following dialogue in "Henry V." (iv. 1):

"*King Henry.* Give me any gage of thine, and I will wear it in my bonnet: then, if ever thou darest acknowledge it, I will make it my quarrel.

Williams. Here's my glove: give me another of thine.

King Henry. There.

Williams. This will I also wear in my cap: if ever thou come to me and say, after to-morrow, 'This is my glove,' by this hand, I will take thee a box on the ear.

King Henry. If ever I live to see it, I will challenge it.

Williams. Thou darest as well be hanged."

Again, in " Troilus and Cressida" (v. 2), Diomedes, taking the glove from Cressida, says:

> " To-morrow will I wear it on my helm,
> And grieve his spirit that dares not challenge it."

And in " Richard II." (v. 3), Percy narrates how Prince Henry boasted that—

> " he would unto the stews,
> And from the common'st creature pluck a glove,
> And wear it as a favour ; and with that
> He would unhorse the lustiest challenger."

The glove was also worn in the hat as the memorial of a friend, and in the " Merchant of Venice" (iv. 1), Portia, in her assumed character, asks Bassanio for his gloves, which she says she will wear for his sake:

> " Give me your gloves, I'll wear them for your sake."

When the fashion of thus wearing gloves declined, " it fell into the hands of coxcombical and dissolute servants." [1] Thus Edgar, in " King Lear" (iii. 4), being asked by Lear what he had been, replies : " A serving-man, proud in heart and mind ; that curled my hair ; wore gloves in my cap."

To throw the glove, as the signal of a challenge, is alluded to by Troilus (iv. 4), who tells Cressida :

> " For I will throw my glove to Death himself,
> That's there's no maculation in thy heart "

—the meaning being, says Johnson : " I will challenge Death himself in defence of thy fidelity."

The glove then thrown down was popularly called " a gage," [2] from the French, signifying a pledge, and in " Richard II." (iv. 1), it is so termed by Aumerle :

---

[1] Nares's "Glossary," vol. i. p. 371.

[2] The verb "to gage," or "to pledge," occurs in " Merchant of Venice," i. 1 :

> " but my chief care
> Is, to come fairly off from the great debts
> Wherein my time, something too prodigal,
> Hath left me gaged."

Cf. " 1 Henry IV.," i. 3.

> " There is my gage, the manual seal of death,
> That marks thee out for hell."

In the same play it is also called "honor's pawn." Thus Bolingbroke (i. 1) says to Mowbray:

> " Pale trembling coward, there I throw my gage,
> Disclaiming here the kindred of the king;
> And lay aside my high blood's royalty,
> Which fear, not reverence, makes thee to except.
> If guilty dread hath left thee so much strength
> As to take up mine honour's pawn, then stoop."

And further on (iv. 1), one of the lords employs the same phrase:

> " There is my honour's pawn;
> Engage it to the trial, if thou dar'st."

It is difficult to discover why the glove was recognized as the sign of defiance. Brand[1] suggests that the custom of dropping or sending the glove, " as the signal of a challenge, may have been derived from the circumstance of its being the cover of the hand, and therefore put for the hand itself. The giving of the hand is well known to intimate that the person who does so will not deceive, but stand to his agreement. *To shake hands upon it* would not be very delicate in an agreement to fight, and, therefore, gloves may possibly have been deputed as substitutes."

Again, the glove was often thrown down as a pledge, as in " Timon of Athens " (v. 4), where the senator says to Alcibiades:

> " Throw thy glove,
> Or any token of thine honour else,
> That thou wilt use the wars as thy redress,
> And not as our confusion."

Whereupon Alcibiades answers: " Then there's my glove." In " King Lear " (v. 2), Albany thus speaks:

> "Thou art arm'd, Gloster:—let the trumpet sound:
> If none appear to prove, upon thy person,

---

[1] " Pop. Antiq.," vol. ii. p. 127.

Thy heinous, manifest, and many treasons,
There is my pledge; [*Throwing down a glove*] I'll prove it on thy
    heart."

In "Troilus and Cressida" (iv. 5), Hector further alludes to
this practice:

"Your quondam wife swears still by Venus' glove:
She's well, but bade me not commend her to you."

Scented gloves were formerly given away as presents.
In "Winter's Tale" the custom is referred to by Mopsa,
who says to the Clown (iv. 4): "Come, you promised me a
tawdry lace, and a pair of sweet gloves;" and Autolycus is
introduced singing:

"Gloves as sweet as damask roses."

In "Much Ado About Nothing" (iii. 4), Hero says:
"These gloves the count sent me; they are an excellent
perfume." Trinity College, Oxford, not ungrateful to its
founder and his spouse, has many entries, after the date of
1556, in the Bursar's books, "pro fumigatis chirothecis," for
perfumed gloves.

Kiss. In years past, a kiss was the recognized fee of a
lady's partner, and as such is noticed in "Henry VIII."
(i. 4):

"I were unmannerly to take you out,
And not to kiss you."

In "The Tempest" (i. 2) it is alluded to in Ariel's song:

"Come unto these yellow sands,
    And then take hands:
Court'sied when you have, and kiss'd,
    The wild waves whist,
Foot it featly here and there,
And, sweet sprites, the burthen bear."

There is probably a veiled allusion to the same ceremony
in "Winter's Tale" (iv. 4), where, at the dance of shepherds and shepherdesses, the following dialogue occurs:

> "*Clown.*   Come on, strike up!
> *Dorcas.* Mopsa must be your mistress : marry, garlic,
> To mend her kissing with.
> *Mopsa.*   Now, in good time!
> *Clown.* Not a word, a word; we stand upon our manners.
> Come, strike up!"

In an old treatise entitled the "Use and Abuse of Dancing and Minstrelsie" we read:

> "But some reply, what fools will daunce,
>   If that when daunce is doon,
> He may not have at ladyes lips,
>   That which in daunce he doon."

The practice of saluting ladies with a kiss was once very general, and in the "Merry Wives of Windsor" to kiss the hostess is indirectly spoken of as a common courtesy of the day.

In "Romeo and Juliet" (i. 5) a further instance occurs, where Romeo kisses Juliet at Capulet's entertainment; and, in "Henry VIII." (i. 4), Lord Sands is represented as kissing Anne Bullen, next to whom he sits at supper.

The celebrated "kissing comfits" were sugar-plums, once extensively used by fashionable persons to make the breath sweet. Falstaff, in the "Merry Wives of Windsor" (v. 5), when embracing Mrs. Ford, says: "Let it thunder to the tune of 'Green Sleeves,' hail kissing comfits, and snow eringoes."

In "Measure for Measure" (iv. 1, song) kisses are referred to as "seals of love." A Judas kiss was a kiss of treachery. Thus, in "3 Henry VI." (v. 7), Gloster says:

> "so Judas kiss'd his master,
> And cried 'All hail!' when-as he meant all harm."

Lace Songs. These were jingling rhymes, sung by young girls while engaged at their lace-pillows. A practice alluded to by the Duke in "Twelfth Night" (ii. 4):

> "O, fellow, come, the song we had last night.—
> Mark it, Cesario; it is old and plain;
> The spinsters and the knitters in the sun,

> And the free maids that weave their thread with bones
> Do use to chant it."

Miss Baker, in her "Northamptonshire Glossary" (1854, vol. i. p. 378), says, "The movement of the bobbins is timed by the modulation of the tune, which excites them to regularity and cheerfulness; and it is a pleasing sight to see them, in warm, sunny weather, seated outside their cottage doors, or seeking the shade of a neighboring tree; where, in cheerful groups, they unite in singing their rude and simple rhymes. The following is a specimen of one of these ditties, most descriptive of the occupation:

> "'Nineteen long lines, bring over my down,
> The faster I work it, I'll shorten my score,
> But if I do play, it'll stick to a stay,
> So heigh ho! little fingers, and twank it away.'"

Letters. The word Emmanuel was formerly prefixed, probably from feelings of piety, to letters and public deeds. So in "2 Henry VI." (iv. 2) there is the following allusion to it:

> "*Cade.* What is thy name?
> *Clerk.* Emmanuel.
> *Dick.* They use to write it on the top of letters."

Staunton says: "We can refer to one MS. alone, in the British Museum (Ad. MSS. 19, 400), which contains no less than fourteen private epistles headed 'Emanewell,' or 'Jesus Immanuel.'"

Another superscription of a letter in years gone by was "to the bosom" of a lady. Thus Hamlet (ii. 2) says in his letter to Ophelia:

> "In her excellent white bosom, these."

And in the "Two Gentlemen of Verona" (iii. 1), Proteus says:

> "Thy letters may be here, though thou art hence;
> Which, being writ to me, shall be deliver'd
> Even in the milk-white bosom of thy love."

This custom seems to have originated in the circumstance of women having a pocket in the forepart of their stays, in which, according to Steevens, "they carried not only love-letters and love-tokens, but even their money and materials for needlework."

Livery. The phrase "sue my livery," which occurs in the following speech of Bolingbroke ("Richard II." ii. 3),

> "I am denied to sue my livery here,
> And yet my letters-patents give me leave;
> My father's goods are all distrain'd, and sold,
> And these, and all, are all amiss employ'd,"

is thus explained by Malone: "On the death of every person who held by knight's service, the escheator of the court in which he died summoned a jury, who inquired what estate he died seized of, and of what age his next heir was. If he was under age, he became a ward of the king's; but if he was found to be of full age, he then had a right to sue out a writ of *ouster le main*, that is, his livery, that the king's hand might be taken off, and the land delivered to him." York ("Richard II.," ii. 1) also says:

> "If you do wrongfully seize Hereford's rights,
> Call in the letters-patents that he hath
> By his attorneys-general to sue
> His livery."

Love-Day. This denoted a day of amity or reconciliation; an expression which is used by Saturninus in "Titus Andronicus" (i. 1):

> "You are my guest, Lavinia, and your friends.—
> This day shall be a love-day, Tamora."

MILITARY LORE. *Fleshment.* This is a military term; a young soldier being said to *flesh* his sword the first time he draws blood with it. In "King Lear" (ii. 2), Oswald relates how Kent

> "in the fleshment of this dread exploit,
> Drew on me here again,"

upon which passage Singer (vol. ix. p. 377) has this note: "Fleshment, therefore, is here metaphorically applied to the first act which Kent, in his new capacity, had performed for his

master; and, at the same time, in a sarcastic sense, as though
he had esteemed it an heroic exploit to trip a man behind,
who was actually falling." The phrase occurs again in " I
Henry IV." (v. 4), where Prince Henry tells his brother:

> "Come, brother John, full bravely hast thou flesh'd
> Thy maiden sword."

Swearing by the Sword. According to Nares,[1] " the singular mixture of religious and military fanaticism which
arose from the Crusades gave rise to the custom of taking
a solemn oath upon a sword. In a plain, unenriched sword,
the separation between the blade and the hilt was usually
a straight transverse bar, which, suggesting the idea of a
cross, added to the devotion which every true knight felt for
his favorite weapon, and evidently led to this practice."
Hamlet makes Horatio swear that he will never divulge
having seen the Ghost (i. 5):

> " Never to speak of this that you have seen,
> Swear by my sword."

In the " Winter's Tale " (ii. 3), Leonato says:

> " Swear by this sword
> Thou wilt perform my bidding."

The cross of the sword is also mentioned to illustrate the
true bearing of the oath. Hence, in " I Henry IV." (ii. 4),
Falstaff says jestingly of Glendower, that he " swore the
devil his true liegeman upon the cross of a Welsh hook."[2]
On account of the practice of swearing by a sword, or, rather, by the cross or upper end of it, the name of *Jesus* was
sometimes inscribed on the handle or some other part.

Mining Terms. According to Mr. Collier, the phrase
" truepenny" is a mining term current in the north of England, signifying a particular indication in the soil, of the

---

[1] " Glossary," vol. ii. p. 858; see Dyce's " Glossary," p. 431.

[2] A Welsh hook was a sort of bill, hooked at the end, and with a
long handle. See Dyce's " Glossary," p. 497; and Singer's " Shake-
peare," vol. ix. p. 168.

direction in which cre is to be found. Thus Hamlet (i. 5) says

> "Ah, ha, boy! say'st thou so? art thou there, truepenny?"

when making Horatio and Marcellus again swear that they will not divulge having seen the ghost.

Patrons. The custom of clergymen praying for their patrons, in what is called the bidding prayer, seems alluded to by Kent in "King Lear" (i. 1):

> "Royal Lear,
> Whom I have ever honour'd as my king,
> Lov'd as my father, as my master follow'd,
> As my great patron thought on in my prayers."

Sagittary. This was a monster, half man, half beast, described as a terrible archer; neighing like a horse, and with its eyes of fire striking men dead as if with lightning. In "Troilus and Cressida" (v. 5), Agamemnon says:

> "The dreadful Sagittary
> Appals our numbers."

Hence any deadly shot was called a sagittary. In "Othello" (i. 1) the barrack is so named from the figure of an archer over the door.

Salad Days. Days of green youth and inexperience. Cleopatra says (i. 5):

> "My salad days,
> When I was green in judgment:—cold in blood."

Salt. The salt of youth is that vigor and strong passion which then predominates. The term is several times used by Shakespeare for strong amorous passion. Iago, in "Othello" (iii. 3), refers to it as "hot as monkeys, as salt as wolves in pride." In "Measure for Measure" (v. 1), the Duke calls Angelo's base passion his "salt imagination," because he supposed his victim to be Isabella, and not his betrothed wife, whom he was forced by the Duke to marry.[1]

Salutations. God-den was used by our forefathers as

---

[1] Brewer's "Dictionary of Phrase and Fable," p. 782.

soon as noon was past, after which time "good-morrow" or "good-day" was esteemed improper; the phrase "God ye good den" being a contraction of "God give you a good evening." This fully appears from the following passage in "Romeo and Juliet" (ii. 4):

> "*Nurse.* God ye good morrow, gentlemen.
> *Mercutio.* God ye good den, fair gentlewoman."

Upon being thus corrected, the Nurse asks, "Is it good den?" to which Mercutio replies, "'Tis no less, I tell you, for the bawdy hand of the dial is now upon the prick of noon."

A further corruption of the same phrase was "God dig-you-den," as used by Costard in "Love's Labour's Lost" (iv. 1): "God dig-you-den all!" Shakespeare uses it several times, as in "Titus Andronicus" (iv. 4), where the Clown says: "God and Saint Stephen give you good den;" and in "King John" (i. 1) we have "Good-den, Sir Richard!"

Another old popular salutation was "good even and twenty" ("Merry Wives of Windsor," ii. 1), equivalent to "twenty good-evenings." Mr. Halliwell-Phillipps quotes a similar phrase from Elliot's "Fruits of the French" (1593), "God night, and a thousand to everybody."

We may also compare the phrase "good deed" in "Winter's Tale" (i. 2)—a species of asseveration, as "in very deed."

Servants' Customs. The old custom of the servants of great families taking an oath of fidelity on their entrance into office—as is still the case with those of the sovereign—is alluded to by Posthumus in "Cymbeline" (ii. 4), where, speaking of Imogen's servants, he says:

> "Her attendants are
> All sworn and honourable." [1]

Gold chains were formerly worn by persons of rank and dignity, and by rich merchants—a fashion which descended to upper servants in great houses—and by stewards as badges of office. These chains were usually cleaned by be-

---

[1] See Percy's "Northumberland Household Book," p. 49.

ing rubbed with crumbs. Hence, in " Twelfth Night " (ii. 3),
Sir Toby says to the Clown:

> " Go, sir, rub your chain with crumbs."

In days gone by, too, it was customary for the servants
of the nobility, particularly the gentleman-usher, to attend
bare-headed. In the procession to the trial in " Henry
VIII." (ii. 4), one of the persons enumerated is a gentleman-
usher " bare-headed." On grand occasions, coachmen, also,
drove bare-headed, a practice alluded to in Beaumont and
Fletcher's " Woman-Hater " (iii. 2):

> " Or a pleated lock, or a bareheaded coachman,
>   This sits like a sign where great ladies are
>   To be sold within."

Sheriffs' Post. At the doors of sheriffs were usually set
up ornamental posts, on which royal and civic proclamations
were fixed. So, in " Twelfth Night " (i. 5), Malvolio says:
" He'll stand at your door like a sheriff's post." " A pair
of mayors' posts," says Staunton, " are still standing in Norwich, which, from the initials T. P., and the date 159–, are
conjectured to have belonged to Thomas Pettys, who was
mayor of that city in 1592."

Shoeing-Horn. This, from its convenient use in drawing
on a tight shoe, was applied in a jocular metaphor to other
subservient and tractable assistants. Thus Thersites, in
" Troilus and Cressida " (v. 1), in his railing mood gives this
name to Menelaus, whom he calls " a thrifty shoeing-horn in
a chain, hanging at his brother's [Agamemnon] leg."

It was also employed as a contemptuous name for dan-
glers on young women.

In the same way " shoe-tye " became a characteristic name
for a traveller, a term used by Shakespeare in " Measure for
Measure " (iv. 3), " Master Forthright the tilter, and brave
Master Shoe-tie, the great traveller."

A Solemn Supper. In Shakespeare's day this was a phrase
for a feast or banquet given on any important occasion, such
as a birth, marriage, etc. Macbeth says (iii. 1):

> "To-night we hold a solemn supper, sir,
> And I'll request your presence."

Howel, in a letter to Sir T. Hawke, 1636, says: "I was invited yesternight to a *solemne supper* by B. J. [Ben Jonson], where you were deeply remembered."

So, in "Romeo and Juliet" (i. 5), Tybalt says:

> "What! dares the slave
> Come hither, cover'd with an antic face,
> To fleer and scorn at our solemnity?"

And in "All's Well that Ends Well" (ii. 3), the King, on the conclusion of the contract between Helena and Bertram, says:

> "The solemn feast
> Shall more attend upon the coming space,
> Expecting absent friends."

Statute Caps. These were woollen caps enforced by Statute 13 Elizabeth, which, says Strype, in his "Annals" (vol. ii. p. 74), was "for continuance of making and wearing woollen caps in behalf of the trade of cappers; providing that all above the age of six years (excepting the nobility and some others) should on Sabbath-days and holy-days wear caps of wool, knit thicked, and drest in England, upon penalty of ten groats." Thus, in "Love's Labour's Lost" (v. 2), Rosaline says:

> "Well, better wits have worn plain statute-caps."

Jonson considered that the statute caps alluded to were those worn by the members of the universities.

Theatrical Lore. At the conclusion of a play, or of the epilogue, it was formerly customary for the actors to kneel down on the stage, and pray for the sovereign, nobility, clergy, and sometimes for the commons. So, in the epilogue to "2 Henry IV.," the dancer says: "My tongue is weary; when my legs are too, I will bid you good night; and so kneel down before you:—but, indeed, to pray for the queen." Collier, in his "History of English Dramatic Poetry" (vol. iii. p. 445), tells us that this practice continued in the commencement of the 17th century.

Tournaments. In " Coriolanus " (ii. 1) Shakespeare attributes some of the customs of his own times to a people who were wholly unacquainted with them. In the following passage we have an exact description of what occurred at tiltings and tournaments when a combatant had distinguished himself:

> " Matrons flung gloves,
> Ladies and maids their scarfs and handkerchers,
> Upon him as he pass'd : the nobles bended,
> As to Jove's statue ; and the commons made
> A shower and thunder with their caps and shouts :
> never saw the like." [1]

An allusion to the mock tournaments, in which the combatants were armed with rushes in place of spears, is used in " Othello " (v. 2):

> " Man but a rush against Othello's breast."

Trumpet. In olden times it was the fashion for persons of distinction, when visiting, to be accompanied by a trumpeter, who announced their approach by a flourish of his trumpet. It is to this custom, Staunton [2] thinks, that Lorenzo refers in the " Merchant of Venice " (v. 1), where he tells Portia :

> " Your husband is at hand ; I hear his trumpet."

WAR-CRY. " *God and Saint George !* "—the common cry of the English soldier when he charged the enemy. " Richard III." (v. 3). The author of the " Old Arte of Warre," printed in the latter end of Queen Elizabeth's reign, formally enjoins the use of this cry among his military laws (p. 84): " Item. That all souldiers entring into battaile, assaulte, skirmishe, or other faction of armes, shall have for their common cry-word, ' Saint George, forward, or upon them, Saint George !' whereby the souldier is much comforted to minde the ancient valour of England, which with that name has been so often victorious ; and therefore he who upon

---

[1] See Singer's " Shakespeare," vol. vii. p. 350.
[2] " Shakespeare," 1864, vol. i. p. 61.

any sinister zeale shall maliciously omit so fortunate a name, shall be severely punished for his obstinate, erroneous heart and perverse mind."

"*Havoc!*" To cry "havoc" appears to have been a signal for indiscriminate slaughter. The expression occurs in "King John" (ii. 1): "Cry havoc, kings!" In "Coriolanus" Menenius says (iii. 1):

> "Do not cry havoc, where you should but hunt
> With modest warrant."

And in "Julius Cæsar" (iii. 1):

> "Cry 'Havoc!' and let slip the dogs of war."

"*Kill, kill, kill, kill, kill him!*" This was the ancient cry of the English troops when they charged the enemy. It occurs where the conspirators kill Coriolanus (v. 6).

Leet-Ale. This was the dinner provided for the jury and customary tenants at the court-leet of a manor, or "view of frank-pledge," formerly held once or twice a year, before the steward of the leet.[1] To this court Shakespeare alludes in the "Taming of the Shrew" (i. 2), where the servant tells Sly that in his dream he would "rail upon the hostess of the house," and threaten to "present her at the leet."

Aubrey, in his MS. History of Wiltshire, 1678, tells us, too, how "in the Easter holidays was the Clerk's ale for his private benefit, and the solace of the neighbourhood."

---

[1] See page 312.

INDEX.

THE END.